# CHARLES DICKEN

C000094547

Dickens's rise to fame and his worldwi
inevitable. He started out with no clear careei in ......
out of the theater, journalism, and editing before finding unexpected
success as a creative writer. Taking account of everything known
about Dickens's apprentice years, Robert L. Patten narrates the fierce
struggle Dickens then had to create an alter ego, Boz, and later to
contain and extinguish him. His revision of Dickens's biography in
the context of early Victorian social and political history and print
culture opens up a more unstable, yet more fascinating, portrait of
Dickens. The book tells the story of how Dickens created an authorial
persona that highlighted certain attributes and concealed others about
his life, talent, and publications. This complicated narrative of
struggle, determination, dead ends, and new beginnings is as gripping
as one of Dickens's own novels.

ROBERT L. PATTEN, Lynette S. Autrey Professor in Humanities at
Rice University, has published widely on Victorian literature and
culture. He has previously published with Cambridge *Literature in
the Marketplace: Nineteenth-Century British Publishing and Reading
Practices* (edited with John O. Jordan, 1995). He is Scholar in
Residence at the Charles Dickens Museum in 2011–12, and Senior
Research Fellow in the Institute of English Studies, School of
Advanced Study, University of London.

Charles Dickens, oil painting by Daniel Maclise, engraved by William Finden.
Frontispiece to *Nicholas Nickleby*, 1839

# CHARLES DICKENS AND "BOZ"
# THE BIRTH OF THE
# INDUSTRIAL-AGE AUTHOR

ROBERT L. PATTEN

CAMBRIDGE
UNIVERSITY PRESS

# CAMBRIDGE
## UNIVERSITY PRESS

University Printing House, Cambridge CB2 8BS, United Kingdom

Cambridge University Press is part of the University of Cambridge.

It furthers the University's mission by disseminating knowledge in the pursuit of education, learning and research at the highest international levels of excellence.

www.cambridge.org
Information on this title: www.cambridge.org/9781107470316

© Robert L. Patten 2012

First published 2012
Paperback edition 2014

Printed in the United Kingdom by Clays, St Ives plc.

*A catalogue record for this publication is available from the British Library*

*Library of Congress Cataloging-in-Publication Data*
Patten, Robert L.
Charles Dickens and 'Boz' : the birth of the industrial-age author / Robert L. Patten.
p.   cm.
ISBN 978-1-107-02351-2 (Hardback)
1.  Dickens, Charles, 1812–1870–Criticism and interpretation.    I. Title.
PR4588.P38 2012
823'.8–dc23
2011043659

ISBN 978-1-107-02351-2 Hardback
ISBN 978-1-107-47031-6 Paperback

*For Seth*

# *Epigraphs*

The brave man carves out his fortune, and every man is the son of his own works.
— Miguel de Cervantes, *Don Quixote*

We ask authors to answer for the unity of the works published in their names; we ask that they reveal, or at least display the hidden sense pervading their work; we ask them to reveal their personal lives, to account for their experiences and the real story that gave birth to their writings. The author is he who implants, into the troublesome language of fiction, its unities, its coherence, its links with reality.
— Michel Foucault, "The Discourse on Language"

The meaning of "Literature" is not to be understood until we have felt its meaning for the author who wanted to be a part of it.
— Kathryn Chittick, *Dickens and the 1830s*

The writer's audience is always a fiction.
—Walter J. Ong, *Orality and Literacy*

# Contents

| | | |
|---|---|---|
| *List of illustrations* | | *page* viii |
| *Acknowledgments* | | ix |
| *Prologue* | | xiii |

1 Christening Boz (1812–1834): the journalism sketches     1

2 Characterizing Boz (1834–1837): *Sketches by Boz*     47

3 Writing Boz (1836–1837): *The Pickwick Papers*     78

4 Hiring Boz (1837–1839): *Bentley's Miscellany* and *Oliver Twist*     134

5 Paying Boz (1838–1839): *Nicholas Nickleby*     178

6 Rewriting Boz (1839–1841): *Master Humphrey's Clock* and *The Old Curiosity Shop*     226

7 Unwriting Boz (1841): *Master Humphrey's Clock* and *Barnaby Rudge*     279

*Notes*     329
*Bibliography*     382
*Index*     396

# Illustrations

Charles Dickens, oil painting by Daniel Maclise, engraved by
William Finden. Frontispiece to *Nicholas Nickleby*, 1839

Chapter 1.  Charles Dickens, Thomas Unwins sketch, 1831                1
Chapter 2.  Charles Dickens, miniature by Rose Emma
            Drummond, 1835, later engraved by Edwin Roffe              47
Chapter 3.  Charles Dickens, "Phiz" sketch, 1837                       78
Chapter 4.  Charles Dickens, George Cruikshank sketch,
            April 1837                                                 134
Chapter 5.  Charles Dickens, Samuel Laurence drawing, 1837             178
Chapter 6.  "Boz," Samuel Laurence drawing, 1838                       226
Chapter 7.  Charles Dickens, Samuel Drummond portrait,
            c. 1840                                                    279

All illustrations listed above are reproduced by permission of the
Charles Dickens Museum, London.

Figure 1.   The communications circuit by Robert Darnton.
            Reproduced by permission. From *The Kiss of
            Lamourette: Reflections in Cultural History*
            (New York: W. W. Norton, 1990), p. 112.                    4

# Acknowledgments

In the fifty years I have been thinking about Dickens as an author, I have incurred more debts to other scholars, students, librarians, research assistants, foundations and granting agencies, and university administrators than I can ever acknowledge or by any fraction repay. This particular iteration of my lifetime obsession began when, in 1991, I was introduced to book history by Simon Eliot and Jonathan Rose at a Dickens Universe summer conference held at Kresge College, University of California Santa Cruz. To my first mentors and to their collaborator and Director of the Dickens Project at UCSC, John O. Jordan, I owe my conversion to a novice book historian. In the two decades since, members of the Society for the History of Authorship, Reading and Publishing (SHARP), which was founded at that summer conference, have provided a continuous fountain of instruction and advice, information about cognate subjects, the location of important documents and scholarly works, and, most important, generous encouragement.

Over that score of years, several institutions have been willing to chance my trying out some ideas on their faculty and students. I am grateful to Bucknell University for inviting me to deliver the Robbins lecture in 1995, to Worcester Polytechnic Institute, which hosted a conference of the Dickens Society in 1996 on the occasion of the accession of a major Dickens library, to Texas A&M University at Laredo for the ESFA 1996 lecture, to the Graduate Center of CUNY for their spring colloquium in 1998, to SHARP and the Gutenberg Institute for the History of the Book at the Johannes Gutenberg University in Mainz for their splendid observation of the 600th anniversary of the birth of Gutenberg, and to Gettysburg College for the Morris W. Croll lecture in 2003. Trial versions of portions of the chapters on *Pickwick*, *Oliver Twist*, and *The Old Curiosity Shop* were delivered at Dickens Project summer conferences in 2007, 1998, and 2003 respectively. I've incorporated as much of the feedback from audiences as possible, and this work is much richer for their insights.

In addition, invitations to compose entries for other books on Dickens helped to clarify and extend my initial arguments. To Paul Schlicke, editor of the *Oxford Reader's Companion to Dickens*, and John O. Jordan, editor of the *Cambridge Companion to Charles Dickens*, I extend warm thanks both for the opportunity to write entries and for their manifold editorial skills.

As part of their graduate training at Rice, Ayse Celikkol, Anne Dayton, Amanda Ellis, David Messmer, Janna Smartt, and Leah Speights were at one time or another subjected to stints of researching and reviewing parts of my messy and incomplete drafts. At the end, Sophia Hsu and an *SEL* research assistant, Michael Hart, checked every fact and transcription and tried to correct my multiple errors. They are in no way responsible for those that remain as a result of further rewrites; those I claim as my misreadings, hoping there might be some Blooming virtue in one or two of them.

Other Rice undergraduates and graduates have discussed Dickens with me in class and out. I can't list them all, but a few deserve special mention: Searcy Milam and Ben Ratner, my two Centennial Scholars who spent two years each on Dickens projects, and doctoral students Duncan Hasell, Jeffrey Jackson, Kara Marler-Kennedy, Kevin Morrison, Victoria Ford Smith, Elizabeth Coggin Womack, and at UCSC Jon Varese. These doctoral students were among the most recent who did not entirely avoid Dickens in their graduate study and dissertations. Several now completing the Rice doctoral program were faithful attenders at the year-long Andrew W. Mellon seminar on late Dickens and authorship sponsored by the Rice Humanities Research Center, and even in most cases at a preceding semester seminar on early Dickens: kudos to Kattie Basnett, Heather Elliott, Maggie Harvey, Heather Miner, and Joanna O'Leary for their amazing contributions to the seminar and this book, and thanks from all of us to the Director of the HRC, Professor Caroline Levander and her matchless staff.

The Internet creates one huge family, and the Dickens relatives are among the most convivial and verbal. I must single out the Dickens Fellowship Philadelphia Branch and their longtime president, Patricia A. Vinci, for innumerable courtesies and invitations always welcomely received. Others who should be named include scholars both professional and superbly amateur: Peter Beal, Rosemarie Bodenheimer, H. Philip Bolton, John Bowen, Logan Browning, Jerome Charyn, Eileen Cleere, Philip Collins, Pamela Dalziel, Lew Eatherton, David Finkelstein, Kate Flint, Ian Gadd, Jonathan Grossman, Leslie Howsam, Christine Huguet,

Stephen Jarvis, Juliet John, Frank Kermode, Patrick Leary, Sally Ledger, Valerie Browne Lester, Thad Logan, William F. Long, Helena Michie, J. Hillis Miller, Catherine Robson, Florian Schweizer, Paul Schlicke, Catherine Seville, Michael Slater, Linda Spiro, Lisa Spiro, John Sutherland, Kathleen Tillotson, and Andrew Xavier. The two anonymous readers for Cambridge University Press provided quite different, happily complementary, assessments: one responded with broad suggestions for the larger implications of the argument, the other spotted details that were either simply wrong or substantially contradicted my thesis, especially the parts about Michel Foucault. I'm a much smarter, if still fallible, author for their discrete and merciful interventions. Authorship is, as I try to show, always collaborative; I regret that I cannot name these anons.

To the principals at the Sunstone Press in Santa Fe, James Clovis Smith Jr. and Carl Daniel Condit, heartfelt thanks for providing me with a room of my own in which to draft this book, and lots of encouragement. I am, if anything, even more indebted to Warwick Gould, Director of the Institute of English Studies in the School of Advanced Study, University of London. First, he invited me to give the third John Coffin Memorial Lecture, on "Anon.," in 2006; then he and his colleagues tendered me an appointment (*sine die*!) as Senior Research Fellow. That honor provided me with the opportunity to spend 2011–12 in residence at the IES perfecting and proofing this book, among other projects. Enabling me to obtain a visa, an office, and research support, were Peter Niven and Sarah Allan of the School of Advanced Study, and Wim van Mierlo, Conor Wyer, Zoe Holman, and Jon Millington of IES. Working with them has been a joy.

Without a "golden handshake" from Rice University, arranged by Allen J. Matusow and seconded by Eugene H. Levy and Nicolas Shumway, I could not have afforded any such research adventure. I hope this book supplies intellectual capital balancing to some extent Rice's generous "real" capital expenditure.

At Cambridge University Press I have had, for twenty years, the inestimable privilege of working with (and for) Linda Bree, surely one of the most alert, discerning, and energetic of commissioning editors. The production staff has been resolutely determined to help my faltering steps reach the finish line: thanks be to Maartje Scheltens, Christina Sarigiannidou, Jacqueline French, and Mike Leach. I acknowledge with gratitude permission from Robert Darnton to reproduce his diagram of the "Communications Circuit," as it has appeared in several iterations of his seminal essay "What Is the History of Books?"

All illustrations were provided by the Charles Dickens Museum, which opened its extensive library of portrait images to me. Curators' notes on some of the photographs discuss sources and disagreements about authenticity. In some cases I have chosen ones that are controversial precisely because the debate adds another element to issues about the material embodiment of the author, whether Charles Dickens or Boz. The image at the beginning of Chapter 2, etched from a miniature painted by Rose Emma Drummond, Dickens gave to Catherine as an engagement present in 1835. It is therefore the face he wanted to show to her, if not yet to the world. The sketch of Dickens for Chapter 3, and an etching of it, are signed "Phiz" but Browne denied them; however, that rejection may have occurred after the break with Dickens in the 1860s. As Chapter 5 discusses, photographs of the facsimile of the Samuel Drummond portrait given to the Museum are inscribed on the back of two images with diametrically opposed opinions about its authenticity. On one a curator notes that the original did not appear in the Burdett-Coutts sale of May 1922, and refers to [B. W. Matz], "Some Gifts to the Dickens House," *Dickensian* 31, 2 (April 1925): 76, announcing its acquisition. On another image of the facsimile there is attached to the frame a printed legend that traces the history of the picture (reproduced in F. G. Kitton's 1902 *Charles Dickens: His Life, Writings, and Personality*, opposite p. 182) and its authentication by Kate Perugini in 1923, according to B. W. Matz. A different inscription now appears on the frame, citing the appendix to Charles C. Osborne's edition of *Letters of Charles Dickens to the Baroness Burdett-Coutts* (London: John Murray, 1931). The evidence seems conclusively to point to the Drummond original as being a portrait of Dickens. I am grateful to Dr. Florian Schweizer, Julia Ziemer, Shannon Hermes, and Fiona Jenkins for their help in researching and supplying these illustrations.

Finally, a word about the wrapper. The watercolor and pencil of Dickens was executed by the artist and art historian Joel Isaacson in 2000, and I am grateful to him for allowing me to reproduce his picture. At that time, painting small portraits of Impressionist artists, he became interested in beards and in "the opportunity to use their forms as fields for abstraction" (email, July 2, 2011). When I first saw the image on a website, it struck me as the perfect representation of Dickens both coming into existence as a corporeal being and being unfinished, if not erased. That his beard featured so prominently spoke to me of the older Charles Dickens whose middle-aged beard is such a constant in his portraiture, not the young, beardless Boz. So the watercolor stands here as another way of seeing the confluence, separation, and protracted birth of the authors Charles Dickens and Boz.

# *Prologue*

During the academic year 1963–64, I studied in London as a Fulbright scholar. Kathleen Tillotson of Bedford College, University of London, was my British supervisor. E. D. H. Johnson of Princeton was directing my dissertation on plot in Dickens's first monthly and weekly serial. My interest was essentially New Critical: I believed passionately that Dickens was an artist, and not an irresponsible, irrepressible writer who just dashed things off for money. If I could show, through a study of whatever manuscripts and proofs still existed, evidence of Dickens's planning and artistic concerns even in two early books that seemed to exhibit little evidence of those features, then I might help clear the way to look more closely at what I felt was a complex interweaving of themes, images, and variations on character embedded in and characteristic of Dickens's art. John Butt and Kathleen Tillotson's *Dickens at Work* was my bible.[1]

One day while working in the Victoria and Albert Museum Library, I chanced upon an entry in a ledger recording additions to the collection that Dickens's best friend and authorized biographer, John Forster, bequeathed to the V&A. It signified that the account books of Chapman and Hall and Bradbury and Evans, Dickens's longtime publishers and printers, had been absorbed into the Forster Collection. After a few days' study, I thought I might have found hitherto unstudied evidence of Dickens's sales and profits that could be used, paradoxically, to strengthen the case for his not prostituting his art for money. Madeline House and Kathleen Tillotson were using these records as resources in annotating the Pilgrim edition of the *Letters*, but these were early days in that heroic project: the first volume, covering Dickens's correspondence through 1839, appeared in 1965. Besides, the publishers' records covered a later period in Dickens's career, from 1845–46 forward, the time at which his contractual arrangements for publication finally settled down to a standard routine with two major firms. I proposed that on finishing the thesis I would publish these records, but no American academic press was interested.

Fortunately, Oxford University Press believed that an account of Dickens and his publishers might have merit. Jon Stallworthy, a wonderful mentor, showed me how to convert tables of figures into narrative and to round out an account of Dickens's professional life. The conclusion I reached was that Dickens's various modes of sales, from weekly or monthly parts through volumes, cheap editions, authorized translations, public readings, and collected works, supplied enough different copies and price points for him to be owned by households of varying incomes and degrees of literacy. As I said in closing,

> Working closely with a succession of enterprising publishers at home and abroad, Dickens democratized fiction ... That Dickens wrote for money should be at the very least a neutral fact, and not a reason for calling his artistry or integrity in question. How it became possible for Dickens to write for money, on the other hand, takes us into the very heart of nineteenth-century culture and into all the intimately reciprocal connections between the artist and his age.[2]

I completed that study in 1975, and it was published three years later. At the time, I was entirely ignorant of developments in bibliography, print culture, and history of the book initiated in France and gathering practitioners across Europe, Britain, and North America. In the thirty-six years since, I have tried to educate myself about these disciplines, which deal so directly and with such finesse with the "connections between the artist and his age." So this book is either an old man's garrulous retelling of favorite stories, or if it does contribute something new to the understanding of Dickens and his times, it does so by attempting to bring several intellectual disciplines and practices together, not so much "in conversation" as in an enhanced, multivalent reconsideration of Dickens's authorial beginnings.

The disciplines I engage in this expanded narrative include, first of all, book history, comprising everything from bibliography to print culture.[3] I have certainly not mastered any of these sub-disciplines, but I have combined evidence from the paratextual surrounds of Dickens's fiction (e.g., advertisements, wrappers and casings for his books, title pages, prefaces to original and reprinted editions), from his correspondence about his writings and his diaries, and from publishers' records and histories,[4] with the history of copyright across Europe and North America up to Dickens's era, theorizations of the "communications circuit" and the place of the "author" within it, and brief mentions of the careers of his fellow authors who paved the way or illuminated the stony path for writers. I have tried to incorporate the perspective of the "sociology of texts" advocated by the late D. F. McKenzie as well as William St. Clair's more recent call for a "political economy of reading."[5] In addition, the important statistical work initiated by Simon Eliot on the nineteenth-century British book trade and David McKitterick's magisterial collection of essays on *The Book in Britain* from 1830–1914 have provided essential grounding for my sense of the publishing context for Dickens.[6] Finally, introductions and anthologies of essays attempting to cover the history of the book supply overwhelming evidence of the complexity and variations of these subjects; they have cautioned me against generalizations. I've not ventured to go beyond Dickens, to other male writers, to women whose relation to commercial publication and the marketplace seems generally to differ from that of men in the Victorian and preceding periods, or to European or North American writers – except to instance their situations in particular contexts as comparisons and contrasts to Dickens's choices and rewards.[7] For me, the devil is in the details, and each writer's situation differs, even though some careers achieve the status of paradigms. Dickens's has.

A second broad discipline to which this narrative pays attention is history, especially the contemporary history, registered for the most part as "news" in the periodicals of the period 1830–40, that Dickens contributed to in a small way through Parliamentary and other kinds of reporting. For his first conceived, sixth published fiction, *Barnaby Rudge*, ostensibly about the Gordon riots of 1780, he also studied older history, including newspaper articles, memoirs, historical reconstructions of the events and of the topography, architecture, and civic governance of London, and interviews with survivors. While the politics of Dickens's early journalism isn't easy to detect or systematize, it is important to recognize that he published in periodicals appealing to very different audiences and political persuasions, and that the editorial "we" he fashioned incorporated numerous overlapping but sometimes politically opposed sectors of the reading public. Much of this study concentrates on the metamorphosis of that "we" as Dickens reinvents his relationship to his pen names, his audience, and his versions of contemporary and past British history.

An extensive, indeed dominating paradigm for this study derives from biography, and especially those notions of biography which understand that many of us live prospectively, inscribing our dreams for our future; simultaneously live in the present with all its triumphs and vexations exaggerated by momentary, largely unreflective feelings and impulses; and also live backwards, composing our lives retrospectively in order to make their end points concurrent with, and in some way a deliberate outcome of, past practices and ambitions. When recounting book history – especially the proliferation of minor projects and publications that litter Dickens's desk and wastepaper basket in the early years – my narrative may sometimes plod – necessarily, I think, because Dickens is searching for something substantial to do and be, and piles on commitments without much discrimination or planning. But whenever he writes about his life, however fictional that account proves to be, it pulses with his energy, his emotions, his dreams, and the rewards and disappointments of his nascent career. I cannot help seeing Dickens's invention of a kind of "industrial-age" authorship, in which he attempts to gain control over the means and ends of his writing, as centered in his own life-writing during the middle years of Britain's all-encompassing industrial revolution.

And that takes me to two other dimensions of the topic. One is the reception of his works. Reception theory and history are, like the other disciplines I've mentioned, complex and proliferating subjects.[8] In Dickens's case, as I write it out, they include the responses of his friends, family, advisors, and publishers; the reviews; the sales and profits of his works; theatricalizations, imitations, parodies, plagiarisms, translations, sequels, and republications of the original texts in new formats for new tranches of buyers; the ways in which actual receptions and anticipated ones shape possibilities and agreements for future works; the increasingly distinguished company he keeps and the increasingly distinguished receptions, dinners, and celebrations that are given to honor his work; and the ways in which Dickens has been read by his literary and academic biographers and critics. Authorship is not a one-way street: genius delivers, the demos receives. Dickens's various publics played a significant role in shaping his career.

Finally, what may be most venturesome – and most unequal to the range and power of Dickens's literary achievements – is my effort to read within Dickens's fictions for signs of his own anxieties about authorship. What, for instance, did he have to say? When faced with a blank piece of paper and an urgent deadline, what prompted his imagination? Oddly, death, along with the improvisatory nature of industrializing urban life and the deterioration of certain kinds of once more stable significations of identity and character: names, faces, speech, occupations, family connections and obligations, and a social ethos forming and maintaining communities. In tracking Dickens's authorial concerns, I trace the devolution of the humorous narrative voice of "Boz" to its 1841 endpoint, when Dickens stops writing and publishing, having killed off his last narratorial embodiment, Master Humphrey. While the evidences of his anxieties about his career are the main subject of these interpretations of his fiction,

I have tried not to make them tendentious. That is, I see the disguised and displaced representations of and reflections on authorship within the larger thematic contexts of the whole fiction, and want always to illustrate how embedded personal issues are part of complex ideological, structural, material, and affective architectures that work together to create the marvels of Dickens's imagination and artistry.

The multiple epigraphs to each chapter stand as instances of the ways different disciplinary perspectives have dealt with those writings of Dickens treated therein. The varied textual incarnations of Dickens's most familiar pseudonym, Boz, prove to be another way of organizing and articulating these many threads of narrative. Creating the name; deploying it as an essayist, or novelist, or editor, and sometimes as the person of Dickens himself; finding it unhelpfully adopted and adapted by others; attempting to reshape the character and occupation of Boz; and eventually trying – rather unsuccessfully – to put pseudonyms aside and establish himself, his patronym and body and voice, as the author of his works are the stages in Dickens's projection of Boz that organize the following chapters. I cannot concentrate on one title at a time, but must instead recount Dickens's authorial career across many projects at the same time, and as particular ones such as *Pickwick* and *Oliver Twist* operate over long stretches of time to enable and constrict his subsequent publishing options. Readers may feel uncomfortable or dislocated in encountering more about *Sketches by Boz* in the middle of a discussion about *Barnaby Rudge*, or in reading that something Edward Lytton Bulwer published three years before anything of Dickens went into print might have constrained Boz's mode of presenting domestic and national villainy in *Master Humphrey's Clock*. And yet it is all of a piece. That we now usually read Dickens novel by novel, taking each title on its own, insulated especially from its cumulative creative and commercial contexts, is at once the triumph of his artistry and of his capacity to teach us the limited set of contexts in which he wants us to appreciate each endeavor.

This story deals only with the "birth" of the industrial-age author. "Births" can be protracted events, and usually comprise naming the child and telling the story of its familial origins. During childhood, that birth story may change; the child may adopt a different name; its family affiliations may alter; its associations may develop in unexpected directions; and it may not live the life forecast at its birth. Those are all aspects of birth recounted here. For the adolescence and maturity of the industrial-age author, one must seek out other stories.

# CHAPTER I

# *Christening Boz (1812–1834): the journalism sketches*

Charles Dickens, Thomas Unwins sketch, 1831

Despite the proliferation of biographies of great writers, the basic conditions of authorship remain obscure for most periods of history ... What was the nature of a literary career, and how was it pursued? How did writers deal with publishers, printers, booksellers, reviewers, and one another? Until those questions are answered, we will not have a full understanding of the transmission of texts.
                              – Robert Darnton, "What Is the History of Books?"

"Literary men," says Mr. Bulwer, "have not with us any fixed and settled position as men of letters ... We are on a par ... with quack doctors, street-preachers, strollers, ballad-singers, hawkers of last dying speeches, Punch-and-Judies, conjurors, tumblers, and other 'diverting vagabonds.'"
                              – Thomas Hood, "Copyright and Copywrong"

[T]his solitary mortal endowed with an active imagination, always roaming the great desert of men, has a nobler aim than that of the pure idler ... He is looking for that indefinable something we may be allowed to call "modernity" ... the transient, the fleeting, the contingent; it is one half of art, the other being the eternal and the immovable.
                              – Charles Baudelaire, "The Painter of Modern Life"

Dickens's career came to be seen, then and since, as a kind of epitome of nineteenth-century authorship.
                              – Patrick Leary and Andrew Nash, "Authorship"

I

On Friday, November 9, 1838, the London publisher Richard Bentley issued a three-volume illustrated novel entitled *Oliver Twist; or, The Parish Boy's Progress.* The title page prints the author's name as "Boz." John Forster, serving as Dickens's literary advisor and acting on his behalf while Dickens was in Wales and Liverpool, had forwarded to Bentley on the preceding Saturday night, November 3, Dickens's instructions about the title pages of each volume: "I forgot [in a previous letter written earlier that evening], by the bye, to leave instructions respecting the title page. Let it stand thus | Oliver Twist | in 3 vols | By Charles Dickens author | of the 'Pickwick Papers' &c. (not Boz) | Bentley."[1] Bentley had no time then to change the title pages, as the work had been advertised for some days as being published on the seventh, and was to be subscribed by the trade on the sixth. As it was, he had to push the date of issue back to Friday the ninth. But by the following Friday, Bentley, following Dickens's instructions as relayed by Forster, had cancelled the title pages of all three volumes of most of the remaining copies and reissued them with new title pages, naming the author "Charles Dickens."[2] That day, November 16, 1838, is as good as any for approximating the birthday of modern authorship, the industrial-age authorship that allegedly died little more than a century later.

"Industrial-age authorship" terms a set of publishing and more general cultural conditions that coalesced during the first half of the nineteenth century in Britain, and shortly thereafter in other parts of Western Europe. It comprises an enormous range of manufacturing inventions that made printing cheaper and faster; improvements in transportation that enabled printed matter to be distributed from any print shop to outlets within a country and, by the 1850s, around the world; legal and governmental provisions that secured property in written materials to their originators and reduced the cost of purchasing such materials; increasing literacy and leisure time; industrial and cultural efforts to educate a workforce and shape it to the perceived needs of the state; the business of governing that depended upon writing as a principal activity (or barrier to activity); and various modes of publicity that stimulated the public's desire for more from the most celebrated figures of the age. By the 1860s reading was a common occupation of "civilized" peoples. The producers of that body of books, magazines, reports, advertisements, pamphlets, ballad and music sheets, and printed ephemera stood to gain, and sometimes did gain, substantial fortunes as a result of a print commerce that traversed classes, frontiers, national borders, and in notable cases even religious and philosophical identities. It became possible to produce writers of worldwide renown and commercial viability.

Why is "authorship" an important component of the print culture industry? Our current understanding of what Robert Darnton has dubbed "the communications circuit" locates particular figures who interact in a linear and circular fashion (see Figure 1 on p. 4).[3]

While Darnton's schematic diagram is conceptually useful, it is neither a description of the book trade at any historical period nor a pattern of the interactive influences among the various players.[4] For instance, "Intellectual Influences," "Economic and Social" conditions, and "Political and Legal Sanctions" were not just contexts for authors and publishers; they were often the impelling forces readjusting the influence and relationships among all the print participants. To comprehend the situation when Dickens, in the 1830s, tried to become an "author," we must briefly and broadly sketch how these interactive elements in the communications circuit developed historically.

At various times since the widespread adoption in Western Europe and North America of printing from moveable type onto rag, plant, or later

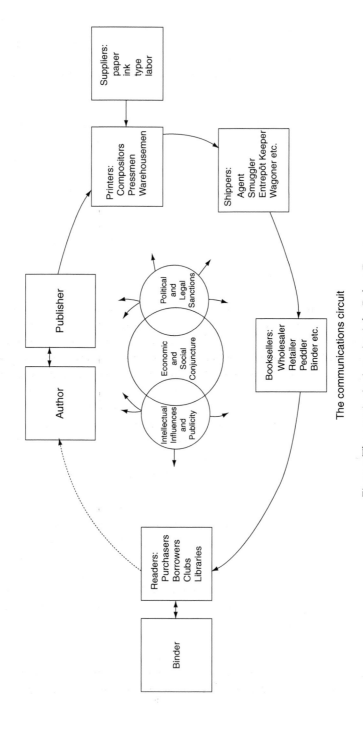

Figure 1 The communications circuit by Robert Darnton

wood-pulp paper and gathering the sheets into folios of one kind (e.g., newspapers, circulars) or another (e.g., bound books and magazines), each of the principal agents in Darnton's model has been thought of, in law, the trade, and by the general public, as the initiator and controller of the process of publishing. But the author became paramount only late in the history of Western print culture.[5] A basis for the whole communications circuit is some form of legal enablement, usually a right to print and sell copies. British copyright has been historically based on four principles: royal prerogative, propriety, property, and public benefit. The priorities and status of these principles have shifted over the centuries, and sometimes one interest has combined with another, while at other times they have collided. The earliest permissions to print copies of texts (e.g., royal proclamations and statutes, bibles) were granted by the throne, sometimes to recognize or seal political and religious alliances. These might establish very profitable monopolies – the right to produce almanacs was a cash cow for centuries. Early royal printing licenses were held at the monarch's pleasure and could be inherited, reassigned, or sold in reversion at the death of the current holder. By the eighteenth century such privileges in effect became a property of the licensee and his heirs, something that could be sold by one proprietor to others in shares or alternative arrangements. After the Civil War, while some older royal patents continued in force, few significant new ones were granted. Almanacs became a principal part of the English Stock of the Stationers' Company, yielding annual profits for the booksellers who shared in the reversion to the company of many print monopolies instigated by the Crown. Authors, however, had no particular standing in these matters.

Various commentators on copyright have stressed some principles more than others, and tracked the entangled relations among them when practiced by the trade, interpreted by the courts, amended by Acts of Parliament, influenced by intellectual, political, and commercial developments at home and abroad, and evaded by all sorts of blatant or ingenious subterfuges. By Dickens's time, as John Feather, one of the principal historians of British copyright, puts it, "British copyright law was thoroughly unsatisfactory. The law had always lagged behind practice, but now there was an accumulation of statute, precedent, trade practice and cultural assumptions which was becoming extremely difficult to use at all."[6]

While Dickens didn't know the detailed history of British copyright, that history impacted everything he did as a writer. Royal Letters Patent in the Henrician and Tudor period granted privileges to the book trade so that "essential" texts (e.g., religious, school, and law books, important scholarly treatises) could remain available. During Queen Mary's reign, in May 1557, the old guild of text writers and scriveners was reconstituted as the Stationers' Company. This organization of book producers, so named because for centuries they had established places of business, "stations," around the precincts of St. Paul's Cathedral, received from the Queen a virtual monopoly over printing throughout the reign. (Certain other bodies, such as the universities of Oxford and Cambridge, obtained special privileges outside this arrangement.) Elizabeth I confirmed this monopoly. But the book trade recognized that such royal patents protected only a small (though profitable) minority of titles being published. So in 1559 Elizabeth issued a set of Injunctions that delegated to the Stationers' Company authority to see that all titles were properly licensed and permitted to be printed because they did not offend against the state or its agents. As an article in the *Westminster Review* in January 1836 explained, "The monopoly granted by the Crown to the Stationers' Company, was made the instrument of exercising an absolute authority over the press through the extraordinary jurisdiction of the Star-Chamber, from the incorporation of the company in 1556 [*sic*, for 1557], to the year 1640 [*sic*, for 1641] when the Star-Chamber was abolished."[7] This summary simplifies and overstates the connection between Star Chamber and the Stationers' Company, but on occasions it or the Privy Council called upon the master and wardens of the Company to enforce state policies. The Stationers' Company was by its Charter "to make search whenever it shall please them in any place."[8] In effect, then, this book trade guild might perform the function of censor (legally vested in the Privy Council, Star Chamber, Bishops of the Established Church, and other state functionaries). It also in time became the registrar of property (the right to print and the printed product) and regulator of the trade (being empowered to list all presses and to nominate successors or leave the position vacant and thus reduce the number of presses, the competition, and the dispersal of printing shops beyond centralized authority's purview).

Initially printers and those who hired them (in a sense, publishers) dominated the Company. But within decades the owners of the right to print a copy, generally London booksellers who bought that right from whoever produced the text – author, previous owner, patent holder, theatrical company, etc. – gained the upper hand. Until the middle of the seventeenth century, booksellers continued to strengthen their control over the trade; authors had very little influence and almost no legal status.

Any member of the Stationers' Company who entered a title in the Company's register was effectively the owner of the right to copy that book – presumably for all time. And while just exactly what constituted a new book – e.g., an anthology of extracts, a condensation – might be disputed, the Company had the means of settling most disagreements.

Under James I the royal prerogative to license patents was extended not so often to classes of books as to individuals for particular titles, something that his predecessors had done as well. This was an early recognition that the originator of the book licensed for copying might have some claim to participate in publishing and its economic rewards, but there was no statute granting authors per se any legal standing in the print process. There were particular issues deriving from plays. Might copyright be granted to an edition that cleaned up a corrupt text printed with or without entry in the Stationers' Register, possibly from prompt texts or parts copied out for actors?[9] This issue touched on licensing requirements, but also in some cases on propriety, broadly conceived. A foul copy might reflect badly on the nominal author's reputation. John Heminge and Henry Condell published the 1623 Folio of Shakespeare's works to replace with a proper text the "diverse stolne, and surreptitious copies, maimed, and deformed by the frauds and stealthes of iniurious imposters."[10] By the beginning of the seventeenth century, some authors were practically, if not statutorily, recognized as having some rights in what they wrote, and once that writing was transferred to a member of the Stationers' Company, the Company would police the copyright, protecting the member's property (the right to copy) against any illicit publication ("pirated edition"), and when necessary the reputation of the author.[11]

Up to the Civil War, penalties for issuing unacceptable books tended to be assessed against the publisher, copyright holder, and/or the printer, not the author. Having stationary premises, bulky machinery, apprentices, and stock, printer/publishers were easy to find and fine. A 1637 Star Chamber decree ordered that the author's name be provided as well as the publisher's, and in 1642 the Commons also considered requiring the publication of the author's name; but nothing much came of that order once war commenced. At its conclusion, all legislation of the interregnum lost its force, and the print trade found itself without clear authority. A 1662 Act compelled registration in the Stationers' books, but the Company's role in licensing publications was somewhat overshadowed by the surveillance of the newly created government office of Surveyor of the Press, which lasted only a short time, from 1663 to 1688. Again, largely what was at issue during these unsettled postwar years were the property rights of copyright owners (largely booksellers who were principals in the Stationers' Company) and the propriety and prerogative rights of the Crown and state. Authors subsisted as minor players in the communications circuit, except insofar as they produced works that might command attention and sales. (Milton, for his defense of the Commonwealth and regicide, almost was executed; his controversial writings kept booksellers interested in buying up his manuscripts, even though no one expected that a long poem glossing the first chapters of the Book of Genesis would generate income for centuries.)

By the end of the seventeenth century, two forces impelled change. The first was widespread opposition to the monopoly powers of the Stationers' Company, coming from many quarters. Even though there was general agreement that somebody had to prohibit certain kinds of publications, there was no general consensus that the Stationers' Company should be that somebody. In effect, the Company lost its monopolistic control over the print business by the 1690s, and thus booksellers had to figure out how to operate in a more unregulated market. They petitioned for, and eventually got, a new statute under Queen Anne that ostensibly reinforced their property rights. The second force derived from Lockean and post-Lockean theories of natural rights. An individual, John Locke reasoned, had a right to the products it made. It seemed clear that if a body could be punished for the products of its brain (in the case of heresy, for instance, when martyrs were burned at the stake), a body should also be rewarded for beneficial ideas. Several concepts useful to print culture play into this theory of natural law: the idea of an individual, useful in establishing contracts between a seller and a buyer; the idea of an originator with whom the right to copy (or, for the sake of propriety, to prevent print copying) first lodged, necessary to identify the chain of ownership from its start; the idea that an intellectual product was property that could be sold and bought; and, though it took another hundred years for this concept to gain primacy, the idea that such intellectual products might be important to the state and its subjects, who therefore had an interest in seeing that such products were encouraged, protected, and eventually released into the public domain (where they might be reproduced more cheaply than by the monopolists hitherto claiming exclusive right to copy).[12]

While it was not Locke's arguments that were the only or perhaps most important influence on MPs, in February of 1695 the Commons rejected a Bill renewing previous legislation essentially controlling the print industry through the Stationers' Company. Whereas until then the right to copy a text had been sutured to policing the content of publications, after February 1695 everything changed: no restrictions on numbers of printers, journeymen, or apprentices; no restrictions on the importation of books; no obligation to enter a title in the Stationers' Register; no guarantee that the courts would uphold the property rights of booksellers who had invested in copyrights; no pre-publication censorship. As John Feather summarizes the situation post-1695, "[m]uch of the superstructure of protection which the Stationers' Company had so carefully erected and so assiduously defended was swept away."[13]

It took another fifteen years to reconstitute the regulation of printed materials. The Act of 8 Anne c. 19, receiving royal assent on April 4, 1710, seemed to restore to the owners of copyright, if not to the Stationers' Company, some of their prior standing. Before this Act, according to the 1836 *Westminster Review* article, "it was usual to purchase from authors the perpetual copyright of their books, and assign the same from hand to hand for valuable consideration, and to make the same the subject of family settlements for the provision of wives and children."[14] But over the sixty-four years after the passage of 8 Anne, battles carried on in the courts contesting the meaning of statutes that had been drafted in the most ambiguous way (partly in order to pass the Bill, partly because it was assumed that trade practice would clarify meanings) snarled print culture and copyrights in red tape and conflicting legal opinions. The 1710 Bill started out as legislation protecting the rights of authors (for the first time) and encouraging publication of books useful and good. The final draft assumed that authors might have some rights and the public a stake: it was misleadingly and purposefully entitled the "Act for the Encouragement of Learning" to gain votes. But the Act of Anne made explicit only that owners of copyright in preexisting books would continue to hold exclusive right to copy them for twenty-one years, while new books duly registered would be protected for fourteen years, renewable upon re-registration for a second term of the same length. Thus books first published before or during 1710 would become freely available to any printer or bookseller/ stationer after 1731 in the first instance and 1738 in the second. What was nowhere explicitly addressed was whether any version of perpetual copy-right, either granted by royal patent or as a common-law right, was modified by the term limits imposed on owners' exclusive rights to copy.

That conflict between perpetual copyright and statutory copyright was fought out in the courts. But copy owners manipulated their property in other ways as well. The most powerful ones organized in "congers," associations of "trading booksellers" usually comprising six to eight persons (or firms), which attempted to impose their will on everything from ownership of copy (one could only sell to others in the conger) to marketing (naming the price and the shops where their books could be sold). By 1710 payment to authors for their works was a general practice, but the sums paid were small: Samuel Simmons gave Milton £20 for *Paradise Lost* and Jacob Tonson paid John Dryden the same sum for his version of *Troilus and Cressida*.[15] As the eighteenth century progressed, some authors, notably Alexander Pope, were assiduous in exerting their personal authority to dictate the terms of publication or non-publication of their works; and by the time of Dr. Johnson it is said that professional men of letters could live entirely on the sale of their writings. But this claim needs to be nuanced by three qualifications. First, there was still an extensive company of Grub Street hacks barely able to subsist by grinding out nonce materials; as Oliver Goldsmith complained, "It is the interest of the [bookseller] to allow as little for writing, and of the [author without patrons] to write as much as possible ... In these circumstances, the author bids adieu to fame, writes for bread, and for that only."[16] Second, writers continued to appeal, until well past mid-century, for patronage – at first from individuals, and then in collaboration with their publisher by raising a subscription for the work prior to its initiation or publication, a practice begun after the Civil War. Third, authors forged complex agreements through which they might, without necessarily bene-fiting from legal authority, establish to their apparent advantage relation-ships with producers of print copy. Samuel Richardson printed and sold his own writings; Pope surreptitiously entered into the book trade himself and frequently granted his publishers – for a high fee – only the right to copy a limited number of books for a limited time.[17] He also colluded with Edmund Curll to issue a "pirated" edition of his own letters, then sued Curll for violating Pope's copyright. The decision established in case law the author's right to grant or withhold permission to publish mater-ials, leading to the finding, still applicable in many countries, that copyright in unpublished materials belongs to the author and heirs in perpetuity, and is only converted into a statutory and limited right when the materials are first printed and published. That Pope was so successful asserting authorial rights in the absence of substantial support from natural, statutory, or case law also has to do with celebrity. In his day some authors mastered publicity, and were entertained lavishly by their booksellers at dinners and other festivities widely reported in the press, while satirical verses castigating the reputations of competing authors and editors further raised writers' visibility even as it sometimes destroyed their credibility. The use of copyright to protect reputation got a thorough workout in the Augustan age.

Scottish and Irish book dealers regularly printed works published either with or without proof of registry by British firms, especially after the term limits for copyrights allegedly expired beginning in the 1730s. Scottish law never adhered to the theory of perpetual copyright, and in attempting to enforce their property rights copy owners in Britain litigated time and time again against "piracies." The case for perpetual copyright rested on the Lockean basis that those rights were property deriving from the labor of its original creator (the author), which the state could not take away from its owner and heirs. The case for a limited, statutory right claimed that the 1710 Act overrode any formerly existing common-law right, an argument that dovetailed with the notion that all copyrights derived from the sovereign's power to create (a monopoly for instance), grant (patents are one example), or seize property, all of which belonged to the Crown.

After decades of conflicting, indecisive rulings, abortive Bills introduced into Parliament but never passed, trade practices that grew up and were enforced by print proprietors in the absence of certain guarantees of ownership, and the decision in 1769 by Lord Mansfield and his fellow judges in King's Bench that the Act of 1710 simply specified temporary protections for a common-law permanent right to copy, too many conflicting interests were involved for the uncertainty of perpetual versus statutory rights to continue. An Edinburgh bookseller, Alexander Donaldson, reprinted James Thomson's *Seasons*, the very book whose reprinting by Robert Taylor in defiance of the owner Andrew Millar's claimed perpetual rights had been quashed by King's Bench in 1769. In the light of that case Chancery granted the plaintiff, Thomas Becket, successor to Millar, an injunction preventing Donaldson from printing or selling his edition. Donaldson then appealed to the House of Lords.

In 1774 the twelve law Lords initially took the case. Lord Mansfield, whose irreplaceable library of personally annotated law books was burned down during the Gordon riots of 1780, an event Dickens both regrets and celebrates in *Barnaby Rudge*, recused himself throughout because he had rendered judgment in the 1769 case that nearly duplicated Donaldson's second attempt to cancel perpetual copyright. Eventually five questions were formulated. The Lords found seven to four that authors had a common-law perpetual copyright (that applied to works not yet published). But they also decided that the Act of Anne took it away, by a vote of six to five. Had Lord Mansfield voted, and voted consistent with his ruling two years previously, there would have been a tie. Moreover, on the next question, "Whether the Author of any literary Composition, or his assigns, had the sole Right of printing and publishing the same in perpetuity by the Common Law?" the vote was tied five to five, with two abstentions. Once these rather confusing decisions were reached, the rest of the Lords got into the act, eventually forcing a vote of the whole House in which twenty-two supported Donaldson (that is, that the Act of Anne cancelled perpetual copyright) and eleven supported Becket. Dr. Johnson thought "[t]he Judgement of the Lords was . . . legally and politically right," but the booksellers immediately petitioned the Commons to restore their property, that is, their copyrights.[18] Members of the trade not part of the cabal of major London firms – Scots and provincial booksellers for instance – opposed any legislation that would reestablish perpetual copyright, and their view prevailed.

This reorganized the communications circuit and the book trade in many ways, establishing over time the conditions for print circulation that obtained when Dickens began to write. John Feather summarizes the changes:

The opening up of the trade copies to all comers created a new trade in low-priced reprints, while the copy owners were forced to find new books to publish, and to exploit them to the full during the limited term of copyright which now existed. This gave authors a far stronger position *vis-à-vis* the trade, and enabled them to begin to make new demands. No longer satisfied with outright sales of their newly defined rights, authors began to look for profit-sharing arrangements, or even for income related to the number of copies sold. Out of this there emerged two recognizably modern groups: publishers and professional authors.[19]

These developments didn't happen overnight and were still nascent in the 1830s. During the intervening years, publishers and booksellers (more than authors) had a comparatively free run, and some of the great houses that continued well into the twentieth century gained pre-eminence, including Longman (founded 1724) and John Murray (1768) in London, and Constable (1795) and Blackwood (1804) in Edinburgh. Copyrights continued to be defined by 8 Anne, although practice and rulings had nibbled at marginal questions, such as, is an annotated edition of a copyright work, or an abridgement, eligible for statutory copyright? In these cases, the answer was "yes." Exactly the status of parodies, sequels, and other texts depending on, but differing from, a copyrighted work was not clear. It was these domestic "piracies" that aroused Dickens's wrath early on. The one change from the Act of Anne that Dickens could benefit from was an 1814 extension of the period of copyright from fourteen to twenty-eight years or the lifetime of the author, the first time the body of the author figured significantly in what had hitherto been legislation about the property right of the owner of "copy."

Against some interpretations of the concept of property, there was a countervailing pressure within the episteme of the Enlightenment and Romantic periods to grant primacy to the originating mind that produced a text, not the one that manufactured or sold it. Authors had gained acclaim, notoriety, and social influence under Anne; some advanced even further under the Hanoverians. As patronage declined, booksellers assumed some of its functions for established authors. Moreover, the notion that authors were inspired by higher powers gained widespread acceptance. And so, while there had been authors, of both sexes, printed and published for centuries, authorship began to take on more commercial connections, more drawing power, and more mystical access to sources.

A few writers transcended the need for publishers' patronage: Sir Walter Scott and Lord Byron most spectacularly, but to a lesser extent William Wordsworth and some of the political, philosophical, and scientific authorities of the age. While the most popular authors such as Thomas Campbell sold thousands of copies of each volume of poems, however, the religious societies gave out millions of copies of the Bible and denominational tracts. God's word may not have outsold *Don Juan* in any year, but it was present and read in many more homes than any other book. Probably second to scripture on domestic and library shelves was John Bunyan's *Pilgrim's Progress*.

For Victorian publishing, novelists, and Dickens in particular, it was Scott's history that dominated thinking about authorship. Scott, wanting to manage the production and distribution of his writings, entangled his authorial share of making printed matter with those of his printer, James Ballantyne and Sons, and his publisher, Archibald Constable. When the banking crisis of 1826 hit, credit seized up, London firms such as Hurst, Blackett collapsed, and the ripples spread to Scotland. Within a short time Scott's printer and publisher were both insolvent, and Scott escaped bankruptcy by pledging to write his way out of the accumulated debts of all parties. While he might have been, at the time, the most popular writer in Europe, authorship did not grant him exemption from the consequences of a perilous marketplace. It did, however, involve him and his agents in devising new ways to "work" old copyrights (through collected editions – with revised texts, notes, and in some cases illustrations – that were eligible for separate copyright) in order to make the back stock yield income as well as the new stories. The author, in Scott's case, functioned as a publisher as well, devising strategies for marketing his wares. Among other things, he composed prefaces that explained the origin of his novels and why they were grouped and sequenced. After the fact, in other words, and partly to sell collected editions, he scripted a narrative of his productions.

Scott's ambition exceeded the boundaries of authorship as it was articulated in 1769 by Lord Mansfield, deciding *Millar* v. *Taylor*.[20] There Mansfield expressed his belief that "by the common law an author is intitled [*sic*] to the copy of his own work, until it has been once printed and published by his authority" (p. 91). Moreover, an author should have the right to prevent another from using his name without his consent; to choose the time and manner of publication, or to refuse publication; to select the person to whom he will entrust "the accuracy and neatness of the impression," and "in whose honesty he would confide" (p. 94). And he should have the authority to prevent unauthorized additions to his text and to be able to amend faulty editions. Authors, in other words, had rights over their text, name, and reputation, but not necessarily any power over the printer or publisher once those disseminators of the author's copy were chosen.[21] Printers might decide the format, styling, print run, publicity, timing of release and reprints, and most manufacturing and accounting matters without any consultation with the author. Mansfield recognized that after first publication "the author is no more master of his name, he has no controul over the correctness of his work." For this and many other reasons, Mansfield thought it "just and fit, to protect the copy after the publication" (p. 94). His views continued, especially for conservative theorists and copy holders, to define authorship until the end of the Georgian era, but few concessions were granted to the author to "protect the copy after the publication." Dickens was fiercely to contest these limitations, from early on in his writing life.

By the close of the Revolutionary wars, the status of copyright in those other countries where it existed at all was often limited, confusing, and sometimes contradictory. Until 1793 in France the King controlled all licensing of copies; copyright was a privilege, a right first created by royal patronage and then regulated by "social concession," that is, the laws regarding those rights passed by Parlement.[22] Yet prohibitions of copyright were evaded by printers, distributors, and booksellers throughout the reigns of Louis XV and XVI. Once the Republic was proclaimed, all previous laws were cancelled. The Assembly on July 19, 1793 rectified this situation by privileging the author, who was granted copyright through his lifetime and for ten years thereafter in all the territories of France, whether that author was a citizen of France or elsewhere, resident or not. Spain, under French control for a few years, followed suit. Post-1815, the German Confederation consisted of the eleven divisions of the Austrian Empire, the six of Prussia, and thirty-nine other kingdoms, duchies, principalities, and free cities: consequently there was no encompassing intellectual property act until 1870, after unification. Similarly, Italy was so divided among remnants of French, Holy Roman, and Austrian empires that there was no national copyright until 1865.

Belgium, gaining independence from the Netherlands in 1830, profited mightily from having no laws regulating copy produced in other countries. Belgian piracies of French books infuriated France for decades. "Books which under the restoration sold 4,000 copies," Balzac complained in the *Chronique de Paris*, "do not sell more than 1,000, and of those that heretofore sold 1,000, not 300 can be disposed of." Why? "Because," the *Athenaeum* explained to its readers in January of 1837, "all these works are reprinted in Belgium. Germany, England, America, the Colonies, the whole world, except France itself (and hundreds of copies are sold even there), are thence supplied. We are told that the trade is so profitable, and carried on so extensively, that the Belgian Government would not dare to become parties" to any international copyright treaty.[23] Even though King Leopold, cousin-in-law and uncle of Queen Victoria, appealed to his adopted countrymen to respect others' copyrights, he lost out to the entrepreneurial energies of his subjects.[24]

Like France, the United States disposed of its inherited intellectual property laws when it overthrew the monarchy. Thereafter, in the federal Constitution of 1788, Congress was invested with the power "to promote the progress of science and useful arts, by securing for limited times to authors and inventors, the exclusive right to their respective writings and discoveries." In a 1790 Act, Congress secured to the author and his assigns exclusive right of publishing for fourteen years, renewable for a second term of the same extent if the author were living then. The Act of 1831 extended the first term to twenty-eight years, with an extension for another fourteen available to the author or, if dead, to his assigns. But these Acts applied only to US citizens. No foreign authors had any rights in the USA. And no Act prevented American citizens from printing works copyrighted in other countries or exporting books across the border to Canada, which tried unsuccessfully to keep out the competition, whether from American presses or French ones. There was some activity in Britain and France in 1837 to reconsider copyright legislation, especially – for Britain – because the lack of reciprocal protections in the USA and UK was injurious alike to both. A French Commission actually offered a law prohibiting the copying in France of any work to which the foreign author objected, so long as a similar provision obtained in the author's country.[25] And C. E. Poulett Thomson, a Manchester Whig MP and President of the Board of Trade, managed in 1838 to push through Parliament a Bill authorizing the government to provide British copyright to foreigners in cases where the foreign author's country provided reciprocal protection for British authors. But all such revisions, including ones proposed by Prussia to the German Diet and Thomas Noon Talfourd's 1837 Commons Bill to extend copyrights to sixty years beyond the author's lifetime, failed either to pass or to be effectively enforced.[26]

So, in practice through the 1830s, though the cultural concept of authorship, and theories about the equity and appropriateness of rewarding writers, circulated throughout Western Europe and North America, most authors were still selling their copyrights outright to publishers for small sums, and getting nothing for large sales or reprints. Few had the clout to insist on sharing in the revenue from their writings; and those who did were often suspicious of publishers' accounts, which much like the balance sheets of film companies in the twentieth century, seemed to go long on expenses and very short on net profits. There was increasingly, from many quarters, and for many reasons, the sense that authors should be major players in the book trade. As it became larger and more profitable, the justice of authors' claims to share in the prosperity received more and more assent, even from conservative legal theorists who anchored their reasoning to the concept of property.[27]

When Dickens came of age in the 1820s – he was fourteen when the banking crisis that wiped out Scott occurred – multinational copyright was virtually unknown, and in Britain "authorship" was a peculiarly unstable and variegated concept. At one end of the spectrum, authors inspired by the Muses or Nature or God were, as Shelley claimed in the 1820s, the unacknowledged legislators of the world or, as Carlyle was to proclaim in the early 1840s, the inspired prophets who delivered the vision of what might and should be in a renovated world.[28] But those notions of power held their own danger. Believing in the power of writers to mold public opinion and incite the people to action, repressive postwar governments threw writers into jail. Intent on eradicating the last vestiges of republican and secular sympathy, successive ministries believed that advocating for votes, democracy, citizens' rights, empathy for the poor, or criticizing the State, the monarch, or the Church, or proposing any limits on the power of Parliament, the Crown, or property, was dangerous. In fact such repressive measures could also increase writers' capacity to influence events, whereas in ordinary circumstances most writers barely earned enough to rent cheap lodgings, wear second-hand clothes, and buy sufficient alcohol to drive their pens.

Jump forward to the middle of the twentieth century. By then it seemed to some sociologists and students of print culture that authors dominated the print industry. Best-selling writers could dictate the terms of their next book, its publicity campaign, the writer's lecture tour, the book's transformation into other media, its foreign translations and reprints, and even its interpretation and call for action. Critics with a different "take" on what the book might mean were admonished, corrected, or dismissed. At the same time, students of language and philosophy, among whom were William K. Wimsatt and Monroe K. Beardsley, observed that "the design or intention of the author is neither available nor desirable as a standard for judging the success of a work of literary art."[29] So many forces contributed to this conviction: for example, the Freudian notions of the unconscious and its semiotic eruptions; work in linguistics that led to conceptions of language as always embedding its history, and thus to the impossibility of delimiting meaning to a single intention; questions arising out of modern poetry – T. S. Eliot for instance – about the "intention" behind quoting or alluding to prior works; the ways in which particular texts were transformed by such publishing-house editors as Maxwell Perkins; the success of adaptations that brought out some themes and characters, while suppressing others, for alternative media (think of 1939's two great film adaptations, *Gone With the Wind* and *The Wizard of Oz*); the very formats in which books were issued, Alfred Knopf standing for impeccable cultural distinction while Faulkner's paperback editions had, until well after he won the Nobel Prize, lurid low-brow covers marketing him as a "poor man's Erskine Caldwell"; and the alternative readings generated by translations into the language and history of other cultures.[30]

In the late 1960s two French theoreticians in particular discussed the death of the author – at about the same time that God's obituary was published. Some theologians mourned the loss of a spiritual consciousness and urged a turn away from materialism. Others saw in the growing secularism and sectarianism of postwar cultures a liberation, of many modes of worship and of the individual who might choose what to believe and practice, if anything. Celebrated in particular was freedom from the kinds of Judeo-Christian injunctions that had guided or shackled Western cultures. An analogous freeing of the individual from authority energized theoreticians of writing and reading.

The author whose obsequies were reported in this era was conceived of not only in the most Romantic of ways, as an inspired, prophetic transmitter of divine wisdom, but also in more ethnic or commercial conceptions as the historian of a culture or subculture, the transcriber of "real" life and speech, and when successful as the all-powerful CEO of print. Roland Barthes hailed the "death of the author" because it released the reader from the dictatorship of the author who supposedly controlled every aspect of his book's production, reception, and signification.[31] Barthes's obituary was fashioned in order to free him to read texts as he chose: "the birth of the reader must be at the cost of the death of the Author."[32] Foucault was less invested in the mortuary, more in locating historically and defining those revenant aspects of authorship – some inherent in linguistic formations themselves – that seemed to exercise control over the work's origin, unity, and "hidden sense pervading" the work even in the absence of a personalized and controlling author.[33] Whereas Barthes objected to giving the text an author and assigning to that person the power to impose and limit interpretation, Foucault was concerned to unpack the implications of connecting an author to a work. He argued that many manifestations of "authorship" inhere in the discourse about writing; the author is not the origin and creator of something new, but rather the product of writing. The name of the author signifies a discrete historical individual and a body of work assigned to that figure. Such an interpellation supplies a number of limit functions. For instance, it leads to including some works and excluding others (think of the disputes current today about Shakespeare's collaborations), and it encourages projecting onto the named author the responsibility for the work's unity, its pervasive hidden sense, and its connections to the author's life (and vice versa, as only those aspects of the author's life in concordance with the work receive attention). Thus by the 1960s "authors" were by some critics projected as having authority over their texts, whereas for Foucault those authorial functions were inherent in certain discursive formations. (We don't expect the teller of a legend or fairy tale to be personally in control of its origin and hidden sense, but we tend to believe that of authors of poetry, fiction, essays, drama, and some other kinds of works.) So while Barthes celebrated the birth of the reader over the corpse of the author, Foucault displaced the author onto linguistic and cultural functions, freeing the work from imposed biographical determinants. In different ways both Barthes and Foucault "killed" the author as a living entity, displacing that figure with the agency of individual readers and of language itself.

There never was such an author or such control, of course. Nor did either Barthes or Foucault put a date on the birth of this omnipotent "author," although Foucault deployed historical analysis whereas Barthes tended to rely more on a conceptual and reception-oriented methodology.[34] Scholars in subsequent decades have delved deeply into the question of how much authority a writer ever had, whether females could or did want to compete in the marketplace, how manuscript circulation may have instantiated more authorial control than print, and what it means to speak about "originality" or "plagiarism." In comparison to the status and agency of authors in previous centuries, nineteenth-century British writers of all kinds – scientists such as Charles Darwin, historians such as Thomas Babington Macaulay, poets such as Alfred, Lord Tennyson, and writers of imaginative fiction – did through a variety of means consolidate formidable cultural and economic agency. Writers, benefiting from improvements in the production of paper and printed materials, copyright legislation, steam transport that facilitated worldwide circulation, reductions in "knowledge taxes," increases in the percentage of literate subjects and in the quality of their literacy, court decisions and trade practices favorable to authors and book dealers, cheaper products sold in a variety of formats, international publicity, prodigious output, and the establishment of organizations that promulgated the author as a professional public servant, came to occupy a central place in Britain's domestic, colonial, and imperial spheres.[35] (There could hardly be a clearer instance of this than the career of Benjamin Disraeli, who wrote novels both before and after he served as Prime Minister.) The development of the "industrial-age author" occurred first in Britain, and first with men, but authors of other nationalities, and women, used British precedents whenever they could to strengthen their own position within print culture.

II

This book tells a story about the hit-and-miss, trial-and-error beginning of an authorial power that would both fuel and stand up to capitalist material and cultural production during the heyday of British industrialism, and that would eventually extend its powers and benefits to writers around the world. The story centers on Charles Dickens. He was, it can be argued, the first to discover and exploit those Victorian developments that conduced to the creation of an identity as author centered in and managed by a writer. Certainly there had been writers paid for their work previously. On rare occasions they were able to supervise the translation of their manuscripts into type inked and pressed into paper, to control the circulation of those printed sheets, and to be famous in their lifetime as the authors of those texts. But as a review of publishing and copyright history demonstrates, more often writers were part of a production sequence that circumscribed their autonomy and oftentimes concealed their participation in that production.[36] Dickens and his fellow authors and successors aimed to do what Michel Foucault identified in 1971 as the distinguishing characteristics of "authors": "answer for the unity" of their books, display "the hidden sense pervading their work," and reveal "the real story that gave birth to their writings." I will argue that in the Victorian period, and paradigmatically in the career of Charles Dickens, we see the formation of what Foucault was to call the "author function": the personalized "he who implants, into the troublesome language of fiction, its unities, its coherence, its links with reality."[37]

For well over a hundred years, Dickens has with considerable success controlled how we read him. In the manuscripts and biographical materials John Forster preserved, in the thousands of letters that the Pilgrim editors have annotated, even in the memoirs of Dickens's agents, publishers, family, and friends, he has to a rare degree fashioned his public image. He has become a prototype of the artist "wounded into art."[38] Dickens's servitude in a blacking warehouse when he was twelve and his parents were imprisoned for debt has often been taken to found not only Dickens's career but also all writers' careers, insofar as artists create out of a need to compensate for childhood traumas.[39] Contrary judgments – to the effect that Dickens did not have an unusually rough upbringing; that he was not always sympathetic to the poor or the middle class; that he could be authoritarian, arbitrary, and reactionary; that he does not in fact display many happy nuclear families; and that he could be murderously savage to his characters and his opponents – while known, are rarely subscribed to by critics or the general public.

Insofar as a "birth" of an "industrial-age" author takes place in the nineteenth century, the "birth" of another "industrial-age" author, the misshapen, unhappy monster of Victor Frankenstein's invention, might come to mind. And insofar as Mary Shelley's novel inscribes the terrible costs of having to remake oneself, to find a place in the world for one's misbegotten, alien, lonely, intelligent, and desiring corpus, Dickens's story is at many points not unlike the monster's. (*Frankenstein* was a major intertext for Dickens's last bildungsroman, *Great Expectations* – perhaps by 1860 he was far enough removed from his originary pains to be able to incorporate the distancing and critiquing effects of Shelley's prototype of the wounded author.) What Dickens does over his lifetime is not only discover the vocation of authorship and practice it with unprecedented success but also retrospectively write up the story of that discovery and that vocation, in ways that achieve several ends. First, he authorizes his status and knowledge. Second, he locates his success within himself more than within social, industrial, cultural, and educational conditions that conduced to, if they did not produce, that success. Third, he assimilates his own career not to paradigms of luck (that David Copperfield is born with a "lucky" caul turns out to be of doubtful value in his life) or family nurture (Josiah Bounderby in *Hard Times* unwrites his parents' support in his effort to represent himself as self-made), but to Protestant bourgeois paradigms showing how hard work leads to deserved success. And fourth, Dickens constructs authorship as an all-encompassing vocation. It implies mastery over every aspect of the production and circulation of his writings, control over his public and private images, the legal right to determine where and how his work will appear, authority over the ways in which it will be received, and management over the corpus of writings even after his own death. Moreover, this control is not simply a fantasy, however much it is projected by Dickens in his fictions of authorship; it is also an achieved fact, a domination of the discourse of Dickens that in some ways has yet to be relaxed. Dickens not only wrote, he wrote himself.

This volume can only begin the tale. It focuses on Dickens's earliest decade as a writer, and on his inability to decide on, characterize, exploit, or suppress pseudonyms in favor of his own patronym. The narrative must juggle five elements. We need to attend to Dickens's chronological development from ambitious but aimless adolescent to the world's most celebrated living author. Simultaneously, we must look at the formative moments in this progress retrospectively, from the perspectives provided by the versions Dickens inscribed and promulgated about earlier experiences. His lived experience and his public accounts of that experience differ in important ways that indicate his fashioning of a writerly identity. Next, we need to see both the life lived forward and the life written retrospectively in the context of the options available to Dickens through his cultural inheritance and historical moment. For he not only selected from prior models of authorship, he also adapted them to the rapidly changing conditions of mid-nineteenth-century printing, publishing, and

literary consumption. Fourth, Dickens's adaptation of preceding authorial self-inventions included absorbing, rewriting, and effacing the texts
that shaped his imagination and conception of a writer. As much as he
credits earlier writers' influence, he also sometimes suppresses his indebtedness. And fifth, in his fictions Dickens projects all kinds of conditions
and outcomes for authorship. Many of them, in the early portion of his
career which this book studies, were trajectories to be laughed at and
avoided, even while (and because) they were analogs to his own provisional writing and writerly identities. Also, in each of these early works
Dickens inscribes anxieties about authorship that express both his personal concerns and those of his society about the power of words. In short,
to narrate the protracted parturition of the industrial-age author we must
look forward, backward, around, and into the fictions simultaneously.

The first chapter ponders the indeterminacy of Dickens's authorial
beginnings. Most lower-middle- and working-class children entered the
workforce in early adolescence. But after his blacking warehouse employment, Dickens gained some additional schooling and did not hold down a
regular job until he was fifteen. He came of age at a time when writing was
a central occupation of the industrial era: writers inscribed everything
from Parliamentary debates to instruction manuals, from business orders
to valentines, from legal documents to journalism, and from editions of
classical texts and anthologized extracts of standard literature to inexpensive tracts and penny dreadfuls. The cultivation of literacy was a central
educational aim throughout the century.[40] The written word, it could be
argued, was as important to the governance of the British Empire as its
army and industrial prowess, its naval and merchant marine fleets, its
colonization and its trade. That all of Dickens's early choices – law,
theater, reporting, transcription, and writing sketches – were centered in
print culture may partly be owing to his father's elocutionary influence.
But also, given his limited education and social background, opportunities for doing something with writing within a metropolis were abundant
and entry was not difficult. What was hard for Dickens was discerning
which might be the most promising outlets for talents he was barely aware
he might possess. This chapter closes with meditations on the pseudonym
that Dickens adopts for some of his early periodical pieces: Boz.

Continuing the history of Boz, Chapter 2 studies the issues involved in
Dickens's formation of nominative and narratorial identity. As "Boz" he
found increasing public and commercial receptivity to brief sketches
of scenes and characters he was observing in lower-middle-class circles
and was adapting from popular illustrated urban fiction and demotic

pantomime, comedy, and farce. What it meant for Dickens to write pseudonymously, how "Boz" both shaped and threatened to restrict his creativity and audience, how he managed to produce narrative out of apparently dead beginnings and ends, and what he feared could be the dead ends of his beginnings, comprise the subjects of this chapter. The "birth" of Boz occurred multiple times, in multiple personations and impersonations, until it climaxed in the exceptionally successful republication of his journalistic fiction in three illustrated volumes of *Sketches by Boz*.

Chapter 3 tracks the evolution of "Boz" from author to editor, with its consequent apparent distancing of the writer from his materials. *The Pickwick Papers* was initiated with very limited input from Dickens, who as Boz claimed to be editing the posthumous papers of the club. From the outset Boz's serial anatomized and critiqued the locutionary and elocutionary protocols of the day. Finding a way to get beyond stereotypical characters and redactions of the words and ideas of others was the challenge Dickens overcame brilliantly. But this success threatened to be brief, snatched away by others who could imitate his style under pen names approximating his own. And given the circumstances under which he began this publishing venture, his control over its publication rights depended almost entirely on the benevolence of others. While Chapman and Hall released the first volume edition of *Pickwick Papers* under the name of Charles Dickens, the author was in fact as much the recipient of charity as of contractual obligation for his remuneration, and the press continued to denominate the author of *Sketches* and *Pickwick* as Boz.

That contractual relationship with Boz – a more commercially viable name than Charles Dickens – bound the author to editing and writing multiple new works simultaneously. Escaping into pseudonyms or anonymity to burst these legal bonds proved unsatisfactory in many ways. The fourth chapter explores Dickens's fraught relationship with the publisher Richard Bentley and with thefts of identity that make the titular character of his next book, *Oliver Twist*, an illegitimate orphan and the product of others' writing about him. Oliver is a boy and story offered for sale over and over, then stolen, and then reclaimed. The Bentley part is a familiar one, but in this retelling the aspect investigated is less the contractual disputes than the conflicting ways Dickens imagined himself as playwright, journalist, editor, author, and novelist during the period 1837–39, and imagined that his success as a writer might be temporary, reversible, and never under his control or voice. Even after all the acclaim for his *Sketches*, *Pickwick*, and early episodes of *Oliver*, Dickens was not certain that he could sustain a career as editor or author. He was only certain that he had not successfully controlled his productions or his identity, and he was determined to do so in the future, enlisting the very imperfect mechanisms of copyright law and his increasing public fame and commercial value to support his efforts. Moreover, European efforts to internationalize copyright and Talfourd's successive, unsuccessful efforts to amend British national copyright raised the consciousness of both print and general culture about these issues. Dickens engaged with these discussions years before his ill-fated advocacy for international copyright during his 1842 visit to the USA.

Charity and contracts do not provide the basis of authorship conceived as a vocation promoting public benefits. Dickens initiated his next serial with the notion of exposing the cruelty of Yorkshire schools. Through brilliant satire and humor, he mounted an attack on perversions of education, that fundamental building block of industrial literacy. Quickly, however, the novel, *Nicholas Nickleby*, took off on other forms of verbal culture: advertising, Parliamentary rhetorical evasions, sentimental "silver fork" fiction, dramatic adaptations from Britain's past and France's present, testamentary provisions as a way of controlling families, and finally financial accounts as an alternative basis for commercial and domestic relations. Now a family man supporting his wife, servants, sister-in-law, parents, and sometimes his siblings, Dickens had wrested a contractual authorial identity and attempted to stabilize, authenticate, and guarantee his brand name. But in life as in fiction such arrangements are vulnerable and in many ways inadequate to the emotional and imaginative as well as financial needs of an author. At the conclusion of *Nickleby*, Dickens tries to project an image of himself, rather than Boz, as the writer of stories, and to affirm the faithfulness of his relationship with his readers, a relationship that might be implicitly commercial but that exceeds purely monetary value.

So, in Chapter 6, we revisit Dickens's decision to return to editing, not writing. He proposes to publish stories, some by himself, some by others, stories that he will then organize and insert in a periodical partly his own, but one in which illustrations dropped into the text of the weekly parts will also be a strong selling feature. Dickens imagines himself as conductor of a complex organization of writers, artists, printers, publishers, distributors, and readers. This is an identity as editor very much enlarged over what he could do editing *Bentley's Miscellany*. In that instance his publisher was also an interfering co-editor who exercised the right to commission and insert stories by other authors, to dock

Dickens's authorial pay when he came up short on his monthly contributions, and to insist that the columns Dickens more or less filled in the *Miscellany* could not be counted as the novels he was contracted to supply in addition to his editorial responsibilities. In 1840 Dickens wanted "editor" to be proprietor, publisher, printer (insofar as he specified the location of the illustrations within the text and vigilantly proofed each issue), master of ceremonies introducing the stories, and investor profiting from the labors of many others. This fantasy was exposed as a fantasy even before *Master Humphrey's Clock* commenced publication. The wrestles Dickens had with his collaborators and most of all with his own writerly identity during the twenty months that the *Clock* ticked instance once again that he had no certain vocation, limited authorial authority, ambiguous and confusing public identities, and inconsistently effective strategies and tactics for making the success of his previous writing and his various narratorial and writerly instantiations pay. The narratives generated out of death that had been a hallmark of his career thus far climax in Nell's trajectory. Simultaneously Dickens's earlier projections of narratorial identity as the middle-aged perambulating bachelor "Boz" devolve into an old man and his aged friends who gather by the clock at night to read their and others' stories.

Chapter 7 explores the ways in which Dickens cancels his career to date. He breaks decisively with Bentley, winds up the anonymous commissions for Chapman and Hall, dispenses with Henry Colburn's project to raise money for the family of his deceased first publisher, John Macrone, and signs no Agreements for writing or editing of any kind. The fictions of an editorial "we" are critiqued and deconstructed, both within the surrounding frame of the clock society and within the narrative of the Gordon riots. The hidden pasts that families uncover in prior stories are disclosed in the course of *Barnaby Rudge*, but in ways that lead as often to dead ends as to a renovated society. The fundamental comedic plot of a rising generation overthrowing a declining older one is seriously disrupted. The empathetic *flâneur* of *Sketches* morphs into a murderous outcast haunting streets and houses. And in the end, Dickens shuts down the *Clock*, pleading (quite legitimately) exhaustion; propounds no future written work of any kind; and pledges his very life to his publishers for a chance to break free.

For Dickens in 1841, although lionized throughout the United Kingdom, in parts of Europe, and in North America, authorship is still an empty promise of a vocation. That's not the way Dickens taught his generation, and all later ones, to read his history. He rewrote it in retrospect and prospect, to fashion himself as born to be a writer. We will see how the greatest story Dickens ever told, that of his own life not as he lived it but as he fashioned it for public consumption, became the story of how authors are born and bred to writing in the industrial era. But in this retelling, we can only fully revisit the earliest years of his career.

III

When Dickens started out in life, he had no clear plan. Having spent portions of his twelfth and thirteenth years at the menial task of tying labels on bottles of shoe-blacking, he determined to establish himself in some more exalted position, and thought that education was the key to advancement.[41] The lessons he learned working for his distant cousin George (aka James) Lamert (or Lamerte) were manifold: he intensely disliked associating with lower-class colleagues, he found the wages insufficient to sustain even a minimal standard of living, and he felt humiliated at being on display behind the window of the shop. Or so he says in an autobiographical account he wrote around 1847 after he became famous and, for the first time, was beginning to earn a comfortable income.[42] He gave that autobiography to John Forster, the man already chosen to be the official biographer although Dickens was only in his mid-thirties. This account was revealed to Dickens's family and the public for the first time in 1871, when the initial volume of Forster's three-volume *Life of Charles Dickens* was published.[43] Although suppressed during his lifetime, this autobiographical fragment, recalling his days in the blacking warehouse, was part of a concerted, lifelong effort by Dickens to understand, and in so doing inscribe and promulgate, a narrative about how authors are born. To read its information back into a more "objective" account of Dickens's development is to employ fabricated evidence as "factual" and to engage in circular reasoning: because Dickens said this, retrospectively and for eventual public consumption, about his past, we should take this information as the truth about his history. Nonetheless, it seems clear from many kinds of evidence, including his suppression of the blacking warehouse humiliation and possibly his empathy for working-class children, that his employment at Warren's Blacking was not the kind of job he wanted to continue or the sort of career-beginning he felt appropriate – except as a traumatic event impelling him to other kinds of work. He wrote many spoofs of Warren's famous advertising jingles and referred humorously to the warehouse often in his early writing, even in *David Copperfield* locating the Peggottys and Micawbers in a tumbledown pub across the street from the Hungerford Stairs blacking factory before they embark for Australia. Still, Dickens clearly felt resentment about being abandoned to demeaning industrial labor by his parents. Since in *Copperfield* (1849–50) Dickens rewrites his childhood, he may have to some degree discharged his anger and reconsidered the trauma in those pages. David learns that all the abuses and neglect he experienced in childhood have made him what he is, a loved and successful author. Failure establishes the grounds for success.[44]

When Dickens left the blacking warehouse, he attended Wellington House Academy, in Mornington Place, as a day boy. He believed that his mother, though she had sometimes taught him, "was warm" for his remaining at work and that it was due to his father that he received further education instead.[45] The quality of that education is uncertain: William Jones, the Welsh headmaster, bears some resemblance, in ignorance and sadism, to Mr. Squeers, headmaster of Dotheboys School in *Nicholas Nickleby*. "[B]y far the most ignorant man I have ever had the pleasure to know," Dickens told the guests at the Warehousemen and Clerks' Schools fourth anniversary dinner in 1857, "whose business it was to make as much out of us and to put as little into us as possible."[46] Although in 1838 Dickens told a German biographer that he finished his education "at a good school in London," the extent of Dickens's exposure to Latin or any other formal learning is debatable.[47] He recalled lighter aspects of those schooldays – friends, pets, teachers – in *Copperfield* and most concertedly in "Our School," published in the October 11, 1851 issue of *Household Words*. In that article Dickens depicts himself as a promising lad who won prizes for translating Virgil and who attained the "eminent position of first boy."[48] One of his schoolfellows recalled that Dickens dressed very neatly and held his head high "like a gentleman's son, rather aristocratic than otherwise."[49] After Dickens's death in 1870, two of his former schoolmates, writing to Forster, confirmed and repositioned Dickens within the Wellington House community. The whole article is "very mythical in many respects," one fellow graduate reported, "more especially in the compliment [Dickens] pays in it to himself."[50] He was remembered as a small boy of high spirits, somewhat smart in dress, who wrote "small tales" and led amateur theatricals, including a memorable production of *The Miller and His Men*. (The last scene, when the mill blows up, was a favorite of the boys.) But there was nothing remarkable about Dickens as a "genius." "I cannot recall anything that then indicated he would hereafter become a literary celebrity," one classmate told Forster; and the other said "his wonderful knowledge and command of the English language must have been acquired by long and patient study after leaving his last school."[51] While enrolled, Dickens began his journalistic career by providing "penny-a-line stuff" for his father and the press more generally.[52]

At the age of fifteen, in May 1827, Dickens entered the employ of attorneys Ellis and Blackmore, in Gray's Inn. His mother, who knew the junior partner, Mr. Edward Blackmore, probably arranged this opportunity. But many years later Dickens told Wilkie Collins that the solicitor was "a friend of my father's."[53] (The rewriting of his parents' lives to rehabilitate his father and blame his mother occurs in the 1840s, but while in the autobiographical fragment he judges his mother harshly, it was she whom he entrusted with the tasks of checking out potential holiday housing, staying with Catherine during her confinements, and in general making accommodations, temporary or permanent, attractive and homey "at a much less expence than I could.")[54] While a great favorite at the office, Dickens wasn't a particularly assiduous junior clerk. He dropped cherry stones from a second floor window onto the hats of passers-by; made colored drawings on office time; ran errands to many of the more than 150 public offices connected to the law; and spent his shillings on half-price theaters, cider cellars, and metropolitan rambles.[55] According to Frederic G. Kitton, he and another clerk named Potter sometimes even took small roles in nearby minor theater productions.[56] Unlike Uriah Heep, he did not devote solitary evenings to swotting up Tidd's *Practice*,[57] and though he seemed genial enough he hardly distinguished himself or inspired his employers to sponsor his legal career. He left the law, he told Collins decades later, because he "didn't much like it."[58]

John Dickens may have set his son a professional example when, after retiring from the Navy Pay Office in March 1825, he taught himself Gurney's shorthand and joined the *British Press* as a reporter. The paper failed seventeen months later, at the end of October 1826. Several of Dickens's maternal relatives were also reporters, and one, John Henry Barrow, a barrister in Gray's Inn, started in 1828 a rival to Hansard, recorder of proceedings in Parliament, called the *Mirror of Parliament*. Dickens did himself, with Barrow's help, also study and master Gurney's stenographic system; in *Copperfield* that mastery is represented as an heroic feat achieved by the young protagonist who is determined to earn a respectable living so he can marry his love, left destitute after the sudden death of her father.

Dickens's own progress was much less single-minded.[59] From 1827 to 1835 he shifted from job to job. After a brief stint clerking in Charles Molloy's law office following his defection from Ellis and Blackmore in

November 1828, he perfected his skill in transcribing Parliamentary oratory until he was the most accurate and speedy stenographer in Parliament. Like recording depositions and testimony or acting, this too was a way of learning how to ventriloquize others' words. The rhetoric of civic discourse permeated Dickens's imagination, while the histrionics of Parliamentary debate, like the histrionics of the low theaters, fitfully aroused his critical and humorous faculties. By 1829 Dickens was periodically employed as a freelance shorthand writer at the Consistory Court of Doctors' Commons (a site memorably represented in *David Copperfield*); a few years later, he advanced to a job transcribing Parliamentary debates for his maternal uncle's paper, the *Mirror of Parliament*, just when politicians were agitated over impending electoral reform.[60] In that same year, 1831, however, he also contemplated emigrating to British Guiana.[61] In 1834, through the influence of a friend, he obtained a position at the liberal, Whig-owned *Morning Chronicle*, second only to *The Times* in circulation. The editor, John Black, sent Dickens out to cover events throughout Britain; the cub reporter relished the coach races home to beat competitors into print. In October of that year, Dickens began contributing theater reviews and sketches, first to the daily *Morning Chronicle*, and from January 1835 also to the tri-weekly offshoot, the *Evening Chronicle*, edited by Dickens's future father-in-law George Hogarth.

Thus by 1833, when he was twenty-one, Dickens might have picked among several careers: newspaper journalism, leading perhaps to a career as editor, editorialist, and political spokesperson, possibly even an MP for a metropolitan constituency; theater, in which he would write, act, direct, or produce plays and musical entertainments; or more general writing, of kinds, subjects, and genres not yet clear. He had experience as a shorthand reporter at Doctors' Commons, had provided tips and brief accounts of accidents, fires, and police reports for his father (for which Dickens did, in fact, get paid a penny per printed line if the story got published), had read good literature and some mild pornography at the British Museum, and kept looking about him for opportunities. He also wrote light verses, some of them extolling Warren's Jet Blacking; was an entertaining guest at domestic parties; fell in love and was jilted; got up a few amateur theatricals for which he served as writer, producer, director, designer, and star; perused lots of magazines aimed at urban male youths; and in general had a pretty good time despite his family's financial instability and their need to provide for his siblings. The premium for boarding and educating the eldest, Frances Elizabeth ("Fanny"), at the Royal Academy of Music cost about 10 percent of John Dickens's income,[62] and there were five other children to provide for: Charles, Letitia Mary, Frederick William, Alfred Lamert, and Augustus. After Augustus's birth in 1827, the family was evicted from their home and Fanny had to withdraw from the Royal Academy. Charles's clerkships and his subsequent employment as a reporter at least covered most of his expenses.

At many times during these exploratory, rambling years, Dickens thought of becoming an actor. "I had been a writer when I was a mere Baby," he told Collins in his "first" statement of biographical "particulars" in 1856 – it was not his first – "and always an Actor from the same age."[63] Early in 1832, around his twentieth birthday, he scheduled an audition at Covent Garden Theatre. But at the appointed hour, he was "laid up" with "a terrible bad cold and an inflammation of the face."[64] He told the management he would apply again next season, but he never did so. The outcome suggests that he was not deeply invested in acting as a career.[65] While, on the contrary, it might be possible to read his funking the audition as a sign that he was overly invested, Dickens's iron determination to pursue whatever he wanted makes it unlikely that he was on this occasion just too shy or too anxious about failure to follow through. More plausible is the explanation that he just didn't want to do it. Maybe he didn't want to appear in ridiculous guises before the public; maybe, already, he didn't want to impersonate people in ways that would suppress his own identity; maybe he preferred to take his own way rather than being directed by someone else. So he drifted for another few years, aiming alternately at a legal career or one as a reporter.

When in 1832 Dickens began working as a Parliamentary reporter for the *True Sun*, a Radical evening paper, writing down in shorthand the debates he heard from up in the gallery, his fellow-stenographers were for the most part aiming for careers at the bar and if possible the consequent status of gentlemen.[66] Dickens told Collins in 1856 that his "calling" was "pursued by many clever men who were young at the Bar," a description that elevates a menial employment into a vocation and puts him in the company of "clever men."[67] Nevertheless, Dickens was not a gentleman, and though on at least one occasion his father in a baptismal register inscribed himself as a "Gentleman," probably could never be a gentleman, at least according to conservative definitions.[68] And he was so poor that he sought any kind of extra work, even shorthand transcription, during Parliamentary recesses. He did keep apart from his colleagues. James Grant, who knew Dickens when they worked together on the *Morning Chronicle*, says that as a reporter Dickens was "exceedingly reserved in his manners," and that even in 1835–36, after three years in Parliament, "his name was not generally known among the reporters in the gallery of the House of Commons." Nonetheless, in Grant's estimation "a more talented reporter" never existed.[69] "The important thing to realize about Dickens's choice of profession at this time," Kathryn Chittick reminds us, "is that he was above all ambitious, regardless of what form that ambition took."[70]

IV

During the Parliamentary recess in the summer of 1833, Dickens wrote a "tale," a prose version of a non-patent theater comedy about a fortune seeker and his disastrous attempt to curry favor with his rich relative. (Dickens was already canny enough to imagine the delights of an unearned inheritance, to critique the fantasy, and to adopt the register of humor to vent, bind, and disseminate the conflicting emotions engendered within and by the story.) In the summer of 1833, he dropped his "first effusion . . . stealthily one evening at twilight, with fear and trembling, into a dark letter-box, in a dark office, up a dark court in Fleet Street."[71] To it he may not have attached any name or address. If so, he could not readily receive editorial feedback, or payment, or name recognition, for this "tale."

This was not quite as quixotic an act as it sounds. The *Monthly Magazine*, like other periodicals in the days before the penny post, communicated with correspondents by printing cryptic rejoinders in the magazine. "The Editor's Letter-Box" at the front of the March 1833 issue tells "G. A." that he is "inexperienced, but possessed of some talent," and invites further samples of his "Views of Rural Life in Scotland." This is followed by a criticism: "He strives at too much effect." The next entry encourages another unsuccessful contributor: "T. E. M. is not quite up to the mark yet. He may, however, 'try again.'" These may not, in all cases, have been genuine communications; they might be "hooks" to encourage submissions. In any event, such entries cease to be a feature of the *Monthly* during the summer of 1833, when its ownership changed hands. The June issue indicates that in future editorial correspondence will be conducted privately, and thereafter the "Editor's Letter-Box" does not appear again until December, after the magazine had once again gained a new proprietor. Whether Dickens knew about this change in policy, whether he provided a real or feigned name, whether he supplied an address, we do not know.

Nor do we know why Dickens picked the *Monthly*. He may have thought of submitting to another journal, the *Metropolitan Magazine*.[72] The half-crown *Monthly* had been one of the respectable journals of the age but was going through a difficult period financially; the publisher Charles Tilt sold it for £300 to Captain J. B. Holland in October 1833.[73] So far as we know, at the time of his submission Dickens knew no one connected to the financial, editing, publishing, or circulating dimensions of the journal. We might presume that he looked for a response, if it were to come at all, by buying, or borrowing, copies, his heart sinking as each successive month passed without any communication or publication.

Apparently unbeknown to Dickens, the article was printed in the December 1833 issue. One early December day Dickens stopped by 186 Strand, the shop of booksellers and minor publishers Edward Chapman and William Hall, to buy a copy of the *Monthly* from Hall. And, as Dickens recounted the event in the 1847 preface to the Cheap Edition of *Pickwick Papers*, he was so moved by finding himself a published author his eyes teared as he read his printed tale in retirement away from the thoroughfares: "I walked down to Westminster Hall, and turned into it for half-an-hour, because my eyes were so dimmed with joy and pride, that they could not bear the street, and were not fit to be seen there" (p. 884).

There are many odd features of this account. At the time he penned a very different narrative of his situation to his friend Henry Kolle; we will read that in Chapter 2. The story Dickens tells to the public in 1847 seems a little overwrought – the tears and retirement are externalizations of the extreme pleasure and anxiety of being published. Other authors, on seeing their work in print, might celebrate with friends, but Dickens depicts himself as turning away from the streets, and walking into Westminster Hall – part of the Houses of Parliament where he served as a reporter. There is something about being published that requires him to retreat into the scene of his "calling" – the vocation that was paying the bills and introducing him to members of the governing class. Instead of bragging to the other reporters, however, he seeks to cultivate solitude and anonymity. It seems an odd proceeding, if one wants to be a writer, to rejoice privately upon learning that one has published anonymously. Why would Dickens, who was "ambitious," to use Chittick's word, and whose work was accepted without revision and published, feel impelled to hide from public scrutiny? Was there something about authorship that was shameful? Was the potential promise of authorship as a way of becoming rich and famous too potent, and perhaps illusory, for him to share it? Does the telling of this story in 1847, at the same time he was composing his autobiographical fragment and his best friend John Forster was recuperating Oliver Goldsmith's reputation in a new biography, invest the writer with a tender sensibility, conceal the egotism, emphasize his youth, and appeal to readers' sympathy for one so "green" and solitary that his success causes him tears and withdrawal? It may do all these things. It may register the complex of emotions writers might feel on such an auspicious occasion. Or it may be Dickens's own shaping of an authorial persona, coming after the financial and critical success of *Dombey and Son* (in which a neglected heir dies and a parentless boy is shipped off by his employer to die), and before *Copperfield* (in which a neglected boy lives and becomes a famous author).

Dickens's retrospective and touching representation of the author at his birth into print establishes his character – vulnerable, modest, proud of his achievement, surprised by it, and destined. Destined, because when Dickens tells this story he is informing his multitude of readers how he became a writer. For the upshot of the purchase of the December 1833 *Monthly* from Hall was that when Hall called on Dickens twenty-six months later, in February 1836, to propose a book, Dickens recognized Hall as the one who sold him his first printed piece, hailed this coincidence "as a good omen," and immediately got down to business (p. 884). Hall's re-emergence in Dickens's life he takes to be the sign that he was fated to become a writer.

However, that's a version of Dickens's early career, his version, and it leaves out a lot. The intervening years are at issue now, but we should note that nine days before Hall's visit Dickens had been told by somebody in Chapman and Hall's office to finish off two articles he owed to them for publication in their new monthly magazine, *The Library of Fiction*.[74] So Hall's appearance in Furnival's Inn in February 1836 wasn't quite the thunderclap of fate Dickens in 1847 presents it as being. However, it may have "felt" that way to Dickens in 1836 or in retrospect more than a decade later. The issue is not one about veracity but one about memory and creativity: how Dickens remembered his authorial beginnings and how he fashioned them for public consumption.

v

When Dickens looked around him in 1833, as we must now do, what virtues might anonymity conceivably have had for him? Writers suppress their names for a variety of reasons. Fear of the consequences motivates many writing on political, religious, and social topics during periods of unrest. Contrary to widespread belief, British law has not required that the author be identified for copyright purposes except for a brief period of time in the mid-seventeenth century (1637–62).[75] It was much easier, in time of trouble, to locate and prosecute those who produced and distributed the material product – they had apprentices, journeymen, leases on commercial premises, and inventory to seize. But even in relatively stable times, anonymity was the rule rather than the exception: James Raven estimates that nearly 70 percent of all novels published in the last thirty years of the eighteenth century were issued anonymously.[76] And in the nineteenth century, anonymity continued to be common throughout Europe.[77] "Many writers began their career in this way," Adrian Room observes, "believing that if what they wrote was worth reading, the public would buy it for its own sake, irrespective of whoever the author might be . . . But there is a snag. If your work has no name to it, how can the public obtain more if they want it?"[78]

Another reason some authors concealed their identity was to maintain a distinction between their "day job" and their books. Writing was not always considered a dignified occupation. "In truth," Walter Scott told his friend John Morritt in July 1814, chuckling over the rumor that Francis Jeffrey wrote *Waverley* to relieve the tedium of a transatlantic voyage, "I am not sure it would be considered quite decorous for me as a Clerk of Session to write novels[.] Judges being monks[,] clerks are a sort of lay-brethren from whom some solemnity of walk & conduct may be expected."[79] In a postscript Scott identified two other motives for concealing his identity: "I think an author may use his own discretion in giving or withholding his name. Harry Mackenzie never put his name in a title page till the last edition of his works . . . I gain . . . only the freedom of writing trifles with less personal responsibility and perhaps more frequently than I otherwise might do." Many other authors have exercised that same discretion, some of them in order to write in a less elevated genre or style or to publish more often.

Dickens's choice to submit anonymously, to a journal that published materials without attribution, may have been a casual, even thoughtless, one. Or he may have still wanted to preserve a wall between his material identity and his writerly one, in case he eventually opted for the law. In November 1834 he explained to the Steward of New Inn that although his "whole time is at present devoted to literary pursuits," he intended "entering at the bar, as soon as circumstances will enable me to do so."[80] It is unlikely Dickens chose anonymity because he had so many manuscripts in his desk that he feared overwhelming the public if they were all published under his name. Nor was he, at this stage of his life, submitting anonymously in order to test the legitimacy of editorial gate-keeping, as later authors have done. Indeed, whether in response to a call paid by Dickens or on their own initiative (in which case Dickens must have let them know somehow how to reach him), by December 10, 1833 the "Monthly people" had requested more papers. The point is that Dickens first published anonymously, and that choice reflects on the options available to him as an author in 1833 and on his motivations for and conceptions of a career as writer.

If amid all the emotions of seeing his story – though not his name – in print, Dickens felt that he might have a future publishing stories, the push into authorship was far from decisive. He kept his day jobs as a shorthand reporter for the *Mirror of Parliament* and the *True Sun* and joined the staff of Parliamentary reporters on one of the best newspapers, the *Morning Chronicle*, in August 1834. Moreover, and this is odd for an "ambitious" lad, Dickens went on submitting anonymously to the *Monthly*, which paid nothing, for another fourteen months. Between December 1833 and February 1835, Dickens had eight stories printed in the *Monthly Magazine* and one in *Bell's Weekly Magazine*, all unsigned.[81] He also wrote a one-act burletta, "Cross Purposes," "long before I was Boz."[82] For someone as impatient for fame as Dickens was, and as needy for money, this seems a curious proceeding, although he later told John Forster that he liked the distinction he earned in the reporters' galleries of Parliament and "didn't want money."[83] Moreover, as Chittick points out, these magazine tales were mentioned in some forty reviews, whereas the later "sketches," signed "Boz," got no notices.[84] Wouldn't an ambitious writer, once a story was reviewed, attach his name to it somehow, or at least attach it to the succeeding stories? Perhaps the calling of writer or journalist was still to Dickens ambiguous, slightly unsavory, smelling of Grub Street and shabby genteel life. That was the condition of London urban writers.[85] The great Romantic bards and critics were, for the most part, dead; those still living enjoyed sinecures providing income that supported their pens. Many would have scorned the notion of being a writer for hire.

Dickens was not wrong or preternaturally doubtful or excessively ambitious in worrying about what status he might achieve as an urban sketcher. Writing was for the majority who filled the pages of the periodicals and churned out novels in three volumes or verse in slender duodecimos and glossy annuals a hand-to-mouth, up-and-down, kind of living. Pierce Egan had in the 1820s commanded large sums and enjoyed the patronage of the king because of his knowledge about and depiction of London pleasures, but he and his imitators found the market for such wares much leaner in the 1830s. The decade has been described "as an interregnum" between Romanticism and Victorianism.[86] And while reporting on Parliament during the tumultuous days surrounding the reforms of the late 1820s and early 1830s taught Dickens a great deal about government, law, bureaucracy, and life, there was a general feeling that being a reporter was incompatible with the status of gentleman, the acquisition of wealth, or a reputation for respectability.[87]

VI

In August 1834, nine months after his initial submission, Dickens published his first piece – later designated a "sketch" rather than a "tale" – under a name. It was not his name, but rather the pseudonym "Boz," "the nickname for a pet child, a younger brother" (p. 886). Pseudonyms mark the author of a text in a variety of ways that conceal and reveal material identity. In Dickens's case, Kathryn Chittick speculates, it "distinguished his sketches from his work as a reporter in two ways. It kept the sketch-writer's fancy separate from the reporter's reputation for accuracy, and removed the sketch-writer from the ranks of anonymity."[88] Many eighteenth- and nineteenth-century books appeared with only an indication of the status of the writer on the title page: "By a Lady," "A Clergyman," "An American." These identificatory gestures often supplied some measure of authority to the text, though it was sometimes spurious authority. (For instance, "A Lady" was sometimes male, and an "American" actually a subject of the British Crown.) A minimal marker of authorial identity is an initial, such as the "A" with which Matthew Arnold signed himself on the title page of *The Strayed Reveller, and Other Poems* (1849). Authors played with this convention: the Scots physician David MacBeth Moir signed periodical articles with the Greek delta and Jonathan Swift used "T. R. D. J. S. D. O. P. I. I." = "The Reverend Doctor Jonathan Swift, Dean of Patrick's In Ireland."[89] Even Dickens did it, signing one early letter with the mysterious (and as yet undeciphered) cognomen "Charles. I. B. L. K. Y. N. Dickens."[90] And at the end of September 1849, after composing the sixth number of *David Copperfield* in which Dickens recounts David's school days at Doctor Strong's Academy – the first chapter of that number is entitled "I am a New Boy in More Senses than One" – Dickens refers to himself as "the inimitable B."[91] It is as if, with the "B," he is returning to an earlier and only partially erased identity as Boz, a time when he himself was making another beginning as a new boy, a writer.[92]

Such initial playfulness may extend to partial concealments of the writer's real identity, by dropping parts of a name (Anthony Hope for Anthony Hope Hawkins) or translating it into another language (e.g. Joseph Conrad for Jósef Teodor Konrad Korzeniowski), or by playing around with the first names or initials, often to disguise gender, as the Brontës did with Acton, Currer, and Ellis Bell. Some women writers adopted men's names, and a few males cross-dressed as female authors. A single pseudonym often signals exceptional fame: classical writers (Homer, Virgil), religious and civil rulers (Pope John, Queen Elizabeth), and cultural luminaries in music, dance, theater, and letters (Farinelli, Rachilde, Elia) are sometimes known by one name only.

In many cases a pseudonym conceals the author's material identity from strangers but reveals it to family and friends. Dickens's "Boz," a single name, not only bids for a kind of fame but also reveals the author to his immediate family. In 1847 Dickens told his public that the name was the "pet nickname" for his youngest brother, Augustus. "Boz" was a corruption of "Moses," the Christian name of Moses Primrose, a character in one of Dickens's favorite eighteenth-century novels, Oliver Goldsmith's *The Vicar of Wakefield*. When Dickens said "Moses" nasally, as if he had a bad cold, it came out sounding like "Boses." But somehow – neither Dickens nor Forster explains how – this became pronounced "Bozz" "to rhyme with 'Loz' as in the word lozenge" (L. Frank Baum is said to have paid tribute to Dickens by naming a magical realm after him) rather than "Bose" to rhyme with "rose."[93] When Dickens was casting about for a pseudonym for his first "sketch" he lit upon "Boz," and so Boz was, in a sense, born.

The point of this story is that it has no point. Nobody when Dickens first began writing had any idea about the derivation of the name. Pseudonyms were the rage in the 1830s, for authors and artists. Francis Mahony was "Father Prout"; R. H. Barham, canon of St. Paul's in London, used the pen name of "Thomas Ingoldsby." More than one author could publish under a single pseudonym. "Bon Gaultier," a phrase connoting "good fellow" taken from Rabelais's prologue to *Gargantua*, was the nom de plume of William Edmonstone Aytoun and Theodore Martin. The latter was knighted in 1880 for his five-volume biography of Prince Albert – so pseudonymity may have preserved his real name for a more dignified fate. Charles Robert Forrester and his younger brother Alfred Henry Forrester drew and wrote under the name Alfred Crowquill. Thackeray, writing for his life as Carlyle

said, adopted multiple pen names, playing with the conventions of authorial identity in a variety of ways. Michael Angelo Titmarsh was an art critic,
Charles James Harington Fitzroy Yellowplush an illiterate footman
recording events upstairs and down.

   Authors were not the only ones who invented names. Caricaturists
loved to etch pseudonyms that parodied their own or another's pseudonym or name. George Cruikshank signed himself once as "Poor Shanks."
Rival artists tried to capitalize on his fame and to associate their images
with his: hence they signed plates "Straightshanks," "Shortshanks," and
"Stoutshanks."[94] Hablot Knight Browne, Dickens's principal illustrator,
in 1836 signed his first illustrations for Dickens "N.E.M.O.", that is, "no
one, nobody" – a moniker his son Gordon Frederick Browne adopted
("A Nobody") on the title pages of three books of nonsense rhymes he
composed and illustrated.[95] Then Browne switched to "Phiz," short for
physiognomy, the pseudo-science that inferred character from the con-
tours of the face and cranium. "Phiz" drew the "phizzes," the faces, of the
characters Boz described in words; "Phiz" as the artist's pseudonym
chimed with "Boz" as the author's pseudonym.[96]

   "N.E.M.O." suggests that a pseudonym is rather like a null set, an
empty placeholder that can be filled up later. That is exactly what
happened to "Boz." Dickens may have started out concealing his real
name to protect against failure. If his fiction did not succeed, no one
would know that the failed writer "Boz" had any connection to the young
journalist and Parliamentary reporter Charles Dickens. But naming oneself anew had other advantages: one could invent a persona, fill up the null
set of "Boz" by giving him a character, a personality, a range of interests,
and an idiosyncratic take on things.

   Boz was a name that in its own right got talked about; it created
mystery. Even after the secret of Boz's identity was widely known within
literary circles in London (by December 1836) and Edinburgh (by April
1837), Dickens published in the periodical he was then editing a quatrain
that further exploits the indeterminacy of his writerly identity:

> Who the *dickens* "Boz" could be
>    Puzzled many a learned elf;
> Till time unveil'd the mystery,
>    And Boz appear'd as DICKENS' self![97]

This poem, which seems to identify Boz with Dickens, and Dickens's
explanation that the name derived from childhood play, have directed our
understanding of Dickens's pseudonym. Authorized by Dickens himself,

in *Bentley's Miscellany* and the 1847 preface to the Cheap Edition of *Pickwick*, his explanation of the pseudonym foreclosed exploration of other possible resonances in "Boz." Let us ask some questions the "official" version of the origin of Boz pretermits, and try to determine better what this particular pseudonym, like others vaguely referential, encoded, and unifying the miscellaneous articles so "authored," might signify.

It is striking that Dickens only explains the origin of his pen name in 1847, more than a decade after Boz had become famous. Indeed, at that period in his life Dickens was trying to put what Boz stood for behind him. Instead, he strove to foreground his real name, which he wanted to stand as the name of the author of more varied, serious, and masterful fictions than the mainly improvised early writings. And he explains the name at the same time he is composing the autobiographical fragment that will a year or so later be incorporated in *Copperfield*, the novel that fictionalizes Dickens's version of the birth of an author. By the matter-of-factness of his deceptively uninformative explanation, Dickens seems to supply the necessary derivation of his pseudonym and thereby shuts off further investigation: "'Boz,' my signature in the Morning Chronicle, appended to the monthly cover of this book [*Pickwick Papers*], and retained long afterwards, was the nickname of a pet child, a younger brother, whom I had dubbed Moses, in honour of the Vicar of Wakefield; which being facetiously pronounced through the nose, became Boses, and being shortened, became Boz."[98]

Why did Dickens take the nickname of his youngest brother, who in 1834 was only six years old? Augustus Newnham Dickens was born in November 1827. Earlier that year, in March 1827, Dickens had had to leave his "good school in London," Wellington House Academy, because his father "was not a rich man" and he "had to begin the world."[99] (Dickens did not explain, in his first autobiography, penned in July 1838 for publication in a German reference work, that the newspaper his father worked for had failed, that his family had been kicked out of their lodgings, and that his sister had had to quit her music lessons. He makes it seem as if leaving school was a natural consequence of not having a rich father.) "Beginning the world," as Dickens explains it to his public in 1847, meant clerking for Ellis and Blackmore; his parents were more than usually hard pressed as they anticipated yet another mouth to feed. Is Augustus somehow tied up in Dickens's subconscious with disappointed expectations, having to go into law as an office boy rather than as a future partner? Why did Dickens call Augustus "Boz"? What was the significance of the application of Moses Primrose's identity to this younger brother?

Some commentators suppose that it was because Augustus was as feckless as Moses, but at the age of six he had hardly had time to develop such a character. And why did Dickens take the name over in this disguised, infantilized form?

Moses Primrose is the second son of Oliver Goldsmith's eponymous Vicar of Wakefield. Goldsmith is a part of Dickens's literary inheritance that has been slighted. A hobbledehoy, Goldsmith scraped together a university education, busked his way through France playing Irish tunes on his flute, eked out a living in Grub Street, and had a talent for gathering ideas from others and reducing them to clarity, rather like a Parliamentary shorthand reporter. Goldsmith "wrote like an angel," David Garrick said, "but talked like poor Poll."[100] Yet Goldsmith succeeded in drama, Dickens's first projected profession, essay writing (Dickens's second profession), editing (his third), and fiction (his fourth). Dickens's best friend and literary advisor, John Forster, published a biography of Goldsmith in 1848, enlarged in 1854, that helped to restore Goldsmith's fading reputation. He records that Goldsmith's schoolmates thought him "a stupid, heavy blockhead, little better than a fool."[101]

However much Dickens associated with the author of and characters in the *Vicar of Wakefield* in the early 1830s, he didn't then, or later, want to be remembered that way. Nor as Samuel Johnson remembered Goldsmith: "No man was more foolish when he had not a pen in his hand."[102] But Johnson, an ardent supporter of Goldsmith, added, "or more wise when he had," and by the middle of the nineteenth century Goldsmith's lyric poetry, comic drama, sentimental domestic fiction, amiable humor, generosity, and improvidence had once more made the author and his works favorites not only of readers and writers but also of painters.[103] When Dickens finished reading Forster's life of Goldsmith, he told him: "I don't believe that any book was ever written, or anything ever done or said, half so conducive to the dignity and honor of literature, as the life and Adventures of Oliver Goldsmith by J.F. of the Inner Temple."[104] By 1847–48, Dickens was more ready to acknowledge his indebtedness to Goldsmith, but he still preferred to occlude that relationship.

The pseudonym and the writer "Boz" therefore pay tribute to Goldsmith, beloved in the Dickens household. His *Citizen of the World* was one of the books Dickens kept in his little attic room in Chatham, and on his last night there his teacher William Giles presented him with a copy of Goldsmith's short-lived periodical *The Bee* (1759).[105] But "Boz" also conceals the connections. And that writing out of Goldsmith continues – possibly in the many explanations of the origin of Oliver Twist's name that do not mention Oliver Goldsmith's name, and certainly in the unpublicized ways Dickens's periodical, *Master Humphrey's Clock*, imitates *The Bee*. Indeed, it was only with the publication of Forster's *Life* that the public knew Henry Fielding Dickens, born January 15, 1849, was almost christened Oliver Goldsmith.[106]

Additional implications of Dickens's first pseudonym, Boz, take us further into the construction of authorial identity. Moses Primrose might be appropriate as the identity of an amusing younger brother. Although his two betrayed sisters were more often the principal subjects of canvases, Dickens's friend Daniel Maclise exhibited *Olivia and Sophia Fitting Out Moses for the Fair* at the Royal Academy in 1838 and returned to the topic with *The Gross of Green Spectacles* in 1850. Moses is far from an ideal role model. A bookish son who receives a "miscellaneous" education at home from his father, at the fair Moses exchanges virtually the only remaining paternal asset, one of two decrepit horses, for a "groce of green spectacles" whose silver rims turn out to be varnished copper, and worthless.[107] How could Dickens, "ambitious" to escape from his family's improvidence, relate to this character and his bankrupt father, except as negative, apotropaic, examples? And if Moses, like Augustus Dickens, is something to grow out of and away from, why adopt it as one's authorial pseudonym?

Moses is christened by his father, the Vicar; the association of feckless son with unfortunate father is another aspect of Boz's history Dickens doesn't feature. The Vicar's family, according to Forster, was like that described in the *Citizen of the World*, another Dickens favorite. The children "were perfectly instructed in the art of giving away thousands, before we were taught the more necessary qualifications of getting a farthing."[108] The resemblance to John Dickens's instruction is unmistakable. So to adopt the pseudonym "Boz" as a coded allusion to the Primrose family is to acknowledge and suppress simultaneously Dickens's private situation as the second child (first son, but his elder sister Fanny got the education he lacked) of an impractical if philosophically uplifting parent.

Moses is also a common first name of Jews – and above all it is the name of the Old Testament patriarch.[109] So the Christian name Moses is also a Jewish name, and pronounced through the nose as stage Jews (and Fagin and Barney in *Oliver Twist*) do, it comes out sounding like "Boses." Might there be a tincture of anti-Semitism operating within the cultural contexts of name and pronunciation? And if so, how does one unpack those implications? The empathy with Fagin that the narrative develops in the last chapters of *Oliver Twist* might suggest that insofar as Jews were another class of outcasts, reviled objects of public gaze, "Boz" complexly and obscurely registers affiliations between Jews and authors. Moreover, such a name might fuse references to a negative example, the feckless sons Augustus Dickens and Moses Primrose, with references to an ideal figure, Moses, a foundling who led his people out of captivity and took dictation (Parliamentary reporter to a higher House of Lords). "Boz" might, on this reading, be another way to signify Dickens's "ambition" as well as its connection to his domestic origins and sometime sense of parental abandonment.

In the Preface to the Cheap Edition of *Pickwick*, Dickens goes on to explain that "'Boz' was a very familiar household word to me, long before I was an author, and so I came to adopt it."[110] Once again, the story of the birth of Boz ostensibly connects the pseudonym to the domestic sphere while obscuring its associations with other writers and their offspring. The term "household word" may be simply a common locution. But coupled with "familiar" the term appears three years later, in 1850, as the title of Dickens's new serial, *Household Words*. At the head of each weekly part stands a quotation slightly modified from Hal's Saint Crispin's day speech (*Henry V*, iv.iii.52): "Familiar in their Mouths as HOUSEHOLD WORDS." In this instance, the "household words" are familiar because written by Shakespeare, the canonical English writer, spoken by one who, in the mid-Victorian period, was held up as a paragon of kingliness, and heard or read over the centuries by millions. So "household words" and public fame are conjoined; they are not alternatives. And, moreover, the single syllable "Boz" bids for single name celebrity, like Shakespeare and Hal.

How far we are entitled to read backward, from 1850 *Household Words* to the 1847 *Pickwick* preface, and thence to the origin of Dickens's authorial pseudonym "Boz" in 1834, may depend on how willing one is to posit an unconscious or preconscious and a persistent, continuing identity. From the evidence of Dickens's text, his mind was complexly and continuously associative. Some of the patterns of association surface early; in increasingly complicated and resonant combinations, they are reinscribed throughout his lifetime. While it may be a stretch to claim that Dickens had Shakespeare in mind when he chose the pseudonym "Boz," it is plausible to detect connections among that choice in 1833, his explanation of the choice in 1847, and the title of his 1850 periodical. Moreover, *Household Words* was, as the first page and bound parts declared, "Conducted" by Charles Dickens. "Conducting" is itself a metaphor for editing, used by Dickens's friend George Cruikshank when he depicted himself as the "Conductor" of *George Cruikshank's Omnibus* (1846). And "editing" is what Dickens and his "Sub-Editor W. H. Wills" did for *Household Words*. Conducting/editing, then, also connects to "Boz," Dickens's pseudonym while editing *The Pickwick Papers* (1836–37) and *Bentley's Miscellany* (1837–39). It is another chain of associations linking Dickens to Goldsmith the editor. So "Boz," a household word, has long associations with Dickens's household, authorship, editing, and words.

"Boz" did, as a pseudonym, develop something of a personality in its own right. As his "Street Sketches" for the *Morning Chronicle* and "Sketches of London" for the *Evening Chronicle* were produced, "Boz" took on the character of a "speculative pedestrian," "lounging about the streets" practicing a little "amateur vagrancy," observing city life but not engaged in what he watches.[111] Deploying both a "panoramic" survey of metropolitan precincts and repeated recognition of the possibilities, indeed even the moral imperative, of sympathetic identification with particular individuals, Boz still keeps his distance, using irony to insulate himself and his perceptions.[112] Irony prevents him from falling into imaginative identification with the plight of those he observes. Boz is thus very different from the kind of sentimental narrator found in Goldsmith and later eighteenth-century fiction. Moreover, Boz is apparently a bachelor, married only to the streets and to his isolation. Walking the streets and observing the life therein keep loneliness and death at bay, but at the same time these sketches express loneliness and reveal a fear that death comes at the end of every perspective.

Boz, this "speculative pedestrian" Dickens invented, shares many of these personal traits with a whole line of bachelor observers, beginning with Charles Lamb's "Elia" and running down through the narrators employed by the great Continental realists Honoré de Balzac, Stendhal, and Anton Chekhov to the middle of the twentieth century, to the personae invented by Caesar Pavese, Walter Benjamin, and Roland Barthes.[113] Baudelaire identified the "flâneur" as the quintessential modern artist, and thought of him as a new type, an observer of the emerging petty bourgeoisie. So when Dickens developed this authorial persona, "Boz," he jumped early into what has become an important tradition of modern representation, a figure recording at a distance, and with some melancholy as well as humor, the evanescence of modern life.

The persona of "Boz," in other words, got filled in with a character as Dickens wrote more and more "sketches," and that character, in turn, took over the street sketches of previous graphic artists and participated in a developing practice regarding urban representation. In Chapter 2 we will read the sketches in order to identify stages in the development of this persona and of Boz's narrative imagination. When Dickens gathered up previously published writing, anonymous and pseudonymous, for republication, he identified authorship with a particular subset of his journalistic pieces, the "sketches" rather than the tales or portraits of characters, and with his pseudonym. Hence, after mooting several other titles, Dickens settled on *Sketches by Boz.*

Reviewing this title in 1836, the *Court Journal* identified Boz as "a kind of Boswell to society – and of the middle ranks especially."[114] One might argue, with some justification, that the series of anonymous "tales" in the *Monthly Magazine*, which commences with a story about a priggish bachelor who has £10,000 in the funds, dealt with a higher economic sphere than the *Chronicle* "sketches."[115] But the *Court Journal* was reviewing tales and sketches as published together under the pseudonym "Boz," thus applying Boswell to the persona of the anonymous *Magazine* tales as well as the *Chronicle* sketches. Sydney Smith, on the other hand, believed that the very name of "Boz" signified "Vulgarity."[116] And on one occasion Dickens, in a humorous mock advertisement sent to the portraitist William Behnes, identified himself as "A remarkable Dog ['a *Setter*'] answering to the name of BOZ."[117]

Names and pseudonyms often conflate generations, father and son, begetter and begotten. The John Murray and William Blackwood publishing dynasties are instances of the perpetuation of name, and to some extent therefore of identity, from generation to generation. Frankenstein and his monster are commonly given the same name. Dickens may have adopted "Boz" in order to keep Charles Dickens separate from his authorial personification – separate and under control, to be claimed or denied depending on how the writing fared. But as Victor Frankenstein and countless "seniors" have discovered, "junior" does not remain under parental authority. Boz began to collect his own circle of readers, to accrete his own identity as a middle-aged, disillusioned Boswell. At the same time, since "Boz" was clearly not the Christian name of a living writer, but a lexical marker, who "Boz" was in real life "[p]uzzled many a learned elf" and stirred up gossip in Grub Street. It was not hard for those in the publishing world to discover who "Boz" was, but the "mystery" was in 1835 not yet sufficiently developed for a public *éclaircissement.*

Moreover, and this now becomes extremely perplexing, between September 27, 1835 and January 17, 1836 Dickens published twelve "Scenes and Characters" in *Bell's Life in London*. These were all signed "Tibbs," not Boz, even though Dickens's "name" was being made as Boz, and the first two volumes of the collected *Sketches by Boz* were already being planned, printed, and advertised. "Tibbs" is the husband of Mrs. Tibbs, proprietress of "The Boarding House." This setting in Great Coram Street and these shabby genteel characters had appeared more than a year earlier in two tales about the "Boarding House" published in the May and August 1834 issues of the *Monthly Magazine*. These were the first publications in which Dickens deals with his own class and adolescent experiences of barely respectable lodgings and characters. Perhaps of significance is the fact that Dickens first attaches his Boz pseudonym to the second installment, in some complicated psychological if not public way connecting his "sketches" with his own life. But his second pseudonym, "Tibbs," puts a great distance between his material and psychic self and the narrator/author Tibbs. In the *Monthly Magazine* stories, which readers of *Bell's Life* may never have read, Tibbs is a long-faced, short-legged, henpecked husband exiled to a turn-up bedstead in the kitchen. He "rarely spoke; but, if it were at any time possible to put in a word, when he should have said nothing at all, he had that talent." He has one long story, beginning "I recollect when I was in the volunteer corps, in eighteen hundred and six," which no one ever heard him finish (pp. 273–75).

Why should Dickens change from a pseudonym that was becoming well known and commercially valuable? What is accomplished by naming, as putative author, an inarticulate character who appears in one anonymous story and a second installment pseudonymously authored by "Boz," both published months earlier in another journal? Given the fleeting nature of Fleet Street fame, would Dickens have counted on readers recognizing the pseudonym "Tibbs"? If he counted on their *not* recognizing it, why use it? When "Boz" is becoming known for his street "sketches," what does Dickens gain by changing to "Tibbs" and to "Scenes and Characters" for his contributions to *Bell's Life in London*? There would not have been any legal problem about Dickens's publishing sketches by "Boz" in more than one journal, and it doesn't seem evident that he adopted another pen name for fear of appearing in print too often as Boz. He published under that pseudonym in three places besides the *Morning* and *Evening Chronicle*, both before and after *Sketches by Boz* First Series was issued. And though "Tibbs" does tell stories about indoor scenes and characters at Christmas and New Year, "Tibbs" also authors two of the best street sketches, "Seven Dials" and "The Streets at Night." So "Tibbs" is not a mark identifying characters within domestic settings versus characters observed by a speculative pedestrian, or scenes rather than sketches. Granted, Dickens is partly being playful in a way only close friends would recognize. Explaining to Kolle in April 1834 that the *Monthly Magazine* publishers have his manuscript of the first part of "The Boarding House," and that he will lend it to Kolle as soon as it is returned, he speaks of himself as "the Proprietor" of that boarding house.[118] "Tibbs" is already in some ways another alter ego of Boz/Dickens. And yet, to complicate matters further, as we've seen, it is the second installment of "The Boarding House" of which Tibbs is nominal proprietor that Dickens, for the first time, signs as Boz. It might be that George Hogarth advised Dickens to choose another pen name for *Bell's* because Boz was becoming identified with the *Chronicle* pieces; but that is speculation only, and in any case doesn't account for the *choice* of Tibbs.[119]

The very name that Dickens is making for Boz, as a roving journalist who is a Boswell of the streets, is blurred and obscured not only by anonymous tales issued in literary magazines but also by the invention of a second pseudonymous author who writes about the same street scenes and farcical characters for newspapers. Dickens undercuts the advantages of a created authorial persona by replicating his material under another name, though not under another voice. For a further puzzle in this conundrum is that Dickens doesn't use the persona of Tibbs at all in the narrative voice of the *Bell's Life* "Scenes and Characters." "Tibbs" the writer is, if anything, the opposite of the inarticulate basement-dwelling husband of the boarding-house keeper. What was Dickens trying to achieve with these pseudonyms in 1834–36? To what extent has Boz been born, and why does he get a sibling competing in the marketplace for authorial acclaim?

# CHAPTER 2

# *Characterizing Boz (1834–1837):* Sketches by Boz

Charles Dickens, miniature by Rose Emma Drummond, 1835,
later engraved by Edwin Roffe

"Magazine work," declared [Thomas] Carlyle in 1831, "is below street sweeping as a trade."
– Michael Slater, *Douglas Jerrold: A Life*

Novel writing has been considered by many as a low pursuit, exceedingly unintellectual and unphilosophical ... but the novel writer needs not only to describe that which is, but that which ought to be and that which may be.
– *The Athenaeum*, November 9, 1833

Dickens's transformation into a novelist during the years 1833 to 1841 was not the inevitable matter it is usually taken to be.
– Kathryn Chittick, *Dickens and the 1830s*

I have taken with fear and trembling to authorship. I wrote a little something, in secret, and sent it to a magazine, and it was published in the magazine. Since then, I have taken heart to write a good many trifling pieces. Now, I am regularly paid for them. Altogether, I am well off; when I tell my income on the fingers of my left hand, I pass the third finger and take in the fourth to the middle joint.
– *David Copperfield*

The fictional sketch of the early nineteenth century ... constitutes one origin of the Victorian novel.
– Amanpal Garcha, *From Sketch to Novel*

I

So Boz the writer was born – anonymously at first, then under pseudonyms. However, his parent, Charles Dickens, continued his protracted scrabble for gainful employment. After leaving Ellis and Blackmore in November 1828, Dickens had clerked in the office of Charles Molloy, later his solicitor who negotiated some of the contracts with the publisher Richard Bentley. When in the early 1830s he was taken on as a newspaper reporter, first by his maternal uncle on the *Mirror of Parliament* and then by the *True Sun*, a sevenpenny evening paper, politics were heating up. Discussions about reforming the franchise had been going on since 1827, and they intensified in 1831, when the first debate on the Reform Bill occupied Parliament from March 1 through 9. Dickens was one of those who transcribed the proceedings for the *Mirror of Parliament*. In 1865, during a speech to the Newspaper Press Fund, he recalled these days with nostalgic pride:

I have worn my knees by writing on them on the old back row of the old gallery of the old House of Commons; and I have worn my feet by standing to write in a preposterous pen in the old House of Lords, where we used to be huddled together like so many sheep [laughter], kept in waiting, say, until the woolsack might want re-stuffing.[1]

But at the time his fatigue was a more serious factor, especially during the first onslaught of Reform Bill debate, when he wrote that he was "so exceedingly tired from my week's exertions that I slept on the Sofa the whole day."[2]

In 1832 and 1833 Dickens explored careers in the theater and as a creative writer, while working as a reporter and continuing to think about the law. Though he funked his March 1832 Covent Garden audition, he did produce amateur theatricals in his parents' Bentinck Street house. On the first occasion, shortly after his coming of age in February 1833, he played in J. H. Payne's opera *Clari* and in the succeeding comedy and farce. In the autumn of that year, he completed and staged his burlesque operatic travesty of Shakespeare, *O'Thello*, again at his parents' house. He may have hoped to see it published or professionally produced; at least he showed a fair copy to his friend Henry Kolle the following April. When Dickens spotted his first sketch in the December 1833 *Monthly Magazine*, he immediately sent in a second submission, "Mrs Joseph Porter 'Over the Way,'" a tale about an amateur production of *Othello* that promptly appeared in the January 1834 issue. By April of that year, the *Monthly* had published two more pieces, though these were still not signed. Henry Mayhew's twopenny *London Weekly Magazine* had reprinted the first *Monthly* sketch for free, and the *Monthly* wasn't paying anything at all. Dickens was, though anonymous, a published author. Yet that "status," if such a grand description applies at all, yielded nothing in fortune or fame, and the theatrical career seemed even less likely to result in either.

At this juncture Dickens was ready for any opening. Exhilarated by his first publication, he had a very different reaction in December 1833 from that of the shy writer retreating to Westminster Hall that he recounted to the public in 1847. Around December 10, Dickens told Kolle that he would submit two other papers to the *Monthly*. The first, "Private Theatricals" (that is, "Mrs Joseph Porter") must have been in hand already, as it was submitted, accepted, and published within twenty days. But the second, "London by Night," didn't appear until two years later, in January 1836, and then in another journal, *Bell's Life*, as No. 12 of a series that had been running for four months, called "Scenes and Characters." Further, Dickens anticipated starting "a series of papers ... called The Parish." This eventuated in six episodes of "Sketches of London" in the *Evening Chronicle* more than a year later (February to August 1835). "Should they be successful & as publishing is hazardous, I shall cut my proposed Novel up into little Magazine Sketches." This novel, clearly already discussed with Kolle, might have been *Oliver Twist* (1837–38) or *Gabriel Vardon, the Locksmith of London* (eventually printed in *Master Humphrey's Clock* in 1841, retitled *Barnaby Rudge*).[3] Even the outlet for these ambitious plans was uncertain: "Should I not settle with this Periodical [the *Monthly Magazine*], I shall try 'The Metropolitan.'"[4] Little of this came to pass in the way Dickens anticipated. Yet, even though the *Monthly* continued to be "'rather backward in coming forward' with the needful," he went on sending in copy and seeing it in print.[5] And so far as the surviving evidence indicates, he didn't approach the *Metropolitan*. In short, for Dickens at this stage authorship meant getting his writing into print. But the only sources of payment for such publications were the journals on which he was working as a reporter. While many of Dickens's immediate predecessors and contemporaries had been journalists and independently published authors simultaneously, he was still looking for some way to make money beyond his newspaper salary.[6]

II

In August of 1834 Dickens was taken on as a regular reporter by the *Morning Chronicle*, edited by the bluff and eccentric Scotsman John Black, who took a strongly reformist and Benthamite line. Over the next two years, until November 1836, one of Dickens's principal occupations was writing newspaper stories and drama criticism for this paper, engaged in a fierce rivalry with *The Times*. Sometimes he (and often a co-reporter) traveled far out of town to cover an event, racing back to beat the competition with the longest, best, or earliest account. Both at the time and thirty years later, Dickens thought of these strenuous engagements as exhilarating fun, taxing but exciting to a venturesome young man: "I have pursued the calling of a reporter," he told those attending the second anniversary dinner of the Newspaper Press Fund in May 1865,

under circumstances of which many of my brethren at home in England here, many of my modern successors, can form no adequate conception. I have often transcribed for the printer from my shorthand notes, important public speeches in which the strictest accuracy was required, and a mistake in which would have been to a young man severely compromising, writing on the palm of my hand, by the light of a dark lantern, in a post chaise and four, galloping through a wild country, all through the dead of night, at the then surprising rate of fifteen miles an hour.[7]

We may never identify all these anonymous articles and reviews.[8] Dickens covered many meetings about reform, went with Thomas Beard to Edinburgh in September 1834 to report on a banquet given for Lord Grey, attended a reform meeting in Birmingham in November, traveled to Essex and Suffolk to file stories about the January 1835 general election, and in May of that year went down to Exeter with Beard to transcribe Lord John Russell's speech, delivered in "a pelting rain" so that "two good-natured colleagues, who chanced to be at leisure, held a pocket handkerchief over my notebook after the manner of a state canopy in an ecclesiastical procession."[9] He and Beard went to Bristol in November to cover another of Russell's speeches, and once they had dispatched the first part of their account via the Express night coach to London, they sped on to Bath to report on a political dinner honoring two of the local MPs.[10] Dickens also reviewed many theatrical events, often not knowing what his assignment would be until the last minute, and staying up late after the playhouses closed to write his review and sometimes to finish other pieces as well. In addition there were meetings and dinners in town, Parliamentary debates, a disastrous fire at Hatfield House in December 1835 that killed the Dowager Marchioness of Salisbury, and numerous other assignments that meant he was hardly ever, "by the mercy of Black, and the Chronicle proprietors, at home" of an evening.[11]

Hard work, and very professionally done. But it paid scantily. And in November 1834, just when Dickens was starting his stint at the *Chronicle*, his father was once again arrested for debts, of a quantity and extent unknown to him, except that the principal claimants were Shaw and Maxwell, wine merchants in Russell Square. The break-up of the family that resulted led Dickens to take three third-floor rooms, a cellar, and a lumber-room under the roof, at 13 Furnival's Inn, in December 1834, housing his younger brother Fred who served as a general factotum.[12] He managed to extricate his father from Sloman's sponging house but could not pay a bill coming due and barely succeeded in persuading the broker to renew for two months. His salary "for a week or two" was "completely mortgaged" by furnishing his rooms, and he was "most desperately hard up." Tom Beard and Thomas Mitton advanced pounds and shillings repeatedly.[13] Adding to his frustrations as a fledgling author, Dickens discovered that his unpaid-for sketch of "The Bloomsbury Christening" had been dramatized (without acknowledgment or payment) by John Baldwin Buckstone and was settling in for a long run at the Adelphi Theatre.[14] Dickens good-humoredly reviewed the opening night performance for the *Morning Chronicle* (October 14, 1834), but was a little less charitable in his letter to the editor of the *Monthly Magazine*:

[A]s I contemplated a dramatic destination for my offspring, I must enter my protest against the kidnapping process.

It is very little consolation to me to know, when my handkerchief is gone, that I may see it flaunting with renovated beauty in Field-lane; and if Mr. Buckstone has too many irons in the fire to permit him to get up his own "things", I don't think he ought to be permitted to apply to my chest of drawers.

Just give him a good "blow up" in your "magazine", – will you?[15]

Things turned around rather quickly. By January 19 his father had been reunited with the rest of the family in lodgings at 21 George Street, Adelphi. The next day George Hogarth, just appointed co-editor of the *Evening Chronicle*, a thrice-weekly offshoot of the morning paper, asked Dickens to supply a sketch for the first number. When employed on the staff of the *Morning Chronicle*, Hogarth had admired a series of five sketches, signed "Boz," that Dickens had contributed between September and December of the previous year. In reply, Dickens asked "whether it is probable that if I commenced a series of articles under some attractive title for the Evening Chronicle, its conductors would think I had any claim to *some* additional remuneration (of course of no great amount) for doing so?"[16] This was an opportunity to combine journalism with sketch writing and to get paid for both. Even though Dickens was placatory about the additional payment, he did ask for it, and over the summer he received an increase in weekly salary from five to seven guineas, raising his nominal annual salary from around £273 to just over £382 – actually a middle-class income.[17] All in all, he supplied twenty "Sketches of London" between January 31 and August 20. At the end of September, he commenced yet another series, "Scenes and Characters," which ran in *Bell's Life in London* through twelve installments between September 27, 1835 and January 17, 1836. *Bell's* paid something for these contributions, although when Dickens's celebrity skyrocketed in late 1836 it reprinted stories from the *Morning Chronicle* without acknowledgment or remuneration.[18]

Even with the additional income, Dickens was sometimes hard pressed to meet his increasing expenses; he wanted to marry but could not get out of his lease on No. 13 and into more suitable quarters at No. 15 until December 1835. Meanwhile, the combined jobs of reporting and writing fiction for several publications at the same time stretched him to the limit. Many of the surviving letters from 1835 were saved by Catherine "to shew the world that Dickens once loved her."[19] While he doesn't usually complain to others about being exhausted, he repeatedly cancels engagements with her for that reason. In June he is "rather tired" and "completely worn out"; in July he suffers from "excessive fatigue" and is "very tired"; in

August he is "too tired, and dispirited, to write more than a very brief note."[20] Although the burden of executing so many commissions was heavy (and, one suspects, sometimes a convenient excuse), Dickens continued to sign up for others. A major one came from his sometime publisher, John Macrone, who from January to August of 1834 had co-owned the *Monthly Magazine*. Macrone proposed, and Dickens eagerly accepted, collecting his sketches and issuing them in volumes with illustrations by the well-known older graphic humorist, George Cruikshank.

III

But this agreement gets us ahead of our story about the many ways Dickens was conceiving of himself as a writer, actor, producer, and potential lawyer in the early 1830s. One question that needs to be addressed is what kind of political beliefs Dickens held during these tumultuous years of reform and unrest in agricultural and industrial sectors. It is not an easy one to answer, as of course he was writing for editors who in turn were publishing journals with very different philosophies and audiences. The *Morning Chronicle*, purchased in mid-1834 by three ardent Whig financiers, was a serious daily determined to cover both domestic and foreign news and to defeat the principal journalistic opponent of Reform, the Tory *Times*. One of Dickens's never-collected contributions, "The Story Without a Beginning (Translated from the German by Boz)," published December 18, 1834, is in Michael Slater's words a "fierce response to William IV's sudden dismissal of the reforming Whigs."[21] The companion newspaper, the *Evening Chronicle*, was published only three times a week; though it trumpeted "a Metropolitan as well as a Country circulation," like all evening papers of the time it catered primarily to a provincial, non-urban readership.[22] Thus when Dickens's sketches appeared in the *Morning Chronicle* they were, by many readers, assimilated into the politics of liberal social reform and the manufacturing interests. Stories in the *Evening Chronicle*, however, though purportedly accounts of experiences shared with other Londoners, actually reached a predominantly rural audience the first time they were published; only when republished in the *Morning Chronicle* did the author's editorial "we" speak to fellow cosmopolitans.

*Bell's Life* was a different publication altogether, appealing to a huge range of readers, drawn from high life and low, and predominantly male. Like the *Chronicles*, *Bell's Life* provided fashionable intelligence, but it also specialized in sporting and games, theatrical news, and comics.

Threepenny reprints of comic cuts from the paper sold hundreds of thousands of copies, and the regular circulation averaged some 30,000 copies weekly.[23] So when Dickens took his urban sketches and tales from the *Chronicles* to *Bell's Life*, he not only increased his pay, he also substantially increased his audience's size and range of classes and interests.

The last journal to which Dickens sold sketches, long after *Pickwick* was up and running, was the shilling weekly, the *Carlton Chronicle*. It began on June 11, 1836 as "a vehicle of sound conservative doctrines" with a special eye to colonial possessions and an equal concern for literature. It lasted less than a year. In writing for this journal, Dickens reached upmarket Londoners. The editor, Percival Weldon Banks, became intimate in the circle around Harrison Ainsworth to which Dickens was introduced at this time. In August of 1836 Banks asked Dickens to contribute a series of sketches, which he agreed to do, "as they will be very short, and the terms long."[24] Dickens contemplated imposing codex coherence on his miscellaneous journalism: he thought of calling his *Carlton* pieces "LEAVES FROM AN UNPUBLISHED VOLUME BY BOZ (which will be torn out, once a fortnight)."[25] Although Banks repeatedly solicited Dickens for material, only two new sketches appeared in the series. One, "The Hospital Patient," is the story of a young woman fatally beaten by her brutal husband, who nevertheless refuses to testify against him in the last moments before she dies (a prefiguration of Nancy's devotion to Bill in *Oliver Twist*); it would seem oddly inappropriate for this society magazine. But maybe Westenders enjoyed reading about violence so long as it was domestic and confined to the East End and hospitals. The *Carlton*'s subsequent Bozzes were apparently only unauthorized reprints.

Appearing in Tory, Whig, down-market, and upmarket periodicals, Boz had to keep a low profile. Whereas Dickens as anonymous reporter sometimes let his partisanship show, Boz in his sketches seldom forthrightly addressed the raging controversies of the day.[26] Instead, he preferred to offer sympathetic commentary on the difficult lives experienced by many types, soliciting varying degrees of compassion not only for the upstanding and the middle class but also for cantankerous landladies, pugnacious slum dwellers, abusive husbands and wives, the destitute, frauds, criminals, and the dying. When the publisher Richard Bentley hired Boz to edit his new magazine, he did so in the conviction that Boz would gather humorous contributors, not politically overt ones. The journal promised from the beginning to avoid politics. (More about this in Chapter 4.) The author of that policy was William Maginn, then editing a rival publication, *Fraser's Magazine*. In an otherwise scathing August 1836 review of Grantley Berkeley's new novel, Maginn praised "Boz the magnificent" precisely because he was not political: "what a pity it is that he deludes himself into the absurd idea that he can be a Whig! – Mr. Pickwick was a Whig, and that was only right; but Boz is just as much a Whig as he is a giraffe."[27] Many reviewers praised Boz for being a humorous and faithful observer of contemporary life, eschewing caricature in favor of "matter-of-factness."[28] After *Pickwick* had been appearing for some months, the comparisons to William Hogarth and Henry Fielding became almost commonplaces; but there was very little commentary about Boz's own political causes even though Hogarth's and Fielding's were well known.

The national political context was similarly blurred. After the repressive postwar measures of the Liverpool administration, which put down popular radicalism and demonstrations in support of Queen Caroline, the mid-1820s ushered in a brief period of quiet. The designations of Whig and Tory, originating as terms of abuse in the seventeenth century, gained wider currency and acceptance by then, though "liberal" and "conservative" were being used as adjectives – not yet as proper names – for advocates of civil and religious liberties (Whigs) versus ardent upholders of law, the established church, and tradition (Tories). Liverpool, felled by a stroke in February 1827, had to resign just as debates about restrictive import duties (Corn Laws) and Roman Catholic emancipation commenced. Various bipartisan coalitions of Ministers failed to cohere. Wellington and Peel had a difficult time forging a workable majority to pass legislation extending religious and civil liberties to Catholics and dissenters. The Whigs returned to power after twenty years and in 1832 passed the first Reform Act by consolidating liberal opportunism and exploiting Tory internecine feuding. Prime ministers, leaders in the Commons, and Cabinet members reshuffled throughout the 1830s. William IV dismissed Melbourne, but in the subsequent election Peel and the Tories could not win a majority, so Melbourne returned as leader of the Cabinet with no mandate or inclination to do much of anything. The 1834 Poor Law Amendment Act reformed state charity and the 1835 Municipal Corporations Act reorganized local governments, but while Melbourne's ministry thought it politic to be active in passing uncontroversial measures, it was "attacked on both sides, by radicals who demanded more thorough reforms and by Tories who accused the Whigs of going too far too quickly."[29] In such circumstances, it is understandable that Boz chose between 1833 and 1836 to write more about local than national issues, and to temper his advocacies so as to appeal to all sides.

IV

While Boz veiled his political sentiments, he still had a lot of stories to write, stories that were different from the articles Dickens submitted about by-elections, banquets, fires, and crime. What were those stories, out of what materials did he spin his early narratives, and what voice did he strive to establish as his own? Initially, the acorns didn't fall far from the tree: the sketches treated subjects Dickens knew from his experiences in law, reporting, theater, and daydreaming of success. "How fill the paper," *Fraser's* asked in a review of Dickens's career up to 1840, "but by reports of debates, meetings, societies, police-offices, courts of justice, vestry-rooms, and so forth" – the stock in trade of a reporter and drama reviewer.[30]

The very first story, "A Dinner in Poplar Walk," not signed Boz, is, as we have seen, about a potential heir hoping that if his rich relative enjoys a convivial dinner in the suburbs amidst demonstrative domestic harmony, inheritance will be secured.[31] As in the farces of the period, this dream of riches becomes for both parties a nightmare. Augustus Minns, a well-to-do clerk at Somerset House, loves order above all things; he hates dogs and children. While breakfasting on dry toast and "the columns of his morning paper, which he always read from the title to the printer's name" (p. 308), he receives a call from his cousin, Octavius Budden, a corn-chandler living in a cottage near Stamford Hill with his wife Amelia and their eight-year-old prodigy, Alexander Augustus Budden, to whom in a weak moment Minns consented to serve as godfather. Budden brings with him an unruly dog that snatches buttered bread from the table, spoils the curtains, and when exiled to the landing scratches the paint off the nicely varnished door. Budden dusts his boots with a cloth napkin, helps himself to breakfast, hacks the ham to pieces, yet secures his cousin's presence at dinner in Poplar Walk the following Sunday. For Minns the journey is uncomfortable; the coaches are late; he is greeted by his host and a dozen friends invited to see the Lion; the Lion not only doesn't roar or divulge any Somerset House gossip, but hardly speaks throughout the meal. Then Master Alexander is introduced, and precociously both answers Minns's question about his age and asks his interlocutor "How old are you?" "[F]rom that moment" Minns "internally resolved he never would bequeath one shilling" to his godson (p. 313). When the toasts commence,

Dickens exploits his acquaintance with after-dinner and Parliamentary rodomontade to give mercifully brief examples. Responding to the toast given in his honor, Minns, in confusion, rises, "but, as the newspapers sometimes say in their reports, 'we regret that we are quite unable to give even the substance of the honourable gentleman's observations'" (p. 314). Another toast promises to retell a story about the Irish dramatist and MP Richard Brinsley Sheridan. But it is interrupted by the announcement that the stage is about to leave. Heavy rain has set in, Minns misses his umbrella and the last coach, and he finally arrives home to Tavistock Street, Covent Garden, at three in the morning,

cold, wet, cross, and miserable. He made his will next morning, and his professional man informs us, in that strict confidence in which we inform the public, that neither the name of Mr Octavius Budden, nor of Mrs Amelia Budden, nor of Master Alexander Augustus Budden, appears therein. (p. 315)

The Covent Garden and Stamford neighborhoods, the layout of newspapers, the miseries of coaches, the shortcuts to which journalists resorted in reporting after-dinner speeches, and the legalities of wills, private but publicly communicated, all are familiar to Dickens; their combination in a farcical story replicates standard theatrical fare. A significant feature of this story is the role of communicating: the orderly sequence of reading the paper contrasts to the disruptions of Budden (christened Bagshaw in the original version in the December 1833 *Monthly Magazine*), the reciprocal inquiries about age determine Minns's testamentary provisions, the toasts are related in reporter fashion, and a lively anecdote about a celebrated playwright and radical MP is cut short by bad weather. The story ends by conveying the information of a "professional man" that Minns did not write three names into his will. The vulgarity of the names Bagshaw and Budden (recall that Sydney Smith thought "Boz" itself signified vulgarity) also suggests their character: moneybags that do not get filled, hopes for a budding offshoot that are drowned by misfortune and miscalculation.[32]

Dickens's remaining contributions to the *Monthly* were also tales, but over time he produced several others types of narrative that in the final assemblage of his early works were identified as "Seven Sketches from Our Parish," "Scenes," and "Characters." "Mr. Minns and His Cousin," which Dickens withheld from the first two volumes of the collected *Sketches by Boz* (published in February 1836), was retitled and substantially rewritten for the second series, in one volume (published in December 1836). Like many of these early printed effusions, Dickens wrote without prior planning, trying out whatever happened to inspire his pen or his patrons.

By January 1835, when Dickens began his "Sketches of London" pieces for the *Evening Chronicle*, his journalism ranged widely. He might be asked at the last minute to review a theater program, which would be published anonymously as a short piece. He wasn't particularly notable in this subset of duties. He was often sent to write up political events at home and on the hustings; still anonymously, but sometimes his own Whiggish sentiments seeped into the report. Late that year, covering a Kettering by-election in December, Dickens was so opposed to the Conservative bullying of electors that when the Tory candidate came top of the poll on the first day, Dickens's report characterized the voters as "ignorant, drunken, and brutal" men fed and herded to the polls like swine. Two days later, when the Tory victory was confirmed, the *Chronicle* sent a different reporter to cover the candidate's speech.[33]

The latitude Dickens was given to write in different modes both as anonymous reporter and as Boz widened more as he composed the series of "Street Sketches" for the *Morning Chronicle* from September of 1834 and then commenced the *Evening Chronicle* series, "Sketches of London" (reprinted irregularly in its sister paper) the following January. These did become identified with Dickens's alter ego, Boz. And Boz spoke familiarly to his readers about the constraints of publishing. These asides were nonce features of the columns, cut when Dickens rewrote for the volume reprints. And so they have not been handed down to posterity, with the result that his *Sketches by Boz* stand clear of their original context, including Boz's solicitations of his readers and his editors. In their first print instantiation, for instance, Boz lamented the limitations of space imposed upon him, a rhetoric that implied both that he had lots of material in reserve and that his readers ought to be clamoring for more. "We have attained our usual limits, and must conclude our paper," Boz informs his readers in the second sketch of "Our Parish" (*Evening Chronicle*, May 19, 1835). At the conclusion of "The House," first published in the *Evening Chronicle* on March 7, 1835, he promises more portraits of MPs in a succeeding article: "We have exhausted our space, and must therefore reserve [the portraits] for our next sketch, which will be entitled Bellamy's." The curious thing is that both statements appear when the sketches are reprinted in the *Morning Chronicle* some time later: the "Our Parish" sketch of the curate, the old lady, and the half-pay captain on July 16, and "The House" on March 19. Presumably the "space" available in the two papers differed: the *Evening* cut Dickens's copy to fit the make-up of that issue, while the *Morning* editions inserted Boz's previously printed contributions verbatim in spaces assigned to reproduce the whole article, so there was no editorial or material limit to complain about. Dickens continued to confide in his readers that he was coping with management's constraints. In "The Parish," the first of that series published February 28, 1835 in the *Evening Chronicle* but nearly two months later (April 20) in the *Morning Chronicle*, Boz explains that "[o]ur space . . . is limited; and, as an editor's mandate is a wholesome check upon an author's garrulity, we have no wish to occupy more than the space usually assigned to us." Exactly whom this apologia addresses is unclear: Hogarth, the *Evening* editor, Black, the *Morning* editor, or readers who are given a portrait of a conscientious scribbler who does not want to offend by garrulity either bosses or customers.

Similar invocations of solicitude for the audience continue to emphasize that Boz is a considerate correspondent. "We are sensible that we owe some apology to many of our readers," he declares at the end of "Bellamy's" (*Evening Chronicle*, April 11; *Morning Chronicle*, April 14). Boz fears that "for the second time" he may have selected "a subject involving allusions which they may not understand." Yet on this, and at least two other occasions, Boz defends his subject matter, in spite of the possibility that his readers might object. In "Bellamy's," he concludes that "it always has been, and always will be, our subject to sketch people and places which all our readers, in common with ourselves, have had opportunities of observing." This formula of appeal is varied in "The Parish": "It is generally allowed that parochial affairs possess little beyond local interest. But, should we be induced to imagine that the favor of our readers disposes them to make an exception of the present case, we shall vary our future numbers, by seeking materials for another sketch in 'our parish.'" A third confession merging Boz's journalistic constraints with his opportunities to enlighten readers terminates "Thoughts about People" (*Evening Chronicle*, April 23; *Morning Chronicle*, June 9):

There are so many classes of people in London, each one so different from the other, and each so peculiar in itself, that we find it time to bring our paper to a close before we have well brought our subject to a beginning. We are, therefore, induced to hope that we may calculate upon the permission of our readers to think about people again at some future time.

Boz thus identifies metropolitan "classes of people" which he and his readers share an interest in observing, and while he repeatedly articulates a concern for his reader's interest and patience, he also kicks a bit against the editorially imposed confinement of columns. Here is another distinctive difference between the professional reporter producing copy that is inserted or not, rewritten and made to fit, as part of a collaborative process of putting together a newspaper, and an authorial figure who reaches out beyond the usual lines of print to solicit an audience wanting further (and longer) stories about their neighbors than conventional news reports and news proprietors might otherwise allow.

V

What we see, then, in Dickens's apprentice writing is a congeries of issues: news as fiction; private lives made public through report, enactment in the streets, or reporters' published investigations; classes of people interpreted as individuated groups; reportorial and editorial back-chat; and the power of communication, especially writing, to create or erase identity and fortune through a recognizable style and space in public print. These issues often are consolidated around moments of suspension or deletion. Many of the sketches begin or end in death or analogous termination.[34] The "Sketches from Our Parish," as they were revised and assembled for the 1839 serial edition of *Sketches by Boz* begin by unpacking "those two short words – 'The Parish!'" "[W]ith how many tales of distress and misery, of broken fortune and ruined hopes, too often of unrelieved wretchedness and successful knavery, are they associated!" (p. 5). Succeeding sketches often conclude with imminent mortality. The parish schoolmaster holds his situation "long beyond the usual period"; he has been forgotten by his former pupils and his own memory is impaired; but he will continue to hold office "until infirmity renders him incapable, or death releases him" (p. 10). The old lady and the half-pay captain "agree very well in the main" (p. 15), but he takes every opportunity to denounce the way that things are conducted in the parish and completely effaces her name from the brass door-plate in his attempt to polish it. "The Election for Beadle" commences with the death of the incumbent and concludes with the triumph of the half-pay Captain Purday and his candidate Bung. The supporters of the old beadle system are defeated; the fate of their candidate, Spruggins, is "sealed"; and even the mother of his ten small children "failed to be an object of sympathy any longer" (p. 26). The nomination speeches in the parish church trade derogations of the opponent in the form of denials of speech: "he would not say, that that gentleman was no gentleman; he would not assert that that man was no man" (p. 24). This is the "celebrated negative style adopted by great speakers," and known as "parliamentary style" (p. 24) of which Dickens had heard so much. By using the figure of *paralipsis*, speech itself is eradicated by speech.[35] "The Broker's Man" sees farther into the lives of the family whose house is put in execution than anyone else.[36] He observes, even in the moment when the execution is paid out, that the wife, bearing her humiliation silently, has reached the end: "if ever I saw death in a woman's face, I saw it in hers that night" (p. 25). An Irish orator invited by one of two contending parties in "The Ladies' Societies" overcomes the audience with his invocations of Eden, life, and death: "He talked of green isles – other shores – vast Atlantic – bosom of the deep – Christian charity – blood and extermination – mercy in hearts – arms in hands – altars and homes – household gods" (p. 40). The other party, dedicated to holding public examinations of the parochial schoolchildren, is defeated, and "the child's examination is going fast to decay" (p. 40). And the final story in the sequence, about the transient tenants of the narrator's next-door neighbor, concludes when the latest renters, a "young lad of eighteen or nineteen" and his very poor mother, struggle with intense privation and his increasing illness until, during a visit the narrator pays, the boy rouses up from the sofa, beseeches his mother to "bury me in the open fields," and falls back. The last sentence is "The boy was dead" (pp. 46–47).

It is extraordinary that Dickens manages, time and again, to unreel a narrative from a moment of stoppage, or direct the story's trajectory to that end. "A Passage in the Life of Mr. Watkins Tottle" begins with an observation about matrimony (a conventional ending to fictional plots) and ends when "the body of a gentleman unknown was found in the Regent's canal" with "a matrimonial advertisement" in its trousers pocket (p. 446). Yet Dickens thought even this ending might admit of further development. In the *Monthly Magazine* version, but not subsequently, the narrator informs us that Tottle (the disappointed lover) left papers with his landlady that she has given Boz to arrange and publish, in expectation that the proceeds will repay his board and lodging charges. Since no further installments of the Tottle archive appeared in the *Monthly* (which wasn't defraying Dickens's board and lodging either) or elsewhere, the story concludes in succeeding iterations with a different allusion: when Tottle disappears, though before his body is identified, "A bill, which has not been taken up, was presented [by his landlady] next morning; and a bill, which has not been taken down, was soon afterwards affixed in his parlour window" (p. 446). Insofar as this is a version of a tenant gone missing and a "to let" sign substituted, the promised continuation of the story, the edited Tottle archive, might be said to be Pickwick's story in the papers edited by Boz shortly thereafter. In both, matrimonial intimations lead to vacant lodgings, departed lodgers, signs in windows, and papers to be edited and published.

While these departures of tenants, either living or dead, are not unusual in communities, the columns of newspapers, parishes, and *Sketches*, they were not a common experience to Dickens in these years. Tenants who stayed with the Dickens family, such as Mary Allen Barrow, Elizabeth's sister, left to get married, not to flee or die. And as for life terminations, in the experience of Dickens these were few compared to many other families. The death of his grandmother in April 1824, when he was twelve, occurred a month before his father was discharged from the Marshalsea after declaring himself an insolvent debtor; John Dickens's inheritance all went toward paying his debts, not cleared for another two-and-a-half years. Two of Dickens's younger siblings died in childhood. But otherwise Dickens's immediate relatives survived and were generally healthy. Frances, "Fanny," died of consumption in September 1848, fifteen years after the sketches commenced; Letitia, born in 1816, although ill through much of her early life, lived the longest of all the siblings, dying at seventy-seven. We cannot therefore account for this strong connection between death and writing through biography.

VI

In his essay asking "What Is an Author?" Michel Foucault postulates that writing and death are closely connected in the modern era:

Writing is now linked to sacrifice and to the sacrifice of life itself; it is a voluntary obliteration of the self that does not require representation in books because it takes place in the everyday existence of the writer. Where a work had the duty of creating immortality, it now attains the right to kill, to become the murderer of its author. Flaubert, Proust, and Kafka are obvious examples of this reversal. In addition, we find the link between writing and death manifested in the total effacement of the individual characteristics of the writer; the quibbling and confrontations that a writer generates between himself and his text cancel out the signs of his particular individuality.[37]

This may not all seem to apply to Dickens, or some of it may apply only negatively. After all, Foucault is describing modern authorship, not Victorian. But certainly the *effect* of Boz's early writing was to produce a kind of "immortality" both for classes of persons previously uncommemorated – one being the London shabby genteel – and for Boz. The *Metropolitan Magazine* singled out his "perfect picture of the morals, manners and habits of a great portion of English Society," going on to explain that that portion "does not reach higher than . . . the best of the middle classes, but descends with a startling fidelity to the lowest of the low."[38] Boz's sketches led *Chambers's Edinburgh Journal* to predict that "he can scarcely fail to become a successful and popular author,"[39] a prediction quickly fulfilled that seems both aligned and not aligned with Foucault's concept of the "immortality" of earlier works: many of Dickens's characters, beginning with Pickwick, have been hailed as "immortal," but so has the author. And whereas Foucault's modern authors sacrificed their lives to their works, Dickens, as we will see, tries to kill off his surrogate Boz.

Moreover, Foucault's notion that the "link between writing and death" effaces "the individual characteristics of the writer" is worth pondering. One of the standard lines about Dickens's apprentice works is that he developed a particular voice, the "Boz" voice. That perambulating middle-aged voyeur, sympathetic yet distanced from what he observes, enjoying the funny and sad scenes around him and the opportunities to tell about them to an eager audience, has been spotted at the front of a genealogical lineup of bachelor narrators descending into the present. Foucault's effacement points to an opposite characterization of the narrator: an absence, a disembodied voice, a product of discourse rather than personal vision, a "dead man" in the game of writing.[40] Dickens's narrator in the sketches is more than a consequence of syntax, but Boz is not always a *flâneur*, a pavement patroller. He frequently is an absent presence at private scenes of suffering and death, and in that aspect seems occasioned more by conventions of grammar and narrative than of verbalized person-hood. Even when Boz deploys not the personal pronoun but the more ambivalent plural "we," he can either assimilate himself into a larger print community or occlude his presence in that society and narrative syntax.

There are various ways that the first-person plural pronoun used by Boz summons readers' concurrence.[41] The editorial "we" invokes a minatory, knowing, authoritative voice; the comradely "we" assumes a company similarly inclined (and aged); the ethical "we" underscores the standards of a society; the authorial "we" collects like-minded writers as a group over against other kinds of writers; the sympathetic "we" interpellates a community of caring urban dwellers; the guide "we" "buttonhole[s] the reader";[42] and the repetitious "we" signs the instability and protean nature of "Boz." Moreover, the "we" segues into a pluralized identity – in the newspapers it might seem to speak for the politics of the proprietor and his public, in the context of content it might assimilate this author's voice to traditional forms of expression about this subject matter. Furthermore, the "we" that draws the print proprietor, the journal's editors and writers, and its readers into a community would, as we have seen, constitute very different communities when Boz published or republished his pieces in politically, socially, aesthetically, and commercially distinct publications.

Boz's "we" speaks both as a characterized persona and on occasion as almost an effaced narrator. As the effaced narrator has received less commentary than the characterized one, let us examine an instance. In Dickens's final ordering of *Sketches by Boz*, "The Broker's Man" immediately follows Bung's election for beadle.[43] The narrator introduces the tale using forms of the plural personal pronoun: "our parish," "we are enabled." This usage at once speaks from an individual and a collective perspective; by hailing the parishioners and by extension the readers "to devote our attention" to less public events and characters, the narrator conflates three separate categories of experience: his own (it seems clear "he" is a "he"), the parishioners', and potentially the readers'.[44] But the "we" is suspended after a couple of paragraphs in which we are made acquainted with Bung, as he is and as he was "[s]ome few months before he was prevailed upon to stand a contested election for the office of beadle," when "necessity attached him to the service of a broker" (p. 27). Bung worked for a functionary of the court employed to value the assets of a debtor, in this case staying by court order in the residence of the debtor so that nothing of value could be removed before being inventoried, seized, and sold. In such cases the private hearth is invaded by public officials, and the hitherto sometimes concealed embarrassments of poverty become the conversation of the neighborhood.

The narrator has, upon further acquaintance, found Bung to be "a shrewd, knowing fellow, with no inconsiderable power of observation." Further, the narrator is struck "(as we dare say our readers have frequently been in other cases)" by Bung's power "not only of sympathising with, but to all appearance of understanding feelings to which they themselves are entire strangers" (all, p. 29). In other words, the narrator discovers in Bung the very powers of observation and empathy that in other stories he demonstrates himself, and that, by using the plural pronouns, he attributes also to his readers. Having thus transferred any characterological nature from himself to Bung and the reader, the narrator withdraws from the narrative, thinking "on reflection," that the stories Bung related to him "will tell better in nearly his own words than with any attempted embellishments of ours" (p. 29). Ostensibly, this move transfers narrative control, authority, vision, and vocabulary, to another teller, whose account has been transcribed, as Dickens was doing often in Parliament. Indeed, the sketch is sometimes seen as one of Dickens's early efforts to render working-class speech.[45] There is both a Wellerism and a Sairey

Gampism in Bung's account, though these two characters will have quite different voices when they appear fully fledged in *Pickwick Papers* (1836–37) and *Martin Chuzzlewit* (1842–43) respectively. However, the effacement of the narrator is somewhat incomplete. These are "nearly" Bung's "own words"; they *ostensibly* lack "any attempted embellishments of ours"; yet they are also entitled by the narrator, "Mr. Bung's Narrative," thus enclosing the ventriloquized voice within that of the supervening narrator, however minimal or communal it might be. Further, like a playwright indicating stage directions, this narrator intervenes several times to decipher through Bung's body language his emotions and sincerity: for instance, "'But this is the bright side of the picture, sir, after all,' resumed Bung, laying aside the knowing look, and flash air, with which he had repeated the previous anecdote" (p. 31).

Thus in some pieces Boz makes way for other voices, fully situated as alternative narrators or, more often, simply loquacious storytellers within the story. One might look for evidence of linear development as Dickens practices his craft. He tries one strategy, elaborates on it in the next contribution, reverses it in a third, then discovers a further potential in the topic or treatment, and thus grows and improves with each successor. The chronology of the *Sketches* is, however, so complicated; the pressures on him to produce were so irregular and at times acute; the competition between reporting and sketching was so continuous and intertwined; and the revisions over time were so extensive and different for each entry in the collected volumes; that linear development, even if it could be minutely tracked, is unlikely to be the paradigm of Boz's artistic trajectory. Minns was the first story published and one of the last to be revised and inserted in the Second Series of *Sketches*. The parish sketches popped up in the *Evening Chronicle* between February 28 and August 20 in 1835, in the same order, it should be noted, that they followed in volume 1 of the First Series of *Sketches by Boz*, February 8, 1836; but "Our Next-Door Neighbours," which after 1837 became the seventh and last episode about the parish, was written after the First Series was published, appearing in the *Morning Chronicle* on March 18, 1836.[46] It was republished in the Second Series released in December 1836 and was only attached to the other six parish sketches when both series were reorganized and published in twenty monthly parts between November 1837 and June 1839. With each reappearance of these pieces, Dickens had an opportunity to revise for a new context, a changing sense of Boz's voice and audience, and when married to George Cruikshank's illustrations a clearly collaborative and sometimes contestatory print instantiation.[47]

What is more possible to pick out, as Dickens dashes off quires of script both factual and fictional, are those preoccupations that generate multiple narratives. One of these is names and the way changes of nominative identity articulate and expose class movement.[48] "The Bloomsbury Christening," an early anonymous tale published in the April 1834 *Monthly Magazine*, supplies a kind of back story to the previously published "Poplar Walk": Nicodemus Dumps, like Minns a well-to-do bachelor with a miserable and cross disposition, agrees to serve as godfather to his nephew's first child, largely because Charles Kitterbell is such "an admirable subject to exercise his misery-creating powers upon" (p. 448). The christening and party that succeeds it go off badly, as these comic engagements usually do in Dickens: heavy rain, bad transport, too many guests, all variants on the Budden Sunday dinner. Dumps, who patronizes the Society for the Suppression of Vice because it advocates "putting a stop to any harmless amusements," delivers a christening toast dwelling on the future calamities that might befall the infant – "premature decay" and "lingering disease" (pp. 448, 461). If these are not enough to summon all the cambric handkerchiefs to staunch the ladies' tears, Dumps happily concludes with the consoling thought – borrowed from *King Lear* – that, should the boy survive, it is to be hoped that his parents will not "experience that distracting truth, 'how sharper than a serpent's tooth it is to have a thankless child.'" "It need hardly be added," the effaced narrator inserts, "that this occurrence quite put a stop to the harmony of the evening" (pp. 641–62). When a subsequent Kitterbell baby boy is about to make an appearance, his parents require that, to qualify, any potential godfather must promise not to make a speech after supper or have any connection with "the most miserable man in the world." Hence a christening party quenches the possibility of inheritance just as the Buddens' party did.

Another instance of names afflicting fortune comes in "The Tuggses at Ramsgate," a late sketch that appeared in the April 1836 *Library of Fiction*, illustrated by Robert Seymour; simultaneously Dickens was composing the first number of *Pickwick*. Joseph Tuggs is a grocer who, when a "long pending lawsuit respecting the validity of a will, [is] unexpectedly decided," inherits £20,000 (p. 330). The shop is shut up "at an unusually early hour" (p. 330) so that the family might settle on their future. One of the first things decided upon is change of name. ("Tuggs" is another of those vaguely vulgar names with which Dickens christens his middle-class characters, but here the joke is underscored when Master Tuggs, attempting to direct an uncooperative donkey by "sundry uncomfortable tugs at the bit," fails [p. 338]. So too do the Tuggs fail to direct their fate.)[49] Henceforth the parents will be called "Ma" and "Pa," while the simpleton son Simon renames himself "Cymon" and his sister calls herself "Charlotta." She adds, "and Pa must leave off all his vulgar habits" (p. 330). Of course their attempt at rising in class is both laughable and disastrous. They are bilked by a couple, the Waters, who first compare them to aristocracy: Cymon "is very much like the Marquis Carriwini," Mrs. Tuggs is "the very picture of the Dowager Duchess of Dobbleton," and Charlotta is "the *facsimile* of a titled relative of Mrs Belinda Waters" (p. 332). After this buttering-up, Mrs. Captain Waters carries on a flirtation with Cymon that ends when he is discovered by the third member of the fleecers, the ominously named Captain Slaughter (it chimes with Waters although the two parties seem to be quite different), hiding behind curtains in a room formerly occupied only by the simpleton and the married lady. A successful suit by the outraged husband for crim. con. transfers £1,500 from the grocer to the captain. The story ends with a variant of the last sentence of "Poplar Walk," publishing names: "The money was paid to hush the matter up, but it got abroad notwithstanding; and there are not wanting those who affirm that three designing imposters never found more easy dupes, than did Captain Waters, Mrs. Waters, and Lieutenant Slaughter, in the Tuggses at Ramsgate" (p. 344).

There are other cases where characters substitute pseudonyms for real names or are associated with the patronyms and titles of upper-class society figures as they unsuccessfully strive for higher station. Signor Billsmethi, the master of a "not . . . dear" dancing academy on Gray's Inn Lane (p. 253), was surely christened plain Bill Smith. His daughter's hopes for marrying up to a gentleman "with a little money, a little business, and a little mother" who manages his commercial and social affairs (p. 253), are soon crushed. After her intended, Mr. Cooper, chooses another young lady as his dancing partner at the grand dress ball, the Billsmethis commence an action for breach of promise, settled by Cooper's mother taking £20 from the till to pay them off. The "mysterious, philosophical, romantic, metaphysical Sparkins" (p. 358), who in the story entitled "Horatio Sparkins" seems to the nouveaux-riches Maldertons and their tuft-hunting friends to bear a resemblance to Lord Byron and the Honourable Augustus Fitz-Edward Fitz-John Fitz-Osborne, is as illegitimate as the latter personage, being in fact the junior partner in a shabby and slippery linen-draper's shop, and another Mr. Smith, Christian name Samuel.

Naming thus has complicated connections to class, with Boz and his readers on the whole siding with those who do not pretend to be other than they are, or seek through nominative gestures to improve their family's fortunes. (What is to be made of the "vulgarity" of Boz, juxtaposed to the heraldic figure on Dickens's bookplate?) Little sympathy is extended by the narrator, or evoked by Boz in the sentimental hearts of his readers, for the unfortunate Buddens, Kitterbells, and Tuggses, or for their rich relatives Minns and Dumps. In fact, another of the persistent themes running through three years of sketches is the disappointment of great expectations. (One of Dickens's most memorable similes appears when David Copperfield is describing the "arbitrary characters" in the stenographic system: "a thing like the beginning of a cobweb, meant expectation, and . . . a pen and ink sky-rocket stood for disadvantageous" [p. 465]. Throughout his career Dickens was intensely aware of the sequence from hopeful expectations to bad endings.) Whether anticipating an offer of marriage or an outing at Ramsgate, Boz's dramatis personae rise to elevated spirits only to fall precipitously into recriminations and regrets. In "The Boarding House," chapter 1 begins with a lyrical description of "decidedly, the neatest [house] in all Great Coram Street" (p. 273). It is managed to perfection by Mrs. Tibbs, to whom her husband "was to his wife what the 0 is in 90 – he was of some importance *with* her – he was nothing without her" (p. 273). (Yet, as we have seen, Dickens adopted him as his second nom de plume, without her.) By the end of the second chapter of this tale, the misadventures of the tenants have ruptured and ruined everything. The Tibbs are separated, with Mr. swallowing his annual income in a Walworth tavern and Mrs. disposing of her exquisitely maintained furniture by public auction. In "The Steam Excursion," Percy Noakes's arrangements are greeted "with the utmost enthusiasm" (p. 372). Despite some contretemps along the way to the launch, once on board the party members have a wonderful time telling stories, singing, dancing, and flirting, until it is time to return to the dock. Then a heavy storm soaks and rocks the boat, materially interfering with the enjoyment of the lavish repast set forth in the cabin. When the guests debark in the middle of the night, they are fractious, inclined to quarrel, "dispirited and worn out" (p. 387). An analogous declension occurs in the "Scene" at "Astley's," an amphitheater successfully specializing in melodramas and circus acts featuring equestrian feats.[50] The narrator, very much in his Boz persona, opens by vicariously delighting in the anticipatory excitement of the families who attend but closes with melancholy reflections on the daytime stage-door loungers in their threadbare clothes, so unlike the personages they perform of evenings "with all the aid of lights, music, and artificial flowers" (p. 111).

There are lots of moments of fun, and despite the melancholy terminations of many scenes and characters and tales, the public took to Boz as a humorist.[51] But Boz is often in the Dumps, with Nicodemus. Though not a patron of the Society for the Suppression of Vice and harmless amusements, Boz is acutely aware of the necessity of and immense lifting of spirits occasioned by a holiday or treat, as well as of the brevity and transience of happiness. Again and again the narratives trace the trajectory doubly inscribed in one of the last sketches Boz wrote, "Meditations in Monmouth Street," published in the *Morning Chronicle* on September 24, 1836, nearly seven months after *Pickwick* began. Boz loves to visit this "emporium for second hand wearing apparel," or as he reformulates it in an instance of rhetorical declension, "these extensive groves of the illustrious dead" (p. 76). While he stands there contemplating the shop displays that spill out onto the pavement, he imagines the biography of a poor but indulged boy who grows up and out of his carefully tended secondhand outfits and into the suit of an idle ruffian with a dog at his heels (prototype of Bill Sikes who makes his first appearance in *Oliver Twist* ten months later), and who ends his days wearing a "coarse round frock, with a worn cotton neckerchief" (p. 80), facing prison, banishment, or the gallows. This imagined fall is succeeded by cheerier fancies about shoes, culminating in terpsichorean feats and romantic competition. But these are put to flight when the proprietress of the shop recalls Boz from his dreaming, sharply reminding him "that in the depth of our meditations we might have been rudely staring at the old lady for half an hour without knowing it" (p. 82). (In this late sketch Boz is clearly a person in his own right, not some necessary piece of syntax providing barely more than stage directions.)

VIII

It is often said that the darkening of *Pickwick*, when after the trial Mr. Pickwick discovers the world of debtors' prison, owes something to Dickens's recollections of his parents' time in the Marshalsea, something to his overt critique of law and poor laws initiated in *Oliver Twist*, and something to the sudden death of his young sister-in-law, Mary Hogarth, in May 1837. These debts may indeed account in part for the Fleet Prison chapters; but it should have come as no surprise to Boz's readers that happy beginnings may have sad endings, and even that the circuit of life so often imaged in the 1820s and 1830s renews its course every day, when, as in "The Streets – Morning," the last drunks and vagrants have disappeared "and the chosen promenades of profligate misery are empty," just before the cold desolation of the thoroughfares slowly warms up and fills with life "and the day begins in good earnest" (pp. 41, 52).[52] That succession of contrasting scenes repeated over and over was indelibly inscribed on Dickens's consciousness by his own ups and downs, the brief flares of acclaim and celebrity as actor or author or crack newsman, the sudden descents into poverty and debt, the weary days and nights of struggle, and the ecstasies and despairs of his first love affair.

Dickens also learns that Boz's public shares his interest in these scenes of alternating glee and misery, even while he was persistently hailed as a new "realist," jovial and intimate, inviting his readers and characters to join him as friends and share in his "entertainments." And as he begins to collect, arrange, and shape his scattered short fictions into volumes for John Macrone, he is increasingly drawn to stories that grow out of, or into, death. He tells Macrone at the end of October 1835 that he has long projected sketching the interior of a prison – not the Marshalsea or the Fleet, perhaps too close to his own personal story to be rendered as fiction, yet. Instead, Dickens asks his editor, Black, to get him admitted to Newgate. Accompanied by Macrone and an American journalist, Nat Willis, Dickens visited both Newgate and Coldbath Fields, Clerkenwell, on November 5; Willis remembered that Dickens was silent throughout the tour of Newgate.[53] He studied the setting and the condemned men carefully, but told Catherine three weeks later that he was having "much difficulty in remembering the place."[54] However, in two days he wrote "A Visit to Newgate," and afterwards he proudly showed it around and asked George Hogarth, Macrone, and Harrison Ainsworth for their opinions.[55]

The conclusion of what Dickens eventually categorized as a "Scene" stretches Boz even further than ventriloquizing Bung. He enters the mind of a condemned man during his last night alive. The transition from Boz's personal voice to his readers' imaginative apprehension and then to the felon's delusions is accomplished swiftly. Boz guides his readers to the condemned cells through a succession of preceding spaces and scenes. He not only walks his readers into the building, past inmates and visitors in the courtyards, he also pauses at the schoolroom to note fourteen young pickpockets with "such terrible little faces" (very unlike the variety and geniality of Fagin's boys) and carefully surveys the prison chapel with its conspicuous "*condemned pew*" (pp. 204, 206). Passing through the press-yard, as if the progress through the prison were a kind of synecdoche for the life of the prisoners and the increasingly serious crimes they committed, Boz comes at last to the condemned cells, his

journey there being suddenly couched in the present tense and assimilated
to that of a prisoner who after the warrant for execution is received "is
removed to the cells and confined in one of them until he leaves it for the
scaffold" (p. 208). The next paragraph begins, "We entered the first cell."
This "we" is both Dickens and his companions on the November tour
and Boz and his readers thereafter. The rest of the paragraph describes the
minimal contents of the stone dungeon.

The succeeding paragraph begins in the imperative: "Conceive the situation of a man, spending his last night on earth in this cell" (p. 208). It is an
appeal to the reader, but also to the writer – one of those moments when the
author in a sense imagines his own death so that a narrative may be generated.
The next sentence continues with the past tense describing the condemned
man's three previous days, but midway through its successor time and tense
move again into the present, this time of the felon's consciousness, the
narrator's story, and the reader's experience: "now that eternity is before
him . . . now that his fears of death amount almost to madness . . . he is lost
and stupefied" (p. 209). The chiming hours mark the passage of hours: seven
left, then six. But the narrative, largely generated out of the prisoner's
deranged senses, jumbles past with present. He sleeps and in his dreams
returns to the pleasant settings and times when he and his wife were in love;
then the scene "changes" to the courtroom and he hears the verdict. The next
dream seems to realize his determination to escape; he runs away far into the
country, surely safe from pursuit, and plans to sleep until morning.

The final paragraph begins in the voice of the effaced narrator:
"A period of unconsciousness succeeds." A necessary piece of information
perhaps, but it does not jar or wrench the narrative from its intimate
engagement with the condemned man's mind and the readers' present
participation. "He wakes, cold and wretched" (p. 210). Confused by his
dreams, he recovers from momentary uncertainty by seeing that every
object in the narrow cell is "too frightfully real." "He is the condemned
felon again, guilty and despairing"; and after a semicolon, the narrator
ends the sentence (in several senses of the word): "and in two hours more
will be dead" (p. 210). Garrett Stewart has observed that the experiential
void of death must during the final transitional interval be spoken
through life's terms. In early versions of this ending, Dickens's prose
attempts to inhabit both the mind of the living and in the phrase "he is
a corpse" (instead of "will be dead") the transformation of vital body into
something we can only name as non-human, non-living.[56]

This is another of those interventions, like that at the end of
"Monmouth Street" (written ten months later), when the narrator's

imaginative world is terminated by the interjection of reality; but unlike the indignant old clothes dealer chastising her surveiller, here the narrator and the narrow barren cell combine to recall prisoner and reader to life and its finality. Dickens was excited by this dramatic ending. Although some months later he apologized to Macrone for not being adept at extravagant self-advertising – "I really cannot do the tremendous in puffing myself" – the announcement that Dickens drafted for the February 4, 1836 *Morning Chronicle* extols "a very powerful article, entitled 'A Visit to Newgate.'"[57]

Not only was Dickens pleased with his story, not only was it immediately praised by his father-in-law George Hogarth and his employer John Black when he showed it to them in manuscript, but also he told Catherine the day after finishing it that "an extraordinary idea for a story of a very singular kind occurred to me this morning, and I am anxious to commit it to paper before the impression it made upon me is lost."[58] Under pressure from Macrone, who "has urged me most imperatively and pressingly to 'get on,'"[59] Dickens is at this moment in late November 1835 fully caught up in identifying himself (especially to the Hogarths) as a professional author. His language incorporates the language of printing: committing a story to paper under pressure, "pressingly," before the impression (of story in his mind, of type on a page) is lost. He is thinking, conceiving of his writing, and speaking about it, using the vocabulary and processes of print production. It is a telling instance of his beginning to articulate himself as a publishing author.

That second story, "The Black Veil," becomes a sequel to the last night in Newgate. Rather than writing the back story for a previously composed tale, as he did with Dumps, Dickens extends the Newgate sketch beyond what one might imagine was the definitive end of every story (as it is of many of his other stories, such as "The Drunkard's Death"): the living body transmogrified into a corpse. In this second story, uncharacteristically set back to 1800, so nothing Boz ever witnessed, a heavily veiled woman asks a young medical practitioner on a winter's evening to attend the next morning to a dying patient. He assents, and when he sees the body in an upper room of an isolated and poorly maintained house in Walworth, he knows the patient has died as a result of violence. Indeed, the victim, son of the veiled widow, was hanged earlier that day for an unspecified crime, while his companion, "equally guilty with himself, had been acquitted for want of evidence" (p. 367). It may be that the surgeon is correct in condemning the punishment as murder,[60] but the boy has the same story as Boz will imagine a year later in Monmouth Street about the indulged child who turned bad. "The history was an everyday one. The mother was a widow without friends or money," and the boy, unmindful of her caring, "plunged into a career of dissipation and crime" (p. 367). The corpse cannot be revived. The mad widow lives out the rest of her days comforted and supported by the doctor, whose first patient affords him the opportunity to extend charity abundantly repaid to him in honors, rank, and station. (Later in his career Dickens would speak about his vocation in medical terms, as diagnosing and attempting to treat societal disease; this could be an almost unconscious prefiguration of the hoped-for reward for extending charity and comfort to those suffering from mental illness.)

That Dickens can find a sequel to death is remarkable enough. That in subsequent republishings the sequel connects to stories written afterwards marks the skill he is acquiring in unpacking an already-printed text further. Dickens will do so with unmatched inventiveness in *Pickwick* and *Oliver Twist*. That he returns to the story of a cosseted child who goes bad prefigures episodes in *David Copperfield* where David wonders whether he will be rescued from the privations his stepfather imposes after his doting mother's death, or turn into another vagabond, thief, or donkey boy. It will be a long time in his writing career before Dickens can credibly imagine that a nurturing childhood yields a mature and respectable adult; it will be equally long before he glimpses the possibility that suffering can anneal character rather than melt it. Death holds the keys to many possibilities, for Boz and Dickens. In shaping his first book, Boz deploys it again and again to open and close narrative.

IX

While death is generating supplementary texts, the life of Boz, separate from Dickens, begins in 1836 to develop beyond his control. Writing under a pseudonym could allow an author to create an alter ego, a persona whose character, personality, opinions, gender, and age might be constructed. Many of Boz's readers believed in the transparency of his narratorial identity. They thought Boz was a middle-aged, solitary, melancholy figure. When at the premiere of his operatic burletta *The Village Coquettes* on December 6, 1836 Boz appeared on stage, the audience was surprised to see a young man, with curly hair, flashing eyes, and high spirits: the disjunction between pseudonym and person startled.[61] More than a year later, the lawyer Serjeant Ballantine met Boz at a quadrille and was startled by his youthfulness: "looks quite a boy."[62] What advantage was there in maintaining this discordance between authorial Boz and authorial body? It was a question Dickens mulled for many years.

If "Boz" was an arbitrary signifier, it might be altered. And altered by others as well as by Dickens. When Macrone republished Boz's newspaper sketches in volume form accompanied with illustrations by George Cruikshank, the composite product took on something of a life of its own. For one thing, at Macrone's suggestion the projected titles linked author and illustrator. Macrone proposed something like "Bubbles from the Bwain of Boz and the Graver of Cruikshank," alluding to an 1834 book by Sir Francis Bond Head entitled *Bubbles from the Brunnens of Nassau, by an Old Man.*[63] If this conjectural title is correct, Macrone too imagined a connection between the writer Boz and "an old man." Dickens suggested two alternatives; the one chosen was much simpler and less reconditely allusive. "Sketches by Boz and Cuts by Cruikshank" echoes John Leech's 1835 *Etchings and Sketchings by A. Pen Esq.*,[64] and Washington Irving's *Sketch Book of Geoffrey Crayon, Gent.*, which Michael Slater points out "Dickens had soaked himself in" as a child.[65] In 1819, when Dickens was seven, Irving was living in England where John Murray published a British edition in order to quash piratical copies of the American one. It was a great success, Irving became a celebrity in England and Paris, and Dickens proposed in 1838 that he and Irving exchange the stories each was publishing at that time (*Oliver Twist* in *Bentley's*, Irving's sketches in the *Knickerbocker Magazine*).[66] Coincidentally, Irving was also an admirer of Goldsmith and published in the USA a biography in 1849, just after Forster released his biography in Britain. But the aspect of the title that initially identified the volumes was the conjunction of writer and artist, "Sketches by *Boz* and Cuts by *Cruikshank*" (my emphases). The "co-adjutors," as Dickens's father-in-law George Hogarth called them, become conflated: "Boz" identified a particular attitude toward the urban environment of London thought to be expressed by both the letterpress and the etchings of these newly illustrated pieces. Hence Dickens's titles that conflated "Sketches" and "Cuts" implied either that the two mediums said the same thing or that they were a composite whole. (In fact, Dickens and Cruikshank, while enjoying many of the same attractions of the city, also appreciated some quite different things about the metropolis and its inhabitants; not all the illustrations express the same sentiments as the corresponding text.[67])

Cruikshank's frontispiece to the Second Series of *Sketches by Boz*, published in one volume in December 1836, picks up the metaphor of the book's being a "pilot balloon" that Dickens used in the Preface to the First Series (February 1836).[68] It shows Boz and Cruikshank ascending in the car of a hot-air balloon: two passengers rising to lofty heights from which to look down on London. The balloon metaphor could be construed as belonging more to the visual than the verbal realm, as panoramas of the city had become quite familiar from balloon-perspective prints as well as from views displayed at the London Coliseum and obtained from the top of the Monument. On the other side, in *Dombey and Son* (1846–48) Dickens imagines taking off the rooftops in order for the writer/voyeur to peer down inside the houses from above. So the balloon complexly reiterates the double perspective of the composite Boz, a writer and artist who together perceive both at ground level and from on high.

However, Dickens struggles in his Preface (p. [xxxix]) to make the book his even though he shares the credit. He says that "the Author of these volumes throws them up as *his* pilot balloon" (emphasis added). A second paragraph elaborates: "in this one it is very possible for a man to embark, not only himself, but all his hopes of future fame, and all his chances of future success." Given that risk, the author – not Macrone, who actually suggested and negotiated the deal – secured "the assistance and companionship" of a "well-known individual, who had frequently contributed to the success, though his well-earned reputation rendered it impossible for him ever to have shared the hazard, of similar undertakings." This may allude to an illustrated predecessor of Dickens's London fun, Pierce Egan's *Life in London* (1821–22), done in collaboration with Cruikshank and his older brother Robert. "The application was readily heard, and at once acceded to: this is their first voyage in company, but it may not be the last." After this graceful bow to his companion and covert appeal for applause from his audience – the whole passage reads like an after-curtain speech – Dickens concludes the Preface with repetitive iterations of *his* authorship. The author notes the "very favourable reception" which several pieces received in their prior (and unillustrated) print instantiations; he entreats "the kindness and favour of the public"; he explains that his object "has been to present little pictures of life and manners as they really are"; and "he hopes to repeat his experiment with increased confidence, and on a more extensive scale." No word here about his balloon companion, but some expression of Dickens's present authorial insecurities and an indication that the next balloon might be piloted "with increased confidence" by only one. Or perhaps not, since the last phrase promises a future release on "a more extensive scale," implying more text and possibly more pictures. The whole preface betrays authorial pride mixed with uncertainty ("no inconsiderable feeling of trepidation") and self-publicity (even if Dickens "cannot do the tremendous in puffing") moderated by terms such as "prudent course" and "devoutly and earnestly hoping" that the balloon may *"go off well."*

Cruikshank never reaped much benefit from being associated with "Boz." Since laws governing copyright in pictures did not protect illustrators, Macrone owned the plates outright. He could reprint or sell them without the artist's permission and without sharing any profit. As he did. But Dickens got a certain amount of additional celebrity as the collaborator in producing "Bozzes" – that peculiar conflation of word and line, tone and attitude, setting and class, with which the *Sketches* became identified by critics and the public.[69] The marginal increase in reputation was no doubt gratifying to Dickens, though the "joined-at-the-hip" association with Cruikshank bedeviled them both later in life. But it also blurred the connection between Dickens and Boz; added, as it were, another person to the persona.

Thus "Boz" came to name a genre as well as an author. People referred to "Bozzes," meaning sketches similar in tone and subject to Dickens's. But "Bozzes" named not the newspaper tales and sketches but the illustrated ones gathered in the three volumes of *Sketches by Boz*. In time, this genre became more generalized. Since *Pickwick Papers* was also attributed to "Boz,"[70] "Bozzes" named a kind of illustrated serial representing contemporary middle- and lower-middle-class life, chiefly about London, and narrated with humour, sympathy, and more than a modicum of distancing coolness and irony. This was a genre of writing and publishing that could be imitated, and it was, since imitations were alternative modes of writing not prohibited by copyright. Consequently there were knockoffs of Boz's serialized parts, plagiarisms of his titles, and permutations on his name. The alteration of a single letter, from "z" to "s," made the pseudonym seem more like what critics supposed it to be, a shortened form of "Boswell." "Bos" might be extended to anyone, and was. T. P. Prest used "Bos" as his moniker for imitations of all the early novels, which were entitled using names as close to Dickens's works as possible: *The Sketch Book by Bos, Pickwick in America, The Life and Adventures of Oliver Twist, the Workhouse Boy*, and so forth. Another parodist altered the first letter: "Poz." This might stand for "positive" or "possibilities" or merely as a misprint for "Boz." Dickens's eponymous heroes had their Christian and family names slightly altered: Oliver Twiss, Nickelas Nicklebery, Mister Humfries, Barnaby Budge. Even titular formulas were revised: *The Posthumous Papers of the Wonderful Discovery Club* and *The Posthumourous Notes of the Pickwick Club* are two examples of the imitations that flooded the market. Changes of name that in the sketches signified aspirations to class ascent, in the print world became ways of appropriating, marketing, and cashing in on another author's commercial value. The middle-aged observant pedestrian Boz may not have resembled his twenty-something creator, but there was a legitimate, if complexly figured, relationship between them. Not so the others adopting chiming names: they took Boz down-market, flooded the book-stalls, threatened to turn Bozzian simulacrums into waste paper for sale in bulk to mix in vats with the old clothes in Monmouth Street in order to manufacture new blank quires.[71]

Finally, "Boz" recycled within Dickens's own family. When his first child, a son, was christened in St. Pancras New Church, Woburn Place, on December 9, 1837 – more than eleven months after his birth on January 6 – Dickens determined on honoring his maternal great uncle, Thomas John Culliford, an insurance broker who might, like Minns or Dumps, bequeath something to his young relative. At the moment in the service when the minister asked the parents to name the child, Dickens pronounced "Charles" – after himself of course – and "Culliford." And then his father John shouted out "Boz"! So Charley, subsequently to be saddled with the further soubriquet of the Snodgering Blee, became nominatively not only the echo of his father Charles Dickens, not only the recipient of a wealthy relative's patronym, but also the holder of his father's pseudonym. The author, Charles, and his father name his son after one of several pen names under which he was publishing. Some of these pseudonyms he claimed or rechristened (the Tibbs sketches were silently reassigned to "Boz" for volume publication, for instance), and others he disclaimed, as we shall see. But the upshot of all these christenings was that Boz was appearing in paratexts, plagiarisms, pluralities ("Bozzes"), authorial personae, and in person, in the person of Boz's own son.

# CHAPTER 3

# *Writing Boz (1836–1837):* The Pickwick Papers

Charles Dickens, "Phiz" sketch, 1837

It is the fate of all authors or chroniclers to create imaginary friends, and lose them in the course of art. Nor is this the full extent of their misfortunes; for they are required to furnish an account of them besides.
– *Pickwick Papers*

There is no doubt that this sudden taste for crowding upon the sunny side of the road, was originally generated by a facetious gentleman who, for some months, escaped detection under the name of "Boz."
– "Some Thoughts on Arch-Waggery, and in especial, on the Genius of 'Boz,'" *Court Journal* 10 (April 1837)

The *Pickwick Papers* may be called an extension of one of [Dickens's] bright sketches. *Oliver Twist* may be called an extension of one of his gloomy ones.
– G. K. Chesterton, *Appreciations and Criticisms of the Works of Charles Dickens*

Dickens is creating *Pickwick* and himself as a novelist against and through his contemporary legal world.
– Jonathan H. Grossman, *The Art of Alibi: English Law Courts and the Novel*

Coming to terms with death was a necessary element in the idea of greatness.
– Sir Frank Kermode, "Fiction and E. M. Forster"

I

On the eve of publishing *Sketches by Boz*, First Series, the twenty-four-year-old Dickens had few relevant models of authorship by which to steer his own course. There were some journalists who had achieved distinction – notably, William Hazlitt, employed by the *Morning Chronicle* in 1812, briefly their theater critic in 1814 (he was dismissed in May of that year for being unreliable about fulfilling assignments), freelance journalist and liberal, attacked for his support of the "Cockney school of poetry" by John Gibson Lockhart in *Blackwood's Magazine* (a cautionary example if Dickens were thinking of a career as a book reviewer), and from 1820–22 a regular contributor of essays and theatrical reviews to John Scott's admirable *London Magazine*. Several collections of Hazlitt's periodical essays were successfully reissued. However, Hazlitt began his working life as a portrait painter and copyist of old masters, not as journalist. Later he wrote books on philosophy, politics, and economics, a grammar textbook, translations, fine studies of contemporary and English Renaissance dramatists, biographical memoirs of Thomas Holcroft and Napoleon, a history of English comic writers, and an account of a prolonged and unfortunate love

affair, *Liber amoris*, that, though published anonymously, soon was identified as Hazlitt's and ridiculed in the conservative press for his infatuation with
his landlord's daughter, who entered into a faithful though unmarried relationship with a handsome aspiring lawyer. Dickens, caught up in an energetic
if also rather bossy courtship of his employer George Hogarth's daughter, was
not inclined to pursue the sorts of romantic entanglements that had been both
the glory and the downfall of so many Romantic period predecessors. Nor was
Hazlitt's end inspiring. Despite the substantial and often brilliant books he
had written, especially his portraits of contemporaries evidencing *The Spirit of
the Age* (1824) and essays about the theater and popular entertainments – both
high (Shakespeare) and low (boxing) – Hazlitt's income declined precipitously in the 1820s. Ill and penniless, at the age of fifty-two he was writing
begging letters far more desperate than those Dickens penned at the beginning
of his career. To Francis Jeffrey of the *Edinburgh Review*, Hazlitt tersely
described his situation: "I am dying; can you send me 10£, and so consummate your many kindnesses to me?" He died insolvent on September 18, 1830.[1]
A great writer, but not a career model for Dickens.[2]

The most successful British author of the early 1830s was a man of
Dickensian energy born into considerable wealth and status: Edward Lytton
Bulwer. By 1836 he seemed to have done and had it all. A graduate of
Cambridge, for a brief time the lover of Lady Caroline Lamb, and "a
monied young blood" in the words of Andrew Brown (*Oxford Dictionary
of National Biography*), after college Bulwer alternated between dissipation
and omnivorous reading in Paris and Versailles. In August 1827, despite the
vehement opposition of his mother, he married the impoverished and
willful Rosina Wheeler and set up a luxurious residence at Woodcot
House in Oxfordshire that probably required many times their combined
annual income. In order to finance their extravagant style, during the
next decade Bulwer produced twelve novels, double that number of
short stories, several plays, a long narrative poem, a history of Athens, an
important analysis of English culture (*England and the English*, 1833), and
hundreds of periodical essays and reviews. He edited and contributed
monthly columns to the *New Monthly Magazine* for two years (1831–33),
and climaxed this extraordinary decade of production with *The Last Days of
Pompeii* (1834), immediately translated into at least ten languages, dramatized frequently in several countries, and reset as an opera at least twice. He
then followed up with another historical novel, *Rienzi, Last of the Tribunes*
(1835), less successful as a commercial venture but effective in rehabilitating
Cola di Rienzi's reputation as a visionary hero in strife-torn early Renaissance Rome (Petrarch had praised him; Friedrich Engels later wrote a play

about him) and inspiring Richard Wagner to his first successful opera, begun in 1838 from Bulwer's novel, premiered in 1842. (Giuseppi Verdi also contemplated an opera about Rienzi.) Dickens reviewed John Baldwin Buckstone's theatrical adaptation of the novel premiering at the Adelphi Theatre in the *Morning Chronicle*, February 4, 1836. From 1831 to 1841 Bulwer was also an MP with a splendid London house just off Park Lane. His fame crossed the English Channel and the Atlantic: in 1834 the *American Quarterly Review* declared that he was, "without doubt, the most popular writer now living."[3] Yet no matter how successful Bulwer was politically, as a novelist and theorist of literature, as a social critic, and as a playwright, "he was extraordinarily sensitive to criticism," Catherine Seville reminds us, and "felt undervalued . . . slighted and misunderstood."[4]

While Dickens had already written poems, plays, essays and reviews, and journalism, and apparently had plans for an historical novel about the Gordon riots (London, 1780) and/or a novel about thieves and fences around the Seven Dials area of London (a setting of one of the *Sketches by Boz*), he certainly hadn't produced anything close to this quantity or quality of output, nor received anything like Bulwer's payments for his writings. Moreover, two of Bulwer's novels, *Paul Clifford* (1830) and *Eugene Aram* (1832), treated criminals sympathetically; these Newgate novels provoked extensive recriminations from John Gibson Lockhart and William Maginn. Both the morality of the stories and the hypocrisy of the author were reprehended by most of the literary journals – reviews that didn't dampen sales but made even Bulwer hesitant about continuing in that strain. Nonetheless, Dickens and Bulwer shared many affiliations, including liberal political opinions and close friendships with John Forster and the actor-manager William Macready, who produced two of Bulwer's blockbuster plays, *The Lady of Lyons* (1838) and *Money* (1840). They were friendly enough by December 1837 for Bulwer to invite Dickens to dinner, unfortunately on the day Charley was to be baptized. Their intermittent exchange of compliments ripened into intimacy in 1850.

A third author, closer in background and career, who also wrote historical and Newgate fiction, was William Harrison Ainsworth, Manchester born, London-based author, editor, publisher, dandy, and popular lion in the circle around the Countess of Blessington and the Holland House set. Ainsworth was admitted to the bar in 1826 but preferred to pursue a literary career abetted by his fashionable dress (Samuel Rogers thought he put Count D'Orsay in the shade). Separated from his wife, in 1835 Ainsworth moved to Kensal Lodge near Willesden, from which he circulated freely among social and literary circles. John

Macrone proposed to issue a fourth edition of Ainsworth's popular novel about the eighteenth-century highwayman, Dick Turpin, and hired George Cruikshank to do the illustrations. The connections forged by this publication led to Ainsworth's meeting Dickens and introducing him to the other participants in what proved to be a very successful venture. The two authors rapidly became friends, with Dickens emulating to the best of his scanty means the dandified wardrobe Ainsworth sported. (Nat Willis, visiting Dickens in Furnival's Inn, remembered in later years that Boz was "dressed very much as he has since described Dick Swiveller, minus the swell look. His hair was cropped close to his head, his clothes scant, though jauntily cut, and after changing a ragged office-coat for a shabby blue, he stood by the door, collarless and buttoned up, the very personification, I thought, of a close sailer to the wind.")[5] Ainsworth prospered both from the notoriety, republications, and equestrian and theatrical adaptations of his Newgate novel, and from his striking presence and social gifts. Dickens was certainly not on the same level of fame, fortune, or sociability, and given the simmering, not yet flaming, controversies over Newgate fiction, composing novels sympathetic to criminals didn't seem a strategic career choice. (Dickens's two Newgate stories in *Sketches* skirted the polemical controversy about exculpating criminals; he could "puff" "A Visit to Newgate" without endangering his reputation as a political moderate.) Riding or walking with Ainsworth around the countryside and exuberantly planning for future success was all well and good, but Dickens still had no adequate income, fixed authorial identity, or steady goal.[6]

Lying behind these authorial precedents was a more remote and distinguished model whose life provided inspiration and warning: Sir Walter Scott. Dickens's prospective father-in-law George Hogarth had practiced as a Writer to the Signet (as had Scott) in Edinburgh during the first decades of the century. When his sister married Scott's printer, James Ballantyne, Hogarth came to know the author (also secretly proprietor of the printing firm), and in time became his trusted advisor. Indeed, Hogarth, Scott, and Ballantyne bought the *Edinburgh Weekly Journal* in 1817. Scott may have met his future son-in-law, John Gibson Lockhart, through Hogarth; Dickens met Lockhart in 1837 at George Cruikshank's. After leaving Edinburgh for London in 1820, Hogarth struggled for a few years to secure a lasting editorial job, which he did achieve at the *Morning Chronicle* in 1834. It was then that he got to know Dickens, and in subsequent years the families, joined by marriage, often spent time together. Dickens learned much not only about Scott's legal, antiquarian, and writing careers, but also about his entangled finances. When in 1838

Lockhart's biography of Scott blamed James Ballantyne for the 1826 bankruptcy of Scott, his publisher Constable, and his printers, and Ballantyne's Trustees and son published a pamphlet refutation, Dickens took Lockhart's side in three increasingly heated *Examiner* reviews, explaining to the editor John Forster that "I have thought it better not to make use of anything I know from the Hogarths" – that is, from George and possibly also his sister Christian who was James's widow. The Pilgrim editors note that Dickens's "support for Lockhart clearly sprang both from his admiration for Scott and from the way Scott *v.* the Ballantynes typified Author *v.* Publisher" – this was, after all, 1838, a year in which Dickens's relations with his publisher Richard Bentley were very rocky indeed.[7]

II

So, looking around at the beginning of February 1836, Dickens could see various possible tracks forward. He wanted to get married – indeed, as we have seen, at Christmas he had leased a larger flat comprising three third-floor front chambers and a basement kitchen at No. 15 Furnival's Inn. He needed assurance of a steady and enhanced income, and he saw that others who wrote for a living wrote journalism, fiction, poetry, drama, essays, biographies, history, philosophy, literary criticism, reviews, and political pamphlets. It would have been easy for him to conclude that the genre of writing was less important than the quantity, quality, and impact of whatever kind of publication he put forth. While ambition spurred him toward the glittering examples of Bulwer and Ainsworth, the catastrophic declines of Hazlitt and Scott served as warning that literary fame was a fickle thing often deserting writers and leaving them destitute. (That was sadly to be the trajectory of Ainsworth's career as well.)

Moreover, writing was not in 1836 a vocation that necessarily required full-time attention. Authors might have substantial occupations as artists, editors, journalists, publishers, lawyers, physicians, civil servants, or politicians. (In the 1841 census authors were listed as "Other Educated Persons." They did not get their own category until 1861, when 687 persons were identified as "authors, editors, journalists.")[8] It might be expedient for Dickens to keep open other options: some form of participation in the theater as playwright, producer, director, or actor; some connection to journalism even if he chose to become more a freelancer; or some kind of legal practice, whether as a proctor or advocate within the by-ways of Doctors' Commons and other venues he had experienced or in more standard ways as a solicitor or barrister. In time, he might even contemplate running for Parliament.

The point of all this is that Dickens was still poor, poorly educated, ambitious, and on the lookout for opportunities. And, though it may be more apparent to us in retrospect than to him at the time, he had arrived in London at just the right moment, when the energy, talent, money, and connections that had forged such an extraordinary intellectual and print culture in Scotland in the eighteenth century were migrating rapidly southward to the north bank of the Thames. Dickens would have had a hard time contemplating, much less choosing, among options as a writer if he had lived in the country, as did Mary Russell Mitford, or in the Bath/Hampshire region (as had Jane Austen), in the industrializing North from which Ainsworth emigrated, or in Ireland, though there was a middling print culture in Dublin and Belfast, and still in the mid-1830s, in Glasgow and Edinburgh. The hegemony of London (reinforced by major academic and small commercial publishers nearby in Oxford and Cambridge) increased throughout the century. Within fifteen years of Dickens's start, though, authors might live in Manchester (Elizabeth Gaskell), Haworth (the Brontës), the Isle of Wight (Tennyson), or the Continent (Charles Lever, Charles Reade, Thomas Adolphus Trollope, the Brownings), and thanks to the postal service still send their manuscripts to be published in the nation's capital and distributed from that transportation center to Britain, the Continent, North America, and the colonies. London was not just Dickens's place of residence; it was the best place in all of Europe for him to venture on authorship.

At the opening of February 1836 Dickens was juggling many things. He had just finished the last scenes of his sentimental comic opera, *The Village Coquettes*. Collaborating with John Pyke Hullah, like Fanny Dickens a pupil at the Royal Academy of Music, Dickens started writing at the beginning of the year a "simple rural story," which recollections of old English Operas inspired him to prefer to the kind of Venetian confections to which Hullah had initially been drawn.[9] Even before starting this script, he mentioned to Hullah that he had another "little story by me which I have not yet published, which I think would dramatize well."[10] He still had his regular duties for the *Chronicle*s, the reporting side of which would ramp up when Parliament resumed meeting on February 4. His engagement with the *Morning Chronicle* had turned uncertain; some dispute had arisen between reporters and the chief proprietor John Easthope ("Blast-Hope" to his subordinates), and Dickens was in the thick of negotiations. He and his colleagues were prepared "to accept the first annual Engagement elsewhere" if their demands were rejected.[11] He also had reviewing assignments, including the premiere of *Rienzi* on February 3. He had agreed to provide sketches for the *Carlton Chronicle*, but no longer had any commitment to *Bell's Life*. Thinking he might put his frequent attendance at theaters to some further profitable use, he wrote to George Cruikshank on the first of February proposing another collaboration. "I should like to spend ['a spare half hour or so'] with you in talking over the idea you suggested sometime since relative to a little Satire on the class of pieces usually presented, at the Theatres in these times. I think I could turn it to the account you desire – a good one."[12] Nothing came of this venture, but the kind of exchange mooted here makes it plausible that Dickens would listen to his illustrator nine months later when casting around for what to write for *Bentley's Miscellany*. And, as someone at Chapman and Hall reminded him at the first of the month, he had promised two articles for their new *Library of Fiction*. These proved difficult to write. He told Catherine on the fifth that he thought "the weather makes me stupid. I have been poring over my desk the whole day, and have only perpetrated ten slips, or in other words one fifth, of the whole Article"[13] – which would become "The Tuggs's at Ramsgate," published in the first, April, issue.[14] The second, probably "A Little Talk about Spring, and the Sweeps," later included in the Second Series of *Sketches* under the title "The First of May," didn't make it into the May issue, presumably because Dickens was late with copy; it appeared instead in the June number.

There was, then, both a lot and very little on Dickens's plate. He was busy, though not necessarily producing the kinds of writing that promised quick success. Though solvent, he wasn't saving. He wrote at odd times of the day and night, in between attending Parliament and plays. Among other things, during the first week of February he dashed off notes to "several private friends both in London and Edinburgh" to be enclosed in copies of *Sketches* as soon as they appeared.[15] On the eighth booksellers at last had copies, and within two weeks a number of highly favorable reviews appeared, including George Hogarth's "beautiful notice" praising the volumes as "evidently the work of a person of various and extraordinary intellectual gifts."[16] Dickens assiduously cultivated the editors of literary journals and kept Macrone apprised of reviews standing in type or promised shortly. He did everything he could, despite his reluctance to puff his own work, to help the book sell.

Still, the situation was dicey. Easthope might fire him and any theatrical venture was uncertain. When William Hall paid a visit to Dickens's rooms on Wednesday, February 10, two days after the release of *Sketches*, Dickens might well have expected to be spurred once again to finish "The Tuggses at Ramsgate." Indeed, Hall probably did set a deadline, since Dickens told Catherine that evening that "the story cannot be any longer delayed – it must be done tomorrow."[17] That seems to be a principal reason for Hall's visit. It is apparent from Dickens's note to his fiancée that they had discussed these overdue assignments. "I have had a Visit from the Publisher," he told her. They both must have known that Hall managed the business side of things; and if so, then Dickens had been in contact with Hall on previous occasions.

However, the conversation veered round to other matters. Hall presumably expressed some expectation that turning in the story right away could lead to other things, since Dickens somewhat mysteriously tells Catherine that "[a]s there are more important considerations than the mere payment for the story, involved too, I must exercise a little self denial, and set to work." This sentence doesn't sound too different from others he had written during the past year breaking tentative engagements because of the press of work.

Whether the next paragraph is an explanation of those "more important considerations," or simply another, if extremely important, proposal made by Hall during this visit, is difficult to tell. "They (Chapman & Hall) have made me an offer of *£14 a month* to write and edit a new publication they contemplate, entirely by myself; to be published monthly and each number to contain four wood cuts." This information is misleading in many ways. Dickens may never before have heard about this project, even though he picked up a lot of gossip about literary matters in the course of reporting, reviewing, and partying with other Grub Street denizens. Still, it had been circulating for months. Robert Seymour, a talented comic artist under considerable financial strain, wanted to do a set of plates about Cockney sporting mishaps. He needed someone to write the letterpress leading up to the climactic incidents, and someone else to finance, produce, and sell the book. He had been turned down several times and was a bit desperate. The firm of Chapman and Hall, only six years old, was not accustomed to publishing this kind of illustrated sketchbook, but the *Library of Fiction* venture had started to introduce them to artists like Seymour, hired to illustrate "the Tuggses." When Charles Whitehead suggested "Boz" as a possible scribe, they acted.[18] Seymour had already drawn a number of plates for his project.

But Dickens didn't hear – perhaps Hall didn't make entirely clear – that there was a prior originator of this publication. Instead, probably because he was excited and because he did so want Catherine and her family to think of him as a success, and not dismissed as someone unworthy to join the family as the Beadnells had done, he represented the offer as "to write and edit a new publication they contemplate, entirely by myself." On the other hand, when in accordance with Hall's agreement Dickens took a day to think about the offer and then replied, Chapman and Hall's February 12 letter spelling out the terms of their agreement makes no mention whatsoever of Seymour, his plates, or Dickens's obligation to write up to the characters and incidents the artist supplied.

Hall did say during his visit that there would be four plates to each installment and that the parts would be issued monthly. In his report to Catherine, Dickens called them woodcuts (as he had Cruikshank's etchings in the provisional titles for *Sketches*, being uninstructed in the technologies of illustrative reproduction), so he knew about them. But he evidently jibbed at what Hall described – with who knows what degree of specificity or vagueness – as the subject, theme, and setting of these installments. Neither Dickens nor Boz (nor Tibbs for that matter) knew anything about Cockney sporting mishaps, though they were frequently depicted in the albums and cartoons of the period. The double verb "to write and edit" may simply be Dickens in his exhilaration magnifying the commission, or it might acknowledge that he could edit the material Seymour had already submitted and write up new incidents for the artist to depict in subsequent numbers, entirely by himself. Whatever reservations Dickens might have expressed about his qualifications, being a city and not a country boy, were voted down by the publishers, who specified on February 12 that he was hired "for a book illustrative of manners and life in the Country."[19]

Whether for Catherine's reassurance, or her parents', or for himself, Dickens particularly emphasizes the financial incentive. Fourteen pounds a month added 50 per cent to his ca. £28 a month from the *Chronicle*. Should he keep both jobs, his income exclusive of any freelance writing would be £504 a year, sufficient to support a middle-class standard of living in London for a married couple with servants and young children. (On the other hand, if the *Chronicle* let him go and the serial didn't succeed, his alternative sources of money were scanty indeed. To marry on the strength of this offer was almost as risky in prospect as several of Dickens's parents' schemes.) "The work will be no joke," he concluded to Catherine, significantly underestimating how he would fit more creative writing into his already crammed days and nights, "but the emolument is too tempting to resist." That may be the truest clause in the whole letter. Chapman and Hall proposed increasing his recompense for writing. How much per month, due when, for how long? These conditions were spelled out in the publishers' February 12 letter: "We propose to pay you at the rate of nine guineas per sheet of 16 pages demy 8vo containing about 500 words in a page – of which we should require one sheet and [a] half every month." That would mean 12,000 words monthly, for which Dickens would receive £14.03.06 – slightly more than the £14 he told Catherine, and by being couched in guineas, the higher-class denomination, a more flattering rate of pay. Moreover, there was the potential for a raise: "Should the publication prove very successful we shall of course be happy to increase the amount in a proportionate degree." This was not only a happy thought and a considerate gesture; Chapman and Hall lived up to it when the book was a runaway success. Their behavior contrasted favorably to Richard Bentley's stinginess in upping Dickens's salary when, a year later, the circulation of *Bentley's Miscellany* rose substantially under Dickens's editorship. So it was a clause in an informal epistolary contract that, when embedded in more formal agreements about later books, would become a test of the publishers' willingness to recompense their author beyond the contractual amount if sales soared.

On the other side of the ledger, Dickens's dilatoriness over supplying copy for *The Library of Fiction* prompted his publishers to incorporate stringent deadlines for future manuscripts: "you ... engage to provide copy for the first number by the first of March [sixteen days ahead] and sufficient for the second by the 15th [of March] and that the future numbers should be always in our hands *two months* before the date of publication." These expectations were not met, could not be met in the first instance. In reply Dickens objected to the exigency of the deadlines, especially as he was about to move into No. 15: "I think the time you propose as the period during which the copy for every number should be in your hands, is too long. You will not object, I think, on consideration, to reduce it a little."[20] It was too long for Dickens, with his other commitments; but probably not unreasonable for the illustrator who needed to design (or if already designed, as Seymour had done for the initial images, refine), etch, and print four plates, while the compositors set, the printers printed, the binders bound, the shippers shipped, the advertisers advertised, and the publishers solicited orders for the next number. Dickens, whose primary experience of publishing was newspaper work, and not the full circuit of printing and distributing Darnton schematizes, thought five weeks' advance sufficient, and he slipped to two or even just one within a year. Still, these negotiations about the timetable for manufacturing a serial part set a pattern for every subsequent contract, in which Dickens was supposed, at least before publication commenced, to get several months ahead, and thereafter to turn in his copy by mid-month so that the illustrator could make the plates and the production team set, proof, print, bind, and ship the monthly number before the end of the month. (The noxiously short month of February often caused headaches all round.)

Two other provisions of this letter established the template for most of Dickens's serials. Payment "for each number to be made always on the day of publication, which is understood to be the last day of every month." This was terribly important. It meant that Dickens could count on a regular salary for his contractual writing, and not wait until it was printed, sold, and assessed for profits before receiving his share. For most of his career, he almost always got a payment per month for writing the current installment; at intervals thereafter, as the parts and volume profits accrued, he also received a percentage of the net beyond his monthly pay.

The other provision turned out to have several important implications. "A Prospectus we shall be glad to have as soon as possible in order to prepare for its immediate issue." Before launching, any book must have a title; a description; perhaps an image forecasting its subject, characters, theme, or general spirit; a retail price and discounts for bulk purchases; a format; date or dates of publication; the name of the publisher if not also of distributors; and anything else that might encourage wholesalers and retailers to subscribe for copies and the general public to seek them out in the bookshops. In the case of this first project, whether it was Dickens's idea or Chapman and Hall's (it seems less likely to have been Seymour's), the title was announced to run for "about twenty numbers" at a shilling a number.[21] For thirty years that was to be the format of Dickens's monthlies.

The other thing that assigning Dickens the task of composing a Prospectus did was, in the end, crucial to the development of *Pickwick* and to Dickens's writerly identity. It let him characterize the contents. The prose is a fantasia on travel to spots relatively close to London: Middlesex, Surrey, Essex, Kent, the Thames and Medway, Birmingham, and the borders of Wales. With the exception of the last venue, to which Mr. Pickwick – according to the announcement – journeyed "in the height of summer," there is little here to suggest the misadventures of nouveaux-riches urbanites encountering the perils of hunting, shooting, fishing, hiking, riding, and the like, to which the extended title in an eighteenth-century style makes reference: "the Perambulations, Perils, Travels, Adventures, and Sporting Transactions." A second allusion to an eighteenth-century tradition, surviving on a reduced scale in the 1820s and 1830s, is to the fiction of a club of amateurs who record their experiences. Dickens's Prospectus sets the Pickwick Club's founding in 1822 and declares that all the correspondence, minutes, and other records of Pickwick "and his enthusiastic followers" were collected in the Transactions of the Pickwick Club – presumably when it ceased to exist – purchased, and put into the hands of Boz.[22] This is even less like Seymour's Cockney sporting sketches, being set in an earlier decade and within a club that had already disbanded as a Corresponding Society (though not like one of the Radical Corresponding Societies of the Revolutionary period – no politics here!). Whatever contemporaneity Seymour planned to reflect in his plates, as he had done in previous books and cartoons on the current scene for Gilbert Abbott à Beckett's *Figaro in London*, got suppressed by the shifting backward in time and by the folding up of the society prior to the first installment of its history.

Finally, in a detail jammed with implications for the future, according to the Prospectus these archives had been entrusted to Boz. Dickens's name appears nowhere in this announcement or in any of the novel's twenty parts. And Boz is defined as "the author of 'Sketches Illustrative of Every Day Life, and Every Day People'" (p. xxi). Remember this Prospectus is written by Dickens. He changes the title of the two volumes Macrone has just published, emphasizes "sketches" and is quite ambiguous about the medium ("Illustrative" could be verbal or visual), and foregrounds the "Every Day" rather than adventures and perils. The publishers have given Boz these transactions to arrange and place before the public "in an attractive form." The fiction that the papers exist (Dickens must first write them) and that he must then arrange them attractively (i.e., edit them) may be what Dickens had in mind in telling Catherine that he was being hired to "write and edit ... entirely by myself." With this advertisement, perhaps because of the prior existence of Seymour's drawings and the unknown role he might play in future monthly parts, he was changing the nature and function of Boz from a *flâneur* and sometime effaced narrator into the alleged "editor" of an archive. It is not remarkable for authors of the period to edit scholarly documents: Scott pre-eminently did it. But, as we have seen, some authors put a distance between their serious and their comic work by issuing them under different names, distinguishing the character of each genre by a distinctive patronym or pseudonym. With this advertisement Dickens fuses Boz the writer of sketches with Boz the editor of transactions. Moreover, when the first numbers appeared, no one knew what to call them. The installments didn't seem like a novel; they weren't short comic incidents; the characters did continue from part to part; and yet the whole seemed very miscellaneous and directionless. The best that reviewers could come up with was that Boz was editing a new periodical. Journals took the "editing" function seriously enough to infer the genre from the title of the producer.

Finally, to revert to Foucault's observation that modern literature occasioned the death of the author, we should note that something rather like this occurs with *Pickwick*. While it is the "papers" that are posthumous, the secretary of the club is not asked to edit them, nor is he referred to after the first installments. Though one of the authors (along with those sending in correspondence and field reports), and according to the Prospectus the organizer, preserver, and transmitter of all the records, the secretary might as well be dead; the editor brings his reports, and all the other papers, back into circulation. Even though the fiction that these papers written by others existed and were edited by Boz was neither sustained in the text nor believed by the majority of Dickens's readers, who credited the installments to Boz, the fiction that they had been written and Dickens/Boz had been hired to edit them appears in Dickens's first report to Catherine: "write and edit." To overstate the situation: Dickens the writer is suppressed by Boz the editor.

### III

The story of the origin of *Pickwick* has become a legend. While the details have seldom been parsed for their implications, the general drift of the narrative goes something like this: on the heels of the great success of *Sketches by Boz* (actually the book had only been available for two days, with no reviews yet), Chapman and Hall offered Dickens an agreement for a monthly serial. This seemed the sign that Dickens was waiting for. From the beginning he insisted on taking his own way; he won every argument over the format, subject, style, content, illustrations, and illustrators; and its runaway success after Dickens got his hands on every aspect of the production made him the literary sensation of the age. This legend already instantiates Foucault's three expectations for a "capital A"

Author: "The author is he who implants, into the troublesome language of fiction, its unities, its coherence, its links with reality."

That version of authorship Dickens promulgated when he composed the Preface to the Cheap Edition of *Pickwick*, published in 1847 when Charles Dickens was arguably the world's most famous living author and when the origin of his fame in *Pickwick* was already the foundation of the narrative of a writer's rise to stardom. In this preface he rewrites the history of *Pickwick*'s origin, remembering it, and recasting it, in the light of the terrific success the novel enjoyed and the equally terrific changes it made in Dickens's career, his publishers' fortunes, and the public's expectations for Boz as editor of a comic periodical.

It's a charming preface (pp. 883–88). The author is sure of his reception, can downplay any obtrusive puffing, and is still able to assert an authoritative version of events that have been narrated by others over the intervening decade, accounts "which have, at all events, possessed – for me – the charm of perfect novelty." Opening with an analogy of himself to a man stopping his friend at a theater door "to entertain him with a personal gossip before he goes in to the play," Dickens thus apologizes without apologizing for having "much to communicate." In so doing, he once more blurs the genre of the work he is prefacing: it is in this analogy rather like a play. In any case, what he recalls in the subsequent paragraphs is that Chapman and Hall, attracted by the *Morning Chronicle* pieces and their collection "in two volumes, illustrated by my esteemed friend MR. GEORGE CRUIKSHANK," called "to propose a something that should be published in shilling numbers." (It probably had slipped Dickens's mind by 1847 that Hall had also called to prod him into finishing that much-delayed story for their first issue of *The Library of Fiction*.) Dickens repeatedly refuses to identify the genre – evidently the publishers wanted something other than the "pieces" he was publishing in newspapers, but the "something" in shilling numbers recalled "certain interminable novels in that form, which used, some five-and-twenty years ago, to be carried about the country by pedlars, and over which I remember to have shed innumerable tears, before I served my apprenticeship to Life." This is an even more obfuscatory description of the "something": fiction, "interminable," sold not in bookstores and stationery shops (such as Chapman and Hall's in the Strand) but by peddlers roaming the countryside, and evidently full of sentimental scenes over which he "shed innumerable tears." These were more likely to have been cheap reprints of eighteenth-century fiction than original works; so the format of shilling numbers aroused expectations that the publisher wanted a "something" that was long, narrative, sentimental (not necessarily humorous), like but not identical to *Sketches*, and possibly intended for both the urban and the country market.

At this point in Dickens's account, the proposal seems to be for something not very grand. The next paragraph, however, transforms this modest opening almost as if the unexpected stranger knocking at the door turned into the harbinger of great fortune. For upon opening the door to the "Publisher," Dickens "recognized in him the person from whose hands I had bought, two or three years previously, and whom I had never seen before or since, my first copy of the Magazine in which my first effusion – dropped stealthily one evening at twilight, with fear and trembling, into a dark letter-box, in a dark office, up a dark court in Fleet Street," etc. (p. 884) – the description of the episode studied in Chapter 1 that resulted in Dickens's withdrawal to Westminster to hide his tears of joy and pride. It is rather unlikely that Dickens hadn't seen Hall since, as he was the managing partner who dealt with authors, their commissions, their pay, their deadlines, and so forth. Just a few days before, someone at the publishers' office had prompted Dickens to get on with his assignments. There weren't all that many other employees who were in a position to convey this message with authority, though conceivably it was communicated by letter rather than in person. Whatever the case, this visit is in 1847 cast as a fortunate coincidence "which we both hailed as a good omen; and so fell to business."

The third paragraph of the Preface fills in the blanks of Dickens's letter to Catherine and exchange of terms with Chapman and Hall. It hedges a tribute to Seymour, "that admirable humourous artist," who might have suggested "a 'NIMROD Club,' the members of which were to go out shooting, fishing, and so forth, and getting themselves into difficulties through their want of dexterity," as the best way of introducing and connecting the artist's illustrations (pp. 884–85). But that notion might have come from "my visitor [Hall]," to which Dickens adds parenthetically "(I forget which)." To most readers this would simply be an honestly uncertain recollection of an idea that in the end had little impact on the success of the project, though it initiated the Pickwick Club. But to Seymour's widow, who had twice already during the 1840s begged Dickens for support after her husband died and the publication he initiated proved a gold mine, the possibility that the sporting club was not her husband's invention was yet another insult to his creativity and memory. So it wasn't an entirely innocent bit of writing on Dickens's part.[23]

Adding to her sense of injury, but only to the reader's store of apparently factual information, Dickens follows on by explaining that he told his publisher he "was no great sportsman" (modesty that also preempts Seymour's idea),[24] that "the idea was not novel, and had already been much used" (ouch!); and that it would be far better for the plates to respond to the text (in which case Hall's proposal for a longer lead time looks even more reasonable). In response to the "idea propounded to me ... that the monthly something should be a vehicle for certain plates" by Seymour, Dickens declares, "I objected." He then goes on to four complex compound clauses, each asserting more forcibly the author's determination to command the project. He concludes this litany of objections by declaring that "I should like to take my own way, with a freer range of English scenes and people, and was afraid I should ultimately do so in any case, whatever course I might prescribe to myself at starting" (p. 885).

This is the version of Dickens's authorial authority to which he is laying claim in 1847, shortly after the success of *Dombey and Son* and the first time in his fourteen-year career when any publishing venture of his has cleared him of debts. He is, frankly, feeling his oats and celebrating his vocational triumph. (Simultaneously, but secretly, he is writing the autobiography that reveals how deeply injured he felt as a child neglected by his parents and sent to work rather than to school. So this *Pickwick* preface at some level offsets the self-image of the wounded and impotent child – though it is the only side of Dickens's construction of authorship the public sees.) Its most full-throated assertion immediately follows his predisposition to take his own way regardless. "My views being deferred to, I thought of Mr Pickwick, and wrote the first number; from the proof sheets of which, MR SEYMOUR made his drawing of the Club, and that happy portrait of its founder, by which he is always recognized, and which may be said to have made him a reality" (p. 885). The closing clause seems another handsome tribute to Seymour, who made Mr. Pickwick real, but it isn't true, and neither is much of the preceding verbiage.

IV

As we have seen, the extant documents recording the exchanges between Hall and Dickens between February 10 and 16, 1836 contain no reference whatsoever to the subject of the proposed serial, or to Dickens's objection to writing about sporting mishaps, or to his views being deferred to. The Prospectus that he dashed off by the eighteenth enshrines Seymour's (or Hall's) notions of a club, of sporting transactions, and of journeys and adventures, and it was the advertisement Chapman and Hall inserted into the newspapers the week before the first number was released. The design, wood-engraved for the wrapper by John Jackson, that Seymour immediately began working on instantiates all the topics of the Prospectus: in his image there are creels and quivers, nets and shotguns, punts and fishing poles; an incompetent marksman (Mr. Winkle) misses shooting a robin, while a somnolent angler (Mr. Pickwick), dozing in a punt moored on the Thames off Putney Bridge, ignores the "tugs" on his fishing line.[25] So between February 18 and the end of March, there had been no substantial change in the subject or direction of the "something" about to be launched that was still closely connected to the proposal and plates Seymour had showed Chapman and Hall months earlier.

Dickens began the first chapter on February 17 and told his publishers it would be finished by the nineteenth, eagerly demonstrating that he was trying to meet if not anticipate the exigent timetable for the first installments. If that chapter was ready by the nineteenth, it was surely not quite the same text that got printed six weeks later. For it turns out that Seymour's notion for the presiding officer of the Nimrod – rechristened Pickwick – Club was of a thin man. Something of that conception, of a touchy, irascible amateur scientist, remains within the character of Mr. Pickwick in the first installments. But when Edward Chapman got involved in the production of this monthly something, he thought Pickwick should be fat, not thin, because good humor and corpulence had been associated since the days of Falstaff.[26] This intervention, which Chapman set down in writing to substantiate a version of Dickens's account of the book's origins over against the increasingly shrill and frustrated assertions of Mrs. Seymour, indicates that some discussion of the nature of the serial (it was to be good-humored rather than satirical, or at least the lead character was to have the capacity to laugh at his incapacities) had taken place, probably in the Strand. Though Seymour was not present at any discussion between the publishers and the author, he must have been visited by Chapman soon thereafter. Chapman had in mind as a model for the serial's protagonist a friend, a fat genial beau who lived upriver at Richmond and sported drab tights and black gaiters. This was a type Seymour knew and had drawn previously, so the two concepts harmonized well enough for the project to go forward without animosity – except, of course, from Mr. Blotton of Aldgate. In the course of writing, the Richmond beau's tights and gaiters stayed with Pickwick while the romantic bachelor became more a model of Tracy Tupman, especially after Pickwick's unfortunate misunderstanding with the widow

Bardell. It is certainly the case that Dickens could not, and did not, on his own and instantly, think of Pickwick and write the first number. Equally certain, however, is that the notion of a genial fat humorous fellow descended from Falstaff, rather than from Seymour's Islington neighbors incompetently attempting to emulate the squirearchy, derived from Dickens's draft of the first chapter, Chapman's elaboration of that idea, and Seymour's indelible first portrait of Pickwick – which still limns a phrenology combining a "gigantic brain" with inspiring firmness and a capacity to be aroused to reject any calumny directed personally at himself.

The first number was an amalgam of many ideas. In general the text parodies Parliamentary proceedings, especially an exchange in 1828 between Henry Brougham and George Canning comically reprised in the resolution of the dispute between Pickwick and Blotton.[27] The characters, on the other hand, start out as versions of the original project. The revised Pickwick appears dozing in the punt at the bottom of Seymour's wrapper design, which must have been drawn, engraved in wood, printed, and distributed as further advertising to book dealers well before the text was printed and bound. The "sporting Winkle," Dickens explains, was put in expressly for Seymour. Put in even on the wrapper, but less elaborated in the first chapter than the "too susceptible Tupman" whose romantic disposition, somatotype, and costume are detailed. Snodgrass gets little description beyond "the poetic Snodgrass" who wears "a mysterious blue coat with a canine-skin collar," perhaps because he doesn't fit anybody's notion of what these sportsmen will do. Winkle, exactly to Seymour's type, is clothed in "a new green shooting coat, plaid neckerchief, and closely-fitted drabs" (p. 5). Clothing, at this point in the creation of the Club, make the man.

It's never been clear exactly what Dickens was writing up to, of Seymour's already composed plates, nor what changes he made to the narrative of the first installment that deviated from the artist's drawings. The opening picture of Pickwick at the Club apparently is the product of negotiations following Dickens's submission of the chapter. "The Pugnacious Cabman," illustrating chapter 2, might have been an image already supplied, although the incident recalls similar confrontations between customers and cabmen in *Sketches*. It also includes many figures Seymour had often represented.

The second chapter also introduces Alfred Jingle, who will grow into one of the most important characters for Dickens's reconceptualization of the fiction. Seymour might not have objected to this unanticipated addition, since Jingle suddenly turns to Winkle and inquires, "Sportsman, sir?" The modest reply offers an opportunity for Jingle to tell the story of Ponto, the sagacious dog who wouldn't enter into an enclosure posted with the gamekeeper's warning that trespassing dogs will be shot. When Mr. Pickwick asks permission to make a note of this fascinating story, the text supplies a footnote, inserted by the editor Boz, assuring readers that Jingle's anecdote "is not one quarter so wonderful as some of Mr. Jesse's 'Gleanings.'" This is a reference to three series of *Gleanings in Natural History* written by Edward Jesse (1780–1868), Surveyor of Parks and Palaces, who in the third volume (1835) supplied thirty pages of anecdotes testifying to the sagacity of dogs. The *Gleanings* were very popular. Seymour may have already prepared an illustration on the subject, or called Dickens's attention to it, and may have drawn his thin Pickwick from portraits of Jesse. (Dickens met Jesse in late autumn 1841.) So the introduction of Jingle, not otherwise anticipated by the Prospectus and concept of a Nimrod Club, gets fused into Seymour's conception seamlessly.[28] This long second chapter contains three of Seymour's plates – the cabman, the sagacious dog, and a third image, "Dr. Slammer's defiance of Jingle," that grows out of a case of mistaken identity engineered by Jingle during a charitable ball at the Bull Inn, Rochester. Rochester was familiar territory to Dickens; romantic complications during a social event, with ensuing threats, were scenes he had sketched previously; and a proposed duel might have been part of Seymour's and Dickens's ideas for "Adventures" involving the club. At any event, Seymour did draw a picture of Dr. Slammer's challenge to Jingle. And Dickens, without deferring to the artist's sensibility at all, drew over the sketch Seymour sent to him his own idea of how Slammer's arm ought to be thrust out in order to achieve a more comical effect.[29]

This analysis demonstrates that all the parties involved in getting out the first number of *The Pickwick Papers* were working together to produce a "something" that no one had complete control over. Despite his complaints of overwork, despite the stock characters and situations, Dickens was catching fire. Two days after finishing the first chapter, he told Catherine – in another letter canceling an evening date – that he liked "the *matter* of what I have done to-day, very much, but the *quantity* is not sufficient to justify my coming out to-night." He had got the Pickwickians rescued from the cabman and onto the Rochester coach "in company with a very different character [Jingle] from any I have yet described, who I flatter myself will make a decided hit."[30] Nearly a fortnight later, though he had been "writing, every morning," he was not so sanguine. "Pickwick is not yet completed. The sheets are a weary length – I had no idea there was so much in them."[31] He had promised the first number would be handed in by March 7, but didn't make the deadline; and he was barely through with the second before the end of the month. However, he also over-calculated the weary length of the sheets, writing so much in chapter 2 that the conclusion stretched onto a twenty-fifth page. Seeing no other solution, the printers added a leaf, beginning chapter 3 up to the start of "The Stroller's Tale." *Pickwick* Part 1 filled twenty-six rather than the stipulated twenty-four pages.

Charles and Catherine married on April 2, spent a brief honeymoon in a cottage at Chalk near Gravesend, and returned by the fourteenth of the month. Awaiting him were Seymour's drawings for the second number, including "Mr. Pickwick in Chase of his Hat" at the Rochester review; "Mr. Winkle Soothes the Refractory Steed" on the way to the Wardles' manor farm and an unetched alternative, "The Runaway Chaise"; and "Arrival at Manor Farm," clearly designed to be the last illustration in the number but never etched. These three plates supply further evidence that Dickens and Seymour were working collabora- tively. Seymour sent Dickens pencil and wash drawings, even offering alternatives, for the manuscript that Dickens had dashed off prior to his nuptials. The motif of older urban males of distinct, almost humours, types, getting into scrapes because they do not understand military maneuvers and horses, stays true to the originating notion of Cockney sportsmen. Their reception at Manor Farm either owes something to Seymour or seemed such a good idea as a place of refuge for the incompetent Pickwickians that the artist drew the scene in the kitchen without complaint. (The Wardles, in their carriage, accompanied by Mr. Tupman, had been witnesses to Mr. Pickwick's runaway hat – thus they had appeared in the first full chapter of the number, but not as major characters whose features Seymour needed to detail too carefully – although the fat boy was unmistakable dozing on the box of the barouche.) All this material seems further evidence of ongoing co- operation through the end of March and the first two weeks of April, when Dickens was away.

However, the story that opens the second number was not part of any previous abstract of the venture. It was a tale, told by Jingle's "friend" Dismal Jemmy, about a low pantomime clown dying of acute alcoholism. Dickens revisits scenes he had portrayed in *Sketches*, once again construct- ing a narrative rushing to death; this time, however, not Boz but Jem Hutley is the ostensible witness of the actor's last hours. The story didn't appeal to Seymour, but he gamely tried to illustrate it. When Dickens saw the drawing immediately after returning from his honeymoon, he wrote to Seymour.[32] He opens by expressing his gratification for the "pains" the artist has taken with "our mutual friend Mr. Pickwick" – a rather patronizing compliment that elides all the influences that contributed to portraying the eponymous hero and that might also have struck Seymour as alluding to the change from his conception of the hero to Chapman's and Dickens's. Then Dickens comes to the heart of his message. "I am extremely anxious about 'The Stroller's Tale' – the more especially as many literary friends, on whose judgment I place great reliance, think it will create considerable sensation." This is a formula very like what Dickens articulated after getting opinions regarding "A Visit to Newgate," and it seems less well justified as he had barely finished the manuscript before marrying and traveling to Chalk. Conceivably George Hogarth had seen the script before Dickens sent it to Chapman and Hall, but there may have been few other readers. In any case, Dickens *was* anxious, especially as the tale was not what anyone expected to be included in this miscellany of posthumous adventures. Having seen Seymour's design, Dickens explains that while it is "extremely good," "still, it is not quite my idea." Well, no; the story comes out of Dickens's head, not Seymour's. Dickens proposes a "glass of grog" on Sunday at his place, with Chapman and Hall. I suspect that he anticipated resistance from the touchy artist and sought reinforcement from the publishers, who may already be feeling that Dickens is the rising, Seymour the falling, star in this constellation.

"The alteration I want," Dickens continues, "I will endeavour to explain. I think the woman [the dying clown's wife] should be younger – the 'dismal man' [Jemmy] decidedly should, and he should be less miserable in appearance. To communicate an interest to the plate [which presumably lacked interest in Seymour's rendering], his whole appearance should express more sympathy and solicitude." How Seymour was to guess this from Jemmy's introduction at the end of part one is impossible to say. Jemmy is there described as an "uncouth-looking person," "care-worn," with a "sallow" face, "deeply sunken eyes," matted and disordered black hair hanging halfway down his face, unnaturally bright eyes, high prominent cheeks, and a long lank jaw (p. 40). The sympathy and solicitude for others less fortunate are aspects of Jemmy's character within the story he narrates, but not inferable from his barroom appearance. "[A]nd while I represented the sick man as emaciated and dying," Dickens continues, "I would not make him too repulsive." His closing sentence probably was not intended to slap as resoundingly as it has seemed to do to subsequent readers of this letter: "The furniture of the room, you have depicted, *admirably.*"

All the foregoing incidents regarding the origins of *Pickwick* have been retold many times. To review them again requires some different perspective. What we can notice as we investigate Dickens's development of an authorial persona and self-definition is how quickly he moves to take charge of a project that is fluid, ill defined, and irresistibly lucrative. That fresh from his honeymoon he was so energized and full of his plans for the novel he could write this kind of letter to the artist who initiated the venture dramatizes how high he could get when feeling good about his work. It is important to recognize this is one moment in a four-week period (mid-March to mid-April) during which Dickens seesawed up and down, swinging from despair to joy and back again. The notices about *Sketches* were good, he assures Macrone on a Friday afternoon; "I am tired and worn out to-day, mind and body," he informs Catherine two days later.[33] And he was, for Parliament was sitting very late and he had his regular stint of reporting to do when called upon. Nor was he on any more comfortable financial footing. With buying decanters, glassware, and china jars, planning the wedding, reception, and honeymoon, and being "hard at work" morning, noon, and night, Dickens still was not clear of debts or certain of steady income. Paying off one loan just days before the wedding, he explains that he has "had many heavy and pressing demands upon me, during the past year; and ... although I have been indefatigable in industry and perseverance, the numerous Irons I have been putting in the fire, for the last twelve months, are only just beginning to get warm."[34] He owed £5.10.0 to the mother of his friend Henry Austin.

Dickens may have been a bit over the top in his expectations that Seymour could, or would happily, meet his demands for new drawings. The artist tried, though the revisions don't get much closer to Dickens's ideas.[35] Seymour was himself distraught, and while the conclusion of the second number at Manor Farm may have been part of his own idea of Nimrods in the country, the general direction and supervision of the *Pickwick* project seemed to be slipping from his hands. After redesigning and etching the clown plate, he took inventory of his effects and prospects. He burnt his correspondence about the *Pickwick* project, which he had been circulating to publishers for more than half a year, and he deliberately turned his last etching for Part II to the wall.[36] He then wrote a note to his "[b]est and dearest of wives," assuring her that no one "has been a malicious enemy to me" – an assurance that sounds as if such a charge had been considered between them in previous weeks – and afterwards, early in the morning of Wednesday April 20, he walked out into his little back garden and shot himself.[37]

v

*Pickwick* was not a commercial success at this point; it barely sold a few hundred copies monthly. If it had stopped then, with a second number containing three instead of the promised four plates plus the twenty-four pages of letterpress, no one would have noticed, and this Boz effort, like most of his plays and all of his poems, would simply have disappeared into the farthest margins of his curriculum vitae. Knowing the subsequent history of this publishing phenomenon, brilliant critics such as G. K. Chesterton, W. H. Auden, Steven Marcus, and J. Hillis Miller have found in these opening chapters a history of gods gone wandering in England, re-enactments of the Garden of Eden and the Fall, a novel of transcendence, and "the age-old motif of the quest."[38] My own version forty years ago was a less Christianized version of Auden's: the novel recounts numerous variants on the invasion from without or within of an ideal, "Edenic" place, whose perfection can be reinstituted but never entirely renewed.[39]

In those cases, praise be for decontextualization, for reading the novel as a whole, not disfigured by its ambiguous and often derivative beginning. What needs to be stressed in this retelling has nothing to do with denigrating the wonderful book Dickens completed, but rather everything to do with how chancy the venture was, how little Dickens or his publishers could call on in the way of tradition or other support for a feeble little paper trifle, and how much Dickens willed the project to succeed, gaining authority unrecognized by any statutory or contractual provision, with a very shallow track record of success behind him and an ever-increasing set of competing obligations ahead. Even when Dickens was most powerful at asserting his control over the unity, direction, and meaning of *Pickwick*, he was acting without any of the foundations that would have supported such assertions. He willed an authorial authority into effect, and got away with it – for a while. It may have helped that he had written so many stories imagining narrative after death.

One of the fortuitous circumstances that contributed to Dickens's authority was the youth and inexperience of his publishers. While older by nearly a decade than Dickens, they were comparatively fresh and flexible, still in the early days of the publishing side of their stationery and bookselling business. William Hall was around thirty-six, Edward Chapman thirty-two. Had Dickens been working with two of the most established metropolitan fiction publishers, he probably would have encountered much more resistance. Henry Colburn, initiator of the first collected sets of reprint fiction issued at the rate of one title per month, was born in 1784 or 1785. In 1836, just over fifty, he had recently concluded an acrimonious divorce from his former partners, Samuel Bentley who printed the works, and his brother Richard Bentley, who sold them. One of the terms of the separation pledged Colburn to remove his business twenty miles beyond London, which he did for a few years, relocating in Windsor. In June 1836 – just when the *Pickwick* troubles reached their height – Colburn paid Bentley to release him from his pledge, and then immediately relocated in Great Marlborough Street. There he competed with Bentley for such fashionable authors as Benjamin Disraeli, Catherine Gore, and Frances Trollope. Colburn was a king of puffers, but he also cut his losses when a product didn't sell.

Richard Bentley was younger, at forty-two, but had been raised to the business of manufacturing and selling print products from childhood, as his father, uncle, and older brother were all in the printing business. He too was a believer in extravagant advertising for the right products, and he too started a collection of reprinted UK and US fiction. Yet, like his former partner, he probably would have simply abandoned a venture selling only a few hundred shilling copies monthly and yielding, at best, only a pound or two of profit after expenses. Some other major publishers were way out of Dickens's league: Blackwood or Constable in Edinburgh, John Murray in Albemarle Street or Longmans in Paternoster Row, London, or for sumptuously illustrated books, Rudolph Ackermann in the Strand.

Chapman and Hall, with some experience issuing serialized print products such as *Chat of the Week* in partnership with other small firms, and which had just launched the monthly *Library of Fiction*, treated Seymour's death as a serious, but not fatal, blow to their faltering venture. Boz was still a name worth marketing. So they asked John Jackson, the wood-engraver who had cut the block for the *Pickwick* wrapper and was engraving the illustration for Dickens's contribution to the June issue of the *Library of Fiction*, to recommend a replacement artist. Jackson suggested Robert William Buss, who had just designed the cut Jackson was engraving. Buss was at this time primarily a painter of theatrical portraits. He set aside that work and etched a reductive version of "Mr. Pickwick at the Review" from Part II to demonstrate to the publishers that he could both design and produce the plates. (Buss's father was an engraver.) When offered the job, he worked up preliminary sketches for the material Dickens had supplied for Part III, due out at the end of May, dated June. He also drew illustrations for incidents to appear in the fourth number, indicating that Dickens had somehow got ahead with his writing. And, hopeful that the rest of the serial would be "Illustrated by RW Buss," he designed a vignette for *The Transactions of the Pickwick Club* – a drastic condensation of the wrapper title: this shows fame blowing her trumpet and holding a laurel wreath over Mr. Pickwick's head, while circular bust portraits of the four Pickwickians dangle from chains attached to a rock (radically diminished in size from Mount Parnassus, which may or may not cast aspersions on the distinction of these illustrious personages). Once hired, Buss and Dickens must have exchanged comments about his proposed images, though no record of those interchanges survives. Uncomfortable with etching despite his demonstration of competence to Chapman and Hall, Buss brought in an expert who translated his drawing into stiff lines and then botched the biting-in. The results were so unsatisfactory that Buss was peremptorily fired by the publishers. He never held that misfortune against Dickens, who may not have been a party to the decision. However, Buss felt it for decades. He made handsome amends with his wonderful though only partially completed large watercolor, *Dickens' Dream* (Charles Dickens Museum) after the author's death in 1870. In it he gracefully and accurately replicates the portraits of Dickens's characters made by his successful successors, especially Phiz.[40]

It was also at this juncture, with the parts still selling in anemic quantities, that Dickens and his publishers reconsidered the format of their undertaking. Though he had only experienced the production of two installments, Dickens had grasped the economics as well as the mechanics of producing monthly parts. Why not reduce the number of illustrations from four to two per issue? Etchings were expensive, so the cost of production would decrease. With two fewer images to write up to, the deadlines for supplying the artist with copy relaxed. If the revamped installment were still to sell for a shilling, however, something would have to be added to make up for the lost images. Why not increase the letterpress from a sheet and a half, or twenty-four pages, to two sheets, thirty-two pages, still printed with approximately 500 words on each page? From a production standpoint, it was slightly easier to print two sheets than one at full length (sixteen pages) and one on which the type was impressed twice and cut in half, making two eight-page gatherings. From the writer's standpoint, it was a 25 percent increase in his monthly obligation. Dickens asked for, and received, an increase in his stipend proportionate to the addition – from £14.03.06 for a sheet and a half at nine guineas per sheet to "Twenty Guineas for the two sheets."[41] But a further advantage, perhaps dimly understood from Dickens's experience over writing the first installment when he really got his narrative and comedic steam up, was that he would only have to produce a good subject for illustration once every sixteen pages, rather than once every six. Instead of inventing a new mishap every 3,000 words, the length of some of Dickens's sketches, he could luxuriate in the development of more complex scenes, characters, and plot, having 8,000 words at his disposal per image. And he would not need to send the first of those incidents to the artist in order for him to work up preliminary drawings until around the tenth of the month, with the other subject coming in the second half of the installment, completed some time between the fifteenth (ideal) and the twentieth of the month.

It is instructive to reflect on this proposal. In recommending improvements to the rather indeterminate "something" that the first numbers of *The Posthumous Papers of the Pickwick Club* represented, Dickens and his publishers proposed stabilizing the format. The first number had contained twenty-six pages and four illustrations, the second twenty-four pages and three illustrations. They were not tampering with the subject matter, characters, humor, incidents, or general situation indicated in the preliminary announcements and the title, but rather with the physical product. And it was that physical reformatting, not any change in the tenor of the text, to which announcements from the publishers and Dickens referred in notifications inserted in the paratexts to the second and third installments.

The report of Seymour's death in Part II comes without any identification of the announcer, though the "we" deployed throughout would seem to be Boz speaking in the editorial plural (p. 879). But as editor, he feels called upon to voice the publishers as well: "Some apology is due to our readers for the appearance in the present Number with only three plates." The death of the illustrator, the Address continues, has left a "void" which could not immediately be filled up; "the blank his death has occasioned in the Society, which his amiable nature won, and his talents adorned, we can hardly hope to see supplied." After explaining that Seymour was working on the embellishment to the Stroller's Tale "up to a late hour of the night preceding his death," the announcer concludes with a promise that "[a]rrangements are in progress which will enable us to present the ensuing Numbers of the Pickwick Papers [already the title has been semi-officially shortened to what it would thereafter be in familiar parlance] on an improved plan, which we trust will give entire satisfaction to our numerous readers." Those arrangements were very much still "in progress": the announcement is dated "April 27th, 1836," the same day as Dickens's letter to Chapman and Hall responding to the proposal they had made to him the night before.

By May the format had stabilized and Dickens was writing 16,000 words per month. The Address from the Publishers inserted in the June issue (Part III) tweaks the facts more than Dickens as Boz as Editor may have wanted (pp. 879–80). It claims that "influential quarters" have suggested the altered arrangements, the addition of eight pages "of closely-printed matter" (no skimping here!), "and two engravings on steel" (no mention of the reduction from four), from designs by MR. BUSS – a gentleman already well known to the Public, as a very humorous and talented artist." Moreover, the publishers continue, this change entails "a considerable expense" (it didn't, even taking Dickens's raise into account), "which nothing but a large circulation would justify them in incurring." Well, any increase in circulation as a result of this change in format and artist would be welcome. In closing, Chapman and Hall do their own bit of relatively restrained self-promotion: "the rapid sale of the two first numbers [some of the print run had been returned unsold], and the daily-increasing demand for this Periodical [not evidenced yet, though hoped-for] enables them to acknowledge the patronage of the Public, in the way which they hope will be deemed most acceptable." One has to credit the obscuring rhetoric for enlisting the support of the public for fewer illustrations and more of the tightly packed print and for making the non-existent rapid sale and not-yet-expanding customer base the occasion for acknowledging the public's patronage. From sow's ear to silk purse in one sentence.

An odd "Postscript from the Editor" follows. It purports to reprint a correspondent's letter, punctuated by full stops different from, but not too dissimilar to, Jingle's breathless dashes, reprehending, on behalf of those concerned for "the amelioration of the Animal Kingdom," the carelessness, bad taste, and "bad English!!" of the paragraphs recounting the cabman's treatment of his horse. Like other periodical letters to the editor, some perhaps genuine, many spuriously invented to stir up interest and controversy, this addendum would seem to be the introduction of yet another feature into the *Pickwick* miscellany. "We shall be happy to receive other communications from the same source," Boz concludes, and then takes back his generosity, "and on the same terms; that is to say, post paid." What were readers supposed to make of this addendum? Might letters from readers be added to the editor's redaction of the Pickwick Club transactions? Might the serial encourage a print version of a chat room or blog? Had someone complained about the apparent lack of feeling for the horse, criticized Boz for being funny about a serious and pathetic case of abuse? How does this bit of nonsense fit with the mixture of Gothic and farce established by the expanded letterpress, that curves from the melodramatic tale of the convict's return to the comedy of the Muggleton cricket match to Jingle's wonderfully farcical and successful seduction of Rachel Wardle by arousing her suspicions that she has a younger rival for Tupman's affections:

> "He'll sit next her at table."
> "Let him."
> "He'll flatter her."
> "Let him."
> "He'll pay her every possible attention."
> "Let him."
> "And he'll cut you."
> "Cut *me*!" screamed the spinster aunt. "*He* cut *me*; – *will* he!" and she trembled with rage and disappointment. (p. 123)

This may be a scene out of lower-class theater, but it works extremely well and sets in motion a succession of travels and romantic entanglements that become a leading motif of the rest of the installments. Here Dickens is getting his groove on, so to speak. Why then publish the silly, distracting, and misleading correspondence, as if future episodes of the work would become subject to readers' commentary? It's one of the many indications that nobody involved in the venture quite understood its potential. By Part xv (July 1837), when according to the advertisements the numbers were selling at least 20,000 per month, letters to the editor of *Pickwick* had become a real nuisance: "We receive every month an immense number of communications, purporting to be 'suggestions' for the Pickwick Papers," begins a "Notice to Correspondents" following an "Address" dated and sent from Chapman and Hall's shop, 186 Strand. "[A]s we really have no time to peruse anonymous letters, we hope the writers will henceforth spare themselves a great deal of unnecessary and useless trouble" (p. 882). In later retrospect, after the book became one of the most enjoyed publications of the decade, as many of these false notes were expunged as possible. It is important to recapture them here precisely because they are not wonderful, not necessary, but all too evidently the result of indeterminacy on everybody's part. Telling the story of *Pickwick*'s triumph, and Dickens's consolidation of certain dimensions of authorial power, forward, produces a very different narrative from the hindsight view from which most accounts are situated.

Part III still was produced within the parameters of the Seymour–Chapman–Hall–Dickens conversations about their monthly "something." Buss did not insist on changing the direction or character of the publication. But Dickens, using Jingle, "who I flatter myself will make a decided hit,"[42] develops in this installment a rather different direction to the narrative. The seduction and abduction of a propertied spinster doesn't seem to be the sort of event anticipated in any previous discussion or announcement about the Club and sporting transactions. At the end of the number, it seems as if the misunderstandings about Tupman's attentions to Rachel Wardle have been cleared up to the satisfaction of her brother (because Jingle has directed Tupman's behavior to achieve this effect), and while Snodgrass is still jealous of Tupman, Jingle and Miss Wardle are also in high spirits "for reasons of sufficient importance in this eventful history to be narrated in another chapter." Not only do this and other hints suggest that Jingle and Rachel are hatching plans to elope, but this also drops – for the moment at least – the fiction of editor, papers, and Transactions of the Club. The narrative has become an "eventful history" – a start at least toward the transformation of the papers from edited records to continuing narrative divided into chapters. This anticipation of further developments is strikingly different from the conclusion of Part I, in which Dismal Jemmy prepares "partly to read, and partly to relate," an incident "which we find recorded on the Transactions of the club as 'The Stroller's Tale.'" It is different, too, from the end of the second part, which while not insisting that the arrival at Wardle's Farm is transcribed from the Transactions nonetheless signals the entry, after many vicissitudes on the road, of the exhausted Pickwickians into safety and hospitality: "Welcome," says Mr. Wardle, "gentlemen, to Manor Farm." While neither of these endings necessarily promises a continuing narrative in the next installment, the end of Part III does. And that's important, because once again the story of *Pickwick*'s success told retrospectively implies that with Part IV the sales picked up because Dickens was fully in charge of the narrative and the number was successfully illustrated by yet a third artist. It seems likely that some at least of the few buyers of the previous installments found the promise of a continuing story incentive to buy the next one before they saw it or encountered Sam Weller and Phiz for the first time.

Encountering Phiz was another stroke of good fortune, but not necessarily one in which Dickens played a large part. The publishers fired Buss and hunted around for another artist. William Makepeace Thackeray applied, thought he had the job, and took his friend Hablot Knight Browne out to dinner to celebrate. Later he learned than neither he nor any other applicant, including John Leech, had been successful. The publishers hired twenty-one-year-old Browne, who had studied etching and engraving at Finden's, a fine firm for teaching apprentices and for printing engraved volumes especially on architectural subjects. Whether Dickens ever met any of the aspiring artists at this time is unknown. But as soon as Chapman and Hall found their man, Dickens must have sent Browne manuscript material for his two plates, since Buss had already seen some of the manuscript for Part IV and there were only a couple of weeks left before publication day. From the July number on, *Pickwick* began to flourish. Dickens took the Pickwickians back to London on another journey full of mishaps, and Browne, who signed his first plates N.E.M.O., "nobody," produced memorable representations of Mr. Pickwick clambering out of an overturned carriage and meeting Sam Weller at the White Hart Inn.

VI

Of course Dickens didn't yet know that this unfortunate serial was going to be the hit of the decade. He knew he had committed himself both to writing 16,000 words a month on an exigent schedule and in some ways to participating in the fortunes of the production – asking for more money if it succeeded, promising to do all in his power not to let it fail. In these first months of *Pickwick*'s travails, Dickens addressed three challenges. One had to do with employment, authorial identity, income, and career choices; a second concerned how he was going to carry Seymour's humours characters through twenty numbers; and the third was how to transform the "something" into some kind of continuing story with at least a rudimentary plot. He was probably less conscious of the last two, as they concerned the writing that, whenever he could get down to it and feel his inspiration driving him forward, he did so fluently.

To deal first with the issue of being a writer. Dickens didn't want to give up any of his other commitments. Before Parliament recessed for Easter on March 30 (the day *Pickwick* was launched), Dickens wrote to the proprietor of the *Morning Chronicle*, Easthope, begging in the most convoluted way for a commission to continue the "Sketches of London," the last of which had appeared in August 1835 in the *Evening Chronicle* with the note "To be continued." Dickens kept writing and submitting sketches, but none seems to have been accepted. Nor had his solicitations to readers to ask for more moved his editors. Since there had been that dispute between the reporters and the management of the paper, Dickens knew his was a delicate position. Easthope wrote a courteous reply, but no further sketches appeared in the *Morning Chronicle* until autumn, when four of the very best, gathered into the one-volume addition to *Sketches* Macrone published in December, appeared. Meanwhile, Dickens continued as a reporter, running to Ipswich in late May to report on Daniel O'Connell's speeches, covering the trial of Lord Melbourne for adultery on June 22 (Dickens filled more than twenty-six columns of the *Morning Chronicle* the following day, and brilliantly adapted the feeble evidence of brief notes introduced by the plaintiff, the Hon. George Norton, into the trial scene of *Pickwick* published in March 1837). After covering the House of Commons debates on Sir Andrew Agnew's Sabbath Observance Bill in May, Dickens dashed off *Sunday Under Three Heads. As It Is; as Sabbath Bills Would Make It; as It Might be Made.* Chapman and Hall published the pamphlet, which Dickens issued under yet another pseudonym, Timothy Sparks, at the end of June. In this case, concealing Dickens's name had to be a decision made jointly by publisher and author, probably because his impassioned political attack might otherwise have compromised Boz's more apolitical and genial authorial persona.[43]

At the beginning of May 1836, just after the second number of *Pickwick* was issued and only two weeks after Seymour's suicide, Dickens accepted £200 from Macrone for a three-volume novel, "Gabriel Vardon, the Locksmith of London," to be written between May and November 30, 1836, in addition to any *Chronicle* sketches and articles and the monthly *Pickwick* installments. The agreement limited Macrone to printing 1,000 copies; beyond that limit, the profit on any additional copies sold would be split fifty-fifty between publisher and author, who was in effect leasing his copyright for a limited number of copies paid at two different rates, while retaining the copyright.[44]

Through the spring, Dickens was also tinkering with the script for *The Village Coquettes*, the comic operetta he and Hullah had been working on for some time and for which they had designed the leading role for John Braham, a popular tenor. The music publisher Cramer's bought the score in early May, and Macrone bought the copyright after hearing the first act in a trial rendition at the end of July. The opening night was December 6, and – possibly owing to strained relations with Macrone over other commitments – Dickens got Richard Bentley belatedly to publish the script on December 22. Writing in late August, Dickens told Bentley that "'Boz's' first play – an old English story, and an attempt to revive the rustic opera – would, I think be purchased, if it were published at any reasonable price."[45] During the final rehearsals Dickens "was so worried" with the production he could hardly think or write, but indeed – as we shall see in a moment – he had several other projects concluding simultaneously. Meanwhile, Dickens also had adapted the sketch of "The Great Winglebury Duel" into a burletta (a play with songs), *The Strange Gentleman*, which he worked over all summer, which premiered on September 29, and which ran more than fifty nights.

As if these various engagements were not enough, Dickens spent an increasingly frantic autumn collecting, revising, and creating new sketches for *Sketches by Boz*, Second Series, one volume, issued in mid-December. He met with, or postponed meeting with, Cruikshank or Macrone, concluded by the beginning of October that he could not possibly get out a second volume before Christmas, and had a blow-up with his illustrator in mid-October. Cruikshank's desire to "have the privilege of suggesting any little alterations to suit the Pencil" Dickens scotched in exasperation, telling Macrone: "[m]ost decidedly am I of opinion that he may just go to the Devil . . . I think it a great question whether it requires any illustrations at all, but if so, I think my Pickwick man had better do them, as he is already favorably known to the public, by his connection with that immortal gentleman."[46] This contretemps was quickly resolved; indeed Cruikshank had already commenced the plates for the first volume, and Dickens never got time to write a second one. Their relations were even more amicably restored when they were hired for yet another project in late 1836.

Over the summer, Richard Bentley, facing renewed competition from a London-based Colburn, became a very important new source of potential income and publishing. On August 22 Dickens agreed to supply Bentley with an original novel in three volumes "of 320 pages each and 25 lines in each page" for £500 paid in complicated steps – on delivery of the manuscript, two promissory notes for £200 each, payable at six and nine months' date, and the final £100 being payable "upon the sale of the said work reaching to 1450 Copies" in yet another promissory note of six months' date. Further, Dickens pledged that Bentley would have his next three-volume novel on the same terms, and that "no other literary production shall be undertaken by the said Charles Dickens Esqre until the completion" of the first of these novels.[47] At this point Dickens was fulfilling his obligation to Chapman and Hall for *Pickwick*, hadn't started to write the three-decker for Macrone, was engaged with two theatrical productions, was still a reporter on the *Morning Chronicle*, was composing more sketches for that newspaper and for inclusion in the second series of *Sketches by Boz*, and now was promising at least one, and possibly two, other three-deckers, each extending to at least 250,000 words.

And still Dickens, almost ungovernable in his manic mood, took on more. On November 4 he agreed to edit a new magazine Bentley was launching in January of 1837, to consist of at least six sheets or ninety-six pages per month, with Dickens himself supplying material for one of those sixteen-page sheets. For editing, Dickens was to receive £20 a month, and for the writing, twenty guineas – a difference of only one pound, but in terms of prestige the writing is clearly of higher status than the editorial duties.[48] This Agreement begins to sort out the difference between Dickens as editor and Dickens as author in ways never before calibrated. We'll go into that more in the next chapter.

This plethora of letters, formal agreements, publications, pseudonyms, and genres testifies as much to the insecurity of authorship as to its power. Dickens really wasn't sure what project would succeed, which ones fail. He had no long-term plan to be one thing or another – reporter, polemical pamphleteer, writer of sketches, editor of miscellaneous publications, playwright of comic dramas, writer of books and lyrics for musical theater, or something else. If the mélange of responsibilities represented the way other self-made writers had entered into the profession of authorship and succeeded, well and good. Dickens had no agent to negotiate his contracts, nor any single publisher to whom he was fully committed. Moreover, he possessed no stable name as author. He was still "Boz" on the title page of most publications, though Tibbs and Sparks took credit for some of them. While his nominative identity as Charles Dickens was known in print circles within London, his writerly identity was universally "Boz."

Moreover, most of the arrangements were entered into through friendship and networking. The most stable partnership was with Chapman and Hall, though the contractual obligations were minimal and constantly being modified in practice. After the various reformattings of *Pickwick*, they began raising Dickens's salary and allowing him considerable license about turning in his monthly budget of writing on time. By the end of *Pickwick*, Dickens received the equivalent of £100 per number, up from the nine and a half guineas at the start some twenty-two months previously. Chapman and Hall slipped in the political pamphlet by Timothy Sparks without undue negotiations, and signed Dickens up for another serial in the same format on the same terms, though with increased stipends per part. At the other end of the spectrum, Richard Bentley's first two agreements were finicky about details – dates of production and payment, number of words to be written each month, restrictions on Charles Dickens's writing anything else until he had produced two novels for Bentley as well as editing and contributing monthly to his *Miscellany*. In between came John Macrone, young, impetuous, financially stretched, striving to make it in the London market with inadequate capital but lots of contacts and some good ideas about marrying an illustrious graphic artist such as George Cruikshank with rising literary stars such as Boz and Ainsworth. Dickens had half-a-dozen "arrangements" with Macrone; almost all of them needed to be haggled about and revised in the course of production. The date of the First Series of *Sketches* slipped from pre-Christmas 1835 to February 1836; the two volumes of the Second Series shrunk to one in order to catch the holiday trade in December 1836; the rustic operetta migrated from Macrone to Bentley; and the three-volume novel became a cause of bitter contention when Dickens could not fulfill his commitment to produce copy by November 1836. Compared to Chapman and Hall, Macrone had neither the resources, legal contracts, nor personal skills to cultivate an occasionally touchy but incomparably gifted author. For the most part, however, his family and Dickens's remained friendly, both having small children and wives who experienced post-partum difficulties. Compared to Bentley, Macrone simply wasn't a stickler for details and deadlines. He got out his products as best he could whenever author, artist, and printer finished the job.

VII

That, for the moment, summarizes Dickens's first challenge as a twenty-four-year-old married man making a living by writing and gaining, monthly, a more enthusiastic and expanding audience for his Boz sketches, his edited Pickwick Club papers, his plays, and his miscellaneous reporting. However, he had, as we noted earlier, three challenges to solve. The first concerned the business of writing just discussed. The second and third arose as consequences of Seymour's death and Phiz's addition as a compliant and effective successor. What could Dickens do with a cast of characters based on physiological types going back to Aristotle and

Renaissance humours (he produced and acted in several of Ben Jonson's plays in the 1840s), and reified into distinctive and predictable personalities according to the pseudo-science of phrenology and the artistic and theatrical principles that connected somatotypes and physiognomies to particular personalities?[49] Winkle=sportsman, Tupman=lover. Clothes, head and face, body, gestures and motions, all bespoke their type. But it would be impossible to produce more than 600 pages of "closely-printed type" reiterating these predictable personalities in repetitive mishaps. The last challenge, to be discussed shortly, was how to invent and develop a sustaining narrative.

In introducing Jingle, Dickens threw over the whole characterological "given" of Seymour's proposal. Graphic artists can accommodate pictorial representations to external signs of internal character. But what if exterior signs do not bespeak the person's nature? In what circumstance might there be a division between appearance and – understanding the word loosely – "reality"? Acting. "The Stroller's Tale" addressed that issue at the very start of the second number; no wonder Seymour felt the subject uncongenial. While theatrical companies still hired personnel based in part on body types and ages, there was inevitably latitude in the kinds of roles the ingénue or the bulky villain might play. Jingle is that principle in its most protean aspect. First introduced by a long passage (p. 13) describing his clothing that simultaneously identifies the history of every garment (as Boz will do in the "Monmouth Street" sketch) and indicates the impercipience of the bespectacled Pickwick, Jingle confounds expectations that any material manifestation, body or clothing, equals the man. Of middle height, his thinness renders his appearance taller. His green coat, once smart when worn by a shorter man, now, buttoned to the neck, hides the absence of a shirt beneath his stock. His scanty trousers shine from long service, and strapped over mended shoes they ineffectually conceal dirty white stockings. His hair "escaped in negligent waves" (which could mean his hair was untrimmed and uncombed); his bare wrists gape between the too short coat sleeves and his glove tops. Thin and haggard, "an indescribable air of jaunty impudence and perfect self-possession pervaded the whole man." This description foregrounds the fact that concealing and revealing both serve their own and opposite functions, that the character's contradictions make typing him difficult. The main problem the Pickwickians have is an inability to perceive Jingle beyond whatever type he presents himself as being, and thus, though they are unsure, they do not register the entire discontinuity between appearance and substance.

Dickens gets much play from this new character, especially because Jingle can deploy words to project any kind of person: a traveler, sportsman, courtier, Pickwickian (wearing Winkle's bright blue dress coat with the gold "PC" buttons), confidant, friend, lover, and adventurer. Love may be the easiest of the "humours" to migrate from one type to another; by the third number Jingle is performing the role of suitor while directing Tupman to play the role of disinterested guest and Rachel Wardle to feign temperate feelings toward both men. In short, Dickens introduces theatricality into Manor Farm and the *Papers*, oversets stock characters while at the same time deploying them (the disappointed spinster appears often in *Sketches*), and reformulates Seymour's principle of character types without losing any of the comedic and interpretive benefits that come from including one-dimensional figures such as the Fat Boy, whose very girth and apparent somnolence at once confirm and disprove his singularity.

While Jingle's self-presentation is often a matter of language, and in his uses of language to create character he enacts all sorts of beings he is not, Dickens's imagination, as so often throughout his life, leaps to the inside-out, upside-down contrary when he introduces Jingle's antithesis and double, Sam Weller. Sam, who has progressed from carrier's boy to waggoner's helper to boots at the White Hart Inn, likes clothes as much as Jingle and knows that the "two suits" Pickwick provides for his servant will render him a higher class of individual than his "coarse-striped waistcoat" and "old white hat" that was "carelessly thrown on one side of his head" (p. 137): "If the clothes fits me half as well as the place, they'll do," Sam says in accepting the situation (p. 176). Sam also knows what clothes signify, as late in the novel he demonstrates in the footmen's "swarry" at Bath. And Sam, like Jingle, creates his character through his stories. There's really not much difference between Jingle's account of a coach passing through a low arch in London and Sam's narrative of his father's coaching accident, after getting bribed to dump opposition voters in the water:

Jingle: "other day – five children – mother – tall lady, eating sandwiches – forgot the arch – crash – knock – children look round – mother's head off – sandwich in her hand – no mouth to put it in – head of a family off – shocking, shocking!" (p. 14)

Sam: "on the wery day as he came down with them woters, his coach *was* upset on that 'ere wery spot, and ev'ry man on 'em was turned into the canal . . . I rather think one old gentleman was missin'; I know his hat was found, but I a'n't quite certain whether his head was in it or not." (p. 188)

The difference between Sam and Jingle is that Sam is what he speaks himself to be. The Cockney accent is not feigned, nor does it change, though perhaps it moderates a bit after long acquaintance with the more standard speech of the Pickwickians (and lawyers). So Dickens creates two characters whose contrasting ways of using words to define themselves mark the rupture with physiognomical psychology and the substitution of the indeterminacies of theatrical speech, costume, and behavior. Dickens took full advantage of the more flexible representations of character in a prose fiction work that this latter conception allows. When people like Sam and Pickwick's lawyer, Mr. Perker, acknowledge the benevolence of their employer, they speak not as an actor mouthing a script, but from what this story sets forth as the core of their character.[50] And it is still, more than a century and a half later, in these skeptical times, immensely moving. Sam's testimony is genuine, not acted:

"I never heerd, mind you, nor read of in story-books, nor see in picters, any angel in tights and gaiters – not even in spectacles, as I remember, though that may ha' been done for anythin' I know to the contrairey; but mark my vords, Job Trotter, he's a reg'lar thorough-bred angel for all that; and let me see the man as wenturs to tell me he knows a better vun."
(p. 704)

The comparison is obvious, but only Shakespeare besides Dickens shows such a capacity to take one set of material determinants, such as an old Richmond buck devoted to tights and gaiters, and turn them into markers of an almost metaphysical transformation.

The other great narrative advantage Dickens gains from reforming characters around language is the capacity to critique further kinds of speech, whether it be the Rev. Mr. Stiggins's hypocritical sermons, the bullying tactics of attorneys, or the artifice of valentines.[51] Dickens places at the core of these *Papers* the very language in which they were allegedly transmitted. And in metamoments such as the controversy over "Bill Stumps, His Mark," Dickens opens the text and his readers to all the possibilities of use, abuse, misuse, misunderstanding, misapplication, misdirection, disguise, and genuine feeling that language can express. He not only shifts character from graphic fixities to linguistic varieties, he transforms "Transactions" and "Sporting Adventures" into a sustained, buoyantly funny, sometimes terrible, sometimes realistically homely, and sometimes harsh, account of how events are transcribed, edited, and received as stories.

VIII

The third challenge Dickens met and triumphed over through the writing of *Pickwick* was to find and develop a plot. In one way, the presence of Tupman, as we have seen, enabled Dickens to invent a whole series of lovers, overwriting the other humours characters so that Winkle and Snodgrass turn into suitors, as does Sam, while Tony Weller, Sam's father, regrets his impetuous remarriage, and other characters such as Mr. Dowler and Bob Sawyer suspect the Pickwickians of amorous designs on their women. There is also an underlying homosocial plot originating in the Pickwickians' joint excursions and focused when Mr. Pickwick's proposal to hire Sam as servant is understood by Mrs. Bardell as a proposal of marriage to her. Dickens was certainly quick to make use of the absurd proceedings in the *Norton* v. *Melbourne* case to thread a breach of promise suit from the fourth through sixteenth numbers.

But the other surprising and lasting discovery Dickens makes in *Pickwick* is that death can be mined for even more kinds of narrative than he explored in *Sketches*. *The Posthumous Papers of the Pickwick Club* is a text suffused with death, from its inception (the originator's suicide) to its title – "posthumous" – to its composition, contents, conclusion, and reception. We do not know when the adjective "posthumous" was first appended to "papers of the Pickwick Club." The March 26, 1836 advertisement in the *Athenaeum* refers to the "Pickwick Travels, the Pickwick Diary, the Pickwick Correspondence – in short, the whole of the Pickwick Papers, [which] were carefully preserved, and duly registered by the secretary, from time to time, in the voluminous Transactions of the Pickwick Club." These records, purchased from the secretary and placed in the hands of "Boz," are, the announcement continues, being arranged by the editor to be placed "before the public in an attractive form," enhanced by plates drawn by Robert Seymour "illustrating the beauties of Pickwick" (pp. xx–xxi). Thus from well before the first number was printed, Dickens and his collaborators conceived the ending of the serial, at least the sentence "The Pickwick Club exists no longer" (p. 871). For those, and they may have been few, who read the installments within this predetermined context, the narrative's ending was foreordained. Furthermore, if the papers are posthumous, does that imply that the secretary who inscribed those papers is also dead? Is Boz the surviving transcriber, along with Snodgrass who is credited with some of the entries? Has Boz at some level, and for only that part of the text which sustains the fiction of edited papers, lived beyond Dickens? Another way of asking this question is, did "Dickens" write the papers and Boz posthumously edit them? At one level this inquiry is silly and irrelevant; at another, we've already intimated the answer in our allusion to Foucault's comments about modern authors; but at a third level, that of the novel's own theorization of its textual production, it is both relevant and unanswerable.

Besides Seymour's suicide, two other deaths in real life occurred over the nineteen months of the serial run. These were the sudden death of Mary Scott Hogarth and the long anticipated death of King William IV. Both occurred in the summer of 1837, when Dickens was writing the later numbers of *Pickwick* and early installments of *Oliver Twist* and also editing *Bentley's Miscellany*. Mary's death on May 7 so deeply affected Dickens and his household ("the saddest and most severe affliction" [1837 Preface, p. xcix]) that he could not complete the June portion of *Pickwick* or *Oliver Twist*. On this occasion a death in the family occasioned, as Seymour's had, another "blank" in the society of consumers of "Boz"'s fiction; but the void was filled up within another month, by a number that Dickens predicted "will bang all the others."[52] The Fleet chapters of Part xv earned John Forster's vehement praise in the *Examiner*: "the author has achieved his masterpiece ... It is devoted chiefly to a delineation of the interior of the Fleet prison, of its various inmates, and of the scenes of misery and profligacy that may still, to the shame of our legislature, be witnessed daily within its walls ... We recognise in this fine writer a maturing excellence, which promises, at no distant day, the very greatest accomplishment."[53] Many critics, from Forster onward, have identified the Fleet chapters, perhaps as a result of Dickens's mourning for Mary, as a place where the serial unmistakably moves from the project's caricature and comedic beginnings to something approaching the social commentary and detailed sociological observation of a Henry Fielding. How much this transformation was due to Dickens's grief has, I think, been exaggerated. *Pickwick Papers* had been transforming for many months, and the Fleet chapters tapped into Dickens's intense, unresolved subsurface feelings about his family's incarceration in the Marshalsea twelve years earlier. (There is something a little uncanny about the numbers here: Dickens was born in 1812; his father was imprisoned in 1824; he began *Pickwick* in 1836 – all twelve-year intervals.)

William IV expired on June 20, 1837. Dickens had little to say about the Sailor King apart from Boz's fury at his attempt to oust the Whigs expressed in his December 1834 "Story Without a Beginning," never republished. However, Dickens had reported the general election campaign in 1834–35, and the scenes he observed then may have influenced the

Eatanswill episodes. With the advent of Victoria and the return of Melbourne's government, there was a kind of hopefulness in the air that Dickens could have sensed. From the start the young Queen took her duties seriously. Her strength of character won over the worldly Melbourne, who, in the words of Asa Briggs, suddenly "watched his language – usually 'interlarded with damns' – sat bolt upright rather than lounged in his chair, and greatly restricted the range of his anecdotes."[54]

So *Pickwick* appears in monthly parts within a context of deaths that threaten its existence and enable its transformations. As we have it, the book – "something nobler than a novel" in Chesterton's unavoidable phrase – seems to be a comedy and to emit "that sense of everlasting youth" – Chesterton again – "a sense as of the gods gone wandering in England. This is not a novel, for all novels have an end; and 'Pickwick,' properly speaking, has no end ... we know [Pickwick] did not stop [in Dulwich]. We know he broke out, that he took again the road of the high adventures; we know that if we take it ourselves in any acre of England, we may come suddenly upon him in a lane."[55] Chesterton's response flatly contradicts everything we have been saying about the novel's "posthumous" genesis and determination to conclude, a determination Dickens reiterated in the tenth number, where he announced "that it is his intention to adhere to his original pledge of confining this work to twenty numbers." In that notice Dickens held out hope of further episodes: "The Author [not 'Editor'] merely hints that he has strong reason to believe that a great variety of other documents still lie hidden in the repository from which these were taken, and that they may one day see the light" (pp. 881–82). But when Dickens did revisit the idea of papers hiding in a repository, being dragged into the light and edited, and did revive Pickwick and Sam in the pages of *Master Humphrey's Clock*, Chesterton's sunny prediction that we might "come suddenly upon [Pickwick] in a lane" in all his everlasting youth proved unfounded. The resurrected modern Don Quixote and Sancho Panza had none of the vitality Cervantes imparted to his twin heroes in the second part of *Don Quixote*. Rather than reviving, *Master Humphrey's Clock* buried Pickwick and Sam fathoms deep in ineffectual prose.

There are, therefore, good reasons for maintaining that the paired Samuels, Pickwick and Weller, live only within the pages of these posthumous papers, and that, unlike characters in the novels of Anthony Trollope, Margaret Oliphant, Anthony Powell, and others composing series of interconnected fictions, they could not be revived. What we now must do is look at the context within which Mr. Pickwick so vividly and memorably survives, and ask what it is about these posthumous papers that allows Dickens's comic powers such scope that his protagonist seems immortal. Here we confront an apparent paradox: *Pickwick Papers* is riddled with death, many more deaths than one encounters in the bloodiest contemporary thriller, or, I venture to guess, in any of Dickens's subsequent fictions. There are four deaths of actual persons mentioned in the text: the decollation of King Charles I is alluded to early on; Mr. Justice Nupkins fears he might meet the fate of Caesar and Spencer Perceval; and the Wellers observe the death of St. Valentine. But these are comparatively trivial references. Of the characters who take their place on stage, or just off, at least seventeen expire. Some of these are incidental: Sam's mother, the gentleman who killed himself over Bill Stumps, the deceased Eatanswill MP whose passing necessitates the by-election, Susan Clarke's "dead-and-gone" husband who leaves her a "widder," Solomon Pell's wife – herself a widow. Some deaths are imagined rather than actual: Tupman's decease from Winkle's misplaced shot, Jingle's fatal trajectory before being rescued in the Fleet as well as his supposititious demise from yellow fever in Bengal, and Boffer's predicted suicide by slashing his throat or hanging himself, an eventuality that Wilkins Flasher and Mr. Simmery wager on. When Winkle is let loose with his gun, he may slaughter partridges, game, even the gamekeeper and his boy. And pre-ceding generations haunt the precincts of Dingley Dell at Christmas. These are light-hearted and slight mortalities.

But some characters' deaths, as clouded as the "dark shadows on the earth" (p. 874), are narrated with affecting and effective rhetoric. Parental opposition, Mr. Wardle allows, could force unfortunate young lovers to choose between "clandestine matrimony or charcoal," that is, asphyxi-ation (p. 830). Susan Weller's deathbed repentance is both humorous and touching. There is, however, nothing funny about the Chancery prisoner's death in life. "'Twenty years,' he gasped, 'twenty years in this hideous grave. My heart broke when my child died, and I could not even kiss him in his little coffin. My loneliness since then, in all this noise and riot, has been very dreadful. May God forgive me! He has seen my solitary, lingering death.' 'He has got his discharge, by G – !' said the [turnkey]. He had. But he had grown so like death in life, that they knew not when he died" (p. 688).

The bills of mortality are even lengthier for persons who expire in the stories characters tell, in the intercalated stories, to be sure, but also in the anecdotes that Jingle, Sam, his father, and others relate. At least sixty-seven persons succumb in tales and songs, and that sum does not include the hundreds who die, shrieking loudly and shrilly in the tempest-tossed ocean or whose bones lie scattered at his feet, in Heyling's dreams of revenge following his wife's death.

There is also a tremendous amount of parent–child abuse in this novel. Parents kill children, children kill parents. John Edmunds beats his wife. His namesake son kills her by his criminal behavior, and on his return from fourteen years' transportation he assails his father who dies of a ruptured blood vessel. Their identical names and behaviors suggest they are doppelgängers, each incarnating the evil twin of the other, and that when son kills father he also kills his own embodied guilt and fury. For the remaining three years of his life he "was truly contrite, penitent, and humbled" (p. 93). Lovers, too, are an endangered species: Winkle for apparently carrying on criminal conversation with Mrs. Pott and eloping with Arabella without parental consent, Snodgrass for similar deceptions played on Mr. Wardle regarding Emily. In stories, characters sometimes tell about mild ruptures that attend romantic escapades. Nathaniel Pipkin, like Snodgrass, conceals himself behind a door in a futile attempt to escape discovery by the father of his beloved, but unlike Snodgrass he does not win the bride, only her father as a friend. Tom Smart does expose and exile his rival and thus gain the hand of the buxom widow and the flourishing business of her roadside inn. The madman, on the other hand, descended from a long line of insane progenitors, is not the courting but the courted party, sought – as many a widow is wooed – because he is rich. Father and brothers sacrifice their daughter and sister for money; she, her father, and her eldest brother all die in consequence.

When we catalogue the communities in *Pickwick*, biological and otherwise, in intercalated tales, anecdotes, and the main narrative, we find that most are riven by internal or intergenerational conflicts. Mr. Blotton of Aldgate temporarily destroys the hearty unanimity of the Pickwickians in chapter 1, and while that contretemps concludes in cheers resulting from the redefinition of humbug so as to "bear a Pickwickian construction," Mr. Blotton resurfaces at the end of Part IV "with a mean desire to tarnish the lustre of the immortal name of Pickwick" (p. 168). By the end of the novel, the Club "has suffered much from internal dissensions," so that "the withdrawal" of Pickwick's name from its roster occasions "its dissolution" (p. 871). The redefinition of the patronymic – also observable in the substitution of Boz for Dickens – or its withdrawal as name or person, often precipitates disaster. With their husbands deceased, widows are vulnerable to matrimonial or economic attack; the substitution of another male in place of the father, as, for example, in the case of the Deputy

Shepherd, can produce domestic discord; the illicit introduction of a potential son-in-law, Mr. Charles Fitz-Marshall for instance, threatens to tear the family of Justice Nupkins apart; and the abduction of the young heiress by the son of the Marquis of Filletoville and rescue by the Bagman's uncle result in two deaths and perpetual bachelorhood.

In sum, there is a lot of rage and killing circulating through this book. Much of the violence occurs within families and close-knit communities, congregating in a club, parish, inn, pub, prison, home, or manor house. Within the Fleet chapters Dickens may well deserve the accolade Forster bestowed, of drawing attention to injustices in advance of Parliamentary remedies. But I suspect that Dickens is also, in these passages overtly and throughout the serial more covertly, reinscribing his tortured feelings about his own family, their follies about money, their sacrifice of him to their improvidence and distractions. Psychically he arranges a space, more easily accomplished after Seymour's death, in which to express these emotions. He occludes his own name and agency, substituting "Boz" for the patronymic Dickens and "Editor" for Author. These strategies enable Dickens to disclaim ownership of the incidents while retaining credit for their being "brought to light." Within the text, male anger against males gets acted out directly through threats, beatings, and murder; male anger against females comes out more indirectly, through widowing an exceptional percentage of the cast of characters, through violence inflicted on or by women, through abandoning them (for instance, Mrs. Bardell and her friends are absent from the last four numbers), through ridicule of the erotic ambitions of elderly females, and through severe policing of the emotional, occupational, and expressive conduct of eligible young ladies. Fleet and family are alike places where violence is quarantined. Indeed, inside and outside are pretty much the same: "money was, in the Fleet, just what money was out of it" (p. 651). Yet, as Sam observes, imprisonment affects the inmates differently – an observation that also applies to marriage. Some lounge about, others suffer. "It's unekal," Sam declares, "and that's the fault on it" (p. 633).

IX

Thus far we have uncovered the deadly strain that runs through these monthly numbers: eighty-seven named corpses, and hundreds unnamed, populate the narrative. Many, though not all, of these deaths occur as a result of interfamilial and intergenerational violence; one stubborn exception would be the man who ate crumpets on principle. Death seems to be a common speculation endemic to many of the book's imagined narratives: Pott will be the death of Mrs. Pott and hopes Winkle will choke himself, Tony Weller advises Sam that if he ever gets to fifty and feels disposed to marry, "jist you shut yourself up in your own room, if you've got one, and pison yourself off hand" (p. 345). On the other hand, Sam predicts that Winkle will drown himself or put extra lead in Ben Allen's head if Arabella doesn't agree to see him (p. 606). Winkle seems a perpetual threat, not only to partridges and game and Tupman and Ben Allen, but also to Dowler, who has threatened to "cut his throat – give me a knife – from ear to ear" (p. 568). "Heavens!" Winkle speculates, "if I should kill him in the blindness of my wrath, what would be my feelings ever afterwards!" (p. 584). While one implication of Winkle's reflection, comic in its assertion of his valor, is that he would feel remorse, other feelings lasting ever afterwards motivate Heyling and possibly could have motivated Winkle. (These experiences do change people: Tupman "never proposed again" [p. 875].) Indeed, Winkle is the biter bit, the hunter whom everyone hunts, the "prior attachment" that must be severed, as Ben Allen demonstrates when he seizes "a poker, flourish[es] it, in a warlike manner above his head, [and] inflict[s] a savage blow on an imaginary skull" (p. 590). We learn of others done away with by the hangman (Sam notes that Jack Ketch does his prisoners in regular rotation [p. 145]) or the executioner, including Master Bardell's worry, in court, that he will be "immediately ordered away for instant execution" (p. 514). The ivy-covered grave is the terminus of every life story. The acme of poetry is a (hilarious) funeral ode:

> Can I view thee panting, lying
> On thy stomach, without sighing:
> Can I unmoved see thee dying
>      On a log,
>      Expiring frog! (p. 216)

While death terminates life and stories, it seems also to be a metaphoric presence within life. The commercial room at the Peacock is ornamented with "the mortal remains of a trout in a glass coffin" (p. 198). Death is like the end of school term: "Death, self-interest, and fortune's changes, are every day breaking up many a happy group and scattering them far and wide; and the boys and girls never come back again" (p. 457). The Bagman's uncle encounters "decaying skeletons of departed mails" (p. 753) and postal customers like dead letters. Those principally assigned responsibility for forestalling death are ominously denominated: "Sawyer, late Nockemorf" (p. 586). These dubious physicians, Ben and Bob, are first encountered dissecting pork and fowl after cutting up a muscular child's leg, putting in for an arm, clubbing together for a subject, and longing for a whole head. They find practicing their anatomical exercises stimulating: "Nothing like dissecting, to give one an appetite," Bob Sawyer declares (pp. 447–48). At the trial of *Bardell* v. *Pickwick*, a chemist picked for jury duty worries that the errand-boy left in his shop "is not much acquainted with drugs; and I know that the prevailing impression on his mind is, that Epsom salts means oxalic acid; and syrup of senna, laudanum" (p. 513).

The most persistent metaphor of mortality, which W. H. Auden stressed half a century ago, is the Garden of Eden and the Fall.[56] Enclosed gardens are everywhere in Pickwick, as are serpents. I noted some of these manifestations of Paradise and its depopulation forty years ago, so I will supply only a single instance of garden, serpent, and expulsion here. One of the first Edens, the product of the lion hunters and the *Eatanswill Gazette*, is the Eastern Fairy-land of Mrs. Leo Hunter, filled with "a blaze of beauty, and fashion, and literature" (p. 221) to an extent never before attained. This exalted setting must, unhappily, represent a fallen world, in which the costumes rented from Mr. Solomon Lucas are a little dirty but "more or less spangled" (p. 219), while the music of the "something-ean singers" is chiefly composed of three grunts and one howl, and the atmosphere – a "Perspiring Fog" Count Smorltork quips mistakenly – darkens occasionally as romantic or professional discords threaten. Into the midst of this acre and a quarter of beauty comes a version of the serpent, one who can talk his way into any community, a music-maker of superficial harmony, one Jingle, who immediately upon confronting the Pickwickians rushes away. At the conclusion of the chapter, itself another kind of enclosure vacated as a result of disruption, he is pursued by Pickwick, whose tights and gaiters lead the juvenile observers to suppose they "were some remnants of the dark ages," and his servant Sam, who compares himself to a "Living Skellinton" (p. 229). Note that these two identifications place the protagonists, like Mrs. Leo Hunter, Minerva, and Mr. Pott, a Russian officer of justice, simultaneously in the ancient past and in the 1820s, when the Frenchman Claude Seurat, fearfully emaciated, exhibited himself as "anatomie vivante; or, living skeleton" in Pall Mall.[57] We'll return to this point in a moment.

Typically, Dickens in this early fiction smashes the elements of the narrative of the Fall and rearranges them in fractured pieces that recall and retell the story: in this case, of a community, however factitiously consti-tuted out of animals, Turks, cavaliers, Charles the Seconds, philosophers, poets, brigands, troubadours, and living skeletons disrupted by the entrance of one whose feigning is less apparent, less charitable, less obvious to superficial sight, and far more dangerous to hospitality and amity, than the slighter impersonations of the costumed guests. Again and again in *Pickwick Papers*, readers encounter serpents in the garden. In one way this imagery, which does often intimate a serious breaking-up of happy communities, climaxes when Mr. Pickwick, a portly serpent chaperone, climbs a tree in order to persuade the immured Arabella Allen to escape from her Bristol garden with Winkle. This is the most explicit enactment of the Fall, and yet it serves a quite different story.

x

Even if there are many more deaths, some of them quite tragic, than we remember or expect in a comedy, we need to find an explanation for why so many of them cause a snigger or a chuckle or a laugh. As Chesterton put it, the two primary dispositions of Dickens were "to make the flesh creep and to make the sides ache."[58] These dispositions were immediately recognized by Dickens's contemporaries, one of whom issued a plagiarism connecting death and humor: *The Posthumorous Notes of the Pickwick Club.*[59]

In archetypal comedy, as Northrop Frye defines it, the focus is on a social group that often enforces laws prohibiting the young hero from achieving his desire.[60] Aided by his tricky servant, the somewhat naive hero manages to overcome the opposition of the elder generation, rivals, and imposters. He also encounters buffoons who both block and assist the festivity, and rustics – either peasants or country squires – who both sponsor and delimit saturnalias. As with the Fall narrative, Dickens decomposes the elements of generic comedy and reassembles them. Pickwick is not a young hero, out to make his fortune and find a wife, "ordinary in his virtues, but socially attractive" like the hero of New Comedy.[61] He is a rich bachelor, old, stout, and foolish. His desire is not to marry but to see the world, for which he will discover a need for corrective lenses, both optical and cognitive. His servant and mentor is tricky at first, but learns principle from his master. While there are heavy fathers blocking the next generation's marriage plans, one of them, Wardle, is also the country squire hosting the Christmas saturnalia and sensibly maintaining limits to foolishness, whether committed by lovers or Mr. Pickwick himself, who sometimes ventures onto thin ice. Frye emphasizes the importance of community to comedy, a genre that has at its center the transformation of one social group into another, often defined as a younger, fertile generation that in the end receives a transfer of wealth from the seniors. Gullibility and illusion characterize the elderly characters before they are enlightened and, through educative deception, they learn to read reality. In the end, the older generation is incorporated into the renovated society. These features *Pickwick Papers* replicates – at least in part.

At the heart of generic comedy, then, is conflict: intergenerational and interfamilial. That conflict often leads to serious, indeed apparently fatal, consequences. Recall the opening of some of Shakespeare's comedies: Rosalind, named a traitor like her father, and Celia are banished from the Court at the opening of *As You Like It*; Sebastian is presumed dead at the start of *Twelfth Night*; Hermia is condemned to death or to "live a barren sister" all her life (1.i.72) if she refuses Demetrius when the Duke of Athens pronounces sentence at the beginning of *A Midsummer Night's Dream*; and in the late Romance *The Tempest* all the mariners drown.[62] The American novelist Jerome Charyn makes the point succinctly: "Behind any great comedy is a sense of fear."[63]

Moreover, the disputes between the two generations constituting society in comedy take on the character and structure of trials, "not unlike the action of a lawsuit," Frye observes, "in which plaintiff and defendant construct different versions of the same situation, one finally being judged as real and the other as illusory."[64] Jonathan H. Grossman has elaborated perceptively on this point. He argues that the case of *Bardell* v. *Pickwick* "structures the novel's actions," setting up a trajectory that also requires previous events to be reviewed, thus incorporating formerly detached incidents such as Pickwick's innocent presence within inappropriate settings (girls' school garden, maiden's bedroom). Further, Grossman points out that the lawyers in the novel enact authorial roles, writing different characters for Pickwick based on their interpretations of limited evidence. The legal profession, like authorship, is "immersed in writing and reading, in orchestrating discourses, and finally in telling stories for money," connections that Dickens both underscores and obscures.[65] One of those connections is made by the date on which the minutes of the Club are first quoted: "May 12, 1827." It is, as Steven Marcus first pointed out, the month in which Dickens "began the world" as a clerk with Ellis and Blackmore.[66] Thus the intergenerational struggle of New Comedy that leads to marriage and the transfer of power to a younger generation maps onto the formalized forensics of trials, in which alternative interpretations or narratives are the essential weapons, and maps also onto the task of writing itself, a "profession" practiced for pay that requires producing many versions of character and events, conflict, and in the Victorian period at least, concluding resolution. In these ways *Pickwick* indirectly articulates Dickens's burgeoning apprehension of the possible imbrication of his legal interests with his writerly ones. The latter, of course, also includes theater, which, though Grossman does not dwell on it, is precisely the medium and setting in which the trial for breach of promise of marriage is staged.

Another feature of many generic comedies is expulsion – a forced journey from home base to the country, the forest, an island, a strange city, where the protagonists learn new things about themselves and their former homes. Once again Dickens adapts conventions to his own comic design: the Pickwickians choose their ramblings, rather than being impelled to them, although in the course of those journeys quick escapes from tight spots and ladies' chambers are sometimes required. Moreover, their illusions are shattered not just in the country, but also on home base, in Goswell Street and the Fleet. So conflict has two dimensions: the overcoming of blocking figures who would deny the social group of Pickwickians their desires, and the overcoming of their own ignorance and illusions about the world. Into this latter category Dickens brilliantly inscribes not only the innocent protagonist, whose "heart must ha' been born five-and-twenty years arter his body, at least" (p. 611), but also the tricky and cynical servant, who comes to know "Pickvick and principle" (p. 374).[67]

Conflict, then, is essential to comedy. The threats to society must be real for their conquering to matter. Blotton may be temporarily reintegrated by linguistic play, but words are not the primary element within the story, though they are the only element in such papers as the editor makes available to the reader. (That this narrative is nothing but papers, and simultaneously everything including papers, is another way Dickens brilliantly converts the givens of his original commission into something almost post-structuralist – yet much funnier and richer.) But words are not substitutes for real bodies, flesh, bones, or furniture, bodies that get bruised and bloodied, ground up and decapitated, "get rheumatic about the legs and arms," or go crazy (p. 208).

Consequently, if Pickwick were as immortal as he is said to be by the editor in the first sentence of chapter 1 or as he is later denominated by Chesterton, there would be no comedy. The assumption that he is immortal, that he cannot be damaged or killed, precludes any kind of comic action, from simple verbal reparation ("humbug in a Pickwickian point of view" [p. 7]) to physical recovery in a wheelbarrow and a pound, to privation and limited spiritual recovery in and after the Fleet, and finally to the muted comedy deriving from Mr. Pickwick's decline of vitality that prompts him for the future to "spend many quiet years in peaceful retirement; cheered through life by the society of my friends, and followed in death by their affectionate remembrance" (p. 871). All the bashings and shootings, the suicides and murders, establish a mortal context within which individual and communal benevolence, constructive engagement with and emotional and financial support of others, become essential to the reformation of society. "Unekal" circumstances must, insofar as possible, be rebalanced, as they will be by death if not through the efforts of the living.

If comedy is about the renovation of a social group, the purging of troublemakers and the incorporation of members from all generations, families, and classes, then transformation becomes the primary dramatic action, reiterated however many times, in however many ways, that the story requires to complete its cure, or in twenty numbers to complete the commercial bargain between producers and consumers of these *Papers*. Transformation is at the heart of *Pickwick Papers* too. To instance just one example: Mr. Perker metamorphoses from a "little high-dried man, with a dark squeezed up face," who is "baffled" by Sam's repulses at the White Hart Inn, to Samuel Slumkey's agent dispensing bribes. Finally, moved by Mr. Pickwick's example, he turns into an attorney who declares to his client that whether or not Job and Jingle make use of, or repay, Mr. Pickwick's loan to enable them to start a new life in Australia, "your object is equally honourable" (p. 819).

Not all transformations are integrative in the best way, even when comic. Consuming sausages containing human remains does not integrate one into community: "the little old gen'lm'n, who had been remarkably partial to sassages all his life, rushed out o' the shop in a wild state, and was never heerd on artervards!" (p. 465). Indeed, many transformations, from that of the Dying Clown forward, track a misanthropic trajectory, leading to hatred and even murder of fellow human beings. It is this trajectory that at the middle of the story the Goblins attempt to reverse for the morose and solitary Gabriel Grub. Unlike most undertakers, who are "the merriest fellows in the world" (p. 432), the sexton and grave-digger Grub "eyed each merry face as it passed him by, with such a deep scowl of malice and ill-humour, as it was difficult to meet without feeling something the worse for" (p. 432). "You a miserable man!" the goblin shouts indignantly (p. 441). After reviewing many scenes in the comedy of life,

Gabriel concludes "that it was a very decent and respectable sort of world after all" (p. 443). That's a transformation which is meaningless unless Grub, the Pickwickians, and the reader, had previously confronted, in life and in print, the very real challenges to that belief which must be overcome.

XI

Maybe, however, the challenges in *Pickwick* are too easy. Maybe, instead of its being a book suffused by death, we would be more sensitive to the book's effect if we said that it is hard to take any Pickwickian bad news seriously. Certainly critics from the time of first publication have striven to insulate and bracket the intercalated tales, denigrating them as bad writing, inartistic filler, and isolated from the surrounding fun. The Fleet passages, too, have been cordoned – explained as the result of Mary Hogarth's death or the influence of *Oliver Twist* or an eruption of Dickens's social conscience intruding on the "real" substance of *Pickwick Papers*. I have been trying to make the opposite case: that these dark shadows are essential to Dickens's art, his comedy, his affect. *Pickwick* and Dickens's art grow up from *Sketches* precisely because they explore further the source of narrative in death and the bond between persons in the repeated recognition and experience of disappointment and loss. But now it is necessary to nuance that argument a bit. At the heart of *Pickwick Papers*, metaphorically and literally – coming in Part x of the twenty parts, is the Dingley Dell Christmas, a time and a place where, "[i]f any of the old English yeomen had turned into fairies when they died, it was just the place in which they would have held their revels" (p. 422). (Notice the theme of transformation – yeomen into fairies.) The January number, recounting events of the preceding month, incorporates the anti-Christmas at the Marquis of Granby, where the presiding clergyman substitutes the letter for the spirit of religion,[68] then moves on to Manor Farm and a wedding and dance under the mistletoe, with much mildly erotic licensed foreplay, and concludes with the tale of Gabriel Grub, another way of showing mankind how to take and perpetuate the season.

But Christmas in Dingley Dell is so idealized as to seem vaguely unreal. Suffused in nostalgia and recollection, the season incorporates memories of many hearts that have ceased to beat, many bright looks that have ceased to glow, many hands that have grown cold – all somehow prompts to cheerfulness. As the Pickwickians start their journey, they are "brisk as bees, if not altogether as light as fairies" (p. 408). Their excursion is marked by effervescent bustle, heralded by bugle calls, impeded by exchanges of packages and persons, threatened by excessive speed and sharp twists in the road, freezing cold and warm walks: all the traditional elements of a portentous journey leading to climactic discoveries. Even after arriving, their access to paradise is somewhat barred by the ill humor of the grande dame of the family. Her gradual transformation under the blandishments of Mr. Pickwick is marked by her first looking "fierce as might be," then exhibiting "great dignity," feigning deafness, "rapidly giving way," and manifesting a quivering lip and "infirmities of temper." Finally, after seeing Isabella's loving face and experiencing "Mr. Pickwick's affectionate good nature," "she was fairly melted . . . and all the little ill-humour evaporated in a gush of silent tears" (pp. 411–12). This is pleasant, if not persuasive; indeed the editor cannot say exactly what precipitates the change. And while it stands synecdochically for the transformative pattern of the story, Mrs. Wardle's transformation and the Christmas number's repeated acts of social reintegration don't engage in the depth of passion, resistance, inequality, and violence we encounter elsewhere. Part x may mark both the epitome and the trivialization of Dickens's theme.

John Bowen makes a suggestion that helps us to understand the disparity between the communions of the fairyland in Dingley Dell and the reality Pickwick encounters elsewhere in the world. Citing the three kinds of time Frank Kermode identified in his *Sense of an Ending,*[69] Bowen identifies aevum, an "intermediate order" situated between cosmic aeons and diurnal moments, as "the time of the angels and of novelists, of creatures who live in time but who are nevertheless eternal."[70] That's a useful way of thinking about comedy which registers at one and the same time the cruelties and inequalities of the world and the sense as of gods gone wandering in England. To revert to an earlier point, the aevum of *Pickwick Papers* includes brigands and Apollos, St. Valentine, and a "love-sick Pickwick," in its fancy-dress fiction of "creatures who live in time but who are nevertheless eternal." The time of aevum registers both the eternal, archetypal movements of the universe – the beginning with the word, the rising and setting of the sun, the Fall – and the diurnal tick-tock of the clock that measures out mortal days. *The Pickwick Papers* begins with a cosmic beginning: "The first ray of light which illumines the gloom . . . derive[s] from . . . [an] entry in the Transactions of the Pickwick Club" – light and the word together illuminate "the earlier history of the public career of the immortal Pickwick" (p. 1). *The Pickwick Papers* ends very much in human time: Winkle, Snodgrass, and Trundle settle into marriage and children; Tupman parades on the Terrace at Richmond, but only in the summer; Bob and Ben suffer fourteen attacks of yellow fever in India; Tony Weller retires; Mr. Pickwick's housekeeper dies; Sam and Mary wed and have "two sturdy little boys"; and the "immortal" Pickwick becomes "somewhat infirm" (pp. 875–76).

No one knew at the time of publication, nor yet quite knows, what to call *Pickwick Papers*. By setting its action in that intermediate time between the cosmic and the diurnal, Dickens violates the canons of bourgeois realism gradually asserting themselves as the hallmark and justification for the novel. Chesterton thought it something "nobler than a novel," and many others have thought it simply an improvisational mess, a set of disconnected sketches repeating a tiresome and misogynistic plot. To early Victorian Utilitarian minds, angels and fairies consort ill with the urgent need for material and spiritual reforms. However, there is another way of thinking about the canons of realism that puts *Pickwick* into the genre. If we think of realism as the overt refusal of convention, the anti-generic prejudice, then the disclosure of imposture is the mark of realism as well as of comedy. "We think this way, we think these things, we imagine these possibilities," the realist novel tells us, "but we are being imposed upon by the conventions we adopt without thinking, conventions that others (for instance, actors and lawyers) use to impose upon us." Protesting against the moral imposed by fictional conventions and public censors, Thackeray once declared that "[s]ermons and snapdragon do not go well together." When reality shows us genius and virtue in penury, and knavery filching reputation, he complains, "how can sublime moralists talk of goodness and gold together? . . . I should like to see a novel where all the rogues prosper, and all the good men go to gaol."[71]

Dickens does provide sermons and snapdragon. He foregrounds and yet contains mortality. His fiction incorporates many kinds of physical and psychic violence known to his contemporaries, not as isolated or insulated episodes cut off from the main text, but as essential parts of life and our mortal expectations and stories. Death is not the end of tales or the extinguisher of humor and benevolence: it is the condition of their creation. Coming to terms with death in all its manifestations is, as Frank Kermode remarked with respect to E. M. Forster, "a necessary element in the idea of greatness."[72] Only within the context of bruised minds and bodies and the possibility of human intervention and comfort can the mingled joy and sadness of this book and its termination pulse:

[Mr. Pickwick] is somewhat infirm now, but he retains all his former juvenility of spirit, and may still be frequently seen contemplating the pictures in the Dulwich

Gallery, or enjoying a walk about the pleasant neighbourhood on a fine day. He is known by all the poor people about, who never fail to take their hats off as he passes with great respect: the children idolise him, and so indeed does the whole neighbourhood. Every year he repairs to a large family merry-making at Mr. Wardle's; on this, as on all other occasions, he is invariably attended by the faithful Sam, between whom and his master there exists a steady and reciprocal attachment, which nothing but death will sever. (pp. 876–77)

We can't quite stop with "sever," changed to "terminate" from 1847 onward. There are many aspects of this idyllic retirement that Dickens will change in his later fictions: the obsequious deference of the poor is reinscribed as resentment, fear, distrust, murderous anger, in *Our Mutual Friend*; Trabb's boy does not idolize the newly minted Pip in *Great Expectations*; and the homosocial ideal of master and man Dickens derives from ample precedent and reformulates movingly here is reconsidered both in terms of the power disparities of employer and employee – think of Tattycoram in *Little Dorrit* – and of the domestic coziness of male friendships, belied by the many rival lovers in the late novels. But even to skeptical hearts and minds, there is something lasting and loving about the fantasy of "a steady and reciprocal attachment, which nothing but death will sever."[73]

## XII

So lasting was it that subsequent authors tried to kill it off. A certain Captain Brown dies indirectly as a result of being absorbed in the latest number of Dickens's *Pickwick*. That incident appears in the first number of Elizabeth Gaskell's novel *Cranford*, which ran in irregular installments in Dickens's new weekly journal, *Household Words*, from December 13, 1851, just before the Christmas issue, to May 1853. Dickens was not happy about being featured in this way, so he exercised his editorial prerogative and changed the offending author to Thomas Hood. But when Gaskell revised the novel for volume publication, she restored her original version, which set Johnson and Augustan rhetoric against the early Dickensian age of coaches and charity. Gaskell's fictional critique of both authors functions in complex ways that Hilary M. Schor has acutely analyzed: "by absorbing and rewriting Dickens," Schor maintains, "Gaskell begins to stake out the territory of technology, history, and narrative for the woman writer; she begins to ask how the woman writer will reread all of literature, and what force she will capture and reabsorb to make real her own literary and social vision."[74] The train, representative of industrial modernity, death, and financial exigency, comes to Cranford, along with magicians who cannot transform themselves successfully and Arabian nights' fantasies that are miraculously fulfilled. There is an atmosphere of aevum about *Cranford* as well as *Pickwick Papers*, but Gaskell had to extinguish the associations with Dickens's immortal fiction in order to create her own. As Garrett Stewart puts it, "The novel within which the Victorian death scene enjoyed its first major try-out [the death of the Chancery prisoner] is now the novel around which, and in part because of whose distracting fascination, the legacy of fictional dying is maintained."[75]

Likewise, William Makepeace Thackeray, having been turned down by Dickens as successor illustrator of *Pickwick*, and writing desperately for money in Paris and London, killed off Pickwickian sentiments in an early monthly serial published in *Fraser's Magazine*, the *Yellowplush Correspondence* (1838). Yellowplush is servant to a scoundrel barrister, Algernon Deuceace. If the heart of Dickens's narrative, as Mark Cronin expresses it, is "a remarkably optimistic story of reconciliation and redemption, brotherhood and community," Thackeray rewrites every element of the earlier book, turning Mr. Pickwick into Deuceace, a marital schemer and snake, Sam into Yellowplush, a prying, disloyal servant, and the ending into a parody of affection and deserved rewards. Thackeray, Cronin shows, refashions *Pickwick Papers* by supplying "a dark mirror exposing the perversions and corruptions that threaten to overwhelm the Pickwickian spirit."[76]

Likewise, when Wilkie Collins commenced as a writer of fiction at age nineteen, he penned a critique of early Dickens. John Bowen tells us that Wilkie Collins's first short story, "The Last Stage Coachman" (1843), resembles *Pickwick*'s "Story of the Bagman's Uncle." "Collins's sketch shares a concern with its precursor[] in its portrayal of the loss of a wild and romantic life of the past, as the old gives place violently to the new," Bowen remarks. But unlike Dickens's wistful and melancholy regret for a passing age, Collins's conclusion "becomes a powerfully vengeful one," as the superannuated coach and coachmen "come back, powerful, undead and clothed in human skin, violently avenging themselves on their presumptuous successors. It is a story that both borrows from what comes before and fears its uncanny and murderous return."[77]

Writers tried to kill off *Pickwick Papers* by train, parody, and ghosts, the latter not revenants returning to life as fairies but in Collins coming back as vampires and living skeletons reclaiming the age of coaches from the clutches of the new. Gaskell, Thackeray, and Collins testify to the power *Pickwick Papers* had to live in their own present lives. All three needed to kill the immortal Pickwick in order to have a space and time for their own tales of travel and adventure. So did Walter Besant, far outside the time frame of our narrative, who wrote a short story entitled "The Death of Samuel Pickwick." Of course these murderous acts had no effect on the Pickwickians, even though over time these newer generations of writers better met the spirit of the new age: "[t]he world would not take another Pickwick from me, now," Dickens mused a decade later, at the start of *David Copperfield*.[78] He was not to repeat the novel himself. Rather, in advance of his successors, by degrees, in different novels, over time, he rewrote, erased, and killed off many of the features of *Pickwick* that at the time so appealed to his readers and still do to many readers today. With *Pickwick* Dickens learned to exploit and improve the sources that inspired the best of his *Sketches*. But a consummate artist before he was a coherently created author, he also spotted the weaknesses of his strengths, and exploited them in subsequent fictions.

We are left with at least three paradoxes. First, a novel for which death figures in the inception, title, composition, contents, conclusion, and reception registers it as essential to comedy and greatness. Second, a tale flexibly set in both angelic and human time seems inextinguishable even by succeeding authors, notwithstanding that on the last page of the last number the final words are "death will sever." Third, Boz, transparently disguised as an editor, wins a huge following as a humorist and chronicler of contemporary middle-class metropolitan life. Yet, midway through this print manifestation of Boz, he does become an actual editor as well as a contributor of monthly articles that deconstruct the settings and benevolent society of his ongoing serial. His next long work moves forward and backward simultaneously to narrate the prequels and sequels to death and life in London.

# CHAPTER 4

# *Hiring Boz (1837–1839):* Bentley's Miscellany *and* Oliver Twist

Charles Dickens, George Cruikshank sketch, April 1837

"Stop thief! Stop thief!" There is a magic in the sound.
                                                    *– Oliver Twist*

[*Oliver Twist* is] out of place in a magazine that started, professing to
dedicate its space to wit and humour.
                                        *– Sunday Times*, April 8, 1838

I began the Sketches of Young Gentlemen to-day. One hundred and
twenty five pounds for such a little book without my name to it, is
pretty well. This and the "Sunday" by the bye, are the only two
things I have not done as Boz.
                        – Charles Dickens, Diary, January 8, 1838

Perhaps we would do best to speak of the *anticipation of retrospection*
as our chief tool in making sense of narrative.
                            – Peter Brooks, *Reading for the Plot*


I

When on November 4, 1836 Richard Bentley engaged Dickens "as Editor"
of *The Wits' Miscellany*, Bentley was consciously and deliberately hiring
"Boz," in spite of the fact that "Charles Dickens" was the name of the editor
and the author who also agreed "to furnish an original article of his own
writing, every monthly Number, to consist of about a sheet of 16 pages." Or
rather, Bentley was hiring several versions of Boz. Boz the editor was an
extension of Boz the nominal "editor" of *The Pickwick Papers* that Dickens
had been hired to "write and edit." Bentley could imagine that the Boz of
*Sketches*, increasingly connected to journalists and aspiring writers, would
be capable of enlisting other rising authors and executing the responsibilities
of a periodical editor. He spelled out five of them in the Agreement:

1. "to correspond generally with Literary men, contributors to the publication or likely to become so";
2. "to read the articles forwarded for the use of the Miscellany & to give
   his judgment upon their eligibility";
3. "to revise & correct, when necessary, such articles as are accepted or
   intended to be used";
4. "to do his utmost to provide for the adequate & timely supply of the
   monthly Number, to consist of six sheets demy 8vo. so as to enable the
   printer to go to press on or before the 24th of every month"; and
5. "to correct the proof sheets and to send them for press."[1]

With this Memorandum of Agreement, the fiction of Boz as editor
becomes a fact. Boz accepts responsibility for recruiting, selecting, editing,

and proofing the contents of a ninety-six-page magazine to be printed and sold as a half-crown (2*s.* 6*d.*) monthly. He bears no direct responsibility for other elements of the publishing process – the printing, advertising, selling, warehousing, or accounting for the periodical. All these tasks are implicitly retained by Bentley to execute himself or by outsourcing, and were, since the time of Lord Mansfield, not normally within the author's remit. But indirectly, of course, the contents of the magazine will be a leading factor in selling it. Bentley expects Boz to reach the same customers as the *Sketches* and *Pickwick*: that is, a population of middle-class and governing class, urban and country readers who seek out funny and affective stories about contemporary life primarily set in the home counties.

Boz had proved himself adept at appealing to a wide range of social and political readers, and Bentley expected him to continue to tap into that non-partisan, sentimental, comic market. But being an experienced, somewhat authoritarian proprietor who had been burnt by other publishers, editors, and authors, Bentley took several steps to circumscribe Boz. First, he assigned the primary task of articulating the new journal's editorial principles to William Maginn. Maginn, an irrepressible, alcoholic, and sometimes irresponsible Irish-born journalist, had come down to London from Edinburgh and started a humorous magazine of the sort Bentley hoped to replicate, called *Fraser's Magazine*. For Bentley, Maginn penned paragraphs promising that in Bentley's new periodical there would be no politics whatsoever; it was not intended to take sides in any of the debates of the age or to align with any faction, party, or other leading daily or monthly publications, such as the *Morning Chronicle*, *The Times*, or the three competing Edinburgh-based quarterlies. "Our path is single and distinct. In the first place, we have nothing to do with politics. We are so far Conservative as to wish that all things which are good and honourable for our native country should be preserved with jealous hand. We are so far Reformers as to desire that every weed which defaces our conservatory should be unsparingly plucked up and cast away."[2]

Moreover, the journal was not to capitalize on Boz's name, but the publisher's. Bentley decided to alter the title from *The Wits' Miscellany* to *Bentley's Miscellany*. That did more to associate the contents of the periodical with the publishing house – a very strategic move, since authors Dickens brought to the journal, if successful with their contributions there, might be persuaded to choose Bentley as their publisher for longer works. Buttering up his new employer, Dickens from his sick bed told Bentley that "I am greatly better. The alteration of the title would have restored me [to health] at once, had I been worse."[3] (Of course, the japes about the alteration mildly compromised the value of Bentley's trade name: "What need was there to have gone to the opposite extreme?" asked William Jerdan, or R. H. Barham, or Douglas Jerrold, all of whom have been credited with the witticism.[4]) Another clause in the Agreement specified that any submission to the journal, whether accepted for publication therein or not, "shall be considered as belonging to the said Richard Bentley." That is, he could arrange to publish rejected articles in other ways without Boz's editorial intervention. The other security against Boz's effecting unwonted editorial changes was that Bentley "shall have the right of exercising a Veto on the insertion of any article in the Miscellany."

At the time these provisions were unproblematic to Dickens. He was much more concerned about the amount of work he would have as editor, on the one hand, and as a contracted contributor for sixteen pages of original letterpress a month in addition (the equivalent to half a monthly number of *Pickwick*). He specified that he retained the right to pen *Pickwick* and "a similar work which he has undertaken to write for the same publishers" at the conclusion of that novel. Bentley granted that. But in return he insisted, and Dickens agreed, that Dickens "shall not enter into any arrangement to conduct or write for any other periodical publication whatever." "To conduct or write" is another version of Dickens's "to write and edit" and seems to comprehend any other form of writing or editing for any other publisher or publication.

If Dickens was going to agree to limit his literary efforts to publications for Bentley and Chapman and Hall exclusively, he could not fulfill any further assignments for Macrone or for any of the periodicals he had been supplying with sketches. Accordingly, he resigned from the *Morning Chronicle*, receiving in return from Bentley a guarantee that even if the new magazine failed after less than a year, he would receive his editorial stipend of £20 for each of the remaining months of the contract, along with the twenty guineas a month he was to receive for the sixteen-page original article. However, these sums would be "deducted as a set off" from the £500 he was to receive for the three-volume novel he had committed in August of 1836 to write for Bentley. In sum, Dickens's Agreement as editor and author focused his career, but it also circumscribed it and placed equal weight on his real (as opposed to fictional) editorial duties and his creative ones. He was to be a discoverer and developer of literary talent, a copy-editor, and a politically uncontroversial humorist as well. And Boz was subordinated to Bentley as the originator and proprietor of the publication he edited.

Bentley bought "Bozzes" as well. As soon as he signed the Agreement with Dickens he hired George Cruikshank as the illustrator of his periodical, at first for only one plate per month at twelve guineas, and from May onward for two, one being the illustration to Dickens's contribution.[5] He thus brought together the author and artist of Macrone's successful *Sketches* (the third volume, published in December, hadn't even yet been issued). He did not go after Phiz, illustrating *Pickwick*. Maybe Bentley thought the Boz–Phiz combination was too closely identified with Chapman and Hall. Maybe he reasoned that Macrone had no claim on Cruikshank, whereas Chapman and Hall had an Agreement not only for another year of *Pickwick* but also for a second serial of the same kind pairing Boz and Phiz. But it is also the case that even in November 1836, Boz was probably more celebrated for the *Sketches* than for *Pickwick*, although the latter publication was gaining fervent adherents every month. Bentley collectively grabbed for his *Miscellany* the "Bozzes" represented by the combined pen and pencil sketches about contemporary metropolitan life. And he advertised the coup, featuring the editor and illustrator in his notices about the forthcoming periodical and in Cruikshank's wrapper design.

Dickens had a lot of commitments to fulfill or cancel in order to meet the terms of his Bentley Agreement. In addition to resigning from the newspaper in early November, he had to back out of supplying "Leaves From an Unpublished Volume By Boz" for the *Carlton Chronicle*, forgo the £100 Thomas Tegg had offered for a short Christmas book, "Solomon Bell the Raree Showman," which, "[f]or many reasons I should agree with you, in not wishing the name of 'Boz' to be appended," complete the second series of *Sketches by Boz*, produce *The Strange Gentleman* and *The Village Coquettes* (published December 22 as by "Boz"), and meet with Cruikshank whenever possible to plan the last plates for *Sketches* and the first plate for *Bentley's*. A week before Dickens signed the *Miscellany* Agreement he told Thomas Beard that he had been unable to wrest a lucrative engagement from the *Sunday Times*, and so he expected to be working as a reporter in the Gallery of the House of Commons until at least Easter of 1837.[6] That of course didn't happen. The Bentley arrangement clarified and simplified many aspects of his accelerating authorial career. However, it turned out to complicate, frustrate, and injure his career as well.

So swamped was Dickens in the autumn of 1836 that he simply couldn't count on a moment free from distractions. He was running so far behind that Macrone decided to limit the *Sketches* to a single illustrated volume to be issued on December 17. As Dickens explained to Cruikshank on November 28, "[f]or the last fortnight I have been very unwell – unable for many days to put pen to paper, and the unlooked-for extent of the preparations for the opera [*The Village Coquettes*], occupies my whole day. I cannot do more than one pair of hands and a solitary head can execute, and really am so hard pressed just now that I must have breathing time."[7] The Dickenses and Cruikshanks were scheduled to attend the often-postponed opening of the operetta whenever that occurred – on December 6 eventually. Meanwhile, author and artist met on November 30 to settle "on a capital subject for the first illustration," "Ned Twigger in the Kitchen of Mudfog house," illuminating Dickens's original article in the January number of the *Miscellany*.[8]

Four days previously Dickens had no idea what he might write to fill his sixteen pages. "[I]f anything should occur to you as a good illustration," he told Cruikshank, "I shall be happy to adopt it." Looking ahead, Dickens was conscious that his serial Agreements had specified the time by which the illustrator needed to have copy in order to design and etch the plates. He therefore promised that he would "arrange so that next month you may have the MS by the 5th. and so on for the future."[9] At this point, so far as the surviving evidence indicates, neither Dickens nor Cruikshank was thinking in terms of a continuing story. They were collaborating on a single tale completed in the January number, and on other such tales, perhaps further "installments" of Mudfog incidents, in the future. At least, by the time Dickens's story was set in type, it concluded with the possibility that "[p]erhaps, at some future period, we may venture to open the chronicles of Mudfog."

The controversy over the origins of *Oliver Twist* has been extensively reviewed, during Dickens's lifetime and thereafter. Here a summary will suffice, as our focus is on Dickens's set of choices rather than on the retellings by others of these events. It is likely that Cruikshank, in response to the invitation to suggest "a good illustration," proposed a topic he had long wanted to illustrate. That was a modern version of William Hogarth's *Industry and Idleness* (1747), in which the upwardly mobile career of Francis Goodchild contrasts to the downward trajectory of Tom Idle. Eventually Goodchild, Lord Mayor of London, sentences his one-time fellow apprentice to be hanged. Cruikshank thought in terms of simple polarities, with the good apprentice to be called Frank Foundling or Frank Standfast, and although falling among thieves he would resist all the temptations of a sinful city. (Hogarth's plates are far more ambiguous about the respective moralities of the contrasted protagonists.)[10] There were things about Cruikshank's proposal that could have struck a chord in

Dickens's mind – they both knew about thieves, criminal haunts around Seven Dials, the secondhand markets near Field Lane and Monmouth Street, pawn-shops, shabby-genteel people, and young men who went bad. These were subjects they had jointly depicted in their Bozzes.

But Dickens may also have heard something rather different in Cruikshank's suggestion. The first monthly article is about a provincial town some distance from London called Mudfog and, as we have mentioned, at its conclusion Boz tentatively projects a series to be drawn from the annals of the town – Mudfog papers rather than Pickwick papers. Nicholas Tulrumble, the reformed ex-Mayor, is said to have requested Boz to write this "faithful" narrative.[11] If this potential chronicle supplied an idea for a "capital illustration" to the start of a series, it and the series were stillborn. For Dickens, imagining monthly for *Pickwick* the narrative of an elderly, innocent, well-to-do bachelor whose heart was born twenty-five years after his body, began (as he so often did) midway through one serial to ponder what kind of story could be generated by inverting the founding premises of his current tale. What if, for a protagonist, the story dealt with a boy born unprotected into the world, to be raised by bureaucratic officials and subjected to the cruelties imposed by parochial and civil authorities?

In trying to disentangle himself from excessive commitments so that he could concentrate on editing *Bentley's* and write a monthly original article, Dickens was both helped and impeded by others. His dramas fared poorly. The press blew "their little trumpets against unhappy me, most lustily."[12] Forster hated the *Village Coquettes*, most reviewers disparaged the text and lyrics as beneath Boz, and the *Weekly Despatch* predicted, ominously, that Dickens "will most probably blast his reputation as a periodical writer by attempting to become a dramatist."[13] Dickens arranged in mid-December for Phiz to provide a frontispiece to the publication of *The Strange Gentleman* (by "Boz"), published by Chapman and Hall early in 1837, but thereafter retired from the theater for a time.

He was so pressed by the triple tasks of writing his *Pickwick* install-ment; accepting, rejecting, and arranging articles and front matter for the first numbers of *Bentley's*; and writing his own contribution for the opening number, ready for distribution by January 3, 1837, that he hardly had time to knit up any loose ends. And as editor dealing with touchy authors, he assumed a new character. He explained to Bentley about his conduct at a party of potential contributors on December 1, 1836, "I kept very quiet, purposely. Since I have been a successful author, I have seen how much ill will and jealousy there is afloat, and have acquired an excellent character as a quiet, modest fellow." He then adds, quoting

*Hamlet* as a way of not-entirely disclaiming his performance: "I like to assume a virtue, though I have it not." In truth, it is hard to imagine anyone, even at this stage in his career, thinking Dickens a "quiet, modest fellow," though he might strategically hold his tongue on occasion.[14]

On other occasions, however, the rough edge showed. In some ways the most difficult task he faced in clearing his desk was to settle with Macrone about the *Sketches* and the promised novel. The third volume of *Sketches* went off quickly and seems to have been well received. Even before it was printed, Dickens proposed through Macrone's intermediary, the publisher T. C. Hansard, to sell his copyrights to Macrone for £400. But he also wanted Macrone to stop advertising the three-volume *Gabriel Vardon*, which in May of 1836 he had promised to deliver to Macrone by November 30, and on which he had made barely a start. Since Macrone was not one of the publishers excepted from the exclusive contract with Bentley, Dickens was caught in a cleft stick: he had an Agreement with Macrone that by his later Agreement with Bentley he could not fulfill. This dilemma was not resolved for nearly six months, and then as much because Macrone was in terrible financial straits, all his popular authors leaving him, as because Dickens had any rights to assert. Except one: if he didn't write the novel, there was little a publisher who had paid no advance could do to force him to produce. In the end, since both parties were in weak positions, they settled: Dickens accepted £100 for the full copyright of both series of *Sketches*, in return for which Macrone released him from the commitment to write a novel.[15]

It is worth reflecting on these details for a moment. Dickens was in demand as a writer; more people wanted more original material from him than he could possibly generate. However, he had enough experience with publishers already to know that some promises weren't kept, and so through the autumn of 1836 he continued to pile up commitments in part because he couldn't be sure every one would eventuate in a profitable publication. Then when Bentley offered an arrangement that bound Dickens as editor and writer to one publication, for which at the time there was no title, editorial policy, or track record of success, Dickens took the gamble, cut off other sources of income, and threw himself into his new role. He lacked any advisor who might have suggested a more moderate kind of commitment or a more substantial safety net. If the journal failed, all Dickens could count on was payment for an unwritten novel, reduced by a few months of termination stipends. As editor, he had to negotiate with touchy authors, some of them loyal to other periodicals, and – as he discovered over the course of the next few months – an even touchier publisher and boss. As author, he had to compose 16,000 words monthly in time for Phiz to execute two plates for *Pickwick*, and simultaneously write another 8,000 words in time for Cruikshank to etch an illustration to that piece, not imagined as a continuing story but rather as a set of miscellaneous articles like the *Sketches*. (It is probably more difficult to design plates that each deal with a different subject than ones that depict continuing characters whose bodies, physiognomies, clothing, and environs have been established in previous images.)

At the beginning of January 1837, Dickens certainly was working more as an editor and miscellaneous writer than as a reporter, playwright, theatrical producer/director/actor, or shorthand transcriber of Parliamentary debates. But he was still an "author" in only a very limited sense, without much control over the other elements of the communications circuit or even over the ways in which his own products were marketed. His responsibility for the "unity" of a work was dependent on collaboration with his illustrators and publishers, and neither in *Pickwick* nor *Bentley's* was "unity" a paramount desideratum. Variety, comic incidents, and Pickwickian adventures constituted the recipe for the shilling monthly numbers, and a selection of miscellaneous essays on topics ranging from history to drama, songs of the month to biographies of writers and extended fictions was the formula for the half-crown monthly magazine.

As if all this weren't enough for Dickens to handle, on Twelfth Night, 1837, Dickens's "son and heir" was born. Kate did not recover quickly, and Dickens suffered from "a violent attack of God knows what, in the head."[16] Authors were complaining about how their effusions were being edited and printed in the journal. And while Dickens found time to consult with Cruikshank about the February *Miscellany* installment, he could not write more than eleven of his sixteen pages. In subsequent months he tried to make up the deficit, but couldn't. And then he tried to make these installments also count as the first of the promised two novels. At that point Bentley struck back hard.

His continuing editorial interference, his Scroogish deductions for Dickens's missing pages, his grudging payment of bonuses for the *Miscellany's* increased circulation, and general temperamental discord with his highly temperamental star: in all these ways Bentley conducted himself as a micromanaging publisher ready at any moment to take legal action to enforce his will. In the course of twenty-eight months, he had his attorneys draw up, and Dickens sign, five Agreements regarding Boz's commitments as editor and writer for the *Miscellany*: (1) November 4,

1836, (2) March 17, 1837, (3) September 28, 1837, (4) September 22, 1838, and (5) February 27, 1839, terminating Dickens's editorship and arranging to lease *Oliver Twist* for three years and thereafter to jointly own the novel's copyright with Dickens.[17] Some of these Agreements run to a dozen or more clauses; the fourth contains twenty-five.

The details of these documents are fascinating – if only to print culture specialists and to the lawyers and contending parties on both sides. What they reveal is the paucity of standard practices and legal precedents for managing author–publisher relations, when both the kinds of publications issued – newspapers, periodicals, serials, etc. – and the kinds of relationships between writers and publishers multiply during the industrial age. Enlarging markets, improved mechanisms for the production and distribution of printed materials, heightened publicity, the development of a celebrity culture, all refashioned the conventional templates of authorship. The simplest, and even through most of the nineteenth century in Britain the most common, arrangement for fiction writers was to sell copyright outright for a few hundred pounds.[18] Those authors who could command any kind of power over against publishers, however, devised dozens of ways to leverage the value of their products. And attorneys tried to understand how these new kinds of arrangements, of which serial issue and leases of copyright were especially significant, might fairly balance the rights and customary privileges of purchasers and sellers.

There is at the British Library, catalogued but in 2010 not yet released for general access, a huge cache of materials about Dickens's negotiations with his publishers throughout his lifetime.[19] As Dr. Peter Beal, then head of Sotheby's "English Literature and History" division, said at the time the collection was assembled, it was "the most important archive of Dickens materials which has appeared in living memory." It is especially rich in documents exchanged by Bentley's and Dickens's lawyers, in which, for instance, the particular items disputed between the parties are set out and the legal arguments for and against granting the case are minuted.[20] While these archives deserve the attention of scholars versed in copyright law, it is possible even now to infer that the quarrels between Bentley and Dickens over the *Miscellany*, editorial and authorial obligations, and remuneration were more than simply personal, as biographical treatments tend, understandably, to assume.[21] Their disputes were symptoms of a larger crisis in early Victorian print culture. As Beal says, "the legal arguments over *Bentley's Miscellany* and *Oliver Twist* were in part attempts to find legal frameworks for unprecedented situations."[22] There were no contractual templates or printing house practices that adequately accommodated rapid authorial success, entrepreneurial publishing, the opening up of vast new markets through innovative formats and serial release of titles, and the opportunities for Continental and North American sales developed outside the restrictions of British author–publisher Agreements. Dickens's time with Bentley was also the time when Boz became marketable so far afield that provisions had to be made, awkwardly, contentiously, imperfectly, and on some occasions in excruciatingly rigid detail, for the working of copyrights and fame in an industrial world.

Let us look, hopefully not in too exhausting detail, at the fourth Agreement, to see the particular issues that had to be negotiated. In general, Bentley thought he had hired an up-and-coming writer who would help to produce monthly numbers of a successful half-crown miscellany, who would provide original material for one-sixth of the printed content, and who would at the same time write a couple of three-volume novels that Bentley would publish. Dickens thought he was in charge of a new publication that could quickly command notice in the literary marketplace. He believed in his ability to stream monthly articles while also writing four novels – *Pickwick*, its successor for Chapman and Hall, and the two promised to Bentley – or five, if the one contracted to Macrone wasn't cancelled. He underestimated the amount of time and energy copy-editing demanded: midway into the first month of full-time editing, he told Bentley "I am hard at work cutting down [William] Jerdan's paper," "Biographical Sketch of Richardson the Showman."[23] Two days later, adopting the voice of the meek hired hand, he explained to Jerdan that "I have been compelled by great press of matter to cut [the article] a little here and there, but I hope you will not think the effect of the paper impaired thereby. I have been obliged to perform the same kind office to my own articles, and was last month at the very greatest disadvantage."[24] This seems disingenuous, since he told Bentley three days later that he couldn't write *enough* of his own original article for the February number, not that he was cutting out over matter. Never mind. The dual voices of hard-working employee and deferential editor articulate the stresses on Boz, sitting in the editor's chair. "It *is* hard work indeed" Dickens insisted.[25]

So what chafed each partner? Well, the original Agreement had been for a year, with provisions in case the venture failed. When within a twelvemonth it turned into a resounding success, both parties wanted an extension of the Agreement. So clause one of the September 22, 1838 articles extended the contractual affiliation for three more years, clause two upped Dickens's editorial pay by 50 percent, to £30 a month, and in clauses eleven and twelve Dickens got a bonus for increased sales and the right to inspect Bentley's books to be sure he was getting appropriately rewarded. A number of clauses simply reiterated those in the original Agreement pertaining to editorial responsibilities, Dickens's obligation to supply sixteen pages of original material each month, the prohibition against his publishing for anyone else excepting Chapman and Hall's previous and current monthly serials and an unspecified annual volume (*Boz's Annual Register and Obituary of Blue Devils*, an octavo volume to be issued at Christmas 1838, for which Dickens was to be paid £300,[26] but which annual series never got started), Bentley's right of veto ("except such articles as shall be written by the said Charles Dickens," a new provision), and his ownership of all submissions.

The remainder of the clauses attempt to combine Dickens's monthly contributions with his promised novels, while still giving Bentley enough of an interest in something he is paying for twice over. Dickens's "Original Articles" stuck at twenty guineas each (clause six). At the expiration of three years "from the appearance of such Original Articles respectively in the said Miscellany," Dickens and Bentley would jointly own the copyright and would be at liberty to publish the whole or a selection "in a collected form." A problem here. First, Bentley retained the right to sell or reprint back *Miscellany* issues containing these articles; that provision doesn't seem to alter the date after which Dickens owns half copyright, but it introduces an ambiguity about how the three years is calculated, and that ambiguity becomes even greater if after three years the articles can be collected and published in a new form. Since beginning at the thirty-seventh month only one article per month becomes available for separate publication in a collection, when would enough be available to make up a volume? Or was the general understanding that after three years *all* the articles up to that point might be reassembled and sold, sort of the way that the *Sketches* were put together from articles published between thirty-seven and two months previously? This is one of the little wrinkles in leasing and transferring copyright after an original date of ongoing serialization that simply hadn't been worked out thoroughly or tested in the courts. The date for copyright had been established in the preceding century: if the title was properly entered in the Stationers' Register, copyright started on the day the first installment of a serial was published. All other installments (volumes, quires of a reference work, weekly or monthly parts, etc.) carried the copyright date of the initial publication. But Dickens's "Original Articles" were not necessarily, in these legal arrangements and in the principals' minds, the same thing, for copyright purposes, as *Oliver Twist*, a novel in three volumes. So the date at which Oliver's life began wouldn't necessarily cover all the subsequent installments as well – especially as the last third of the novel ran in installments for six months after they had been published in the three-volume first edition, which had its own copyright status.

And there was more, much more. Since the monthly "Original Article" had become instead a continuing story about a parish boy's progress, Dickens after considerable travail wrested from Bentley the concession that the articles would also suffice as the material for the first of the two novels he owed. Here we see the power of Dickens's writing. Bentley gnashed his teeth and growled, but gave in. Dickens promised to have "the remainder of the series of original papers" sufficient "so as to complete such work" delivered to Bentley by October 25, 1838, one month from the date of the Agreement. (All summer he had been frantically writing ahead to finish what was in effect the third volume of *Oliver Twist*.) In return, Bentley would not only continue to pay Dickens the twenty guineas per month for the periodical article, but also four hundred pounds for a three-year lease of Dickens's copyright permitting him to print the novel in three post-octavo volumes but prohibiting him from reprinting it in Bentley's Standard Novels – a cheaper rendition that could depress sales in the other formats and depreciate the novel's prestige.[27] At the expiration of the thirty-six months, Dickens and Bentley would jointly own the copyright; in effect Bentley's temporary lease of restricted copyright converted into half ownership, with restrictions about format no longer mentioned. Bentley got "first option of printing and publishing" subsequent issues – presumably subject to the other copyright sharer's approval though that isn't stated, and the right, unless Dickens bought a moiety of the unsold *Miscellany* and three-volume stock remaining at the end of the third year, to sell the remainders for his own profit.

There is one little phrase in paragraph seventeen that dramatically contrasts Dickens's authorial power, however circumscribed it was, to Cruikshank's artist's power. The twenty-four illustrations to *Oliver Twist* are simply mentioned as adjuncts to the putative unsold volumes: if Dickens declines to buy into the remaining stock "together with the engravings or etchings published therewith," Bentley can sell the prints as well as the text for his own benefit. By the laws of the time, illustrations were purchased by and owned thereafter by the publisher; the artist had no residual copyright or claim of any sort on the ways in which those images might be retouched, reprinted, or otherwise reproduced. There was no need to rewrite any Agreement with Cruikshank.

Clauses seventeen through twenty-one essentially establish the same terms for *Barnaby Rudge*; it will run in the *Miscellany* for a minimum of eighteen successive months as Dickens's contractual "Original Article," after which time Dickens will complete it at a length suitable for publication as a three-volume novel, which Bentley will publish on terms similar to those for *Oliver Twist*. Clause twenty-two specifies that if Bentley wants to get out of his obligations during the initial three years he must offer to Dickens first, and clause twenty-three reverses the proviso should Dickens want to withdraw. Finally, clause twenty-four prevents Bentley from publishing these works in any other format, and the final paragraph specifies that if Bentley falls more than a month behind in his payments to Dickens, the author "shall have power by notice in writing to put an end to this agreement, and every clause herein contained," except that those portions of the works already published by this time shall continue to be controlled by the terms of the Agreement.

Robert Bayly Follett, Bentley's solicitor, and Thomas Mitton, Dickens's, had under instructions from their clients spent almost as much effort providing for cancellation strategies as for the modification of previous terms in order to incorporate the Original Articles as novels. Yet ownership and power of choice were still muddled. If Dickens simply didn't, or couldn't, write, there was no clause punishing him. (This indeed proved in the case when Mary Hogarth died in May 1837 and Dickens could not compose either the *Pickwick* or the *Twist* installment. And four months later Dickens declared that Bentley's editorial interference was so intolerable he would edit the journal and write the paper for the October issue and then "decline conducting the Miscellany or contributing to it in any way.")[28] The timing for the completion of *Twist* so that it could be released in three volumes in November 1838 was not coordinated with the release of the monthly installments, so that readers of *Bentley's Miscellany* did not finish the story until April of 1839, five months after its dramatic concluding chapters were available in book format. Another perhaps unintended consequence of these microdetailed provisions is that Dickens could have been paid for monthly *Miscellany* installments between December 1838 and April 1839 that he had already written and Cruikshank had already illustrated. Finally, while the clauses prohibiting publication in other formats managed the near-term, they precluded taking advantage of the new form of monthly serialization that Chapman and Hall were promoting. It wasn't until 1846 that *Oliver Twist* was released in ten monthly shilling parts (it is about half as long as the twenty-part novels), and then neither Bentley nor Chapman and Hall had a share in the publication, because Dickens had broken off relations with both houses.

It wasn't just author, publishers, and lawyers who were interested in Dickens's contracts and finances. *The Durham Advertiser* for January 26, 1838 ran "a brief Autobiography [*sic*]" of Dickens by R. Shelton Mackenzie, the first paid European correspondent for any US newspaper (the New York *Evening Star*), to which Dickens took exception. "Dr. Mackenzie whoever he may be, knows as much of me as of the meaning of the word autobiography." Dickens then proceeded to enumerate for the editor of the newspaper the misinformation contained in Mackenzie's account:

[W]hen I commenced the Pickwick papers I was *not* living on five guineas a week as a Reporter on the Morning Chronicle [he got seven guineas for the combined work on the morning and evening papers] – that Messrs. Chapman and Hall were never persuaded with some difficulty to become the Pickwick publishers [what about after Seymour's death?] but on the contrary first became known to me by waiting on me to propose the work [not quite true, as Dickens was already contracted to them for *The Library of Fiction*] ... that by the Pickwick Papers alone I have *not* netted between £2000 and £3000 [he had received the lower amount and was scheduled to gain more when he began sharing in the copyright] – ... that I am *not* now in the receipt of £3000 a year [that was the price for the whole of *Nickleby*, paid in monthly £150 installments during the serial run; only £1800 would be received in a calendar year, but adding in the salary as editor and writer for the *Miscellany* and other nonce income Dickens was earning not very far short of Mackenzie's sum], and that Mr. Bentley does *not* give me £1000 a year for editing the Miscellany [only £270 in 1837] and twenty guineas a sheet for what I write in it [exactly what Dickens received].[29]

Mackenzie apologized (probably for more than he needed to), and Dickens accepted the "frank and manly letter." What really annoyed him was his "private affairs being dragged before the public," although Dickens continued the sentence less justifiably with "and stated incorrectly in every particular."[30] Clearly Mackenzie had done some research. Even more clearly, the publication of that research was thought by newspapermen to be of interest to their readers, and was thought by Dickens to be an unwarranted disclosure of his personal life. It would also, had Mackenzie's paragraphs been widely circulated in other papers, have made Dickens's role as editor negotiating with authors for the parsimonious Bentley more difficult, and made his persona as Boz, a middle-class figure, less credible.

II

In the period we're considering at the moment, 1836–39, Chapman and Hall treated Dickens quite differently from Bentley. Granted that they had composed a letter about *Pickwick* in February 1836 that specified details regarding length of contribution, time of delivery, date of payment, and so forth, but they didn't rewrite these terms when the serial shot up like a rocket, in this case not a "disadvantageous" development. (William Jerdan's statement at the dinner celebrating the conclusion of *Pickwick* "that there never had been a line of written agreement" about the book overstated the fact, but not the feeling, that publishers and author had dealt through handshakes rather than contracts.)[31] Instead, they volunteered raises in the monthly stipend, from nine and a half guineas for twenty-four pages at the start to £21 for thirty-two pages from June 1836, to £25 from November as circulation and profits swelled, with a bonus of £500 on the anniversary of the first number (April 1837) and a dinner celebrating the serial's success on April 8.[32] When Mary Hogarth died and Dickens couldn't write the June number of *Pickwick*, Chapman and Hall behaved with sympathy and discretion. They didn't press Dickens for copy, and at the end of July, when he had completed the installment for August, they sent him a set of six Pickwickian punch ladles. In his reply Dickens not only thanked them for what he intended to be an heirloom "for my boy to shew *his* boys – and girls likewise," but also for the "delicate and warm-hearted feeling" they had exhibited over the preceding three months, and that he said "touched me deeply."[33] If any similar consideration was extended by Bentley during these difficult months, no letter acknowledging it has survived. While Chapman advanced money to Dickens to help him pay household and funeral expenses when he got no monthly stipend for his *Pickwick* installment, all Bentley's communications with Dickens have to do with business: the *Miscellany*, a burgeoning quarrel over Bentley's attempt to bid for Macrone's copyrights to *Sketches*, and the renegotiation of the Agreement for Bentley to purchase and publish Dickens's next two novels.

By November of 1837 *Pickwick*'s monthly print run was 40,000 copies. Chapman and Hall topped up Dickens's payment to £2,000, the equivalent of £100 an installment. (The publishers netted £14,000.)[34] In a double indenture prepared by Chapman's brother William and signed in November, the language couches the Agreements for *Pickwick* and *Nickleby* in a most tactfully flattering way, making it seem as if Dickens was giving his publishers a portion of the copyright, rather than that they were ceding some portion back to him. Indeed, Dickens got one-third of the *Pickwick* copyright after five more years, and while during the first five years after *Nickleby*'s serialization Chapman and Hall had full rights, thereafter entire ownership reverted back to Dickens. A few other provisions of the *Nickleby* arrangements will be considered in the following chapter. The main point to be stressed here is that whatever legal Agreements Chapman and Hall obtained for these first serials – and over time it is true that Dickens took a dislike to Edward Chapman's brother William, the firm's attorney[35] – their instinct to treat Dickens liberally without renegotiations, and to pay thoughtful tribute to him with presents and delicate forbearance – extending loans to him and, quietly, to his father – created the feeling among the three partners of warm friendship and generous regard.

And Chapman and Hall did extend forbearance on more than one occasion. By November of 1836, when as we have seen Dickens was drowning in overcommitments to the theater, journals, and publishers, he wrote an apologetic letter "assuring" Chapman and Hall that the "lingering disease under which Mr. Pickwick has recently laboured, and . . . the great aggravation of the symptoms which has gradually taken place," that is, copy being dispatched to illustrator and printers later and later in the month, was about to be remediated. Piling on the compliments intended to alleviate his publishers' unease, Dickens assures them that he has no desire to dissolve their "most pleasant and friendly connection," and names them his "periodical publishers" until he is "compressed" into his "last edition – one volume, boards, with brass plates." (Another lightsome allusion to death as story.) He closes the letter "by saying how much – how very much – I feel your honorable conduct."[36] And *the very next day*, Dickens writes to Bentley accepting his offer to edit the *Miscellany* and write an 8,000 word original article for it every month, "feeling perfectly satisfied that it will not interfere with Pickwick."[37] It's hard not to see this new commitment as a betrayal of his existing ones, even though Dickens believed himself capable of prodigies of creativity and often proved it. That Chapman and Hall never complained about Dickens's going to work for Bentley or contracting for two unwritten novels with their rival is probably the most striking proof of their willingness to do whatever it took, excepting going to law, to cultivate Boz.

III

Control over copyright, which includes control over the right to copy and to prescribe the kind and number of copies impressed, at what price, and over what period of time, was at the heart of the Dickens–Bentley Agreements. No wonder. For in other dimensions of Dickens's writing, he found himself with little control and much vulnerability. To look forward a year before concentrating on Dickens's "Original Articles," aka *Oliver Twist*, we should consider the kinds of twists he got into with other of his literary properties.

Whereas Chapman and Hall were free to exploit monthly shilling numbers, and Bentley was not, nobody had any control over Macrone.[38] He had bought all rights to *Sketches* for a hundred pounds. The success of *Pickwick* in parts and *Oliver Twist* in monthly magazine installments inspired him to propose, in June of 1837, re-issuing *Sketches* in twenty shilling parts with all the illustrations and a wrapper design by Cruikshank. Macrone had overspent in buying up prestige authors and publications, bidding for Benjamin Disraeli, Robert Browning, and Thomas Moore among other writers, and the *Westminster Review* and the *London Review*, which he merged in 1836. So long as Ainsworth and Dickens were solidly in his stable – Dickens even put his "very quick and steady" younger brother Frederick into Macrone's counting house[39] – Macrone's extravagant ambitions and commitments seemed affordable. But when Dickens reneged on *Gabriel Vardon* and Ainsworth dried up, Macrone had few expedients left. He sold Ainsworth's unfinished novel *Crichton* to Bentley for £1,000 and the *London and Westminster Review* to Henry Hooper. Serializing *Sketches* was a last throw of the dice.

When Dickens heard of this venture on June 9, 1837, he fired off an angry letter to John Forster, a new friend rapidly becoming Dickens's principal advisor in all matters pertaining to his writings. "I need not tell you that this is calculated to injure me most seriously, or that I have a very natural and most decided objection to being supposed to presume upon the success of Pickwick, and thus foist this old work upon the public in its new dress for the mere purpose of putting money in my own pocket."[40] Dickens's echo of Iago's repeated advice to the love-struck Roderigo in the first act of *Othello* – "put but money in thy purse ... fill thy purse with money" and wait until Desdemona forgets the Moor before wooing her – seems an odd context, perhaps an unintentional one. It also obscures what Dickens has already done with Macrone, namely dressed up his old sketches in new attire in order to profit from them a second time. He goes on to adduce another objection: "Neither need I say that the fact of my name being before the town, attached to three publications at the same time, must prove seriously prejudicial to my reputation."

This sentence needs a lot of parsing. To begin with, as we have already seen, what does Dickens mean by "my name"? He publishes *Sketches* as Boz, edits *Pickwick* as Boz (though on the November 1837 title page he is identified as Charles Dickens), edits *Bentley's* as Boz, and writes *Oliver Twist* as Boz. When attempting to lease a house in February of 1837 (not Doughty Street for which he offered in March), Dickens advised Bentley that he was a potential reference "to testify to my being 'sober and honest,' &c – to testify in short to my being Boz."[41]

Boz, much more than Dickens, is the name known by the majority of his readers. *Bentley's* versified the situation. For the April 1837 issue, Maginn composed a "Song of the Cover" that once more pairs Boz and Cruikshank, this time adding Bentley:

> Bentley, Boz, and Cruikshank, stand
>     Like expectant reelers –
> "Music!" – "Play up!" – pipe in hand,
>     Beside the *fluted* pillars!
> Boz and Cruikshank want to dance,
>     None for frolic riper,
> But Bentley makes the first advance,
>     Because he "pays the piper."[42]

And the previous month the *Miscellany* had played with the revelation of the identity of Boz and Dickens, as we have seen:

> Who the *dickens* "Boz" could be
>     Puzzled many a learned elf;
> Till time unveil'd the mystery,
>     And *Boz* appear'd as DICKENS' self![43]

The flip-flopping of real name and pen name continued. The playbills advertising *The Village Coquettes* named Boz as author through April 7, 1837. On that date Dickens asked Harley to alter them so as to "omit all mention of our respectable friend 'Boz.'" Withdrawing from identification with "this most unfortunate of all unfortunate pieces," he "was not anxious to *remind* the Public that I [as 'Boz' not Dickens] am the perpetrator."[44] He did not, however, disclaim Boz's responsibility for the more successful *Strange Gentleman*, whose lavender paper wrapper for the rare 1837 edition declares that it is "BY 'BOZ.'"[45] The quotation marks around the pseudonym was a feature from the first series of *Sketches* forward, typographically marking it as something special, a brand name or soubriquet, that is, "a nickname or a fancy name, sometimes assumed, but often given by another. It is usually a familiar name, distinct from a pseudonym assumed as a disguise, but a nickname which is familiar enough such that it can be used in place of a real name without the need of explanation."[46] That Dickens has been deploying Boz instead of his "real name," and that in some cases he didn't want that nickname to be associated with himself or his works, further complicates our already complicated sense of what he wanted Boz to stand for.

Moreover, he anticipated publishing other works by Boz: all the parts novels through 1841 avowed Boz as editor or author in some paratextual locations, though in others such as volume title pages and some advertisements, Charles Dickens appears. The *Annual Register . . . of Blue Devils* was to be "*Boz's*." Dickens sometimes referred to himself as Boz, "usually in the context of a convivial outing or a comic point" as Kathryn Chittick observes, and occasionally he even signed a letter with this nickname.[47]

At the same time, he suppressed the name, telling Tegg he didn't want to be identified with "Solomon Bell," which never got published anyway. Though Chapman and Hall commissioned *Sunday Under Three Heads*, Dickens adopted another pen name, "Timothy Sparks." Perhaps in this case it was because he didn't want another title besides the two serials appearing under his cognomen at the same time. And when he signed up with Chapman and Hall to do two booklets capitalizing on their publication of Quiz's [Edward Caswall's] *Sketches of Young Ladies* (1837), he suppressed his name altogether. That was because by writing these he violated his Agreements with Bentley. Or did he? The relevant clause in the September 22, 1838 Agreement with Bentley that we have just analyzed specifies that "the said Charles Dickens shall not edit, conduct, or write for any periodical publication whatsoever" excepting *Pickwick*, *Nickleby*, the *Blue Devils*, and Bentley's productions. But if Dickens doesn't put his own real name to something, is he within bounds in actually producing other books anonymously or under a pen name? In doing so he was gratifying the wishes of his other publisher, Chapman and Hall, and making some money. He got £125 for *Sketches of Young Gentlemen* (1838) and presumably the same for *Sketches of Young Couples* (1840).[48] Moreover, Bentley himself broke existing Agreements by hiring Dickens to edit, as Boz, *Memoirs of Joseph Grimaldi*, published in February 1838. So what the clause about not editing, conducting, or writing for any periodical publication meant in fact, whether it applied to other volumes as opposed to periodicals, whether it applied to Dickens's pseudonyms, and whether Bentley was prepared to enforce it when Dickens strayed or when Bentley himself wanted to ignore it, became more and more unclear as events unfolded.

The next part of Dickens's objection to Macrone's scheme for republishing *Sketches* in monthly numbers also requires reflection. If Dickens, *in propria persona*, anonymously, or as Boz, didn't want to appear before the public as author of so many different titles, why was he signing contracts right and left, with Tegg for an annual, with Chapman and Hall for three additional books, and with Bentley for the *Memoirs*?

Presumably because neither he nor his publishers yet understood the market consequences of the combination of brand name, quantity of production, quality, and value. Dickens may have been right to fear that another issue of *Sketches* would damage his reputation. But in the end he was forced into it. There was no way to stop Macrone except by buying him out. That was exceedingly costly. Macrone had purchased the entire copyright for £100 on January 5, 1837; Chapman and Hall bought it back six months later, on June 17, along with 850 unsold copies of both series of *Sketches* and Cruikshank's twenty-eight copper plates, for £2,250.[49] They adopted Macrone's plan and issued the *Sketches* in twenty shilling monthly parts between November 1837 (when *Pickwick* concluded) and June 1839; Cruikshank designed a pink wrapper in which "BOZ" is prominently displayed, enlarged some of his previous etchings, and supplied thirteen new ones. So Dickens had three serials running simultaneously: the re-republished *Sketches*, *Oliver Twist* in *Bentley's*, and from April 1838 *Nicholas Nickleby*, and a fourth, *Pickwick*, available as one volume or probably still in parts in order for purchasers to complete sets. Whatever legitimacy there was to Dickens's fear that three concurrent publications would be "seriously prejudicial" to his reputation, he had to settle for more than that. What from one perspective looks as if Dickens was taking the town by storm, from another reveals how imperfect was his control over the number, format, and nature of his publications.

And, equally important, note how many permutations of "Boz" he was allowing as his authorial avatar (from the Sanskrit word for "a form of self"). For in addition to all his other projects, he agreed at the end of November 1837 to edit as "Boz" the autobiography of the great clown Joseph Grimaldi, which Bentley had bought and which had been incompetently revised by Thomas Egerton Wilks. And a year later, in August 1838, Dickens contracted with Henry Colburn, Bentley's former partner and now rival, to recruit for and edit as "Boz" a three-volume collection of articles, entitled *Pic Nic Papers*, for the benefit of Macrone's widow and family. This Agreement specified that Dickens would write a story of about 16,000 words ("two sheets" or thirty-two pages at twenty-eight lines to a page), solicit other well-known authors for contributions, get two etchings from Cruikshank and two from Phiz (who actually contributed six), and compose a preface.

It is astonishing enough that Dickens would himself parody Boz's edition of the *Pickwick Papers* in the title, having so often complained about copycat authors doing the same thing. Even more astonishing is the proviso that if Dickens and the other contributors don't submit sufficient material to make up the three volumes, "[t]he papers for the remaining volume and a half are to be furnished by the said Henry Colburn, and to consist partly of the 'Charcoal Sketches' – published in America."[50] These were the work of Joseph Clay Neal, a Philadelphian, and they were inserted without payment as the second half of the three-decker. Dickens apparently didn't even jib at Neal's title, echoing as it did Boz's *Sketches*. Mackenzie, with whom Dickens had intermittent and sometimes disputatious relationships for over thirty years, published one of the first posthumous biographies of Dickens in 1870, and asserted in it that Dickens had failed to give Neal credit for his part in the volume. True. Dickens told Edmund Yates in March of 1859 that he didn't know anything about this expedient for filling out the volumes.[51] But while he may have forgotten details of an Agreement made twenty-one years earlier, the contract specifically says Colburn may include Neal's work.

Dickens was careful to keep his own connection to this charitable endeavor at a distance – the Agreement insists that "no advertisement shall be preceded by the words 'New work by Boz' – or 'New work by Charles Dickens', but that the words 'Edited by Boz' – or Charles Dickens shall always be inserted." (As published, the title page says "Edited by Charles Dickens" while the back of the cloth binding stamps "Edited by Boz.")[52] Even so, his allowing the volumes to be made up with what, had the republication gone from Britain to the USA rather than the other way round, Dickens would have roundly denounced as a "piracy," makes his animadversions against the practice of uncompensated reprintings in other nations seem a bit hypocritical.[53] By way of extenuation, one should note that Dickens exhibited little interest in the undertaking, which dragged on for several years, and in the end he detested Colburn, who "accepted and rejected Papers at his most literary will and pleasure," then held the copy so long in press that Dickens "damned his eyes (by implication and construction) at the same time; and declined to hold any further correspondence with him, on any subject."[54] Nonetheless, we cannot overlook the fact that whereas Dickens objected to Macrone hawking a serialized version of *Sketches by Boz* because it would be injurious to his name, Dickens himself by 1838 had signed contracts for ten books to be issued as by "Boz."[55]

IV

Adding to his vexations were the numerous offshoots of his works, issued under variants of "Boz." We've mentioned some of the takeoffs on

*Pickwick*, and seen Dickens attempt to be gracious about the "theft" of "The Bloomsbury Christening" by Buckstone for dramatization in April 1834. The longer *Pickwick* continued and the greater its circulation, the more imitations tried to capture the market: *The Posthumous Papers of the Cadger Club*; another about the *Wonderful Discovery Club*; the *Posthumous Notes of the Pickwickian Club. Edited by "Boz,"* with 132 engravings; the *Pickwick Gazette* illustrated by Robert Cruikshank, plus extra illustrations by Kenny Meadows, William Heath, Alfred Crowquill, Thomas Onwhyn, Thomas Sibson, and others; songsters, almanacs, jest books, "selected beauties," tricks, shadows; *Mr. Sam Weller's Scrap Sheet, with 40 wood-cut Characters*; sequels such as Reynolds's *Pickwick Abroad* illustrated with forty-one plates by Alfred Crowquill and another about *Pickwick in America*; and the *Penny Pickwick* in 112 weekly numbers with a woodcut every four pages.[56]

Stage versions abounded. In March 1837, Edward Stirling mounted a dramatization at the City of London Theatre that transferred by July to the Franklin Theater in New York City.[57] When only eight monthly parts had been issued, in November 1836 William Leman Rede composed a three-act drama, anchored on Jack Bamber's "Tale of the Queer Client" in the October installment. It did not get to the stage, however, until April 1837. It played at the Adelphi, in the provinces, and then at the Surrey, and was published later that year.[58] The program for Rede's adaptation, *Peregrinations of Pickwick*, a three-act "Serio-Comic Burletta ... interspersed with music," claims that the "*comic dialogue ... extracted*" from the serial was done with "*the express permission of the Author, C. Dickens, Esq., better known as 'Boz'.*"[59] This version, which interweaves comedy and "a serious story" "in the most favorable dramatic form," in the second act jumps from the White Hart Inn, where Sam Weller is introduced, directly to the Marshalsea Prison. Yet Mr. Pickwick does not enter into the Fleet (*not* the Marshalsea of Dickens's unhappy memories) until the May number published at the end of April, after the play opened. Consequently the playwright invented a scene consisting of "Destitution. – Unforgiving Father. – Generous Hibernian. – Catastrophe," followed by a contrasting comic scene, a banquet of country and cockney sportsmen. Although the Marshalsea episode is the product of the playwright's imagination, in Dickens's subsequent numbers destitution (the Chancery prisoner, Job and Jingle, the Poor Side), unforgiving father (Sam and Tony's performance to enable Sam to join his master in prison), generosity (on Pickwick's part, if not on any Hibernian's), and catastrophe, Mrs. Bardell's imprisonment for not paying Dodson and Fogg's charges, all figure. No wonder Dickens was aggravated by stagings that anticipated, and thereby sometimes precluded, his own plots. (A production of *Oliver Twist* early in that serial's run particularly exasperated him.) And in June 1837 W. T. Moncrieff's *Sam Weller; or the Pickwickians* opened at the Theatre Royal, Strand, a production memorable for the performances of Jingle by John Lee and Sam Weller by W. J. Hammond. Dickens protested this adaptation. Moncrieff defended himself in a long advertisement, pointing out that however bold his plagiarism was, it was "at all events quite legally" done.[60]

The usual accounts of Dickens's writing at this time say little about these versions, which probably had a dual effect: further publicizing Dickens's own productions while cultivating customers who might otherwise have been his and Chapman and Hall's. Over the next several years the "pirates," as Dickens termed them, became increasingly annoying and possibly injurious to his own interests. But at this moment he inclined to take little notice of them. On one occasion, however, when he heard about a City Theatre hireling, ensconced in a meager room too close to a gin-mill and struggling between tots of gin to produce seven melodramas for five pounds by any means whatsoever, Dickens forgave him his plagiarized *Pickwick.* "Well; if the *Pickwick* has been the means of putting a few shillings in the vermin-eaten pockets of so miserable a creature, and has saved him from a workhouse or a jail, let him empty out his little pot of filth and welcome."[61] The laws governing permissions to print and sell alternative versions of copyrighted books, as we have seen, were so complex and inconsistent within the different parts of the United Kingdom that demanding enforcement of the copyright of an "original" was often chancy. Things didn't change much through Dickens's lifetime. In 1878 the Royal Commission on copyright described the law as "wholly destitute of any sort of arrangement, incomplete, often obscure, and even when it is intelligible upon long study, it is in many parts so ill-expressed that no one who does not give such study can expect to understand it."[62]

As we saw in Chapter 1, British authors had virtually no copyright protection of any kind in other countries, which could print and sell versions in English or translation with impunity.[63] An edition of *Pickwick* with lithographic impressions of the original illustrations was sold in eighteen serial parts, 1837–38, and in two volumes thereafter, by William Rushton in Calcutta; in Van Diemen's Land Henry Dowling had a complete edition on sale by 1838. There was a five-volume German translation originating in Leipzig in 1837 and a French translation by Mme. Eugénie Niboyet published in Paris the following year: Dickens had copies of both these editions in his library. Galignani sold a two-volume English version (1838) in Paris to English-speaking Frenchmen and to British subjects on the Continent; and a year later Frederick Fleischer in Leipzig sold a two-volume English version to British travelers and Anglophone Germans. In none of these cases did Dickens have any control over the publications or translations or receive any remuneration.

While no reciprocal copyright agreements existed between Britain and other countries in the 1830s, one American publisher, and one German one, acknowledged an obligation to British authors in one way or another. Carey, Lea and Blanchard of Philadelphia wrote to "Mr. Saml. Dickens" in June of 1837 offering a bill for £25 payable in four months for the twelve parts of *Pickwick* they had already published in three volumes, four parts in each. ("Samuel" was a mistake; the "Advertisement" preceding the first part of the volume declares that the "author under the fictitious name of Boz, is Mr. Charles Dickens." This would mean that "Boz" was widely known as Dickens in the USA by November 1836.) While "the times" had been hard on publishers – land speculation and a run on banks had destabilized an already fragile US economy – Henry Charles Carey, the managing partner, promised to "continue the papers" and expressed the wish that Dickens would accept the payment "as a memento of the fact that unsolicited a bookseller has sent an author, if not money, at least a fair representative of it."[64] (In August of 1837 Dickens drafted a conversation between Mr. Brownlow and Oliver about what profession the boy might choose; Oliver declines being a "book-writer" and replies after some consideration that "he should think it would be a much better thing to be a bookseller."[65] Wise beyond his years, Oliver seems to know that booksellers, not authors, owned most of the copyrights protected by law.) Dickens didn't get round to replying until the end of October, being caught up in the press of other work (and quarrels with Bentley). He refused the payment – although thirty years later another partner, H. C. Lea, intimated that he did take it[66] – and instead requested a copy of the work "which – coupled with your very handsome letter – I shall consider a sufficient acknowledgement of the American sale." Subsequently the firm paid an additional £50 for *Pickwick* "in acknowledgement of the success" it had achieved. In fact, Carey had – typically of publishers – minimized in his original letter to Dickens the profits the book might yield if the market steadied. By December 1837, 6,250 copies of the five-volume edition had been sold; in January 1838 the firm issued 5,000 copies of a one-volume edition, illustrated by "Sam Weller, Jr." (Thomas Onwhyn) and Alfred Crowquill. Carey noted in the firm's account book that all the costs of this production would be recouped on a sale of 1,600, leaving "the remaining 3400 – all profit."[67] In subsequent years the Philadelphia firm sent further payments to Dickens for advanced sheets of *Master Humphrey's Clock* and to Bentley and Dickens for the manuscript of chapters forty-four on of *Oliver Twist*.[68] Such pecuniary acknowledgments to the British author or publisher did not carry any weight with American publishers, of course. While "trade courtesy" was a practice in which, if one house took out an advertisement announcing the forthcoming publication of a title by a foreign author, other houses might desist from issuing a competitive edition, such courtesies did not prevail when any particularly popular work was at issue, especially if it was going to be sought by a newspaper or firm such as Harper's which issued magazines and books.

The other foreign publisher with whom Dickens enjoyed cordial relations for many years was Bernhard Tauchnitz of Leipzig, who arranged with British authors for permission to print English versions of their works for sale on the Continent. Even though the Fleischer edition was issued the same year, Tauchnitz selected *Pickwick* to be published as volumes two and three (1839) of his "Collection of British Authors," which by 1900 ran to several thousand titles.[69] Tauchnitz published most of Dickens's works, and even at Dickens's request took Charley under his wing for some months in 1853. As with Carey, Lea and Blanchard, the remunerations were small, but Dickens all the more appreciated the gesture of pecuniary acknowledgment because it was voluntary. When in the 1850s Britain began to sign reciprocal copyright treaties with several European nations, however, Dickens took full advantage of the commercial opportunity to license reprints and translations for significant fees.

However, in January 1837 Dickens had little control over his burgeoning literary production. John Forster was beginning to give advice on literary and legal matters – Forster credits himself with proposing the "deed" which resulted in Chapman and Hall's granting Dickens a third share in the copyright of *Pickwick* five years after the serial ended.[70] But, as we have seen in detail, Dickens's publishing affairs were complicated, entangled with one another, restrictive, and at the same time often so lax in spelling out what ownership of copyright entailed, that he was unable to keep up with his British, much less his international, circulation. Moreover, he still had to edit other writers and produce his own copy each month in order to earn the income that, all sources considered, might bring in well more than £1,000 a year. That sum can be translated in various ways to express contemporary equivalence: about £76,000 in 2008 purchasing power, and ten times that much compared to average earnings.[71]


V


On January 9, 1837 Dickens wrote to Cruikshank to say that "the bustle *et cetera*" of Charley's birth had put him behindhand, and that he needed more time before settling the subject of the February *Miscellany* illustration. (He also had to get the subjects to Browne for two *Pickwick* illustrations and complete that 16,000-word installment.) Whatever happened in the next week, besides vexations about Bentley's interference with his editorial duties ("I must beg you once again, not to allow anybody but myself to interfere with the Miscellany"), he decided not to extend the Mudfog papers, but instead to begin a story, which might continue through a few or many months, commencing once more with death.[72] As Burton Wheeler puts it in a classic essay, the novel grows out of "a conjuror's trick which converts a serial of uncertain length into a novel with the superficial appearance of a unified plan."[73] A young woman in labor is brought by an overseer's order to the Mudfog work-house – in subsequent editions, denominated a public building "in a certain town, which for many reasons it will be prudent to refrain from mentioning" (p. 1), thus further distancing Oliver's birth from Ned Twigger and the Mayor of Mudfog. She gives birth to "an item of mortality," and dies. "It's all over," the parish surgeon declares. No story can be generated from her appearance or possessions: "where she came from, or where she was going to, nobody knows," the aged attendant reports. Looking at the corpse's left hand, the surgeon terminates the inquiry into his late patient's past: "'The old story,' he said, shaking his head: 'no wedding-ring, I see. Ah! Good night!'" (pp. 2–3). With one surgical stroke, he imposes a standard life history and brings it to a final conclusion.[74]

We've seen Dickens do this often, in *Sketches* and *Pickwick*. Here, at this moment, it is doubtful whether he knew himself what that "old story" might comprise, since the greater interest of surgeon, attendant, author, and readers is directed towards the newborn. He too hovers between silence and story: "For a long time after it was ushered into this world of sorrow and trouble, by the parish surgeon, it remained a matter of considerable doubt whether the child would survive to bear any name at all" – naming being another of the obsessions out of which Dickens had generated previous tales and his own shifting authorial identity.

Or, had the nameless boy died, "it is somewhat more than probable that these memoirs would never have appeared; or, if they had, that being comprised within a couple of pages, they would have possessed the inestimable merit of being the most concise and faithful specimen of biography, extant in the literature of any age or country" (p. 1). Birth and death equally generate and terminate stories. Bodies, dead or alive, write themselves and their life narratives: Oliver Twist yields *Oliver Twist.* The nameless item of mortality, after a struggle, breathes, cries, and thereby announces "a new burden having been imposed upon the parish" (p. 2). The narrator then adds another theme familiar from previous stories and Thomas Carlyle's recently serialized *Sartor Resartus*: the power of clothing to express class. Had Oliver been wrapped in an anonymous blanket, "he might have been the child of a nobleman or a beggar." But wrapped in a workhouse calico robe, "he was badged and ticketed, and fell into his place at once – a parish child – the orphan of a workhouse – the humble half-starved drudge – to be cuffed and buffeted through the world – despised by all, and pitied by none" (p. 3).

A wonderful beginning, inconspicuously packed with hidden implications that will come to light many chapters later, when the tokens of Oliver's identity concealed in his mother's clothing establish both her story – not an old one, or at least a variant on the old one – and his "proper station in society." In many ways *Oliver Twist* is a classic instance of Peter Brooks's observation that fiction's master trope is "the *anticipation of retrospection*," the structure of narrative, as opposed to news, being to discover the events behind the story's opening that determine it. Dickens went on in the next chapter to "treat" of "Oliver Twist's growth, education, and board," generally exfoliating the prediction of the previous chapter's last sentence, that if the infant "could have known that he was an orphan, left to the tender mercies of churchwardens and overseers, perhaps he would have cried the louder." The subject of Cruikshank's plate, "Oliver asking for more," is a perfect picture of starving boys (hair cropped close to control lice) with huge eyes and meager limbs, being challenged by corpulent, balding, incredulous authority dispensing "tender mercies" indeed. A very restricted diet was a principal component of the New Poor Law that attempted to regularize provisions for paupers throughout the British Isles.[75]

It is impossible for us today to register the impact of this beginning, in this magazine declaratively humorous and apolitical. Boz, whose sketches appeared in periodicals appealing to the whole spectrum of political opinion, issues without warning what he calls in a letter to Thomas Beard "my glance at the new poor Law Bill," that is the Poor Law Amendment Act of 1834, which Dickens had heard debated in the Commons when he was a Parliamentary reporter.[76] *Pickwick* was entertaining "the whole reading public," governing classes as well as general readers.[77] As Mary Russell Mitford told her Irish friend Emily Jephson, "a lady might read" this book about "London life" "all *aloud*." "All the boys and girls talk his fun – the boys in the streets; and yet those who are of the highest taste like it the most. Sir Benjamin Brodie [a leading surgeon] takes it to read in his carriage, between patient and patient; and Lord Denman [Lord Chief Justice] studies *Pickwick* on the bench while the jury are deliberating."[78] As G. H. Lewes summarized, "all classes, in fact, read '*Boz*.'"[79]

But with *Oliver Twist, or, The Parish Boy's Progress*, the narrator's satirical attitude toward parish and workhouse authorities, and the outright condemnation of the official attitude toward and provisions for the destitute – "Oliver was the victim of a systematic course of treachery and deception" (p. 3) – began to alarm some of Bentley's associates. Its "Radicalish tone" and strongly partisan bias might alienate middle-class readers, Canon R. H. Barham of St. Paul's Cathedral warned his old St. Paul's classmate.[80] Hired at £10 a month to advise Bentley, who also paid him a pound per page for his literary contributions published under the pen name of Thomas Ingoldsby, Barham excelled in composing comic and grotesque legends and poems abounding in puns, crimes, the supernatural, and Byronic rhymes, but without any hint at contemporary politics.[81] While over the next several months, as Dickens developed his story and moved away from Oliver's parish childhood to boyhood in London, the attack on the Poor Law faded, Bentley's discomfort with the unexpected direction Boz had taken may underlie both his insistence on inserting stories of his own liking into the *Miscellany* by way of compensation – especially Barham's – and his inconsistent but sometimes overbearing efforts to keep Dickens in line.[82]

VI

In any event, Dickens had more things in mind for Oliver than the workhouse. The novel has often been identified as the first of the three "autobiographical" accounts, all carefully disguised and displaced, that Dickens wrote – the other two being *David Copperfield*, his "favourite child," and *Great Expectations*. Obscure allusions to Dickens's own London boyhood may be discovered in the novel, including the adoption of the name of the boy, Bob Fagin, who cared for Dickens when he suffered a severe attack while working at Warren's Blacking, for Oliver's rescuer, kidnapper, surrogate parent, teacher, and spiritual tempter.[83] And Dickens told Forster in the autobiographical fragment, that "for any care that was taken of me" during the blacking warehouse days, he "might easily have been ... a little robber or a little vagabond."[84]

Less, however, has been said about the ways in which Dickens's current situation and anxieties are embedded in the text, along with some general cultural concerns widely voiced at the start of Victoria's reign. Prominent among these are issues about identity: its character and fixity, portability, theft, relation to inherent body and spirit, connection to one's life story, and class status. It is with these issues that we must now deal.

Cruikshank had suggested narrating the progress of twinned protagonists, one good, one bad, with the good one surviving adverse circumstances. In the course of an improvised and somewhat incoherent plot, Dickens makes Oliver his own twin – a raggedy thief and prisoner with Fagin, a promising young lad when with Brownlow and the Maylies.[85] Dickens also provides Oliver with multiple doubles: his half-brother the self-consuming Monks, his companions Charley Bates and the Artful Dodger, his "sister" and "brother" Nancy and Bill Sikes, his early friend little Dick, and his fellow apprentice and bullying companion Noah Claypole. Oliver is none of these, has in fact no biological connection to any of them excepting his half-brother Edward Leeford ("Monks"), but he is associated with them all and identified by many with his felonious companions and physiognomy: a boy who "will come to be hung" (p. 12).[86]

Like Boz, Oliver's name is invented – by Bumble, on an alphabetical principle. (Cruikshank claimed that Dickens heard the name uttered by a bus conductor and took a liking to it;[87] Patricia Ingham has pointed out that "Oliver" is thieves' slang for the moon, and Oliver goes out to Chertsey when the moon is dark.[88] Crime can only be committed when "Oliver" is eclipsed. And there's Boz's suppressed connection to Oliver Goldsmith.) Like "Boz," "Oliver" is believed to stand for multiple and contrary things, criminal and honorable, guilty and innocent. When he is recovering at the Maylies' cottage after the attempted break-in, Rose Maylie asks the doctor who comes to minister to Oliver's wounds, "can you really believe that this delicate boy has been the voluntary associate of the worst outcasts of society?" To which the surgeon replies by shaking his head, "in a manner which intimated that he feared it was very possible" (p. 191). Once again, a tiny detail in Dickens's text, easily read as simply a piece of realism, or stage-business passing as realism – the doctor's wordless reply – opens up an immense issue in this story that pertains to Oliver and, as we will see, also to Dickens.

For Oliver cannot tell his story, and cannot be read rightly by others. Repeatedly, silence even silences the counternarratives, as in the case of the surgeon's head shake. Oliver hasn't any narrative history, at first – or rather, the swaddling clothes in which he's wrapped could bespeak one of two "old stories," ones Mark Twain told delightfully as the prince and the pauper (and a gang of thieves). But when Oliver is interrogated in his later years, by a magistrate or a beadle or a benevolent caregiver, he rarely gets a chance to speak. He can't utter his name, which, for the court, becomes Tom White, the intimation of innocence nominatively supplied by the "kind-hearted thief-taker" (p. 64). Oliver usually faints, or others tell their version of his life. For instance, Noah's taunt: "Yer know, Work'us, it carn't be helped now; and of course yer couldn't help it then; and I'm very sorry for it; and I'm sure we all are: and pity yer very much. But yer must know, Work'us, yer mother was a regular right-down bad un" (p. 36). On this occasion, Oliver's spirit is "roused at last ... his whole person changed, as he stood glaring over the cowardly tormentor who now lay crouching at his feet: and defied him with an energy he had never known before" (p. 37). But even here, in the undertaker's basement, Oliver says nothing verbally to contradict another version of his family's "old story," which gets told in spite of any evidence supporting or confuting it.

At first, as a result of the courtroom mistake, Brownlow believes Oliver's name is Tom White, and when Oliver insists that he is "Oliver Twist," for a moment Brownlow suspects him of a falsehood. But, on peering into the boy's face, Brownlow concludes that "[i]t was impossible to doubt him; there was truth in every one of its thin and sharpened lineaments" (p. 72). However, when he asks to hear the child's story, "Oliver's sobs checked his utterance for some minutes." And then, "when he was on the point of beginning to relate how he had been brought up at the farm, and carried to the workhouse by Mr. Bumble, a peculiarly impatient little double-knock was heard at the street-door," and the interview is interrupted by the arrival of Mr. Grimwig (p. 86). "And when are you going to hear a full, true, and particular account of the life and adventures of Oliver Twist," Grimwig asks after dinner. "To-morrow morning," Brownlow promises (p. 89). That never happens.

Again and again Oliver's story is narrated only through the testimony of others, always colored by their own assumptions and prejudices, and equally by what they expect their auditor wants to hear. That Brownlow, on first seeing Oliver, thinks "[t]here is something in that boy's face" that "touches and interests" him (p. 61), indicates that already, by the July 1837 installment, Dickens had imagined the back story of Oliver's parents and intended in future that someone – not Oliver – would discover and tell it, proving Oliver's innocence.

But instinct and prejudice usually twist Oliver's story. Sometimes for the good. Oliver does, weakly and haltingly, tell his story to the Maylies and Dr. Losberne – but not to the reader, who has as yet never heard Oliver's own version of his experiences. However, moving as the story is to his Chertsey auditors, the doctor doesn't think it would stand up before the constable, the Bow Street Runners, or in court: "I don't think it would exonerate him," he tells Rose, "either with [the officers], or with legal functionaries of a higher grade. What is he, after all, they would say? A runaway. Judged by mere worldly considerations and probabilities, his story is a very doubtful one" (p. 198). Believing it themselves, Dr. Losberne and the Maylies so bully the servants about Oliver's part in the robbery that the Bow Street Runners conclude he was not guilty: indeed, each has another culprit, with a long "old story" of criminal conduct, in mind: Conkey Chickweed or the Family Pet.

More often, the story pinned on Oliver is a bad one, beginning with the workhouse board member who predicts that Oliver "will be hung."[89] When Oliver is abducted in public by Nancy, she tells the bystanders that "he ran away, near a month ago, from his parents, who are hard-working and respectable people; and went and joined a set of thieves and bad characters; and almost broke his mother's heart" (p. 96). Brownlow offers five guineas reward for "such information as will lead to the discovery of said Oliver Twist" (p. 110). Bumble, happening to be in London on business, reads the notice and supplies Brownlow with his version of Oliver's character, which he says betrays "no better qualities than treachery, ingratitude, and malice." On hearing this, Brownlow says "sorrowfully" as he hands over the five guineas, "I would have given you treble the money, if it had been favourable to the boy." The narrator adds that had Bumble known this, "he might have imparted a very different colouring to his little history" (p. 112).

And that's a central truth to the stories told in this book. They are all bought and sold. Oliver is offered up for sale twice, at five pounds each time, through an advertisement. His first potential employer, Gamfield the chimney sweep, attempts to exonerate himself from responsibility for the death of other young apprentices so he can obtain the money and incorporate Oliver into an "old story" of the death of sweeps. As memorialized by William Blake, Tom Dacre dreams "that thousands of sweepers,

Dick, Joe, Ned, and Jack, / Were all of them locked up in coffins of black."[90] Both Gamfield and Oliver's subsequent employer, the undertaker Sowerberry, appreciate that Oliver's body is small from the privations he has suffered, thus being the perfect size for squeezing up stove flues, sleeping in black coffins, or walking at the head of a funeral procession, a "mute in proportion" "for children's practice" (p. 29). Bodies and life stories are commodities, and not just for Oliver. Monks's mother tells the "wretched cottagers" who are bringing up Rose "the history of the sister's [Agnes, Oliver's mother] shame, with such alterations as suited her," and thus blights the adoptive relationship (p. 355). Later, Rose's "tainted" association with her deceased sister forces Harry Maylie to give up his hopes for a Parliamentary career and the influential patronage of wealthy relatives. Fagin pays Noah to spy on Nancy and tell her story. Thieves sell one another up to the authorities for cash. So does an "old gentleman" in the crowd surrounding Sikes on Jacob's Island, who promises "fifty pounds to the man who takes him alive" (p. 346). And of course for at least a century, the prison chaplains had made money hawking criminals' last testimony as the crowds watched them being hanged.

Stories are told not according to any fixed "truth" or even in accord with traditional narratives, "the old story," but for payment or reward. The convoluted history of Edwin Leeford's two relationships – the forced mercenary marriage to Monks's mother and the loving though illegitimate association with Oliver's – his will (mysteriously both destroyed and somehow still available)[91] that requires one life-history or another to be told in order to allocate the inheritance, and the long story Brownlow recounts to Monks, in Oliver's presence and the reader's, in order to clear up the hitherto suppressed back story, all connect life accounts to financial accounts. It is the new utilitarian law of capitalism, which Fagin, the nighttime, nightmare capitalist, fully understands.[92] Everyone is bound by the same law: taking care of number one, which means that "a regard for number one holds us all together, and must do so, unless we would all go to pieces in company." To reinforce his lesson to Noah, Fagin tells a long story about "the magnitude and extent of his operations; blending truth and fiction together, as best served his purpose" (p. 294). A similar use of stories is of course the basis of legal proceedings, demonstrated memorably in the trial of *Bardell* v. *Pickwick*. When Fagin thinks it is time to protect himself as number one, he can so inflect a story about another as to cut him or her off from the company. Stories are told for gain and gold, not truth.

That Dickens was, partly consciously, partly unconsciously, discomfited by the extent to which his own stories were shaped and rewarded according to the wishes of the one paying him can be seen not only in his correspondence but also in the ways in which he tells the story of a boy who also names the life narrative Dickens sells twice over to Richard Bentley. That he was vexed by the multiplication of Bozzes, variant names also constructed on alphabetical principles (Bos, Poz, etc.) seems reflected in Oliver's case. That neither Oliver, pseudonymously named and never actually given a patronym (it couldn't be Leeford, he is "adopted" by Brownlow "as his own son" but doesn't seem to take his new father's name [p. 365], he's a Fleming descendant but can't take that name as even his mother and aunt have suppressed it), nor Boz can stabilize a genealogy of descent or a singular character speaks too to a concern that is growing for Dickens, trying through stories carefully crafted to particular audiences to establish his own writerly identity without supplying an explanatory back story about Boz or himself. As we have seen, in providing a biography for a German publication in July 1838, Dickens completely skips over his family's Marshalsea experience; he says that he began a rambling education in Chatham and finished (!) "at a good school in London – tolerably early, for my father was not a rich man, and I had to begin the world."[93]

This anxiety about the possibility of losing one's identity in a rapidly growing metropolis is the dark side of all those comic stories in *Sketches* about folks pretending to be other than they are, and the somewhat more ambivalent stories told by Jingle as part of his impersonation of others, or about Pickwick as he is misrepresented time and time again, from the opening chapter through his breach-of-promise trial, even by Sam, who steals his name to sign a valentine "your love-sick Pickwick." It was also, as Richard Stein has pointed out in *Victoria's Year*, a concern of the mid-1830s.[94] Massive shifts of population from villages to large conurbations meant that the kinds of ways neighbors knew one another, living, working, worshipping together, going in and out of one another's houses and shops and recognizing family resemblances and traits, no longer applied. As Dickens's *Sketches* dramatized repeatedly, identity in the city can be assumed and performed, using language, haberdashery, cosmetics, bodies filled out or cinched in to alter appearance, manners, and feigned associations to create a persona. Those marks of identity can also be taken away, as Fagin's pupils pick out the initials on handkerchiefs and Oliver's suits of clothing are recycled, leading both to the loss of his identity as a gentleman's son and to the discovery of his residence in a gentleman's house. Simply put, urban life upsets the stability and reliability of bodily and behavioral markers of identity. A stolen child can be recast as another's – and many of the novels published at the opening of Victoria's reign dealt with precisely that situation. Those "old stories" recounted the history of lost heirs and faked identities. And while in fact few children were ever kidnapped, the fear of losing one's child or identity, Stein maintains, pervaded the culture and its stories "of shifting classes, families shattered, titles falsely claimed and innocent people tricked into dangerous courses of action"; stories "in which the confusions of identity endanger the stability of society and of all the individuals within it."[95]

Boz was Dickens, his son, and his books. And the latter were being stolen all the time. Peter Murphy reminds us that these issues are much more intense in a written culture than in an oral one. In the oral tradition "accusations of theft . . . are rare because such incidents do not appear to qualify as theft. In the modern world the written self may appear to be more capricious and free [than an oral self that reproduces ancient and formulaic texts known to the auditors], but that self is sutured ever closer to the bodily self, since its career generates profits that the bodily self wants, and which culture becomes ever more capable of overseeing and collecting."[96] Old stories can be retold by griots and bards without loss of authority or remuneration, but new stories that are written, printed, purchased, and read need to be able to claim originality and an originator. This was one of the principal reconstitutions of the idea of copyright coming out of the eighteenth century: the need for an origin of the copy that was an original text. Out of the infinite recombinations of words and narratives, an author must establish a claim to having produced something unique, and as a single entity. Copyright gives the right to copy to *an* entity: a printer, a publisher, an author. It doesn't, it can't distribute that right to a whole congeries of writers, a dozen Bozzes who produce a dozen imitations of the same new or old story. And yet in Britain both the law and the courts had allowed parodies, sequels, adaptations, abridgements, and some kinds of imitations also to be protected by copyright. Moreover, since copyright inheres in the originality of the text's presentation, and not in facts publicly known, different arrangements of the same facts – for instance, a directory alphabetically organized by the name of the inhabitants in one case and in another arranged by consecutive street address – could both be eligible for separate copyrights. So it was not clear how much might be done to an existing text, editing it or "correcting" it or rearranging or condensing or dramatizing it, in order for it to gain its own copyright rather than being punished as an infringement on another copyright. And in cases where the legitimacy of the imitation was challenged, even if the plaintiff won the case, court costs alone often exceeded the resources of the defendant, as Dickens discovered to his great disgust when asserting his copyright to *A Christmas Carol* in the 1840s.

The widespread practice of marketing a similar product without permission which so vexed Dickens and so marked *Oliver Twist* was usually stigmatized by one of two names: piracy or plagiarism. Both in law and in public opinion the two terms, while often used interchangeably, had different histories and affective connotations. Pirates literally stole people and property, sometimes ransoming them, sometimes not returning them at all. There is no validity to the assertion that Americans "pirated" British authors. As there was no bilateral copyright agreement, works copyrighted in England were simply unprotected in other places, and vice versa. So while by analogy it felt as if the books had been stolen for the US market when they were reprinted on American presses without payment to the original British copyright holder, there was no piracy or theft involved – unless multiple copies of a title printed in the UK got smuggled into North America. (Sometimes books produced in the USA got smuggled across the border into Canada, which had its own restrictive laws as a British colony about importing printed materials manufactured in other countries, and an especial resistance to Francophone books that did not originate in France.) Piracies had been a plague to booksellers and copyright owners for centuries. They were a principal concern of the Stationers' Company, which, however, never was able to eliminate the copying of titles registered in the Company's books by others who either noted irregularities in the registration, or produced copies in places outside the Company's reach (Ireland, for instance), or found other loopholes, or simply went ahead like buccaneers and took their chances on being caught. Moreover, pirates had a somewhat romantic reputation. Sir Francis Drake and Martin Frobisher were technically pirates.[97] And pirates from one perspective might be heroes from another: those who ran blockades in order to import prohibited or heavily taxed products were often abetted by legions of civilians who helped to smuggle the goods from the ports of landing past excise officers and into the interior for distribution. Several of Scott's novels, and G. P. R. James's 1845 novel *The Smuggler*, exonerate these evaders of government oversight because they provided highly desirable imports, usually – for those products also sold legally – at more affordable prices. From one perspective, at least, pirates acted in the public interest.[98]

Pirates functioned in another way as well: they often ransomed their captives. In the eighteenth and early nineteenth centuries, there were a fair number of such pirate tales, and while some emphasized the sufferings of those captured, others portrayed the pirate captains as merciful and gentlemanly, at least to the women prisoners. Sometimes the pirate company contained both kinds: think of Mozart's *Abduction from the Seraglio* and *The Magic Flute*, in both of which cases the overseer of the captives is ferocious while the leader proves to be enlightened (Sarastro) or merciful (if vengeful, as is the case with Pasha Selim Bassa). Thus the pirate and the highwayman get conflated as gentlemanly criminals; and in the 1830s Bulwer, as we have seen, Ainsworth's *Rookwood*, which turned Dick Turpin into a hero, and *Jack Sheppard*, which granted more worth to Jack than to the police who were themselves profiting by thieving and thief-taking, refurbished the image of the attractive criminal.

Although publishers and authors perennially complained about pir-acies, the complaint didn't reach down into the fundamental roots of intellectual law and order. Indeed, for centuries one of the most effective remedies for print piracy was for the copyright owner to buy up and destroy the offending stock, or even bring the pirate bookseller into a conger or other partnership and divvy up the market. These piracies infuriated Dickens because of their commercial damage and supposed effect on his reputation – though in the latter case there's always some truth to the adage that no publicity is bad publicity. He was also right to protest on behalf of the Americans: Washington Irving and James Fenimore Cooper were as hurt by British reprints of their novels as Dickens was by reprints of his early works in America.[99] Nonetheless, piracy, while widely denounced, was often a term used to designate perfectly legitimate reprints where the writ of copyright did not run, was a practice that booksellers had learned to live with for hundreds of years, and was often tinged with a certain fondness, especially if it made desirable goods available on the cheap. Piracies may have cut into Dickens's sales and vexed him, but they were a recognized and to some extent tolerated part of his print culture.

Even so, efforts were often made to restrict the practice. In 1835, Bentley and two other publishers brought actions for piracy, and the *Athenaeum* predicted that if all publishers would follow these examples, piracy "will be put an end to in six months."[100] Of course, that didn't happen, in part because the booksellers didn't all join together to prevent it. Piracy, in any direct way, does not figure in the text of *Oliver Twist*, but Dickens strongly condemns piracies both in his preliminary advertisements for *Nicholas Nickleby* and in his attack on those who adapt novels for the theater, as we will see in the next chapter.

Plagiarism, on the other hand, has a less illustrious and more mixed history.[101] Augustine Birrell distinguishes piracy from plagiarism, the former being a felony, the latter a "moral offence":

The intent to steal, the unscrupulous determination to benefit by another's labours (that other being a "protected" author) without independent work of one's own, this is to be a pirate at law. If the extraneous matter is not protected property, the offence is the moral offence of plagiary.[102]

From early on in the history of copyright, as we saw in Chapter 1, the right to copy was conceived of, by those in the print industry and by the Crown, as property. And property was one of the most important concepts enshrined in British law. Property is inheritable. Products of the author's body and brain are property. And nothing the body produces is more valuable than an heir. To alienate that heir, to disrupt that transmission from parent to child, from body to offspring, was to undermine the whole structure of society. (Except, of course, we must acknowledge that the system worked in the opposite way too: to acknowledge the products of one's body, if those products were not lawfully conceived, would be to disrupt the canonical chain of succession. So kings and lords and commoners often disclaimed those "naturally" conceived but unlawful products – bastards. They also sometimes created heirs not of the body, through the means of legal fictions such as adoption or testamentary bequest. It turns out that succession can be as much a matter of paper and ink as of egg and sperm.) To take a lawfully as well as bodily conceived offspring away from its parent is to kidnap it. The Latin word *plagiarius* means "one who abducts the child or slave of another"; *plagiare*, the verb, means to kidnap. Alternative etymologies suggest that the word "plagiarism" may derive from the Greek *plagios*, meaning oblique, slant-wise, which becomes in Latin *plaga* – a net; one kind of combatant in Coliseum games trapped his enemy by throwing over him a weighted net.[103]

There are fascinating implications of this alternative etymology for the tropes we use about language, about being caught in the web of words as James A. H. Murray was caught making the *New English Dictionary on Historical Principles*.[104] But we can't explore them now. I want to concentrate on the simple idea that "plagiarism," deriving from the Latin, became a serious crime because of the way copyright came to be defined, as wholly personal property, the "immaterial" product of the body and brain of the author. Any appropriation of that product was stealing, kidnapping. Either derivation, *plagiarius* or *plaga*, sustains the notion that a plagiarist is one who captures the person of another. This is a different kind of theft from piracy, and the theft is often extended from the body to the identity of the victim. A plagiarist thus appropriates a bodily heir of the family, disrupting the lineage, and frequently the nominative identity as well. A plagiarist can redirect the inheritance of name and family, as Bos and Poz redirect purchasers of Boz's work to their own, and Monks tries to redirect half his father's fortune from Oliver to himself. So while plagiarism is like piracy a kind of stealing, the most pernicious and lasting effect is to steal not just *a* property but a whole inheritance. And plagiarists don't ransom their captives or ever return them unharmed to their rightful families. Moreover, plagiary is harder to prove. All writers borrow from their textual inheritance. Some of those borrowings are socially approved and legally protected: for instance, parodies, sequels, condensations and abridgements, and anthologies of quotations. In the case of textual plagiarism, as opposed to personal kidnapping, the only recourse, if any court judges that the theft was unlawful, is to destroy the remaining copies of the offending text and demand damages. But most plagiarists were fly-by-night operators with no assets to seize, unlike pirates who might still have booty hidden away. And an identity, once stolen, is hard to recover, as victims of identity theft discover. Thus a plagiarist commits a kind of crime for which perfect restitution is impossible.

What Dickens does is to take both models of infringement on intellectual property and embed them in a net (*plaga*, if you will) of associations within his novel. Oliver is, as we've remarked, boy and book. Boy is arrested for stealing a handkerchief (from which the identifying marks would later be picked out): a white cloth stitched with initials, not dissimilar to a page made from boiled and pressed cloth and imprinted with type.[105] (The connections between handkerchiefs and publications were widespread. In the 1833 *Athenaeum* article about dramatic copyright, the anonymous writer concludes by imagining that the judge will in future instruct theatrical managers who stage plays without authorial permission that "you may keep your present stock of pocket-handkerchiefs [i.e., previous theatrical scripts taken from dramatists' publications or actors' reconstructions], whether you have picked out the marks or not [i.e., the original author's name and claims]; but, in future, you must respect property, and keep your hands from your neighbours' pockets.")[106] Boy is not the thief, but is so identified by the real thieves, who impose their identity on the innocent bystander. And the cry is then taken up by the mob. At court, boy is too weak to speak, so a compassionate jailer tells the judge his name is Tom White – another, apparently adventitious, allusion to the white surface on which any name can be imprinted or erased. Moreover, boy's theft allegedly occurred while the victim was reading a book at a stall outside a bookseller's store, and which book in the subsequent confusion the customer took without paying for, another theft. Boy and books are stolen again when Oliver carries £5 and some books back to the shop in repayment. This sequence of events enacts plagiarism almost literally. And it is replicated in other keys by the old nurse Sally who steals from Oliver's mother's corpse the material tokens of her identity, her ring engraved with her Christian name and a gold locket containing two entwined strands of hair; by Mrs. Corney who takes the pawn ticket from Sally's dead hand, recovers Agnes's property, and negotiates its sale to Monks for £25; and by Monks who throws ring and locket into the millrace. Here many participate in the abduction of identity, just as in the communications circuit it takes more than an author to steal another's identity: it takes printers, binders, publishers, booksellers, and customers who all pick the forged or erased identity (Bos, Poz) over the real one.

Dickens waxes wroth about piracies; but even so allows some. Plagiarism, however, seems a subtly different matter: stealing property is one thing, and infuriating, but stealing identity, authorial identity, is virtually a capital crime, the abduction and ruination of heirship and lineage. That descent of lineage is often signified on the title page, advertisements, and other paratexts by the phrase "By the author of . . ." If that chain of associations is broken, it is almost like killing one's child – or parent. While Dickens's first books were "edited" by "Boz," and thus presumably the text was not generated, only adjusted, by the editor, by the time Bentley advertises *Oliver Twist* in volumes it is by Charles Dickens, the author of all the preceding titles, whether published by his firm or another, whether ostensibly edited, or actually edited, under a pseudonym. For Oliver not to be able to lay claim to his name, not to be able to control in any way the circulation of stories about him for which many get paid, is to experience what it is like to be an author plagiarized. And that is one reason why Oliver would rather be a bookseller than an author. Furthermore, since plagiarism is, in metonymic terms, the very center of the novel's plot, Dickens's insistence on having his name, rather than Boz's, printed on the title page seems such an important event: Dickens is claiming his books for himself, not for Boz or other factitious writer. Dickens's identity is as much at risk in urban, capitalist London as Oliver's, and the author's anxiety is deeply embedded in his parish son's story.

Hiring "Boz," paying him for editing or writing, and negotiating copy-rights on the materials so produced, involves a larger historical and social context that we need to consider at this point. Dickens wasn't just working for money – indeed he continued to contemplate a number of occupational options, as we have seen and will see again in the next chapters. He also desired a particular status, cultural, ethical, and intan-gible: membership in the genteel classes. Industrial Britain could not hang on to a single category of "gentleman," meaning among other things someone who received income (especially from land, its agricultural production, and also if applicable from canals or railway rights of way or mining) but did not depend on manual work for his living. Since, as Robin Gilmour emphasizes, "it was leisure which enabled a man to cultivate the style and pursuits of the gentlemanly life," the gentleman both underwrote a traditional class hierarchy and troubled the case being made by nouveaux riches for the dignity of labor.[107]

Industrial Britain was constantly revitalizing the genteel classes with entrants from trade, finance, agriculture, and the professions. Some professions argued that though they worked, they served public interests and should be recognized as not self-serving. Certain classifications of labor sought, and got, legal recognition and enhanced status as self-regulating professional bodies during Dickens's lifetime.[108] The status of those in the legal profession was extremely variable, ranging from law lords down to country attorneys whose practice might be as self-serving as Samuel Dockwrath's in Anthony Trollope's *Orley Farm*. Yet it was possible to earn a living, not just live off investments, and be considered a gentleman. And it was to that station that Dickens aspired. In the 1830s and 1840s, a heated national and Parliamentary debate ensued over how to evaluate, guarantee, and defend intellectual products, especially literature. To understand the stakes in that debate, and then to connect Dickens to the issues being raised, we need to recognize, as we saw in Chapter 1, how in Britain copyright was always about money, but also about reputation and control over print products.

There were at least two large cultural issues underlying Dickens's discomfort with the way he sold his works, and his works were sold to the public. One was the sense that he was still, and only, a hired hand, not much different from other Grub Street hacks or retail clerks selling new or used goods. In glancing critically at the New Poor Law, Dickens was, probably only semi-consciously, enhancing the basically non-political entertainment Boz was so loved for by adding a social critique that implicitly claimed for literature another, perhaps higher, role, one of educating the public and moving it to reconsider its provisions for charity. (The prisons and workhouses that Scrooge identifies as those basic charitable provisions were not the solution to "respectable" poverty, though individual charity doesn't reach the collective poor either.) In changing the subjects, tone, and objects of "Boz"'s rhetoric, Dickens is also changing his self-presentation as a writer, to someone – as he defined it late in his career in *The Uncommercial Traveller* – as an *un*-commercial traveling salesman for the Human Interest Brothers.

That Chapman and Hall expressed their financial transactions as compliments to Dickens's talent and as gifts to his genius seemed to Dickens a much better way, in the absence of any arrangements that would entirely disprove his being paid per word, to acknowledge that he was more than a hireling. Similarly, though he may in the end have taken Carey's money, he projected himself in his letter to the firm as preferring to be paid with a copy of the book, the product of his intellectual labor even though manufactured and sold in another country. Appreciating what was deeply, psychologically and socially, at stake in Dickens's publisher relations with his two principal publishers helps to understand how devastating it was to him to have William Hall come, some years later, to invoke a clause in a subsequent contract that deducted money from Dickens's monthly stipend. Suddenly Chapman and Hall were bankers, lawyers, merchants, and he was a hireling and debtor.

Dickens in 1837–38 can't imagine how anyone can earn money and be a gentleman, though he would like to do the one and be recognized as the other. In the early novels, inherited status trumps earned status. The Pickwickians don't work, and while they aren't culturally of the governing class they are in some sense gentlemen, and received by an undoubted gentleman, Wardle of Manor Farm. Mr. Brownlow is a gentleman. Oliver's father, on his own and by his marriage to an heiress, was a gentleman, but Agnes could never be a gentleman's wife, and her story as told by Monks's mother prevents her sister and husband from a secure role in the genteel classes. Nancy, who understands the workings of the power of class (she can perform Oliver's respectable sister to bystanders, and, like the staff in the hotel where Rose stays, instinctively knows and defers to higher classes while trying to protect them from lower ones), and the narrator, refer to Brownlow as the "gentleman" in the passage quoted a few pages back.

Fagin is also, in text and captions, called a "gentleman," usually the "old gentleman." At one level, this term is parodic – he is Jewish, not gentile, and neither he nor his gang acts gentlemanly when they exploit Oliver's naiveté and abuse his body. At another level, it is satiric. The narrative defines Fagin as an inverse capitalist: he inculcates stern lessons about earning a living, taking care of number one, being thrifty and saving, and doing a good job. He inhabits the abandoned houses of prior upper classes. And though, as a Jew, he would not be received as a gentleman under any circumstances in the 1830s, his taking in the stranger fallen by the side of the road at once repeats and perverts the charity of the Good Samaritan, whose image graces the parish insignia. Brownlow, another rescuer of Oliver after his courtroom trauma, owns a painting of the Good Samaritan that hangs over the fireplace in Mrs. Bedwin's sitting room. Surely at first it seems to emphasize the contrast between Oliver's first Samaritan, Fagin, and his second; but skeptical readers have wondered at times whether Brownlow's domestic protections (and vanishing residence) aren't more of a fantasy and a bore than Fagin's gang and changing residences.

The critique of being a gentleman (think what Harry Maylie is forced to abandon because of Rose's sister) runs through *Oliver Twist*. It is one of the deepest of Dickens's contemporary autobiographical concerns. How can he not sell out Oliver, as a charity child, but sell *Oliver Twist* (twice over); how can "Boz" morph from entertainer to social critic while remaining a humorist, be an editor and an author, and be both a projection of Charles Dickens, his creator, and a separate identity not to be confused either with his improvident parent surreptitiously taking his son's money or any of the others making money by plagiarizing Dickens's name and products? And how can Dickens, as editor, aggrandize his class status and not decline into a paid clerk with pretensions to grandeur, like Horatio Sparkins, the upmarket pseudonym of Samuel Smith, assistant at a shop selling cheap goods (inexpensive fabrics, but not unlike magazines and shilling serials compared to three-volume novels beautifully bound in leather).

The "editing" Boz takes up for "real" when he joins Bentley has its own contradictory class and professional attributes. On the one hand editing is a kind of writing for pay – very working class. It distances creative writing from invention, which can be dangerous, out-of-control (e.g. Bill Stumps, madmen); editors edit copy, correcting grammar and spelling and cutting prolixity and mixed metaphor. Editors insist on their gatekeeping and propriety-keeping functions, even though "Boz" as the writer of an "Original Article" each month supplies a "Radicalish" story that disturbs Bentley and his conservative readers. Editing replaces writing with rewriting; it bleeds into office management. On the other hand, editors have power over other writers and writings (and to a degree over illustrators, advertising and publicity, and public reception). Some historical editors gained scholarly (e.g. Samuel Johnson) or journalistic (e.g. Francis Jeffrey) social cachet. Editing internalizes the surveillance and punishment of writing. And, as was the case with Oliver's "editors," editors tell the story their way, to suit their personal, professional, and commercial purposes. So was "Boz" as editor a way forward, toward more respectable status within print culture, or a way of staying secondhand, polishing others' stories according to formulas devised and enforced by superiors?

In October 1837 Dickens penned the dedication of *Pickwick* to his friend, the attorney Thomas Noon Talfourd. His play *Ion* had been the dramatic hit of 1836: an imitation Greek drama that centers on the kidnapping and fateful recovery of Ion, the heir to the throne of Argos, an abduction that dooms the hereditary line and blights the kingdom – a variant on *Oedipus* that once again enacts the fatal consequences of *plagiarism*. The two writers were bound by many things, including a commitment to elevate the status of authorship and provide an expanded legal context that would guarantee remuneration for writings for many decades, far beyond the author's death. Talfourd first introduced his copyright Bill into the House of Commons in 1837. It extended the period of copyright to forty-two years and seventy years past the death of the author, thus a right that would be inherited just as property was. The Bill didn't pass. It wasn't until 1842, when Talfourd was no longer an MP, that a compromise version of his legislation was voted into law. In the meantime, printers, publishers, and authors vigorously debated its premises and terms in the public forums. And Boz, Dickens, and his publishers issued another twenty-part serial, allegedly autobiographical and presumptively a novel, that anatomizes what it means for human relations to be governed by what Carlyle in 1839 called the "cash nexus," the conversion of all human relationships to capital and labor rewarded by pay.

CHAPTER 5

## *Paying Boz (1838–1839):* Nicholas Nickleby

Charles Dickens, Samuel Laurence drawing, 1837

"Boz" has been puffed into the belief that he ought to occupy a much higher station in our literature than he does; he has been classed with Fielding and Smollett, and, no doubt, in consequence, believes that he is equal to those great novelists; but endeavouring to "be like" them, he will ruin himself.

– *Bell's New Weekly Messenger*, April 8, 1838

If the author is the guarantor of the text (*auctor*), this guarantor himself has a guarantor – the publisher – who "introduces" him and names him.

– Gérard Genette, *Paratexts*

It was well for Dickens that, whatever his defects in the conception and in the practice of his art, he possessed in a high degree the artist's conscience.

– George Gissing, *Critical Studies of the Works of Charles Dickens*

Just as the uncle becomes the vehicle of exogamy and exchange for the closed, nuclear family, the avunculate marks the intersection of feudal, paternalistic culture with newly developing nineteenth-century discourses of economic individualism [and] free trade.

– Eileen Cleere, *Avuncularism: Capitalism, Patriarchy, and Nineteenth-Century English Culture*

[I]t was in these years [from roughly 1840 to around 1880] that the nature of gentlemanliness was more anxiously debated and more variously defined than at any time before or since.

– Robin Gilmour, *The Idea of the Gentleman*

I

At the end of 1837, it seemed as if 1838–39 should be banner years for Boz. As we've seen, *Pickwick* sold nearly 40,000 copies of its final double number at the beginning of November 1837.[1] Immediately Chapman and Hall bound reprints of early parts with newly printed, unsold copies of later parts and issued a one-volume edition that also did well. While Boz as editor and writer for Bentley struggled for independence, Charles Dickens was becoming well known and advancing rapidly into the higher ranks of Britain's London-based intellectual and social circles. At the *Pickwick* dinner Dickens hosted (and paid for) on November 17, 1837, his guest list included his father (but none of his brothers); Chapman and Hall and their foreman printer Charles Hicks; both Dickens's illustrators – Browne and Cruikshank; Ainsworth and several of his circle, including the wealthy book collector Thomas Hill and William Jerdan, the powerful editor of the *Literary Gazette*; the actor and producer William Macready, rapidly becoming one of Dickens's closest friends;[2] and the Irish miniaturist and novelist Samuel Lover, who had helped to start *Bentley's* and was intimate with Lady Blessington and the Holland House set. Foremost among these was John Forster, by now Dickens's mentor, promoter, and best friend, literary advisor to Chapman and Hall, influential critic, and man about town who introduced Dickens to Talfourd, Bulwer, Leigh Hunt, and other notables. Not all those invited could attend. To Talfourd's toast Dickens replied, in Macready's opinion, "under strong emotion – most admirably."[3]

While the editorial Boz was still an indistinct, often imitated, and inconsistent persona, Charles Dickens was effectively building a network of highly placed supporters, though significantly none of those associated with his newspaper career, not even his father-in-law, Thomas Beard, or John Black, was asked to this celebration.[4] Although *Pickwick* started as just another periodical, it had by November of 1837 become – even if G. K. Chesterton overstates the case – "something nobler than a novel," and it was with persons connected with higher callings than mere reporting that Dickens now often associated.[5] Elected to membership in the recently founded Garrick Club under the sponsorship of Bentley, one of the founders, "cum multis aliis" on January 21, 1837, Dickens was also elected to membership in the Athenaeum on June 21, 1838, having been proposed by Spencer Hall, librarian of the club and younger brother of Dickens's other publisher William Hall. "[A] remarkable honor for a 26-year-old author," Robin Gilmour comments.[6] Whereas the Garrick was established as a place where theater people and "men of education and refinement might meet on equal terms," the Athenaeum aimed higher. Dickens was selected under the Club's Rule 1: "Individuals known for their scientific or literary attainments, Artists of eminence in any class of the Fine Arts and Noblemen and Gentleman distinguished as liberal Patrons of Science, Literature or the Arts." Elected with Dickens were Edwin Chadwick, Charles Darwin, George Grote the historian of Greece, George Lyttleton, 4th Baron Lyttleton and Gladstone's future brother-in-law, Macready, and Richard Monckton Milnes, first Baron Houghton from 1863, traveler, poet, MP, and enthusiastic supporter of Talfourd's Copyright Bill.[7]

During the first months of 1838, Dickens zipped up two minor contracts, one with Chapman and Hall for *Sketches of Young Gentlemen* (published anonymously), and one with Bentley who hired Boz to edit *Memoirs of Joseph Grimaldi*. As we have already seen, this was a project to which Boz was not attracted. He did it for the money. When the task was first mooted, he told Bentley, "I have thought the matter over, and looked it over, too. It is very badly done, and is so redolent of twaddle that I fear I can not take it up on any conditions to which you would be disposed to accede. I should require to be ensured three hundred pounds in the first instance without any reference to the Sale." This requirement both freed Dickens from participating in the marketplace and made him simply an editor for hire – contradictory, but not incompatible, constructions of authorship. One other provision marks his sensitivity, after the Macrone/ *Sketches* contretemps, to exploiting serialization excessively: "and as I should be bound to stipulate in addition that the work should never be published in Numbers, I think it would scarcely serve your purpose."[8] But Bentley did think hiring Boz to edit would serve his purpose. The Agreement signed a few days after the *Pickwick* banquet, on November 29, specified that the work could be enlarged or abridged so long as it formed no "less than two volumes post Octavo," that it should be publicized as "Edited by Boz" but should not in any manner "state either by himself or his Agents that the said work is written by the said Charles Dickens or that he is the Author thereof such being contrary to the fact." These clauses clearly divided Dickens from Boz – something both author and publisher seemed eager to effect. However, surprisingly, Bentley and Dickens also made Dickens a partner in the project, giving him half profits on the sales after all publishing expenses, and his £300 editorial payment, were recouped.[9] Hence when the sales mounted to 1,700 copies within a few weeks of publication in March 1838, Dickens exulted, telling Forster that "*the demand increases daily!*" followed by thirty more exclamation points. Actually the sales stuck there; Bentley printed 3,000 and still had 920 copies on hand in 1840, which he tried unsuccessfully to offload on Dickens.[10]

Because Dickens's father transcribed his son's abridgement, rumors circulated that John had done the editing – adding another person to the lengthening list of "Boz" personifications.[11] And to some Grimaldi fans, Dickens's abridgement evidenced Boz's ignorance. Dickens opted to draft a letter from Boz "To the Sub-editor of *Bentley's Miscellany*" (a non-existent entity) admitting that since he – that is, Dickens, not Boz, despite the signature – only saw Grimaldi perform three times when he was very young (7, 8, and 11), the "recollections of his acting are – to my loss – but shadowy and imperfect." But he penned an elaborate denial of the proposition "that to write a biography of a man (having genuine materials) or to edit his own notes it is essential that you should have known him." Scott and Hazlitt did not know Napoleon though they wrote fine biographies of the emperor, Lord Braybrooke successfully edited Pepys's memoirs two centuries after he died, etc. Even these examples got to be too labored, so Dickens cancelled further instances.[12] Eventually, Forster says, "it was thought best to suppress" the letter. Surely one could read that Forster thought it best, though thirty-three years later he quotes extensively from the unpublished letter[13] – another instance of the ways in which the construction of authorial identity in 1838 differs from that Dickens created in subsequent decades and Forster canonized. One must not make too much of this cobbled-together project and its aftermath, but it does illustrate once again how fluctuating, uncertain, indefinite, and inconsistent Dickens and his publishers were about using, introducing, or suppressing the editorial "Boz" and the authorial Dickens, and how ambiguous his status was as editor, author, and copyright sharer.

Another instance of this muddle involves early portraits of Dickens. His likeness appeared on posters displayed in omnibuses by October 1837, and in the advertising leaflet for *Bentley's Miscellany*.[14] He highly recommended the portraitist Samuel Laurence (exactly Dickens's contemporary, born in 1812) to Bentley: "I should like you to see his illustrious work."[15] Dickens sat for Laurence on several occasions – in October 1837 and March 1838 as he was just beginning *Nickleby*. Laurence's two chalk and crayon pictures capture Dickens's youthful vitality, but they also illustrate the interchangeableness of his identity. The 1837 one Dickens signed with his legal name, and Laurence, who liked it exceedingly, hung it over his mantelpiece until his death. (It is now at the Charles Dickens Museum.) This may well be the picture that Georgina told J. W. T. Ley was "of all the innumerable portraits of Dickens . . . the best." The problem with this identification is twofold: Ley refers to it as an 1836 drawing, presumably a mistake for 1837 and not yet another drawing (Laurence had drawn Dickens's sister Fanny in 1836), and if it resided on Laurence's mantelpiece Georgina may not have had much occasion to see it, as opposed to the 1838 drawing.[16] This later one, which Dickens disliked, he inscribed with his pseudonym "Boz" and gave to his sister Fanny. It is, however, the one that was lithographed both by Laurence and by another artist, Weld Taylor, and was the first portrait sold to the public – as a picture of Boz.[17] Thus the picture signed with Dickens's name precedes that assigned to Boz, or, to put it another way, Boz comes after Dickens.

There is in the Charles Dickens Museum, to further complicate the issue, a portrait of Dickens by Samuel Drummond ARA (1765–1844), "[p]ainted in the majestic style of Sir Thomas Lawrence [*sic*] RA,"[18] very

Byronic in look – dark curling hair, heavy-lidded eyes, large nose – that for a century was not recognized as of Dickens. Drummond never so far as we know had a live sitting from Dickens, but Dickens did sit to his daughter, a miniaturist, for a portrait he gave Catherine at the time of their engagement in 1835. Angela Burdett-Coutts, who bought Drummond's painting, never doubted the likeness, but owing "to a number of errors made in the earlier part of the 20th Century," the Dickens Museum reports, "its authenticity has long been questioned, principally because it offers an image unwelcome to Dickens Scholars." Unwelcome to scholars, because not nearly so complimentary to Dickens: this figure seems overfed, complacent, and if not particularly meditative then also not curious or animated.

Part of the point of these early portraits is simply that one version of Dickens as Boz was in 1838 lithographically circulated and deemed iconic. But that one version wasn't the only likeness drawn by artists in the Dickens circle. Cruikshank sketched Dickens one afternoon while they collaborated on *Oliver Twist*. Yet only the one that seemed consonant with a public apprehension of who Boz might be reached the public, and images that contravened this impression were rejected by fans for over a hundred years. (For the volume edition of *Sketches by Boz*, Cruikshank had also etched Dickens and himself, accompanying Chapman and Hall: the illustration to "Public Dinners" shows all four men escorting charity children into a fundraising dinner. But since it illustrated a prose sketch, the figure of Dickens was not identified as such.) We will shortly see that portraiture becomes a central feature of the text, paratexts, and publishing context of *Nicholas Nickleby*, and that faces, like voices and bodies and names, no longer in Dickens's writing signify as certain indices to identity or status, as they did in *Oliver Twist*. This is another of the many recognitions that he as author must make about the instable relationships among name, physiognomy, public image, and authorial identity.

II

To return now to the promising opening of 1838 and Dickens's develop-ing, though still incoherent, construction of himself as author, we must take note of his confirmation of a newer strand in Boz's writerly identity. The political satire at the beginning of *Oliver Twist* had surprised many. For Dickens, however, the association of his voice with outrage at inhumane treatment of charity children seemed a part of his growing reputation worthy of further development. At the end of January, he and

Phiz took a short trip to Yorkshire to investigate schools that advertised "no vacations" – a not-too-subtle appeal to families with illegitimate offspring, or stepchildren, or other infant impedimenta.[19] He says very little in the surviving correspondence about his motives for exploring these schools, but in the Preface to the Cheap Edition of 1848, Dickens takes an opportunity to foreground his reformist impulses:

> I cannot call to mind, now, how I came to hear about Yorkshire schools when I was a not very robust child, sitting in bye-places, near Rochester Castle, with a head full of Partridge, Strap, Tom Pipes, and Sancho Panza; but I know that my first impressions of them were picked up at that time, and that they were, somehow or other, connected with a suppurated abscess that some boy had come home with, in consequence of his Yorkshire guide, philosopher, and friend, having ripped it open with an inky penknife. The impression made upon me, however made, never left me. I was always curious about them – fell, long afterwards, and at sundry times, into the way of hearing more about them – at last, having an audience, resolved to write about them.[20]

This retrospect emphasizes two kinds of continuities that the mid-career Dickens builds into the construction of his identity: first, his devotion to eighteenth-century picaresque fiction and Cervantes – which comes out strongly in the early numbers of *David Copperfield* – and second, his lifelong concern for the mistreatment of children. While both are true, both too are brought forth in the 1840s as part of his continuing fashioning of a public persona. For it is much less clear in the 1830s that either picaresque fiction (with the exception of *Don Quixote*) or child abuse was foremost in mind when he began writing.

The episode of the inky penknife, which he evidently heard from a Chatham neighbor in 1817 or 1818, was contravened in 1886 by John Crosse Brooks, who claimed to be the boy Dickens refers to. He says he himself was trying to lance a pimple, and that his schoolmaster always treated him well.[21] As for the cruelty of schoolmasters in the vicinity of Greta Bridge and Barnard Castle, in both the preface to the serial edition of the novel in October 1839 and in the Cheap Edition preface (1848), Dickens takes pains to iterate that Squeers "is the representative of a class," and that he "and his school are faint and feeble pictures of an existing reality, purposely subdued and kept down lest they should be deemed impossible." He then goes on to refer to trials seeking damages for the injuries inflicted on the pupils, and letters testifying to atrocities "very far exceeding any that appear in these pages" (pp. 3–4 [1839], 8 [1848]).

However, the only trials that surface as having to do with these schools are two featuring William Shaw, owner of Bowes Academy.

In his Diary for February 2, 1838, Dickens writes: "Shaw the schoolmaster we saw to-day, is the man in whose school several boys went blind sometime since, from gross neglect. The case was tried, and the Verdict went against him. It must have been between 1823 and 1826. Look this out in the Newspapers."[22] Two trials took place in the Court of Common Pleas, October 30 and 31, 1823, and in each case the parents of the afflicted child received £300 damages. In fact, Shaw's school, one of the largest in the district, suffered from an epidemic of ophthalmia (conjunctivitis caused by bacterial or viral infection), which some believed spread and became virulent because of Shaw's neglect, bad health practices, poor nutrition, and miserable living conditions. Others defended Shaw in court and again after *Nickleby* so unmistakably reproduced Shaw's features on Squeers; and in awarding damages in 1823, the judge also held that "there was nothing to impeach the general conduct of Mr Shaw in the management of the school."[23] In addition to paying damages in both suits, Shaw hired a London specialist for another 300 guineas to advise ways of stopping the epidemic or at least silencing his critics. As Philip Collins comments, "this episode must, therefore, have cost [Shaw] at least a thousand pounds, yet he was able to stay in business. His school must have been very profitable, cheap though it was."[24]

At the time of *Nickleby*'s publication and ever since, correspondents have agreed or disagreed with Dickens, with the identification of Shaw as Squeers, with the cruelty of the Yorkshire schools, and with whether Dickens gave a "faint and feeble" picture of an "existing reality, purposely subdued and kept down," or exaggerated for commercial effect. While his insistence that the exposé of these schools was long motivated does not appear publicly until 1848, Dickens writes to Anna Maria Hall in December of 1838 about the "truth" of his "little picture," providing several of the stories he incorporates into his preface a decade later.[25] So once again, while the full account of Dickens's social mission appears only in the late 1840s, a time when he was very much involved in speaking out about and working for charitable causes, he was interested in exposing the Yorkshire schools at the start of *Nickleby* just as he had exposed the cruelties of the poor laws at the start of *Oliver Twist*. And, in both these early cases, the social satire quickly morphs into humor and other topics. As Collins so astutely notices, "[d]iscussions about Squeers's 'original' often ignore the obvious fact that no Yorkshire master could have been so funny as Dickens's creation, nor so complete and word-perfect in his vulgar effrontery."[26]

In short, whatever reformist leanings Boz was taking on, they achieved their effects more through humor than jeremiads. And the Yorkshire school episodes, though forming part of the backbone of the Nickleby family story, do not themselves occupy a substantial portion of the whole narrative. So Dickens could both deploy his pseudonym as a crusader and retain his reputation for comedy. This was to be one of the writer's unique contributions to Victorian social reform, even after Boz was buried while Charles Dickens grew massively alive. Dickens's style usually solicits through pathos and comedy, rather than by means of thunderous Carlylean denunciations, Ruskinian reasoning, Thackerean satiric sentimentality, or George Eliot's deeply felt philosophical humanism.

The often keenly perceptive G. K. Chesterton identifies *Nickleby* as coinciding with Dickens's "resolution to be a great novelist and his final belief that he could be one."[27] If neither the resolution nor the finality of belief can be observed in the events leading up to and during the writing of *Nickleby*, it is nevertheless true that Dickens was at the time thinking more about how he should construct his persona and career. In retrospect he did his best to make this fourth venture a major bid for distinction as a writer concerned for the public welfare. Moreover, by 1848 he was able to point out, simply and without taking undue credit, that at the time the novel first appeared there were "a good many cheap Yorkshire schools in existence. There are very few now." Educational reform was the rage in the 1840s, and Dickens anticipated and contributed to that movement.

Furthermore, Dickens conceived *Nickleby* as a "novel," whereas his previous publications had been sketches, papers, or successive squibbets of a story that nevertheless contractually remained a series of monthly articles. The public likewise considered his works to be generically uncertain. *Pickwick* was called a "periodical," a "magazine," a "very droll miscellany," and "a series of monthly pamphlets."[28] It was not, in the opinion of Edward S. Morgan, Bentley's assistant, a novel. Instead, Dickens was hailed as a "monthly producer of public entertainments."[29] *Oliver Twist* was a set of "Original Articles" in Bentley's Agreements and a "clever series of articles" to reviewers. During its serialization its generic indeterminacy became even more pronounced: it was a "romance, novel, history, or narrative, or whatever else it may be called."[30] Not everyone agreed that carrying characters and situations forward from month to month was a good thing; there was a fair amount of griping about continuations that seemed to fill up periodical pages and weary the reader with old stories. Those running in *Bentley's Miscellany*, often excepting *Oliver Twist*, were particularly subjected to criticism, especially, as in the case of Captain Marryat's early fictions printed in his periodical, the *Metropolitan Magazine*, when the serial installments were then re-issued complete in one or more volumes. The *Weekly Dispatch*, for instance, protested "against the publishing a long story, bit by bit, in a Magazine, and then reprinting the whole in the shape of a novel" – a shape that belied its episodic serial character.[31] This stigmatization of his piecemeal publications was another aspect of his authorial identity Dickens hoped to silence with *Nickleby*, even though it was slated to appear in the same monthly format as *Pickwick*.


III

While *Nickleby* was coming into being for Chapman and Hall during the spring and summer of 1838, Dickens enjoyed a fairly pleasant spell as Bentley's colleague. For the most part Bentley proved amenable to modifying Dickens's editorial and novelistic commitments; they seemed to agree about the contents of the magazine; the families socialized together; at Dickens's suggestion Bentley published George Hogarth's two-volume *Memoirs of the Musical Drama* (June 1838); and payments arrived on time. That is, until the end of May, when Dickens was furious to discover that Bentley was deducting from his twenty guineas per installment of *Oliver* pages and half pages cut out in proof to accommodate other *Miscellany* materials.[32] But that accounting storm blew over quickly, and Dickens never thereafter fell short of filling all sixteen *Miscellany* pages. To complete *Oliver* in time for publication in three volumes in November, Dickens asked Bentley if he might skip a month's contribution to the *Miscellany*; granted. In September Forster and Mitton negotiated with Bentley and Follett the extensive September 22, 1838 Agreement discussed in the previous chapter. During the time these negotiations were underway, Dickens chafed and grew irritable: not surprising, since he was trying to finish *Oliver* (including giving subjects for the final illustrations for Cruikshank to etch), keep up his *Nickleby* numbers (and Browne's instructions for plates), edit the *Miscellany*, cobble together the *Pic-Nic Papers* to alleviate the financial distress of the Macrone family, respond to other friends and charitable solicitations, attend sporadically to his own family's needs (after Mary's birth in March Kate was indisposed), and get Bentley to count *Barnaby Rudge* as his *Miscellany* monthly Original Article following *Oliver* as well as the second three-decker.

When all the minute details were worked out and inscribed in twenty-five articles, Dickens felt he had won a major battle – proof that while legally his authorial and editorial rights rested on a weak foundation his reputation and commercial value empowered him. He told Mitton that "everything (except one or two mere matters of *words*) was settled in my favor."[33] He then, in prose whose compliments are matched by undertows of resentment, wrote to Bentley to repair the ill will erupting during the negotiations. "While I have most unfeigned pleasure [surely a Freudian locution disguising a modicum of feigning on his part] in saying that the arrangement you have consented to is alike highly satisfactory to me and highly creditable to yourself ... I feel sure [that is, doubtful] you will acknowledge that it embodies no unreasonable or unfair proposal of mine, but merely [litotic diminution of lengthy and strenuous drafting of clauses] carries out the wishes and intentions which have been expressed or implied between us on many occasions." The apology he adds is, as only Dickens could do it, not an apology at all. I add italics to underscore the ambivalence of the formula: "That this arrangement *should have been so long delayed* I very much regret, – the more especially *as its postponement had greatly chafed and irritated me*, and so *led to expressions of feeling on my part which I should be hurt if I supposed likely to give you any pain*." After that almost Squeers-like rodomontade, Dickens compounds his victory with a veiled warning: "Let me assure you with real [as opposed to feigned?] sincerity that in our future intercourse all proposals *emanating from you in a spirit of fairness and candour* will be most cheerfully and cordially responded to by me; and that it will be my endeavour *as I feel assured* [doubtful] *it will henceforth* [but not hitherto] *be yours* to make our connection a source of mutual pleasure and advantage."[34]

Richard Bentley was not an easy colleague. He had his convivial moments hosting *Miscellany* dinners in his Burlington Street shop for many of the top literary talents of the day. But he was stubborn, slow, imitative of other publishers, and inclined to stand upon his editorial rights and dignity even to his cost. Una Pope-Hennessy's disparagement of his character, "purblind and mean of soul," overstates the case, though it may more nearly apply to Bentley's breakdown in the 1840s and 1850s; but while he had integrity, he had what W. H. Prescott called a "tricky spirit" and always insisted on his own judgment in business and literary matters.[35] Dickens's letter needs to be understood in the context of the publisher who still controlled his fate. If it is assertive, passive-aggressive, and sounds a bit like a cock crowing, those very attributes betray the fragility of the Agreement and the grounds for continuing partnership. (It was, in fact, an Agreement superseded five months later by two others terminating the editorial relationship, renegotiating the ownership of

*Oliver Twist*, and fixing the sale of *Barnaby Rudge*.) As a writer Dickens attempts to inscribe Bentley's lines – a playwright forcing dialogue on an actor: "you will acknowledge," "proposals emanating from you in a spirit of fairness and candour," "it will henceforth be your[] [endeavour] to make our connection a source of mutual pleasure."

Yet Dickens is a multifaceted man activated by an inexhaustible imagination, and he is as sincere in wishing for a happy continuation of relations as he is anxious, distrustful, and aggrieved. No one voice speaks for all his feelings. "Will you help me to put a less formal termination to our differences," he asks in closing, "by dining with me on Wednesday at five o'Clock? – long before which time I hope we shall have forgotten them all." (Bentley's office manager, Edward S. Morgan, attributed many of these differences to Forster, who could butt heads with the best and who was much less politic and multifaceted in his communications than Dickens.)[36] Bentley accepted the invitation. Dickens immediately wrote to Cruikshank, the other named principal on the *Miscellany* wrapper and in advertisements: "Bentley and I have at length come to a cessation of hostilities and made a fair and most satisfactory arrangement respecting Oliver Twist; to celebrate which long-deferred event he dines with me on Wednesday at five o'Clock. My Missis's love to your'n and will she join us with you?"[37]

That Wednesday ratification of peace, involving the Bentleys, Cruikshanks, and Dickenses, took place on September 26, 1838. It is important to remember it. Because little more than a month later a blow-up occurred that has for over 150 years been the basis for asserting that Cruikshank and Bentley both seriously offended Dickens on the eve of publishing *Oliver Twist*. What happened was that on October 29 Dickens and Browne began an excursion to the Midlands and North Wales, stopping at Leamington, Stratford, Shrewsbury, Llangollen, Bangor, Chester, and Manchester.[38] Forster stayed behind in London to see the last quires of the third volume of *Oliver Twist* through the press. It had been advertised to the trade as available on November 7. Pressmen at Whiting's and Bentley's, who divided the copy, worked with "prodigious exertion," even all day Sunday, to meet the deadline,[39] but by Monday, November 5, though Forster had been reading proofs until 4 a.m. that morning, it was clear a further postponement was necessary. Forster traveled to Liverpool to deliver this news to Dickens, and probably to impart his impression of some of the changes that still should be made. Dickens told Kate he would return to London on Thursday the eighth, and Forster asked Bentley to have revised proofs of all three volumes at Doughty Street by

2 p.m. on that day.[40] When they arrived, Dickens made some minor alterations; the exact number and kind are inferred from the fact that the manuscript of the third volume was sent from Liverpool to Lea and Blanchard in Philadelphia for setting the conclusion of their one-volume edition, dated 1839 but finished in December 1838.[41] Some of the variants between the Philadelphia edition and Bentley's presumably record American readings of Dickens's handwriting, difficult under the best of circumstances to interpret.

What Forster says was most disturbing were Cruikshank's final illustrations; he disliked all eight, though Dickens had already seen three in print in the *Miscellany* and approved designs for some of the others. Forster's disparagement of "Fagin in the condemned Cell" was not shared by Dickens, contemporary reviewers, or posterity; the scene of "The Last Chance," Sikes about to hang himself from the rooftop on Jacob's Island, was – despite Dickens's doubts about whether it could be represented – a triumph of narratorial perspective and served as the prototype for theatrical sets; and there were those then and since, including Richard Ford in his *Contemporary Review* notice and Thackeray in his 1840 essay on Cruikshank's oeuvre, who much admired "Sikes attempting to destroy his dog," whereas Forster disparaged the depiction of Bull's-eye as a "tailless baboon."[42] In the end, Dickens did ask Cruikshank to etch a new plate to replace the domestic scene of "Rose Maylie and Oliver" by the fireplace with Mrs. Maylie and Harry looking on. It is not a bad plate; and the substitute, Rose and Oliver looking at Agnes's memorial tablet in the church, is considerably more static and boring. In requesting "whether you will object to designing this plate afresh and doing so *at once*," Dickens deploys the same impositional rhetoric he had used with Bentley: "I feel confident you know me too well to feel hurt by this enquiry, and with equal confidence in you I have lost no time in preferring it."[43] Cruikshank complied, reluctantly at first, but quickly enough so that a second edition came out with the substitute within a week.

Kathleen Tillotson, building on a long tradition of Dickensians who blamed Cruikshank for disfiguring the novel and attempting to wrest credit for it from Dickens, asserts that Dickens returned home because "his chief concern was with the illustrations."[44] If we look at the surviving evidence through the spectacles of print culture, however, it is evident that Dickens and Forster were also, perhaps even more, bothered by some aspects of the text and paratexts. Indeed, Forster's request that a "pull" of the entire book be sent to Dickens's home indicates that they wanted to look at the proofs of much more than the last chapters and illustrations.

In addition to some textual emendations, Dickens wanted two substantial changes. One had to do not with the text itself but with the paratext, specifically, Bentley's announcement on the verso of the half title in the first volume of *Oliver Twist* that *Barnaby Rudge* (not yet written) would be appearing "*forthwith.*" Well, according to the Agreement between Bentley and Dickens, installments of that new fiction should have started in the *Miscellany* immediately after the concluding chapters of *Oliver*, scheduled to appear in the April 1839 number. And Dickens might have made that deadline, since he had been tinkering with *Rudge* for at least four years. Still, Bentley's repeated notices in the *Miscellany*, as well as in the volume edition of *Oliver*, Forster thought not "exactly prudent."[45] When Bentley advertised *Barnaby* as a new work of fiction in three volumes in his January publication to the trade, *Bentley's Advertiser*, Dickens was so furious that he asked Ainsworth to negotiate his withdrawal from all further association with the publisher. Thus the notice in the first volume of *Oliver* about *Barnaby* was a matter of considerable import and consequence, not a trivial slip. It committed Dickens to a future of writing he was not yet ready to contemplate or meet.

From Bentley's perspective, touting a new novel as he issued the current one was simply good business practice. For many readers the volume issue of *Oliver Twist* was a reprint rather than first publication because they had read most of the *Twist* installments in the *Miscellany* from February 1837 on. At the beginning Bentley had bought Dickens for three things: continuing editorship of a magazine, a monthly sixteen-page article, and sequential publication of two three-volume novels. Why not advertise the forthcoming title? Indeed, since *Oliver* was already well known, building the public's expectation for something really new was almost a necessity, or at least a perfectly legitimate and even prudential notice that Dickens would continue to churn out fiction that Bentley would publish. It was good publicity for the public and for the trade.

The second change that Dickens wanted connects to this first one in ways that also dramatize the differing interests of publisher and author. Evidently he had decided several days previously, perhaps before or as soon as Forster arrived in York, that he did not want *Oliver* going forth in volumes as authored by Boz. Forster had mentioned this to Bentley in a note, but the proofs arriving in Doughty Street still had "By 'Boz'" (in quotation marks) on the title page that was used for the first issue. This, along with the desire to cancel the notice about *Barnaby* and to substitute for Cruikshank's last plate, was the subject of Forster's "Private & Confidential" letter to Bentley of November 8, the day before publication.

"Pray *lose no time* in affixing the new title page to Oliver Twist, as soon as ever the first impression, which I hear is indispensably necessary, shall have been worked off. You have my last note? 'Oliver Twist. By Charles Dickens. 3 Vols. Bentley.'"[46]

Bentley did his best to comply, but he also added something to Forster's title page paratext: "By Charles Dickens. Author of 'The Pickwick Papers.'" This "Charles Dickens" issue was on sale by November 16, but the binders gathered sheets rather haphazardly, so that some copies have Dickens as author on the title page in one volume, Boz in other of the volumes, and some Boz issues have the "Church" plate that substituted for the "Fireside" illustration, while all the Dickens issues examined by Tillotson contain the "Church" plate.[47] It would be convenient to date the conversion of Boz to Dickens to November 16, 1838, as I did tentatively at the opening of this study. But subsequent printings of the title page in the UK and the USA confound that. Bentley's 1840 edition reverts to Boz; and the Lea and Blanchard editions of 1838 and 1839 have "By Charles Dickens, (Boz!) Author of 'Pickwick Papers,' 'Nicholas Nickleby,' 'Sketches of Every day life,' &c."

These title page variants speak to many issues. From Dickens's standpoint, identifying the author by his name clearly was a deliberate attempt to distinguish the Boz of *Sketches*, *Pickwick*, *Grimaldi*, and the soon-to-resign editor of *Bentley's* from Charles Dickens. In that sense, Chesterton's observation that *Nickleby* was Dickens's bid to be a "great novelist" applies as well to this change of writerly identity. Dickens, not Boz, belonged to the Athenaeum; and Dickens (more associated with Boz at the Garrick) resigned from that club in sympathy with Macready in November of 1838, rejoining in 1844 when he was a world celebrity known as both Boz and Dickens. To Bentley the distinction may also have been instrumental. He wanted to connect the writer to his works and fame. Interestingly, Bentley didn't mind attaching Dickens's name to publications from another firm: "Author of 'The Pickwick Papers' and 'Nicholas Nickleby'" appeared on the 1840 title page. "Author of" became in the Victorian period the usual way for publishers to hook one title to other titles *by the same writer*. It was the expedient adopted of necessity for books published anonymously or pseudonymously, which could still be identified as to type and likely style by listing the former titles by the (allegedly same) author. (Pseudonyms might disguise the fact that the "author" was more than one person either writing collaboratively or sequentially.) Thus, as Genette says, the author as guarantor of the text is guaranteed by the publisher, "who 'introduces' and names him," or her, even if anonymous or pseudonymous.

IV

The not-entirely-coordinated or successful effort on the part of Forster, Dickens, and Bentley to resituate *Oliver*'s authorial paternity replicates the situation within the book where Oliver had such difficulty establishing his own name. Indeed, he never does get any biologically or legally determined surname other than the Twist Bumble invented on an alphabetical principle. (Surely it's only a coincidence that the parallel is to **A**nonymous, **B**oz, **C**harles, and **D**ickens!) But the effort starts a decade-long campaign by Dickens to reformulate his writerly cognomen, to establish his authorial credentials within his own patronym and to begin to associate the majority of his books with that name. (Of course he has already suppressed Tibbs and Sparks, the anonymous author of *Young Gentlemen* and *Young Couples, The Village Coquettes* and other fugitive pieces, while gathering *The Strange Gentleman* within his authorial ambit.) As part of this erasure, he notes in his Diary that *Sunday Under Three Heads* and *Sketches of Young Gentlemen* "are the only two things I have not done as Boz."[48] Demonstrably, the change in the title page of *Oliver Twist*, while from a printing and editing standpoint relatively insignificant, was as a declaration of a new authorial identity a very important act. Its consequences far outweighed any alteration in an illustration or even the premature announcement of a forthcoming fiction – which Bentley never published.

However much Dickens, or at this stage, probably Bentley, wanted to stitch Dickens's literary productions together, Dickens was unable to do so, being prevented by various contracts from acknowledging some products (several of which he wished to suppress anyway) and still not having enough of a sense of who and what he was as an author, or how his intellectual property and reputation could be made to count in the early Victorian era. An amusing, and centuries-long, dispute centers on another false move he made around this time. Cruikshank had long been known for his hilarious rendition of "The Loving Ballad of Lord Bateman." Thackeray too knew and performed a version of it, and at some point Dickens got into the act. Thackeray began to set down the lyrics and sketch illustrations, Dickens got his brother-in-law Henry Burnett to transcribe the score complete with Cruikshank's idiosyncratic wavers and quavers, then at Cruikshank's request he wrote a preface, and Cruikshank found a publisher, Charles Tilt, and then . . . Dickens realized that both by contract and by virtue of his higher aims he must not be connected in any way with this publishing product. (Cruikshank retrieved the manuscript from the printers because Dickens's handwriting would have established his contributions to the Preface and notes.)[49] Ever since, partisans of each of the three collaborators have claimed that *he* was the originator, author, producer, or secret principal behind the scene. In fact there was nothing wrong with Dickens's participation except legally; his preface was funny and the whole thing was a lighthearted *jeu d'esprit* and tribute to Cruikshank's verbal, visual, and thespian eccentricities. But to many Dickensians the possibility of the Master's participation was either delightful or delinquent. Charles Dickens stood for something more elevated and responsible.

So we see the glimmerings of an authorial identity that, while far from the royal "we," still had the beginnings of a reputation as the originator answerable for the unity, tenor, sources, and application of the writing. How misjudged it would be to backform a fuller notion of authorial control onto Dickens's 1838 writing is easily demonstrated. For all the claims, at the time and afterwards, that he intended with *Nickleby* to expose Yorkshire schools, his "research" occupied only a couple of days. His later fame produced two diametrically opposed effects: some in the northern counties resented his ruining a thriving educational enterprise, while others bragged that he stayed in their inn, visited their homes, interviewed them, and was intimate with many in the community for months. A kind of "Washington slept here" phenomenon.[50] Dotheboys Hall occupies less than a quarter of the book.

Despite Dickens's claims to have intended to write a reformist novel, most critics take their cue from the "*Nickleby* Proclamation" issued a few weeks before the first number went on sale. In it Dickens threatens the "pirates" (more about this hereafter) and, using the editorial first-person plural characteristic of Boz, promises "THE PUBLIC" that "in our new work, as in our preceding one [presumably, since this is a Chapman and Hall publication, the episodic *Pickwick* rather than the more plot-driven *Oliver* is the referent], it will be our aim to amuse, by producing a rapid succession of characters and incidents, and describing them as cheerfully and pleasantly as in us lies."[51] Gissing thought that "to attack the 'Yorkshire schools' was [Dickens's] one defined purpose when he set down to write," but that the material "proved rather refractory" because, "as always, in dealing with social abuses, Dickens had to reconcile painful material with his prime purpose of presenting life 'as cheerfully and pleasantly as in him lay.'"[52] Chesterton thinks that the best things in the book are Mrs. Nickleby, always postponing the plot by her monologues about what he asserts is the essential thing, that experience is "one of the gaieties of old age," and the "[p]erfect absurdity" of Mr. Mantalini, while Mark Ford in his introduction to the Penguin Classics edition says that the book "is made up … of all manner of different kinds of writing – melodrama, political satire, class comedy, social criticism, domestic farce – while its loose, episodic narrative style allows Dickens to push the story at almost any moment in whatever direction happens to appeal."[53] Indeed, the huge success of David Edgar's redaction of *Nickleby* for the Royal Shakespeare Company depends on exploiting that range of writing, the essentially miscellaneous subject matter, episodic narrative, and melodramatic style: the large cast of characters – *as* characters – gave the RSC their Crummles moments to exploit the talents of the entire company.[54] And against the energy of Nicholas and the pathos of Smike, John Woodvine played a Ralph Nickleby of such restraint and – toward the end of the eight-hour performance – deeply conflicted and powerful emotions, that his realistic portrayal brilliantly set off the contrast to everyone else, a private and tragic figure surrounded by the noisy colorful crowd filling the Aldwych to the rafters and exits.

That has been the profile of the *Nickleby* phenomenon for over a century: a bustling succession of entertainments flawed by the introduction late in the novel of Madeline Bray, Arthur Gride, and the deaths of Smike and Ralph. The novel's theatricality has been understood as a reflection of Dickens's own thespian aspirations and affections – to such an extent that if anyone questions whether the theater really is highly commended in the novel, partisans are shocked.[55] Dickens's dedication to Macready, who was advertising his own efforts to reform the English stage, seems to reinforce the notion that the book is a kind of Victorian vaudeville in prose, even though Macready's forte was the re-staging of Shakespeare, not Grimaldi.

v

For all the miscellaneousness of *Nickleby*, readers have tried to locate a unity behind "the rapid succession of characters and incidents." In 1958 Hillis Miller saw a multitude of unique grotesques, a kind of philosophical nominalism in which "the character really exists as a kind of generalized form or abstract idea of himself." The collision of these figures within an urban space yields "sheer chaos, an inextricable jumble of objects and people in ceaseless motion, multiplied inexhaustibly, without order or direction." Picking up on the presence of morbid moments and morbidity in the early works (Chesterton defined them as "gloomy"), Miller declared that "The city is, for Dickens, a Dance of Death."[56] Seven years later Steven Marcus proposed that the novel contrasts the prudential with the anti-prudential, siding with the latter: "[t]he aggressive force of intellect in the novel is directed against prudence – the conception which holds that life should be lived close to the vest, that incessant work, cautious good sense, deliberate action and sobriety are the principal indications of virtue and the principal assurances of 'success.'"[57] This attitude toward work of course involves Dickens in terrible conflicts: on the one hand, he justifies his own success repeatedly in terms of "truth" and unceasing labor, and on the other, he cannot decide whether his parents' conviviality and imprudence constitute a beneficial legacy or not. In the late 1830s John Dickens was still borrowing using his son's credit, and was not yet the exemplary reporter Dickens praises in the late 1840s. His mother, too, represents to him – as we have seen – both imprudence and a thrifty way of arranging domestic spaces that he highly admires.

So in the 1960s searches for unity and connections to the author's own history produced some attempts to weld the characters and incidents into a whole. In the 1970s and 1980s, much attention was paid to Dickens's theatricality and grotesquerie: one of the most influential studies – markedly influential to this chapter – is Paul Schlicke's *Dickens and Popular Entertainment*.[58] Coming, as we have seen, out of several years' deep immersion in various kinds of dramatic experiences, Dickens certainly was in a position in 1838 to exploit those experiences touched on in *Sketches*, and to shape a serial that aimed to amuse and move his "public." Such aims were not incompatible with advocating reform; indeed, in Dickens's hand lobbying for the correction of abuses was a form of entertainment. His passionate and funny prose stands over against the inanities of the silver-fork school of novels so deftly skewered in the scene where Kate reads from *The Lady Flabella* to her employer: "'Sweet, indeed!' said Mrs. Wititterly, with a sigh. 'So voluptuous, is it not – so soft?' 'Yes, I think it is,' replied Kate, gently; 'very soft.'"[59]

More recently, a new generation of scholars has begun to think about *Nickleby* in a different way, as a novel in which the family is forced into commercial circulation. In 1996 Joseph N. Childers proposed that "it is a novel about doing business," and that in the end the Cheeryble brothers, who combine business with family, "succeed[] where Ralph has failed to control Nicholas."[60] Eileen Cleere in her 2004 study of *Avuncularism* draws attention to the connection between "uncle" as a quasi-patriarchal family member and "uncle" as the nickname for a pawnbroker, who converts private possessions into retail products: "under industrial capitalism, a socioeconomic philosophy founded upon the law of the father was threatened by a competition-based commercial code that took its shape from the law of the uncle."[61] Helena Michie amplifies this insight, concentrating both on the uncomfortable ways Dickens manages "issues of family, age, and sexuality by having his characters undergo shifts from the category of the sexually inappropriate to that of the sexually appropriate," and on the ways in which Nicholas's highly emotional and violent protection of his sister's innocence and his uncle's personal attraction to Kate's purity and commercial potential activate deep fissures in the construction of a fatherless family. I note that Uncle Ralph as the capitalist agent sells son, nephew, and niece in the marketplace.[62] And Jon Varese, in a densely argued dissertation chapter, "Making and Breaking Contracts in *Nicholas Nickleby*," has recently cogently demonstrated the extent to which throughout the novel contractual relations govern many facets of Nicholas's life. He argues that Dickens's protracted and stressful negotiations with Bentley and other publishers are reflected in the agreements and commitments kept and broken within the text.[63]

I would like to expand on these recent reinterpretations of the novel, to which I am deeply indebted. For it seems to me that at the heart of *Nickleby* is Dickens's observation about a pervasive heartlessness disseminating through British culture, and his demonstration of the various manifestations of that phenomenon through all the characters and incidents of the story. *Nickleby* anatomizes the substitution of capitalist and commercial relations for older, less money-centered ones. The novel begins with a family and a country estate, both of which are divided because of the financial ambitions of the two brothers: a faint and unmistakably fractured rendition of Eden, Cain, and Abel, an origin which Dickens will take up again in the opening of *Martin Chuzzlewit*.[64] Thenceforth virtually every relationship entered into within the novel has an economic element. The obvious cases are those pertaining to Nicholas, Kate, and Ralph, in which Nicholas is sold several times over, and Kate nearly so both as a model (and potential mistress) at the Mantalinis and in Ralph's mercenary negotiations with Lord Frederick Verisopht ("very soft" as Kate remarks of his fictional counterparts, and a self-deceiving sophist to boot, but not very sophisticated) and Sir Mulberry Hawk (one who spins silken threads to bind and swoops down on victims). But this pattern is everywhere repeated, with variations. Mrs. Nickleby, entranced by Ralph's attentions to her daughter, launches into anecdotes about "young ladies who had accidentally met amiable gentlemen of enormous wealth at their uncles' houses, and married them" (p. 227). The Kenwigses' financial expectations from their uncle Lillyvick – an extended reprise of those two stories about disappointed heirs in *Sketches* – affect all their relationships – social, with their neighbors; hospitable, in their entertaining; pedagogic (hiring Nicholas to teach the children French and calling in their uncle and Henrietta Petowker to witness the lessons); and dramatic, when Lillyvick's marriage to Miss Petowker threatens to disinherit them. The disposal of Madeline Bray's hand in marriage is itself a banking arrangement, and the Cheeryble brothers' attempt to alleviate her poverty is couched as a commercial transaction:

the best course would be to make a feint of purchasing her little drawings and ornamental work at a high price, and keeping up a constant demand for the same. For the furtherance of which end and object it was necessary that somebody should represent the dealer in such commodities, and [since both brothers are known to Madeline's father] after great deliberation they had pitched upon Nicholas to support this character. (p. 568)

This scheme pretends to be business, and in "keeping up a constant demand" for Madeline's product it has affinities with Ralph's strategy for increasing the price of Muffin shares. But the Cheeryble business is in fact a theatrical act, the commodities are art not intended for resale though the brothers hope to persuade Madeline that "we made a profit" from them (p. 569), and the "dealer in such commodities" is playing a "character." The whole effort at financial rescue derives from generous, but also romantic and subtly erotic motives stemming from Charles and Ned Cheerbyble's long-ago love for Madeline's mother and her sister. Operating through Nicholas's agency as benevolent uncles, and through the somewhat less tainted exchange of money for art, they attempt to support the Brays and, not incidentally, to preserve Madeline's chastity from sale to Arthur Gride, who proposes quite simply to buy her from her father. Commerce affects all these transactions, but those inflected by artifice, secret agents, role-playing, and generationally displaced erotic impulses appear more ethical than Gride's straightforward purchase of Madeline's body for the price of canceling the debts piled up by her father's improvidence, selfishness, and self-indulgence.

In this context, Squeers's business is a splendidly pertinent example of the buying and selling of bodies, and another elaboration of incidents Dickens broached in earlier fiction. Where Oliver was put up for sale by the parish at the age of eight or nine, to work as a sweep or an undertaker's mute, in *Nickleby* Dickens turns the previous givens upside down and inside out. The boys at Dotheboys School are ostensibly paid for, sent by benevolent parents to be educated, with the school offering room, board, and a "practical mode of teaching" (p. 100) in exchange for an annual tuition. That many are boarded to be gotten rid of, that their education consists of the practical more than the cognitive ("C-l-e-a-n, clean, verb active to make bright, to scour. W-i-n, win, d-e-r, der, winder, a casement. When the boy knows this out of book, he goes and does it" [p. 100]), that their board is little more nourishing than wood, that their housing is frigid, their good clothes exchanged for rags (as Fagin does with Oliver's suit), and their entertainment nonexistent – that, in short, their bodies have been made over to a more grown-up kind of baby farm than Oliver was sent to as an infant, reduces all interchange between parent, child, and schoolmaster to sale and theft (they are often synonymous). When the thief, Squeers, cries "thief!" on Smike and Nicholas, it is the same transference of guilty identity Oliver experiences when Brownlow is robbed. Squeers can not only steal the boys' tuition, possessions, and presents, he can also impose on them his own extravagant misappropriations and misidentifications ("here's richness!" he says, so memorably and comically, of the watered milk served for breakfast in London [p. 58]).

Fanny Squeers and Matilda Price engage in another form of rivalrous commerce that has at its "heart" also a set of material concerns: who has the most extensive wardrobe and the largest number of admirers are two examples. When Nicholas "jilts" Fanny, her inimitable letter of complaint accuses him of stealing her mother's garnet ring but begs that "the thief and assassin" be let go because "he is sure to be hung before long, which will save us trouble, and be much more satisfactory" (p. 177; more echoes of *Oliver Twist* in "thief" and "hung"). By contrast, John Browdie gives Nicholas money without any expectation of reward, simply because it is clear he will need it to get Smike and himself out of harm's way. The contrast between the motives governing the two sets of lovers may not be subtle, but it is wonderfully funny and at the same time affecting. What can't be calculated or monetarized has great power to move.

Bodies are themselves a chief commodity. Readers don't know until the end that Ralph unknowingly through an intermediary sequestered his son at Dotheboys, but early on they see examples of that transaction effected in other families, and in the complicated maneuvers leading up to the denouement Snawley enacts a parody of fatherhood as commerce. Mrs. Wititterly gains social cachet because she is "very delicate, very fragile; a hothouse plant, an exotic" (p. 262); Miss Knag loses place because though she "still aimed at youth," she "had shot beyond it years ago" (p. 209); Mantalini secures large sums of money by flattering his wife's beauty – the examples multiply as the novel proceeds. Rejected by his furious wife, he threatens to fill his pockets with coins and drown in the Thames, after mailing a letter to tell her where his corpse is. "She will be a lovely widow. I shall be a body" weighted with halfpence (p. 411). There are, however, some complications to the immorality of connecting bodies with commerce, and these take us to art, itself both implicated in commodity exchange and in some ways quarantined from its worst effects.

Miss La Creevy makes her miniature portraits from bits and pieces of bodies she picks out when looking at the passing parade from her window. She understands that she can only sell a portrait that meets the expectations of the sitter, and those expectations seem to exceed the actual material conditions. She corrects facial features, introduces dresses and uniforms superior to the rank and station of her sitters, and gives them not a picture of nature, not even a Reynolds idealized portrait of a type, but rather a collage that represents her client's image of a best self, in some cases given to a wealthy relative in hopes of expectations. Portraiture can only limn externals, but it understands those externals as predicting character and fate and as locating the figure in its material social context. That she is a generous and loving friend to the Nicklebys, and that at no point the novel disparages her pictures, complicates any understanding of the value of the art she practices. As it complicates Dickens's own appreciation of his portraits, including the miniature painted by Drummond's daughter that he gave Catherine in 1835; Laurence's and Georgina's admiration of the Charles Dickens drawing rather than the Boz one; the public's consumption of the Boz portrait instead; and the refusal for a century of Dickensians to accept the Drummond image even though Angela Burdett-Coutts thought it most accurate. Most of all, La Creevy's miniature artistic plastic surgery reflects back on the whole tradition of physiognomical caricature that Cruikshank and Browne grew up in and that Seymour and Dickens inherited at the start of *Pickwick*. Faces, or representations of them in portraits, Dickens's fiction now recognizes, are not necessarily any more reliable indices to character, identity, or worth than clothing or language. The upset to any stable markers of identity that Jingle introduced into the Pickwickian world now can encompass physiognomy as well as somatotype and words; cranial and facial elements may not convey the essential and permanent nature of the subject. Dickens and Browne still, on the whole, associate pleasing features with pleasing character. Yet the power of art (perhaps still relegated by Dickens to the miniature and the feminine) to manufacture a likeness that is the image of what the subject wants to be destabilizes the last material claim for fixity and truth.

And that's what the theater understands so well. Every member of the Crummles troupe specializes in roles for which their physique is a widely understood sign: Folair is the slender young mischief-maker, pantomimist, dancer, and comedian – a rather protean character who personifies the (eventually tamed) Indian Savage in the terpsichorean act of "The Indian Savage and the Maiden." His colleague Lenville takes the tragedy parts, not only because he looks tragic, but also because of his make-up: "his face was long and very pale, from the constant application of stage paint" (p. 284). But Ninetta Crummles, at least fifteen, squeezes herself into the body of a ten-year-old (her Christian name suggests nineteen and nine), an "Infant" phenomenon she performs well past her time, especially as the maiden who reforms the savage Folair.[65] Her "comparatively aged countenance" – presumably botoxed with heavy applications of cosmetics – may be a result of having been "kept up late every night, and put upon an unlimited allowance of gin-and-water from infancy, to prevent her growing tall" (p. 283). In sum, the theater takes the bodies and faces, as well as the personalities and voices, of its thespians and shapes them into the characters they both portray and become.[66] Acting as practiced in the early Victorian period *presented* a character by deploying conventions shared by visual artists, writers, and the theater; artifices of gesture, costume, vocal inflection, and movement into which gifted actors such as Edmund Kean could introduce original touches; and "stage business" that was passed down from generation to generation. The stage did not require an actor to lose himself in the part, but rather to project that character across the footlights by means of vocabularies of body, visage, dress, and motions shared with the audience.[67] (Smike, hungry all his life, has to be taught to rub his stomach "in compliance with the established form by which people on the stage always denote that they want something to eat" [p. 318].)

A version of the "studio system," the Crummles company does not, in this novel's world, so crassly rename and reconstruct decorated bodies for sale as a milliner's or dressmaker's shop. Mantalini (né Muntle), a marked contrast to Crummles, "married on his whiskers, upon which property he had ... recently improved after patient cultivation by the addition of a moustache, which promised to secure him an easy independence; his share in the labours of the business being at present confined to spending the money" (p. 130).

The theater not only produces illusion, it trades in it, although somehow not in the same ruinous way that bodies are commodified in other settings. As Dickens and his illustrators have shown repeatedly, the stage is a liminal place where persons may become who they want to be (as subjects of Miss La Creevy's portraits see themselves being), can project that fantasy over the footlights, and can by doing so provide entertainment, not fraud. Even the payment for these illusions is slightly disguised: tickets for "benefit" nights, where the proceeds sequester in the pockets of the star, are solicited through social calls and abject catering to the varied tastes and desires of the sponsors.

Two other participants in the Crummles's commercial venture need mention: Smike and Nicholas. For me the casting of Smike as the apothecary in *Romeo and Juliet* is inspired and heartbreaking.[68] To begin with, he is already physically the embodiment of the character: Romeo "late noted" him

> In tattered weeds, with overwhelming brows,
> Culling of simples. Meagre were his looks.
> Sharp misery had worn him to the bones.[69]

Shakespeare's character is so desperate that Romeo says to himself,

> An if a man did need a poison now,
> Whose sale is present death in Mantua,
> Here lives a caitiff wretch would sell it him. (v.i.50–52)

And so he resolves to solicit poison from this apothecary because "this same needy man must sell it me" (v.i.54). Smike is needy too. He wants to earn something toward his keep. And so with Nicholas's patient tutoring he manages at last to memorize the six-and-a-half lines of his part. Significantly, though Romeo believes that poverty has cancelled any moral concern that the apothecary might have, either for his customer or for his own sake in a Mantua that would execute any dispenser of poison, Shakespeare's figure protests that "My poverty but not my will consents," to which Romeo replies, "I pay thy poverty and not thy will" (v.i.75–76). So even in this scene the commercial transaction is hedged by immaterial counter-interests.

Like the apothecary, Smike has little character. He exists as a loving blank, nothing in his own right except as he can serve and be loved by others. (A redemptive version of Tibbs's zero?) His homosocial good fortune is to find Nicholas as friend: "You are my home," he says to Nicholas. "'May I – may I go with you? . . . I will be your faithful hardworking servant, I will, indeed. I want no clothes,' added the poor creature, drawing his rags together, 'these will do very well. I only want to be near you.' 'And you shall,' cried Nicholas. 'And the world shall deal by you as it does by me, till one or both of us shall quit it for a better. Come!'" (p. 162). This "deal" is not worldly.

For Smike companionship, love, and death are compatible, if not inevitable. Clothing, the very thing that people don to establish class position and that actors use to impersonate roles, is what Smike, like Lear nearly naked on the heath, can go without; he is no more or less than what you see, "[u]naccommodated man" as "no more but such a poor, bare forked animal" (*King Lear*, iii.iv.95–97). And Nicholas, like shelter on the heath, is his home. He vows to go with Nicholas "anywhere – everywhere – to the world's end – to the churchyard grave" (p. 162). (And he does so by the novel's end.) That partnership to death is ratified not by money but by affection. By having Smike play apothecary and deliver the poison that kills Romeo, while in real life he is Nicholas's loyal friend and servant and dies for love of Nicholas's sister, Dickens mixes many things. A living if shadowed homosocial relationship combines with a hidden and deadly heterosexual desire; a dispenser of poison to a lover metaphorically takes that poison to himself; a needy *pharmakon*, in Jacques Derrida's formulation, is both the cure and the killer; an insider within the community must be denied closer relationship for the health of the whole.[70] And within the context of *Nickleby*, it is important to register that neither the play's commercial transaction, nor Smike's remuneration as a member of the troupe, is entirely pecuniary. Other values enter into the exchange.

Nicholas, though forced to work for pay by circumstances, his father's improvidence, his mother's passion for speculation, his uncle's venality, Kate's vulnerability, and his own and Smike's needs, is never quite bought.[71] He rebels against his employment at Dotheboys School. Then he rejects serving the hypocritical MP Gregsbury who, among other discreditable things, opposes "any preposterous bill" that would give "poor grubbing devils of authors a right to their own property" (p. 197). For the first half of the novel, Nicholas finds his most satisfactory arrangement with the Crummles troupe. Yet what he does there, dashing off new scripts in a few days and translating French farces under a pseudonym (Mr. Johnson), is very like what Dickens deplored, both in his own life, when at times he felt as if he was Sisyphus (not the Camus heroic version), always laboring, never achieving his goal, and in the lives of others who adapted his fictions even before he finished them and "stole" them for the stage. That Nicholas's pseudonym points unmistakably to Dickens (John's son) is only one of many instances of Dickens's investment in Nicholas's story and stories. And Nicholas, though impecunious, asserts his equality with the gentry: "I am the son of a country gentleman," he declares to Sir Mulberry Hawk, "your equal in birth and education, and your superior I trust in everything besides" (p. 399).

VI

*Nickleby* bids to establish Dickens as a distinguished author by distancing his work from other kinds of writers and writing and stories: wills disappointing expectations, false advertising, announcements of jobs, the mixed authorship of the theater, legends on tombstones and in glass, Mrs. Nickleby's endless recollections, forgeries and business correspondence, Parliamentary and electoral proceedings, IOUs, journalism, legal documents, and translations. Having been directly or indirectly involved with most of these modes of communication, Dickens is more and more concerned to define his own contributions to print culture against those misuses that he believes contaminate and misrepresent the truth and steal from his own veracious fictions. *Nickleby* fuses New Comedy, Aristophanic death and rebirth, melodrama, and pantomime; it incorporates and rewrites the plots and characters of his literary inheritance and earlier works.[72] And in turn it was quickly and frequently imitated.

By the end of *Nickleby*, at least twenty-five adaptations of Dickens's writing had been appropriated by other writers and produced, usually in non-patent theaters catering to the middle to lower classes in London and provincial theaters south and west of the metropolis.[73] He was perhaps most peeved by the repeated "piracies" of W. T. Moncrieff, very much a theatrical hack and proud of it, whose increasing blindness did not prevent him from adapting current serials into popular dramas – over 200 of them in his lifetime.[74] He, Forster, and Dickens sparred over his *Pickwick* dramatization, *Sam Weller; or, the Pickwickians* (1837), and Dickens responded to his adaptation of *Nickleby* (in which he anticipated Dickens's climax by identifying Smike as Ralph's son) by placing him among the guests at the Crummles's dinner celebrating their embarkation to the United States: "there was a literary gentleman present who had dramatised in his time two hundred and forty-seven novels as fast as they had come out – some of them faster than they had come out" (p. 597).

The conversation between this literary gentleman and Nicholas gets quite testy. While Nicholas concedes that Shakespeare "derived some of his plots from old tales and legends in general circulation," he goes on to attack his interlocutor. "[Y]ou take the uncompleted books of living authors, fresh from their hands, wet from the press, cut, hack, and carve them to the powers and capacities of your actors, and the capability of your theatres, finish unfinished works, hastily and crudely vamp up ideas not yet worked out by their original projector ... all this without his permission, and against his will; and then, to crown the whole proceeding, publish in some mean pamphlet, an unmeaning farrago of garbled extracts from his work, to which you put your name as author" (p. 598).

Moncrieff replied "to the Public" (and thus, publicly, to Nicholas, Dickens, and Boz) in a long printed *Address* dated June 5, 1839, arguing that he did what many others did.[75] (And did it in many cases quite well: his version of Pierce Egan's *Tom and Jerry* was a brilliant adaptation of both the linguistic and the social excursions of that story and ran for over 300 nights.) "I willingly admit," Moncrieff wrote in his defense, "that the common practice of dramatising works before their original authors have completed them is an unfair and vexatious one; but it did not originate with me."[76] Nor was Dickens always savage about adaptations. He rather liked Edward Stirling's stage version (which opened at the Adelphi on November 19, 1838), starring Frederick Yates whose "glorious Mantalini is beyond all praise." Dickens attended the production at least twice, and withdrew "all objection to its publication"; Stirling dedicated the play to Dickens, and Chapman and Hall published it.[77]

The restrictions on transforming narratives into theatrical pieces were so trifling that many did what Moncrieff excelled at doing. Especially in the late 1830s and 1840s, translations and adaptations of French drama, particularly comedies, filled the non-patent theaters; scripts could be produced quickly, a production using the stock company mounted with minimal expense, and the takings, small or large, at least kept the company together until another new play, or a revival, was mounted to amuse the public. Copyright laws did not cover works originally published in other countries, and so while what Nicholas did for Crummles was legal, he – and Dickens – disapproved. Although lacking the legal power to prevent theatrical adaptations, Dickens attempts to assert an author's moral right to prevent such plagiarisms; and Moncrieff in return tries to reestablish their equality or equivalence as authors inscribing works for public consumption.

So Dickens writes himself into the text as a version of a theatrical adapter and writer for a minor company (his own efforts being produced for the most part in better theaters by better managers and actors), attacks a fellow dramatist engaged in this same practice, and by the midpoint of the novel, the last chapter in Part x, draws Nicholas away from the greasepaint and footlights.[78] The novel deals very delicately with the Crummles: they do more than simply "buy" Nicholas. While they are amateurish in many regards and conceited in most, they work hard at their business organized along the lines of a family, not simply a congeries of "employees"; they do not sabotage the success of Henrietta Petowker; and they do eventually make it up to London before emigrating – to the United States, where it is hoped they will find better fortune than Martin Chuzzlewit does. (Was Dickens already contemplating a similar move, two years before he proposed it?)

But Nicholas's heated retort at the Crummles's farewell dinner exposes Dickens's continued chafing at his authorial situation. The *"Nickleby* Announcement" had threatened "PIRATES" with hanging, because "these kennel pirates are not worth the powder and shot of the law, inasmuch as whatever damages they may commit, they are in no condition to pay any." The notion that "cheap and wretched imitations" of Boz's "Works" were thefts, piracy, Nicholas reiterates: "show me the distinction between such pilfering as this [adapting another's text and putting one's own name to it as author], and picking a man's pocket in the street" – clearly reverting to the connection between handkerchiefs and authorial identity in *Oliver Twist* – "unless, indeed, it be, that the legislature has a regard for pocket handkerchiefs, and leaves men's brains, except when they are knocked out by violence, to take care of themselves" (p. 598). The dramatic adapter's argument from survival, "[m]en must live, sir," inspires Nicholas's fiercest *ad hominem* retort: "if I were a writer of books, and you a thirsty dramatist, I would rather pay your tavern score for six months – large as it might be – than have a niche in the Temple of Fame with you for the humblest corner of my pedestal, through six hundred generations" (p. 598). It is a flare-up moment, all the more passionate, perhaps, because Nicholas as Mr. Johnson has indeed participated in similar kinds of unauthorized adaptations.

VII

Can anyone live without payment? Newman Noggs exemplifies the deformations and compromises to which a ruined gentleman is reduced. It is perhaps the least mad thing Mrs. Nickleby's wooer does to romance her with cucumbers and vegetable marrows: at least he engages in an exchange that potentially nourishes without cashing out. Whether he knows it or not, she has always been materially inclined; indeed, her husband's insolvency was occasioned as much by her greed as by his incompetence. So produce tossed over a garden wall as tangible proof of affection may indeed be a strategic way of soliciting a relationship between materialists while evading the contaminations of pounds, shillings, and pence.

The pre-eminent example of an alternative economy is of course the Cheeryble Brothers. Much was made by Dickens of their real-life prototypes, successful cloth merchants. But he doesn't stress that he met them only once, at a dinner party given in Manchester by a friend of Ainsworth's, Gilbert Winter. And met them on the Tuesday night, November 6, 1838, the same day he heard from Forster of the troubles over the proofs of *Oliver Twist* and told Kate he planned to return to London Thursday. It was, in other words, a potentially charged meeting, in that any hint that Daniel and William Grant might conduct their robust business on something other than hard-nosed commercial practices of the sort Bentley engaged in, could inspire Dickens to elaborate that hint into an entire alternative system of keeping accounts and employees. While the first time Nicholas visits the Brothers' offices he passes through "a warehouse which presented every indication of a thriving business" (pp. 430–31), their bookkeeping seems to consist in writing rather than numbers. In anticipation of his employment, Nicholas spends two weeks "acquiring the mysteries of book-keeping and some other forms of mercantile account" (p. 448). But when it comes to the test, the fastidious bookkeeper Tim Linkinwater extols not Nicholas's double-entry accounts but his penmanship: "His capital B's and D's are exactly like mine; he dots all his small i's and crosses every t as he writes it" (p. 449). (Dickens's unconscious gives himself away here: B for Boz and D for Dickens? Small i's for the minor characters' egos? T's crossed so that false accusations of theft, as well as true ones, can be made legible?) Even after his death, Tim exults, Nicholas's neatness will keep the ledgers just as tidy: "there never were such books ... nor never will be such books – as the books of Cheeryble Brothers" (p. 449). Arthur Gride's "dirty old vellum-book" recording sums lent and owing, by contrast, is his only book, "all true and real ... as its gold and silver. Written by Arthur Gride – he, he, he! None of your story-book writers will ever make as good a book as this, I warrant me. It's composed for private circulation – for my own particular reading, and nobody else's" (p. 660). But in the end Dickens's circulating serials are not more publicly conned than Gride's ledger, and while they are sold, they are not written by a miser or a merchant.

While the brothers seem benevolent and charitable, they operate by participating in a series of financial interventions. Those attempting to rescue Madeline are unsuccessful; her father's death releases her. Those rewarding Nicholas with an occupation and what amounts to a tied house are happier, though patronizing. Those testing their nephew Frank, while manipulative and on occasion apparently unfeeling, prove him worthy of joining the business. And in the end Nicholas and Frank are taken on as partners, while Tim Linkinwater and Miss La Creevy quietly register a different kind of partnership. Nicholas's fortune derives from his wife's inheritance from her maternal grandfather and its investment in the Cheeryble business, not from inheriting through Ralph's intestacy; and Kate's financial comfort is secured by Frank's share in the business. But what that business is, or how anyone living in Dorset can pursue it on a regular basis while enlarging a family and the old homestead, the text doesn't say. The novel does imagine an alternative to payment, but it cannot provide the realistic context for such an alternative except to insist in the paratexts that the Grants do live. So necessary to Dickens's "truth" was their existence, that in the 1867 Charles Dickens edition of the novel he mentions that "those who take an interest in this tale, will be glad to learn that the BROTHERS CHEERYBLE live," and one paragraph further on admits, in a single-sentence paragraph, "The Brothers are now dead."[79] No wonder that Dickens was drawn to fairy godfathers who "grant" wishes without adverse consequences: a cheery ability indeed. They were not a hit with Dickens's contemporaries, however. *Fraser's* called them "unredeemed and irredeemable idiots," "insufferable bores," "such fault-less monsters which the world ne'er saw," and "pot-bellied Sir Charles Grandisons of the ledger and day-book." Whenever they, or Tim, or Frank, appear, the reader should "skip the page with the utmost possible activity."[80]

The latter half of the novel also rewrites Dickens's earlier serials, as if in acknowledgment that he still cannot get the relationship between money and worth right. Ralph Nickleby tells Charles Cheeryble that he "is not an angel yet, to appear in men's houses whether they will or no" (p. 720). So much for the reality of Pickwick as an angel in tights and gaiters dispensing charity and forgiveness and arranging marriages. In Ralph's opinion, such behavior amounts to unwarranted meddling. Newman Noggs tells Ralph a few moments later that he did more work and suffered more hard words "than any man you could have got from the parish workhouse" (p. 726) – a ruined gentleman not an orphan boy reduced to demeaning servitude because of his own earlier profligacy. Shortly thereafter, Squeers declines to have stories told about him without answering back – something Oliver cannot do – and then in a more domestic version of Fagin's maxim, declares that the image of his family "short of vittles" cancels every other consideration: "the only number in all arithmetic that

I know of as a husband and a father is number one" (p. 733).[81] And the romance between Tim Linkinwater and Miss La Creevy prospers through genuine articulation of the mercenary argument Pickwick used so clumsily to Mrs. Bardell and Bumble used so cynically with Mrs. Corney, that two might live as cheaply as one. In this case, it's companionship, not savings, that matters: "why shouldn't we both be married instead of sitting through the long winter evenings by our solitary firesides?" Tim asks. "Why shouldn't we make one fireside of it, and marry each other?" (p. 761). Something has radically altered the economic and charitable calculations of Dickens's prior fictions. As Amanpal Garcha, putting things in a more theoretical perspective, justly formulates the problem: capitalism's destructive force registers on Smike and the other victims of Dotheboys School, while the good characters seem somehow exempt from the industrial impress of the age. The Cheerybles and Nicholas remain, in a sense, in another world and time. "*Nickleby*'s paradoxes," Garcha concludes, "represent, for Dickens and his readers, a simultaneous acknowledgment and mystification of the market's effect on those participating in it."[82]

VIII

Juxtaposing *Nickleby* (1838–39) to Carlyle's *Chartism* – written as an "Article on the working people" in the autumn of 1839, then published as a pamphlet in December – discloses substantial parallels in the two works' analysis of the economic condition of England. Carlyle starts from the assumption that there are two primary forces in British society: an aristocracy whose responsibility is to govern, and a laboring class whose responsibility and freedom lie in work. Reviewing recent history, including falling wages, strikes, demonstrations, rick burning, and other signs of social distress, Carlyle declares that it is time to abandon *laissez-faire* policies and return to governing. He defends the New Poor Law on the grounds that laborers should work, and that no government should make idleness more comfortable than a job. But he recognizes, too, that while in agricultural and feudal communities there was always work to be done, in industrial societies the influx of hundreds of thousands of unemployed men (from Ireland in the late 1830s) drives wages down and, when laborers congregate in urban spaces, they locate where there is little or no work to be had. From these premises Carlyle then identifies what he believes to have disrupted former relations between lords and labor: the "cash nexus."

How much the Upper Classes did actually, in any way the most perfect Feudal time, return to the Under [Classes] by way of recompense, in government, guidance, protection, we will not undertake to specify here ... Yet we do say that the old Aristocracy were the governors of the Lower Classes, the guides of the Lower Classes; and even, at bottom, that they existed as an Aristocracy because they were found adequate for that. Not by Charity-Balls and Soup-Kitchens; not so; far otherwise! But it was their happiness that, in struggling for their own objects, they *had* to govern the Lower Classes, even in this sense of governing.[83]

This ideal sense of feudal relations, of what the aristocracy owed to their tenants and laborers, and where the happiness of each class was located, became one of the tenets of Disraeli's Young England a few years later. At this moment, Carlyle is unable to specify exactly what feudal lords did "by way of recompense, in government, guidance, protection," and it would take a pretty Romantic and ahistorical imagination to suppose that such governance, by lords temporal and spiritual, worked always, or even sometimes, for the larger public good.[84] But, unable at this juncture to define exactly the kind of society coming into being in the industrial age, Carlyle was conscious after completing his three-volume *French Revolution* that older forms of feudal government had failed the people and justified resistance: "These Chartisms, Radicalisms, Reform Bill, Tithe Bill ... are *our* French Revolution: God grant that we, with our better methods, may be able to transact it by argument alone!" (p. 42). Carlyle does shrewdly identify a key force upsetting contemporary political and social affairs:

[i]n one word, *Cash Payment* had not then grown to be the universal sole nexus of man to man; it was something other than money that the high then expected from the low, and could not live without getting from the low. Not as buyer and seller alone, of land or what else it might be, but in many senses still as soldier and captain, as clansman and head, as loyal subject and guiding king, was the low related to the high. With the supreme triumph of Cash, a changed time has entered. (p. 58)

Five years before Friedrich Engels published *The Condition of the Working-Class in England in 1844* (1845), Carlyle memorably articulated the disruption of class interaction engendered by the substitution of one measure of value and relationship, cash, for all the others – loyalty, hierarchical collaboration, kinship and clan fealty – that had once bound persons of greatly different economic circumstance together.

To a limited extent, Carlyle seems to concur with Locke's influential analysis of property, that each person has inalienable property in himself, his body and its products. If "Society 'exists for the protection of property,'" Carlyle reasons, the poor man's property is his labor. The eighth commandment, "Thou shalt not steal," is the essential "definition of the rights of man. *Thou shalt not steal, thou shalt not be stolen from:* what a Society were that; Plato's Republic, More's Utopia mere emblems of it! Give every man what is his, the accurate price of what he has done and been, no man shall any more complain, neither shall the earth suffer any more" (p. 59). Theft then, of kinds Dickens anatomized in *Oliver Twist*, becomes the fundamental inversion of social relations. But Carlyle dematerializes the definition of property: it is, fundamentally, life imbued with Soul.

*Chartism* does not aim to analyze particular conditions, but to articulate the major relationships among social and political bodies and to argue that without a responsible governing class and the opportunity for the laboring classes to work, there must be revolution. For "poor Sanspotatoe peasants [the Irish], Trades-Union craftsmen, Chartist cotton-spinners, the time has come when [*laissez-faire* governance] must either cease or a worse thing straightway begin, – a thing of tinder-boxes, vitriol-bottles, second-hand pistols, a visibly insupportable thing in the eyes of all" (p. 68). One of the cases Carlyle dwells on in exemplifying the need for better laws is that of intellectual property. He acknowledges that "there are so many things which cash will not pay!" And then he instances Johnson, who might have been worthy of higher returns for his literary and lexicographical labors. "Nay is not Society, busy with its Talfourd Copyright Bill and the like, struggling to do something effectual for that man; – enacting with all industry that his own creation be accounted his own manufacture, and continue unstolen, on his own market-stand, for so long as sixty years?" Conditions that render it impossible for impatient writers, "half-made inflammable Rousseaus," to earn a sufficiency, "you may drive too far"; "discrepancies on that side" – that is, an enormous disparity between the value of the work produced by writers and its remuneration – "may become excessive." Society may be right to intervene in the free marketplace and adjust the balance since not simply "supply and demand" but other valuations as well justify giving an author the right to his product, "unstolen, on his own market-stand, for so long as sixty years" (p. 67). That Carlyle chooses to shift the terms of his social contract from feudal to commercial, and specifically to the imbalances between writers and publishers, brings his analysis and critique of the cash nexus right to the heart of print culture.

In closing, Carlyle returns to his theme that radicalism will break out when the governing classes do nothing:

Everywhere, in these countries, in these times, the central fact worthy of all consideration forces itself on us in this shape: the claim of the Free Workingman to be raised to a level, we may say, with the Working Slave; his anger and cureless discontent till that be done. Food, shelter, due guidance, in return for his labour: candidly interpreted, Chartism and all such *isms* mean that. (p. 89)

## IX

The incendiary potential glowing below the surface of contemporary European social relations in Carlyle's analysis seems far removed from the mainly comedic episodes of *Nickleby*. But at some level Nicholas's violence at Dotheboys and on Hawk manifests not just what Dickens – unnecessarily, in my judgment – apologized for in his 1848 preface, that if "Nicholas be not always found to be blameless or agreeable ... He is a young man of an impetuous temper" (p. 9). It might also be read as a manifestation on the local and personal level of the result of the same kind of cruel disparities between masters and men that inflamed the citizens of France in 1789 and that were, not coincidentally, inflaming Europe at the time of the second preface, 1848. Indeed, that Carlyle brings the past and potential social conflagrations erupting between the upper and working classes down to a case deserving remediation, namely, the extension of copyright protection to authors, demonstrates how widely applicable was his mountain-top analysis of the condition of England to life in streets, homes, and commercial houses. When the Royal Shakespeare Company collectively researched the historical context for *Nickleby* prior to David Edgar's writing the adaptation, they concluded that the era Dickens evoked was a period of change, industrialism having "taken nature by the throat and commanded it to bend to its will," while "the old certainties ... were dissolving ... True, the out-moded hierarchies and snobberies were swept away by the winds of change; but something else had gone too: the idea of a social hierarchy which not only granted immeasurable rights to the powerful, but imposed obligations on them too."[85] This analysis could not be more in line with Carlyle's contemporary one.

In other, very recognizable respects, Carlyle's emphasis on the need for working men to find jobs paying at least a minimal wage sufficient to purchase food and housing applies to Nicholas and Kate, who are, however, not victims of *laissez-faire* rulers, but of a manipulative member of the governing classes who does not intend their welfare. That jobs are so much at issue in this novel, for everyone from Newman Noggs to Smike, makes those scenes when Nicholas studies the notices in the window of the Register Office (and through which he meets his future – heiress – wife) not merely another episode in a succession of arbitrary incidents, but a center of the novel's economic analysis.[86] It is, after all, called the General Agency Office as well, and certainly serves as the agent of employment for many persons dependent in the new era of industrial capitalism on work to survive as well as establish or maintain their class status. It also advertises opportunities to invest capital in estates and businesses, and, "in short," placards "opportunities of all sorts for people who wanted to make their fortunes" (p. 427). That Nicholas and Kate seek positions with persons of the governing class who do not govern – Wititterly and Gregsbury – further instances the *laissez-faire* attitude toward political and social responsibility that Carlyle deplores. That greedy, tyrannical, and fraudulent paymasters (Squeers, Ralph, Gride, Hawk) provoke rebellion reinforces the novel's insistence that human relations need to be conducted on different terms than the cash nexus.

There are many instances of those different terms, often ones associated with the "heart" rather than the pocketbook. But, as always, Dickens thinks beyond binaries. Mrs. Nickleby combines a modicum of heart, especially for her children, with a modicum of materiality. It may be that her loquaciousness and digressions mark the inability of narrative so balanced between love and greed to travel to any terminus. Many in *Nickleby*, in life and in the theater, act from mixed motives, whether selling poison unwillingly, stimulating townspeople for the "last" performance of a play, or entertaining a rich uncle. Clearly in this story the "cash nexus" has already, in a multitude of ways, altered the calculus of friendship and mutuality. Carlyle's appeal to an idealized medieval world (however much he cautions that people acted imperfectly then as now) may even be relevant to Dickens's insertion into *Nickleby* of two stories that seem a throwback to *Pickwick*'s intercalated tales and irrelevant to the Nickleby family saga. Set in the rule of Henry IV, "The Five Sisters of York" shows that familial loyalty, abiding love, and handcrafted art can sustain siblings through all the distresses of life better than taking the veil, marrying, or competing for advancement at court. "There are shades in all good pictures," observes the merriest of the travelers listening to this narrative, "but there are lights too, if we choose to contemplate them" (p. 77). This gentleman then proceeds to amuse the company with "The Baron of Grogzwig." Also set in a feudal era, the Baron and his retainers live a "merry life" until he marries, fathers thirteen children, and succumbs to the rule of a wife who cleans up his act to such an extent that in middle age "he had no feasting, no revelry, no hunting train, and no hunting – nothing in short that he liked, or used to have" (p. 81). He also discovers that he is broke. To that calamity his initial response is to commit suicide. But after a conversation with the Genius of Despair and Suicide, who inadvertently loses a victim by asserting that a man killing himself because he has too much money is "no better than a man's killing himself because he has got none or little" (p. 84), the Baron decides to rectify his life, and once having made up his mind to common sense, he quickly brings his wife and in-laws "to reason," enjoys in moderation his pleasures (a swig of grog among them), and dies, "not a rich man ... but certainly a happy one" (p. 85). In different ways, and in generic keys contrasting to the mercenary scenes Nicholas is about to meet at Dotheboys Hall, these interludes show societies sustained by relationships unmediated and undetermined by the cash nexus. Seen in the light shed by Carlyle's analysis of the condition of England, the miscellaneous elements of *Nickleby* seem much more artistically and relevantly related.

x

Neither Dickens nor Carlyle yet understood what Engels glimpsed, and Marx thirty years after *Nickleby* analyzed, capitalism, and its economics of alienated labor and irresponsible capital. Unable to imagine a fully credible benevolent yet successful London commercial enterprise, Dickens offers the Cheerybles. Their business is unsubstanialized, translated to a kind of financial writing, and their benefactions are paternalistic and unevenly effective. But another way of characterizing them points to a strength rather than weakness in Dickens's imagination: their commerce is symbolic as much as tangible. That money is a sign, not necessarily a substance, is demonstrated in the second chapter. The floating of stock in the United Metropolitan Improved Hot Muffin and Crumpet Baking and Punctual Delivery Company does not really participate in the cash nexus. The point of the rally isn't to sell muffins or stock per se; it is to create an illusion of prosperity and future gains that will allow the privileged current stockholders to sell their shares, regardless of whether the enterprise for which real cash was paid for shares ever makes a profit or feeds the hungry. That the resolutions to restrict competition – not *laissez-faire* economics but its opposite, monopolistic capitalism – are roundly seconded by an Irish and a Scots MP indicts Carlyle's governing class both with imposing unfavorable market conditions for the sale of bread (an oblique allusion to the Corn Laws?) and with rigging conditions within metropolitan England from outside. Ralph and his fellow investors understand that whipping up enthusiasm for an as-yet undelivered product is better than actually making anything material: he "whispered to his friend that the shares were thenceforth at a premium of five-and-twenty percent" (p. 30). With this incident in the second chapter, following the narrative of the disastrous speculations of Ralph's brother and sister-in-law leading to death and the sale of their landed possessions, the novel commences not only by establishing the economic terms of a cash economy, but also by pressing those terms further, to the realm of the insubstantial, shares whose value relates only to demand, not to anything substantive.[87] (The rest of the novel insistently stresses "bread," the insufficiency of which, in Yorkshire or London, causes real misery, whether the substance be food or its slang synonym, cash.) The insight that value in a cash economy can be determined by manipulating public sentiment rather than manufacturing a product, that it may be even more remunerative to sell an illusion than an actuality, is then reinforced time and again: by Squeers's advertisements, by Miss La Creevy's miniatures, by Ralph's pimping of Kate's beauty, by assumptions of class privilege asserted especially by Hawk and Verisopht, even by the fiction that one owns, and can sell, a son, something in which Ralph, Snawley, and Squeers trade. In short, Dickens's novel seems to see that cash itself, while necessary to living – to lodging, eating, and clothing oneself – is not equivalent in value to the thing it purchases. Illusions, fictions, may yield more profit than half-pints of watered milk or French lessons or dresses. It is not always a bad thing to trade in illusions, but it is very bad and often ruinously expensive to confuse illusion with reality.

## XI

Which observation takes us back to Dickens's own situation as an author making a living writing fictions that he defends, as he strenuously defends his depiction of Nancy in *Oliver Twist*, as "true." For he seems to do something very like what he most vehemently reprehends: steal another's possession, his life, and make it his own. That theft takes place in the paratexts, the same location that he insisted on altering in November 1838 for *Oliver*'s three volumes.[88] The wrapper design of *Nickleby*'s monthly parts declares that this print product is *The | Life and Adventures | of | Nicholas Nickleby | containing | a faithful account of the | Fortunes, Misfortunes, Uprisings, Downfallings, | and | complete career of the Nickleby family | Edited by "Boz." With illustrations | by "Phiz."* It is impossible to reproduce the typographical design of this text. Note that the title of the novel does not have an end stop until after "Edited by 'Boz'." That seems to imply that the "Life" and its editing by Boz are parts of the same whole. Browne's plates are mentioned afterwards in a phrase that has no syntactical connection to the preceding clauses, though the "with" with which it starts expresses the sense that the illustrations accompany the text; and in the wrapper, they surround, and through typography even declare, the novel's title.[89] The first page of the first shilling part simplifies the title to "Life and Adventures of Nicholas Nickleby, Chapter I," and the succeeding parts skip even that abbreviated title, beginning simply with the chapter number. When the parts are bound into the first one-volume edition, the half title and title adopt the simplified *Life and Adventures of Nicholas Nickleby.* There is a full stop at the end of that title. Then centered and encased in rules some lines below, in small caps, "BY CHARLES DICKENS." – not "Edited by 'Boz'" as all the wrappers declare. Another full stop. Followed by, in smaller caps and no rules, "WITH ILLUSTRATIONS BY PHIZ" – Phiz not in quotation marks, and not followed by a full stop.

Now printing house practices varied from book to book, even within books, and these title pages were set and printed quickly, both to be bound in as part of the sixty-four pages of the final double number and to be supplied to the book-binding trade when customers wanted their shilling numbers reorganized and encased in boards or leather. We have seen with Forster's instructions to Bentley about the title page for the second issue of *Oliver* that even though Dickens wanted his name substituted for Boz, Bentley took other liberties with the title page paratexts to which neither Dickens nor Forster objected. So we shouldn't make too much of all these typographical niceties – except to notice them and to credit them with articulating in type what the compositors, author, publisher, and publisher's advisor (Forster) thought represented the case by October 1839. This was a book by Dickens, though in serial form it declared itself a Life and Adventures edited by Boz. With illustrations.

Not, one might think, a big deal. The editorial Boz and the authorial Dickens had been vying for primacy now for at least three years. Yet the situation in this case is rather different from that in *Pickwick*, papers declaratively edited by "Boz" in paratexts, advertisements, and reviews, though not on the title page of the first volume issue. This book purports to be the story of Nicholas Nickleby's life, indeed, according to the wrapper, the story of the "complete career of the Nickleby family." Such stories were often produced and sold as memoirs, such as Grimaldi's, and edited by some competent writer not affiliated with the writer of the memoir. If this text records the Nickleby family history, why should Dickens rather than a Nickleby be the author? Why shouldn't Boz remain in his rightful place, in the volume title page, as the editor each green wrapper proclaimed he was?

What would readers have imagined the relationship among Nickleby, Boz, and Dickens to be? As we saw in the case of a fellow author, Moncrieff, he was moved to refute charges made by Nicholas, a fiction, to another author, also fictional, and to bring Dickens (and inferentially Boz) into the conversation as well. If "Mr. Johnson," Nicholas's playwright pseudonym, is John's son, and Boz is Dickens's self, pseudonym, and son, then the ontological distinction between real person, writer, editor, and biographical subject gets effectively erased. This does not seem to have bothered anyone much. It demonstrates the way Victorian readers read and how even Dickens presented himself sometimes. For instance, writing to the sculptor William Behnes in June 1839 about making an appointment for him to come down to Elm Cottage, Petersham, which Dickens had taken for the summer, he fashions a mock advertisement for a lost animal:

A remarkable Dog
answering to the name of
BOZ.
He had on at the time a white collar, marked with the initials "C.D."[90]

In this instance, and for a portraitist to boot, Boz is a dog sporting a dog collar marked with Dickens's initials.

If narratives seemed "real" to Victorian artists and readers, it was partly because the gap between text and life hardly existed. As far back as the pages of the *Morning Chronicle*, when "Sketches of Our Parish" stood on the same page, in the same type, for a statistical count of Irish church attendance and one of Dickens's early sketches of "Our Parish," novels were news and news might be fiction. The distinctions we seek to make today beleaguer our brains and probably for most readers do not exist. Books tell us about life; they are true, even when the writer of a biography of the Nickleby family isn't a Nickleby, and the editor of the Nickleby story hasn't the same name as the person depicted in the frontispiece.

So what Dickens did in having the title page identify him as the author has more to do with his increasing attention to establishing that identity than it does with stealing the text from Nicholas or Boz – though to some degree it does a bit of that too. A larger deviation from accepted practices comes with the frontispiece, not, despite the title page, one of Browne's illustrations. For the frontispiece of *Pickwick* he had designed a fine complex image: theatrical curtains parted by imps of comedy and tragedy to reveal Pickwick and Sam at a library reading table before a bookcase surmounted by a shield, helmet, and sword evocative of Don Quixote and Sancho Panza. This image brilliantly incorporates the multiple levels of the novel's fictional ontology: its forebear by Cervantes; its application of the dangers of believing what one reads, that addled the Don's brain, to Mr. Pickwick; its overt recognition of the bookness of the book, in a library, being read, but being depicted visually in an appendage to that text; and the whole being revealed as a theatrical scene by fantastic characters representing – what? The author's, editor's, or reader's imagination? The genre of melodrama or picaresque fiction? Serialized texts, whose covers are opened monthly to disclose another installment of scenes and characters? There's no need to pin any of this down. More important is to recognize that, in 1836–37, author and illustrator were very well aware of the complexities of the novel's ontology and epistemology. They could play with those overlapping entities. They didn't see them as "problems" but as amusing resonant associations to be explored, exploited, foregrounded, reinscribed in words and pictures, and taken in by readers who could mix them up with their own lives, reading, and experience.

However, it is likely that middle-class readers who purchased volumes of "Life and Adventures," replaced by the soberer and more ontologically "truthful" "Life and Letters" biographies of mid-century and after, expected that a frontispiece would depict the subject of the volume, as, for all the playful additions, the frontispiece of *Pickwick* gives another glimpse of Sam and Pickwick in retirement. Instead, Chapman and Hall went to great lengths to supply something quite different. They commissioned an oil portrait from Daniel Maclise, a young Irish painter who was rapidly becoming another of Dickens's favorite companions (not a "retainer," such as the Baron has, but enjoying some of the benefits of clan affiliation, as so many of Dickens's friends did). Now this was a considerable extra expense, though the novel was earning a fortune for the publishers. There were, as we have seen, several portraits that could have served, one of which, of "Boz," had been lithographed and widely distributed. It didn't appeal to Dickens or members of his family; but the other Laurence portrait might have been reproduced, and it did appeal to the author and his relations. Yet the decision was made to commission a new portrait, for which Dickens agreed to sit. Once more, and in a different medium, the publishers introduced the author to his audience.[91]

We don't know who said what about this commission, but we can see the result. It is a painting Chapman and Hall presented to Dickens at the banquet celebrating the novel's conclusion that belongs to the Tate and is on loan to the National Portrait Gallery. It was not intended to be reproduced except in an engraving offered as the frontispiece to *Nickleby* and for sale separately. It is not Boz, but Charles Dickens.[92] That of course raises its own problems. His exceptionally mobile face seemed, according to Leigh Hunt, to have "the life and soul in it of fifty human beings," and we know that at least six contemporary renderings differed significantly in representing him. Yet, Jane Carlyle quipped, he also seemed "made of steel."[93] He was slight in stature, nothing like as impressive a body as John Brodie's. A seated rather than standing pose, with no adjacent object that might provide a scale diminishing him, was called for. In his early Boz days, while a reporter, Dickens's wardrobe was according to visitors to Furnival's Inn shabby and limited. Though as he progressed in his career he complained often about the cost of fitting up dwellings, he must have spent some money with tailors and bootmakers, even if on credit (the usual practice, especially among the upper classes). He gained a reputation as something of a dandy, not in the league of Ainsworth or D'Orsay, but one who sported "a swallow-tail coat with a very high velvet collar; a voluminous satin stock with a double breast-pin; a crimson velvet waistcoat, over which meandered a lengthy gold chain; beneath the crimson vest one or sometimes two under-waistcoats; [and] 'Cossack' trowsers for morning dress."[94] The clothing chosen for Maclise's portrait is conservative: a dark brown coat, black in the shadows, with large lapels, dark green trousers, two under-waistcoats, and a dark grey satin stock secured by the "double breast-pin" and chain. Dickens's neck-length curly hair frames a wide forehead (still a sign of intellect for physiognomists), dark straight eyebrows, bright eyes looking left to something outside the picture frame (another person, an idea or Muse?), a long straight nose and full, shapely lips. His chin is adequate, but not prominent or squared to any degree. (Prognathous jaws were to become markers of Irish genes and devolution back toward apes in subsequent decades.)[95] He sits on an elaborately carved gilded chair upholstered with an embroidered red fabric.

The oval shape of William Finden's engraving cuts off significant details. As in Maclise's portrait, Dickens sits in an upholstered armchair half turned to the right of the picture plane; his body twists in the opposite direction. His right arm rests on the chair's arm, and his white right hand with curled fingers, as if he were about to grasp a pen, stands out against his coat's dark fabric. Less successfully, in Finden's engraving his left arm simply scoots off beyond the frame. Maclise has it possessively and authoritatively poised above thin printed sheets (a monthly part?) on a writing desk, with a quill pen beside them and five leather-bound books (decidedly not cheap paper publications) resting on the desk at the rear. But Finden's frontispiece eliminates those objects that domesticated and professionalized Maclise's setting. George Henry Lewes makes a patronizing comment on Dickens's Doughty Street library in an 1872 memorial: "A man's library expresses much of his hidden life," he says, and Dickens's bookshelves held "nothing but three-volume novels and books of travel, all obviously the presentation copies from authors and publishers, with none of the treasures of the bookstall, each of which has its history, and all giving the collection its individual physiognomy."[96] Well, the books of Dickens's childhood had probably been pawned years before, and perhaps those he now treasured were stored elsewhere in the house. In any case, no bookshelves appear in either the painting or the engraving, and no books at all are displayed in the frontispiece to the *Nickleby* text.

So here is Dickens, not Nickleby.[97] Not a hot-headed boy of nineteen, not an idealized self-portrait of Dickens as a young man protecting his sister Fanny, nor the sober businessman of middle years with a Devon estate and large family. In this frontispiece we see Dickens unconnected to any other person, or even to writing or books. As Kathryn Chittick remarks, "that Dickens was now no longer advertised as Boz but actually had his portrait as the frontispiece to the volume publication [*sic*] of *Nickleby* gives some idea of how far the cult of a Dickensian personality or sensibility had gone."[98] He seems a comfortably off middle-class chap, but we don't know anything about his surroundings besides the heavy drapes and the nearly baroque chair (which, had he been Miss La Creevy's client and impecunious, he might have hired for the sitting). Paradoxically, that says a lot. Nothing about this frontispiece speaks to Dickens's earning a living by his pen, working as a reporter or playwright, or associating with friends as raffish as some of his Garrick Club cronies or as upwardly mobile and respectable as his fellow Athenaeum initiates. He's not associated with publishing, serials, newspapers, scribbled manuscripts, farces, burlesques, operettas, or any political cause. At one and the same time, the portrait drains him of specific affiliations and makes his body available to the public as a young man of breeding and status.

There is even more to this image. This picture of Dickens's face and body is the first time he *in propria persona* offers an uncaricatured image of himself – not Boz – to the public; it becomes his imprimatur. Later writers, Ainsworth among the first, imitate the pose and setting as resonant of authorship. Since *Nickleby*, as I read it, has much to do with commerce, with money and value, it might not stretch interpretation too far to mention that for centuries monarchs had been very concerned with their images on the currency of the realm. Especially as, over time, while the coinage continued to be stamped with the ruler's image as signifier of authenticity and value, the value of the metal within the coin decreased, to the point at which the coin was only symbolically worth its stamped value, and paper bills promising they could be exchanged for the stated equivalent in metal became promissory notes backed by faith, not gold and silver. By the nineteenth century, much banking was done through paper instruments that purported to guarantee their face value, but which were discounted for much less, as Bentley's payments to Dickens were. Likewise, Dickens's green numbers nominally cost, and were worth new, retail, a shilling apiece; but the publisher sold them to wholesalers and retailers for quantity discounts (e.g., thirteen as twelve at some discount on the shilling); and as the century progressed publishers issued cheaper editions sooner and sooner after the first edition, so that the value of a book might decline steeply from 31*s*. 6*d*. for a three-decker to 5*s*. for the same text in a one-volume reprint. Like shares in the Muffin Company, public demand might hold or elevate the price of a promissory note or a text, but different buyers could go into the marketplace and get all kinds of commodities, including printed materials, at various prices.

Dickens knew this all too well, having seen cheaper imitations of his books grabbed up by customers who didn't care about the alphabetic distinctions between Boz and Bos. Part of his effort in 1838–39 was to establish his own identity in his own name, suture it to his own face and body, and *guarantee the value* of the product bearing his name. Of course he was anxious, and sometimes may seem a bit overbearing, in his quest for payment for services rendered in whatever form his writing took. But he also cared deeply that his customers got full measure for their money – and full measure calculated in more than simply monetary terms. He and his publishers had to explain that the expense of reproducing the *Sketches* in serial meant that it came out monthly in twenty-four rather than thirty-two pages, but they hastened to assure buyers that the parts were worth it. With a couple of exceptions, over thirty-six years Dickens always produced copy to the last line of the last page or column. And so this frontispiece portrait in some ways stands as his personal guarantee of value. He may not be a monarch, he may not control the Treasury or regulate the discounts on par as government, bankers, and stockbrokers try to do, but he does stand behind his product and its worth, even if that product is, allegedly, the life of someone else. In this case, Dickens comes out from behind Mr. Johnson, Nicholas, and Boz, none of whom has the same fundamental commitment to supplying value for money.

XII

However, the frontispiece speaks obliquely. Despite being a guarantee of value, the Finden engraving is as divorced from the marketplace as possible. It doesn't say, the book is sold with the full faith and credit of the state, printer, or publisher. It is not one of those Phiz illustrations "with" the text. It conceals whatever "theft" has taken place as Dickens steals Nicholas's and Boz's writing for his own. And it translates the commercial implications still indicated by small print stating that the plate can be purchased separately into another register altogether.[99] The plate is signed – and signatures as we know from within the novel and without are crucial proofs (real or forged) of authenticity. It is also inscribed: "Faithfully yours." To whom and in what terms Charles Dickens is faithful, and to what extent "yours" alludes to his being in thrall to his public for acceptance and completion of the purchase and reading transactions, isn't spelled out.[100] For this argument what is important is the shift from the vocabulary of the cash nexus (1s. per part, 2s. for the final double number, 20s. for the set of parts, 21s. and up for bound copies) to a vocabulary drawn from earlier sets of relationship, to God and to other human beings, "faithfully." It would be Smike's favored term, but Dickens casts himself in a much less dependent relationship. This "faithfully yours" is a professional and personal promise that the author Charles Dickens will maintain the value of his developing relationship with an expanding public, now extending to North America and Europe.

   John O. Jordan has brilliantly dilated on Dickens's deployment of "faithfully."[101] Dickens first uses it in a complementary close to the note he writes to Chapman and Hall on February 18, 1836 informing them that "Pickwick is at length begun in all his might and glory."[102] "From the beginning, then," Jordan points out, "'faithfully yours' carries a commercial and specifically contractual meaning" (p. 3). But thereafter Dickens uses it increasingly as the close to every kind of letter, from business to social correspondence. And the third sentence of his "Personal" address at the opening of *Household Words* for June 12, 1858, declares that he has, throughout the quarter-century of his publishing lifetime, "tried to be as faithful to the Public, as they have been to me."

Moreover, of the four principal implications of "faithful," the notion of being full of faith is the one Dickens tends to subordinate to more secular commitments: firm in adherence to promises be they contractual or personal; loyalty and service of the sort Smike promises to and performs for Nickleby; and truthful, as in a "faithful" story. Faithful, Jordan reminds us, is a strong Protestant virtue, represented in *Pilgrim's Progress* by the hero's traveling companion Faithful. All these senses of the word resonate within Dickens's usage, especially in the context of this frontispiece portrait that is itself a true image (*pace* George Eliot) of the body of the author who signs his christened name and promises loyally to fulfill his commitments to stories, publishers, and readers.

There is one final implication, I believe, to this portrait of a bourgeois subject. Unlike, say, Hogarth's portrait of Thomas Coram, housed just a few squares from Doughty Street, nothing in this engraved frontispiece, as opposed to Maclise's painting, speaks to how Dickens makes money.[103] For this is the trickiest part of dealing in the marketplace and being "faithfully yours" simultaneously. And not only because the value in the marketplace of any Dickens product fluctuates. Even more importantly because, at least as a gentleman was understood in earlier times, gentlemen don't work for a living. As I mentioned earlier, Newman Nogg's history is absolutely crucial to *Nickleby*: it enacts all the troubles caused by the collision between older, post-feudal notions of what the ruling classes ought to do and be, and the rising industrial-based wealthy who valued work and amassed fortunes allowing them to buy into the landed gentry. Even if impecunious, a gentleman ought to be honest and loyal, behaviors incompatible with one another when serving Ralph Nickleby. That Newman chooses unemployment and honesty (an honesty that involves spying and stealing, but on the "right side") shows that as far as character is concerned, he still has class. No wonder he is goggle-eyed: he has to keep the past and the present in sight simultaneously.

Dickens was not alone, or uniquely self-interested, in wrestling with these complex and contradictory formations of authorship's class status. Chris R. Vanden Bossche has discerningly narrated the debates, beginning at the time of *Nickleby* in 1838 and continuing through 1842, over Talfourd's Copyright Bill. Opponents of copyright analogized access to knowledge to access to commodities (and the raging controversy over the Corn Laws); they advocated free trade and public benefit and characterized authors as no more than other laborers. Robert Mudie declared that "what the author of [a] book does is really nothing but labour ... consequently, he can claim his reward only as a labourer."[104] Longman and Co. held that view: "The projector and publisher of an encyclopedia, a review, or other literary works supplied by numerous individuals, should be looked upon in the same light as a contractor who purchases contributions for any great work in architecture, civil engineering &c."[105] As editor or proprietor of a miscellaneous journal authored by many hands, Dickens was in this view merely a hired hand, deserving payment for work done but no further remuneration from sales.

Proponents countered that imaginative literature developed the character of the nation, rather than simply producing evanescent knowledge soon superseded by newer inventions and patents. Authors were not simply slaves to an industrial machine (such as Darnton's "communications circuit") funded by publishers and dedicated to churning out printed copy on demand. They invented new and whole works, not collages of existing knowledge such as encyclopedias and abridgements, and those wholes, while requiring time to be digested by a reading public, remained integral and complete, unamenable to modification. Thus authorial labor produced a unique property that should be conserved and handed down to succeeding generations of the author's family, as a kind of patrimony or landed estate. (Scott effectively turned his copyrights into an estate, that as we have seen he was unwilling to forfeit when his publishing ventures failed.) Furthermore, the public interest cultivated by literature in particular was portrayed as embodying a moral code that could bind the nation together. Dickens felt strongly, all his life, that literature should, and his did, serve this end. Thus a proponent of extending copyright tended to hold two conflicting views of consumers: on the one hand they were hungry for the cheap and potentially immoral amusements which curtailing the length of copyright would produce, and on the other audiences should be led by moral literature to higher ideals and a national culture. The quarrel over the influence of Newgate fiction illustrates and reinforces the extensive arguments about the social effects of reading that raged in Parliament and pamphlets, among publishers, printers, authors, and advocates of inexpensive education for the working class.

In sum, as Vanden Bossche ably formulates it,

What the copyright debate makes clear is that the desire to distance the author from the marketplace was not simply a desire to make authorship genteel or a conservative impulse to remove literature from the processes of history into an idealized realm; it was also a means of managing authors' necessary engagement in commerce by attempting to give them a disinterested moral vantage point. Correlatively, the Victorian emphasis on the social responsibilities of the author was not simply a reaction to the excesses of Romantic egoism, but rather a means to establish the value of the literary author.

In this light, we can see why the making of the Victorian author takes the form of moral training as much as it does of aesthetic education.[106]

Dickens's critique of the cash nexus, his panorama of ways in which families were being put into commercial circulation, and the ambiguity of his own status as editor and author, writer of immoral Newgate fictions that he regarded as true and useful to society, profiter if not profiteerer from the commercial success of his writings, and laborer producing works beneficial to the nation – all these issues implicit in the production of *Nickleby* reflect, comment on, enlarge, and reformulate the concurrent debates about the value of "the literary author."

   One of Dickens's later friends, T. J. Thompson, inherited his grand-father's large fortune derived from West Indian plantations (and thus from slave labor), but only on condition that he did not adopt a profession – which meant in practice that he didn't go to work.[107] (Being a gentleman and a slave owner were not contradictions; the income was generated by live property working the estate.) It was still uncertain in the 1830s to what degree one could rise socially while occupied in a profession. Writers were unlikely to achieve such status, though as we have seen a few did. But if working were a bar to some kinds of gentlemanly class, working faithfully, giving full value for money received, working to tell truth to power and to serve the public's interests: that essentially protestant bourgeois work might make the laborer worthy of his hire and the kind of companion one would wish for on the journey through books and life. And it is that kind of work, both obscured and in other ways advertised by his *Nickleby* frontispiece, that Dickens signed himself "faithfully" to perform. This was another stage in his transformation from a shorthand reporter to a globally honored author. And it didn't last.

# CHAPTER 6

# *Rewriting Boz (1839–1841):* Master Humphrey's Clock *and* The Old Curiosity Shop

"Boz," Samuel Laurence drawing, 1838

The *Sketches*, *Pickwick*, and *Oliver Twist* ... are the only works in which that native force of Mr Dickens' genius has not been weakened by that mixture of the artificial with the natural which ... has made his subsequent works ... to be in the main and on the whole worse than they. These we will call the works of "Boz." By the works of "Dickens" we mean all those written since *Nicholas Nickleby* ... and the world is disappointed.

    – *Parker's London Magazine*, February 1845

[B]iographical renown eventually catches up with literary renown or surrounds it like a halo.

    – Gérard Genette, *Paratexts*

Authorship has become a profession, and like other trades it is greatly overcrowded.

    – *Monthly Review*, December 1839

Bah! what figments these novelists tell us! Boz, who knows life well, knows that his Miss Nancy is the most unreal fantastical personage possible ... He dare not tell the truth concerning such young ladies.

    – William Makepeace Thackeray, *Fraser's Magazine*, August 1840

Alternately void and fiction without ever emerging as cognitive event, death in the novel transforms human enigma to a paradigm of narrativity.

    – Garrett Stewart, *Death Sentences*

## I

In the early months of 1839, Dickens tried to clear his desk and his commitments. Frustrated at not being able to stop Bentley's advertising *Barnaby Rudge* as "forthcoming," he also seems to have felt an obligation to try to fulfill the Agreement. Since *Oliver Twist* was finished and the final chapters were running as his "Original Article" in the January through April 1839 issues of *Bentley's Miscellany*, Dickens had only *Nickleby* as a continuing serial to compose monthly. Thus early on January 4, he told Forster he had "begun" *Barnaby*. "I wrote four slips last night." But then Ferdinand Pickering, painter of literary subjects and a portraitist, was scheduled to disrupt Dickens's morning with a sitting, so he could "do little or nothing 'till evening ... However, the beginning is made, and – which is more – I can go on, so I hope the book is in training at last."[1] Since *Rudge* had first been promised to Macrone by November 30, 1836, it seems odd that Dickens has only now, three months before publication is scheduled to begin, written anything of the novel. We'll look at the consequences of *Rudge*'s long gestation later on. But note now that Dickens has started, and thinks he can go on – on with a story that seems to have nothing to do with the 1780 Gordon riots in London, but instead opens in the parlor of a country inn five years earlier. As these pages must have been written to set up the Haredale mystery plot, which itself involves questions of lineage and descent, they are distant cousins of the openings of *Oliver* and *Nickleby* in that all three begin their stories *in medias res* with a concealed back story about family secrets that will serve as the structural backbone of the whole narrative. Thus Dickens must have had much of the history of the Warren and of the Rudge family already in mind, along with Hugh and his obscured paternity. Steven Marcus says the novel "contemplates only one kind of personal relation – that of father and son."[2] But how these Oedipal beginnings merge with a violent anti-Catholic uprising may not yet have been fully worked out in Dickens's mind.

A couple of weeks later Dickens stopped writing *Barnaby*. Surviving letters do not indicate what so violently turned him against Bentley. On January 9th Dickens writes in his editorial Boz capacity a perfectly cordial note to New Burlington Street making an appointment for the next day "to arrange the Miscellany."[3] Two days later he set off with Ainsworth for Manchester. On his return, Dickens told Forster that he couldn't go on with *Rudge*. Forster insisted that Dickens had a responsibility to live up to the terms of his Agreement. In fact, Forster had told Bentley and his lawyer, Follett, that he "pledged himself ... to see [Dickens's] last agreement ... executed and carried out."[4] Perhaps during the Manchester journey Ainsworth sympathized with Dickens's frustrations, for a few months later Dickens reminds Ainsworth that when "you pressed upon me the hardship of my relations with that noblest work of God, in New Burlington Street," Forster said "he could not and would not be any party to a new disruption between us – *that he was bound to see the old agreement performed*."[5] Then Forster wrote to Bentley warning him that Dickens was dissatisfied, and told Dickens clearly that he was in the wrong.

But Dickens rebelled, penning a letter to Bentley announcing that "for six months *Barnaby Rudge* stands over."[6] "And but for you," he informed Forster, "it should stand over altogether." Why had Dickens changed his mind? Why could he no longer "get on like a house on fire," as he felt he could earlier in the month? The reason he offers to Forster is that he received a "paltry, wretched, miserable sum" for *Oliver*. In fact, he got at least £340 for the *Miscellany* installments, another £500 upon completion of the manuscript, and half-profits and copyright after three years – less than the £2,000 Chapman and Hall paid for *Pickwick* and the £150 per monthly installment and a five-year lease on copyright they were paying for *Nickleby*, but not an inconsiderable sum for material appearing first in a monthly magazine and then repackaged in three volumes, though half the length of the twenty-part serials. Dickens thought his remuneration for *Oliver* "not equal to what is every day paid for a novel that sells fifteen hundred copies at most." However, most three-deckers didn't sell but 500 copies or so, and if the publisher paid for copyright in advance he took all the risk that the title would sell any copies. Furthermore, since *Oliver* had already run in a half-crown monthly for nineteen months, and would finish up there in another five, it would be hard to predict which tranche of readers might choose to purchase the three volumes – those who wanted the novel in a more coherent and permanent form, or new customers.

Besides, Dickens's anger is in some ways contradictory. Part of him wanted to be insulated from the sheer penny-a-line calculations of value for his writing, and yet at this moment his sense of injury because not sufficiently rewarded pains him so much he cannot go on:

the consciousness that I have still the slavery and drudgery of another work on the same journeyman-terms; the consciousness that my books are enriching everybody connected with them but myself, and that I, with such a popularity as I have acquired, am struggling in old toils, and wasting my energies in the very height and freshness of my fame, and the best part of my life, to fill the pockets of others, while for those who are nearest and dearest to me I can realise little more than a genteel subsistence: all this puts me out of heart and spirits.[7]

Forster surely understood the exaggerations in this letter, even if he did not believe them to justify breaking the Agreement. Dickens had not "journeyman-terms" from either Bentley or Chapman and Hall; he was one of the best-paid writers in the world, already. He had certainly achieved for his family "more than a genteel subsistence": his income was enabling him to rise rapidly into the upper-middle classes. Granted that Doughty Street was getting crowded – a third child, Kate Macready, would be born in October of 1839 – and that his parents were proving difficult once more. He would try to remove them to the West Country in March, to get them out of London and his daily life.[8]

Still, the boiling frustration he expresses in this letter voices an author who feels infuriatingly unrewarded by his labor. (That Bentley was a tight wad compared to Chapman and Hall contributes not a little to Dickens's wrath.) "I do most solemnly declare," he goes on to Forster, "that morally, before God and man, I hold myself released from such hard bargains as these, after I have done so much for those who drove them. This net that has been wound about me so chafes me, so exasperates and irritates my mind, that to break it at whatever cost – *that* I should care nothing for – is my constant impulse." Dickens shifts the grounds of his complaint from money ("*that* I should care nothing for") to equity, and uses one of the figures hovering in the etymology of *plagiarism*, the *plaga* or net used by gladiators, to cast himself as a combatant urgent to break free. How many publishers and agents of how many authors, from Dickens's day to ours, have heard their clients protest in similar accents that their writing enriches everyone but themselves? Dickens, as he realizes, hasn't a lot of room to maneuver. For though he should care nothing about money, he does; he wants to maintain his family at more than a subsistence level; and he can't do so without an income, which he can only earn when writing or editing. (By now it had become evident that the stage would not provide him with an alternative livelihood.)

So he resorts to the only alternative he knows, one he's tried with some success previously: requesting a delay of six months on starting *Barnaby*. This, he declares, is "very common in all literary agreements." Writers had from time immemorial been tardy with delivering their manuscripts, but there's no evidence that it was common in literary agreements of the 1830s to allow for substantial deviations from the stipulated delivery date. (Perhaps Dickens was thinking of *Pic Nic Papers*, which Colburn was slow to publish, possibly because the volunteer contributors weren't meeting their deadlines.) In any case, at the heart of Dickens's feeling was the need for space and time to heal from the fatigue of overwork: he wanted "time to breathe" and some "cheerful" summer days in the country that would restore him "to a more genial and composed state of feeling." The psychology of his situation, trapped, enslaved, ill rewarded, had – temporarily he believed – dried up his pen and ink.[9]

It's an understandable condition. That Dickens, seemingly so unprecedentedly successful, acclaimed by the public and reviewers and the governing classes and readers of all kinds, should feel as if he had hit the wall and could not write anything further, is, however, something of a surprise. When he writes the history of *Barnaby*'s composition in 1841 and in the Preface to the Cheap Edition of 1849, Dickens says nothing about this breakdown. He speaks only about the historicity of his account of the riots, citing published references, and in 1849 begins his account with stories about his own ravens, occasioned by the remarkable performance of Barnaby's Grip. These prefaces are the least forthcoming about the origin, progress, and reception of the novel of any he had composed to date. That silence is another indication that Dickens did not want to put himself before the public as an author whose works were influenced by monetary considerations. Or, since he does sometimes crow about how extensively he has been received by the public, Dickens doesn't want to tell about instances where he felt underpaid and abused by his publishers.

Perhaps some other events occurring during the Manchester visit fueled Dickens's wrath. Forster mentions that at this time (1838–39) Ainsworth was an "especially welcome" friend "who shared with us [Dickens and Forster] incessantly for the three following years in the companionship which began at his house" Kensal Lodge.[10] Ainsworth, at the height of his popularity and with no extensive family to support, enjoyed a luxurious and socially glamorous life that must have seemed vividly attractive to Dickens, though beyond his own reach. Did Ainsworth's circulation among the glitterati at Holland House and elsewhere stir up Dickens's resentment about his lesser standing, provoking the complaint that he could provide "little more than a genteel subsistence" for his own family? On Ainsworth's part at this time, there seems to have been no jealousy. When his hometown gave a dinner to honor him, he invited Dickens along. While Dickens's surviving correspondence gives no information about the trip, Ainsworth got the impression that the celebrated guest at the forthcoming dinner had shifted from himself to his friend. "[I]n respect of the public dinner," he wrote to his old law associate and bibliophile James Crossley, "[i]s it to be given to me or Dickens – or to both? Acting upon your former letter, I invited my friend to accompany *me*, imagining the dinner was to be given in my honour; but I have no feeling whatever in the matter, and only desire to have a distinct understanding about it."[11] The visit must have gone off splendidly, further deepening the affection between the two literary lions.[12] But the underlying rivalry and the uncertainty about who was really being honored roiled the waters below the surface. Soon enough a tsunami would erupt.

Forster dutifully carried Dickens's letter to Bentley's office. He "saw Mr. Bentley for a full hour, in his own rooms (a man must be in earnest to do that)" Dickens told Ainsworth. Forster read Dickens's letter aloud and "strongly urged upon [Bentley] the necessity and propriety of some concession." (This is Dickens's account, defending his break to Ainsworth; probably Forster said something like "Dickens is in a rage. You're going to have to mollify him somehow." The "necessity" Forster doubtless stressed, but since he himself didn't believe in the "propriety" of Dickens's request he more likely urged the "prudence" of some concession.) Bentley thanked Forster and arranged for a further conversation. And then, instead of seeing Forster, Bentley wrote directly to Dickens.

In his response, Bentley tried to be accommodating. "[D]esirous as I am at all times to meet your wishes," he began, and then destroyed the good will the phrase might have raised by adding, "even at the expense of my own convenience." He nevertheless consented to postpone all dates regarding *Barnaby* for six months, provided that Dickens write nothing but *Nickleby* in the interim. "I trust the recreation you promise yourself will tend to the improvement of yr. health & strength."[13] In effect, Dickens won.

But he wasn't satisfied. He fumed about this communication, which he stigmatizes in his reply to Bentley as "the lawyer's letter (fairly re-written and signed by yourself)." "I do *not*, and will not receive it [the postponement] as a favour or concession from you . . . I will *not* consent to extend my engagements with you for the additional term of six months . . . I will *not* give you the pledge you so insultingly require – and . . . if you presume to address me again in the style of offensive impertinence which marks your last communication, I will from that moment abandon at once and for ever all conditions and agreements that may exist between us, and leave the whole question to be settled by a jury as soon as you think proper to bring it before one."[14] It is hard to feel that Bentley deserved this reply, having acceded to all Dickens requested. Perhaps the stipulation that Dickens not write for anyone else, intimating as it does suspicion that his author is playing him false, lit Dickens's fuse, although there is no reason to believe that he in fact planned to freelance with another publisher. Or almost no reason; one exception will be discussed hereafter.

In any case, the collaborative relationship between publisher and author was irrecoverable. Ainsworth, Forster, and Dickens spent all day on Monday January 28 talking over the situation and Bentley's offer to pay Dickens £40 a month just to keep his name (or Boz's?) on the masthead as editor; they continued their deliberations over dinner at the Parthenon. Dickens decided to decline even that inducement to continue; after they separated for the night Dickens went home and wrote urging Ainsworth "to offer yourself as the future Editor of the Miscellany" immediately.[15] So agitated was he about the situation, that he sent a messenger out to Kensal Lodge with instructions to deliver the letter "before 7 in the morning." Dickens argues that Ainsworth's friends will rally round him, that Dickens has "yet some lingering interest in the well-being of a periodical which has cost me so much time and so many anxious hours," that Ainsworth is the most likely person to keep the *Miscellany* flourishing, and that "at this critical period of its existence, you will do Mr. Bentley the greatest service (while you do that which is not disagreeable to yourself) that you could by [any] possibility render him." Dickens closes by reiterating the urgency of the moment: "Do not neglect this advice my dear Ainsworth, or lose an hour. And believe me now, as ever, Your faithful friend."

Ainsworth evidently acted on the "faithful" advice. Bentley immediately went to him and concluded for his taking over the editorship of the *Miscellany*. But when these terms were communicated by Ainsworth to Forster and Dickens, they were both astonished and dismayed. Forster warned Ainsworth that if he accepted the Agreement Bentley proposed, "you will be in Bentley's power ... *You can get all you wish from him*, and *hold a superiority over him*, if you do not willfully and willingly put yourself beneath his feet." And like Dickens – though without the "faithfully" – Forster signed off "Your friend as you know me."[16]

There's a lot about this imbroglio that doesn't, from the evidence that has survived, make sense. Dickens's initial request was for a six-month postponement of *Barnaby*; it had nothing to do with Boz's editing, which as late as the second week of January seemed to be proceeding smoothly enough. Dickens's January 26 rejoinder to Bentley's "offensive impertinence" concluded with a threat to "abandon at once and for ever all conditions and agreements that may exist between us, and leave the whole question to be settled by a jury as soon as you think proper to bring it before one." A reasonable reading of that threat would understand it to refer to *Barnaby* and all the consequences relating to extending Dickens's "engagements with you [Bentley] for the additional term of six months." Even so did Bentley interpret it, minuting it as the "letter declaring that no court in England shd force him to fulfil this agreement."[17]

Yet as the conversations among the principals continued, Dickens's outrage seeped over onto his editorial status as well. He couldn't even stand the thought of remaining as the nominal editor at nearly £500 a year, the equivalent of a middle-class income just for lending his name to Bentley's editorial product. While the expansion of Dickens's sense of injury may appear merely the result of a tantrum stoked by Forster and Ainsworth, his refusal of a very considerable sum of money for the use of "Boz" or Dickens as the editor of something Bentley absolutely controlled was a necessary move. He could not entrust his growing reputation as editor or author to the product of Bentley's judgments, sometimes quite at odds with those of editor Boz.

The speed with which Ainsworth was nominated, seconded, and secured as replacement editor also seems unanticipated and overhasty. And from the reaction of Forster to the Agreement Ainsworth accepted, it would seem that Dickens's successor held his editorship on highly restrictive terms. One new clause reinforced Bentley's absolute authority: "The entire control and management of the said Miscellany shall rest with the said Richard Bentley, and the said W. H. Ainsworth shall not interfere in the direction and management ... unless called upon to do so."[18] Ainsworth did immediately begin inserting installments of *Jack Sheppard*, which replaced *Oliver* as the first novel appearing in each issue; and that succession of another sympathetic story about thieves and Newgate within nine months precipitated a substantial row. More on that later. At this moment we must notice that Ainsworth jumps into the editor's chair without even having the editorial discretion Boz exercised. An odd resolution to a set of disagreements that revolved around giving a novelist some leeway about publication deadlines.

Throughout February Dickens's lawyer, Mitton, and Bentley's attorney, Follett, hammered out severance Agreements. That for *Rudge* was astonishingly simple and disadvantageous to Bentley. Dickens promised to deliver the equivalent of 930 printed pages by January 1, 1840, and to write or edit nothing for anyone else excepting the two publications contracted by Chapman and Hall (*Nickleby* and *Boz's Annual Register*) and the Colburn three-decker for the Macrone family. But if Dickens *does* write anything else before turning in *Rudge*, Bentley "shall be at liberty to put an end to this Agreement if he shall think so fit but not otherwise."[19] So at any moment, simply by writing something for another publisher, Dickens could break forever the Bentleian bonds tying himself and *Barnaby* to New Burlington Street, unless Bentley choose to ignore the violation. As incentive to keep Dickens to terms, Bentley promises to pay him £2,000 (in bills at four, six, and eight months) for the manuscript of *Barnaby*, with another thousand pounds if sales reached 10,000, and a further thousand if they reached 15,000. That was a huge increase over the prior Agreement whereby Dickens would have netted only about £800 for the installments and first volume edition. But then by this later Agreement *Barnaby Rudge* would go on sale with no prior publication of any part, so the probabilities of a hefty circulation in an expensive format, with consequently enhanced income, made the alternative arrangement plausible from the publisher's viewpoint.

Concluding the editorship of *Bentley's* was more complicated, because it involved the monthly installments of *Oliver Twist* within the *Miscellany*, and Dickens's share in the copyright after three years. Bentley was prohibited during those three years from releasing *Oliver* in cheaper formats, and the Agreement could be cancelled if he didn't pay Dickens his share of the net on the three-volume edition. But these were comparatively minor points; Dickens for the most part got his way in everything. This prolonged testing of an author's and editor's powers, rights, and abilities to reset the terms and conditions of hire, a testing done with one of the most experienced, well-connected (his brother owned the printing house that produced Bentley's books and periodicals), and influential publishers in London, showed that a determined writer with a strong commercial following and resolute advisors could negotiate favorable contracts. Dickens got paid, participated in determining in what formats, at what price, and when, his writings would be released, obtained a share of the copyright after a limited period of time, and had the right to inspect the publisher's books to ascertain that he was paid fairly on the profits, and in a timely manner. While Lord Mansfield had identified some of these as the rights of an author eighty years previously, the extent and specificity of these last Bentley Agreements were real steps forward in consolidating the commercial parameters of authorship.

But there's always a "but." And in Dickens's case, the termination of his relationship with Bentley didn't end things nearly as cleanly as the lawyers set forth. A month after Ainsworth took over as editor, the *Examiner* published an accusatory article charging Bentley with piracies – including one in the March issue for which Ainsworth was nominally editor – and stating that Ainsworth was only Bentley's puppet. It absolved Ainsworth of writing the "Address" on his assumption of the editorship, while calling that statement cheap self-advertisement.[20] Dickens believed that Ainsworth, to curry favor, had first "by dint of urgent solicitation" procured the unfavorable notice, and then showed it to Bentley "with assumed vexation and displeasure."[21] Unbeknownst to Dickens, someone in the *Examiner* office told Bentley that Dickens had written the article; Barham and Jerdan both heard this directly from Bentley himself. Moreover, Bentley was "going about town stating in every quarter" that Forster, having pledged to Bentley and his attorney to see that Dickens met his obligation under the *Rudge* Agreement, "counselled me to break it and in fact entangled and entrapped the innocent and unsuspecting bookseller – who being all honesty himself had a child-like confidence in others" [sure!]. And, Dickens told Ainsworth, "because you do countenance Mr. Bentley in these proceedings by hearing him express his opinion of Forster and not contradicting him," it is crucial that Ainsworth set the record straight. Furthermore, Bentley had ceased to print two plays by Walter Savage Landor that had been brought to him by Forster, so it seemed as if Forster's conduct toward Bentley was endangering Landor's career.

Dickens's letter to Ainsworth was very forceful, accusing him by not speaking up of seeming to sacrifice Forster to Ainsworth's ambition to remain on cordial terms with his boss. Ainsworth went directly to Bentley's best friend Barham with a draft of his reply to Dickens, which Barham approved although he considered "half an hours conversation settles matters better than a whole volume of correspondence."[22] Ainsworth thereupon offered to go directly to Bentley and persuade him to write to Forster exonerating him of fomenting ill will between Dickens and himself. That he did, and Bentley, in a tightly circumspect declaration, stated in writing to Ainsworth "that in imagining Mr Forster to have been instrumental in causing the ill feeling of Mr Dickens towards myself, I did not come to that conclusion in consequence of anything I ever heard from you."[23]

This didn't address all the issues any more than any of the previous correspondence, half-hour conversations, or legal clauses did. Ainsworth was convinced that Dickens had talked with him about the *Examiner* notice at Macready's. Dickens believed that they had had only one conversation about it, in Doughty Street, "and that *from you* I never heard one word relative to your having shewn it to Mr. Bentley."[24] One of the most significant things about this storm is how much it is fomented by gossip circulating within a small group at the top of the book world. Everyone hears from somebody, but not "you," that Forster did this, or Bentley that, or Ainsworth or Dickens the other thing, and only written declarations, or as Dickens puts it the "formality of a correspondence," can quell the rumors and mistrust. It is one thing to drop a manuscript into a mail slot down a dark alley at night, not having met any of the persons responsible for the magazine. It is a totally different notion of authorship to be insisting, as Dickens does to Ainsworth, that the record of a whole set of contractual and personal interrelationships among publisher, author, lawyers, author's representative, and third parties be amended by statements that might be openly communicated. Dickens's visibility as an author now makes everything he does the potential subject of gossip and public notice, as publication of the Mackenzie "Autobiography" demonstrated. That visibility makes it even more important that he manage his authorial identity effectively, maintaining his integrity both with respect to his friendships and contractual negotiations, and with his public, to whom he intends to remain "faithfully yours."

II

Once more, the contrast between the protracted, angry, and complicated relationship to Bentley, the *Miscellany*, the contracted novels, and
Bentley's associates, with that Dickens enjoyed with Chapman and Hall
spotlighted the accommodation and smoothness of the latter association.
Dickens became friendly not only with Edward Chapman, but also with
his older brother Thomas, a surveyor, and his sisters. He also socialized
with "Little Hall and his little wife," whose wedded life served as the basis for
the "Nice Little Couple," illustrated by Phiz, in *Sketches of Young Couples*.
This ninety-two-page compendium of humorous papers Dickens penned
anonymously for Chapman and Hall, who published it in January 1840,
just in time for the build up to Victoria's nuptials on February 10.[25] In late
January 1838 Charles and Catherine gave a dinner for the Halls, their "big
partner" Chapman, George Cruikshank "and *his* stout lady" Mary, and
Ainsworth, on which occasion the hosts and guests concluded a preliminary Agreement to produce "The Lions of London," a collection of tales
about the old and new metropolis.[26] Nothing came of this immediately,
but the idea surfaced again in the conversations about *Master Humphrey's
Clock* in the summer of 1839.

Dickens had no trouble keeping *Nickleby* going. His reports of
progress are generally cheerful and confident. He complains about the
rush forced by February, "this most fraudulent month of eight and twenty
days," finds himself squeezed again in March because of Good Friday
(March 29) and Easter Week, moans that he is in "Nicklebeian fetters"
often but seems cheerful about it, crows about the numbers ("as good a
Number as the last," "Mrs. Nickleby's love scene will come out rather
unique"), gripes about how difficult it is to wind up in parts, and – after
"pretty stiff work" until mid-September – completes the final double
number on which he has "taken great pains." He has, he tells Forster on
the eighteenth, "now only to break up Dotheboys and the book
together."[27] Surprisingly, he adds, "I have had a good notion for Barnaby,
of which more anon." A "good notion" seems a bit late, if copy for all
930 printed pages is to be delivered in three-and-a-half months to Bentley.
Once again, in the same paragraph, in succeeding sentences, Dickens
implicitly contrasts his situation with Chapman and Hall with that at
Bentley's.

At mid-summer Dickens had ducked another quarrel with his quon-
dam publisher. Cruikshank's *Loving Ballad of Lord Bateman* had been
published by Charles Tilt in June, immediately adapted as a burletta by

Charles Selby, and staged at the Strand Theatre at the beginning of July. A review of the first night in the *Morning Post* on July 2 mentioned that "Boz has the credit and, we believe, justly, of having written the preface and notes" to the book. Next day, Dickens implored Cruikshank to "be strict in not putting this about, as I am particularly – *most particularly* – anxious to remain unknown in the matter, for weighty reasons."[28] The Pilgrim editors speculate that these reasons might have to do with the ballad's being "rather 'low,'" but given some of the "rather 'low'" theatrical productions Boz had previously been associated with, the scale in this case was probably tipped by the Agreement with Bentley; Dickens was not yet willing to forgo up to £4,000 because of a *jeu d'esprit.*

Suddenly, in the middle of July, with *Nickleby* rocketing toward conclusion and *Rudge* somewhere off on the horizon, Dickens – with no agreements for any future work besides *Barnaby* – wraps everything he has done since 1833 in a new package and sends off to Forster a stunning proposal for his next publishing venture. From some perspectives, it looks as if Dickens is abandoning every writing and publishing formula that has proven successful. From others, he seems to be stretching toward a new status as author that would build on prior experience and rectify earlier injustices. The prolonged quarrels with Bentley unmistakably shape his planning, but so too does the generous behavior of Chapman and Hall and the ideal of a non-cash-nexus relationship with others in the communications circuit, particularly his publishers and printers. His admiration of Goldsmith and other eighteenth-century periodical writers plays into his project, making Boz both a more significant marker of his literary forebears and a less significant persona in the proposed new work. In every way, Dickens's letter to Forster of July 14, 1839, with its enclosure to be handed over to Chapman and Hall, decisively breaks Dickens from, and just as decisively reconnects him to, all the elements of his writerly past.

As he did during the prolonged Bentley battle, Dickens sends Forster ahead to Chapman and Hall as his advance man – functioning as a professional literary agent will forty years later on.[29] "I send you … my rough notes of proposals for the New Work." And in the letter, he tells Forster "what I think, when you see Chapman and Hall, you may safely throw out."[30] First of all, Dickens expects a bonus when *Nickleby* concludes; he believes that the publishers cleared £14,000 each on the serialized *Pickwick* and *Nickleby*, without reference to additional profits from the subsequently issued one-volume edition.[31] Under these circumstances, Dickens wants them to behave toward him like the Cheerybles do to Frank and Nicholas. But they aren't the Cheerybles, and therefore

Dickens, as so often in this stage of his authorial career, has to script their role for them and give their lines to an intermediary director, while pretending that his own hand remains invisible. First, he tells Forster to assure Chapman and Hall "that they may admit you into their confidence with respect to what they mean to do at the conclusion of Nickleby, without admitting me." This surely is a fiction. Would any of those involved imagine that Forster wouldn't tell Dickens exactly what his publishers meant to do? Now it could be argued that what Dickens meant was that Forster should sound them out about the completion bonus, and if it seemed insufficient, he could persuade them to up the ante, without telling Dickens about the low ball figure, only the satisfactory enhanced sum. Dickens is still wielding an invisible hand, but under this interpretation doesn't necessarily want to know how the final reward was determined.

Next, Dickens speaks not to the financial rewards his publishers have reaped and to his entitlement to some additional payment on account of the stupendous profits, but rather to the relationship between their apparently unforced generosity, their Cheeryble pecuniary compliment, and his future dealings with them: "I am well disposed towards them, and ... if they do something handsome – even handsomer perhaps than they dreamt of doing – they will find it their interest and will find me tractable." What a ripping of the veil these clauses effect. Chapman and Hall must go beyond anything they planned to do to enhance an Agreement they had already fulfilled to the letter, or else Dickens threatened to become as intractable as he was over the Bentley negotiations. That he had overridden Bentley's assertions of rights and control must have been common knowledge throughout the small community of publishers and authors in central London, so the New Burlington Street contretemps served Dickens well as a warning of what could happen were he undervalued and his wishes crossed. This is still, it must be stressed, a set of author–publisher relations negotiated without benefit of the kinds of precedents and laws that would regulate and regularize these matters. So Dickens thrusts Forster forward to bully his publishers; and Forster was good at bullying.

Then Dickens instructs his agent to use, not the carrot, but the stick, as further inducement to a handsome *Nickleby* settlement. Forster should say that Dickens has had offers from other publishers who would willingly take all the risk and give him from the outset a percentage of the profits. That may be true in a general sense: Colburn and Tilt had both had conversations with Dickens with regard to the *Pic Nic Papers* in the first instance (but Dickens was so mad at Colburn he ceased talking to him) and Dickens might have seen Tilt about the *Lord Bateman* book (but that was essentially Cruikshank's project, and Tilt was too small a publishing house to manage Dickens's business). Who else might have bid? John Murray? Longman's, who published Marryat and whose partners, Thomas and William Longman, were friends of Dickens? An Edinburgh firm such as Constable or Chambers? None of these seems quite suited to the formats, distribution mechanisms (including peddlers traversing the countryside), and clientele associated with Boz – Longman's would be the most plausible bidder. In any event, author and publishers could easily imagine someone else soliciting Dickens's business.

But, he continued to Forster, say to Chapman and Hall that "I am unwilling to leave them, and have declared to you, that if they behave with liberality to me I will not on any consideration, although to a certain extent I certainly and surely must gain by it." The pretense that liberality will be gratuitously and joyfully extended by big Chapman and little Hall is swept away with a stroke of the pen: Dickens authorizes Forster to tell them they must pay to play. And yet, ever the manipulator of rhetoric, Dickens formulates the most naked threat as if he were inevitably going to be the loser: "to a certain extent" he "certainly and surely" would gain from changing firms. (Doubling adverbs and adjectives often signals a claim that could be contested, that isn't self-evident but might gain credence if overemphasized. It's also often a sign that Dickens is rhetorically whipping himself into belief.) In short, Dickens closes this part of Forster's prologue by authorizing him to "hint that when Barnaby is published I am clear of all engagements." Whereas two years before Dickens felt he had to sign contracts right and left to have any security that somebody would publish some of his works for pay, now he offers the bared desktop as the most auspicious indication of future success. So, "if they wish to secure me and perpetuate our connection, now is the time for them to step gallantly forward [still couching the naked financial blackmail in gentlemanly rather than cash-nexus language] and make such proposals as will produce that result." And why does Dickens go to these extraordinary lengths to wrest favorable terms? Because he still believes that only if Forster succeeds in this negotiation might "a very great deal ... be done to recompense your humble for very small profits and very large work as yet." This close is both an affirmation and a kind of collapse: it says in effect "I'm worth a great deal more than I've ever been paid." It's not the strongest argument an advisor would recommend to anyone seeking a better position and higher pay: the obvious rejoinder would be, "we'll pay you what you earned before and see if you're worth more by the quality and success of your work for us."

Once again, as in so many earlier bouts with publishers, Dickens asserts himself by every means at his command to leverage his unquestionable success into more favorable financial circumstances. The great hitch in publishing is, as always, that the author comes selling not a proven product, the backlist, which has already yielded most of its value, but future product, not yet created. (Dickens and his publishers will in the next decade pioneer in wringing a great deal of additional value from that backlist, through a variety of contractual and formatting strategies.) So in this case all these preliminaries about liberality and loyalty lead up to the big sale: what Dickens describes as the "glories of this new project" Forster will disclose. One can imagine that Chapman, the more literary of the two partners, and Hall, the more business-minded, would at this point in Forster's presentation be prepared to stump up to the mark to retain Dickens, perhaps to an extent they hadn't initially aspired to, so long as this next project was going to be as gloriously successful as the two original twenty-part predecessors, and not as comparatively marginal as the serial reprint of *Sketches by Boz*, which had to work hard to repay its £2,250 cost.

What was the new project? A threepenny weekly miscellany. Instead of a shilling monthly, this periodical could reach farther into the pockets of the working poor and possibly further extend Dickens's reading public: especially for folks living week to week, threepence might be an affordable outlay some of the time, whereas a shilling at the end of the month might not be found in pocket, purse, or drawer. For this magazine Dickens would be a proprietor, share profits, and supply "a certain portion of every number." In short, he proposed the arrangement he had with Bentley, this time, however, combining Bentley's roles as proprietor, publisher, and co-editor with Boz's roles as editorial recruiter, gatekeeper, copy-editor, and contributor. This would *not* be one continued story, but a journal about miscellaneous popular subjects on the model of "*The Tatler, The Spectator*, and Goldsmith's *Bee*." And, like other periodicals of the era, Dickens would hire help – even, as the conversations about this idea extended, bring other authors into the magazine after the manner of the Edinburgh quarterlies (fading) and the new London monthlies (rising). Dickens insisted at the outset, however, that any assistance would be "chosen solely" by him, and that "the contents of every number are as much under my own control, and subject to as little interference, as those of a number of *Pickwick* or *Nickleby*." This in itself is an interesting comparison, as in the previous serials Boz was nominally the editor of existing materials. Of course in both cases Dickens had written rather than Boz edited the texts; now Dickens wants to convert the fiction of Boz's editing to fact.

The bottom line, surely apparent to Hall, was that Dickens wanted his publishers to back him as proprietor of a new periodical. Not primarily as the nominal editor Boz or the actual writer Dickens, but as the part owner and conductor of the weekly. Moreover, Dickens would get paid as part of the cost of production, and not as a deduction from the profits that would be split between him and his partners; and if he elected to contribute papers about travels to Ireland or America, the expenses of his trips would again be a cost of production, not a deduction from his salary or the net profits.

Why would Dickens imagine he would enjoy the editorial responsibilities he had just shed, that he could set up and manage a new publication when *Barnaby* remained unwritten – he'd only composed ten pages by November 1,[32] that he could support his family better through initiating a new, untried print product deriving from century-old models than by spinning out another three-decker fiction, and that Chapman and Hall would be so overjoyed at these prospects they would do something far handsomer than they had planned to retain him in their stable? And, most pertinent to this account of the birth of an industrial-age author, how did Dickens conceive of this proprietor-editor-writer as a desirable culmination of his career hitherto? It was, after all, precisely because he was a proprietor as well as author that Scott went bankrupt.

Forster, in the first volume of his biography of Dickens published in December 1871, supplies some of the answers, but they are composed in part by rewriting the original documents to make it seem as if Dickens was in a more assured position from the start, less straining to be credited, and more beholden to Forster for the proposal he presented to Chapman and Hall.[33] Some of the issues troubling Dickens ("I have been thinking the subject over. Indeed I have been doing so to the great stoppage of Nickleby and the great worrying and fidgetting of myself") were, first, that "the public" were "likely to tire of the same twenty numbers over again"; second, "that, by invention of a new mode as well as kind of serial publication, he might be able for a time to discontinue the writing of a long story with all its strain on his fancy"; and third, that he might "ultimately retain all the profits of a continuous publication, without necessarily himself contributing every line that was to be written for it."[34] Another consideration surfacing during the discussions was that by producing weekly numbers Dickens might "baffle the imitators," because the story would advance so quickly there'd be no time to write and produce a play, parody, or sequel before it would have disclosed its own trajectory and denouement.[35]

Still, Dickens realized that to seduce the publishers into backing the venture, he needed to expand on what kinds of popular topics the periodical would treat. It would open, as *The Spectator* did, with an explanation of the origins of the publication, and introduce a little club of characters, including Mr. Pickwick and Sam, whose histories and stories would be carried through the installments. Then it would move on to a variety of essays some of which might be repeated features of the miscellany, such as Chapters on Chambers, descriptions of London then and now related by the Guildhall giants Gog and Magog (a reprise of the "Lions of London" idea); and Savage Chronicles, rather like *Gulliver's Travels* and Goldsmith's *Citizen of the World*, purporting to be from unenlightened lands and supplying satirical renderings of "the administration of justice" and "the magistrates in town and country." The periodical would never leave those "worthies" alone. In fact, this series would engage heartily in politics, instigating a running critique not of Mudfog but of Britain. Dickens held out the possibility that he might add to the popular tradition of books on travel by going either to Ireland (Charles Lever was to mine that vein) or America, and while reporting on his excursions introduce "local tales, traditions, and legends, something after the plan of Washington Irving's *Alhambra*" which Colburn and Bentley, when joined together, had published in 1832. These travel sketches, like the Gog and Magog chapters, could then be gathered together for republication as a volume. In addition, Dickens proposed "to vary the form of the papers by throwing them into sketches, essays, tales, adventures, letters from imaginary correspondents and so forth, so as to diversify the contents as much as possible." All these kinds of materials had appeared in the newspaper and magazine sketches and the early numbers of *Pickwick*. In short, Dickens described as if original and innovative a weekly publication regurgitating a century of periodicals and six years of his own writings.

III

The thing is, Dickens had reanimated corpses many times already. It didn't take too much faith to believe, or hope, or invest, in his performing a resurrection once more.[36] So conversations ensued in which the publishers, Forster, and Dickens worked their way through what might be possible. Dickens got an additional £1,500 for *Nickleby*. Although no mention was made of it in these rough notes, the collaborators decided that the weekly would be illustrated (Charles Knight's illustrated *Penny Magazine* was selling around 200,000 copies each week).[37] Dickens brought Browne into the fold – Cruikshank he was talking to about illustrating *Barnaby*[38] – and added George Cattermole, known for his Clapham Rise studio crammed with antiquated furnishings and accessories and his skill as an architectural draftsman and watercolorist. He was also a fellow member of the Garrick and Athenaeum Clubs, in the late 1830s a jolly good fellow, and when he married in 1839, he became a distant in-law of Dickens. All the risk of the venture was undertaken by the publishers, who paid Dickens £50 per installment, absorbed all expenses, and accounted for each issue separately, so that any loss sustained by one installment was not carried forward. The profits were to be divided fifty-fifty.

On one thing only were the discussants at variance with the major thrust of Dickens's notes. Forster says that "it was felt by us all that, for the opening numbers at least, Dickens would have to be sole contributor; and that, whatever otherwise might be its attraction, or the success of the detached papers proposed by him, some reinforcement of them from time to time, by means of a story with his name continued at reasonable if not regular intervals, would be found absolutely necessary."[39] This smacks of twenty-twenty hindsight. The surviving evidence from early 1840 indicates that Dickens did not think of writing a continuing story until his customers, disappointed that he wasn't producing such a narrative, stopped buying the early numbers. And in his understandable emphasis on Dickens's career, Forster neglects the other contributors – the illustrators.

Pictorializations were much on Dickens's mind at this time – Miss La Creevy's miniatures; the various portrait paintings and prints for which he had been sitting, and which extended his fame and attached a face and body to the twin names of Boz and Charles Dickens; the popularity of illustrated books and magazines; and his friendship with several rising young artists. He signed up Browne for *Master Humphrey's Clock* right away; eventually Phiz designed well over one hundred of the wood engravings. Dickens "propound[ed] a mightily grave matter" to Cattermole on January 13, 1840: "I want to know whether you would object to make me a little sketch *for* a woodcut – in indian ink would be quite sufficient ... the subject an old quaint room with antique Elizabethan [*sic*] furniture, and in the chimney-corner an extraordinary old clock – *the* clock belonging to Master Humphrey in fact – and no figures. This I should drop into the text at the head of my opening page."⁴⁰ While no particular clock has been identified as the original of Master Humphrey's, the owner's name and artifact derive from Dickens's Yorkshire visit, when he met Thomas Humphreys and his son William, clockmakers, at Barnard Castle.⁴¹ Dickens was delighted with the outcome and persuaded Cattermole to contribute more drawings, especially on atmospheric and picturesque subjects containing few or no people.

He also eventually obtained an image from Daniel Maclise (quite out of scale compared with the other plates) and early on, one from the superb wood-engraver Samuel Williams who, rather than Cattermole, executed the picture of Nell asleep "in the midst of a crowd of uncongenial and ancient things" at the end of the first installment of the little child story that developed into *The Old Curiosity Shop*. Dickens thought about commissioning further illustrations from Williams, even though at first try he had got his assignment quite wrong, showing "an exceedingly comfortable" room "and the sleeper being in a very enviable condition."⁴² Dickens also contemplated adding other artists to the project as well, though once the notion of a miscellany was chucked in favor of continued novels wholly by Dickens, there was no need or advantage to have a variety of illustrators.

It is worth emphasizing that the collaboration with artists that had been at least an ancillary part of Dickens's previous publications becomes fully integrated into the plan and format of the weekly serial: letterpress and picture are designed around one another, and sometimes text or image will do the work customarily performed by the other medium.⁴³ As proprietor (Charles Dickens) and editor (Boz, credited on the wrappers of the *Clock* installments as author), Dickens held a supervisory power even over the cost of the illustrations (which were expensive to commission, engrave, and compose with the letterpress) that he enjoyed afterwards only with the 1840s Christmas books. The effects on his prose of thinking about dual-medium fictions (and their adaptability to the stage) have not yet been extensively explored. But it is clear from the outset of the *Clock* that Dickens did have, if not collaborators in writing the miscellany, partners in designing and producing the illustrated text.

As for "those who assist me, and contribute the remainder of every number," Dickens stated in his "rough notes" for his publishers, they never turned up. Dickens ended up doing everything for each installment: writing the first advertisements, instructing the illustrators, designing the pages, composing the text, proofing the copy, dealing with publishers and compositors, examining the accounts, negotiating with Lea and Blanchard for shipping stereotypes of each issue in time for their reprinting in America, retrenching when the miscellaneous contents didn't sell, and once enough issues were printed to collect into a volume, seeing about frontispieces and inditing prefaces. Moreover, the weekly deadlines rolled around incessantly. With monthly installments Dickens usually had at least a few days toward the end of the month with little to do except proofread and party, whereas with the *Clock* he was always winding it up and starting again. The strain over time damaged his health.

IV

There were three major disruptions as he felt his way into the opening installments. First, on the strength of his optimism about the *Clock's* probable profits, Dickens started house hunting for something more substantial. He saw a house in Kent Terrace where Macready used to live, "but larger than his," he told Forster.[44] Elizabeth Dickens had come up to London, first to help with Kate's confinement, then Fanny's, and in between to inspect premises that might be suitable for her son's family. Macready, however, reported that the "stench from the stables" when he resided in Kent Terrace was "so great that they could scarcely breathe."[45] A few days later a "house of great promise (and great premium) 'undeniable' situation, and excessive splendour, is in view," he told Forster. "Mitton is in treaty, and I am in ecstatic restlessness."[46] The property, 1 Devonshire Terrace, York Gate, Regent's Park, was leased from December 1; the rest of November and much of December was occupied in "the agonies of house-letting, house-taking, title proving and disproving, premium paying, fixture valuing, and other ills too numerous to mention."[47] He concluded agreeable terms with his landlord E. W. Banks for vacating Doughty Street by December but paying the rent to March (it was in fact re-let by Christmas), spent much time and money moving into his splendid new home, and then opened it to innumerable visitors. This is a replay, on a much higher level, of previous moves into new quarters; the scale, location, and arrangements contrast markedly with the relocation in Furnival's Inn when Dickens married. Mary Hogarth then admired the "prudent way of beginning," although as we have seen Dickens borrowed repeatedly from friends just to get enough furniture and accessories to make the suite of rooms at number 15 livable. Mary thought "they have furnished them most tastefully and elegantly, the drawing-room with Rose-wood the dining-room with Mahogony furniture."[48] Then Dickens had signed up for enough jobs that might extend over years to risk setting up in marriage. Now, in December 1839, if he doesn't finish *Barnaby* by the first of the year, he will be without any guaranteed steady income, and if the proposed miscellany fails, he will have nothing to fall back on. Yet whereas in 1836 he needed work to advance his career, now his success, fame divided between Boz and Dickens, and cleared desk allow him (and his creditors) to bank on those intangible authorial assets to guarantee the expense of a sumptuous dwelling. Once again an author is living on unearned income, but his name commands money and great expectations.

V

Second, it was all the more galling, therefore, to find in the midst of house moving, *Barnaby* stalling, and *Clock* ticking that his work was being associated with novels by Bulwer and Ainsworth that critics were taking to task for their romanticized criminals.[49] Maginn, editor of *Fraser's* until 1836 and co-author of the Preface to *Bentley's Miscellany* promising that that journal would eschew politics, had kept up a "venomous" battle with Bulwer over his sympathetic depictions of criminals in *Paul Clifford*, which opens with the now notorious and often parodied phrase, "It was a dark and stormy night" (1830) and *Eugene Aram* (1832), based on the life of an eighteenth-century linguist who is caught for the murder decades earlier of his good friend. In both cases Bulwer's fictions teach that "Circumstances make Guilt." When Thackeray entered the fray in *Fraser's* shortly after the start of *Jack Sheppard*, he criticized Bulwer, Ainsworth, and Dickens. His *Catherine*, pseudonymously authored by Ikey Solomons, Esq., Jr. – a reference to the supposed original of Fagin, the London fence Ikey Solomons – began serializing in *Fraser's* in May 1839. Thackeray intended it as a "cathartic" to purge the town of "dandy, poetical, rosewater thieves," and made Catherine, a murderess, morally repellant, but he couldn't help liking her a bit by the end. Meanwhile, every installment attacked Newgate fiction; and in his essay "Horae Catnachianae," published in the April 1839 issue of *Fraser's*, simultaneous with the *Bentley's Miscellany* installment of *Oliver Twist* treating of "The Jew's Last Night Alive," he gave full vent to his objections. Glamorizing criminality was a sham, to begin with. Second, to transfer heroic passions and virtuous sentiments and "place them in the thief's boozing ken – be prodigal of irony, of slang, and bad grammar – sprinkle with cant phrases – leave out the h's, double the v's, divide the w's (as may be necessary), and tragedy becomes interesting once more." But no less inauthentic and morally dangerous. Third, novelists, and Dickens in particularly, cannot and do not tell the truth about the criminal classes, in large part because it would offend public taste and readership. And then Thackeray fires his largest cannon:

> Here is Mr. Dickens about to blaze upon the world with a new novel: may we hear no more of thieves and slang. [No wonder Dickens was so touchy about announcements that *Rudge* was "forthcoming."] Here is Mr. Ainsworth gathering up the ribands of *Bentley's Miscellany*, and driving a triumphant journey with "Jack Sheppard:" we wish it were Jack Anybody else. Gentlemen and men of genius may amuse themselves with such rascals, but not live with them altogether. The public taste, to be sure, lies that way; but these men should teach the public.[50]

At first this bad publicity seems not to have affected Dickens much. He was in April 1839 still planning to release *Rudge* in *Bentley's*, in which case the *Miscellany* would have run, in succession, three Newgate novels illustrated by Cruikshank: the first about the contemporary prison Dickens had visited and been writing about (as "Boz") since 1835; the second about the older prison and the ambiguity of law when thief takers were themselves thieves hired as police (*Jack Sheppard*), and from which Jack makes spectacular escapes; and the third (*Rudge*) dealing somehow with the issue of locks – recall that the title for several years remained *Gabriel Vardon, the Locksmith of London* – and passage across domestic and carceral thresholds as well as the mob's destruction of Newgate Prison. It may have been of some slight comfort to Dickens to know that it was all right for "[g]entlemen and men of genius" to amuse themselves with rascals – certainly Hogarth, Fielding, and Pierce Egan had known the underside of London. But since Dickens more and more aimed at the same sense of moral and truthful art that Thackeray's irony underscores, it was hard to be lumped with writers who allegedly cared more about sensation and pleasing lower-class readers than elevating society's morals.

To run ahead of our story for a moment, Dickens addressed Thackeray's charges in particular, though not by name, in the 1841 "Introduction" to Bentley's third edition of the three-volume *Oliver Twist*. He defends representing "the most criminal and degraded of London's population" because "a lesson of the purest good may . . . be drawn from the vilest evil." In planning his novel, he proposed that Oliver, "the principle of Good," would survive contact with the most seductive of villains, thereby refuting Bulwer's thesis, in particular, that circumstances determined character. He dwells at some length on the allurements that dashing thieves such as John Gay depicted in *The Beggar's Opera* exercised, especially for juveniles. Some readers, Dickens postulates, cannot encounter criminal characters unless they are "in delicate disguise." But Dickens scorns that sort of delicacy, argues that his forthright representations have long precedents in English literature and art, and in particular defends Nancy: "It is useless to discuss whether the conduct and character of the girl seems natural or unnatural, probable or improbable, right or wrong. IT IS TRUE." There were other, more immediate issues in 1840–41 that impelled Dickens to this defense. But think what a different novel he describes in this "Introduction" from what Bentley expected from "Boz" at the start of 1837: disconnected essays that would be funny, apolitical, and deal with the metropolitan population of shabby-genteel people and social pretenders. Dickens morphed his Boz assignment in an unexpected direction, for a time unwelcome to Bentley until the circulation climbed with each installment. But neither Boz nor Dickens nor Bentley could control the way in which the resulting novel got contaminated by its proximity and similarity to other Newgate fiction. However sympathetic in a non-judgmental way the narrator of "A Visit to Newgate" and "The Lifted Veil" had been, he had, at moments at least, attempted to align his affective response with his readers'. Now those appeals to empathize with the suffering of felons and their loved ones, to learn about compassion even for the outcast, have turned rancid and radical.

There's more to this slippage bringing Dickens into the ranks of immoral sensationalists. By October, stagings of the novel were all over town, often using Cruikshank's illustrations as models. Moncrieff, Dickens's nemesis, though nearly blind, designed and scripted a whole play including the songs, and W. P. Davidge hired Cruikshank and Ainsworth to oversee his production at the Royal Surrey Theatre. The most electrifying of the versions was Buckstone's at the Adelphi, in which Mrs. Keeley played Jack as a captivating fellow who danced and sang "Nix my dolly pals" – the thieves' cant Thackeray so objected to – to standing ovations night after night. There was a production in Paris, imitations and sequels galore, references in the early numbers of *Punch*, a cheaper part issue for the lower-income customers, and much celebration of the novel's appeal for more humane treatment of criminals and of its dramatization of the difference between the bad old days and the safety of metropolitan streets under Sir Robert Peel's bobbies. But contrary voices weighed in: the *Athenaeum*, and then Forster in the *Examiner*, picked the novel and its dramatizations to pieces. Moreover, some adaptations seemed to go too far. Thackeray reported to his mother that in the lobby of the Coburg Theatre entrepreneurs were selling replicas of Sheppard's bag of housebreaking tools.[51] Several young men confessed that they never would have contemplated pocket picking or theft had it not been for the play.

And then the influence of the novel turned even worse. Lord William Russell was in June 1840 murdered by his valet, who allegedly said that from reading about Blueskin's cutting the throat of Mrs. Wood in the novel he got the idea for the mode of assassinating his employer. Ainsworth insisted in print that Courvoisier told him he'd never read the book, but the London and Middlesex sheriff riposted that the murderer had learned from a copy of the novel lent to him by the valet to the Duke of Bedford. (Think how innocent the below-stairs gathering of butlers and valets at Bath in *Pickwick* is, and then of Sim Tappertit's club of disaffected servants who do so much damage in *Rudge*. The whole context for depicting working-class solidarity in Dickens shifts between 1837 and 1841.) Another toxic strain to the Newgate novel controversy was public hanging, especially after Courvoisier's execution. Both Thackeray and Dickens protested the brutality and demoralization of such displays, and the gallows tree comes up for criticism through the character and sentiments of Dennis the hangman (a partially invented figure) in *Rudge* in 1841.[52]

No wonder Dickens was having trouble beginning *Barnaby Rudge* in the same months that *Jack Sheppard* was playing and inciting miscreants all over London and beyond. Surely the new beginning (if he'd ever written an earlier beginning), with its covert back story about murder, was designed to shift the novel's moral center away from rosewater criminals – although by renaming it *Barnaby Rudge* Dickens reserves considerable sympathy for one of the principal Gordon rioters. It must have been very difficult for him to plot out exactly how gentlemanly villains such as Sir John Chester, schemers such as Gashford, well-intentioned anti-Catholic enthusiasts such as Gordon, unprincipled muscle like Hugh, and Gothic, ghostly cloaked murderers such as Barnaby's father, Rudge, could apportion responsibility and blame for the destruction not only of Newgate but also of the homes and businesses of respectable and law-abiding subjects. How could the locksmith of London bear all the goodness?

VI

If all this weren't enough to pile onto moving, celebrating the holidays, and rushing around London lining up the crew and customers for the

*Clock*, to be published by arrangement in the USA nearly simultaneously with its UK release, Bentley began in mid-December advertising *Barnaby* as "preparing for publication." Cruikshank had already told him that Dickens would not deliver the manuscript by January 1, but Bentley still wanted to exert what pressure he could, and to keep the trade and the public aware that Dickens was a Bentley author. Moreover, he kept tying the copyrights he possessed to those belonging to Dickens and Chapman and Hall, so that *Barnaby* was connected to *Pickwick* and *Nickleby*. Even worse, given the controversies swirling around *Jack Sheppard*, on October 17 Bentley had inserted a notice in *The Times* announcing that Ainsworth's novel was now published "uniform in size and price with 'Oliver Twist.'"

Dickens had had enough. He informed his attorneys that he would not present *Rudge* on January 1, and that he preferred to let Bentley "avail himself, if he thinks proper, of that penal clause in our agreement (penal as regards me at least) which provides for this contingency."[53] In other words, he was prepared to "sacrifice ... from two to four thousand pounds." This could not have been an easy decision for Dickens to make economically, as he was strapped for funds. But Bentley's practice of forcing the sale of his books by connecting Dickens's name to others and his imitation of the *Oliver Twist* format for Ainsworth's story, issued both in three volumes and fifteen shilling weekly parts starting in December, were simply too much to bear.

When Bentley learned formally that *Rudge* was not to be, he considered applying for an injunction forbidding the publication of any other work by Dickens. But his counsel's opinion, given in February 1840, was that a Court of Equity could not compel Dickens to write something, and thus enforcing only "the negative stipulation" that he couldn't publish anything else, was not likely to be granted. If Bentley wanted, he could sue for damages – but they would be hard to prove and equally hard to value. How much would he lose by not publishing an unwritten novel that might or might not sell? He chose not to go down that road.[54] Having entrusted the case to his attorneys, Dickens was able for the most part to put the dispute aside. Once the *Clock* was fully prepared for launch in the spring, he concluded three Agreements in succession: a rather complicated one about the *Clock* with Chapman and Hall on March 31, 1840; the termination on July 2 of all shared interest in *Bentley's Miscellany* or *Oliver Twist* for which Dickens paid £2,250, with no mention of any outstanding obligation on either the author's or the publisher's side for further dealings regarding *Barnaby Rudge*; and an Agreement written up in July 1840 for Chapman and Hall to issue *Rudge* in ten to fifteen *Nickleby*-sized monthly numbers, with the publishers paying £3,000 on delivery of the manuscript for a six month's lease on copyright dating from the publication of the last installment, but advancing £2,250 for *Oliver Twist*. No date for delivery of *Rudge* is specified. These arrangements cut through the Bentleian bonds but, ever so gently, placed Dickens under even greater obligation to big Chapman and little Hall to write the novel on which they had already advanced more than two-thirds of its purchase price. At this date there was no expectation on either side that *Barnaby* would succeed *The Old Curiosity Shop* in the *Clock*. As was the case when *Rudge* was pledged to Bentley, its appearance in a journal rather than as volumes was decided under pressure when the periodical depended for its sales on a continued story by Dickens. He was the fount of value, but he had to flow steadily forth.

Was he serious about writing the much-postponed novel for Chapman and Hall? It's hard to tell. For the last distraction Dickens encountered in the winter of 1839–40 was his own decision to apply for admission to the Middle Temple and read law. Upon paying the entrance fees on December 8, he was admitted a student. He talked Talfourd and Edward Chapman into signing his bond, assuring the latter that "the responsibility you incur is a very slight one – extending very little beyond my good behaviour, and honorable intentions to pay for all wine-glasses, tumblers, or other dinner furniture, that I may break or damage."[55] This was a furtherance of the plan first mooted back in 1834. Dickens continued to think about being called to the Bar for another fifteen years.[56] Achieving that goal could be done alongside pursuing other occupations – though it takes Tommy Traddles a very long time to make it in *David Copperfield*. Dickens's application at this moment does not indicate his desire to quit writing altogether. But it does signify a number of related things: the possibility that he would one day actually be called to the Bar, as so many of his fellow Parliamentary reporters had planned to do at a time when such a course of action for him seemed impossible; the potential rise in status he might enjoy from being a lawyer; the assistance he could provide to Talfourd in his efforts to pass copyright legislation more favorable to authors; the expertise he would gain about intellectual property rights to arm him in future publication negotiations; and, finally, if he did complete his terms and become a lawyer, he would, like so many other writers including Ainsworth and Forster, not necessarily practice law but move within circles where law and authorship intersected. (We've already seen the two professions intersecting imaginatively in *Pickwick*.) Indeed, the combination was not unusual for many Victorian men of letters. It would be plausible also to interpret his signing up at this moment as another of the "stalling" tactics many artists engage in as they ramp up for a new project; in later years Dickens writes to correspondents about being in the throes of planning his next serial, restlessly working up ideas, trying them out on himself and friends, canceling them, and often taking long walks. (Barbara Hardy, among others, has tied Dickens's Olympic-scale perambulations to the stimulation of his imagination.)[57]

### VII

For the present, nothing came of this beginning. *Master Humphrey's Clock* loomed on the horizon. If it was to be published in the USA simultaneously with its appearance in the UK, the type needed to be set a month ahead of publication date, stereotyped, and shipped overseas. Dickens needed therefore to get ahead with the opening numbers. In doing so, he foregrounded a conception of authorship that had been implicit in his own practice since 1834 but rarely advertised as such: authorship as a collaborative enterprise. Some critics have argued that this has always been the case, and we have seen it apply to Dickens: printers who determined, copied, or originated formats; publishers (Chapman introduced the fat Pickwick); readers who read manuscript before it was set (including illustrators, newspaper editors such as Black, family members such as George Hogarth, advisors such as Henry Kolle early on, and Forster from 1837); copy-editors; in the case of plays various members of the theatrical company (as demonstrated when Mr. Johnson works for the Crummles troupe); early reviewers who might effect revised versions (Thomas Hood for *The Old Curiosity Shop*, as we will discuss shortly) or provoke a prefatory defense of the work (Thackeray *et al.* on Newgate fiction); and adapters and plagiarists of all kinds who could anticipate and thus affect the end of a serial.[58] Indeed, we have been following the dual career of Boz and Dickens, who themselves might be said to collaborate in fulfilling various authorial functions. Moreover, Dickens's early career is embedded in collaborative enterprises: newspapers, magazines, dramas, editing manuscripts composed by others, penning anonymous supplements to another author's book, assembling essays and illustrations for *Bentley's Miscellany* and Colburn's *Pic Nic Papers*.

Another way authorship may be overtly collaborative is through the writer's invocations of predecessors. Dickens does this repeatedly, commending and incorporating Shakespeare, Cervantes, the canonical authors of eighteenth-century prose, poetry, and fiction, Scott, and William Hogarth, among others. In the case of the *Clock*, in the clock case itself reside manuscripts contributed by members of the club, which it was Dickens's intention to have them draw out from time to time and read aloud, so connecting their stories to their own histories. This notion, that the author's own life affects his writings, becomes a more and more central thesis over the course of Dickens's career and is, especially through its Marxist, Freudian, and historicist amplifications, virtually unchallenged today. Authors who declare themselves as such and *in propria persona*, not concealed behind pseudonyms or anonymity, are, as Foucault posited, looked to for the explanation of their work's origin and its connection to their life. Dickens's idea of stories pulled out of a container and read by their writers recalls Anna Laetitia Barbauld and her brother John Aikin's six-volume collection of didactic dialogues, tales, and other materials entitled *Evenings at Home, or, The Juvenile Budget Opened*. The frame for this miscellany is the home of the Fairborne family, a house filled with children and frequent visitors. Often the children would write pieces that, after being reviewed by their mother, were locked in a box. During family holidays it was a great treat for all those in residence to gather together, for one child to rummage in the unlocked box and pick out a story, for someone then to read it, and after all the company had responded to it, repeat the process.[59] Seventy years later Margaret Gatty deployed a similar frame in her story of "The Black Bag." The bag contains stories by the adults and children of Aunt Judy's family. It may be opened by anyone (it is not locked) and the stories read by either generation when they gather together.

Dickens's club of elderly bachelors consists of the crippled Master Humphrey and a deaf gentleman whose name and history are never told, and who produces a "chapter" about Gog and Magog and about ancient Chambers that Dickens had first proposed to publish with Ainsworth and Cruikshank in "The Lions of London" and then to run as a series under his own, or Boz's, name, in the *Clock*.[60] Perhaps that complicated back history of potential collaborators, including Dickens himself, impelled the anonymity of the Gog and Magog narrator, who also, as it turns out, writes the last words of the *Clock*. The other two initial members are Jack Redburn, a Jack of all trades who mismanaged his relations with his wealthy guardian and was disinherited, and who the deaf gentleman suspects may be personally involved in the second novel pulled from the clock case, as Edward Chester. (He would have to be well into his eighties, being a young man in 1780 and the *Clock* story appearing in 1841, but

Dickens, without perhaps knowing what he was doing at the time, made his age indefinite: "I should be puzzled to say how old he is," Master Humphrey remarks [p. 20].) The fourth member of the group is Owen Miles, a wealthy retired merchant, and co-executor (with Mr. Pickwick!) of the estate of Master Humphrey when at the conclusion of the *Clock* he dies. While from the clock case comes a story about a lieutenant in the army of Charles II who murders his nephew, no member of the club is introduced as author or reader of this tale. Master Humphrey begins the next installment with a tale of his "personal adventures," entitled in black letter to emphasize the antiquity, "The Old Curiosity Shop." That number closes with a comic letter from "Belinda." At the opening of the next, number five, Mr. Pickwick arrives and introduces himself to Master Humphrey. He begs admission to the club, offering as his qualification a scroll of papers that turns out to be a story about witchcraft near Windsor during the time of King James the First. Will Marks, hero of the story, is enlisted by his Windsor and Kingston neighbors to discover whether the midnight sounds of witches' orgies really are evidence of witchcraft round a gibbet. He learns that actually a mother and wife come in the dark of night to mourn the execution of their son and husband, but when Will arrives on the scene, the body has been taken down and carried to a private house near Putney. Sympathizing with the grieving women, he is persuaded by another person, a somewhat disheveled, masked cavalier, to take the coffined body for burial at St. Dunstan's in Fleet Street. Though beset by challenges along the way, he fulfills his mission, earns one hundred golden coins, and having been missing for two nights and a day reports on his return to Windsor the most terrifying story about being abducted in a huge copper cauldron. He is acclaimed a great hero and written up in a pamphlet, and he takes care to describe the "witches" so they bear no resemblance to the unhappy family he aided. This is the sort of story Mr. Pickwick might have read during his adventures, but seems very unlikely to have issued from his pen. That it *is* Pickwick's bid for admission succeeds, and that it would be read by most purchasers of the *Clock* as either by "Boz," editor of the *Pickwick Papers*, or Dickens, rather than Pickwick seems likely.

Eventually Mr. Pickwick is inducted into the club, taking one of the two seats hitherto purposely left vacant. Invited to recommend someone to fill the sixth and last chair, he suggests Jack Bamber, teller of the "Queer Client" tale in *Pickwick*, who "has a grave interest [suppressed pun?] in old mouldy chambers and the Inns of court," and is now a close friend. Sam and his father, who accompany Mr. Pickwick to Master

Humphrey's residence, are inducted below stairs into "Mr. Weller's Watch," comprising Master Humphrey's housekeeper and barber, but not before Tony is reassured that the housekeeper is not a widder. After a little by-play in the kitchen, and some anecdotes about barbers that Sam relates, "The Old Curiosity Shop" continues, and it soon becomes the only tale being told. By its conclusion, the members of the Watch have sneaked upstairs and begun listening to the story through the closed door; they are invited into the clock chamber where they too attend to the narrative about the Gordon riots.

These *Clock* circumstances were excised from the published versions of the two novels, so few are familiar with them or care about them. But as evidence of the first conceptions of the *Clock*, they raise interesting issues about Dickens's imagination and authorial construction.[61] The Gog Magog chapters, composed by the deaf gentleman, obviously were designed for continuation: the accidental witness to the giants' coming alive at night, Joe Toddyhigh, resolves to sleep all day and return to the Guildhall so that he might watch the giants reanimate and, presumably, tell more tales. This tale fills the second part of the *Clock*, and is initiated without any introduction of its writer or reader, information filled in during the third number. If Dickens imagined someone else taking over these antiquarian tales, he had no voice or collaborator yet in mind; the deaf gentleman, significantly, cannot hear others speak, writes out his comments, and never discloses his past. This teller and this tale are thus wrapped in silence and secrecy: the giants only come alive at night when the Hall is empty, their Elizabethan love-and-death story is overheard by someone who, like the Chronicles, never reappears, and the deaf gentleman never reveals more about himself or provides any further material from the clock case. The next tale is supplied without any preliminaries about opening the case and drawing forth a manuscript, it is unattributed, and there is no follow-up. It too deals with concealed death. Then comes the tale identified as Master Humphrey's personal adventure, which concludes with his reiterating the striking visual impression of the beautiful child Nell asleep "alone in the midst of all this lumber and decay and ugly age." The story doesn't quite fill an installment, so most of page forty-seven and all of forty-eight of number four are taken up with a letter from a young lady who has been betrayed by the man she believes to be the author of a letter published in number two. Most of numbers five and six are occupied with Mr. Pickwick's tale, with six also describing Master Humphrey's welcome to Sam and Tony Weller. This conversation contains all the missing h's and doubled v's Thackeray complained about as substituting for any deeper representation of rogues. The Wellers aren't rogues, but in this installment they are no more than linguistic tics: in no way do they come alive, and their by-play is but a faint imitation, a poor plagiarism one might justly complain, of *Pickwick Papers*. By Dickens, no less, who could never have substituted some other writer for himself in writing subsequent episodes of "Mr. Weller's Watch."

Finally, once Pickwick is introduced to everyone, the ceremony of the clock commences. And at this moment, though not in earlier episodes when the clock disgorged its contents, Master Humphrey shifts into the third person, explaining, "in treating of the club, I may be permitted to assume the historical style, and speak of myself in the third person." Surely this is nothing more than clumsy preparation for Master Humphrey's removal from narrating anything. The clock society breaks up that evening, without reading any story, and Jack Redburn tells Master Humphrey of the formation of "Mr. Weller's Watch" and promises to report its future proceedings. Then follows the second part of number seven, "The Old Curiosity Shop," still in black letter, and the first indication of a continuing story: "CHAPTER THE SECOND." At the end of the third chapter, in number eight, Master Humphrey announces that having "carried this history so far in my one character and introduced these personages to the reader, I shall for the convenience of the narrative detach myself from its further course, and leave those who have prominent and necessary parts in it to speak and act for themselves."

VIII

This moment wipes out all the prior club fiction. No more does Jack Redburn serve as secretary for the nightly proceedings, no more does Master Humphrey unlock the clock case, no longer does any one of the auditors (including those who steal up from downstairs) comment on the tale that was told. The continuing story that Dickens's customers demanded forced him into harness as the sole narrator. And what at first seems the gloomiest and dreariest compilation of settings and stories, paying unnecessary and not even terribly complimentary tribute to Cattermole, to whom Dickens always deferred, suddenly takes off in the fourth chapter by introducing the reader, without Humphrey's interference, to the lively, erotic, and grotesquely humorous by-play among the residents and guests of Quilp's lodging on Tower Hill. The energy of the story begins here, as it does in *Pickwick* when Dickens quits the miscellaneous vignettes of the first three numbers and begins the continued story entangling Jingle and Sam.

Before we proceed forward, we should ask, is there any indication in these early numbers that Dickens was preparing sections of the *Clock* that might be composed at intervals by others? The Pickwickians below stairs clearly emerge from his Boz voice, while Pickwick's ghost story resembles the intercalated tales attributed in *Pickwick* to other tellers and usually attributed to Dickens writing under great pressure, at his worst; the deaf gentleman is as a narrator a nobody whose place could be filled in by anyone or no one or Dickens; the Charles the Second tale is told by the murderer on the night before his execution, and thus leaves no successor behind to relate further stories. In short, the narrative structure of the opening numbers is so miscellaneous and inconsistent that there seems to be no plan or controlling consciousness, despite Master Humphrey's initial and elaborate introduction of himself as the one in charge.

One other disparity is striking. The *Clock* is "edited by 'Boz.'" Boz was a bachelor, an urban stroller, often walking late into the night and learning the stories of his metropolitan contemporaries. Master Humphrey is an urban pedestrian who gets around with some difficulty and like Boz roams the streets at night. He is a solitary who lives in an old house in the suburbs. He had a melancholy and friendless childhood, and is now an ugly, "mis-shapen, deformed, old man." This description separates Humphrey from Boz physically, constitutionally, emotionally; as Dickens was surprisingly young when first seen as the embodiment of Boz (in person and in the print portraits sold by the thousands), so Boz seems much younger and more cheerfully sociable than this decrepit elder who spends long hours sitting by the clock side. One of the things this muddle of narratorial identities does is begin to separate Boz from Dickens, Humphrey, and the *Clock*. The future of Dickens's authorial voice barely begins to emerge from the complex and incredible multiplicity of figures claiming narrative control over the *Clock*'s miscellaneous content. For unlike *Bentley's* or other edited periodicals, the *Clock* within a short period of time is refigured from a collection of papers by various hands into two consecutive novels by a single, though multiply identified, hand. We need to pay further attention to the difficulties Dickens experienced in trying and failing to establish a coherent narrative persona for this first weekly serial.

Master Humphrey's clock has, it seems, ticked off centuries of death; the pendulum swings and almost by that motion writes the stories stuffed into its casing, all of which concern death usually by unnatural means, and which are consumed by relics of younger days. Even Pickwick and Tony and Sam have aged. It may be true that Forster was the first to mention overtly that Nell should die, but surely one needn't read far into the first volume of the *Clock* to sense that the energy of Quilp and Kit and Dick Swiveller contrast to the material decay and bodily deformation prevalent throughout the story.[62] At the end of *Pickwick*, Boz the editor or narrator observes that "There are dark shadows on the earth, but its lights are stronger in the contrast. Some men, like bats or owls, have better eyes for the darkness than for the light. We, who have no such optical powers, are better pleased to take our last parting look at the visionary companions of many solitary hours, when the brief sunshine of the world is blazing full upon them." If *Pickwick* is a solar myth, *The Old Curiosity Shop* is mired in darkness and artificial lights.

IX

If *Clock* journeys are death marches, who tolls Nell's knell? In other words, who tells Nell's story? At the end of *The Old Curiosity Shop*, an oral narrator is identified: Kit Nubbles. His children, Barbara, Jacob, Abel, and Dick, "would often gather round [Kit] of a night and beg him to tell again that story of good Miss Nell who died. This, Kit would do; and when they cried to hear it, wishing it longer too, he would teach them how she had gone to Heaven, as all good people did." So far, that would seem to be a story, and responses to that story, recognizably in line with what we and Dickens's first readers might have experienced – the story of an innocent girl who dies and goes to Heaven. It's a sad story with a consolatory ending, capped by the last paragraph of the novel: "Such are the changes which a few years bring about, and so do things pass away, like a tale that is told!" (p. 575).[63]

But, as John Bowen reminds us in *Other Dickens*, Kit's children end up laughing, not crying, at Nell.[64] For after telling of Nell's death, Kit relates to his offspring "how needy he used to be, and how she had taught him what he was otherwise too poor to learn, and how the old man had been used to say 'she always laughs at Kit', at which they would brush away their tears, and laugh themselves to think that she had done so, and be again quite merry" (p. 574). We might not think that being "quite merry" was exactly the response Nell's story was designed to elicit; but *The Old Curiosity Shop* is full of sentimental comedy,[65] and one of the most popular excerpts, known from illustrations and paintings as well as words, was Kit's writing lesson (chapter 3). So it is possible to conclude that Kit provides a reasonably comprehensive version of Nell's story – the good she does in life, particularly in the realm of education, stands almost as the proof of her own goodness. This *is* a story about education, about learning life's lessons whether about writing (Kit's letter, Mr. Slum); about history (the Shop furniture, Mrs. Jarley's waxworks); about fighting, winning and losing (Quilp, Tom Scott, Codlin and Short's Punch shows); about schoolmastering, young pupils and old teachers; about brazen- (Brass, or "melted lead and brimstone" [p. 480]) faced law; or about the pleasures and dangers of imagination (Kit at Astley's, Dick and the Marchioness). The last sentence ups the ante on the story's lesson: "things pass away, like a tale that is told." Education, stories, teach us about life's evanescence. The elderly woman widowed shortly after marriage puts it memorably to Nell: "Death doesn't change us more than life, my dear" (p. 138).

But that's not the whole of Nell's story. If it were, it wouldn't be particularly moving or memorable. The years bring changes, things pass away: those are "old stories" producing neither tears nor laughter. And it would be difficult for any one person to tell the whole of Nell's story. Many tell parts of the narrative: Master Humphrey, Mrs. Nubbles (pp. 166–67), Mrs. Jarley, the Marchioness (pp. 497–99), Sampson Brass, the attorneys for the prosecution and defense of Kit, all contribute to the narrative of Nell and Kit. The Single Gentleman (subsequently identified as a younger Master Humphrey) explains Nell's ancestry and relations to Mr. Garland in the carriage as they ride to the rescue at a time when she is unconscious, if not already dead (pp. 542–44). The death of Quilp is unobserved by anyone except an omniscient narrator who pops up when there's nobody else around.[66] And some parts of the whole story, told by participants, were suppressed during print production: for instance, Sally Brass's revelation that the Marchioness is her offspring: "I am her mother. She is my child. There. Now what do you say?" (p. 588). (Dick Swiveller suspects that Sally is the mother and that Quilp might be the father, and Dickens allowed Dick's speculations – after all, he is nominatively another truncated Dickens – to appear in print [p. 572]).

The most notorious narratorial discontinuity is the withdrawal of Master Humphrey from the telling of his "Personal Adventures." But while he leaves it to the other actors in the drama to narrate their parts (a narratorial strategy Wilkie Collins was to perfect in later decades), that doesn't always happen. In the case of Quilp's death, for instance, or the Marchioness's parentage, no actor gets to speak for him- or herself. And Master Humphrey does have to explain how he was related personally to these adventures when the *Old Curiosity Shop* concluded and *Master Humphrey's Clock* resumed. Dickens's manuscript version of this revelation, revised in proof, has Master Humphrey declare to his friends:

Forgive me, if for the greater interest and convenience of the narrative you have just heard, I opened it with a fictitious adventure of my own. I had my share in these transactions, but it was not that I feigned to have at first. The younger brother – the single gentleman – the nameless actor in this little drama – stands before you now! (p. 590)

It's absurd, of course. If the single gentleman had met Nell on the first page, why would he not rescue her then? Why would his elder brother, who on meeting the then nameless narrator takes "an opportunity of observing me more closely than he had done yet" (p. 11), not recognize him? And how can a deformed old recluse who walks the streets by night be reconciled with the vigorous pursuer of Nell, the younger brother of her grandfather who actively engages with others in solving the mystery of her whereabouts? Nothing Dickens could do at the end of the novel to an already printed text that began with no clear plan could account for these narratorial discordances. This whole mis- and re-identification of the narrator seems a clear violation of the "faithful" relationship between teller and reader that Dickens promised in the frontispiece of *Nickleby*. No wonder Master Humphrey asks his clock auditors, and thus the *Clock* readers, to forgive him for passing off a fictitious adventure and feigning an identity.

However, the problem of who tells Nell's story is more than a question of who has access to information or who Master Humphrey might be. This is a novel told by spies who see or overhear crucial scenes.[67] Most of them eventually own up to what they have surreptitiously learned. But some parts of the story are virtually unnarratable, because what they tell is so horrifying no one wants to own up to it, or own it.

For instance, who tells this part of Nell's story? While spending the night (and a very expensive night) at "honest Jem Groves'"s inn, the Valiant Soldier (p. 228), Nell awakes from fitful slumbers to an awareness that a silent shadowy figure has crept into her bedroom.

A figure was . . . there, between the foot of the bed and the dark casement[. I]t crouched and slunk along, groping its way with noiseless hands, and stealing round the bed. She had no voice to cry for help [MS: or commend herself to God], no power to move, but lay still, watching it.

On it came – on, silently and stealthily, to the bed's head. The breath so near her pillow, that she shrunk back into it, lest those wandering hands should light upon her face. Back again it stole to the window – then turned its head towards her.

The dark form was a mere blot upon the lighter darkness of the room, but she saw the turning of the head, and felt and knew how the eyes looked and the ears listened. There it remained, motionless as she. At length, still keeping the face towards her, it busied its hands in something, and she heard the chink of money.

Then, on it came again, silent and stealthy as before, and, replacing the garments it had taken from the bed-side, dropped upon its hands and knees, and crawled away. (pp. 237–38)

It is inconceivable that Kit, or Humphrey, or Nell's grandfather's younger brother, could ever tell this part of Nell's story.[68] This is as close to a rape scene as early Victorian discourse allowed: the para-lyzed female body, the fetid breath and groping hands of the invader, its unceasing gaze upon her, its hands busy in the woman's garments until a chink is grasped and dropped ("she heard the chink of money"), and then the stealthy departure, having secretly secured the woman's value. Moreover, the overheated language of this passage heightens the stakes: "it," the invader, is inhuman, serpent-like: crouching, slinking, silently and stealthily, stealing, watching and listening motionless, crawling away. As with many elements in *The Old Curiosity Shop*, local events are suffused with eschatological resonance: this scene reeks of serpent in the garden intimations.[69] Whereas those were comic in *Pickwick*, this version is not.

The consciousness registering this violation seems to be Nell's and by identification with her, also the reader's – "she had no voice, no power to move, but lay still, watching it." But as the passage continues, the body under threat recedes from the foreground and the creature violating the space, as silent and stealthy as its observers (Nell and the reader), becomes the cynosure. By the end of the passage, all attention is fixed on the creature's departure, known now not by sight but only by sound: "How slowly it seemed to move, now that she could hear but not see it, creeping along the floor! It reached the door at last, and stood upon its feet. The steps creaked beneath its noiseless tread, and it was gone" (p. 238).[70]

This is a primal scene in many senses. The serpent imagery suggests an invasion into Eden; Nell's room, if not a paradise, is yet a place sanctified by her feminine purity. Her person and her clothing should be, as they are not, immune from prying hands. And this is not just the intimation of an ordinary rape; it discloses incestuous rape. The "it" slithering around Nell's room, groping through her clothes, seeking the chink of her money, is her grandfather. He is, we learn, ostensibly looking not for her person but for her coins – money she sewed into the hem of her dress as precaution and ultimate resort. The secretiveness and protective nature of that hoard so proximate to Nell's legs does nothing to defuse the association between his stealing and rape.[71] And it takes the relationships between women's clothing, commodification of the body, and rape broached but never enacted in *Nickleby* to its horrifying climax – even more violently transgressive because, as with uncles, the sexual violation comes from within the family. Rape is the cash nexus enacted on the body.

x

It's worth pausing to reflect on Dickens's narratorial choices and development. For the most part, in *Sketches* Boz either observes the events or is able to reconstruct what he cannot see through the publication of them and the gossip that follows – as when he tells his readers about the terms of the will Minns makes (courtesy of his lawyer) and the pleasure Dumps takes in making his nephew's family miserable (courtesy of his landlady, who "has offered to make oath that she heard him laugh, in his peculiar manner," after his godson's disastrous christening [p. 462]). If the door remains closed, the neighbors and Boz have a hard time determining what is going on inside – as is the case with the four Willis sisters, one of whom (but which?) is married. But in the *Old Curiosity Shop* old curiosity takes over; the narrator can be anywhere despite having been identified as a particular person, Master Humphrey (and another personification, the Single Gentleman, at the end). In this work scenes are not limited to those seen by or told to the narrator (as Bung narrates the "distress" he has witnessed and felt in his time [p. 29]). The narrative, that sometimes proceeds without a narrator, admits readers to every kind of concealment, even those the novel's legion of spies do not observe. Not only admits readers, but affectively engages them as witnesses, as here – when some might feel that the old man, although dehumanized as an "it" and morphed into a serpent, is as much an emotional register and trigger as the transfixed child and her narratorial observer.

Observations which, if true, might lead some to speculate about the moral economy of viewing and desiring in this text. Everyone sees Nell, and consequently wants to do something about, for, with, or to her. She is a universal object of desire. One can imagine her in bed (Quilp), as a wife (Kit), as a living waxwork soliciting customers (Mrs. Jarley), as an heiress (her grandfather), as a beautiful contrast to her gargoyle surroundings (the illustrators), as the source for posthumous rejoicing at the good actions and thoughts her kindness and charity inspired (Kit, the schoolmaster), and as a saintly sacrificial victim (Forster). Many commentators have related Nell's death to Mary Hogarth's, and found warrant in Dickens's own correspondence: "Dear Mary died yesterday," he told Forster, "when I think of this sad story."[72] But as the Pilgrim editors point out, Dickens communicated no thoughts connecting Nell to Mary through the first seventy chapters; and his need to perpetuate the "state *I have been trying to get into*" when writing about her death (my italics) "is evidence against an emotional obsession."[73] What might be the case, however suppressed it was for Dickens and his readers, is that Nell's death preserves her purity. That, in turn, allows the desires of all kinds that shadow and pursue her to prove harmless; she cannot be hurt by the world's material and sexual lusts. And, following that logic, the lusts can therefore be "sinlessly" indulged, released, and sanctified by her perpetual innocence. No wonder there were tears, though again as the Pilgrim editors dryly note, not as many tears as subsequent readers claimed, perhaps in response to their own complex need for Nell's death.[74] The affective strategies of Dickens's novel – and in his letters he often speaks about his delight in Dick, the Marchioness, and Kit – are far more variegated and intense than in some of the set pieces in *Sketches*. They seem to require a more pliable narratorial stance than one limited to a single personalized point of view. One, too, that allows Dickens, Boz, Master Humphrey, and the Single Gentleman to deny any shared empathy for Quilp or Nell's grandfather, while nonetheless, and in some cases (Quilp and Dick Swiveller, particularly, though in different registers) exuberantly to evoke and enact unsanctioned desire. No wonder Dickens felt he had gone too far (or perhaps it was Forster's act of censorship) when Sally Brass declares to her brother that the Marchioness is her child. That conception (in both senses) too explicitly invades the domestic by the unbridled id.

Theodor W. Adorno, a Marxist critic, reads this relationship between Nell and her grandfather differently. He sees Nell almost as a "pre-bourgeois" creature, not yet autonomous or isolated within a bourgeois economic system. She bears "objective factors," "a dark, obscure fate," and "a starlike consolation" but cannot escape from, nor be wholly absorbed by, the capitalist system that both accompanies her, in the case of her grandfather, and strives to overtake her, in the case of all her moneyed pursuers.[75] This may be a valid reading of Nell's fated pilgrimage to escape from a society dominated by money, but it too is not a story available to anyone within the text to narrate. How one can be rich and yet pure – the Cheeryble conundrum – Dickens cannot solve.

XI

There's another set of secrets, partly disclosed during the narrative, and partly disclosed after the narrative ends, beyond any tale that Kit tells his children. It turns out that Nell's grandfather and his younger brother the Single Gentleman were both in love with the same woman.[76] The younger brother gave up his claim so that his much-loved elder brother could marry her. The offspring of that marriage was a daughter whose mother died at her birth. She married a profligate, Trent, who beggared both his own family and his father-in-law. He and his wife die young, leaving two children, Fred and Nell. Thus Nell is the third iteration of the woman both her grandfather/abuser and her ineffectual suitor and rescuer, the Single Gentleman, loved. She is, as the printed text, manuscript, and suppressed proofs insist on several occasions, the living image of her maternal forebears, both in her beauty and in her ailing (cf. pp. 542–43). And therefore, for the two brothers, she is the perpetually deferred object of desired consummation and perpetuation.

Now this genealogical origin of the old man and the girl explains less than it might. And when the younger brother identifies himself to Mr. Garland and the reader, the Trent family composition is revealed as more complicated, but not more clear or safe, than before. Moreover, the story of the desiring males competing for a single female, and of their coming together again at the end of their lives in order to secure the well-being of the granddaughter of that female, which they cannot do, has implications about the connection between storytelling and fictions of origin. As Freud outlined and Steven Marcus and Albert Hutter have foregrounded in Dickens, there are a number of scenes in his novels in which a child gazes on something that may be analogous to the child's own begetting.[77] To put it in layman's terms: we want to know, we are curious, about how we were begotten so that we can ground our stories of our own lives, and yet that knowledge of our parents' sexuality is deeply and elaborately taboo. The scene of sexual origin is one we need to discover and deny. And when, as in Nell's case, that origin is so contaminated by unfulfilled desires and displaced drives, it becomes a story even more impossible to tell, and even more impossibly embedded in Nell's body, the third female in her genealogy whose relationship to her grandfather is an impacted combination of desire, death, profligacy, and commerce. So the bedroom scene would be almost impossible for any character in the story to tell.

Except Quilp, who might smack his lips and bare his teeth at such a delightful prospect as seducing Nell and gaining control over her supposed fortune. Quilp has no qualms about overtly displaying his lecherous impulses and would narrate such a bedroom scene without apology. He is, as it were, an embodiment of all the malformed energies at work over the generations that comprise Nell's history and her story. Displaced from the biological line, he is free to articulate and act out the erotic dance of gaze and seduction, marriage and money, expenditure and consumption, that is so obliquely and disjunctively narrated about Nell. But Quilp, master of the ill quip, the whip, and the seducer's guilt, could never "toll Nell's knell," never honor her or mourn her passing or imagine her Heavenly reward. His is the version of her desirability that no authoritative narrator or reader could produce or own up to. His is the unsanctioned, unsanctionable story, though his leering, groping advances to Little Nell and her treasures of body and inheritance are disturbingly analogous to her grandfather's mode of hoarding: Master Humphrey in introducing the proprietor of the Old Curiosity Shop describes him as one who "might have groped among old churches and tombs and deserted houses and gathered all the spoils with his own hands" (p. 10). (This is, by the end of the novel, Humphrey describing his older brother!)

All these old curiosities are deeply embedded in Nell's story: the curiosity for the knowledge of good and evil that caused the Fall, the curiosity about our sexual origins that produces the tensions between innocence and experience and between mother-love and father-love in the family, the curiosity involving the mysteries of the body and its secret hoards of wealth and increase. But they are unnarratable for a variety of reasons: social taboos, cultural reticence, and a need for this story to unfold a variety of scenes and emotions, not just one primary scene endlessly reiterated. It contains a company of grotesques, some delightfully comic (Dick and the Marchioness), some quietly domestic (the Garland and Nubbles families), some fierce. And they seek to possess their desires in many ways.

For this book is not just about our age-old curiosities, but also about the Old Curiosity Shop, whose inventory consists of an eye-catching miscellany of objects, including "distorted figures in china and wood and iron and ivory; tapestry and strange furniture that might have been designed in dreams" (p. 10). The proprietor has hoarded a warehouse full of stuff that he evidently hopes to sell; goods attractive enough for Quilp, no fool in the commercial department, to lend money against. The manuscript has Nell tell Master Humphrey that she goes out "Selling diamonds" (p. 577), a detail that supports the speculation so many enter into that the old man is really rich. Nell's grandfather is gambling on his gambling eventually returning enough money to repay his loans and set her up for life. He has gathered an assemblage of diverse objects for sale and he has mortgaged the present for a hoped-for future. And yet, excepting Quilp's loans, almost nothing material in this novel is either bought or sold. It seems as if trade has come to a standstill, even in the manufacturing Midlands. Entertainers, especially those who can claim an educational repertory, sell some tickets; but the commerce that counts is personal, abusive in the case of the Brasses, gloriously restorative in the case of Dick Swiveller's reinvention of Sally's maid.[78]

Unlike Master Humphrey's purported older brother, most of those who constitute his company above stairs – the deaf gentleman, Jack Redburn, and Owen Miles – or below stairs, the Wellers and Mr. Pickwick – have a retrospective, rather than prospective, view of life. Whereas Dick Swiveller and others are hopeful that their fortune will turn (a motif that resounds with Sol Gills and Captain Cuttle in *Dombey and Son*, Tommy Traddles and Mr. Micawber in *David Copperfield*, and Richard Carstone in *Bleak House*), Master Humphrey's guests know much about the sunsets to which sunrise prospects often come.[79] They thus serve as a kind of chorus from the future ends of hope.

And that is another complication to telling this story. Those whose hopes are realized, however imperfectly – neither Kit nor Dick nor Quilp gets Nell, but Kit and Dick do achieve domestic bliss with another – can tell, as Kit does, a story that provokes both sorrow and mirth. Death authorizes Nell's narrative, makes it possible for Kit and others to mourn her and toll her knell; they know her story to its end and know nothing will change her in life or death. But those whose fortune and life are still in prospect have no completed tale to tell. And the most important one whose fortune is yet to be made is the principal, but deeply hidden, teller of the tale, Charles Dickens.[80]

## XII

Leah Price has related the rise of the novel to the rise of anthologies of excerpts from poetry and prose.[81] Whereas the novel might demand sustained attention and prolonged reading, the anthology allowed rapid access to high points. On the other hand, the leisurely appreciation of those high points might contrast to the impatient, hurried reading practice of the consumer of novels. And these different reading practices were tied to different modes of producing reading: the epistolary novel, for instance, allowed a kind of reading not dissimilar to that promoted by anthologies. Different classes, with different amounts of reading time and literacy skills, sought different texts; and by the middle of the nineteenth century, novels of plot gave way in the hierarchy of critical opinion to novels with more thoughtful, and more excerptable, passages of reflection and philosophy. Samuel Richardson, George Eliot, and Thomas Hardy all had their novels rifled for anthology moments. Though Price does not focus on the 1840s, when Dickens was producing *Master Humphrey's Clock*, it is well worth placing that publication in the field where anthologies competed with three-volume novels for readers, and when reviews – including those of Dickens's titles, especially *Nickleby* – more often simply printed extracts from the volume or monthly number rather than providing any more substantial analysis of the work.[82] Anthologies, like the Christmas coffee table books edited by Lady Blessington and others, appealed to those who preferred to read closely and think about the philosophy and expression of the excerpts; novels may have appealed to another class of readers more interested in fast-paced entertainment.

Bringing Price's work into conversation with *Master Humphrey's Clock* raises some crucial questions. Clearly, Dickens did not initially plan for the *Clock* to incorporate novels or appeal to that segment of the reading public. It was to be a miscellany addressing issues of the day and architectural and social history, while leavening the mix with shorter pieces that might be humorous or dramatic or fanciful. If two of the functions of the "author" in relation to the text that "author" authorizes are to provide the work's unity and the source of its origin, a miscellany isn't "authored." It doesn't have a unity in the same ways that a novel does; it may indeed, as Dickens planned, be a compilation by various hands. Yet Dickens also wanted to impose a kind of "unity" on the *Clock*: not only did he propose writing much of the text and threading through the whole various repeating materials, but also he wanted control over the contributions of any hirelings. The ambiguity of the conception of the *Clock* – part miscellany, later mainly novel – is signaled in its declaration of authorship. The paper wrappers of the *Clock* parts state that *Master's Humphrey's Clock* is "by Boz." Not "edited" by Boz, as *Pickwick*, *Oliver Twist*, *Bentley's Miscellany*, and *Nicholas Nickleby* were "edited" by Boz, but not written by Charles Dickens, either. The *Clock* was simply "by Boz." And this, in 1840, three years after Dickens began regularly signing his own name to his fictions.

We can now return to the question we started with: "Who tolls Nell's knell, or tells Nell's tale?" The anthology model suggests that, insofar as the genre of the miscellany is concerned, there is no single answer, no single gentleman, necessary to provide the unity and origin of a miscellaneous assemblage of papers under the title of *Master Humphrey's Clock.* So perhaps not being able to find a satisfactory answer to our question simply indicates that it is inappropriate to ask of a miscellany. But Nell's story begins under a subheading to the magazine's title. That subheading reads "Personal Adventures of Master Humphrey." The initial story, as I have argued elsewhere, may have been all Dickens intended to write even though Master Humphrey promises to return to it from time to time. It is a street sketch, not unlike those in *Sketches by Boz* – emphasizing the contrast between the beautiful young child (of indeterminate age in this first chapter) and her grandfather and all the antique furniture – redolent of history – in the Shop.[83]

The question of who tells Nell's story is thus bound up with the question of genre. Insofar as the periodical *Master Humphrey's Clock* was designed as a miscellany, the *Clock* contents, all directed and composed "by Boz," the alter ego of Charles Dickens, nonetheless may without violation of aesthetic or other protocols come from many sources. One of those sources not yet discussed is Thomas Hood, who wrote an appreciative essay about the novel when it was halfway through publication. He identified the kind of "Allegory" that Dickens teased out from the initial chapter.[84]

Look at the Artist's picture of the Child, asleep in her little bed, surrounded, or rather mobbed, by ancient armour and arms, antique furniture, and relics sacred or profane, hideous or grotesque: – it is like an Allegory of the peace and innocence of Childhood in the midst of Violence, Superstition, and all the hateful or hurtful Passions of the world ... How soothing the moral, that Gentleness, Purity, and Truth, sometimes dormant but never dead, have survived, and will outlive, Fraud and Force, though backed by gold and encased in steel![85]

When Dickens gathered the sheets of the *Shop* for reissue in a single volume, he had to expunge intervening *Clock* material. That included the comic letter from "Belinda" to the nominal editor, Master Humphrey, that fills the last page and a half of the number printing the first chapter of the novel. Into this space Dickens inserts four new paragraphs, in the voice of Master Humphrey meditating on his night's encounter:

I had her image, without any effort of imagination, surrounded and beset by everything that was foreign to its nature, and furthest removed from the sympathies of her sex and age ... she seemed to exist in a kind of allegory; and having these shapes about her, claimed my interest so strongly, that (as I have already remarked) I could not dismiss her from my recollection, do what I would.

"It would be a curious speculation," said I, after some restless turns across and across the room, "to imagine her in her future life, holding her solitary way among a crowd of wild grotesque companions; the only pure, fresh, youthful object in the throng. It would be curious to find – "

I checked myself here, for the theme was carrying me along with it at a great pace, and I already saw before me a region on which I was little disposed to enter.

(p. 19)

Since these remarks were written long after Dickens had entered into that region of wild grotesque companions and was thoroughly enjoying the journey, the cutting off of Master Humphrey's speculations at this point signifies yet again the effort the novel makes to focus on Nell as "pure, fresh, youthful," and not on the next words, "object in the throng" of shapes and creatures "furthest removed from the sympathies of her sex and age." Neither Hood nor Dickens specifically identifies the "Allegory," leaving individual readers – and they were the largest aggregation of customers Boz had yet recruited to his stories – to construe the allegory and empathize with either Nell or her pursuers, or both. Thus Dickens adopts Hood's reading, imposing it on Master Humphrey and adding a further collaborator whom he generously acknowledges in his Preface to the 1848 Cheap Edition, while declaring two paragraphs before this acknowledgment that he "had it always in [his] fancy to surround the lonely figure of the child with grotesque and wild, but not impossible companions, and to gather about her innocent face and pure intentions, associates as strange and uncongenial as the grim objects that are about her bed when her history is first foreshadowed" (p. 610).[86] And yet, as with the ambiguities about the tellers and the stories in the *Clock* frame, the text opens up the interpretation of this allegory to its readers, rather than foreclosing it. Here is another instance where Dickens, Boz, Humphrey, are far from the dictatorial author policing readers' own reactions to the story.

The whole style of *The Old Curiosity Shop* seems anthologized. Bulwer told Forster that it "contains patches of the most exquisite truth & poetry," but thought it was not well constructed as a whole.[87] There are passages of narrative that read like uninspired set-pieces of architectural and topographical description or sociological travelogue (think of the journey through the industrial Midlands), and others that seem, in Steven Marcus's formulation, to be "hollow reiteration[s] of ... idyllic life."[88] Nell's adventures on the road comprise a series of chapter vignettes that alternate disruptively with chapters about her pursuers in London.

There are scenes that get reiterated and, in a sense, anthologized, in all kinds of other verbal and visual mediums, including dramas and canvases: Kit's writing lesson and visit to Astley's; Dick and the Marchioness; Nell at the racetrack, which became an incident in William Powell Frith's great painting, *Derby Day*. Other parts of the novel drop out of the text and out of sight – including all the stuff about how the "Personal Adventures of Master Humphrey" might be related to the Single Gentleman and his brother. And there is one scene that everyone alludes to even though it never is shown in the text – namely, the death of Little Nell. This is, in some ways, an incoherent text, inconsistent in tone, jerky in narrative progress, uncertain in its point of view, and dispersed rather than focused in its affect. Our inability to imagine one narrator, omniscient or individual, for all the stories this text tells is a marker of its origin and affinities with the miscellany as well as being the result of the multiple traces of pens and pencils and oral and written stories contributing to the novel's text and context.

## XIII

One other aspect of the miscellany is worth noting. In the 1840s, novels were fiercely contesting with other subject classifications: religion, which still accounted for the largest percentage of titles in the 1840s (20 percent); geography, history, travel, and biography – the second highest (17 percent); fiction and juvenile literature, third at 16 percent; and education, fourth at 12 percent.[89] Publishers and novelists were fighting for customers – readers. Printed commodities sold to various grades of customer, but the two most lucrative markets were the middle class and the upper-working class. The 1840s, with Dickens in the lead, tried to forge kinds of publications that would reach into both cohorts. The consumers of tales in *Master Humphrey's Clock* are imagined to be of two kinds: elderly, deformed bachelors of leisure, ruined and retired gentlemen, upstairs, and a more vigorous but down-market company below stairs. That frame narrative about the clock society models, within the text, Dickens's desire to invite both classes to his clock side by the chimney corner.

To do so successfully, he had to price his wares to fit the exigencies of many size purses. Accordingly, in the most complex marketing scheme Dickens had yet attempted, the *Clock* was published in weekly installments at 3*d.*, monthly parts at 1*s.* for four-week months and 1*s.* 3*d.* for five-week months, and half-yearly volumes. Eventually, the entirety of the *Clock*, comprising two novels, *The Old Curiosity Shop* and *Barnaby*

*Rudge*, plus all the other *Clock* matter at the opening and between the two novels, appeared as if the *Clock* was a three-volume novel, though in an odd oversized format with tall pages, 10.5" × 7".[90] Moreover, the novels were made available immediately after their conclusions as separate one-volume tales complete in themselves, expunged of most remnants of their miscellany origin.

But marketing to many classes depended on more than making the text available at different prices. To begin with, no one could be sure what class bought at what price. Was it easier for the working class to lay out threepence a week or a shilling a month? Could middle-class consumers wait for the monthly installment or had they the leisure to partake of the tale each week as it appeared? And what kind of attention might be paid to the text by various kinds of readers? How would women read differently from men (there were lots of theories circulating)? "While the preference for beauties or for plot has continued to differentiate one class of novel-readers from another," Leah Price remarks, "the shift from a culture in which critics enjoy beauties while ladies devour stories to one where the vulgar appreciate stylistic ornament and the elite demands organic unity makes clear how arbitrary those markers of difference are."[91] How would country residents read differently from urban dwellers, and Midlands readers respond differently – especially to the unflattering portrait of the industrial area – from Scots or residents of the home counties? How could anyone predict the frenzied reaction of the Americans to Nell's saga, so readily assimilable to their own fantasies of their innocence threatened by the old gargoyles of Europe?

Telling Nell's tale, then, requires an audience, requires imagining an audience in advance, as Dickens imagines Master Humphrey's audience, and requires designing a story or stories that would appeal to a variety of tastes, a variety that one might imagine but not dictate. So *Master Humphrey's Clock* and its embedded stories addressed many different kinds of readers by providing many different kinds of reading experiences. The presumption of the canonical critical journals of the period was that a successful novel had an artfully designed plot, complete with beginning, middle, and end, no muddle or loose ends, and a moral enacted by the plot that was socially beneficial.[92] This judgment by the whole was, however, undercut by those same periodicals' practice of excerpting exceptional passages as if they were representative of the whole.[93] The plot of *The Old Curiosity Shop* could hardly be called an artistic triumph: it starts with a static scene of contrast, rather like one of the *Sketches by Boz*.[94] Then its relation to the titular "Personal Adventures" is severed in the third chapter. And thereafter its episodic nature and insistently foreshadowed end preclude the kinds of suspense and surprise that consumers of exciting tales sought. Nor is the moral derivable from the plot very satisfying or striking, however entertaining the story may be to the imagined audience of Barbaras, Jacobs, Abels, and Dicks: "things pass away." Chesterton gave it the best gloss anyone could. He said it was an ironic *Pilgrim's Progress*, in which the travelers flee from the safety that pursues them.[95] That's a part of the story, but by no means all, and it is not a story that would necessarily be thought to attract the novel reader who wanted a pulse-thumping read.

Nell's pilgrimage had uncomfortable overtones for Dickens himself, though only toward the end of his tale. For at some level the story of a single gentleman who loves a woman, gives her up to another, later in life finds her ill and in need, strives to rescue her, and fails, has psychic connections to Dickens own recent past, as many critics have perhaps overemphasized. Yet, as Dickens wrote about the coach ride to Nell's resting place, he "tremble[d] to approach the place a great deal more than Kit; a great deal more than Mr. Garland; a great deal more than the Single Gentleman. I shan't recover [from] it for a long time."[96] He did not so much give up his love to another as, in the case of Maria Beadnell, get jilted, and in the case of the Hogarth sisters, perhaps pick the wrong one. But when a dearly loved young woman became ill, Dickens rushed to her bedside, but could not rescue her from death. If the ironic pursuit of rescuers is the basic plot of the *Shop*, it is also a story that at some personal level, at some point during the construction of the tale, Dickens hates, fears, and needs to tell to exorcise his own guilt and mourning.[97]

Still, however Dickens and his publishers imagined their audiences, *The Old Curiosity Shop* confounded the skeptics. Thackeray thought the new novel "sadly flat," but the last installments of the *Shop* achieved sales approaching 100,000.[98] Whatever calculations might have been made to appeal to one set of customers by providing excerptable beauties, another set by telling stories of chambers and horrors, another by reviving the Samuels, Pickwick and Weller, yet another by supplying amusing snippets of correspondence and other light matter, and still another by composing a tale that appealed to sympathy, reflection, and curiosity, the medley that is the *Shop* hit home beyond anyone's reckoning.

The *Clock* sold; the *Shop* as part of and apart from the *Clock* sold; Nelly sold. Emblematic of her commodity status are the two most famous images of her, in antique beds. She could almost be, in either one, part of a marble monument, like all those funerary sculptures purchased and installed in churches to commemorate the departed. Indeed, the monuments beside her grandfather in the penultimate illustration are all versions of Nell in bed. There is a complex interweaving of temporality, art, sexuality, and commodity in *The Old Curiosity Shop*. Its most succinct formulation, that time is money, that things are made to be sold, and that art, though commodity, may outlast time, comes later in Dickens's career, first in *A Christmas Carol* and next, more elaborately and critically, in *Dombey and Son*. But Nell's life is ticked off, week by week, by the *Clock* that Boz produces and sells; her tale is presumably one of those in the clock case, under the pendulum.

XIV

Nell's status as a temporal commodity once again complicates any answer to the question of who narrates this tale. If the story is a story of failed rescue, it elicited from Dickens's contemporaries frantic efforts to save her or at least to hope for her earthly salvation and snatch up the next installment. But to create this kind of interest Dickens drove her to death. The generation of readers after Dickens's own death reacted to the pawky sentimentality and crass commercialism of this artistic strategy: kill Nell for sales. Ruskin charged that Dickens dispatched characters the way a butcher slaughtered a lamb, for the marketplace. That was one version of Nell's story Dickens or Boz was not going to tell overtly.

Not tell overtly, but covertly. Mrs. Jarley and Mr. Slum, between them, exemplify the proximity of crass commercialism to "art." An acrostic on Warren's Blacking can easily, for three and six in ready money, be changed to one extolling waxworks (p. 220); and a slight adjustment of costume will convert "a murderess of great renown into Mrs. Hannah More" (p. 225). Subjects, even genres can be changed at the audience's whim: Mrs. Jarley knows that representations appealing to the vulgar must be altered if they are to attract "audiences ... of a very superior description" (p. 225). For another aspect of the question "who tells Nell's story" is the power of the consumer. As Barthes has pointed out, the "death of the author," the withdrawal of a singular "authority" from a text, empowers the reader. If we do not get all our information from one third-person omniscient source, if instead "those who have prominent and necessary parts" tell the story, readers are free to interrogate the speaking subjects, to doubt their veracity, to fill in gaps in their stories. In short, readers of *The Old Curiosity Shop* are much in the position of Quilp, the Marchioness, and Nell: they all spy on others in order to construct and consolidate their own stories. In that sense, there is no one story, either in *Master Humphrey's Clock* or in *The Old Curiosity Shop*, and therefore no one teller of the tale. Each reader, like Kit, fashions a story for his (or her) audience, self or others. That Dickens suppresses his own investment in his tale for various reasons has many unexpected outcomes. One of them is that he gives Nell over to her purchasers. It was a story, Forster tells us, that "more than any other of his works" made "the bond between himself and his readers one of personal attachment."[99] Dickens and his readers had the same relationship to Nell and recognized each other's investment. But turning the story over to his audience meant that Dickens forfeited his authority to dictate their response – there were, after all, some including John Ruskin who thought the story quite bad.

Never, in all the revisions of the printed text and explanations in prefaces of his "intention," did Dickens manage entirely to regain authority even over the origin and composition of the text. These prefaces, more than any others that Dickens composed, foreground the notion of "author" as reigning authority. The preface to volume one of the *Clock* opens, "When the author commenced this Work, he proposed to himself three objects" (p. 606). These were (1) "To establish a periodical ... [for] certain fictions which he had it in contemplation to write"; (2) "To produce these Tales in weekly numbers; hoping that to shorten the intervals of communication between himself and his readers, would be to knit more closely the pleasant relations they had held"; and (3) "to have as much regard as its exigencies would permit, to each story as a whole, and to the possibility of its publication at some distant day, apart from the machinery in which it had its origin" (p. 606). Dickens's own letters, Forster's biography, and the numerous cancelled manuscript and proof passages flatly contradict these objects. He did not envision the *Clock* as the container for his continuing fictions; his choice of weekly format was made as much in order to foil the pirates as to knit readers and authors more closely together; and he did not contemplate, even after the first month or so of *Clock* issues, publishing his weekly fiction installments afterwards as a book, though he did imagine that certain repeated features such as the Chapters on Chambers might be extracted for separate release in volume format. The "author" for whom Dickens speaks in the Preface is a rationalization of an outcome the actual writer, editor, and proprietor neither anticipated nor intended. This preface is one of the most blatant instances of Dickens writing himself into being as a professional, not only after the fact but also after the facts.

The preface to the separate release of the sheets containing *The Old Curiosity Shop* also begins with a claim about authorship, this time fashioned not as an authority with three objects in mind, but rather as an innkeeper who must provide for miscellaneous customers by supplying a bill of fare. "'An author,' says Fielding, in his introduction to 'Tom Jones,' 'ought to consider himself, not as a gentleman who gives a private or eleemosynary treat, but rather as one who keeps a public ordinary, at which all persons are welcome for their money'" (p. 4). Dickens goes on to apologize for not providing such a bill of fare, preferring that his story "make its own way, silently and gradually, or make no way at all." But this is hardly a true bill either, since the miscellany was transformed into a continued story precisely because the customers didn't like the variegated eats and entertainment originally proffered. Dickens cannot help recurring to the most vexing issue about the *Shop*, his own published lack of authority over its narration. "To give a text an Author," Barthes observes, "is to impose a limit on that text, to furnish it with a final signified, to close the writing" (p. 147). When no coherent authority for the text is prescribed, a text is instead made up of multiple writings and authorities. There is one place, Barthes explains, "where this multiplicity is focused and that place is the reader, not, as was hitherto said, the author. The reader is the space on which all the quotations that make up a writing are inscribed without any of them being lost; a text's unity lies not in its origin but in its destination" (p. 148).

Well, that may be true of post-modern texts, but it is not entirely true of *The Old Curiosity Shop*, nor of Dickens's intentions as an author who always wants to seem in control of text and audience, whether he speaks in his own name or through a pseudonym. What complicates matters for Dickens in the present instance is his own ambivalence regarding his material. The *Shop*, begun with less advance planning than almost any other of his fictions, and composed under enormous strains – financial, compositional, religious, and psychological – irresistibly tapped into the deepest energies of Dickens's psyche. At no level was he able to master these forces completely; the result is a text with the disorder of dreams, nightmares, fantasy, and fairy tale. And it is marked everywhere by the genre of dream – the blend of the real and unreal that moves the dreamer so powerfully. From the close of the first chapter to the close of the novel, persons and events are likened to dreams. Master Humphrey daydreams all night, obsessively, about "the beautiful child in her gentle slumber," surrounded by "the old dark murky rooms – the gaunt suits of mail with their ghostly silent air – the faces all awry, grinning from wood and stone," and yet "smiling through her light and sunny dreams" (pp. 19–20). Nell's dying is marked by dreams: "They could tell, by what she faintly uttered in her dreams, that they were of her journeyings with the old man" (p. 559). In Dickens, dreams somehow bespeak our elemental nature, but they are not under our control. A dream contests the authority of an author, even when the author imagines the dream.

Dickens was hard pressed to construct even a syntax for narration that excludes the narrator. "Chapter the last" opens with "The magic reel, which, rolling on before, has led the chronicler thus far, now slackens its pace, and stops. It lies before the goal; the pursuit is at an end" (p. 566). The reel is itself an interesting metaphor, anticipatory of cinema and perhaps alluding to the kinds of scenery on rollers used in theaters of the period to give an illusion that actors walking in front of it were moving across a landscape. (This was, not perhaps irrelevantly to note, how *Lord Bateman*'s journeys were staged.) The reel becomes analogous to the story itself, figured in the next sentence as a journey rather in the picaresque mode: "the little crowd who have borne us company upon the road." But the relation of reel to narrator is opaque, indirect. It rolls *before* the chronicler. He is another of those who looks on and then tells his version of the story.[100] But the reel, presumably, holds the whole story, and knows, if anyone does, that the journey has reached its end. That end is the final paragraph, following upon Kit's increasing uncertainty as to where the Old Curiosity Shop used to stand. Time is erasing history. And, the novel concludes, "Such are the changes which a few years bring about, and so do things pass away, like a tale that is told!" Here we have a tale told, without any teller. And a tale that "is told" is both already completed ("things pass away") and in progress, as the odd tense ambivalence of "is told" articulates. Nell's death releases her narrators into retrospection; effectively they have no future in narrative, no further story to tell. With a brief notation of the fate of each character – something Dickens had to make a note about in order to accomplish, because those brief futures were so unintegral to Nell's story – the novel stops.[101] Dreams are a bit like this kind of tale – told without a teller, disjunct, a mixture of the horrific and the idyllic, finished and yet repeated in the mind, very real at the time of dreaming, oddly enmeshed with real life too, and yet fading over time. Dreams, like magic reels, may have a chronicler, but not an author.[102]

A tale that is told is the summative formula for this novel, and one that lexically embeds the problematic of narration I've been addressing. "Tale" and "teller" come from the same Indo-European root. To tell is to disclose something, to divulge it. That something may be in the present, as in "I'll tell my love," or in the future, as in fortune telling. The disclosure may be innocent or not. One can "tell" on someone else – which happens very often in this novel. And one can "tell a tale" meaning speak a falsehood, which also often happens here. One who is told about counts for something. So telling, while it may efface the teller, elevates the subject told about, in this case, Nell – and, through Dick Swiveller's fancy, the Marchioness, who rises from subterranean invisibility to nobility because he tells about her.[103] And finally, telling means not just to count for something but to count, to enumerate or reckon, as in telling beads or serving as teller in a counting house, or telling up points in cribbage. Telling is a way of getting money and status as well as stories, and becomes another of Dickens's euphemisms for the commercial transaction of authorship. Telling can be done by writing or speaking: Nell's tale is both like the manuscripts in the clock case, though it is not one of them, and like Kit's recitals to his children. *The Old Curiosity Shop* is not only generically mixed, its story is recounted in both written and oral testimony. In later years Dickens as international celebrity author will exploit this combination of written and oral, revising excerpts from his own texts for delivery as his own version of Charles Mathews's monopolylogues.

A "tale that is told" effaces or obscures the teller, privileges all those who overhear the tale and retell it, tells the tale retrospectively and in the present retelling, makes the subject of the tale, Nell, count or "tell," tells all the secrets of origins and desires that the teller might not wish to disclose, tells falsehoods (the Trents are rich, Kit stole money) and fictions that are hard to discriminate between, and does all this so that the tale may tell in Dickens's till. What "a tale that is told" does not say is who tells it. Like the eruptions of the subconscious in dreams, we know tales that have no authorized teller, though in fact we are that teller, unacknowledged. As Dickens was, unacknowledged in so many ways, a teller of the material he released into his consumers' minds and authority.

# CHAPTER 7

# *Unwriting Boz (1841):* Master Humphrey's Clock *and* Barnaby Rudge

Charles Dickens, Samuel Drummond portrait, c. 1840

[I]t does not appear from anything that Boz has yet done that he is equal to the demands of a regular novel, or that he is willing to throw himself at once upon a three-volumed production simultaneously published.

– *Monthly Review*, January 1839

*Barnaby Rudge* is Dickens's best constructed story; and, in one sense of the word, the best written.

– George Gissing, *Critical Studies*

By late 1840 the [Gordon] Riots had become a literal and totally appropriate metaphor for the English political situation.

– Thomas J. Rice, "The Politics of *Barnaby Rudge*"

"I loved my father better than any man in the world – in a different way of course . . . I loved him for his faults." Rising from her chair and walking towards the door, she added: "My father was a wicked man – a very wicked man."

– Gladys Story, quoting Kate Dickens in *Dickens and Daughter*

I

In the *Clock*, *Barnaby Rudge* begins with no introduction of any kind. The manuscript, in the Forster Collection at the Victoria and Albert Museum, starts with the two chapters Dickens had penned by February of 1840; these were subsequently divided into the first three chapters of the serial version on January 21, 1841.[1] Which leaves a big gap. What was the novel Dickens had conceived of writing back in 1836, when on May 9, he contracted with Macrone, just as he was renegotiating *Pickwick*'s production and beginning to think about a second collection of *Sketches* to be issued by the end of the year, to also indite enough matter for a three-volume novel by November 30? It *seems* to have been conceived as a narrative of the Gordon riots of 1780, a historical novel in the mode of Scott, and perhaps inspired by the burning of the Old Tolbooth Prison in *The Heart of Midlothian* and the demented, powerful figure of Madge Wildfire. Perhaps at that time Dickens was already connecting the rioters with madness. He told Macrone in June of 1836 that he thought of visiting Bethlehem Hospital (Bedlam) for one of the stories he would contribute to the "New Series" of *Sketches*, but there is no such story in the New Series, nor conclusive evidence that he ever made the visit or that madness was part of his initial plan for the novel.[2]

The most significant clue we have to the earliest conception of the novel is its title, *Gabriel Vardon, or the Locksmith of London*. This figure is partly based on a Moravian blacksmith who, during the riots, refused the mob's demand to free the Newgate prisoners from their shackles. Dickens may already have read Thomas Holcroft's *Narrative of the Late Riots* (1780) and Robert Watson's *Life of George Gordon,* both of which were in his library.[3] In 1836 Dickens might have been thinking back to the storming of the Bastille, to be described memorably the following year in Carlyle's *French Revolution* (1837). More recently, as a reporter he had followed accounts of a series of uprisings in the late 1820s and early 1830s – the agitation over Catholic emancipation that pushed Parliament to enact more tolerant laws despite fierce Protestant opposition, the Swing agricultural riots of 1830–31 anachronistically mentioned in *Pickwick,* and the European revolutions of 1832. As prisons, prisoners, and incarceration policies had been on his mind since his family went to the Marshalsea in 1824, and were to show up with a very sympathetic treatment of debtors, sane and mad, in the March through May 1837 numbers when Pickwick is locked in the Fleet, it seems likely that at the center of Dickens's first ideas for the book were issues about jail, jailers, and whether justice was locking up the right people or, to anticipate Gilbert and Sullivan, making the punishment fit the crime. Evidently the Moravian blacksmith did not think prisoners should have their irons struck off; whether Vardon in this shadow version would have behaved in the same way, or freed unfortunate victims of injustice, simply isn't known; nor does any evidence exist suggesting how Vardon's unsuccessful attempts to secure his own home, shop, family, and servants under lock and key might have contributed to the plot and his character as the titular protagonist.

It is also unclear why Dickens changed his mind about the eponymous hero, although the date of the change is certain. When Bentley first contracted in August 1836 with Dickens for two novels, "the Title" of the first "is not yet determined," and a second, also untitled, was to follow.[4] It seems as if this first novel was the one due to Macrone in November, which Dickens's friends had counseled should be purchased for £500, not the £200 Macrone had promised before *Pickwick* became such a hit.[5] So already *Gabriel Vardon* may have been being reconceived and retitled, although since Macrone had not formally released Dickens from his obligation perhaps the Agreement with Bentley was just keeping mum about what that first novel would be. In November, while still negotiating with Macrone about the contents of the two-volume, reduced to one-volume, second series of *Sketches,* Dickens told him that he wanted to withdraw from their May Agreement.[6] But Macrone refused to back down, having been advised by Ainsworth to say merely "I shall hold you to your agreement."[7] He pressed his case by sending notices that *Gabriel Vardon* was preparing for publication to Bentley for insertion in the *Miscellany* and to Chapman and Hall for the January *Pickwick Advertiser*, and inserted it at the back of *Sketches*, Second Series, published December 17. Some time in January 1837, Dickens and Bentley reached an understanding with Macrone that he would cancel the *Vardon* Agreement as part of a larger commitment on the part of Chapman and Hall to purchase all rights to and stock in *Sketches by Boz*, which as we have seen Macrone had threatened to publish in serial format identical to *Pickwick*. Exactly how all these publishers got together is mysterious, but Bentley was sufficiently confident by the end of January that he now could publish Dickens's novel that he advertised in the February *Miscellany* a "New Work in 3 vols" as forthcoming (a notice that prompted Carey, Lea and Blanchard to treat with Dickens or his publisher for early sheets to be sent to America).[8] By April that new work, announced in the *Miscellany*, had a new name: *Barnaby Rudge*.[9] But it still wasn't considered as the second novel Dickens had agreed to write for Bentley separate from his *Miscellany* monthly installments, and it was not accepted as the second novel, to be published first in the *Miscellany*, until September 1838. At that time its official title, connecting the Gordon riots to the eponymous hero, was "Barnaby Rudge: A Tale of the Great Riots."[10]

So, through the fog of incomplete communications, unsupported advertisements, and undocumented backstage discussions among Dickens, Chapman, Hall, Macrone, Bentley, and their lawyers, we see that early in 1837, while writing the first installment of *Oliver* and before sending Pickwick to the Fleet, Dickens reconceived his Gordon riots novel, substituting Barnaby for Gabriel Vardon, who in the final version becomes Varden. This may mean that whatever opening pages Dickens had drafted from time to time up to the end of 1836 got scrapped as the ingredients of his narrative shifted. In the intervening years, before he actually began writing the final version in January 1840, then postponing it for another year until resuming in January 1841, the applicability of social uprisings dramatically increased. As Butt and Tillotson summarize:

the events of 1836–41 made the novel almost journalistically apt. The Poor Law riots, the Chartist risings at Devizes, Birmingham, and Sheffield, the mass meetings on Kersal Moor and Kennington Common, and most pointedly of all, the Newport rising of 1839 with its attempt to release Chartist prisoners – all these, with their aftermath of trials, convictions, and petitions against the punishment of death, gave special point in 1841 to "a tale of the Riots of '80."[11]

Moreover, in 1839 the Protestant Association was formed, with many local branches run by working-class "operatives"; it held large meetings in Exeter Hall and petitioned the Government against granting Roman Catholics any special exemptions with regard to education. Though the Association rejected social demonstrations, its rhetoric was impassioned, perhaps inflammatory to minds like Gordon's, susceptible to heightened fears of Catholic ascendancy. When in the mid-1830s the Liverpool Town Council tried to institute the "Irish" system of educating both Protestants and Catholics in the same school, while allowing Catholics to use the Douay Bible, Tory and Protestant opponents vigorously campaigned against such toleration. In the General Election of 1837, the *Liverpool Courier* stigmatized Catholic placards, which they claimed were calculated to "call together a mob of the most ruffianly desperadoes in Christendom" who were "the rankest scum of Irish Popery, being non-electors." If Papists were allowed to parade on St. Patrick's Day, the *Liverpool Standard* thundered, "all we can say is that the public authorities of the town are willing to be considered as conniving at treason and the Protestant inhabitants of the town have consented to place their necks under the yoke of Popish tyranny."[12] (Dickens visited Liverpool just a few months after this election, which unseated the Liberal MP and returned two Conservatives. It was from Liverpool that he dashed back to London to oversee the final proofs of *Oliver Twist*.)

Thus events between 1836 and 1841 conspired to reactivate Dickens's journalistic training and to intuit complicated parallels, dangers, and differences between previous national uprisings, the extreme rhetorics of polarized religious and ethnic parties (not all Irish were Catholics but the distinctions between the two were often elided), and the events of 1780. At one root of *Barnaby*, therefore, is Dickens's own background as a reporter and his sustained interest in the relationship between current events, national crises, and his own writings. The alliance of Ultra-Tories (anti-Catholic) and Ultra-Radicals (pro-Chartist) that formed in the late 1830s to overthrow Melbourne seemed to many to reawaken sectarian passions. As Thomas J. Rice observes, "Dickens was exceptional ... in recognizing early the full appropriateness of the Gordon Riots as a political metaphor for the contemporary situation."[13]

Journalism and news merge with another genre of writing, history, particularly the history of a troubled time as retailed in the newspapers of the period and in the memory of survivors. (The exact relation between history and its recounting by a chronicler had not, it seems, been formulated by Dickens, for whom both Nell's story and the Gordon riots are chronicles.) Dickens consulted a number of contemporary accounts of the riots and also interviewed several who had lived through them. And in taking as his subject a formative clash between constituents of the kingdom – Catholics and Protestants, and also government versus the mob – Dickens follows the paradigm of Scott, who sets so many of his historical fictions at just such moments in the long and troubled formation of a United Kingdom. In *Barnaby* journalism, history, and fiction combine. Later in the chapter we will return to this aspect of the book.

II

But the focus on the Gordon riots doesn't entirely account for the change of title, or for the prominence in the first thirty-two chapters of goings-on in the country residences of John Willet at the Maypole Inn and Geoffrey Haredale at the Warren, and in London of Gabriel Varden at his house in a tidy suburb of Clerkenwell and Sir John Chester luxuriating in his rooms in Paper Buildings within the Temple precincts. These are four parallel and contrasting cases of patriarchs exercising various kinds and degrees of despotism over their relations. And two of the four have ancestors who died violently: Haredale's brother, murdered; Chester's mistress, executed. Some of the younger generation have rebelled. Emma Haredale disobeys her uncle in receiving Edward Chester's attentions. Ned Chester resists his father and is finally ordered out of the house. Hugh, his bastard brother, is both aggressively antagonistic to authority of any kind and yet wholly awed by his biological father's social superiority. Joe Willet chafes openly at his father's authoritarianism. And while Dolly Varden on the whole conforms to her father's directions, Varden's apprentice Sim Tappertit is an ardent and ambitious Protestant who sneaks out at night to lead a cadre of potential working-class rebels, the 'Prentice Knights, and Martha Varden's maid, Miggs, sycophantically supports her mistress while sowing ill will and suspicion everywhere in the house – even in the front door lock which she jams so that Sim can't get back in after his night's carouse.

Rebellion is thus inscribed within domestic as well as civic spaces, and builds over the five years between the opening chapters and chapter the thirty-third.[14] A perfect image of the connection between domestic and national issues is the little "red-brick dwelling-house, with a yellow roof; having at top a real chimney, down which voluntary subscribers dropped their silver, gold, or pence, into the parlour."[15] The money goes to support the Protestant Association. Mrs. Varden extracts these so-called "voluntary" contributions from her friends and neighbors. Miggs shrewdly flings her wages down the chimney with loquacious demonstrations of her devotion, knowing she will purchase many times the value in "gifts of caps and gowns and other articles of dress" from her mistress (p. 343). But the house sits on the mantel-shelf of a house divided, as neither Gabriel Varden nor Dolly will deposit down the chimney, while Sim takes the proceeds to finance rebellion against all masters and Catholics, the latter including Dolly's "foster-sister" Emma Haredale (p. 169). At the novel's end, Martha Varden, chastened into permanent amiability by the riots, does not object to her husband's crushing the red house that had been divisive abroad and at home so that harmony might be restored.

Dickens has always been interested in family origins and continuities, especially those that are concealed. Oliver's, Smike's, Nell's, the Marchioness's, Barnaby's, and Hugh's ancestries determine significant parts of their novels' plots.[16] The Nickleby brothers' antithetical handling of their inheritance and offspring initiate that novel and also, later on, contrast to the Cheeryble brothers' treatment of their one nephew, Frank. Disastrous christenings and romantically roaming uncles threaten to disinherit the hopeful collateral descendants. And often it is at the denouement of the novel that the recovery of the past and the restitution of the biological family occur – from the slight drama of Mr. Winkle accepting his son to the protracted unfolding of Oliver's parentage to the fatal identification of Smike's father.

Behind that backbone of Dickens's plots lies a larger set of myths about origins. He seems to favor one of two kinds of stories about how domestic and civil societies are founded. One version pits father against son (Saturn eating his offspring) or son overthrowing father (Oedipus) or father-surrogate/uncle (Hamlet). This is the intergenerational myth that requires the overthrowing of the *ancien régime* in order for a cleansed society to emerge. The other version pits siblings against one another (Cain vs. Abel, Valentine and Orson – which Dickens knew well and references in chapter the fifteenth)[17] or gives each complementary strengths that combine to forge lasting and productive alliances (less common, and often displaced onto cousins, as in Jesus and John, or foster-siblings, such as David and Jonathan). In either of these paradigms, there is potential for overthrow or reconciliation; in some cases both – what Mircea Eliade identifies as the *coincidentia oppositorum*, two figures sprung from the same principle who may be opposed at some time and reconciled at some end time, and in the meantime exhibit, as divinity does, both benevolent and terrible aspects, sometimes at the same time.[18] *Barnaby Rudge* seems, in this final version that Dickens published, to explore both templates and all four outcomes, and to implicate as well as he can the domestic rebellions and alliances in the larger battle between Catholics and Protestants, rebels and loyalists, underclasses and prisoners versus civic authority and honorable leadership. As Ronald Paulson observes, while "Rowlandson's model for riot was the adulterous triangle, Dickens's nuclear crowd is the disrupted family."[19]

III

If these issues were in their deepest configurations narratives of the founding of civilizations, and on a historical level the threats to stability experienced throughout Europe on an international as well as localized scale, they were also relevant to Dickens's unresolved relations to his own family. His father had apparently continued to draw on his son's credit (in both senses, distinction and financial resources); Dickens gave him an allowance to be shared with his wife, but there seem to have been unauthorized draws as well. And while removing his parents to Devonshire distanced them, Dickens found he needed to call on his mother's aid a lot, as we have seen, and so Elizabeth returned to London in 1840 and stayed for a long time. Dickens was in temperament and material possessions the clear head of the family, but he had not, could not, completely throw over his father – and in the next decade indeed his father's industry and accomplishment as a news reporter earned his son's warm respect and praise. Dickens acted as father to his younger brothers, all of whom to some degree seemed "feckless." He got jobs for them in the offices of friends, publishers, and employers; he helped them out finan-cially and advised them on their romantic affairs (though his advice was not always followed, and that produced tensions); he looked out for his sisters and brought a total of three of the Hogarth daughters (Catherine, Mary, Georgina) to live with him; he even helped his father-in-law get his books published.

In his persona as author Dickens enjoyed collaborative, more than commercial relations with Chapman and Hall. He relished almost brotherly relations with Macrone until the disputes over *Sketches* and *Rudge*, but they were amicably settled before Macrone's sudden death, and Dickens tried to raise money for his widow and children. By contrast, he experienced at times intense animosity toward his interfering "master" Richard Bentley; by December of 1839 their relationship was so bad Dickens told Thomas Beard that "[w]ar to the knife and with no quarter

on either side, has commenced with the Burlington Street Brigand."²⁰
This combat between proprietor and editor, owner and employee, senior
and junior members of the publishing fraternity, was joined by Bentley,
his attorneys Gregory and Follett, and his son George, who endorsed
Dickens's flaming complaints to his attorneys Smithson and Mitton
about Bentley's advertising of *Rudge* as "preparing for publication" with
an emphatic defense of his father: "The charges made in this letter, which
I bought up, are false. I do not however destroy the letter. It is a brick in
the building of Dickens' character. He wished to break his agreement, &
so he made up the account contained herein. Dickens was a very clever,
but he was not an honest man."²¹

IV

What is at issue for the moment is not the justice of Dickens's claims or
behavior, but the frustration, anger, and sense of being abused he felt
about his relationships with his family and his professional associates at
this moment in his authorial life. These infiltrated his writing, giving it –
especially but not exclusively in the chapters describing the riots – a
sustained fury never before seen. And that makes *Barnaby* a revolutionary
novel in several senses. Having won the war with Bentley, Dickens sells his
unwritten but long contemplated historical fiction to Chapman and Hall
as a ten-to-fifteen-part serial. Hall does his calculations and figures he can
offer Dickens £3,000 (ten times what Macrone originally paid for the
same unwritten novel!) for outright purchase of copyright.²² Dickens then
overthrows that Agreement, running the novel on in *Master Humphrey's
Clock*, of which he is already part proprietor. So he snatches the whole
copyright away from his Cheeryble-like publishers, thereby giving up the
£3,000 purchase price, turns *Rudge* into a shared property within the
*Clock* and when separately published, and achieves, apparently without
rancor or extended discussions, what it took so many fierce negotiations
and renegotiations to achieve with Bentley: *Rudge* would count both as
the twelve printed pages Dickens was contracted to supply for each issue
of the periodical and as a separate publication thereafter.²³ In fact,
however, the publishers' rancor simmered below the surface for a while.

While these developments are not the equivalent of founding new
civilizations, they are, within the context of Dickens's effort to establish
himself as a professional author earning a substantial income, stages in his
development. And stages that mark progress and peril simultaneously. For
to get his way, Dickens time and again gives up money. He won't lend his

name to the *Miscellany* at any price; he returns the advance and rejects the purchase price Bentley has agreed to pay for *Rudge*; and likewise he rejects the very substantial offer of Chapman and Hall for the same novel.

His situation becomes even more precarious, and rapidly so. The last installments of *The Old Curiosity Shop* secured Dickens a huge fan base in Britain and America. Had he wished, he could have saved Nell and extended her adventures for many more months. Instead, he buried her and shortly thereafter tried to collapse the whole inchoate collocation of narrators who at one time or another were identified textually or para-textually as her biographers. At the same time, he basically shut down the *Clock* framework and started his new story (his oldest story in its latest guise) *with no narrative voice characterized or identified*. After eight years of venturing different rhetorical personae for the tellers of Dickens's sketches, tales, and novels, he plunges into his next novel voiced by a third-person, omniscient, and largely apolitical rhetorician, almost entirely a function of the syntax of narration rather than being a charac-terized figure overtly recounting a story according to his humanly con-strained and biased point of view.

In these pages there is no "Boz," although he remains in the custom-ary place of author in the paratexts of the *Clock* numbers. The few uses of plural pronouns – "we," "us," "our" – are used to establish time. The narrator recounts in the present to his present (1841) readers events that occurred sixty years earlier. It is the chronological homology of narrator and reader in reading the text that the plural pronouns stress: "Leaving the favoured, and well-received, and flattered of the world . . . we follow in the steps of two slow travelers on foot," chapter the twenty-fifth begins (p. 207). And, having located both teller and reader in the present, the narrator can then refer backward to that earlier time, when London looked different and operated in different ways. These retro-spective topographical, architectural, and governmental allusions per-form several of the features Dickens originally proposed for the *Clock*: Chapters on Chambers, "a series of papers . . . containing stories and descriptions of London as it was many years ago, as it is now, and as it will be many years hence," and the Savage Chronicles that exposed contemporary juridical abuses.[24] But contrasts between the bad past and the improved present aren't consistently observed. For instance, at the end of the novel the narrator comments that "It was a long time . . . before there was such a country inn as the Maypole, in all England: indeed, it is a great question whether there has ever been such another to this hour, or ever will be" (p. 685).

There is no limitation to the narrator's range, but in the tradition of storytelling the text does not disclose its secrets until they are discovered by the characters in the story.[25] In his previous novels Dickens had slipped into this familiar and comfortable style of narration, but always before he had at some point pulled back, reminded readers that this was edited or told by Boz or a member of the clock or watch societies, or at least, in *Nickleby*, supplied in the paratext multiple identifications of the source of the narrative: Nicholas himself, Boz, or the faithfully yours author Charles Dickens.

In spite of the temporal distance between the narrator's present and the narratorial past, there is a kind of inseparable intimacy between voice and story. The novel defines its genre as history (p. 370), the narrator as a chronicler (p. 80), or, adopting a slight mockery of the legal system while at the same time the narrator proclaims his veracity, he says that "this deponent hath been informed and verily believes" that Dolly wore very attractive clothes (p. 169). That characterization of the narrator as chronicler works pretty well, although the text mystifies whatever characters do not understand or recall. "Chroniclers," chapter the ninth opens, "are privileged to enter where they list, to come and go through keyholes, to ride upon the wind, to overcome, in their soarings up and down, all obstacles of distance, time, and place" (p. 80). Insofar as "chronicler" derives from "chronos," Greek for time, and identifies a form of narration that privileges temporal succession over interpretation, a "chronicler" is rather like a speaking "reel" of history, a voice articulating the sequence of events (often happening simultaneously, necessitating jumps from one scene to another) without obtruding opinions or reorganization according to an imposed interpretation of causality. This kind of narrative breaks down some by the middle of the novel, when several chapters open with paragraphs of narratorial opinion that lead into the succeeding action. As a particularly pertinent example, take the first sentence of chapter the thirty-seventh: "To surround anything, however monstrous or ridiculous, with an air of mystery, is to invest it with a secret charm, and power of attraction which to the crowd [readers included, surely] is irresistible" (p. 304). But in general even these philosophical reflections keep within the boundaries of an apolitical news-reporting narrative.

While there may not be either a fully characterized narrator persona such as Boz or extensive "editorial" commentary, there are instances of sympathy and criticism distributed across the class spectrum. Dickens brings up the case of Mary Jones in chapter the thirty-seventh and in his first preface, and he elaborates it in the Preface to the Cheap Edition of

1849: a respectable and remarkably attractive young girl of nineteen, she and her two children lived honorably until her husband was pressed into military service when the Government prepared to defend its occupation of the Falkland Islands. Starving and with her children in rags, she took a few pennysworth of cheap cloth off a draper's counter. Though when confronted by the owner she returned the goods, it was felt that an example needed to be set to the numerous shoplifters in the neighborhood, and so she was hanged at Newgate, suckling her youngest until the last minute. On the other hand, the cowardice of the Lord Mayor was equally well documented, and Dickens portrays him no worse than he was in fact, even quoting his own words when let off with a light reprimand after a Privy Council inquiry into his conduct: "such was his temerity, he thought death would have been his portion" (p. 612). Many of the mob are maddened by frustration or drink or general meanness, but there are those eager to rescue family members whose sentences the narrative questions, and while some soldiers are brutal, most behave with restraint and excellent discipline.

Indeed, insofar as an "editorial" accusing or exculpating the rioters is concerned, the narrative backbone is a congeries of images expounding the thesis that fermenting energies too long bottled up cannot but explode. (Ronald Paulson says that Hogarth's "*Gin Lane* haunts the text of *Barnaby Rudge*.")[26] From the rationing of liquor and conversation at the Maypole to Grip's famous popping cork and exclamation "I'm a devil!"; from the Varden breakfast beverage of an uncorked Toby mug of beer with the foamy head resembling a wig (harmless, homely) to the destruction of the Maypole; from the demolition of the Catholic distiller and vintner Thomas Langdale's Holborn premises to the burning of bodies torched by the mixture of alcohol and blood running down the neighboring streets; the novel supplies numerous instances of the destructive effects of alcohol-fueled intemperance. (Religious intemperance both precedes and is exacerbated by liquor.) John Willet, in his obstinate despotism, faults Hugh and Barnaby for bottling up and corking down their imagination, which should have been drawn out (more to get rid of it than to encourage it) as he did when Joe was a boy. Sim has an ambitious soul casked and sealed: "the spiritual essence or soul of Mr. Tappertit would sometimes fume within that precious cask, his body, until, with great foam and froth and splutter, it would force a vent, and carry all before it" (p. 42). And when such outbreaks occur, the bleeding body marks all it touches – Barnaby's wrist, the floor of the Warren, the gutters of Holborn.

v

Excessive authoritarianism – which traditionally British Protestants asso-ciated with the Roman Catholic hierarchy – leads to intemperance, drunkenness, rioting, theft, conflagrations, destruction and theft of sacred and secular property, and loss of limbs or life. A steady and moderate hand is needed at home and in Parliament. Government is administered by honorable men such as Sir John Fielding and Lord Algernon Percy, as well as by Dennis the hangman; in Dickens's version Gordon is misled by the villainous Gashford; and there are exemplary Catholics such as Langdale and Haredale and Protestants such as Varden. In short, as many commentators have noted, sympathy and criticism are expressed toward both sides of the political and religious divide. The vast throng of Protestant demonstrators, the narrator reports when the petition is being presented to Parliament, is "sprinkled doubtless here and there with honest zealots, but composed for the most part of the very scum and refuse of London, whose growth was fostered by bad criminal laws, bad prison regulations, and the worst conceivable police" (p. 407). The most damning single critique may be leveled against the drunken and brutal country magistrate, brother of the timorous Lord Mayor, who, testifying at Barnaby's trial, "turned the wavering scale against poor Barnaby," in recompense for Barnaby's not selling Grip. This is an invented incident and not one that indicts any larger class of persons on either side (though Sir John is much obliged to him for his evidence [p. 622]). Those the novel most condemns are they who combine "private vengeance" with "public sentiment" (p. 206): Gashford and Sir John from different motives attacking Haredale, and Sim and Hugh marking Joe for annihi-lation: "Destroy him. Crush him. And be happy," Sim counsels Chester père (p. 207).

The destruction of old Newgate prison in 1780 was a precursor to the fall of the Bastille in 1789, but from the perspective of 1841 it seems the ghost of a series of past insurrections that tore down prisons and opened the gates of madhouses. *Barnaby Rudge* has rightly been called ghostly – the Warren and Barnaby haunted by Rudge senior and the blood of Reuben Haredale; the Gordon riots themselves concurrent with the American revolution (in which war Joe Willet loses his arm "at the defence of the Salwanners" [p. 651]), a precursor of the French revolutions and the Continental upheavals in 1832, and the ancestor of contemporary Protestant–Catholic controversies in Ireland and Britain. The story is itself a ghostly retelling of these events, not just those sixty years hence (itself an echo of Scott's title for *Waverley*), but also a chronicle incorporating all the subsequent tales told and written, oral and printed, about those past times. "In the end," John Bowen says, "Dickens wants to have nothing to do with ghosts, or at least is determined to lay them to rest" (p. xxvii). The paragraph at the beginning of chapter the thirty-seventh, quoted earlier, promises that Truth and Common Sense will, in time, prevail. And so it seems to. The "ghosts," Bowen continues, "who so trouble the boundaries between public life and private hallucination, between the living and the dead and the virtuous and the evil, will all be exorcized" (p. xxvii). The strange force of the rioters is expunged with the executions of Dennis (unruly rule) and Hugh (unruly ruled – through Chester); the rivalry between Haredale and Chester for the same woman is finally satisfied by a duel in which one is killed and the other dies abroad in a monastery; a new and better Maypole, with an even more potent proprietor, rises from the old; and Varden is restored as "the centre of the system: the source of light, heat, life, and frank enjoyment in the bright household world" (p. 665). The one errant and ghostly element not entirely domesticated is Grip, who, as Bowen so shrewdly notes, is "an enemy of boundaries" (p. xxviii), the one unassimilable element in a binary system of good and bad, males and females, Catholics and Protestants, fathers and sons, soldiers and rioters, the innocent and the guilty.

VI

Unexorcised, Grip exercises a lasting grip (sorry) over the novel, being in fact the only character Dickens speaks about, in the opening paragraph of his prefaces to the Cheap (1849), Library (1858), and Charles Dickens (1868) editions. Grip, it seems, had two descendants in the Dickens household. And while bringing up their presence in the present finesses any more substantial Truth and Common Sense about the novel's origins or the author's intentions as they were briefly stated in the first preface (1841) and later framed by the ravens, they stand in place of order, concealing it in their own familial history. Thus the mad antics of the birds overwrite any of the other madness in the novel, the history it tells, or the history of its telling.

That overwriting by the ravens is another laying to rest of ghosts. Grip, combining devilry ("I'm a devil!") with domestication ("Polly put the kettle on") embodies the melodramatic polarities of Victorian fiction. He is, in that sense, the last speaker, and the essence of authorship. But he's a bird, standing in place for the author of domesticated historical fiction.

And that author, Dickens, like Grip, overwrites virtually everything that he has articulated hitherto. To list all the examples would be tedious and time-consuming. But consider some of the ways previous characters, events, and scenes are un-written, re-constituted as a cancellation of what went before. To begin with, *Rudge* doesn't begin in Master Humphrey's parlor, but in John Willet's bar; and yet the space and company are similar: Gothic rooms occupied by old men. The Maypole cronies don't tell tales, unless invited or terrified; and Willet is much less genial than Master Humphrey in inviting his companions to speak. Whereas Time, signified by the clock case, unfolded its stories in the frame narrative and in the unreeling of Nell's story, in *Rudge* Time ferments the bottled-up spirits until they explode from their own inner force and tell their own stories. At the end of the novel, John in his retirement cottage has his own miniature Maypole, replete with its inhabitants residing in the same location as Master Humphrey's companions: "in the chimney-corner, they all four quaffed, and smoked, and prosed, and dozed, as they had done of old" (p. 686). John dies, bequeathing quite a large sum of money. And one chapter later Humphrey is found dead in his chimney corner, leaving his substantial property to his cronies, to whom Pickwick and the Wellers bid farewell. From Pickwick and Sam together at Dulwich, bound by "a steady and reciprocal attachment which nothing but death will terminate," through the deaths of those who would endanger Oliver and who by dying free him to live with his adoptive relatives, to the deaths of Ralph and Smike that shadow but do not blight the Nickleby country retreat, to the death of Nell that consecrates her life's journey and Kit's family's stories, to the end of community, lives, and stories, is but one unwriting Dickens undertakes.

Another, in which he is abetted by his splendid illustrators, is the reimagining of Newgate, especially the condemned cells. What was at first appearance a silent cell imaginatively populated by Boz becomes in *Barnaby* a series of cells inhabited by noisy, frightened felons begging for release and life, not to be roasted alive inside or "worked off" by the hangman. The woman in the *Sketches* who tries to revive her dead son becomes (in a story that takes place just twenty years prior to "The Black Veil") Mrs. Rudge nursing her condemned son and nearly dying herself, while he, at the last minute, is rescued and restored to life, and they live together happily every after. (This scene and theme – "restored to life" – will be re-enacted near the beginning of Dickens's other story of riots, *A Tale of Two Cities*.) While the Fleet imprisons debtors, not felons, its inhabitants and those in Newgate seem to combine in *Rudge*: all sorts and conditions of men, from hardened villains to innocents, reside within those stony walls, and some, once freed, seek its security and return. Six of the illustrations show these inhabitants, and all the cells bear some resemblance to that in which Fagin spends his last night alive. But instead of a Jewish fence who runs a criminal gang and even gives up some accomplices to the authorities to save his operation, we see Barnaby and Grip, Rudge and Stagg, Barnaby and his father, Dennis chaffing the condemned men, Dennis in the same cell as the animalistic Hugh, Barnaby in the Condemned Cell with his mother, and in the historically accurate variant, Lord George Gordon, not in Newgate where he died thirteen years later, but in the Tower, from which he was released after being found Not Guilty of High Treason. Guilty, innocent, mad, parent, child, blind man, talking bird, centaur: the polyphonic narrative voices are in a sense replicated by the plurality and variety of those locked up to die, unwriting and re-creating the singular stories of Dickens's earlier Newgate prisoners. And, not incidentally, unwriting and rewriting the Newgate novel with its rosewater villains, separating Dickens's fictions from his own previous work, and Bulwer's and Ainsworth's. Moreover, Phiz's illustrations deepen the historical and religious precedents of these riots and their representation: Ronald Paulson notes that "they define the riot by means of typology," and sees the portraits of Gordon echoing *Ecce Homo* compositions by Dürer and Rembrandt, Varden threatened by the mob as a version of *Christ Mocked* scenes, and those who take over the Maypole Inn decked out in mitres and robes as versions of Saturnalia.[27]

Even characters are in some senses rewritten. In the Fleet, Jingle's tears are real; in *Rudge*, Sir John's tears flow copiously, but they lie. The story of Haredale's and Chester's competition for a mistress after being school-mates at St. Omer's in France undoes that of Nell's grandfather and brother for a wife; whereas while living apart they retain affection for one another, Haredale and Gordon bear unslaked enmity for each other because, as Chester tells it, his scapegoat and drudge at school, Haredale, wooed and won a mistress, couldn't keep her, and "threw me in her way to carry off the prize" (p. 249). The story sounds unlike Haredale. But both are younger brothers (as was Ralph Nickleby) with their different ways to make in the world. (Chester displeased his father but married affluence and spent it; Ralph inherited little, married a bit more, and built a fortune; Nicholas's father squandered his inheritance.) So once again the story of brothers is retold, each time with variations on the theme of sexual and/or economic rivalry. At root, those are cognates, as Mrs. Rudge warns her son: "Nothing bears so many stains of blood, as gold" (p. 375).

Other examples of this rewriting of earlier fiction: John Willet advertises for his "young boy," about four feet tall, and promises the same reward of £5 that the parish offers to rid itself of Oliver. Of course, in this case the conditions are in some ways opposite: John wants Joe's return, and Joe is a fully grown man whose maturity and sexuality John simply can't acknowledge, whereas the parish really wants to sell Oliver, who is a very small boy. Another tiny edit altering *Oliver*: on Barnaby's last day at the village in which he and his mother have hidden, he takes a final walk through the woods. Gentle Barnaby has to tell the ugliest of the dogs who used to love to ramble with him all day "to go back in a surly tone, and his heart smote him while he did so." Whereas Sikes couldn't get Bull's-eye to come to him so he can drown his steadfast companion, Barnaby can't get the animal to run away to safety: "The dog retreated; turned with a half-incredulous, half-imploring look; came a little back; and stopped. It was the last appeal of an old companion and a faithful friend – cast off" (p. 387). Further along this line of variants, Nancy's eyes, reincarnated in Bull's-eye's, condemn him; Rudge Sr. is both befriended by, and ultimately abandoned by, the blind Stagg. *Oliver Twist*, whether on account of Cruikshank's advice or because Dickens himself wanted to follow Henry Fielding in writing a Hogarthian narrative, does present versions of industrious and idle apprentices; in Sim Tappertit, Dickens unwrites the binary, making Sim both industrious and idle, master of his company of journeymen and one who kidnaps his longed-for mistress.

## VII

The most striking unwriting, however, is of the narrator. The Boz of *Sketches* is, as we know, a middle-aged bachelor, drawn to the nighttime streets but also perambulating by day. He learns a lot about the disappointments and miseries of life, by observing closely the outward signs (even the outsides of shops and homes tell their stories), and by following crowds who lead him to public quarrels, the bedside of a fatally battered woman, dying sons, the condemned in Newgate, and dead bodies. Not all his ventures are morbid: he attends christenings, engagements, holiday parties, amateur theatrics, parish elections, and out-of-town excursions. But he is a solitary, and his destination is often a scene of death, rendered sympathetically whenever possible. The narrator at the opening of the *Clock* is Master Humphrey himself, another nocturnal pedestrian who leads "a lonely, solitary life" in a silent, shady house full of ancient nooks and crannies and worm-eaten doors. He is accustomed to being suspected and distrusted by his classmates and later his neighbors because of his misshapen body. He generally sits by his fireside reading and reflecting on his melancholy past, though by degrees he has made three friends who join him of evenings to beguile the time by reading aloud old stories. On Christmas Day he dines alone in a tavern where he meets the deaf gentleman who becomes his first friend. And he walks, preferably at night when he can speculate about the characters in the streets, rather than during the day, "which too often destroys an air-built castle at the moment of its completion, without the smallest ceremony or remorse" (4.37).

This is already a devolution from Boz. Humphrey is a more solitary, melancholy, disfigured perambulator, not notable for the humor and hearty appreciation for the varieties of life that the original Boz exhibits. Dickens, by placing Humphrey at the center of his title and as the frame narrator, and by doubling him with Kit as narrators of Nell's history, takes the double character of Boz as the first readers discovered − a middle-aged bachelor and a sparkling, married writer of twenty-four − and splits it up. He also creates distance between himself, unnamed in the serial paratexts, Boz the author of the *Clock*, and Humphrey, who hopes that there will spring up between him and his readers "feelings of homely affection and regard" (1.1). Humphrey thinks of his communication as written, although the stories are allegedly read aloud, and his last words to the reader are also written at the desk where he dies. So he is a creature of manuscript more than oral culture, and this too has its distancing effect, especially as the *Clock* is so sumptuously a print product of image and text artfully composed on the page.

And yet in his preface to the first volume of the *Clock*, made up of the April through September 1840 installments, Dickens once again rewrites the present and the past. He calls himself, not Boz, but "the author" (providing at the end his new address, the house of "excessive splendour" at Number 1 "Devonshire Terrace, York Gate"). He lays out three objects he planned to achieve with the *Clock*, none of them actually the kinds of ideas he proposed to Chapman and Hall in July 1839. So the "author" accounts for the origin and purpose of his publication in ways that are strikingly different from the proposals Dickens made fourteen months earlier. And he separates himself, unnamed but Dickens to those who knew him and his residence, from the Boz of the title page, the Master Humphrey who presides over the clock society, and the alleged authors (the deaf gentleman, Mr. Pickwick, possibly Jack Redburn) of the manuscripts pulled out of the clock case and read aloud. Moreover, the preface continues, "[i]t was never the author's intention to make the Members of Master Humphrey's Clock, active agents in the stories they are supposed to relate" ("Preface" 1:[iii]). What? They are identified *as* the authors, and in the cases of Master Humphrey and Jack Redburn identified as participants in the stories. Instead, Dickens "ghostifies" (would there were such a word!) the auditors, asking readers to imagine "all these gentle spirits" of the clock company – including Mr. Pickwick – tracing "some faint reflection of their past lives in the varying current of the tale" ("Preface" 1:[iii]). The company is itself almost a ghostly revenant of their own past lives and stories. As are the readers addressed. For according to Dickens's preface, it was never the author's intention in reintroducing Pickwick and the Wellers "of reopening an exhausted and abandoned mine" (Pickwick "exhausted" and "abandoned" is itself a staggering claim given his continued popularity, and certainly belies Chesterton's notion of his immortality), but rather to mingle them with the other clock society who have their own "faint reflection" of past lives, and with the readers, who likewise "connect" the Pickwickians, who had been "favourites" of those readers, "with the tranquil enjoyments of Master Humphrey" ("Preface" 1:[iii]).

As we have seen in the preceding chapter, the *Clock* replaces Boz with a ghostly "author" who provides a set of justifications for his print production that cannot be supported by biographical or bibliographical evidence, and assembles the ghosts of former creations to merge with the ghostly clock company whose personal stories may contain "faint reflection[s] of their past lives." (We'll return to this claim later.) Those "faint reflection[s]" include not only the actual events of the Gordon rebellion, but all the memories and stories about it. As John Bowen concludes, "[a]ll writing has a ghostly quality, conjuring up the presence of things when there is nothing there, but historical novels, particularly one as haunted as *Barnaby Rudge*, provide a peculiarly intense version of this experience, a story of ghosts of ghosts of ghosts" (p. xxvi), told, I would add, by ghosts of ghosts.

VIII

Wraiths don't, however, get us to the violent center of *Barnaby Rudge*, some thirty-odd chapters recounting the Gordon riots. They commence rather quietly, as Barnaby and his mother hasten to London to hide once again from Rudge, and become "aware that the stream of life was all pouring one way ... in unusual haste and evident excitement" (p. 395).

From the moment of their encounter with Gashford and Lord George Gordon, Barnaby's fate is determined; the "stream of life" separates him from his mother. He goes to join "this great body," dreaming of adventure and fame, and is "whirled away into the heart of a dense mass of men," while his mother is thrown to the ground by Sim Tappertit and sees her son no more (p. 403). This is the moment when domesticity, familial comfort, and protection, already sadly undermined at every home the novel visits, is abandoned, and the wholly male-led anti-Catholic demonstrations begin.[28]

If these events had been in Dickens's mind for six years, he now had the opportunity to discharge them. And discharge them he did, with a ferocity and speed unprecedented in his writing career to date. Whereas in earlier years he had complained about the length of the sheets for the monthly numbers, wondered what he could do to fill out an early number of *Nickleby*, and wearied of both the incessant routine and the sad subject of the weekly numbers of *The Old Curiosity Shop*, Dickens wrote up to and through the riots in a sustained fit of energy. On January 29, 1841 he reported to Forster, "I imaged forth a good deal of *Barnaby* by keeping my mind steadily upon him; and am happy to say I have gone to work this morning in good twig, strong hope, and cheerful spirits."[29] Over the next several months he got on well, despite many distractions. These included the birth of his fourth child, Walter Landor Dickens, and extensive arrangements – including a public advertisement – to prevent his father from either forging his signature on notes or otherwise getting money in Dickens's name.[30] More often than not, squeezed by the small compass of his weekly installment, he relied on Forster to cut out excess matter. In chapter the seventeenth alone, Forster deleted five sections, several of which he felt overdramatized Rudge's threat to his wife. Yet Dickens also added eight paragraphs in a lighter vein telling about Barnaby's decision to claim the day as his birthday.[31]

During the first half of June 1841, Dickens was "fearfully hard at work, morning, noon, and night," getting enough ahead in the story to allow him a month in Scotland, June 19–July 18.[32] While there he received a letter from Mary Hurnall that contained some objection to Dickens's associating Stagg's disability with immorality. "My intention in the management of this inferior and subordinate character," he responded, "was to remind the World who have eyes, that they have no *right* to expect in sightless men a degree of virtue and goodness to which they, in full possession of all their senses, can lay no claim." Some slight changes in Stagg's character were made in the manuscript of chapter the forty-fifth, and the succeeding chapter elaborates Stagg's defense along these lines. But the Pilgrim editors, trying to reconcile the composition of these chapters with Dickens's activities in Scotland and his reply to Mrs. Hurnall from Devonshire Terrace after his return to London, say that "[i]f CD had written the addition to Ch. 45 and Stagg's defence in Ch. 46 as a result of Mrs Hurnall's letter," then Dickens's statement to her that she would have seen his plan for Stagg "if you could have had the whole book before your mental vision" is "clearly disingenuous. Certainly nothing in Stagg's earlier appearances prepares for it."[33] If Dickens did make changes to accommodate this reader, they were very small; in general he could not be turned away from his story, whether Forster objected to Gordon's character or anyone found fault with any other part of the tale.

Dickens was five or six weeks ahead before leaving for Edinburgh to attend a great fete celebrating him as Scott's successor, and he dashed off two more chapters while touring the Highlands. "I have left [the story]," he told Forster on July 9, writing from Ballachulish, "at an exciting point, with a good dawning of the riots."[34] That was the chapter ending with Mrs. Rudge on the ground and Barnaby whirled away into the "stream of life." As soon as Dickens returned to London in late July, he went "horribly hard" to work, but the writing of the riot chapters, the Pilgrim editors summarize, "came easily to him."[35] He occasionally complained about time pressure and agonized over the confinement of the installments: "Oh!" he exclaims to Forster, "if I only had him [Barnaby/the novel], from this time to the end, in monthly numbers. *N'importe!* I hope the interest will be pretty strong [in the destruction of the Warren and the capture of Rudge] – and, in every number, stronger."[36] And he exulted in his fluency: "I was always sure I could make a good thing of *Barnaby,*" he crowed to Forster from Broadstairs a week later, just before finishing off the chapters narrating Barnaby's arrest and imprisonment. "I am in great heart and spirits with the story."[37]

Dickens's instructions to Cattermole for illustrations are detailed and upbeat. (Browne burned his correspondence with Dickens, so we do not know what kinds of instructions were sent to him.) Dickens worries that the artist might need more supervision than Browne, so he provides compliments and directions in part out of respect and in part because both artists are representing the same characters, settings, and actions. Thus, he tells Cattermole about the plates for chapters the fifty-fifth and -sixth, "the best opportunities of illustration are all coming off now, and we are in the thick of the story ... Please to observe that the M. F. ['mysterious file,' i.e. Rudge] wears a large cloak and a slouched hat. This is important, because Browne will have him in the same number, and he has not changed his dress meanwhile."[38]

## IX

Although in "the thick of the story," Dickens left London for nearly four months of the summer. The first trip he took was to Scotland. In drafting the proposals for the *Clock*, he had mentioned the possibility of traveling to Ireland or America at the journal's expense to write a travelogue. Nothing came of that notion immediately. But in mid-March of 1841, Dickens learned that Lord Jeffrey, judge and for many years editor of the Whiggish *Edinburgh Review*, was coming to London in April. Jeffrey had been all round Edinburgh "declaring there has been 'nothing so good as Nell since Cordelia,'" and saying to Dickens that Edinburgh wanted "to give me greeting and welcome."[39] This set his mind on Scotland rather than Ireland as the next new place to visit, and he immediately tried to inveigle Forster into joining him: "Think of such a fortnight – York, Carlisle, Berwick, your own Borders [Northumberland], Edinburgh, Rob Roy's country, railroads, cathedrals, country inns, Arthur's-seat, lochs, glens, and home by sea."[40] Note that in this initial stage Dickens is thinking about a tour, and that the invitation itself comes not because he is publishing a historical novel in the tradition of Scott, but because a leading figure in Edinburgh society wept over the death of little Nell.

As it turned out, Forster didn't join the expedition, but Catherine did, and the banquet held in Dickens's honor on June 25 in the Waterloo Rooms was a triumph. More than 250 men attended the dinner, and when Catherine escorted the ladies in after dinner, their company added another 150 to the gallery. It might be thought that by honoring Dickens, Edinburgh was attempting to reclaim its position as a cultural center for publishing. That may be so, but Dickens, shrewdly and movingly, in his fine speeches that evening – the first memorable after-dinner speeches of his illustrious career – ranged much further afield. Indeed, when Jeffrey was too ill to attend and Professor John Wilson (the crusty "Christopher North" who wrote for the Tory *Blackwood's Magazine*) took the chair, the evening turned into a love feast, even between otherwise fiercely opposed political partisans, although Dickens heard that a number of Whigs stayed away because they distrusted the Tory presiders.

Wilson celebrated Dickens's insights into "the common feelings and passions of ordinary men," and Dickens replied by summarizing his authorial ambition: "to increase the stock of harmless cheerfulness."

It must be noted that both speakers were following protocols for these kinds of celebratory occasions: North surely knew that Fagin, Squeers, Ralph Nickleby, Quilp, Sally Brass, and their ilk did not walk along "the common and ordinary paths of life," and Dickens surely knew that "harmless cheerfulness" belittled the passionate desire for sympathy and reform that emerges in *Oliver Twist* and *Nicholas Nickleby*. But he defended even his evil characters, in whom he found "that soul of goodness which the Creator has put in them," and explained that the death of Nell might "substitute a garland of fresh flowers for the sculptured horrors which disgrace the tomb." This too seems formulaic, especially since Nell's deathbed and the last image of her grandfather both incorporate mortuary imagery. After toasts to Scott and Burns, Dickens stood to toast the chair, including his Scots predecessors just mentioned and, a little later on, "other names which are familiar to you: poets, historians, critics, all of the foremost rank," among them Jeffrey, Lockhart, and "Delta," the Scots physician David Macbeth Moir. He then delivered a most moving elegy to David Wilkie, long expected to attend the festive occasion, who had died suddenly on the voyage home from Egypt and been buried at sea. "I think of him as one," Dickens orated, "who made the cottage hearth his grave theme, and who surrounded the lives, and cares, and daily toils, and occupations of the poor, with dignity and beauty." Lastly, in response to Angus Fletcher's toast to Catherine's health, Dickens cemented his identification with Scots culture by reminding the overwhelmingly enthusiastic crowd that she was born in Edinburgh. "I think (ahem!) that I spoke rather well," he told Forster, adding that "both the subjects (Wilson and Scottish Literature, and the Memory of Wilkie) were good to go upon."[41]

This account permits some further observations about Dickens's self-construction as an author at this point in his career. With *Barnaby* losing customers but gaining Dickens's increasingly fervent attention, he goes to the city which had been a center of history and historiography, philosophy, law, poetry, journalism, and fiction for nearly a century. He speaks not as Scott's heir, though he certainly thought often that he needed to attend to Scott's examples both positive and negative, but as a lover of Scottish literature; not as a Whig or Tory, but as a spokesperson for commoners and cottage hearths, like Burns and Wilkie; not, certainly, as the Bozzian London urbanite, but instead – and, since apart from a quick trip to Edinburgh to report on a banquet for the *Morning Chronicle* in 1834 this was his first actual visit, he speaks from his reading and imagination – as a lover of "this capital of Scotland . . . her people, her hills, and her houses, and even the very stones of her streets." The capital responded by electing Dickens a burgess and guild brother; and after a few more days of private engagements, he, Catherine, and Fletcher toured the Highlands for ten days. As Isobel Murray points out, "Scotland was important to Dickens for the literary and popular receptions it offered him" – especially during his reading tours – "rather than any literary inspiration." He visited it twelve times, but sets very few scenes there. Still, the triumphant reception of 1841, less than two decades after Scott had engineered a brilliant visit by the immensely unpopular King George IV, elevated Dickens to stardom: Forster, who heard about the reception principally from Dickens himself, calls it "his first practical experience of the honours his fame had won for him" (p. 175). And, should we need reminding, it was an event prompted by the story of Nell, celebrating not the ostensible editor Boz or the sometime narrators Kit, Master Humphrey, and the Single Gentleman, but Charles Dickens. And Dickens not as he was coming forth with a historical novel, but as he had written about contemporary common life.

x

After returning to London, Dickens took off for Broadstairs, where he spent nearly two months bathing, writing, and entertaining. He didn't need London in order to populate its streets with flaming torches and seething rioters. But from London came infuriating news. Chapman and Hall, seeing no future story in Dickens's plans after the *Clock* stopped, and holding more than £3,000 of Dickens's debts which could not be called in before July 1845, began to feel queasy. On July 31 from Devonshire Terrace, Dickens summarized what he understood to be the arrangement made a year before, a lien in the amount of the loan secured by their joint copyrights and the stock of *Oliver Twist* bought from Bentley, to be paid down by half of Dickens's profits on the *Clock* (steadily decreasing, one assumes, from the fall in sales), and Dickens's endorsement to his publishers of a £2,000 life insurance policy.[42] As the only possibility for a substantial decrease in the loan would be the sale of the three-volume *Oliver* stock, and as Bentley had issued in 1840 another edition partly from standing type and partly reset from earlier issues, which Chapman and Hall marketed in May 1841 as their own "third edition," the likelihood of selling off back stock of earlier editions was slight.

Two days later Dickens sent a private letter to Edward Chapman thanking him for the loan by which they obtained the 1,002 unsold copies of *Oliver Twist* in Bentley's warehouse and the rights to the novel apart from its appearance in the *Miscellany*.[43] So far, so good. The proposals for an agreement about the *Clock*, signed in October 1839 by Dickens, Chapman, and Hall, and witnessed by Forster, were very short and uncomplicated: Dickens supplied the material, the publishers issued and accounted for copies, profits and copyright were owned half by author and half by publisher. Chapman and Hall guaranteed to publish for one year; Dickens was committed to five. The firm could back out at the expiration of that year, Dickens only after five years. When these principles were put into legal form by Edward Chapman's solicitor brother William, however, the March 31, 1840 formal Agreement ran to many pages and contained the same sorts of specifications as Bentley's Agreements about how much content Dickens was to supply each week ("twelve pages [which] shall be original Literary Matter to be contributed and furnished by the said Charles Dickens");[44] how costs and profits were to be calculated, distributed, and paid (including details about the discounts the publishers would offer the trade); how the copyrights were to be shared; the mandate to offer first to the other partner any rights or stock owned by the seller; provisions for the settlement of disputes; and an elaborated specification that the publisher could discontinue after one year but Dickens only after five. This Agreement was signed not only by the principals but also by their respective attorneys, William Chapman of Richmond and Charles Smithson, senior partner in Smithson and Mitton, Dickens's solicitors in London. The Agreement was virtually as lengthy and specific as the most particularized of the Bentley contracts; its greater formality may well have been the result of Dickens deciding to furnish all the *Clock* material himself, and then to fold in *Barnaby*. But even at that point Dickens didn't jib.

However, William Chapman told his brother that the firm needed more security than Dickens's letter, and proposed that Dickens's acknowledgment of indebtedness "be put into law."[45] In a rather disingenuous pleading, Dickens claimed that Smithson, "not in my confidence, and not having much reason that I know of to be partially interested in my proceedings," got hold of a draft of a deed prepared by William Chapman that Smithson told Dickens was "of a most hard, stringent, and overbearing kind ... such as no client of his ... should ever sign with his consent." (Since Smithson had drafted and witnessed the March 31, 1840 Agreement about the *Clock* and was the senior partner in the firm of Smithson and Mitton, he certainly had taken an interest in Dickens's proceedings, even though he and his partner had been differing on matters connected with the firm for some time.) This Deed became a matter of furious contention between the lawyers and the principals.[46] There were meetings of the opposing parties with their lawyers, attempts to reconcile interests with Forster in attendance, correspondence back and forth, a flat refusal on the part of William Chapman to consider Dickens's first statement of the loan arrangements on July 2, 1840 as adequate in law ("the old letter is totally inapplicable to existing circumstances"),[47] and finally a Bond instead of a Deed signed by Dickens on July 31, accompanied by the demand that Edward Chapman return the private letter of commendation Dickens had sent at the beginning of the month. Dickens's fury was aroused by the legalistic proceedings into which his relationship with his "best of publishers" had devolved, but also because, as Chapman tried to explain to Smithson and Mitton, the firm had "consented to sacrifice the profits they expected to derive from the publication of 'Barnaby Rudge'" if, as Forster undertook, Dickens "would no longer object to legal assignments of the Copyrights as Security."[48] Dickens acknowledged on July 31 that his publishers "are to have a lien to this amount [with other loans, it had mounted to £3,019 without any interest accruing] on the property belonging to me," namely his shares in the stock and copyright of previous publications.[49] But somehow in the working out of Agreements based on that concession, Dickens simply hated the idea of signing a Deed provisionally giving up his copyrights. What he consented to do, and Chapman and Hall agreed to accept against counsel's strong advice, was to reiterate his July 31 warrant to use half his *Clock* profits and any sums accruing from the sale of *Oliver* stock toward reduction of the principal. And the Bond added one further clause: "the Condition of the above written Obligation" is that on July 2, 1845 Dickens or his heirs will pay off the total balance remaining.[50] In place even of a "lien," the publishers got a promise to pay (already in effect as a condition of the loan) in the future ... without any certain prospect of any future publication by Dickens. By trying to secure some better legal guarantee, they botched a five-year friendship. And while Dickens was being feted as the greatest living author in Edinburgh, his copyrights were tied up in large debts with small chance of early repayment. The distance between his "fame," as Forster terms it, and his actual legal and financial condition as an author, was greater, and less favorable, than ever.

But Dickens knew how to use the "fame." Somehow he managed to secure from those same deeply indebted publishers extraordinarily favorable terms for a future novel, to be published in parts identical to those of *Nickleby*, starting November 1, 1842, to pay Dickens £200 for each installment chargeable to the expenses of publication, and to give him three-quarters of the net profits.[51] When Forster first disclosed Dickens's plan for "a year's silence," "little Hall and big Chapman [were] knocked down by a thunderbolt." But they came round rather quickly, in ways that did much to repair the frayed relationship of the previous months. They not only (and surely with concealed doubt) agreed that "the effect of the year's silence would be tremendous" (not specifying that it would have a tremendous effect on their income),[52] they also agreed to pay him for the full year between the end of the *Clock* and the beginning of the monthly serial £150 a month, the total of £1,800 to be paid with interest out of those three-quarter profits.

The perilous economics of authorship could not be more starkly rendered than by these summer 1841 negotiations taking place while Dickens was being feted, touring Scotland, and spending two months at Broadstairs. On one side of the ledger, he was famous and loved by high and low, honored by Tories and Whigs, bought by Britons, Americans, other nationalities in translation or Continental English editions, sought out for after-dinner speeches and elite gatherings, living in a splendid house with requisite help for Catherine and his family and provisions for educating the children. In seven years he'd gone from earning £350 per annum to many thousands. On the other side, he was not just broke, but in serious debt: nearly £5,000 (plus the mortgage) by the fall of 1841. Depending on which calculus we use for current equivalence, Dickens owed between £220,000 and £380,000. His income for the succeeding year was borrowed, not earned; "Fame's Trumpet should blow a little more of the wealth arising from the circulation of my works, into the Booksellers' pockets, and less into my own," he complained in response to a begging letter.[53] Although he was getting a year off, he also had to return with enough of a new serial written ahead of time for all the pre-publication matters to be settled – title, wrapper design, advertisements, plus text and illustrations for two or three numbers. While Mitton may have been "quite aghast . . . at the brilliancy of the C. & H. arrangement," he wasn't reading between the lines nor seeing clearly into a future that brought the downsides of these arrangements to the forefront.[54] And it wasn't just money and contractual issues that left Dickens feeling vulnerable, exhausted, and uncertain about his future course. He was no longer sure what voice, Boz, Dickens, or some other persona or persons writing under his direction, would sustain the immensely important engagement between him and his readers, important more for the acceptance, pleasure, and affection they brought to the exchange even than money. In that sense, Dickens never measured his worth or achievement in pounds, shillings, and pence, however shrill on occasion his paeans to an overflowing till. One of the ways in which he is most modern is his need for a clamorous reception from his audience: that, more than money, family, or mistress, was his greatest love affair.


XI

Although Dickens, while in Broadstairs, was caught in the midst of wresting new agreements with his publishers for loans, a vacation, and a new work, those distractions didn't slow him up or divert him from the speeding trajectory of his tale. By September 11 he had "burnt into Newgate" and was about "to tear the prisoners out by the hair of their heads."[55] A month earlier he had exulted to Forster, "how radical I am getting!" Dickens is referring to three anti-Tory poems published in the *Examiner* in successive weeks, August 7, 14, and 21.[56] They were all signed "W," presumably for Whig, and thus tentatively spell out a new pseudonymic and political authorial identity. One of the squibs are the verses entitled "The Fine Old English Gentleman," which Forster quotes "entire" and from which these lines are particularly apposite to *Rudge*:

> The good old laws were garnished well with gibbets, whips, and
> chains,
> With fine old English penalties, and fine old English pains,
> With rebel heads and seas of blood once hot in rebel veins:
> For all these things were requisite to guard the rich old gains
>          Of the fine old English Tory times;
>          Soon may they come again!
>
> .    .    .    .    .    .    .    .    .    .    .
>
> This brave old code, like Argus, had a hundred watchful eyes,
> And ev'ry English peasant had his good old English spies,
>
> .    .    .    .    .    .    .    .    .    .    .
>
> The good old times for cutting throats that cried out in their need,
> The good old times for hunting men who held their father's creed.

The verses go on to note that "the press was seldom known to snarl or bark" and judges' deeds remained hidden in the dark. Yet Tolerance, building slowly, put those times to flight, until with Peel's 1841 electoral victory "the fine old English Tory days" now dawn again. "In England there shall be – dear bread! in Ireland – sword and brand! / And poverty, and ignorance, shall swell the rich and grand."[57] While these animadversions on the old and current times, published in an August 1841 periodical, unmistakably raise the same issues as Dickens's concurrent serial, by the different pseudonym he separates his political squibs from his historical fiction. It will be more difficult for him to keep these two authorial voices separate in the next few years.

Indeed, Dickens was sufficiently agitated to contemplate once again emigrating, this time to the colony of Van Diemen's Land, that is, after 1856, Tasmania. The island had been in the news recently, as Sir John Franklin had been appointed Governor-General in 1836. In consequence, British papers ran the occasional story about the famous explorer and his current residence. "I wonder if I should make a good settler!" Dickens wrote to Forster in mid-August. "I wonder, if I went to a new colony with my head, hands, legs, and health, I should force myself to the top of the social milk-pot and live upon the cream! What do you think? Upon my word I believe I should."[58] He didn't act on this radical change, but the idea got transferred, in a resounding affirmative, to Mr. Micawber's career in Australia at the conclusion of *David Copperfield*.

Dickens is "radical" is a different sense as well. In the chapters he wrote immediately after bragging about his leftish politics, he included the following historically grounded incident:

the mob gathering round Lord Mansfield's house [the one in Bloomsbury Square, not his country home the magnificent Kenwood House on the northern edge of Hampstead Heath], had called on those within to open the door, and receiving no reply (for Lord and Lady Mansfield were at that moment escaping by the backway), forced an entrance according to their usual custom … they then began to demolish it with great fury … involv[ing] in a common ruin the whole of the costly furniture, the plate and jewels, a beautiful gallery of pictures, the rarest collection of manuscripts ever possessed by any one private person in the world, and worse than all, because nothing could replace this loss, the great Law Library, on almost every page of which were notes in the Judge's own hand, of inestimable value, – being the results of the study and experience of his whole life. (p. 551)

The chronicler's sympathy here is unmistakably with Mansfield, not the mob, Mansfield, the judge whose decisions regarding copyright essentially established the very conditions of authorship under which Dickens both prospered and chafed. Though the point of view affectingly describes the "common ruin," the author of this passage was also imagining and writing up the fury of "the mob." Especially after the fall of the Bastille, it was difficult not to think of broken prisons, forced locks, and escapes from confinement as liberating. This narration at once summons up the accumulated assets and wisdom ensconced in the law as personified by one of Britain's greatest judges, and seems at another level, like "W"'s poem, to be "radical" about the punitive consequence of that law, the Newgate residence of misery and in some cases unjustly sentenced inmates contrasting strikingly with the elegant establishment of a leading member of the governing class.[59] On which side of the divide, harassed by the law, hailed by the commons, did Dickens stand? On both? To Forster he confessed, "I have let all the prisoners out of Newgate, burnt down Lord Mansfield's, and played the very devil."[60] As Thomas Rice states it, Dickens's "warning that political extremism of the left or right insures social instability is of enduring validity."[61] But Dickens was not always of the party of stability.

XII

Knowing that he had secured time off after the conclusion of *Barnaby*, Dickens relaxed at Broadstairs to an unprecedented extent. He described himself to Hall as "hideously lazy – always bathing, lying in the sun, or walking about. I write a No. when the time comes, and dream about it beforehand on cliffs and sands – but as to getting in advance – ! where's the use, too, as we so soon leave off."[62] Four days later, to Forster he tells a different story, of having "let all the prisoners out of Newgate ... I feel quite smoky when I am at work. I want elbow-room terribly."[63]

   It may be more than coincidence, especially given the long time Dickens debated the plan in his mind and with others, that just as he was releasing the prisoners he determined to go to America himself, and drafted and redrafted a difficult announcement "To the Readers of *Master Humphrey's Clock*," first printed with the October 9 number, informing them that he would sail west in January 1842 and issue the first part of a new shilling monthly novel on November 1.[64] October was otherwise a horrible month: Dickens had surgery without anesthetic for a fistula on the eighth, Catherine's brother George Hogarth died suddenly on the twenty-fourth, Dickens gave up space adjacent to Mary's grave that he had been saving for himself to his grieving mother-in-law for her son, and he had to finish the last numbers of the novel and the *Clock* for publication at the end of November. Nevertheless, he found it "a wonderful testimony to my being made for my art [even though he believed the fistula had been caused by sitting too long at his desk], that when, in the midst of this trouble and pain, I sit down to my book, some beneficent power shows it all to me, and tempts me to be interested, and I don't invent it – really do not – *but see it*, and write it down."[65] His doctor, the eminent surgeon Frederick Salmon, ordered Dickens to Windsor for recovery, and there, standing up writing, he finished *Barnaby* on November 5, as well as the preface to the last volume of the *Clock* which appeared in the final number, December 4.[66]

This exigent timetable, and Dickens's capacity to write through an enormous number of serious disturbances, both pleasurable and painful, suggest that he was intensely involved with his story no matter what else was happening. Yet virtually no commentators have spent long thinking about the composition of *Barnaby* during its serial run, and the Pilgrim editors devote no words in their preface to volume two of the *Letters* to the novel's progress. It is, however, possible to speculate on the basis of Dickens's correspondence and the text itself on the reasons why this novel, and especially its latter portion, took such hold on him and allowed him to finish it off without any postponements for trips, illness, or the death of a family member.

For, to put it baldly, *Barnaby* doesn't just rewrite Dickens's earlier works; it burns them down as savagely as the rioters torched London. Dickens unwrites himself with a fierce energy and mounting exhilaration at the thought of his impending freedom from the shackles and confinement of serial cells. That this unwriting was partly unconscious and unforeseen, that it was abetted by publishing decisions such as the termination of the periodical and the year's vacation discussed heretofore, and that it was necessary as a consequence of that plan to retire or kill off the characters in both the fiction and the frame, do not entirely account for the manic actors and activity of Dickens's scorched earth narrative.

There are other issues contributing to Dickens's fervor. His predecessor in historical fiction, Scott, loomed large. Dickens had gained much knowledge about Scott and his printing and publishing associates from George Hogarth, and more when John Gibson Lockhart's biography appeared in seven volumes in 1837–38, revised and expanded into ten volumes by 1839. Further, Lockhart's treatment of Scott's printers, Ballantyne, in 1838 provoked a strong rebuttal from the trustees of Ballantyne's estate and his son John Alexander Ballantyne: *Refutation of the Mistatements [sic] and Calumnies Contained in Mr. Lockhart's Life of Sir Walter Scott, Bart., Respecting the Messrs. Ballantyne.* In turn, Lockhart responded with the same mordant satire he had brought to editing the *Quarterly Review*: *The Ballantyne-Humbug Handled* (1839). This provoked another defense, *Reply to Mr. Lockhart's Pamphlet Entitled*

*"The Ballantyne-Humbug Handled"* (1839). Dickens sided with Lockhart in three reviews he wrote for the *Examiner*; of the *Refutation*, published on September 2, 1838, which he wrote not using anything he had learned from George Hogarth or his sister Christian, married to James Ballantyne and mother of Mary Hogarth's dear twin cousins Teenie and Jane; of *Humbug*, March 31, 1839, ending by including the Ballantynes in the "little knot of toadeaters and flatterers" to whose counsel Scott paid too much heed; and briefly and contemptuously of the *Reply*, September 29. The Pilgrim editors believe that, even though Dickens was entangled with the Ballantynes through the Hogarths, he sided with Lockhart's interpretation of Scott because the dispute "typified Author *v.* Publisher."[67] It doesn't exactly, however, both because Ballantyne was Scott's printer, not publisher and because the Ballantyne rejoinders offer substantial proof that Scott himself took responsibility for the firm's bankruptcy. But still, Dickens read into Scott's life and these accounts his own fierce struggle for authorial control over the other agents in the communications circuit.

Dickens was introduced to Lockhart at a dinner hosted by George Cruikshank – another fan of Scott's historical fiction – on December 12, 1837. The meeting went well and the two writers soon became friends. Dickens consumed Lockhart's biography as soon as it appeared: he transcribed Scott's musings after the death of his wife (May 1826) into his own Diary on January 14, 1838 because the thoughts so resembled his own since Mary Hogarth's death. The next day he ended "this brief attempt at a Diary. I grow sad over this checking off of days, and can't do it."[68] Scott's later years, however, haunted Dickens as much as any specter in *Barnaby*. Less than a month after stopping his Diary (temporarily, it turned out), when faced with the prospect of fulfilling his Agreement with Bentley by continuing *Oliver*, at its conclusion writing monthly a sixteen-page Original Article, and also producing at the same time the three-volume *Barnaby*, "writing a little of it when I could," he believed that the triple task would be impossible. He told Bentley that "[t]he conduct of three different stories at the same time, and the production of a large portion of each, every month, would have been beyond Scott himself."[69] Dickens won that argument, but three years later *Barnaby* in the *Clock* installments was draining him beyond endurance while losing subscribers: reporting to his friend and attorney Tom Mitton on August 23, 1841, Dickens accounted for his proposal to stop writing for a time by remembering "that Scott failed in the sale of his very best works, and never recovered his old circulation ... *because he never left off.*" (This really wasn't the case: Dickens has read Lockhart's account in his own terms.) He then goes on to say that his success in serial publication had "spoilt the novel sale" of fellow authors such as "Bulwer, Marryat, and the best people," and then that his "great success was, in a manner, spoiling itself, by being run to death and deluging the town with every description of trash and rot."[70] He knows that *Clock* sales have dropped over 50 percent, and while 30,000 a week is still "a sale wholly unprecedented and unknown, even in Scott's case, that sale is *shaky*, and trembles every day." Thus Scott became Dickens's watchword, more as an overworked and oppressed writer – if we believe the correspondence and reviews contain most of his response to Scott – than because of Scott's legacy to historical fiction. But part of the intensity of *Rudge* derives, I believe, from Dickens's self-appointed challenge to take up and revise that legacy, especially insofar as Scott's novels tend to conclude with reconciliation between opposing sides and the restoration of domestic and civic harmony. Dickens's novel portrays the carnage and death occasioned by the riots as more destructive, and the recuperation of families thereafter as more "shaky" – to apply his term about sales – than many of Scott's stories.

Scott's legacy was coming under reconsideration in ways that Lockhart's contentious biography does not explore. The competition between historians, biographers, and novelists for the right, the cultural authority, to tell the past was keen. At the center of that contention was Bulwer, the same Bulwer whose Newgate novels first catalyzed opposition to that genre. In the paratexts surrounding his 1835 novel *Rienzi*, about the fourteenth-century "last" of the Roman tribunes, Bulwer speaks about his own archival research. That research in turn authorizes him to attribute a different, nobler character to his protagonist than other biographers and historians, who judged Cola di Rienzi superficially and crudely. Moreover, Bulwer rejected the notion of writing a straightforward biography because he believed that the laws of fiction permitted, indeed demanded, understanding and presenting the deeper impulses motivating his hero, the spiritual side to which the current age seemed blind. That repurposing of the history of Rienzi to suit the present had its own precedent in Alessandro Manzoni's 1827 novel *I Promessi Sposi*, often identified as the foundational work for the Italian Risorgimento; and when Bulwer wrote a preface to an 1848 reissue of *Rienzi* he took pride in its influence upon the nationalist movements then gaining traction on the Italian peninsula.[71]

Dickens doesn't connect *Barnaby* directly to this ongoing conversation about the place of history in fiction. Perhaps he didn't want to call attention to another association with Bulwer, as the Newgate novel controversy had done quite enough already to embroil him in sharp stigmatism of socially radical stories. But he does relish, and take advantage of, the opportunity in his novel to invest historical figures with motivations and psychology derived in part from, but in most cases extending beyond, the archival record and, possibly, the interviews he conducted with survivors of the Gordon riots. The Mayor of London speaks from the record. The vintner and distiller Langdale, based on Thomas Langdale (1714–90) who did have his premises destroyed during the riots, becomes not simply a rich merchant vainly seeking help from civic authorities, but also a resourceful and worthy Catholic who shelters Haredale and helps him to escape from the mob. In three other cases, Dickens's imagination imparts quite a lot of character to historical figures more or less well known and biographized. Dickens is more sympathetic to Lord George Gordon than many. "Say what you please," Dickens writes to Forster, disputing the opinion of his friend, also a biographer of historical figures, Gordon "must have been at heart a kind man, and a lover of the despised and rejected [phrases applied in the King James Bible, Isaiah 53:3, to the "Man of Sorrows" understood to prefigure Christ], after his own fashion." In his next sentence Dickens nearly adverts to his quarrel with his own father, always overdrawn even though with his naval pension and Dickens's allowance he drew around £125 a year after giving Elizabeth £40 for her own use.[72] "He lived upon a small income, and always within it [unlike John Dickens and, at times, Dickens himself]; was known to relieve the necessities of many people; exposed in his place the corrupt attempt of a minister to buy him out of Parliament; and did great charities in Newgate."[73] Within the morality of the novel's plot, Gordon gets off lightly, and his subsequent unhappy career is but briefly sketched. However, as Dickens told Charles Ollier, until 1839 one of Bentley's principal staff, "As to the Riot, I am going to try if I can't make a better one" than Gordon did.[74]

In two other cases Dickens deployed his imagination more freely. He may have based the character of Gordon's secretary on Robert Watson (1746–1838), who wrote Gordon's biography and subsequently strangled himself. While some Dickensians dispute the claim that Watson was a model, an inquest on his body held on November 20, 1838 discovered nineteen scars. "Gashford" may be named for this corpse, but Dickens gifts him with his own personality and behavior, not Watson's.[75] He makes Gashford, unknown to Gordon, secretive and sly, skillfully instigating Hugh and his associates to wreak vengeance not only on metropolitan papists but especially on Haredale, who had bested him in romantic contests. After the failure of the anti-Catholic revolt, Gashford turns spy and, like Watson, eventually kills himself, though by poison rather than strangling.

Ned Dennis the hangman is even more complexly rendered by Dickens. There was such an official in 1780 named Ned Dennis, and he did participate in the carnage, but he was reprieved from execution whereas Dickens's Dennis is hanged. He justifies his role in the riots by maintaining that it supports the Constitution: he believes in the rightness of his calling, not least because papists "boil and roast instead of hang," so if they came to power "what becomes of my work! If they touch my work that's a part of so many laws, what becomes of the laws in general, what becomes of the religion, what becomes of the country!" (p. 312). Dennis is the person for whom death is a state-sanctioned terminus of life, and he makes both his living and his stories out of executions. Insofar as Newgate fictional prototypes are concerned, he certainly isn't a rosewater criminal in his own right, nor does he hang such. He does string up Hugh's gypsy mother. Yet like Newgate clergy, novels, novelists, and Boz, Dennis generates his life, status, occupation, and narrative out of death. And when confronted with his own execution, his bravado and professional pride collapse. Surely in several ways this really named but fictionally characterized professional death-dealer stands and cowers as a slantwise critique of Boz's professional interest in death narratives.

These, then, are the historical characters, whose personality, actions, and fate Dickens feels free to alter in varying degrees in order to present an even more faithful reconstruction of events and persons. But what about the principal actors whom Dickens invents? How do they figure in his historical reconstruction and its oblique reflections on the revolutions and rebellions on both sides of the Atlantic from 1776 through 1840? Take the three who besides Dennis participate in the forefront of the riot: the stable centaur Hugh, the ambitious apprentice Sim, and Barnaby. It is worth noting at the outset that they are pushed into leadership both by their own motives and enthusiasm and by those manipulating them from behind the scenes. (The most sinister and successful of the concealed manipulators is of course Sir John Chester – whose case we will take up in a moment.) Hugh, Sim, and Barnaby act not in accord with any historical precedent, but rather in ways that reword prior figures in Dickens's fictions. They alter, not the history of 1775–80, but the past eight years of Dickens's professional career.

Hugh, illegitimate, half-animal, reared in a stable, seems the antithesis of earlier offspring, notably Oliver who, though subjected to a dehumanizing upbringing at a baby farm, in the workhouse, in an undertaker's employ, and in his birth parish, turns up trumps at the end: the child of respectable parents, an heir, and adopted by a generous, loving extended family. Hugh enjoys all the privations of Oliver, and an even more exalted if uneven biological family (lord and gypsy); he grows up strong and illiterate as opposed to Oliver's delicacy and literacy. Gashford's principal agent in furthering destruction, and himself the abductor of Dolly Varden, Hugh incarnates adult male vitality and sexuality unchecked by any correction from employer or society until he meets his father. Then the composure and access to authority that Chester claims thoroughly intimidate, as well as infuriate, Hugh. He has his redemptive moments, especially on the gallows when he appeals for Barnaby's reprieve and asks that someone care for his dog, the only creature that showed sorrow at his mother's death. Hugh is what Oliver never could become, the orphan who is not saintly nor morally or sexually innocent, but insofar as he too is despised and rejected, he has his tender side and is not wholly villainous.

Sim is everything an industrious apprentice should not be: betrayer of his master's home, misuser of his professional skill as a locksmith, petty tyrant, spindle-shanked roué convinced of the quelling power of his "eye," and cruel in little ways. He stands over against another clerk with odd eyes who spies and leaves the office without permission: Newman Noggs. The ethos of the two stories values these characters' actions quite differently: Newman helps to ruin his master, for legitimate reasons, and enters into a late companionable marriage the opposite of Bumble's, while Sim is unable either to defeat his rivals for Dolly, Hugh and Joe Willet, or to demolish his master's home. Between the idle Hugh and the industrious Sim, Dickens thoroughly recasts the Hogarthian-Cruikshankian paradigm of contrasted apprentices and their earlier manifestations in his novels.

And Barnaby? Another child – a barn baby contrasting to Hugh? – born already marked with his paternal inheritance and curse, not a cipher who, wrapped in different cloth, might be the natural son of a lord (Hugh is that, though his clothing never connects him to his father's fashion). But he is loved and protected by his self-sacrificing mother, who lives for her son rather than dying as Oliver's, Dick's, and Smike's mothers do.

Barnaby spends his days and nights as an epochal pedestrian, but more within nature and accompanied by dogs and birds, rather than in the city alone. Barbara Hardy, disagreeing with her longtime colleague Kathleen Tillotson who found Barnaby (person and novel) a melodramatic failure, defines Barnaby as "a true and convincing portrait of the imagination," an avatar of Dickens's own delight in and fear of letting go, "an image and an example of the wildness, delusions and damage of revolution."[76] Barnaby's mind as well as body have been maimed by paternal, one might almost say "original," sin; and he is open to the temptations of money, excitement, and fame. Dickens likewise, at times, figured himself as marked by parental abandonment, and recognized at times his frantic need for money, excitement, and fame. The redomestication of Barnaby at the novel's close circumscribes his wildness and delusions, penning in what Dickens's pen let out. After recovering from the shock of his near hanging, Barnaby "had a better memory and greater steadiness of purpose; but a dark cloud overhung his whole previous existence, and never cleared away." This is too much like Dickens's own experience as narrated in the autobiographical fragment not to be noticed as a parallel. Still, Barnaby's "love of freedom and interest in all that moved or grew, or had its being in the elements [echoing Acts 17:28 about God 'in whom we live, and move, and have our being'] remained to him unimpaired. He lived with his mother on the Maypole farm" – a sentence composed when Elizabeth was very much living with her children in London while John Dickens rusticated in Devon – "and though he was free to ramble where he would, he never quitted Her, but was for evermore her stay and comfort" (p. 687).

## XIV

Dickens and Barnaby have madness in common, but in different degrees and embodiments. Barnaby's imagination is contaminated, and his raven, Grip, is both an infernal and a household familiar. As we've seen, Dickens devotes the whole of *Barnaby*'s Preface in the first and subsequent editions to his own raven and its predecessor: a displacement of authorial madness and ventriloquized speech onto a succession of animal avatars. These are, upon analysis, astonishing moves, once more demonstrating the extent to which Dickens through his characters unwrites prior incarnations and even domesticates the almost superhuman energies released in writing the riot chapters by licensing Grip as the novel's ultimate spokesperson.

So, given that three of the main characters – Gordon, Gashford, and Dennis – are historical to some degree, and not entirely at Dickens's disposal to imagine, and that even the leaders of the carnage, though wholly invented, follow the itinerary and timetable of the historical rioters, what can we make of the rest of the cast? There are two families that evidently formed the core of the first version of the novel – the Vardens and the Willets. In each case these groupings live in their place of business, the Golden Key and the Maypole. Both are patriarchal, as their names imply; whereas Varden's "key" opens and closes locked spaces in a household composed of three women and one other man, the Maypole seems unmistakably a phallic signifier for a community of impotent old men and unruly younger ones (Hugh, Joe, and the unwelcome guest Rudge). As the novel centers on the overthrow of authority, these two families contrast sensible but at first ineffectual paternal authority (Gabriel Varden) to tyranny (John Willet). They are paired with a third house and family, the Catholic Haredales, whose home is haunted by blood, largely in disrepair, and lacking in leadership. Geoffrey broods over his elder brother Reuben's murder, of which he is suspected because of rumors circulated by Sir John Chester, and tries with some severity and inconsistency to raise his niece Emma. This configuration of interrelated families and homes is evidently what Dickens principally brought to bear, tangentially at first, on the metropolitan riots of 1780.

The Gordon riots, the mob's ruinous excursion into the countryside, the destruction of the Warren and the Maypole, the abduction of Emma, are all tied together and furthered by another character of Dickens's invention: Sir John Chester. As much as Gashford, Chester steers the uprising, though without tipping his hand: "you set on Gashford to this work," Haredale charges Chester, referring particularly to the charred ruin of the Warren but also more generally to the riots (p. 677). There is an old connection between Gashford, Chester, and Haredale – the Jesuit school St. Omer's in France – though two become fanatically Protestant and the third remains unflinchingly Roman Catholic. Chester and Haredale hate each other because of a romantic contest in the past (the opposite result from that of Nell's grandfather and great-uncle): Haredale won, but cast off his mistress whom Chester afterwards enjoyed for a brief spell. Haredale hates Gashford. He tells Lord George that Gashford is "a servile, false, and truckling knave" who, among other crimes, "robbed his benefactor's daughter of her virtue, and married her to break her heart" (p. 362). Dickens tightly weaves the enigmatic enmity into the fabric of his story, but it does not register strongly, even in the climactic moment of the duel between the rivals (outlawed in Britain in the 1840s), when Haredale plunges "his sword through his opponent's body to the hilt" (p. 680). The end of the chapter, and the feud, however, comes not with the fatal thrust, but with Sir John's effort to erase from his features his "scorn and hatred," and instead to produce a composed smile so that his death mask will retain the image he fashioned as a living man.

For that is the secret of Chester's power: a superhuman composure that does not crack even when Varden informs him that the imprisoned Hugh is his son. Chester is in one way a tailor's dummy – always impeccably dressed whether at home or in company. In another way, he is the creation of his author-mentor, Philip Stanhope, fourth Earl of Chesterfield, whose cynical letters of advice to his natural son remain the only legacy of the earl's much more complicated and at times politically courageous life. Like father, Chester emulates his mentor; but unlike son, Hugh is overmastered, but not civilized, by his father. Chester lives on nothing a year, having spent his inheritance and his bride's "great wealth" (p. 133); but he does not work. He finds Haredale's accusation that the torching of the Warren is his work inappropriate: "'Work!' echoed Sir John, looking smiling round [the look he hopes to maintain in death]. 'Mine! – I beg your pardon, I really beg your pardon – '" (p. 676). For above all, Chester is a gentleman of the old school, who lives and dies by a perverted chivalric code perfectly summarized by yet another phallic instrument, the sword.

In Chester, then, Dickens rewrites the ideal of the gentleman, showing one whose practiced addresses and flirtatious appeals mask hypocrisy and deadly antagonism. By any traditional measures, still applicable in the late eighteenth century, Chester is a gentleman of taste, breeding, and notable self-control, who without other qualifications is knighted in recognition of his imperturbable deportment. If Noggs personifies what becomes of a ruined gentleman in the cash-nexus age, Chester embodies gentlemanliness at the end of its time. On the surface – for which impeccable exterior he is celebrated – he is one of the *laissez-faire* governing class that does not govern, while beneath that polished, reflective surface his schemes divide and wreck family and country. Like Chesterfield, Sir John perverts the societally imposed constraints that signified cultivated sociability into mechanisms for unlimited self-assertion, even though he seemingly has neither institutional authority nor wealth. For money Chester substitutes his perfectly disciplined body and manners. Barnaby associates gold with sunset: "If we had, chinking in our pockets, but a few specks of that gold which is piled up yonder in the sky," he says to his mother one summer's evening, "we should be rich for life" (p. 373). But Chester gets gold through his body and its products, especially his legitimate son Edward whom he raises to "marry well," to be a "fortune-hunter" like all those in high places (p. 135). And not, incidentally, support his father's fraudulent lifestyle. By inventing Chester, Dickens gains the freedom to rewrite Chesterfield's life and letters, and perhaps thereby to reflect on his own father's contrasting imperturbability and rhetorical flourishes, not to mention Dickens's occasional sense that he too was raised to support his sire. This is yet a further way Dickens manages historical fiction to reflect on his own times and situation as author and John's son.

In these characters that Dickens can freely imagine, then, we see a complicated reconsideration of his own ambitions. Work may or may not define a gentleman; desire for gold may or may not contaminate imagination; education or neglect of offspring may or may not produce a younger generation of moral and obedient subjects. Dickens gains space for these paradoxical propositions by setting his work sixty years earlier: a time when home and business took place in the same setting (Chester works as hard in his chambers at not working while getting dressed as Gabriel in his workshop hammers and forges making keys), and when cash was not the only measure of worth.[77] Indeed, one of the striking things about this story is its economy. There are products bought and sold, particularly the fermenting stock of the Maypole for which Joe Willet pays every quarter. But otherwise cash is scarce: a few shillings dropped down the chimney of the red-brick house, a penny in Joe's pocket, declining income and property at the Warren. The only time money is plentiful is during the riots; then it seems that such shops as dare to open – mainly public houses – treat the rioters or take their recompense in stolen property. When John Willet, senile, retires after the destruction of the Maypole, his spirits are rekindled because Joe gives him a large slate "upon which the old man regularly scored up vast accounts for meat, drink, and tobacco. As he grew older this passion increased upon him; and it became his delight to chalk against the name of each of his cronies a sum of enormous magnitude, and impossible to be paid" (p. 686). This is a mimic, fantastic cash nexus that has no applicability either to monetary exchange or to the factitious value of Muffin shares run up by fictions of future demand.

Instead, the alternative exchange is bodies. And in this economy male potency rather than female pregnancy signifies the production of expendable lives and limbs. Haredale, childless, is for years suspected of killing his brother so as to inherit the estate. Rudge substitutes another body for his own, thus, he hopes, escaping suspicion that he lives. Dennis earns his living by attending to the necks of felons. Dolly Varden's piquant and saucy beauty attracts robbers, kidnappers, and potential rapists within the story, and throngs of admirers among her readers, who bought up thousands of print portraits supplied by several artists as extra illustrations. The quieter distinction of Emma Haredale subjects her to the first two threats, but not to rape or Dolly's degree of public adoration. The cruelest person in this history is the man whose body circulates as his credit, Chester; and he tries to preserve that value even in his death mask. Others pay with portions of their bodies – Stagg's eyes, Joe's arm, Sim's legs – or the whole corpus in the cases of Dennis and Hugh.[78]

In this mercantile economy blood and money commingle, bodies are bought and sold for wartime fodder, corpses hang in the marketplace outside Newgate where their life stories are sold, and flesh is subjected to fierce corporal punishment. Desire can be replaced by sadism. Deprived of any lover and expelled from her sister's loving family, Miggs proves an exceptionally effective turnkey for the County Bridewell (asylum), maintaining impeccable order among her female inmates in part through a number of "useful inventions" she practices, such as "inflicting an exquisitely vicious poke or dig with the wards of a key in the small of the back, near the spine" (a wonderful instance of Dickens riffing on the theme of keys, locks, containment, and surveillance), or "treading by accident (in pattens) on such as had small feet" (p. 685). Sim and Miggs, despite their disagreements (or because of them, even), would be even better matched than Bumble and Mrs. Corney. They both prosper through bodily abuse – Miggs the successful turnkey actively "falling upon" her charges, especially the beauties, on the slightest occasion, while Sim, legless, makes his living polishing the booted nether limbs of the Horse Guards officers. In his domestic life he corrects his wife "with a brush, or boot, or shoe," while she retaliates "by taking off his legs, and leaving him exposed to the derision of those urchins who delight in mischief" (p. 684). Unspoken in this novel is the treatment of those laborers at the West Indies estates where Ned Chester and Joe Willet work and prosper. But the same economy, though offstage, operates there: bodies yield money. And money follows bodies, as the substantial inheritance Joe gains and the prosperity Ned enjoys (despite not having married a fortune as his father commanded) are novelistically celebrated in their numerous offspring and heirs. This is yet another instance of Dickens's being at once a realist about the source of some late eighteenth-century fortunes (in reality, the Marryat family; in fiction, the Bertrams and the Eyres, among others), and a fantasist, since he still can't bring "work" and "worth" together except at the Golden Key, where nothing seems to get sold, and the Maypole, enriched by Joe's paternal inheritance.

XV

*Barnaby Rudge* is as many have noted insistently Oedipal; sons overthrow fathers.[79] Edward Chester and Joe Willet are fictionally rewarded with loving and fertile wives, wealth, and happiness. The older generation dies: Rudge, Chester, Haredale, Willet, and beyond the time of the story, Gordon and Gashford. The last surviving creature is Grip, "and as he was a mere infant for a raven, when Barnaby was grey, he has very probably gone on talking to the present time" about the kettle and the devil.

The novel, along with the *Clock* frame, also in several dimensions enacts both Oedipean and Saturnian supplantations. In real life Dickens tries to allowance, discipline, and exile his parents while in his fiction he's annihilating London and the law; he also neatly oversets Chapman and Hall twice (once over their loan, once over his next project to commence only after a year's vacation) and Richard Bentley, with whom he terminates all contractual arrangements in July 1840. He also, as we'll speak about in more detail shortly, attempts to consume his offspring Boz. But first, it is time to consider in some detail what humans are left talking when the *Clock* winds up. Master Humphrey, after dreaming happily of "sons and daughters, and grandchildren," including one "crippled boy" who rests "upon a little crutch" (Tiny Tim's precursor), is aroused by the clock striking, puts down the pen with which he has been writing these memories down, and dies.[80] He leaves his property to Jack Redburn and the deaf gentleman, naming Pickwick and Owen Miles as executors. Legacies to the housekeeper and barber enable them to retire and possibly to wed, Humphrey having anticipated and approved of such an event should it occur. Mr. Pickwick and the Wellers depart, and thus the company of Mr. Weller's Watch disperses. Redburn and the deaf gentleman live on in his house, but Master Humphrey's room, preserved as at his death, is silent and uninhabited. The deaf gentleman, who anticipates the return of a runaway daughter and her husband to support him in old age, speculates that Jack Redburn may be Ned Chester, but if so, Ned no longer is accompanied by wife and numerous children, since he has lived with Master Humphrey for eight years.

Before *Rudge* begins, the deaf gentleman, inspired by his host's revelation of his part in the preceding story as the Single Gentleman, proposes that in future the writers might "interweave" their own lives with the clock fictions, an article of agreement that is "cordially received" (pp. 695–96). Since this innovation comes after the manuscript Master Humphrey has selected to read was written, there seems no possibility that the personal adventures of a clock society member could have been stitched together with the historical account and woven into *Rudge*, though Master Humphrey thinks that he "detected in one quarter that this was really the case" (p. 696). Thus Dickens prepares a case in February of 1841 for events in *Barnaby Rudge* to be connected to one of the clock company. One can believe either that Humphrey's speculation at the start of the story, and the deaf gentleman's at the December 4 ending of the *Clock*, are implausible and instances of Dickens's incompetence, or that some great misfortune befell John's son. And so "the chimney corner has grown cold: and MASTER HUMPHREY'S CLOCK has stopped for ever."

Although the circulation of the weekly had fallen to 30,000, it was still profitable. For Dickens to silence the *Clock* and to lay to rest so many persons who narrated its contents needs further elucidation. Whereas he dashed through the last portions of *Rudge* with incredible facility, he did chafe at the confinement of the short parts and the necessity of filling another number every week. In taking leave of his readers, after taking leave of his narrators, Dickens complains about the unsuitability of weekly parts.

I have often felt cramped and confined in a very irksome and harassing degree, by the space in which I have been constrained to move. I have wanted you to know more at once than I could tell you ... In a word, I have found this form of publication most anxious, perplexing, and difficult. I cannot bear these jerking confidences which are no sooner begun than ended, and no sooner ended than begun again. (p. 697)

With extraordinary percipience, Edgar Allan Poe a few months later assailed Dickens for his inconsistent management of the mystery, putting some clues into the mouths of mistaken persons, as when Solomon Daisy declares that Rudge's body was found months after the outrage, and averring others misleadingly, as when the narrator continually calls Mrs. Rudge "the widow." Poe recognizes that for the first-time reader these clues, true and false, may not be comprehended "without the key" – another way of thinking about the significance of keys for the novel's apprehension – and that the author may "feel that much of what is effective to his own informed perception must necessarily be lost upon his uninformed readers"; but still Poe judges that while upon re-reading the now informed reader will find these points "break out in all directions like stars, and throw quadruple brilliance over the narrative," that brilliance is "unprofitably sacrificed at the shrine of the keenest interest in mere mystery."[81] In sum, though Dickens and Poe come at the confinement of serial installments and the problematics of authorial revelation from different perspectives, both perceive a disjunction between the novel's murder mystery, begun in the first chapter and not solved until nearly the last, and the substance of its historical narrative.

That is, however, not the only, or perhaps most important, cause for Dickens's abandoning serialization for a time. At a fundamental level he seems to have been carried along, in the course of the rebellions domestic and religious, to a thoroughgoing overthrow of his provisional authorial practices and personae. By November his desk was cleared. And he was considering other alternatives not directly connected to writing. He turned down an invitation to stand for Parliament at Reading in the summer General Election. He thought about it for a few days, especially because there was some social and intellectual property legislation (Talfourd, the other MP for Reading, intended to reintroduce his Bill) that he would have liked to help pass. But Dickens estimated his chances, correctly, as slight and the expenses as heavy; Peel's party won a substantial majority. Interestingly, he doesn't seem to have considered that serving as an MP would cut into his writing time and income; others had combined the two occupations. Or maybe, just possibly, he was tired enough of the constant pressure of writing that another career beckoned. Not politics. Yet he had enrolled as a student in the Middle Temple, where he would have dined close to the location of Chester's rooms – another anti-author of Dickens's serial. Most of all, he simply wanted not to write.

And so, when he concludes negotiations with his publishers for a holiday, he promises in his October announcement to resume publication a year later in monthly numbers, reconceiving the weekly parts not as communing with his audience every seven days, but as necessitating fifty-two gaps instead of only twelve. In other words, whereas once upon a time Dickens had thought weekly serialization would increase his commerce with his readers by contact every seven days, he now counts on the gaps between monthly parts as the better way to maintain the conversation. It's surely an odd conclusion, written in part to conceal the facts that weekly installments made insatiable demands on his time and that they were too short for the fuller development of plot and characters he felt he achieved with the monthly numbers.

Yet beyond that partially concealed confession about authorial practices lies a deeper issue about his authorial persona. As we have seen over the last two chapters, Dickens essentially does away with Boz. The ambiguous old/young narrator/author of the *Sketches* and dramatic pieces, the alleged editor of Mudfog and parish stories and of the life of the Nickleby family, the actual editor of *Bentley's Miscellany*, and the nominal, actual, and yet displaced editor of the *Clock*, all get shoved aside. Boz is replaced by Master Humphrey, himself the crippled relic of his younger days, who pulls out stories composed by others, and spends his declining years by the clock case rather than in the streets. And while Master Humphrey has his sentimental and fanciful aspects, he is not anything like the solitary pedestrian of the urban sketches. Whether in fact, as he writes in his last pages, he has children and grandchildren, or whether these are only dreams, remains undecided; but waking from these dreams, he dies. Either they have sustained him during his life (which allegedly includes the finding of the dead Nell), or their contrast to his lonely existence is insupportable. Either way, he is not the self-sufficient, sometimes cheerfully distanced and ironic, Boz.

If this weren't enough of an erasure of previous authorial and editorial personae and purposes, *Rudge* provides a last version of the nocturnal perambulator: Rudge himself.[82] Like Boz, he walks, he observes, he moves fearlessly within the most dangerous quarters of the city, and he remains unknown to most of those whom he observes and tracks to their ends. But he refuses to inquire into other lives or speculate. Unlike Boz, who has no history, this pedestrian is himself obsessed with his past, not interested in the world around him. He is Boz's haunted shadow, a revenant of his former self died and recalled to a ghastly, ghostly life:

He could be no spy, for he never removed his slouched hat to look about him, entered into conversation with no man, heeded nothing that passed, listened to no discourse, regarded nobody that came or went. But so surely as the dead of night set in, so surely this man was in the midst of the loose concourse in the night-cellar where outcasts of every grade resorted; and there he sat till morning.

He was not only a spectre at their licentious feasts; a something in the midst of their revelry and riot that chilled and haunted them; but out of doors he was the same. Directly it was dark, he was abroad – never in company with any one, but always alone; never lingering or loitering, but always walking swiftly; and looking (so they said who had seen him) over his shoulder from time to time, and as he did so quickening his pace ... The footpad hiding in a ditch had marked him passing like a ghost along its brink; the vagrant had met him on the dark high-road; the beggar had seen him pause upon the bridge to look down at the water, and then sweep on again; they who dealt in bodies with the surgeons could swear he slept in churchyards, and that they had beheld him glide away among the tombs, on their approach. And as they told these stories to each other, one who had looked about him would pull his neighbor by the sleeve, and there he would be among them. (pp. 140–41)

To his wife he identifies himself as a "hunted beast"; in the body he is "a spirit, a ghost upon the earth" (p. 145). In this most *unheimlich* of Dickens's novels, Rudge is the monstrous embodiment of all wretchedness and evil, past and present, his only companion fittingly one who is blind but who sees with his hands and his heart what his traveling partner is. Whereas genial Boz seems someone readers would like to know more about, Rudge is the one whose narrative we would not read or hear if we could, and whose tale is fiercely suppressed by his wife and never comprehended by his damaged son. He doesn't toll anyone's knell, least of all his victims', as he has reincarnated himself as one of those dead men. He is the last wraith-like embodiment of all those mad storytellers interpolating their tales into Dickens's texts. Only Grip is left to utter domestic and infernal asseverations.

We might turn one more time to Foucault's statement about the self-sacrifice of modern authors:

Writing is now linked to sacrifice and to the sacrifice of life itself; it is a voluntary obliteration of the self that does not require representation in books because it takes place in the everyday existence of the writer. Where a work had the duty of creating immortality, it now attains the right to kill, to become the murderer of its author. Flaubert, Proust, and Kafka are obvious examples of this reversal. In addition, we find the link between writing and death manifested in the total effacement of the individual characteristics of the writer; the quibbling and confrontations that a writer generates between himself and his text cancel out the signs of his particular individuality.[83]

This does seem to apply in some degree to Dickens's fictional avatars. In his own life, he has for five years been struggling to subdue his alter ego Boz and supplant it with his own name. He wants to sacrifice the life of Boz to release and copyright the life writing of Dickens. There is thus a sense in which the obliteration of the alternative self "takes place in the everyday existence of the writer," who some days signs himself as Boz and on other occasions demands that the name be cancelled out. Where Boz created "immortality" for himself and Pickwick, he now appears under the shadowy alter ego of a murderer and ghost, immortal only in the sense of revenant; Dickens effectively kills Pickwick in bringing him back to life in the *Clock* where he ends up being executor of the estate of another avatar of the Bozzian narrator, Master Humphrey; and later authors need to kill off Pickwick *and* his readers in order to make room for their very different authorial and narratorial selves. The quibblings and confrontations among all the narrators of *Clock* stories, the withdrawings and occludings of narrative agency, the transformation of personal adventures into a chronicler of the Gordon riots, all seem to execute the same sentence and cancel out authorial personality and identity. At the same time Dickens, by reducing, traducing, and removing Boz, asserts his own authority: this is Oedipal, Saturnian, and sibling overthrow, given Boz's referents to Dickens's writerly precursors, paternal offspring, and paratextual pairings. Of course such opposition isn't consistently maintained, any more than any other mode of rebellion is: Dickens can still sign a mid-summer 1841 letter to Forster, "Always your affectionate friend / Boz." Forster reproduces this close and signature in his biography (1:251). (But there might be a hidden combat here, since Dickens refers to an invitation to another public dinner, in Glasgow, publicly announced in Scots newspapers: at this moment he is clearly more the man of the hour than Forster, whom he invites, with the slightest hint of *de haut en bas*, to join him. Forster fell ill and couldn't – is there a Freudian doctor in the house?) These may seem overblown and over-theorized assertions, but they attempt to associate the clear rebellions within Dickens's fictions to the multiple rebellions, against parents, publishers, fellow authors, fictional genres, Tories, pirates, plagiarists, and his own pseudonymic alternates, that with increasing assertion he stages in his own authorial life.

## XVI

Master Humphrey writes his final entry, and dies. Many of those in the stories die, and the survivors, such as Kit, Dick Swiveller, Joe Willet, and at least the young Ned Chester, while sharing the sometime cheerful spirit of Boz, seem more youthful, hopeful, imaginative, sociable, fecund, and forward-looking. Moreover, those hopes that Boz as narrator, editor, or authorial stand-in express, for living comfortably, ethically, in loving communities, and for being recognized as a member of the respectable middle class, in the reforming parlance of the day being acknowledged as a gentleman who works faithfully at a socially useful trade, seem critiqued and collapsed within the *Clock*. The idea of being a reduced gentleman like Noggs is insufficient though redeeming. The idea of being a successful simulacrum of a polished gentleman and courtier, like Chester, is thoroughly undermined. The idea that writing, words, have power and affect continues to be supported through *Rudge* by Gordon, Gashford, Chester, and others – but their mixed motives and effects are questioned and shown in some cases to be fatally vicious and destructive.

Within *Rudge* and the *Clock*, then, Dickens challenges his earlier creations and writes some of them into extinction. Or tries to. He was known to his friends by his real name, but known much more widely as Boz. But the *Clock* works had insistently separated the earlier apolitical pedestrian Boz from Dickens's material and authorial selves; Dickens was no longer capable of speaking about historical or contemporary events without any apparent political bias or passion. Boz was a past authorial self, a part of that side of Dickens that felt and expressed so much affection for people at all points along the social spectrum. Insofar as authorial names are indices of content, signs used for categorizing and valuing different kinds of writing, the brand Boz and the brand Dickens increasingly stood for different commodities. The former was being phased out although its standing with the public was high; the latter was the brand for the present and future, even if its character and history were uncertain and changing and its guarantee of faithfulness was not yet fully tested.

Dickens went to America as Charles Dickens, author, addressing his public and aligning with other authors on either side of the Atlantic shoreline to advocate for fairer treatment of intellectual property across national frontiers. America expected to see, and for some time did think they saw, only the genial Boz. To the extent that Dickens was a self-made man, not the inheritor of a title and estates, he was "a true hero for the Americans."[84] To that extent he could be received on American class terms, perhaps a bit florid in dress and ordinary in looks; his features showed "more animation than grace and more intelligence than beauty," one reporter opined.[85] But when he spoke about copyright, he crossed a boundary line. "You must drop that, Charlie, or you will be dished," warned the *Boston Morning Post*; you're wrong to intrude "*business* upon those who assemble to do homage" to genius, scolded the New York *Courier*.[86] Even in the New World, authorship and business, writing and copyright, ought to be kept separate. One might be accorded the reception due to a gentleman, although some press thought Dickens was meeting real society for the first time, but he dropped out of the ranks of polite society when he campaigned for restrictions on free trade in books. In some sense the Dickens who spoke for print culture was simply not the author Americans wanted to celebrate. That was Boz.

The stories about Dickens's American tour and its aftermath and how it changed his standing as an author; how he struggled through the mid-1840s to find a new voice, a Dickens voice, a voice that could be political as well as imaginative and sympathetic and reportorial; how he furiously terminated his relationship with Chapman and Hall (a termination that, because of joint copyright ownership, simply couldn't be wholly effected); how with his old printers and new publishers, Bradbury and Evans, he finally struck it rich with *Dombey and Son*; how the passage of copyright amendments and later bi-national copyright agreements consolidated his ownership of and authority over his writings; and how he found his mature voice in the oddest but, on reflection, most obvious of places, that of a neglected boy in *Copperfield*, and in *Bleak House* an imperial voice tolling the present moments and a traumatized but recovered subaltern female diarist reinscribing her past, constitute the narrative of the second phase of Dickens's authorial self-creation. It was in the 1840s that he also positioned himself front and center on social issues, helping to found and edit a daily newspaper on the Whig side, superintending a shelter for the reform of prostitutes, and collaborating with others in efforts to supply authors with fiscal support in desperate cases.

The last phase, beginning in the mid-1850s, once again reidentifies Dickens, now for the imperial age. He owns and edits two highly successful magazines that print his own writing and that of many other contributors, thus melding proprietorship with editorship and authorship; he leases an even more splendid London home and then buys a country house that fulfills a childhood dream; he leaves his wife and thinks that separation deserves national attention and forgiveness, thus massively breaching the boundary between his private affairs and the public to which he paid lip service in prior decades; he supports a mistress and her family and travels often to the Continent and once more to America while consolidating his reputation as Britain's greatest living writer; and he leverages the amateur theatrics started to raise money for indigent authors into a string of plays and public readings that bring him closer than ever to his fans, and yield an estate far exceeding in value those bequeathed by his publishers or any contemporary author who did not inherit (Bulwer) or marry (Disraeli) money. *That* Dickens, the post-Boz one of the many collected editions, of international celebrity, the author whose works, through stereotype, steam transport, bi-national agreements, authors' and publishers' agents, reprints, new illustrators and series of illustrations (some of them running to several hundred separate images) issued through lithographic processes, was a paradigmatic "author" for the industrial era. He did seem to command the narrative of his origins, the sources and unity of his works, and the continuity of his imperative message to practice the charity of the gospels. And this authoritative figure, not the hesitant, overcommitted, under-financed, ambiguously personified writer of Dickens's first phase, became the figure handed down to the next generation, to be celebrated by writers as diverse as Gissing and Chesterton and reviled by the majority of decadent wits such as Oscar Wilde and Edwardians such as the Stephen brothers, their families and friends such as Virginia Stephen Woolf (who did admire much of Dickens) and Lytton Strachey.

What this narrative provides is simply an account of the "birth" – and death and rebirth and christening and rechristening and unwriting – of this paradigmatic and probably earliest full instance of the future industrial-age author. By trial and many errors, over his lifetime Dickens learned to manage all facets of print culture, from formats to fame. And the most triumphant, most lasting achievement of all was, finally, to so suture his writing to his own corporeal identity that he supplied the template for Freud and Edmund Wilson: the writer, whose wounded body and psyche never heal, writes out of that injury recuperative narratives moving readers to believe in, and act on, the faith that it is possible under most circumstances to assemble a loving community bound by trust, our mutual friends if not relations. Dickens shapes that author backwards, from manuscripts and prefaces and speeches and self-presentations that rewrite his early history, his parents, his career choices, his romantic involvements, his wife and children, and his works so that he seems to have been born a writer, not made one while holding options to break out in another life altogether.

The stories about the adolescence and maturity of this industrial-age author have been told many times, following Dickens's lead; and if they need to be retold within the context of the industrial print culture revolution, they require another book or books. Of this story we have, at last, come to

THE END.

# Notes

1 John Butt and Kathleen Tillotson, *Dickens at Work* (London: Methuen, 1957).

2 Robert L. Patten, *Charles Dickens and His Publishers* (Oxford: Clarendon Press, 1978), pp. 343–44.

3 Although Roger Chartier's "General Introduction: Print Culture" precedes a series of "case" and "object" studies that do not include any British instances, his "dual definition of print culture" and defense of the case and object study as ways of speaking about print culture are succinct and thoroughly relevant to this project (*The Culture of Print: Power and the Uses of Print in Early Modern Europe*, ed. Chartier, trans. Lydia G. Cochrane [Cambridge: Polity Press, 1989], pp. 1–10). A useful place to begin studying book history is David Finkelstein and Alistair McCleery, *An Introduction to Book History* (New York and London: Routledge, 2005).

4 I will use Gérard Genette's term "paratexts" to designate both those parts of a book that are generally integral to it, such as title page and preface, and those which are usually produced separate from the text, such as advertisements (a public epitext) or authorial statements in correspondence (a private epitext): "[t]he epitext is any paratextual element not materially appended to the text within the same volume but circulating, as it were, freely, in a virtually limitless physical and social space" (Genette, *Paratexts: Thresholds of Interpretation*, trans. Jane E. Lewin, foreword Richard Macksey [Cambridge University Press, 1997], p. 344).

5 The "sociology of texts" originated in McKenzie's 1984 study of the Waitangi Treaty between white immigrants and the indigenous Maori people of New Zealand, and was elaborated and expanded as a principle in his Panizzi Lectures of 1985, *Bibliography and the Sociology of Texts* (London: British Library, 1986). William St. Clair, *The Reading Nation in the Romantic Period* (Cambridge University Press, 2004), bases his "political economy of reading" on very substantial quantitative evidence about British book production and circulation over some sixty years on either side of 1800.

6 Simon Eliot, *Some Patterns and Trends in British Publishing, 1800–1919* (London: Bibliographical Society, 1994); David McKitterick, ed., *The Cambridge History of the Book in Britain*, vol. VI: *1830–1914* (Cambridge University Press, 2009).

7  A fine study that addresses the situation of women authors in the nineteenth century is Linda Peterson's *Becoming a Woman of Letters: Myths of Authorship and Facts of the Victorian Market* (Princeton University Press, 2009).

8  Founding works on uniformist reception theory include Wolfgang Iser, *The Act of Reading: A Theory of Aesthetic Response* (Baltimore: Johns Hopkins University Press, 1978) and Hans Robert Jauss, *Toward an Aesthetic of Reception*, trans. Timothy Bahti (Minneapolis: University of Minnesota Press, 1982).

## 1 CHRISTENING BOZ (1812–1834): THE JOURNALISM SKETCHES

1  Charles Dickens, *Letters*, ed. Madeline House, Graham Storey, Kathleen Tillotson, *et al.*, The Pilgrim/British Academy Edition, 12 vols. (Oxford: Clarendon Press, 1965–2002), 1:449–50nn3–4. Hereafter *Letters* followed by volume:page.

2  Charles Dickens, *Oliver Twist*, ed. Kathleen Tillotson, The Clarendon Dickens (Oxford: Clarendon Press, 1966), "Introduction," pp. xxiii–xxiv; "Descriptive List of Editions, 1838–1867," pp. [xlviii]–l. Unless otherwise noted, quotations from Tillotson's editorial apparatus and Dickens's text will be to this edition and usually cited parenthetically in the text. Bentley's staff didn't do a perfect job of title page substitution: Michael Sadleir's "Copy II" (UCLA Library) has "Charles Dickens" for volume one and "Boz" for volumes two and three (p. xlix).

3  Diagram from Robert Darnton, "What Is the History of Books?" in *The Kiss of Lamourette: Reflections in Cultural History* (New York: W. W. Norton, 1990), p. 112.

4  Darnton's schema has been criticized for disregarding the book as artifact, though in other of his publications he has been very attentive to the materiality of print, especially the ways it can be smuggled across frontiers. See Thomas Adams and Nicolas Barker, "A New Model for the Study of the Book," in Barker, ed., *A Potencie of Life: Books in Society* (London: British Library, 1993), pp. 5–43.

5  The Chinese first invented and used moveable type in the eleventh century CE. They had plant-based papers by 100 BCE; the Japanese and Koreans perfected these papers as smooth writing surfaces by 700 CE, and paper making was established in Baghdad shortly thereafter. What is important about Johann Gutenberg is less his own Western (re)invention of moveable type than the impetus his products gave to Europeans to exploit the advantages of print over manuscript reproduction. Prior to print the author's name was often the guarantee of authority, especially for works by ancient authors.

6  John Feather, *Publishing, Piracy and Politics: An Historical Study of Copyright in Britain* (London: Mansell, 1994), p. 97. There are a number of important authorities on British copyright. W. A. Copinger published the first edition of the *Law on Copyright* (1870) when he was twenty-three; the latest edition, the fourteenth, has according to the publisher "been fundamentally rewritten

by Kevin Garnett QC and his team": Garnett, Gillian Davies, and Gwilym Harbottle, eds., *Copinger and Skone James on Copyright* (London: Sweet and Maxwell, 2009). Lyman Ray Patterson's books, of which the first was *Copyright in Historical Perspective* (Nashville: Vanderbilt University Press, 1968), are helpful in defining users' rights. For what D. F. McKenzie called the "sociology of texts," Mark Rose's book, *Authors and Owners: The Invention of Copyright* (Cambridge, MA: Harvard University Press, 1993), not only covers the statutory and judicial proceedings but also contextualizes the shifting grounds for arguments in support of various claims about and claimants to copyright. John Feather has also published *A History of British Publishing* (London and New York: Routledge, 1988), a study focusing on the book trade side of things. McKenzie's *Bibliography and the Sociology of Texts* was first presented as the 1985 Panizzi Lectures. Robert Darnton calls him "the greatest bibliographer of our time." See also *Privilege and Property, Essays on the History of Copyright*, available free online as of the end of June 2010, at www.copyrighthistory.org; these essays cover aspects of copyright worldwide since its inception. I rely often in my account on the phrasing and emphases (where correct) of Augustine Birrell, who gave a series of lectures on copyright in 1899 and then published a selection, *Seven Lectures on the Law and History of Copyright in Books* (London: Cassell, 1899). Birrell's understanding of the status of copyright law probably comes closest to what Dickens might have known over the course of his career. James Raven covers all aspects of print commerce in his authoritative *Business of Books: Booksellers and the English Book Trade, 1450–1850* (New Haven and London: Yale University Press, 2007).

7  "Copyright Case in America," *Westminster Review* 24 (January 1836): 187–97, 187.

8  Quoted in Raven, *Business of Books*, p. 71.

9  With respect to play texts, I am particularly indebted to Peter W. M. Blayney, "The Publication of Playbooks," in *A New History of Early English Drama*, ed. John D. Cox and David Scott Kastan (New York: Columbia University Press, 1997), pp. 383–422. My brief synopsis glosses over multiple exceptions and hypotheses that Blayney is scrupulous in identifying and critiquing.

10  William Shakespeare, *Mr. William Shakespeares Comedies, Histories, & Tragedies* (London: Isaac Iaggard and Ed. Blount, 1623), A3 (spelling slightly modernized). As Blayney points out, the Stationers' Company authorities would not care about the authorship or the quality of the text, but rather would require that the new publisher obtain the consent of any member claiming ownership of copyright in a previous edition properly allowed and licensed (p. 399).

11  Feather, *Publishing*, p. 33.

12  Locke and his friends lobbied hard against the renewal of the Stationers' Company monopoly, arguing that the lack of competition and the exercise of its authority over the market made books unnecessarily expensive and exacted profit from the labors of others.

13  Feather, *Publishing*, p. 5.
14  "Copyright Case in America," 188, quoting from *Millar* v. *Taylor* (1769). The article is often inaccurate (for instance, giving 1716 as the date rather than 1769). But it instances what a layperson such as Dickens might have learned from periodicals in the 1830s. The review, on the *Report of the Copyright Case of Wheaton v. Peters decided in the Supreme Court of the United States* (New York, 1834), begins by saying that "the decision in question seems to leave the law in America even in a more unsatisfactory and uncertain state than under the administration of justice in England."
15  Feather, *Publishing*, p. 67. The equivalent in 2009 US currency would be about $4,000.
16  Oliver Goldsmith, *An Inquiry into the Present State of Polite Learning in Europe* (1759), in A. Friedman, ed., *The Collected Works of Oliver Goldsmith*, 5 vols. (Oxford: Clarendon Press, 1966), 1:316.
17  Feather, *Publishing*, p. 77.
18  Samuel Johnson, letter to William Strahan, March 7, 1774, in *Letters*, ed. Bruce Redford, 5 vols. (Princeton University Press, 1992–94), II:129–31, 130.
19  Feather, *Publishing*, p. 94. William St. Clair stresses the importance of the "new trade in low-priced reprints," while Richard B. Sher emphasizes that the resolution of uncertainty over copyright ownership and the affirmation of term limits allowed publishers to ramp up operations in order to exploit their window of opportunity for both reprints and new editions. See Sher, *The Enlightenment and the Book: Scottish Authors and Their Publishers in Eighteenth-Century Britain, Ireland, and America* (University of Chicago Press, 2006), and Raven, *Business of Books*, pp. 243–45.
20  *Millar* v. *Taylor* (1769) 4 Burr. 2303, 98 ER 201; citations from the pamphlet printing the four judges' decision, with Sir Joseph Yates dissenting, appear parenthetically in the text.
21  Ben Jonson strove, through every means at his command – composing prefaces, inductions, and epilogues to guide his audience, overseeing a collected edition of his works in a distinguished format, and entrusting his literary effects to a leading courtier and intellectual – to establish himself as a model professional author at a time when there were few laws or cultural formations supporting such a paradigm. For an authoritative study of Jonson and the emergence of "the bibliographic ego," see Joseph Loewenstein, *Ben Jonson and Possessive Authorship* (Cambridge and New York: Cambridge University Press, 2002).
22  Birrell, *Seven Lectures*, p. 10.
23  "Our Weekly Gossip on Literature and Art," *The Athenaeum*, January 28, 1837, p. 65; the article includes the Balzac quotation.
24  As Adrian Johns notes in his opening remarks in *Piracy: The Intellectual Property Wars from Gutenberg to Gates* (Chicago and London: University of Chicago Press, 2009), "piracy was a property not of objects alone, but of objects in space. A given book might well be authentic in one place, piratical in another" (p. 13).

25  "Our Weekly Gossip on Literature and Art," *The Athenaeum*, February 18, 1837, pp. 121–22, 122; "International Law of Copyright," February 25, 1837, p. 141; "Protection of Copyright," April 8, 1837, pp. 249–50. Thomas Hood published three letters to the editor of the *Athenaeum* supporting Talfourd's Bill, headed "Copyright and Copywrong," April 15, 1837, pp. 263–65; April 22, pp. 285–87, and April 29, pp. 304–06.

26  Feather, *Publishing*, pp. 155–57. Upon its introduction into the House of Commons in the summer of 1837, the prospects for Talfourd's Bill looked promising, according to "Our Weekly Gossip on Literature and Art," *The Athenaeum*, June 3, 1837, p. 402. Also, according to the same column in the issue of May 20 (p. 367), the Board of Trade was preparing to enter into negotiations with France for reciprocal copyright arrangements. For further discussion of the six-year struggle to amend copyright, consult C. R. Vanden Bossche, "The Value of Literature: Representations of Print Culture in the Copyright Debate of 1837–1842," *Victorian Studies* 38, 1 (Autumn 1994): 41–68. In this fine and extensively researched article, Vanden Bossche points out that in these early Victorian debates not only the "originality" and "labor" of the author were commended, but also "the author's value to the nation" (p. 57). See further discussion of this article in Chapter 5.

27  Feather, *Publishing*, p. 123.

28  Percy Bysshe Shelley, "A Defence of Poetry," written in 1821, not published until 1840; Thomas Carlyle, "The Hero as Poet," in *Lectures on Heroes, Hero-Worship, and the Heroic in History* (London: J. Fraser and Chapman and Hall, 1841).

29  William K. Wimsatt and Monroe K. Beardsley, "The Intentional Fallacy," in *The Verbal Icon: Studies in the Meaning of Poetry* (Lexington: University of Kentucky Press, 1954), pp. 2–18, 3.

30  On Faulkner's paperbacks, I am grateful to Gordon B. Neavill, both for his paper on "Bibliographic Evidence and Reader Response: The Modern Library Series," presented on July 9, 2003, at the Society for the History of Authorship, Reading and Publishing (SHARP) annual conference at Scripps College, Claremont, CA, and for further elaborations in an email of May 14, 2010.

31  Roland Barthes, "The Death of the Author," published in English in *Aspen* 5–6 (1967) and in French in *Manteia* 5 (1968), repr. in *Image Music Text*, ed. and trans. Stephen Heath (New York: Hill and Wang, 1977), pp. 142–48. Michel Foucault, "What Is an Author?" first delivered as a lecture before the Society at the Collège de France, February 22, 1969, and published in the *Bulletin de la Société française de Philosophie* 63, 3 (1969): 73–104, then repr. in Donald F. Bouchard, ed., *Language, Counter-Memory, Practice*, trans. Bouchard and Sherry Simon (Ithaca: Cornell University Press, 1977), pp. 113–38, and "The Discourse on Language" (1971) quoted as the second epigraph to this book. At the 1998 Vancouver annual conference of SHARP, Juliet Gardiner persuasively demonstrated that publishers have resuscitated the author as a publicity engine: "the author-fiction lives on in

the circulation and reception of the book, and authorial intention is re-biographized not as an interpretive textual practice but as genre branding and promotional supplement and marketing strategy . . . the watchful nurturing of the reader [by publishers] has served to vivify the Author and recuperate him or her as a guarantor of the book's meaning in the marketplace." A revised version of this address was published as "Recuperating the Author: Consuming Fictions in the 1990s," *Papers of the Bibliographical Society of America* 94, 2 (June 2000): 255–74.

32   Barthes, "The Death of the Author," p. 148. For a strong counterstatement, see Seán Burke, *The Death and Return of the Author: Criticism and Subjectivity in Barthes, Foucault, and Derrida* (Edinburgh University Press, 1998). Barthes himself rethought his views on authorship in his Collège de France lectures, 1978–80; see *The Preparation of the Novel*, trans. Kate Briggs (New York: Columbia University Press, 2011). As Mairéad Hanrahan says in her review of this book, "the most astonishing reversal of all in these lectures is the volte-face they represent in relation to Barthes's previous view of the work. Gone is the valuing of the 'writerly' text which obliges its reader to participate in the creative process: the principal qualities of the desired work are now readability, a clear narrative structure, and a lack of metalanguage or self-reflexivity" (*Times Literary Supplement*, January 21, 2011, p. 5).

33   Foucault, "Discourse," p. 153. Roger Chartier discusses Foucault's conceptions of authorship in "Figures of the Author," in *The Order of Books: Readers, Authors, and Libraries in Europe Between the Fourteenth and Eighteenth Centuries*, trans. L. G. Cochrane (Stanford University Press, 1994), pp. 25–59.

34   Classical scientific authors (e.g., Pliny, Aristotle) and some medieval saints (e.g., St. Jerome) had, as Foucault points out, great authority: their name was essentially the guarantee of their works. By the eighteenth century science depended more on the reproducibility of effects than on the author's name, whereas literary works began to be evaluated by the name of the author. In neither case could the authors of texts answer for their unity and coherence. Even Shakespeare was thought to need a lot of editing, improvement, and adjustment of his corpus.

35   For documentation and detailed discussion of nineteenth-century British print history, consult McKitterick. Importantly, as McKitterick explains in his Introduction, this volume in *The Cambridge History of the Book in Britain* studies not just the manufacture and consumption of books made in Britain, but also the use of books in the British Isles. Book, it should be noted, is for this series a portmanteau term including newspapers, magazines, pamphlets, school texts, government publications, and other forms of print material both new and secondhand.

36   For the earlier history of authorship, see Joseph Loewenstein, *The Author's Due: Printing and the Prehistory of Copyright* (University of Chicago Press, 2002), esp. chapter 1, and Finkelstein and McCleery, *An Introduction to Book History*, esp. chapter 4.

37 Foucault, "Discourse," p. 153. "Author" is first listed as a profession in the 1861 census, but authors were grouped with other educated persons in the 1841 census. See W. J. Reader, *Professional Men: The Rise of the Professional Classes in Nineteenth-Century England* (London: Weidenfeld and Nicolson, 1966), p. 147 and Appendix 1, p. 211.

38 Edmund Wilson, *The Wound and the Bow* (Oxford and New York: Oxford University Press, 1941); the Dickens essay was first dedicated "To the Students of English 354, University of Chicago, Summer, 1939." Wilson never makes the connection between the blacking-warehouse trauma Dickens suffered, discussed in the first chapter of his book, the snake-bite that incapacitates and isolates Philoctetes for a decade in Sophocles' play, discussed in the last chapter, and a Freudian interpretation of writing as an unavailing but unceasing attempt to heal the wounds the ego suffers while growing up. But the implications are latent, and more fully developed by critics in subsequent decades. Valentine Cunningham has pointed out that in 1872 Francis Jacox's *Aspects of Authorship* already makes the connection between trauma and art; it contains "a section on how failed lawyers tended to become writers, with the emphasis on some sort of failure in real life as the key to the art," "Unto Him (or Her) that Hath," *Times Literary Supplement*, September 11, 1998, pp. 12–13, 13.

39 More recently the American novelist Jerome Charyn has proposed that the wound is not the source of creativity; rather, imagination enters into the nothingness that is the gaping hole of the psychic wound and populates the space (personal conversation, September 1, 2003).

40 David Vincent, *Literacy and Popular Culture: England 1750–1914* (Cambridge University Press, 1989).

41 In *Charles Dickens' Childhood* (Houndmills: Macmillan, 1988), Michael Allen established that Dickens worked at Warren's Blacking for about thirteen months, not less than half a year as previous biographers had posited (p. 103). In a revised chronology recently published, Allen proposes that Dickens went to work at the age of eleven, before his twelfth birthday and his father's imprisonment for debt, in September 1823, and that his father removed him from the blacking business a year later, in September 1824 (Allen, "New Light on Dickens and the Blacking Factory," *Dickensian* 106, 1 [Spring 2010]: 5–30).

42 John Forster, *The Life of Charles Dickens*, 3 vols. (London: Chapman and Hall, 1872–74). Hereafter all references, unless otherwise noted, are to the one-volume version edited by J. W. T. Ley (New York: Doubleday, Doran and Company, [1928]), pp. 23–37.

43 Catherine Dickens may have known about it earlier. See Michael Slater, *Dickens and Women* (London: Dent, 1983), pp. 156–57.

44 This argument is elaborated in my "Autobiography into Autobiography: The Evolution of *David Copperfield*," in George P. Landow, ed., *Approaches to Victorian Autobiography* (Athens: Ohio University Press, 1979), pp. 269–91.

45 Forster, *Life of Charles Dickens*, p. 35. In *The Childhood and Youth of Charles Dickens* (London: Hutchinson, 1891), Robert Langton expands on Forster's

narrative of the author's early years; the book is particularly useful in supplying many pasted-in prints of houses, inns, and other sights familiar to Dickens as he was growing up.

46 Charles Dickens, *Speeches*, ed. K. J. Fielding (Oxford: Clarendon Press, 1960), pp. 238–45, 240. Hereafter *Speeches* followed by page numbers.

47 See Forster, *Life of Charles Dickens*, pp. 39–46 and notes, and *Letters* I:423–24, 423.

48 [Charles Dickens], "Our School," *Household Words*, October 11, 1851, pp. 49–52, 49.

49 Forster, *Life of Charles Dickens*, p. 835n.

50 Forster, *Life of Charles Dickens*, p. 43.

51 Forster, *Life of Charles Dickens*, pp. 41, 43.

52 Samuel Carter Hall, *Retrospect of a Long Life, From 1815 to 1883*, 2 vols. (London: Bentley and Son, 1883), I:111 and II:155.

53 *Letters* VIII:130–32, 131.

54 *Letters* I:523–25, 524–25; in this instance, Dickens is entrusting to his mother part of the decoration of the cottage at Alphington in Devon into which in the spring of 1839 he planned to move them. Neither parent liked the country; they returned to London in October 1842.

55 William J. Carlton, "Mr. Blackmore Engages an Office Boy," *Dickensian* 48, 4 (September 1952): 162–67. The cherry stone incident derives from Edward Blackmore's recollections, first printed in Frederic G. Kitton, *Charles Dickens by Pen and Pencil* (London: Sabin and Dexter, 13 initial parts and 5 supplementary ones, 1889–90, then in one volume), p. 129.

56 Kitton, *Dickens by Pen and Pencil*, p. 102.

57 William Kidd, *Practice of the Court of King's Bench*, first published in the 1790s, was a standard text; cf. *David Copperfield*, chapter 16. All quotations from this novel are taken from Nina Burgis's edition, The Clarendon Dickens (Oxford: Clarendon Press, 1981), and will appear parenthetically in the text.

58 *Letters* VIII:130–32,131.

59 Peter Ackroyd believes that Dickens "was planning a new career" as Parliamentary reporter even while at Ellis and Blackmore's: Peter Ackroyd, *Dickens* (New York: HarperCollins, 1991), p. 124. The trouble is, Dickens left the law four years before he became a reporter for the *Mirror of Parliament*. I'm inclined to Kathryn Chittick's view that retrospective reconstructions of Dickens's life, heavily influenced by his own post hoc accounts, make what at the time was uncertain, even accidental, into something fated: Kathryn Chittick, *Dickens and the 1830s* (Cambridge and New York: Cambridge University Press, 1990), p. 9.

60 Most of Dickens's biographers assume that Parliamentary reporters were supposed to transcribe debates verbatim, but in fact many MPs were happy to have their impromptu remarks filtered and edited. See Matthew Bevis, "Temporizing Dickens," *Review of English Studies* 52, 206 (2001): 171–91, the *Review of English Studies* Prize Essay. This densely researched

article on Dickens's engagement with Parliamentary rhetoric was expanded and extended through 1870 as the second chapter of Bevis's book, *The Art of Eloquence: Byron, Dickens, Tennyson, Joyce* (Oxford University Press, 2007).

61 Michael Slater, *Charles Dickens* (New Haven and London: Yale University Press, 2009), pp. 34–35, now the definitive biography. Slater provides many instances where Dickens in subsequent years rewrites incidents in his earlier life; I concentrate on the educational and professional ones.

62 Robert Newsom, *Charles Dickens Revisited* (New York: Twayne, 2000), p. 41, from Allen, *Charles Dickens' Childhood*, p. 110.

63 *Letters* VIII:130–32, 131.

64 Forster, *Life of Charles Dickens*, p. 60.

65 John Glavin, *After Dickens: Reading, Adaptation, and Performance* (Cambridge University Press, 1999): "from the start Dickens was in not quite equal parts thrilled (less) and (more) frightened by the stage" (p. 11).

66 Chittick, *Dickens*, pp. 9–10. This is the best book on the subject of "Dickens's transition from reporter to author" (p. x), and I depend heavily on it in contextualizing this account of Dickens's initial construction of authorship. Part of what I'm adding to Chittick's account is how Dickens subsequently represented his induction into the field of letters.

67 *Letters* VIII:130–32, 131.

68 Chittick, *Dickens*, pp. 13, 16; Slater, *Charles Dickens*, p. 5; Robin Gilmour, *The Idea of the Gentleman in the Victorian Novel* (London: Allen and Unwin, 1981).

69 James Grant, *The Newspaper Press: Its Origin – Progress – and Present Position*, 2 vols. (London: Tinsley, 1871), 1:296, 306, 298.

70 Chittick, *Dickens*, p. 13.

71 Charles Dickens, "Preface to the Cheap (1847) [Edition]," in *The Pickwick Papers*, ed. James Kinsley, The Clarendon Dickens (Oxford: Clarendon Press, 1986), Appendix B, pp. 883–88, 884; hereafter, "Preface to the Cheap Edition." All subsequent quotations to *Pickwick* are taken from this edition and cited parenthetically in the text. The "dark court" is Johnson's Court, and the "dark office" is either A. Robertson's or Baylis and Leighton's; both are listed in 1833 issues of the magazine. Richard Phillips published the magazine from 1796 to 1824, and made it the journal of dissenters and radicals. He sold out to Cox and Baylis in 1824, as the competition from Henry Colburn's *New Monthly Magazine* was too much: Geoffrey Carnall, "The Monthly Magazine," *Review of English Studies* n.s. 5, 18 (April 1954): 158–64. By 1833 a new publisher, Charles Tilt, was losing money on every issue and looking for someone to buy him out; that may explain the inconsistencies in editorial policy during the year. In proof for the Cheap Edition, Dickens changed "stealthily one summer's night" to "stealthily one evening at twilight"; the original reading helps identify the time of year, but may have been altered because Dickens recollected that the event occurred in the autumn instead. See facsimile of proof, from Forster Collection, printed

in Walter Dexter, "The Pickwick Dedications and Prefaces," *Dickensian* 32, 237 (Winter 1935–36): 61–64, 63.

72 *Letters* 1:33–34, 34; cf. Chittick, *Dickens*, p. 44.

73 *Letters* 1:32n3. Holland, veteran of the Napoleonic wars who had been tried in Philadelphia in 1817 for training troops to aid Simon Bolivar, bought the journal, whose circulation averaged 600 per month, to advance his "ardent liberalism" (*Letters* 1:130n4).

74 *Letters* 1:121 and n3. They were supposed to be finished by early February 1836. "The Tuggses at Ramsgate" was published in *Library of Fiction* 1 (April 1836); "A Little Talk about Spring, and the Sweeps" (subsequently retitled "The First of May") was presumably intended for the May issue, but it appeared in June.

75 Robert J. Griffin, "Anonymity and Authorship," *New Literary History* 30, 4 (Autumn 1999): 877–95, 887–88. Griffin's article is an excellent place to begin learning about the issues surrounding anonymity; see also the collection of essays he edited, *The Faces of Anonymity: Anonymous and Pseudonymous Publication from the Sixteenth to the Twentieth Century* (New York and London: Palgrave Macmillan, 2003).

76 Communication to Griffin, "Anonymity and Authorship," cited p. 883.

77 Griffin, "Anonymity and Authorship," pp. 884–85, and Genette, *Paratexts*, p. 44.

78 Adrian Room, *Dictionary of Pseudonyms*, 3rd edn. (Jefferson, NC and London: McFarland, 1998), p. 26.

79 Sir Walter Scott, *Letters*, ed. H. J. C. Grierson, 12 vols. (London: 1932–37), III:477–81, 479.

80 *Letters* 1:43.

81 Chittick, *Dickens*, p. 43; cf. *Letters* 1:692–94 and Charles Dickens, *Sketches by Boz*, in Michael Slater, ed., *"Sketches by Boz" and Other Early Papers 1833–39*, vol. 1 of the Dent Uniform Edition of Dickens' Journalism (London: J. M. Dent, 1994). All subsequent quotations from this title are taken from this edition and cited parenthetically by page number in the text.

82 *Letters* 1:226 and n2. This was probably *Is She His Wife? Or, Something Singular*, eventually staged on March 6, 1837 at the St. James's Theatre. Dickens offered it to J. P. Harley "if you think there is anything in it," and Harley both starred in the production and chose it as the opening piece for his benefit on March 13.

83 Forster, *Life of Charles Dickens*, p. 60.

84 Chittick, *Dickens*, p. 48. For a comprehensive bibliography of early reviews of Dickens's works, consult Kathryn Chittick, *The Critical Reception of Charles Dickens 1833–1841* (New York and London: Garland Publishing, 1989).

85 See Patrick Leary and Andrew Nash, "Authorship," in McKitterick, ed., *Cambridge History of the Book*, pp. 172–213.

86 Chittick, *Dickens*, p. 1.

87 Chittick, *Dickens*, p. 18.

88 Chittick, *Dickens*, p. 57. For a thorough discussion of pseudonyms, see "Notes on Anonymity and Pseudonymity," in James Kennedy, W. A. Smith, and A. F. Johnson, *Dictionary of Anonymous and Pseudonymous English Literature* (Samuel Halkett and John Laing), 7 vols. (Edinburgh and London: Oliver and Boyd, 1926), I.xi–xxiii. Adrian Room expands the discussion by paying particular attention to stage and screen names, and he identifies two of the most pseudonymous authors, François-Marie Arouet (Voltaire), who employed at least 173 pseudonyms, often to escape censorship or jail, and Daniel Defoe, who published under at least 198 (pp. 22, 384). Gérard Genette has a brief but suggestive passage about pseudonymity and anonymity in chapter 3, "The Name of the Author," in *Paratexts*, pp. 37–54. See also John Mullan, *Anonymity: A Secret History of English Literature* (London: Faber, 2008), a book that ranges from the sixteenth century to the present.

89 Room, *Dictionary of Pseudonyms*, and Kennedy *et al.*, *Dictionary of Anonymous and Pseudonymous English Literature*, p. xxii.

90 *Letters* I:31.

91 *Letters* v:615, 619, from Forster, *Life of Charles Dickens*, p. 504.

92 *Letters* v:605, 615, 619; cf. Julia F. Saville, "Eccentricity as Englishness in *David Copperfield*," *SEL Studies in English Literature 1500–1900* 42, 4 (Autumn 2002): 781–97.

93 For the "exact pronunciation," see B. W. Matz's notice (pp. 4–5) in the "When Found" section of *Dickensian* 21, 1 (January 1925): [3]–9. Room lists "Boz" but gives the wrong pronunciation ("Boze").

94 Robert L. Patten, *George Cruikshank's Life, Times, and Art*, 2 vols. (New Brunswick, NJ: Rutgers University Press; Cambridge: Lutterworth Press, 1992, 1996), I:12–15.

95 Room, *Dictionary of Pseudonyms*, s.v. "Phiz."

96 Valerie Browne Lester, *PHIZ: The Man Who Drew Dickens* (London: Chatto and Windus, 2004), p. 51, quoting Browne's comment recorded by Kitton: "I think I signed myself as 'Nemo' to my first etchings . . . before adopting 'Phiz' as my *sobriquet*, to harmonise – I suppose – better with Dickens's 'Boz'" (Frederic G. Kitton, *Dickens and His Illustrators* [London: George Redway, 1899], p. 65).

97 R. J. [C. J. Davids], "Impromptu," *Bentley's Miscellany* 1 (March 1837): 297; *Letters* I:264n1. The first use of "Boz" was in the August 1834 *Monthly Magazine*.

98 Dickens, "Preface to the Cheap Edition," p. 886.

99 *Letters* I:423; cf. Allen, *Charles Dickens' Childhood*, p. 112.

100 Garrick's "impromptu epitaph" is quoted in Ian Ousby, ed., *The Cambridge Guide to Literature in English* (Cambridge University Press, rev. edn. 1993), s.v. Goldsmith.

101 John Forster, *The Life and Times of Oliver Goldsmith*, 2 vols., 5th edn. (London: Chapman and Hall, 1871), I:12. The testimony comes from the curate, Dr. Strean, who succeeded Oliver's older brother in his father's parish, Kilkenny West.

102 Ousby, ed., *Cambridge Guide*, s.v. Goldsmith.
103 More than a hundred paintings from Goldsmith's novel, poems, and plays were executed from 1784, the date of George Morland's picture from the Vicar, to the end of the nineteenth century. Moreover, with the exception of James Thomson, Goldsmith was for art lovers the most popular eighteenth-century author. For further information about pictorializations of Goldsmith's life and writings, see Richard D. Altick, *Paintings from Books* (Columbus: Ohio State University Press, 1985).
104 *Letters* v:288–90, 289.
105 Allen, *Charles Dickens' Childhood*, pp. 68–69.
106 *Letters* v:483, from Forster, *Life of Charles Dickens*, p. 523.
107 Oliver Goldsmith, *The Vicar of Wakefield and Other Writings*, ed. Frederick W. Hilles (New York: Modern Library, 1955), p. 351.
108 Forster, *Goldsmith*, 1:16.
109 "Moses viewing the Promised Land, turns out to be Moses going to the Fair": Charles Dickens, "The Tattlesnivel Bleater," *All the Year Round*, December 31, 1859, subsequently gathered into the first series of *The Uncommercial Traveller*; repr. in Michael Slater and John Drew, eds., *"The Uncommercial Traveller" and Other Papers, 1859–1870*, vol. IV of the Dent Uniform Edition of Dickens' Journalism (Columbus: Ohio State University Press, 2000), p. 23.
110 Dickens, "Preface to the Cheap Edition," p. 886.
111 Dickens, "The Prisoners' Van," *Bell's Life*, November 29, 1835; passage excised from volume edition of *Sketches* but printed in Slater, *Charles Dickens*, p. 53.
112 Deborah Epstein Nord, *Walking the Victorian Streets: Women, Representation, and the City* (Ithaca and London: Cornell University Press, 1995), identifies the panoramic and individualistic perspectives. She focuses on the figure of the sexually tainted woman, viewed by and for a predominantly male audience: "[t]he female figure allows [Dickens] simultaneously to isolate and to expose social misery: he quarantines that misery by sex and yet suggests the threat of contamination that women – particularly fallen women – always represent" (p. 51). Others who have thought a lot about Dickens's perambulations include Michael Hollington, who has written extensively about the topic, beginning with "Dickens the Flâneur," *Dickensian* 77, 2 (1981): 71–87, which connects Dickens to European pedestrians – especially Baudelaire and the observations of Walter Benjamin; Audrey Jaffe, *Vanishing Points: Dickens, Narrative, and the Subject of Omniscience* (Berkeley, Los Angeles, and Oxford: University of California Press, 1991); and Rosemarie Bodenheimer, *Knowing Dickens* (Ithaca and London: Cornell University Press, 2007).
113 Philip Lopate, "Bachelorhood and Its Literature," in *Bachelorhood: Tales of the Metropolis* (Boston/Toronto: Little, Brown and Company, 1981), pp. 249–81.
114 *Court Journal*, February 20, 1836, quoted in *Letters* 1:129n3.
115 As Chittick observes, "one wonders if Dickens's characters simply consist of lower-class persons arbitrarily assigned a higher status" (*Dickens*, p. 46).

116  *Letters* 1:431n5.

117  *Letters* 1:555 and n1: Dickens had evidently arranged to sit for a portrait, and had removed for the summer of 1839 to Elm Cottage, Petersham, Surrey.

118  *Letters* 1:38.

119  Slater, *Charles Dickens*, pp. 52–53.


2  CHARACTERIZING BOZ (1834–1837): *SKETCHES BY BOZ*

1  *Speeches*, pp. 342–48, 347.

2  *Letters* 1:2 and n3.

3  Kathleen Tillotson opts for *Oliver Twist* in her "Introduction" to the Clarendon edition of the novel, p. [xv].

4  *Letters* 1:33–34, 34.

5  *Ibid.*

6  By 1834 Dickens seems to have been earning perhaps as much as £5 a week from his "french Employer" for services not determined (*Letters* 1:45). This could be André Fillonneau, who married Henry Austin's sister Amelia in a double ceremony with Austin and Dickens's sister Letitia at St. George's, Bloomsbury, on July 15, 1837 (*Letters* 1:52 and n1).

7  *Speeches*, p. 347.

8  At present the authoritative source is the "Complete Listing of Dickens's Known Journalism, December 1833–August 1869,", Appendix D in Slater and Drew, eds., *"The Uncommercial Traveller"*, pp. 436–46.

9  *Speeches*, p. 347.

10  According to Matthew Bevis, *Art of Eloquence*, Russell's speech influenced Dickens's subsequent prose.

11  *Letters* 1:84.

12  *Letters* 1:48n5. Hablot Knight Browne, "Phiz," and his etching partner, Robert Young, rented a studio at 3 Furnival's Inn, but Dickens may not have known his neighbors until June 1836, when Browne was hired to illustrate *Pickwick*. Valerie Browne Lester (*PHIZ*, pp. 35 and 41) thinks it likely that they did have at least a nodding acquaintance before then.

13  *Letters* 1:48–49. See also 1:46–48 and nn3–4 about re-housing the family.

14  At this time there was no law prohibiting or regulating dramatic adaptations of other writing. By the end of the century, given some changes in the law, theatrical productions of novels often yielded more income to novelists than their books. The Baroness Orczy converted her unpublished novel into a play, then back into the first of a series of novels about the Scarlet Pimpernel. For a time she lost her theatrical rights, but she gained them back in the 1920s and prospered from both stage and screen versions. But she benefited from a late nineteenth-century law granting authors rights in dramatizations, whereas a few years earlier Mrs. Henry Wood got nothing for stagings of her novel *East Lynne* though it played for years in London and in every substantial provincial city.

15　*Letters* 1:42. This letter suggests that Dickens may already be thinking about material that will appear much later in "Meditations in Monmouth Street," not published until September 24, 1836, and *Oliver Twist*, which doesn't get to the theft of handkerchiefs until the May 1837 issue of *Bentley's Miscellany*.

16　*Letters* 1:54–55, 55.

17　*Letters* 1:55n2.

18　*Letters* 1:188.

19　*Letters* 1:xxi.

20　*Letters* 1:66, 64, 70, 69, and 71.

21　Slater, *Charles Dickens*, p. 44. Matthew Bevis detects a liberal bias in Dickens's reporting of the election campaign of 1834–35 for the *Morning Chronicle* (p. 97), but these reports are not signed, and definitely are not identified with "Boz."

22　Advertisement in the January 10 and 17, 1835 issues of the *Morning Chronicle*, quoted in Richard Maxwell, "Dickens, the Two *Chronicles*, and the Publication of *Sketches by Boz*," *Dickens Studies Annual* 9 (1981): 21–32, 24. Maxwell points out that evening papers could not depend on advertising to the extent of their morning rivals. They were therefore vulnerable to outside influences and political patronage. He speculates that the *Evening Chronicle* may have served its proprietors best simply by adding its circulation to that of its *Morning* sibling, so that in the stiff fight with *The Times*, the *Chronicles'* combined circulation could demonstrate "that Whig policies had public support" (p. 25). The circulation of the papers ranged between 1,000 and 5,000 in the 1820s and 1830s; see Richard Altick, *The English Common Reader* (Chicago and London: University of Chicago Press, 1957), p. 392, and the *Waterloo Directory of English Newspapers and Periodicals, 1800–1900*, Series 1, ed. John S. North (Waterloo, Ont.: North Waterloo Academic Press, 1997).

23　*Waterloo Directory*, pp. 440–41; cf. Donald A. Gray, "A List of Comic Periodicals Published in Great Britain, 1800–1900, with a Prefatory Essay," *Victorian Periodicals Newsletter* 15 (March 1972): 2–39, which cites the paper's claim to have sold 600,000 of the first three issues of collected comic cuts (p. 11); Louis James, *Fiction for the Working Man 1830–1850* (London: Oxford University Press, 1963), p. 21, which quotes an 1831 article claiming that 128,000 copies of an issue of the *Gallery of Comicalities* were sold; and an 1829 article declaring that the Sunday issues of *Bell's Life* circulated 22,000 among "the very lowest part of the population."

24　*Letters* 1:160.

25　*Ibid.*

26　The most extensive recent study of Dickens's journalistic politics is John M. L. Drew's *Dickens the Journalist* (Houndmills: Palgrave Macmillan, 2003). In chapter 2 he demonstrates that Dickens's Radical, pro-Whig, and anti-Tory sentiments sometimes colored his newspaper reports. More often they colored his informal social disputations, with, for example, John Black over the new poor laws. Drew also stresses that for Dickens's most outspoken diatribe, *Sunday Under Three Heads*, he adopts a unique pen name, Timothy

Sparks. While my own account of Dickens's sketches, as distinct from reports, downplays the undoubted political content of simply portraying as worthy of attention the lower-middle class, I agree with Drew's summary conclusion that "Dickens was developing the freelancer's knack of not letting political leanings interfere with writing projects and commercial prospects" (p. 34).

27 Quoted in *Letters* 1:161n1.

28 Philip Collins, ed., *Dickens: The Critical Heritage* (New York: Barnes and Noble, 1971), pp. 27–28.

29 A handy and authoritative summary of this period, and one I have relied on in this paragraph, is provided by Michael J. Turner in "Political Leadership and Political Parties, 1800–46," chapter 7 of Chris Williams, ed., *A Companion to Nineteenth-Century Britain*, Blackwell Companions to British History and The Historical Association (Oxford and Malden, MA: Blackwell Publishing, 2004; paperback 2007), pp. 125–39.

30 *Fraser's* 21, 124 (April 1840): 381–400; quoted in Chittick, *Dickens*, p. 146.

31 It may be difficult for many present-day readers to conceive how extended families constituted economic networks in earlier centuries. The Dickenses were no exception, gaining support from John Dickens's mother and several of Elizabeth Dickens's Barrow relatives. Great expectations, however, often exceeded actual support, and that was a cautionary as well as comic narrative often told in books and theaters.

32 Audrey Jaffe observes that "Boz's characters" are "themselves marked, shrunken in spirit and size, as many of their names – 'Tibbs,' 'Tuggs,' 'Minns,' 'Watkins Tottle' – suggest" (*Vanishing Points*, p. 29).

33 Drew, *Dickens the Journalist*, pp. 30–31.

34 Amanpal Garcha (*From Sketch to Novel: The Development of Victorian Fiction* [Cambridge University Press, 2009]) argues that temporal stasis and plotless style mark the sketch and its appeal; Dickens does interrupt his narratives with descriptive passages. But it seems to me that Dickens redefines death, the ultimate plotless stasis, as the origin of plots, even as he develops stylistically long descriptive passages that stop the rush to death, as in the extended passage about the Newgate chapel to which Garcha rightly calls attention (p. 125). Garcha's chapter on *Sketches by Boz* (pp. 118–43) persuasively and sensitively analyzes and contextualizes Dickens's early "aesthetics of hurry and fragmentation" (p. 145) and the *flâneur*'s "amateur vagrancy" that allows both a sense of superiority to his middling-class subjects and freedom from the temporal pressures of industrial society (pp. 137–38).

35 Bevis, *Art of Eloquence*, p. 89.

36 Several critics have commented on the ways that bankruptcy violates domesticity, citing "The Broker's Man" as an example. See Richard D. Altick, *The Presence of the Present: Topics of the Day in the Victorian Novel* (Columbus: Ohio State University Press, 1991), pp. 638–67, Jeff Nunokawa, *The Afterlife of Property: Domestic Security and the Victorian Novel* (Princeton University Press, 1994), and Andrew Miller, *Novels Behind Glass: Commodity Culture and Victorian Narrative* (Cambridge and New York: Cambridge University Press, 1995).

37 Foucault, "What Is an Author?" p. 117.
38 Unsigned review of *Sketches by Boz*, *Metropolitan Magazine* 15 (March 1836): 77. I transcribe from the text provided by W. D. (Walter Dexter) in "The Reception of Dickens's First Book," *Dickensian* 32, 237 (Winter 1935–36): 43–50, 48–49. See also Collins, ed., *Critical Heritage*, p. 30.
39 Unsigned review of *Sketches by Boz*, *Chambers's Edinburgh Journal* 5 (April 9, 1836): 83; in Dexter, "Reception," p. 50; in Collins, ed., *Critical Heritage*, p. 28.
40 Audrey Jaffe reviews structuralist critiques of the impossibility of omniscience in her "Introduction" to *Vanishing Points* (pp. 1–22) and offers a term originating with Dickens, "a certain SHADOW... a kind of semi-omniscient, intangible creature" (p. 15) that is often deployed in portions of Dickens's text where no characterized individual, but a somewhat characterized voice and perspective, are evoked. What the succeeding discussion attempts to do is connect the perspectival structures and effects of Dickens's early writing with his attempts to establish an authorial persona with which his readers can identify. In instancing Gustave Flaubert, Marcel Proust, and Franz Kafka, Foucault is speaking about the power of the "work" to cost the writer identity, sociability, even life itself, an effacement in reality parallel to the work's envelopment of writerly originality or personality within discourse. One might say that Dickens's late "work" as a reader of his fictions as well as writer of them hastened, if it did not cause, his end. But in the early and middle stages of his career, Dickens attempted with increasing success to establish his voice as a human and present one, not some ghostly shadow of language itself.
41 Wayne C. Booth, in *The Rhetoric of Fiction* (University of Chicago Press, 1961), provides a chapter, "Types of Narration" (pp. 149–65), that attempts "a richer tabulation of the forms the author's voice can take" than simple "first-person" and "omniscient" narrators (p. 150). But he concludes that "terminology for ... distance in narrators is almost hopelessly inadequate," although we can sense that some narrators are reliable and act "in accordance with the norms of the work" while others are manifestly unreliable (pp. 158–59). Booth does not in this chapter explore the kinds of editorial authorial voices Dickens deploys, nor his quasi-effaced narrators; Booth is more interested in the moral and ethical character of the narrator in relation to the tale told by the narrative.
42 Drew, *Dickens the Journalist*, p. 29.
43 The two sketches of "Our Parish" were composed and published successively in July 1835 issues of the *Evening Chronicle*: "The Election for Beadle" on July 14 and "The Broker's Man" on July 28.
44 Compare Jaffe's definition of "semi-omniscient narrator[s]": "they hover between presence and absence, providing a locus for reader identification while remaining diffuse enough to evade the fixed characterizations assigned to other figures" (*Vanishing Points*, p. 15).
45 Dennis Walder, "Notes" to his edition of *Sketches by Boz*, Penguin Classics (London: Penguin Books, 1995), p. 589, note 5 to p. 45 of the text.

46 Originally entitled "Our Next-Door Neighbour," the singular became plural in the 1837 serial edition.

47 For a discussion of the differences between Dickens's sense of the city and Cruikshank's, see Patten, *Cruikshank*, ii:40–49.

48 Geoffrey Hemstedt, "Inventing Social Identity: *Sketches by Boz*," in Ruth Robbins and Julian Wolfreys, eds., *Victorian Identities: Social and Cultural Formations in Nineteenth-Century Literature* (London: Macmillan; New York: St. Martin's Press, 1996), pp. 215–29, speaks about the multiplicity of elements bombarding Boz and all urban dwellers, and about ways in which "Social Being is established, proclaimed, performed, and also tested and exposed, in public places" (p. 224). Virgil Grillo's classic study of *Sketches* and their refraction in Dickens's later fiction identifies a disjunction between the "narrative of the stories" that "explores the ludicrous, false, shallow, pretentious involvements of idiosyncratic characters culminating in a negative vision and a disdainful chortle," and the "narrator" who assures "his readers that though there are some things wrong with the world, there are also things right with it" (*Charles Dickens' "Sketches by Boz": End in the Beginning* [Boulder: Colorado Associated University Press, 1974], p. 83). I don't see this binary as running through all the sketch materials; instead, both the narratorial elements and those who tell stories within the sketches speak from a multitude of ideologies.

49 The edition Slater follows as copytext for *Sketches by Boz* is the 1868 Charles Dickens Edition. For his edition Dennis Walder chooses the Chapman and Hall 1839 volume based on the 1837–39 serial reissue. In this case, the earlier text preserves a pun excised by Dickens or some printer functionary thirty years afterwards: Cymon's donkey felt "uncomfortable tuggs" (p. 400). Paul Schlicke kindly forwarded materials from his forthcoming Clarendon edition of *Sketches*, based on first publication, which I have used in making my arguments, but as his text was not yet in print I forbore to impinge on that copyright by direct quotations.

50 For more on Astley's, see Altick's *Presence of the Present*; and for Dickens's associations with it, consult Paul Schlicke's comprehensive *Dickens and Popular Entertainment* (London: Allen and Unwin, 1985).

51 In "Performance and Control: The Carnivalesque City and Its People in Charles Dickens's *Sketches by Boz*," *Dickens Studies Annual* 35 (2005): 1–19, Ian Wilkinson "argues that Dickens uses his sketches to show Londoners at play, when the streets take on a carnivalesque atmosphere and the street characters emerge as strongly delineated types who counter the adversity found in their lives with a resilience that generates comedy and the spirit of the carnival" (p. 1). I don't deny that the spirit of carnival (in an English rather than Eastern European/Russian way) infuses many of the sketches, but I do maintain that, taken as a whole, the three volumes of *Sketches* are deeply invested in disappointment and terminations. In an as-yet unpublished paper, Jeffrey Jackson demonstrates that Dickens's revisions and reorderings of the sketches through the serial reissue tend to emphasize collapse and death.

52 The cycle of life, the ups and downs of fortune, are a commonplace in the literature and illustrated frontispieces of the late Georgian era: see Patten, *Cruikshank*, esp. 1:chapters 14 and 15.

53 *Letters* 1:88nn1–2.

54 *Letters* 1:97.

55 *Letters* 1:98, 112, 114, 115–16.

56 Garrett Stewart, *Death Sentences: Styles of Dying in British Fiction* (Cambridge, MA and London: Harvard University Press, 1984). Stewart does not discuss death in *Sketches by Boz, Oliver Twist,* or *Barnaby Rudge.*

57 *Letters* 1:123–24 and n5; at the time the practice of two vigorous rival publishers, Henry Colburn and Richard Bentley, to advertise their publications extravagantly had come under attack by *Fraser's Magazine* and the *Athenaeum:* see Royal A. Gettmann, *A Victorian Publisher* (Cambridge University Press, 1960). So Dickens may not just have been being modest; he may also have been trying to elevate the status of his book and himself above vulgar hawking.

58 *Letters* 1:98–99, 98.

59 *Letters* 1:97.

60 Both Dickens in an 1845 letter to Macvey Napier about the death sentence and Thackeray in his 1840 article about the Courvoisier execution refer to public executions as "murder." See *Letters* IV:340–41 and nn, and Thackeray, "Going to See a Man Hanged," *Fraser's Magazine* 22 (August 1840): 150–58.

61 *Letters* 1:210 and n1.

62 *Letters* 1:631n2.

63 *Letters* 1:81–84 and 82n1.

64 *Letters* 1:168–70, 168n4 and 169n4. Dickens met Leech the following year when the artist, at Cruikshank's suggestion, submitted a sketch, "Tom Smart and the Chair," hoping to obtain work as *Pickwick*'s illustrator and to convince Chapman and Hall of his abilities.

65 Slater, *Charles Dickens*, p. 90.

66 *Letters* 1:469 and n1. Dickens and Irving sustained a warm friendship; when Irving broke down attempting to propose the toast to Dickens at the Boz Ball in New York (February 14, 1842), Dickens refused to say anything. Forster explains, "He had so great a love for Irving that it was painful to speak of him as at any disadvantage" (*Life of Charles Dickens*, p. 220).

67 Patten, *Cruikshank*, II:40–49.

68 Since Genette doesn't consider serials, his chapters about prefaces (pp. 161–293) do not extensively deal with the most complicated of prefatorial situations, when the "original preface" is written *after* the text has been published and read by critics and customers. In such cases, the paratextual preface may serve, as it often does for Dickens, multiple functions: as a history of the text's origin and creation, correcting misimpressions; as an authorial statement of purpose (a purpose that may itself be formulated well after writing the text); as a defense of the text's unity; as a corrective to misinterpretations and criticisms of the text; and as an instruction to readers on how to read that text correctly.

In all these ways Dickensian prefaces anticipate the kind of authorial control stigmatized in the 1960s.

69 Ainsworth called Cruikshank's illustrations "Bozzes" (Jane R. Cohen, *Charles Dickens and His Original Illustrators* [Columbus: Ohio State University Press, 1980], p. 19), and Christian Isobel Johnstone speaks in 1838 about "new Bozzes" in "Decline of the Drama," *Tait's Edinburgh Magazine* 21 (February 1838): 112–15, 113. Even after Dickens's death the term remained in currency: see R. Shelton Mackenzie's usage in his *Life of Charles Dickens* (Philadelphia: T. B. Peterson and Brothers, 1870).

70 The *Spectator* announced in April 1836 that "'Boz' has commenced a periodical under the title of the *Pickwick Club*" (*Spectator* 9, 407 [April 16, 1836]: 373).

71 Kathryn Chittick offers a succinct summary of the usages of "Boz" in the *Oxford Reader's Companion to Dickens*, ed. Paul Schlicke (Oxford University Press, 1999). See also "Boz *versus* Dickens," *Parker's London Magazine* 1 (February 1845): 122–28, and Angus Easson, "Who is Boz? Dickens and his Sketches," *Dickensian* 81, 1 (Spring 1985): 13–22. Easson is subtle and observant both in distinguishing "Boz" from Dickens and in connecting their ways of seeing and speaking across Dickens's lifework, all the way to *Bleak House* and *Hard Times*. Recognizing that Boz is a voice Dickens can use or dismiss, even in the *Sketches*, Easson observes that "[t]here are ... three powers of Boz, which are also powers of Dickens, developed in the *Sketches*. These are: the perceiving eye; the responsive mind; the creative imagination" (p. 19).

## 3 WRITING BOZ (1836–1837): *THE PICKWICK PAPERS*

1 For essential facts and judgments about Hazlitt's life, I rely on Jonathan Bate's sympathetic entry in the *Oxford Dictionary of National Biography* (2004).

2 At his death, Dickens owned thirteen books by Hazlitt, three of them published in Hazlitt's lifetime, including *Spirit of the Age* (J. H. Stonehouse, ed., *Reprints of the Libraries of Charles Dickens and W. M. Thackeray* [London: Piccadilly Fountain Press, 1935]).

3 *American Quarterly Review* 16 (1834): 507. Bulwer's enormous productivity, his political career, his personality, and his disastrous marriage and divorce have made it difficult for biographers to portray the "whole man." Michael Sadleir gave up after one volume, taking Edward and Rosina only to 1836. Andrew Brown does an admirable job of summarizing the life, writings, and influence in the *ODNB*; it is the source for most of this information on Bulwer. Dickens's Gad's Hill library contained a twenty-volume collected crown octavo edition plus *King Arthur* and *A Strange Story*. Henry Sotheran mistakenly included Bulwer's son Robert's *Lucile*, published under his pseudonym Owen Meredith, under the entry "Lytton (Lord)," which applied to both father and son (Stonehouse).

4 Catherine Seville, "Edward Bulwer Lytton Dreams of Copyright: 'It might make me a rich man,'" in Francis O'Gorman, ed., *Victorian Literature and Finance* (Oxford University Press, 2007), pp. 55–72.

5 S. M. Ellis, *William Harrison Ainsworth and His Friends*, 2 vols. (London and New York: John Lane, 1911), has been the standard source of information about Ainsworth. The Willis anecdote Forster inserts in his *Life of Charles Dickens* as a footnote, characterizing the author as "notorious," and J. W. T. Ley's endnote asserts that Willis "never met Dickens at all … [t]he whole story was an absolute fabrication" (p. 80n84). But the Pilgrim *Letters* show that in fact Willis was in England in 1835, when Dickens was living in Furnival's Inn, and did not only meet him but visited Newgate and Coldbath Fields with him and Macrone (1:88nn1–2), as Willis recounts in *Dashes at Life with a Free Pencil*, Ephemera section (New York, 1845). For a fuller account of Dickens's early connections to Ainsworth, Macrone, George Cruikshank, Bulwer, and others enjoying the high-spirited Kensal Lodge hospitality, see my *Cruikshank*, II:1–22.

6 Only *John Law, the Projector*, a novel written late in Ainsworth's decline, survived in Dickens's library at his death (Stonehouse).

7 *Letters* 1:428 and nn1–2. The Gad's Hill library sported the eighty-eight volume Cadell *Complete Works* (Stonehouse).

8 Reader, *Professional Men*, p. 147.

9 *Letters* 1:120; 113–14, 113 and nn.

10 *Letters* 1:113–14, 113 and n4.

11 *Letters* 1:122–23, 123.

12 *Letters* 1:122.

13 *Letters* 1:124–25, 125.

14 So titled there; in later versions "The Tuggses at Ramsgate."

15 *Letters* 1:126.

16 *Letters* 1:129–30, 129 and n1; *Morning Chronicle*, February 11, 1836.

17 *Letters* 1:128–29, 128.

18 There's some controversy about what role Whitehead played: Ley says unequivocally that Whitehead "had no hesitation in recommending" Dickens (Forster, *Life of Charles Dickens*, p. 81n86); *Letters* 1:207n7 declares that there is "no authority" for this story; and Slater says Whitehead "probably" recommended him (*Charles Dickens*, p. 61). But if Dickens had not yet written anything for the *Library of Fiction* for which Whitehead was editor, Hall's invitation to Dickens to write something *in addition to* the *Library of Fiction* pieces had to be prompted by some other sample of his writing, in all probability the two-volume First Series of *Sketches by Boz* published two days previously, on February 8. Chapman and Hall may have read some of the *Sketches* when they were first published; but the republication could have consolidated Boz's visibility for the publishers. Dickens himself used the volume publication of *Sketches* as evidence of Boz's celebrity in his Prospectus for *Pickwick*.

19 *Letters* 1:648.

20 *Letters* 1:131–32, 131.

21 Publishers' advertisement dated March 26, 1836, pp. xx–xxi, xxi.

22 According to a footnote in chapter 2, Mr. Pickwick's altercation with the cabman and meeting with Alfred Jingle occurred in 1827 (five years after the alleged founding of the Pickwick Club). That is probably Dickens's way of correcting an error, namely, having Jingle recount his double engagement during the July 1830 revolution in Paris: firing a musket, then rushing into a wine shop to compose lines of heroic poetry, and so back and forth between firing a field-piece and twanging the lyre. This proleptic account exemplifies, according to the note, a "remarkable instance of the prophetic force of Mr. Jingle's imagination" (p. 17n1).

23 For Mrs. Seymour's protracted battle with Dickens for money and her husband's credit, see Mrs. [Robert] Seymour, *An Account of the Origin of the "Pickwick Papers"* (London: printed for private circulation, 1854; repr. for author, London, 1901). In the 1867 preface to *Pickwick*, Dickens added two paragraphs rejecting all the Seymour family claims (p. 886n2).

24 An amusing sidebar: the *Carlton Chronicle*, reviewing Dickens's "dramatic bantling" *The Village Coquettes*, objected to the lines "A winter's day, we're blithe and gay / Snipe-shooting in the snow" (ii.ii). The reviewer corrected the mistake: "for snipe read cock." But Dickens, writing to the editor, defended – not his knowledge of shooting, but his research. "When I am not *practically* certain of the subject I am writing about, I generally take care, and look about me ... [I consulted] a great many undoubted sources. Depend upon it, that in this part of the United Kingdom, *Snipes are only to be found when Ice and Snow are on the ground*" (*Letters* 1:211–12 and 212n1). If Dickens had been yoked with Seymour through twenty months of sporting mishaps, his research would have had to be very extensive indeed.

25 Steven Jarvis, who is going into the circumstances of *Pickwick*'s creation far more carefully than I have done, notes that the far bank of the Thames depicted in the wrapper was territory well known to Edward Gibbon, whose grandfather lived next door to the church beside Putney Bridge seen in the background. A volume of Gibbon's memoirs was published in 1827, and so could have been known to Seymour and Dickens (DICKNS-L, August 22, 2010).

26 Edward Chapman, letter to Forster dated 1849, Forster, *Life of Charles Dickens*, pp. 75–76 and nn, *Letters* v:575n6.

27 Many critics have thought little of the first chapter. Garrett Stewart subjects it to searching rhetorical analysis in the first section of *Dickens and the Trials of Imagination* (Cambridge and London: Harvard University Press, 1974). Bevis (*Art of Eloquence*) makes much of the connections between the Parliamentary oratory Dickens heard and transcribed and the parodic, comedic, and sympathetic representations of that prose in *Pickwick*. Brougham resurfaces, in a sense, as Pott in Browne's portrait of that combative newspaperman attending Mrs. Leo Hunter's reception: see my "Portraits of Pott: Lord Brougham and *The Pickwick Papers*," *Dickensian* 66 (September 1970): 205–24.

28 Kathleen Tillotson identified the connection between Jingle's anecdote and Jesse's *Gleanings*, and the implications of that connection, in "Pickwick and Edward Jesse," *Times Literary Supplement*, April 1, 1960, p. 214.

29 See Joseph Grego, ed., *Pictorial Pickwickiana: Charles Dickens and His Illustrators*, 2 vols. (London: Chapman and Hall, 1899), 1:67, facsimile from the original drawing in the possession of Augustin Daly. According to Seymour's son, Dickens then returned the altered sketch with a letter to Seymour (*Letters* 1:136, headnote to Robert Seymour [?February 1836]).

30 *Letters* 1:133.

31 *Letters* 1:135, 137.

32 *Letters* 1:145–46.

33 *Letters* 1:140–41, 140.

34 *Letters* 1:143.

35 The Pilgrim editors think that Seymour tried to meet Dickens's requirements with respect to Jemmy, but that he failed to render the wife younger and in fact made the dying man "horrifying" and more "emaciated" than before. The facsimiles that Grego reproduces don't, to my eyes, show much difference between versions of the clown's family, although Jemmy's body turns much more in toward his friend and his head is better groomed, better looking, and more sympathetic. But I could not conclude from Grego's evidence that while "Seymour may at first have followed CD's directions … on coming to the clown [he] let his exasperation take control" (*Letters* 1:146n2). This is one of the many ways the notion that Dickens was in control, was issuing "directions" to his artist, and thus demeaning and overriding him, in my judgment overreads the extent to which anyone at this stage of *Pickwick* was sitting firmly in the saddle.

36 Stephen Jarvis, postings to DICKNS-L, January 10, 2007.

37 *Letters* 1:146n3.

38 G. K. Chesterton, *Charles Dickens: A Critical Study* (New York: Dodd, Mead, 1906), p. 79; W. H. Auden, "Dingley Dell and the Fleet," in *The Dyer's Hand and Other Essays* (New York: Random House, 1962), pp. 407–28, 408; Steven Marcus, *Dickens: From Pickwick to Dombey* (London: Chatto and Windus, 1965), p. 15; J. Hillis Miller, *Charles Dickens: The World of His Novels* (Cambridge, MA: Harvard University Press, 1958, second printing 1959), p. 5.

39 Robert L. Patten, "Introduction" to the 1972 Penguin English Library edition of the novel.

40 Kitton, *Dickens and His Illustrators*, pp. 47–57, and Cohen, *Charles Dickens and His Original Illustrators*, pp. 51–58.

41 Dickens's rate of pay stumps many critics, and I'm not sure I've got it right either. If, according to the April 12 agreement Chapman and Hall tendered, he was paid at the rate of "nine guineas per sheet of 16 pages" for one and one-half sheets per month, that would work out to £14.03.06 (*Letters* 1:648). True, two sheets at 9 guineas each would yield 18 guineas or £18.18.0; but he wasn't getting that. So there's a bit of finagling in Dickens's saying to his publishers that "[m]aking it twenty at once, would be an addition of Two Pounds per number." It would be that as the rate of pay assessed per sheet, but not as the stipend Dickens had been receiving. That addition was actually just under £7 per month: from £14.03.06 to £21.

42 *Letters* 1:133–34, 133.
43 For more about this pamphlet, see Drew, *Dickens the Journalist*, pp. 32–34.
44 *Letters* 1:150.
45 *Letters* 1:172.
46 *Letters* 1:183 and n1.
47 *Letters* 1:648–49.
48 *Letters* 1:649–50, 649.
49 For a classic treatment of this subject, consult Judith Wechsler, *A Human Comedy: Physiognomy and Caricature in 19th Century Paris* (University of Chicago Press, 1982), especially chapter 1.
50 Slater, in *Charles Dickens*, says that Sam "can be seen as, among other things, a racier, fully characterised, successor to Boz in Dickens's oeuvre" (p. 76).
51 See the brilliant analysis of "Sam Weller's Valentine" by J. Hillis Miller in John O. Jordan and Patten, eds., *Literature in the Marketplace: Nineteenth-Century British Publishing and Reading Practices* (Cambridge University Press, 1995), pp. 93–122.
52 *Letters* 1:274.
53 John Forster, unsigned review of *Pickwick Papers*, *Examiner* 15 (July 2, 1837): 421–22; repr. Collins, ed., *Critical Heritage*, pp. 36–37.
54 Asa Briggs, *The Age of Improvement* (London and New York: Longmans, Green and Co., 1959), p. 454.
55 Chesterton, *Charles Dickens: A Critical Study*, p. 65.
56 Auden, "Dingley Dell and the Fleet."
57 Altick, *Presence of the Present*, pp. 505–07.
58 Chesterton, *Charles Dickens: A Critical Study*, p. 110.
59 Louis James, "Plagiarisms of Dickens," in the *Oxford Reader's Companion to Dickens*, pp. 443–54, 452.
60 Northrop Frye, "Comic Fictional Modes," in Robert D. Denham, ed., *Anatomy of Criticism: Four Essays*, The Collected Edition of the Works of Northrop Frye, ed. Alvin A. Lee *et al.*, vol. XXII (Toronto, Buffalo and London: University of Toronto Press, 2006), pp. 40–49; in the same volume, see also Frye, "The Mythos of Spring: Comedy," pp. 151–73.
61 Frye, "Comic Fictional Modes," p. 41; Frye is speaking about New Comedy.
62 William Shakespeare, *The Norton Shakespeare*, ed. Stephen Greenblatt *et al.* (New York and London: W. W. Norton, 1997), p. 816.
63 Telephone conversation, June 17, 2007.
64 Frye, "The Mythos of Spring," p. 154.
65 Jonathan H. Grossman, *The Art of Alibi: English Law Courts and the Novel* (Baltimore and London: Johns Hopkins University Press, 2002), pp. 86, 89.
66 Steven Marcus, "Language into Structure: Pickwick Revisited," *Daedalus* 101, 1 (Winter 1972): 183–202, 187. In the original parts issue and first volume issue, however, the year is 1817. It isn't clear whether this is a printer's error or whether Dickens deliberately altered the date in the Cheap and subsequent editions to correspond with his entry into professional life. This might be another instance of Dickens rewriting his life in later decades, though the

evidence for rewriting and connecting to his life is ambiguous and admits of less tendentious explanations.

67 For more on the novel's complicated exemplifications of "principle," see Alexander Welsh, "Waverley, Pickwick, and Don Quixote," *Nineteenth-Century Fiction* 22, 1 (June 1967): 19–30, 28–29.

68 "Lest there should be any well-intentioned persons who do not perceive the difference (as some such could not, when OLD MORTALITY was newly published) between religion and the cant of religion, piety and the pretence of piety, a humble reverence for the great truths of scripture and an audacious and offensive obtrusion of its letter and not its spirit in the commonest dissensions and meanest affairs of life, to the extraordinary confusion of ignorant minds, let them understand that it is always the latter, and never the former, which is satirized here" (1847 Preface to the Cheap Edition, pp. 886–87).

69 Frank Kermode, *The Sense of an Ending: Studies in the Theory of Fiction*; with a new epilogue (1966; Oxford and New York: Oxford University Press, 2000).

70 John Bowen, *Other Dickens: Pickwick to Chuzzlewit* (Oxford University Press, 2000), p. 64.

71 W. M. Thackeray, "A Grumble about the Christmas Books," *Fraser's Magazine* 35 (January 1847): 119.

72 Sir Frank Kermode, "Fiction and E. M. Forster," *London Review of Books*, 29, 9 (May 10, 2007): 15–24, 21.

73 Stewart, *Death Sentences*, pp. 353–54, brilliantly analyzes how this phrase not only concludes the fictional lives but also transforms putative biography's "scriptive sequence to the roundedness of spatial form," that is, "fictional closure seen under the aspect of human mortality." Dickens has here made death not only the end of lives but also the end of stories, and in more subtle, affecting, and lasting ways ("immobilizing but also immortalizing" the characters), than in his previous attempts at merging mortality with narrative terminus.

74 Hilary M. Schor, *Scheherezade in the Marketplace: Elizabeth Gaskell and the Victorian Novel* (New York and Oxford: Oxford University Press, 1992), p. 97.

75 Stewart, *Death Sentences*, p. 102.

76 Mark Cronin, "Thackeray's First Fashioned Response to Dickens: *The Yellowplush Papers* Cast a Cynical Eye on the 'Admiral Boz's' *Pickwick Papers*," *Dickens Quarterly* 10, 4 (December 1993): 191–202, 193, 201.

77 John Bowen, "Collins's Shorter Fiction," in Jenny Bourne Taylor, ed., *The Cambridge Companion to Wilkie Collins* (Cambridge University Press, 2006), pp. 37–49, 43.

78 *Letters* v:527.

## 4 HIRING BOZ (1837–1839): *BENTLEY'S MISCELLANY* AND *OLIVER TWIST*

1 *Letters* i:649–50.

2 See *Letters* i:682–83 for Dickens's draft of the Prospectus, and the *Wellesley Index* 4:6, for the identification of Maginn's contribution; the combined text

appears as the "Prologue" to volume one of *Bentley's Miscellany*. Critics disagree about who – Maginn or Dickens – wrote which part of this Prologue, but the Table of Contents to volume one says "Prologue, by Dr. Maginn," and Dickens's draft Prospectus makes no reference to politics.

3   *Letters* 1:202.

4   Henry Vizetelly, *Glances Back Through Seventy Years: Autobiographical and Other Reminiscences*, 2 vols. (London: Kegan Paul, Trench, Trubner, 1893), 1:202–3. See also *Letters* 1:202n2.

5   Patten, *Cruikshank* II:51, 60.

6   *Letters* 1:185.

7   *Letters* 1:200.

8   *Letters* 1:202.

9   *Letters* 1:198.

10  Ronald Paulson, *Hogarth: His Life, Art, and Times*, 2 vols. (New Haven: Yale University Press, 1971).

11  Two other installments of Mudfog papers were inserted, one in October 1837 when Dickens downed pen to thwart Bentley, and the other in September 1838 when Dickens was frantically trying to finish *Oliver Twist* for three-volume publication in November.

12  *Letters* 1:210.

13  Cf. *Letters* 1:210nn1, 2, 5, and 8.

14  *Letters* 1:206–8, 207.

15  *Letters* 1:647 notes that the Widener Collection at Harvard owns Dickens's receipt for £100 received from Macrone on January 5, 1837 for selling the copyright of *Sketches* to him, and *Letters* 1:653 prints the June 17, 1837 Agreement between Chapman and Hall and Macrone for the purchase of copyright in *Sketches*, now worth £2,250.

16  *Letters* 1:221, 227.

17  See *Letters* 1: Appendix C, and II: Appendix B.

18  For authorial incomes during the Victorian period, consult John Sutherland, *Victorian Novelists and Publishers* (London: Athlone Press, 1976), and Leary and Nash, "Authorship," esp. pp. 176–78.

19  Sotheby's Sale L09209, July 15, 1999, "The Dickens Archive," lots 160–188. With three exceptions, the archive did not sell on that date, but later negotiations brought the rest of the material to the British Library. See my account of the auction, "The Dickens Archive and the Sotheby's Sale," *Dickensian* 95, 3 (Winter 1999): 257–58.

20  See especially lot 163.

21  Peter Ackroyd is only one of the recent biographers who relates these events as a contest between Bentley and a Dickens whose "supreme position in English letters meant that he was literally able to force publishers to do his bidding" (p. 235). Not really, not always, even at the height of his fame. (Ackroyd, *Dickens* [London: Sinclair-Stevenson, 1990; repr. paperback New York: HarperCollins, 1992], p. 235.)

22  Sotheby's Sale, p. 90.

23   *Letters* I:224.

24   *Letters* I:225–26.

25   *Letters* I:224.

26   *Letters* I:379.

27   For a discussion of the relationship of format to prestige, see Pierre Bour-
     dieu, *The Field of Cultural Production: Essays on Art and Literature*, ed.
     Randal Johnson (New York: Columbia University Press, 1993).

28   *Letters* I:308–9, 308.

29   *Letters* I:367 and nn. Note 4 on p. 367 incorrectly states that by February 1838
     Dickens had received "approximately £1300"; *Letters* I:128–29n3 states,
     correctly, that by the close of *Pickwick* Chapman and Hall had paid Dickens
     £2,000.

30   *Letters* I:375.

31   William Jerdan, *Autobiography*, 4 vols. (London: Arthur Hall, Virtue and
     Co., 1853), IV:365.

32   *Letters* I:147, 148n2, 244 and nn2, 5.

33   *Letters* I:288 and n3.

34   *Letters* I:570.

35   See *Letters* II over 1840 and 1841 Agreements with Chapman and Hall, and
     my entry for Edward Chapman in the *ODNB*.

36   *Letters* I:188–89.

37   *Letters* I:189–90.

38   Information about Macrone supplementing that contained in the notes to
     the *Letters* derives from my entry on him in the *ODNB*.

39   *Letters* I:157.

40   *Letters* I:269–70.

41   *Letters* I:238.

42   *Bentley's Miscellany* 4 (April 1837), p. 402.

43   *Bentley's Miscellany* 3 (March 1837), p. 297.

44   *Letters* I:246.

45   That Dickens rushed *The Strange Gentleman* into print may speak to his
     conceiving himself more as author than playwright, since, as an article in the
     *Athenaeum* put it a few years earlier while discussing an "Act to Amend the
     Laws Relating to Dramatic Literary Property," prior to that 1833 Act a
     playwright could license a representation of the play but retain the copyright.
     But of what use was it? "If he printed his play, it was forthwith acted at any
     other theatre in town or country . . . without his being offered, or being able
     to enforce, any pecuniary acknowledgment whatever." And if he did not
     publish it, "a garbled manuscript copy, taken down from the mouths of the
     actors," would be substituted and published, with the profits, if any, shared
     between publisher and provider of text, with nothing for the author. This
     had been the situation since Elizabethan times. The 1833 Act was supposed to
     remedy the case by securing in law authorial control over productions, but
     many doubted that it would be significant or effective (*Athenaeum*, June 22,
     1833, pp. 404–5). Although the play was staged at least three times in the

USA by 1839, it seems not to have been revived in Britain until 1873, when after a few performances at London's Charing Cross Theatre it was withdrawn at the request of Dickens's family (H. Philip Bolton, *Dickens Dramatized* [London: Mansell; Boston: G. K. Hall, 1987], pp. 73–74).

46 This definition, courtesy of Wikipedia, is conveniently apt for my purposes.

47 Chittick, in *Oxford Reader's Companion*, s.v. "Boz"; *Letters* 1:566.

48 Moreover, Dickens was himself indirectly accused of plagiarism for one of these *Sketches*. William Kidd, in his advertisement in *Operative*, November 4, 1838, claims that his publication, *Characteristic Sketches of Young Gentlemen*, by Quiz, Junior, is the original, and that it has been "fraudulently imitated" by Chapman and Hall. Paul Schlicke provided this information, which will appear in his Oxford edition of all three volumes of *Sketches*.

49 *Letters* 1:653. Chapman and Hall paid £300 in cash "on the transfer of Copyright, on June 22nd," and the balance in bills from three to eleven months thereafter. As Macrone died on September 9, presumably the remaining bills were paid to his widow and children, who were very hard up.

50 The Agreement is printed in *Letters* 1:664–65, from a manuscript then owned by Mr. H. C. Dickens. It contains in Dickens's hand one change, and isn't signed by him, so presumably a corrected copy was executed thereafter.

51 *Letters* IX:44–45.

52 John C. Eckel, *The First Editions of the Writings of Charles Dickens and Their Values: A Bibliography* (London: Chapman and Hall, 1913), pp. 158–59.

53 The Lea and Blanchard edition, which identifies Dickens as "Author" of *Pickwick* and *Nickleby*, does not reprint *Charcoal Sketches* because, according to John B. Podeschi, "American copyright ... belonged to another publisher," unspecified. Podeschi, *Dickens and Dickensiana* (New Haven: Yale University Library, 1980), p. 173.

54 *Letters* III:273–74.

55 The tenth book is something of a phantom. Dickens, "long before I was Boz," wrote a one-act comic burletta, *Is She His Wife? Or, Something Singular*. Since the play was submitted to the Lord Chamberlain's office on February 27, 1837 and licensed for production two days later, it seems that whenever Dickens first sketched the piece, he polished it up as a vehicle for John Pritt Harley in February 1837, more than three years after Dickens had become "Boz." The play apparently bore no authorial name initially, but for Harley's benefit performance at the St. James Theatre on March 13 "Boz" is credited with writing lyrics for a solo song performed by Harley as Pickwick, following *The Strange Gentleman* and *Is She His Wife?* Then the script was published, with or without authorial attribution. The only known copy was sold years later by T. H. Lacy, a theatrical bookseller, to an English collector. He, in turn, sold it to the Boston publisher of Dickens, James Ripley Osgood (successor to Ticknor and Fields), who produced an 1877 reprint of the original. Osgood recollected that it was a demy octavo of about thirty pages – the right size for the text of a one act. However, a fire in the publisher's warehouse in December of 1879 destroyed that "something singular," the

original book. There was apparently an earlier English reprint, possibly by Chapman and Hall, and printed either by Bradbury and Evans or Dickens's son Charley, for a short while in the papermaking business with his father-in-law and brother-in-law, both named Frederick Evans, in the 1860s, or more likely after Dickens's death, and thus between 1870 and 1873. Only three copies of this version were known to John C. Eckel in 1913, and the third might be a ghost. Three copies of the Osgood reprint had been auctioned by then. Eckel, *First Editions*, pp. 178–81; *Letters* 1:167n, 226 and n (incorrect in asserting that the first publication was the 1877 Osgood reprint), 233 and n, and 698–700.

56  See Percy Fitzgerald, *The History of Pickwick* (London: Chapman and Hall, 1891), Grego, *Pictorial Pickwickiana*, and Ley's n107, p. 101, to his edition of Forster's *Life of Charles Dickens*. *Letters* 1:350–51n1 gives the publication date of *The Post-Humourous Notes of the Pickwickian Club*, which it identifies as "The Penny Pickwick," as 1842, but the British Library integrated catalogue gives 1837–39. See also James Kinsley's "Introduction" to his edition of *Pickwick Papers*, p. lxxin1.

57  Bolton, *Dickens Dramatized*, pp. 77, 79.

58  Grego, *Pictorial Pickwickiana*, II:12–15, Bolton, *Dickens Dramatized*, pp. 78–79. After twenty performances, "the serious scenes were cut out, and the piece was played as a farce in the shape in which it now appears in print," Rede reported in the Advertisement to the published version (Grego, *Pictorial Pickwickiana*, II:15).

59  Grego, *Pictorial Pickwickiana*, II:12.

60  See Grego, *Pictorial Pickwickiana*, II:16–23 and Bolton, *Dickens Dramatized*, p. 78.

61  Forster, *Life of Charles Dickens*, p. 95, with Ley identifying the dramatist as Moncrieff. Quoted in part in Fitzgerald, *The History of Pickwick*, p. 219, and Grego, *Pictorial Pickwickiana*, II:9. The notes to this quotation in *Letters* 1:304 also identify Moncrieff, sometimes manager of the New City Theatre. Bolton, however, locates Moncrieff's *Pickwick* at the Theatre Royal, Strand, opening around June 12, 1837 (p. 78), and not the New City Theatre, Cripplegate, which Moncrieff managed for some time between 1833 and its demolition in 1836. In view of Dickens's later lashings out at Moncrieff, I'm skeptical that he would have been so lenient to him in this case; it may be another dramatic hack who "was always drunk."

62  Royal Commission on the Laws and Regulations relating to Home, Colonial and Foreign Copyrights; Report, Minutes of Evidence, Appendix C 2036 (1878), quoted in Catherine Seville, "Copyright," in McKitterick, ed., *Book in Britain*, pp. 214–37, 214.

63  Simon Nowell-Smith, *International Copyright Law and the Publisher in the Reign of Queen Victoria* (Oxford: Clarendon Press, 1968).

64  *Letters* 1:652 and nn – Carey's letter; and 322 and nn, Dickens's October 26, 1837 reply.

65  *Oliver Twist*, p. 85; chapter 14 in the September 1837 *Bentley's Miscellany*.

66  *Letters* 1:322n2; 652n3.

67  See Earl L. Bradsher, *Matthew Carey Editor, Author and Publisher*, Columbia University Studies in English (New York: Columbia University Press, 1912), p. 94, David Kaser, *Messrs. Carey and Lea of Philadelphia* (Philadelphia: University of Pennsylvania Press, 1957), esp. p. 111, and Richard Hauck, "The Dickens Controversy in the 'Spirit of the Times,'" *PMLA* 85, 2 (March 1970): 278–83.

68  See Tillotson's edition of *Oliver Twist*, Appendix A.

69  Simon Nowell-Smith, "Firma Tauchnitz 1837–1900," *Book Collector* 15 (1966): 423–36.

70  *Letters* 1:xii.

71  See www.measuringworth.com/indicator.html and "The National Archives," http://nationalarchives.gov.uk/currency/results.asp#mid, both accessed December 7, 2009. The two calculators differ widely, with the National Archives reporting that £1 in 1840 would be worth £44 in 2009, while "Measuring Worth" uses the retail price index to give an 1830 pound a value of nearly £76. The latter figure seems to me a better measure of what Dickens could buy with his money in 1837 – furniture and domestic implements for a five-story London townhouse, servants, ample food and liquor and clothing, support for parents and siblings and sisters-in-law, entertainment, holidays, club memberships, and a plethora of other expenses often prompted by his gregarious and sometimes generous nature. (He could on occasions be quite tight-fisted, too.)

72  *Letters* 1:223–24.

73  Burton Wheeler, "The Text and Plan of *Oliver Twist*," *Dickens Studies Annual* 12 (1983): 41–61, 55. In Chapter 5 I discuss in more detail the issue of genre in Dickens's early works, and whether any of those titles were considered "novels" at the time of their issue.

74  For a different discussion of the "old story" in *Oliver Twist* from the one provided here later, see Robert Tracy, "'The Old Story' and Inside Stories: Modish Fiction and Fictional Modes in *Oliver Twist*," *Dickens Studies Annual* 17 (1988): 1–34. David Paroissien notes that the "Bastardy clauses" in the 1834 Act placed responsibility for supporting illegitimate children on the mother and the parish, and were thought to have contributed to a reduction in the number of children charged on the parish (Paroissien, *The Companion to "Oliver Twist"* [Edinburgh University Press, 1992], p. 39).

75  Paroissien, in "Appendix One" (*Companion to "Oliver Twist*," pp. 294–303) supplies a wealth of detail about the government dietaries of 1836.

76  *Letters* 1:231. For a discussion of the old and new laws and the hybrid nature of their administration in the mid-1830s, see Paroissien, *Companion to "Oliver Twist*," pp. 34–36.

77  [Abraham Hayward], review of *Pickwick Papers*, *Quarterly Review* 59 (October 1837): 484–518, quoted in Collins, ed., *Critical Heritage*, pp. 56–62, 57, and Kinsley, "Introduction" to his edition of *Pickwick Papers*, p. lii.

78 A. G. L'Estrange, ed., *Life of Mary Russell Mitford*, 3 vols. (London: Richard Bentley, 1870), III:78.

79 [G. H. Lewes?], review of Dickens's publications, *National Magazine and Monthly Critic* I (December 1837): 445–49; repr. Collins, ed., *Critical Heritage*, pp. 63–68, 64.

80 R. H. D. Barham, *The Life and Letters of the Rev. Richard Harris Barham*, 2 vols. (London: Richard Bentley, 1870), II:20–24.

81 See Rosemary Scott's entry in *ODNB*, or consult William Guerrant Lane, *Richard Harris Barham* (Columbia: University of Missouri Press, 1967).

82 Kathryn Chittick, noting that both Tories and Radicals objected to the New Poor Law, thinks that the politics of *Oliver Twist* suited both publisher and author (*Dickens*, p. 74). I think Barham's concern would have changed Bentley's mind.

83 One indication of how Dickens redirected the blacking warehouse trauma is his giving the name of the fellow worker who comforted him during one of his "spells" to Fagin: John Bayley observes: "No wonder Fagin the criminal is such an ambiguous figure when the real Fagin's kindness had, so to speak, threatened to inure Dickens to the hopeless routine of the wage-slave" ("Oliver Twist: 'Things as They Really Are,'" in John Gross and Gabriel Pearson, eds., *Dickens and the Twentieth Century* [University of Toronto Press, 1962], pp. 49–64, 53). Another factor in Dickens's displacement is that Bob Fagin, who like Dickens "had attained to great dexterity in tying up the pots" of blacking (Forster, *Life of Charles Dickens*, p. 34), saw him weak and helpless. From time to time throughout his life, Dickens suffered from various incapacitating ailments that he never wanted to acknowledge or to retard his creative or social momentum.

84 Forster, *Life of Charles Dickens*, p. 28.

85 Many years later Walter Besant "rewrote" *Oliver Twist*, providing twin brothers to personify Oliver's double identity: *The Bell of St. Paul's* (London: Chatto and Windus, 1890). Of course, the parallels to Dickens are more suggestive than exact.

86 Dickens's use of doubles is compared to Mark Twain's deployment of twins in Susan Gillman and my "Dickens:Doubles::Twain:Twins," *Nineteenth-Century Fiction* 39, 4 (March 1985): 441–58.

87 George Cruikshank to the Editor, *The Times*, December 30, 1871.

88 Patricia Ingham, "The Name of the Hero in Oliver Twist," *Review of English Studies* 33, 130 (May 1982): 188–89.

89 Joanna O'Leary has pointed out that this prediction could come to pass in two ways: Oliver might be executed for theft, or his portrait might be hung up as a mark of his worth.

90 William Blake, "The Chimney Sweeper," *Songs of Innocence*. Dickens makes brilliant use of coffins – as cheap and profitable containers for starving paupers, as Oliver's bed, as a metaphor for self-centeredness (Brownlow says that though disappointed in love he has not "made a coffin" of his heart), and as a ghostly premonition of death, Nancy tells Brownlow when they

meet at the foot of London Bridge that she is so fearful that when she was reading earlier in the evening she saw "'coffin' written in every page of the book in large black letters, – aye, and they carried one close to me, in the street to-night." "'There is nothing unusual in that,' said the gentleman. 'They have passed me often.' 'Real ones,' rejoined the girl. 'This was not'" (p. 312).

91 On Fagin's last night alive, Brownlow accompanies Oliver to the condemned cell and begs Fagin to give up papers that "for better security" Monks entrusted to him. Fagin reveals that they are "in a canvas bag, in a hole a little way up the chimney in the top front-room" (pp. 364–65). Wheeler believes that these papers are Monks's father's will (p. 57), but that was supposedly destroyed, and in any case Brownlow recites the will's provisions weeks before these papers are recovered, so he must have known about the will either from Leeford himself or from some unmentioned draft or copy. In the succeeding chapter Brownlow decides not to put the will's provisions into effect, but instead, with Oliver's joyful accedence, the remaining property is equally distributed between Leeford's two sons.

92 I develop the notion of Fagin's relationship to capitalism more fully in "Capitalism and Compassion in *Oliver Twist*," *Studies in the Novel* 1 (June 1969): 207–21.

93 *Letters* 1:423–24, 423.

94 Richard Stein, *Victoria's Year: English Literature and Culture, 1837–1838* (New York and Oxford: Oxford University Press, 1987); see especially chapter 4, "The Stolen Child," pp. 135–76. Twenty years earlier Robert A. Colby noted and discussed the "proliferation of orphan tales" in the 1830s: *Fiction with a Purpose: Major and Minor Nineteenth-Century Novels* (Bloomington and London: Indiana University Press, 1967), pp. 119–37, 122.

95 Stein, *Victoria's Year*, p. 176.

96 Peter T. Murphy, *Poetry as an Occupation and an Art in Britain, 1760–1830*, Cambridge Studies in Romanticism (Cambridge University Press, 1993), p. 134.

97 Joan Pong Linton, *The Romance of the New World: Gender and the Literary Formations of English Colonialism* (Cambridge University Press, 1998), p. 31. In *Mimesis and Empire: The New World, Islam, and European Identities* (Cambridge University Press, 2001), Barbara Fuchs observes that pirates were a strategic resource for Elizabethan England, and accorded them "different values at different points" (pp. 118–19). What "'piracy' meant in a variety of generic forms including public drama, broadsheets and ballads, prose romance, travel writing, and poetry" during the late Tudor and early Stuart reigns, is the subject of Claire Jowitt's *The Culture of Piracy, 1580–1630: English Literature and Seaborne Crime* (Farnham, Surrey, and Burlington, VT: Ashgate, 2010). Jowitt's "Coda" looks at a 1554 portrait of a "Gentleman pirate," and concludes that it encapsulates "a range of ideas that would become increasingly important to Britain's national and global understandings in the following centuries" (p. 201).

98 See Johns, *Piracy*, esp. chapter 11, pp. 291–326.

99 Six of the first twenty titles in Bentley's Standard Novels, first series (1831–55) were by Cooper, all published in 1831–32; twelve more were issued by the end of 1845. Michael Sadleir, *Bentley's Standard Novel Series* (Edinburgh: for the *Colophon*, April 1932), fifty copies only, provides the history and achievement of the series in thirteen unfoliated pages, followed by "Complete List of Bentley's Standard Novels" (first series). A revised and more detailed list appears in Sadleir's *XIX Century Fiction* (1951; repr. 2 vols., New York: Cooper Square Publishers, 1969), II:91–104, which includes a revised version of the *Colophon* essay and subsequent series as well. Bentley published a lot of American authors and was also assiduous in prosecuting "piracies" of his own publications. Dickens's association with him from 1837–42 thus further confused Dickens's identity as an author reprehending a practice his publisher both exploited and fought.

100 "Miscellanea. Literary Piracy," *The Athenaeum*, January 3, 1835, p. 18.

101 Ben Jonson is credited with introducing the classical loanword "plagiary" into the vernacular and distinguishing it from legitimate "imitation": see Richard S. Peterson, *Imitation and Praise in the Poems of Ben Jonson* (New Haven and London: Yale University Press, 1981), pp. 2, 3, 17–20; and Ian Donaldson, *Jonson's Magic Houses* (Oxford: Clarendon Press, 1997), p. 203.

102 Birrell, *Seven Lectures*, p. 172; he goes on to instance cases from 1811 onward that attempted to distinguish piracy from legitimate quotation or use of prior texts, and to prescribe limits to free use of quotation without the author's permission.

103 *OED* s.v. plagiary, plaga, plage; Online Etymology Dictionary www.etymonline.com/index.php?term=plagiarism, accessed May 13, 2010.

104 See K. M. Elisabeth Murray, *Caught in the Web of Words: James Murray and the Oxford English Dictionary* (New Haven: Yale University Press, 1977).

105 The classic study of the multiple significations and uses of handkerchiefs in *Oliver Twist* is by John O. Jordan, "The Purloined Handkerchief," *Dickens Studies Annual* 18 (1989): 1–17.

106 *Athenaeum*, June 22, 1833, p. 405.

107 Gilmour, *The Idea of the Gentleman*, p. 7.

108 Throughout his study, Robin Gilmour emphasizes the importance of education – especially reform of the old public schools – and "disinterested" competition by examination for places open to all as part of the mid-Victorian response to pressures exerted by the middle class to expand notions of gentility beyond their aristocratic origins, and to admit those who "worked" to the status of gentlemen.

## 5 PAYING BOZ (1838–1839): *NICHOLAS NICKLEBY*

1 Patten, *Publishers*, p. 68.

2 Forster introduced Dickens to Macready on June 16, 1837 (William Charles Macready, *Diaries*, ed. William Toynbee, 2 vols. [New York: G. P. Putnam's Sons, 1912], 1:399).

3  Macready, *Diaries* 1:426.
4  Beard and his family continued to be close to Dickens's family: see *Letters* 1:404–5 and the balloon ride they shared in June 1838, *Letters* 1:406–7 and nn.
5  Chesterton, *Charles Dickens: A Critical Study*, p. 79.
6  Robin Gilmour, "Between Two Worlds: Aristocracy and Gentility in *Nicholas Nickleby*," *Dickens Quarterly* 5, 3 (*Nicholas Nickleby* 150th Anniversary Issue, September 1988): 110–18, 111.
7  *Letters* 1:399–400 headnotes and nn, 1:508n2, and *ODNB*.
8  *Letters* 1:326–27 and n5.
9  *Letters* 1:662–64, 663. The Agreement also includes specific instructions about how Bentley was to prepare and display his accounting to Dickens. Dickens concluded a rather similar contract with Chapman and Hall in February 1838 for a short Christmas book, *Boz's Annual Register and Obituary of Blue Devils*, for which the publishers would pay £300 upon publication, split the profits equally with Dickens, and receive in return a half-interest in the copyright. Nothing came of this project, but it was specifically exempted in later Bentley agreements from the provision that Dickens was to write nothing for any other publisher.
10  *Letters* 1:391 and n2.
11  *Letters* 1:326n5.
12  *Letters* 1:382–83, 382 and nn.
13  Forster, *Life of Charles Dickens*, pp. 104–5.
14  Gerard Curtis, "Dickens in the Visual Market," in Jordan and Patten, eds., *Literature in the Marketplace*, pp. 213–49, 236.
15  *Letters* 1:334–35, 335.
16  Forster, *Life of Charles Dickens*, p. 129n131.
17  See the entry on "portraits, busts, and photographs of Dickens" by the then curator of the Charles Dickens Museum, Andrew Xavier, in *Oxford Reader's Companion*, ed. Schlicke, pp. 462–65, 462. *Letters* 1:395n1 switches the identification of the 1837 and 1838 portraits; the note acknowledges that the editors were indebted for much of the information to Mr. F. R. Miles. In a *Dickensian* article Xavier quotes a letter in the Gimbel collection at Yale that implies it was the *first* portrait, the one Laurence kept, that was copied for a lithographic print, but it is not certain that Edward Morton's letter of November 2, 1837 eventuated *then* in a lithograph. The print may not have been made until the second drawing was completed the following March. See Xavier, "Charles and Catherine Dickens: Two Fine Portraits by Samuel Laurence," *Dickensian* 92, 2 (Summer 1996): 85–90.
18  From the virtual tour of the Charles Dickens Museum, www.dickensmuseum.com/vtour/groundfloor/diningroom/, accessed January 5, 2010.
19  Lord Robert Grosvenor sent Dickens a copy of one such announcement in July 1838, for Mr. Twycross's school at Winton Hall, Westmoreland. Dickens had not previously encountered this particular advertisement (*Letters* 1:411 and nn).

20 Since as of winter 2011–12 there is no Clarendon Press edition of *Nicholas Nickleby*, I cite the version edited by Mark Ford (London: Penguin Books, 1999). Here, p. 6. Subsequent citations from the novel, its paratexts, and Ford's editorial matter will be contained parenthetically in the text.

21 Philip Collins, *Dickens and Education* (London: Macmillan, 1963), p. 103.

22 *Letters* 1:632.

23 *Letters* 1:482n1.

24 Collins, *Dickens and Education*, p. 101.

25 *Letters* 1:481–83, 481.

26 Collins, *Dickens and Education*, p. 108.

27 G. K. Chesterton, *Appreciations and Criticisms of the Works of Charles Dickens* (London: J. M. Dent, 1911), p. 31.

28 Quoted in Chittick, *Dickens*, pp. 64, 65, 71, 75, 77.

29 Quoted in Chittick, *Dickens*, pp. 71, 78.

30 Quoted in Chittick, *Dickens*, pp. 77, 90. For the leakage of surrounding *Miscellany* material into *Oliver Twist*, and its declared aesthetic affiliation with drama and other literary forms, see my "When Is a Book Not a Book?" *BIBLION: The Bulletin of the New York Public Library* 4, 2 (Spring 1996): 35–63, revised for *The Book History Reader*, ed. David Finkelstein and Alistair McCleery, 2nd edn. (London and New York: Routledge, 2006), pp. 354–68.

31 Quoted in Chittick, *Dickens*, p. 83.

32 *Letters* 1:401–2 and nn.

33 *Letters* 1:435.

34 *Letters* 1:435–36.

35 While my entry in the *ODNB* (2004) condenses and quotes from all that had been published about Bentley at that time, there is a large amount of unpublished material relating to the Bentley firm in US and British archives that begs for attention, and that may modify these judgments about his character and business acumen.

36 The fullest assessment of Forster's career is James A. Davies, *John Forster: A Literary Life* (Totowa, NJ: Barnes and Noble, 1983).

37 *Letters* 1:436.

38 *Letters* 1:634–36, from Dickens's diary.

39 *Letters* 1:449n3, Bentley to Forster, November 3, 1838.

40 *Letters* 1:449–50 and nn.

41 *Oliver Twist*, ed. Tillotson, Appendix A, pp. 372–81, 373–78.

42 *Letters* 1:451n1.

43 *Letters* 1:450–51, 451.

44 *Oliver Twist*, ed. Tillotson, p. xxiv.

45 *Letters* 1:451n1, sent by Forster to Bentley on November 8 after he and Dickens had seen the full set of proofs for the three-decker.

46 *Letters* 1:451n1, Forster to Bentley from the MS in the Berg Collection of the New York Public Library.

47 See the "Descriptive List of Editions," in *Oliver Twist*, ed. Tillotson, pp. xlviii–lvi.

48 *Letters* 1:630. There were to be at least two other anonymous publications by 1841, *Sketches of Young Couples* and his introduction to *The Loving Ballad of Lord Bateman*.

49 Patten, *Cruikshank*, II:105–6.

50 For examples see Collins's *Dickens and Education*, pp. 98–112, Michael Slater's Introduction to the serial reprint of *Nicholas Nickleby*, 2 vols. (Philadelphia: University of Pennsylvania Press, 1982), and Horatio Lloyd, "The Real Squeers," *Times Literary Supplement*, December 19, 2003, p. 17.

51 Mark Ford prints this three-page advertisement in his Penguin edition of *Nicholas Nickleby*, pp. 780–82.

52 George Gissing, *Critical Studies in the Works of Charles Dickens* (New York: Greenberg, 1924), p. 63.

53 Chesterton, *Charles Dickens: A Critical Study*, pp. 116–17, and Mark Ford, "Introduction" to his edition of *Nicholas Nickleby*, p. xiv.

54 See David Edgar, "Adapting *Nickleby*," in Robert Giddings, ed., *The Changing World of Charles Dickens* (London: Vision Press; Totowa, NJ: Barnes and Noble, 1983), pp. 135–47.

55 On a personal note, I recall Philip Collins, with whom I had the pleasure of seeing the opening day performance of the RSC *Nickleby*, being deeply disturbed by later critics who maintained that Dickens was at best ambivalent, and at moments pretty down on, what passed for drama on the London stage.

56 Chesterton, *Appreciations and Criticisms*, p. 30. J. Hillis Miller, *Charles Dickens*, pp. 85–93, 88–89.

57 Marcus, *Dickens*, pp. 92–128, 95.

58 *Nickleby* is indeed the paradigmatic example of Dickens incorporating demotic theater: see Schlicke, "*Nicholas Nickleby*: The Novel as Popular Entertainment," in *Dickens and Popular Entertainment*, pp. 33–86. More recently, Tore Rem has published two articles on melodrama in the novel: "Melodrama and Parody: A Reading that *Nicholas Nickleby* Requires," *English Studies* 77, 3 (1996): 240–54, and "Playing Around with Melodrama: The Crummles Episode in *Nicholas Nickleby*," *Dickens Studies Annual* 25 (1996): 267–85, which discerningly compares the melodramas the Crummles troupe stages to parodies of them enacted unwittingly by other characters: "By parodying melodrama Dickens in fact also parodies other parts and elements of his own novel" (268).

59 I hear in this name allusions to a small, bird-like ("tit") writer ("writerly") who provokes at most "titters."

60 Joseph W. Childers, "*Nicholas Nickleby*'s Problem of *Doux Commerce*," *Dickens Studies Annual* 25 (1996): 49–65, 49, 61.

61 Eileen Cleere, *Avuncularism: Capitalism, Patriarchy and Nineteenth-Century English Culture* (Stanford University Press, 2004), p. 24.

62 Helena Michie, "From Blood to Law: The Embarrassments of Family in Dickens," in John Bowen and Robert L. Patten, eds., *Palgrave Advances in Charles Dickens Studies* (London: Palgrave Macmillan, 2006), pp. 131–54, 136. See also her essay, "The Avuncular and Beyond: Family Melodrama in

*Nicholas Nickleby,*" in John Schad, ed., *Dickens Re-Figured: Bodies, Desires, and Other Histories* (Manchester and New York: Manchester University Press, 1996), pp, 80–97.

63  Jon Varese, *The Value of Storytelling: Dickens, Collins, Eliot, and the Business of Novel-Writing in the 19th Century,* Ph.D. dissertation, University of California, Santa Cruz, 2011.

64  At the novel's conclusion, when brokenness is insofar as possible repaired, Smike in his last moments tells Nicholas that he has awakened from a dream of "beautiful gardens ... filled with figures of men, women, and many children, all with light upon their faces; then whispered that it was Eden – and so died" (p. 717). The "small farm near Dawlish" that Godfrey Nickleby purchases and that Nicholas re-purchases at the end of the novel lies just a few miles from Alphington, to which Dickens's parents reluctantly moved in the spring of 1839. Ralph remembers late in the novel that he was always unfavorably compared to his younger brother (p. 421).

65  Many commentators speculate that Dickens based Crummles and his daughter on the actor and manager T. D. Davenport and his nine-year-old daughter Jean, advertised as a "prodigy" in playbills extolling their March 1837 engagement at Portsmouth. "Ninetta" could therefore be an allusion to the "original" infant phenomenon.

66  For the acting specialties, or "lines of business," of stock companies, see Joseph Donohue, *Theatre in the Age of Kean* (Totowa, NJ: Rowman and Littlefield, 1975), esp. pp. 72–73.

67  In addition to Paul Schlicke's book, Angus Easson supplies a rich discussion of the melodramatic gestures within *Nickleby* in "Emotion and Gesture in *Nicholas Nickleby,*" *Dickens Quarterly,* 5, 3 (September 1988): 536–51.

68  Edgar's account of how Smike became the lynchpin of his adaptation locates the *Romeo and Juliet* performance as the heart of the drama, pp. 139–41.

69  William Shakespeare, *The Tragedy of Romeo and Juliet,* in *The Norton Shakespeare,* ed. Greenblatt *et al.,* v.i.39–41. All quotations from Shakespeare are taken from this Norton Shakespeare edition; citations to act, scene, and lines will be included parenthetically in the text.

70  Jacques Derrida, *Dissemination,* trans. and ed. Barbara Johnson (University of Chicago Press, 1981), pp. 95–117. Mrs. Squeers is another *pharmakon,* administering doses of medicine allegedly for the pupils' benefit, which makes them sick, and being exiled from a community that is itself "broken up" at the novel's end. Mantalini poisons himself at least seven times, according to the caption of plate 27 published with Part xv. For wider applications of the *pharmakon* to *Nickleby,* see Bowen, *Other Dickens,* pp. 130–31.

71  Michael Slater maintains that Nicholas is Dickens's idealized self-portrait: "Introduction" to Dickens, *Nicholas Nickleby,* ed. Slater, Penguin English Library (Harmondsworth: Penguin, 1978), pp. 13–31, 26–27.

72  For the uses to which Dickens puts pantomime in his writings, consult Edwin M. Eigner, *The Dickens Pantomime* (Berkeley, Los Angeles, London: University of California Press, 1989).

73 Bolton, *Dickens Dramatized*, p. 154.

74 *ODNB*, s.v. William Gibbs Thomas Moncrieff, formerly William Thomas Thomas.

75 Responding to comments by a character in a fiction about another fictional (if thinly disguised) character seems a confusion of ontological categories, but that melding of fictional persons and real ones happened all the time in the Victorian era; the presumed "original" of Squeers is just one of hundreds of other examples.

76 Moncrieff's reply is fully reprinted in S. J. Adair Fitz-Gerald, *Dickens and the Drama* (London: Chapman and Hall, 1910), pp. 121–26.

77 In addition to Fitz-Gerald's account, information about this production is contained in *Letters* 1:463–64 and nn.

78 How much should be made of Nicholas's pseudonym, Mr. Johnson? Son of John (Dickens) aligns Nicholas with the author Charles Dickens; and the surname connects Nicholas both to a man of the theater whom Dickens admired (and whose plays he produced and acted in), Ben Jonson, and to Samuel Johnson, the pre-eminent "professional author" in the days before such an occupation technically existed, who famously scorned "patronage" and stated that "no man but a blockhead ever wrote, except for money" (James Boswell, *Boswell's Life of Johnson*, ed. George Birkbeck Hill, rev. and enl. L. F. Powell, 6 vols. [Oxford: Clarendon Press, 1934–50], III:19; dated April 5, 1776). But however much Nicholas would like to be amid that company, he's not; he's a hack. And thus Dickens removes him from such authorial contaminations as theatrical adapters are prey to.

79 In this instance, since Ford's edition does not print the Preface, I quote from the Charles Dickens edition of the novel (London: Chapman and Hall, 1867), p. x.

80 Anon, "Charles Dickens and His Works," *Fraser's Magazine* 21 (April 1840): 381–400; repr. Collins, ed., *Critical Heritage*, pp. 86–90, 89.

81 In early 1838 Dickens, Forster, and Ainsworth formed the "Trio Club." Among its resolutions was the provision that Dickens's "personal Coffee and Muffins" would be provided by and charged to the club and that he draw up seven by-laws, taking "especial and particular care of number One" (*Letters* 1:637 and n3). It is interesting to see how the fictional materials of *Nickleby* and his other works are reformulated playfully in his leisure time. Whether that play mitigates his social and political commitments is, however, doubtful.

82 Garcha, *From Sketch to Novel*, p. 160.

83 Thomas Carlyle, *Chartism* (London: James Fraser, 1840), p. 58. Further references to this copy are inserted parenthetically in the text.

84 Significantly, in this book Carlyle takes no notice of the lords spiritual, surely as little concerned with general welfare and as devoted to *laissez-faire* governance in the middle ages as in the late-eighteenth and early-nineteenth centuries.

85 Edgar, "Adapting Nickleby," p. 138.

86 The significance of this location is noted by Michael Cotsell, who calls it "a potential central symbol"; I assign to it a greater significance, but agree with his analysis of the class, economic, and gender stresses in the novel ("Nicholas Nickleby: Dickens's First Young Man," *Dickens Quarterly* 5, 3 [*Nicholas Nickleby* 150th Anniversary Issue, September 1988]: 118–28, 122). Michael Hollington also calls attention to the General Agency Office in "Nickleby, Flanerie, Reverie: The View from Cheerybles," *Dickens Studies Annual* 35 (2005): 21–43, 27, seeing it as "a magnetic center for [Nicholas] in his street-wanderings." Hollington is interested in the ways pedestrians are absorbed by their own thoughts while walking the streets, and how psychologically acute Dickens can be about these "interior" meditations.

87 On "speculation" and its relationship to a changing British economy, see Titiana M. Holway, "The Game of Speculation: Economics and Representation," *Dickens Quarterly* 9, 3 (September 1992): 103–14.

88 In the section on "onymity," i.e., signing the text with the author's legal name (pp. 39–42), Genette discusses the particular case of autobiography, where the congruence of author with eponymous character is generically presumed. He instances "disguised autobiographies" where the "hero" has a different name from the author, such as Anatole France's "Pierre Nozière" or Colette's "Claudine," but doesn't deal with cases such as *Nickleby* where the serial title declares that the genre is autobiographical, Nicholas's life and adventures as edited by "Boz," while the volume edition gives the author as Charles Dickens.

89 Dickens allowed, without complaining, a number of artists to supplement Browne's illustrations, not seeing in those unauthorized commodities a threat to his identity or income, though they might have diminished Browne's. See Kitton, *Dickens and His Illustrators*, Appendix II, "Concerning 'Extra Illustrations," pp. 227–42. *Pickwick* was a popular text for illustrating, but given the presence of Miss La Creevy, so was *Nickleby*, which generated images by Sir John Gilbert for the Cheap Edition; Kenny Meadows's *Heads from "Nicholas Nickleby"* (portraits "from drawings by Miss La Creevy") – which featured in the center of the advertisement Miss La Creevy painting Kate's portrait, a version of Browne's illustration "Kate Nickleby sitting to Miss La Creevy" (reproduced by Gerard Curtis, "Dickens in the Visual Market," p. 223, with a misleading caption), and on the wrappers in the center Miss La Creevy seated before Laurence's portrait of "Boz," who does hold a quill pen in his right hand (Kitton, *Dickens and His Illustrators*, p. 234; Slater ed., *Nicholas Nickleby*, facsimile edition, 1:facing p. lxxii); Thomas Onwhyn using the pseudonym of "Peter Palette"; three portraits by Frank Stone issued concurrently with the Cheap Edition; Weld Taylor's representation of the Baron of Grogzwig; and anonymous woodcuts issued by J. Cleeve. See Gerard Curtis, who in "Dickens in the Visual Market" discusses the many ways commercial visual materials interact with Dickens's texts. Luisa Calé comprehends the complex interaction of Phiz's plates, Dickens's letterpress, advertisements, and extra illustrations in "Dickens

Extra-Illustrated: Heads and Scenes in Monthly Parts (The Case of *Nicholas Nickleby*)," *Yearbook of English Studies* 40 (July 2010): 8–32.

90 *Letters* 1:555.

91 Images of authors had of course appeared in texts for centuries; a contemporary example is Duncombe's 1835 edition of the complete plays of Douglas Jerrold: at the end of the first volume the publisher supplies "A portrait of the Author": Michael Slater, *Douglas Jerrold: A Life (1803–1857)* (London: Duckworth, 2002), p. 99.

92 Or both Dickens and Boz. Thackeray thought so. Praising the picture, exhibited at the Royal Academy in 1840, he wrote in *Fraser's* that Maclise "must have understood the inward Boz as well as the outward before he made this admirable representation of him" (*Letters* 1:557–58 and 558n1).

93 Quoted in Patten, *Cruikshank*, 11:6.

94 All the descriptions come from Kitton, *Dickens by Pen and Pencil*, p. 19. Nat Willis is the source for the description of Dickens's scanty wardrobe, quoted in Forster, *Life of Charles Dickens*, p. 73n, but dismissed by Ley as "an absolute fabrication" (p. 80n84). However, as we have seen, Willis's acquaintance with Dickens in these early years is confirmed in *Letters* 1:88n, and the visit to Furnivals Inn has been accepted by Edgar Johnson and later biographers.

95 See L. Perry Curtis, *Apes and Angels: The Irishman in Victorian Caricature* (Newton Abbot: David and Charles, 1971).

96 George Henry Lewes, "Dickens in Relation to Criticism," *Fortnightly Review*, o.s. 17 (January–June 1872): 141–54, 152.

97 It is well known that George Eliot hated the "keepsakey, impossible face" of the frontispiece; when she got hold of a photograph taken around 1851, she told Sara Hennell that it offered a "satisfactory refutation" of the Maclise image (George Eliot, *Letters*, ed. Gordon S. Haight, 9 vols. [New Haven: Yale University Press, 1954–78]: v:226).

98 Chittick, *Dickens*, p. 137. She also says, rightly, that "Dickens came to understand that the trappings of reality surrounding his own identity" reinforced "the imaginative world of the books" (p. 138). That's true, but I offer modifications of those "trappings of reality," since Finden's engraving leaves out many of the signs of an author writing for money and middle-class status. The frontispiece was not just for the volume publication; it was the fourth plate for the final double number of the serial as well.

99 I have not seen this statement on the verso of the frontispiece, but Gerard Curtis has ("Dickens in the Visual Market," p. 238).

100 An 1848 reprint by George P. Putnam of Washington Irving's *Sketch Book of Geoffrey Crayon Gent.* opens with a frontispiece portrait of the author autographed "Yours truly Washington Irving 1823": Herbert F. Tucker, "Literal Illustration in Victorian Print," in Richard Maxwell, ed., *The Victorian Illustrated Book* (Charlottesville and London: University Press of Virginia, 2002), pp. 163–208, 183.

101 John O. Jordan, "'Faithfully Yours, Charles Dickens,'" address to the Dickens Universe, University of California, Santa Cruz, August 2005; unpublished paginated typescript hereafter cited parenthetically in the text.

102 *Letters* 1:132.

103 Coram established the first foundling hospital for children; while the novel makes nothing directly of the contrast to Squeers and Dotheboys Hall, the contrast may have been activated in Dickens's mind by his frequent walks through the neighborhood.

104 Robert Mudie, *The Copyright Question and Mr. Sergeant Talfourd's Bill* (London: William Smith, 1838), p. 34.

105 *The Times*, May 16, 1838, p. 7.

106 Vanden Bossche, "The Value of Literature," p. 63.

107 *Letters* 1:416n5, and *ODNB* under Alice Meynell, Thompson's younger daughter by his second marriage.

## 6 REWRITING BOZ (1839–1841): *MASTER HUMPHREY'S CLOCK* AND *THE OLD CURIOSITY SHOP*

1 *Letters* 1:490–91 and nn. The entire letter is housed at the Victoria and Albert Museum. As the Pilgrim editors note, Forster took extracts from it and backdated them to Dickens's "birthday-letter of 1838," applying the news about getting started on the book to *Nickleby*.

2 Marcus, *Dickens*, p. 184.

3 *Letters* 1:491.

4 *Letters* 1:530–32, 530.

5 *Ibid.*

6 *Letters* 1:493–94, 494, to Forster, but summing up the letter he asked Forster to take to Bentley.

7 *Letters* 1:493–94.

8 As mentioned in earlier chapters, Dickens found them a cottage at Alphington, near Exeter; they stayed there, though not particularly happily, until the end of 1842, and then returned to London.

9 The Pilgrim editors add a rather odd note to this letter, which was printed in Forster but did not otherwise survive: "Whether the text in F is as CD wrote it, or to some extent rewritten and heightened by Forster, cannot be known" (*Letters* 1:494n2). Forster did alter Dickens's letters for various purposes, as the editors discuss in the Introduction to the first volume; but this note seems to express something more – a doubt whether Forster really transcribed Dickens's outrage or to some extent created it. Since Forster had been the one pressing Dickens to adhere to his contract, heightening Dickens's fury could serve as exoneration for Forster's apparently taking Dickens's side thereafter; but it also would tend to make Bentley's response more reasonable and politic, after he received such a diatribe.

10 Forster, *Life of Charles Dickens*, p. 130.

11 Quoted by Ley in Forster, *Life of Charles Dickens*, p. 136n133.

12 There's no indication that Dickens saw the Grant brothers while in Manchester 12–17 January, though it is likely they were invited to the dinner, and may have attended. The Cheeryble brothers appear for the first time in chapter 35, the second chapter in the February number written in January and published at the end of that month.

13 Quoted in *Letters* 1:495n2.

14 *Letters* 1:495–96.

15 *Letters* 1:498–99, 498.

16 Ellis, *Ainsworth and His Friends*, 1:387n; partially transcribed in *Letters* 1:531n1.

17 *Letters* 1:496n1, MS Berg.

18 *Letters* 1:498n2, Agreement of February 2, 1839, MS British Library.

19 *Letters* 1:674–75, 675.

20 I have been unable to locate a copy of this Address.

21 *Letters* 1:530–32, 531.

22 *Letters* 1:532n1, MS Berg.

23 *Letters* 1:538n4, MS Forster's Executors.

24 *Letters* 1:538.

25 *Letters* 1:358–60 and my *ODNB* entry for Edward Chapman. Eckel notes that the first page of the advertisements bound in with the text of *Young Couples* was "surely the composition of Dickens" (*First Editions*, p. 111). It trumpets Boz's new work in weekly numbers, "now wound up and going, preparatory to its striking, on Saturday, the 28th March."

26 *Letters* 1:358–60, 358–59 and nn.

27 *Letters* 1:510, 528, 542, 511, 527, 561, 581.

28 *Letters* 1:559 and nn.

29 See, for example, James G. Hepburn, *The Author's Empty Purse and the Rise of the Literary Agent* (London and New York: Oxford University Press, 1968), and a more recent study by Mary Ann Gillies, *The Professional Literary Agent in Britain, 1880–1920* (Toronto and Buffalo: University of Toronto Press, 1997).

30 *Letters* 1:562–63 for the letter, 563–65 for the notes.

31 *Letters* 1:569–70, 570.

32 *Letters* 1:597.

33 Forster transcribes the four paragraphs of Dickens's July 14 letter pertaining to what he might "throw out" to Chapman and Hall as Dickens wrote them, but as if he were simply reminding Forster of facts already known to him (and in some ways owing to his advice). He both condenses and adds to Dickens's text, fortunately preserved in the Victoria and Albert Museum. For instance, where Dickens says the publishers could tell Forster what they mean to do at the conclusion of *Nickleby*, "without admitting me," Forster adds "it would help us very much." (Note the "us.") Instead of enumerating what Forster should advance as arguments, Forster's transcription changes each item to begin "You know," as if Forster had been partner, if not instigator, of these ideas. And where Dickens has "In addition to this, you may expatiate on the glories of this new project," Forster prints "Knowing all this, I feel certain that if you were to put before them the glories of the new

project," the result (not the "negociation" as in Dickens's letter) "will be of the most vital importance to me and mine." It's understandable that more than thirty years later, and in failing health, Forster would rephrase to emphasize how significant the "result" of these deliberations was for Dickens and his family; but the change from "negociation" conceals the fact that *at the time* that future was not secured, and the negotiations might well have come to nothing. Forster then gives Dickens's "rough notes of proposals for the New Work" as if it were a separate letter ("written also in the same month from Petersham"), when in fact it was an enclosure to Forster in Dickens's July 14 instructions, intended first as an *aide-mémoire* for him, "that you may have time to make yourself master of the subject," and then as something that "may be handed over to C & H when the palaver has been holden," in other words, after Forster has inveigled a handsome *Nickleby* bonus and set forth in his own words the plan for the future (Forster, *Life of Charles Dickens*, pp. 139–42; J. W. T. Ley provides no notes glossing any part of this *Clock* proposal).

34  Forster, *Life of Charles Dickens*, p. 139.

35  *Letters* II:7–9, 7.

36  For a fine treatment of the theme of resurrection throughout Dickens's works, see Andrew Sanders, *Charles Dickens "Resurrectionist"* (New York: St. Martin's Press, 1982).

37  See entry for Knight in *ODNB*.

38  *Letters* I:589 and n.

39  Forster, *Life of Charles Dickens*, p. 142.

40  *Letters* II:7–9, 7–8.

41  Dickens told Thomas that his clock had suggested the title of the new book, although there is some uncertainty about this; see *Letters* II:5 and nn.

42  *Letters* II:48–49, 49 and nn.

43  There are many fine studies of the *Clock* illustrations, starting with Kitton's *Dickens and His Illustrators*, and including Joan Stevens's canonical article "'Woodcuts Dropped into the Text': The Illustrations in *The Old Curiosity Shop* and *Barnaby Rudge*," *Studies in Bibliography* 20 (1967): 113–34, John R. Harvey's influential *Victorian Novelists and Their Illustrators* (New York: New York University Press, 1971), the authoritative study of Phiz's work for Dickens by Steig, and in addition to her chapter on all of Browne's plates for Dickens, Jane Cohen's comprehensive chapter on "The Other Illustrators of *Master Humphrey's Clock*," in her *Charles Dickens and His Original Illustrators*, pp. 125–38.

44  *Letters* I:596.

45  *Letters* I:597.

46  *Letters* I:598.

47  *Letters* I:603–4, 603.

48  *Letters* I:689–91, 689.

49  Still the best study of the Newgate novel controversy is by Keith Hollingsworth, *The Newgate Novel, 1830–1847: Bulwer, Ainsworth, Dickens, and*

*Thackeray* (Detroit: Wayne State University Press, 1963). For Cruikshank's involvement – he illustrated three of the suspect fictions – see "Almost in Love with Roguery," chapter 28 in volume II of my *Cruikshank*.

50 W. M. Thackeray, "Horae Catnachianae," *Fraser's Magazine* 19, 112 (April 1839): 407–24, 408, 424.

51 Gordon Ray, *Thackeray: The Uses of Adversity* (New York: McGraw-Hill, 1955), p. 252.

52 An expedition led by Richard Monckton Milnes to watch Courvoisier's hanging left Thackeray dismal and melancholy. The experience weighed upon him, he told his mother, "like cold plum pudding on the stomach" (W. M. Thackeray, *Letters and Private Papers*, ed. Gordon N. Ray, 4 vols. [Cambridge, MA: Harvard University Press, 1946], 1:452–54, 453). Thackeray, "Going to See a Man Hanged," *Fraser's Magazine*, 22 (August 1840): 150–58. Dickens wrote letters about Courvoisier's case to the *Morning Chronicle* that were published on February 28, June 23, and June 29, 1840: see *Letters* II:86–91 and nn.

53 *Letters* I:616–18, passages quoted from throughout the correspondence.

54 *Letters* I:621n8, MS Berg.

55 *Letters* I:646 for payment of fees, taken from Dickens's cheque counterfoil, and I:620–21, for his request to Chapman to sign the bond.

56 See *Letters* I:621n2.

57 Barbara Hardy, *Dickens and Creativity* (London and New York: Continuum, 2008).

58 See, for example, Jack Stillinger, *Multiple Authorship and the Myth of Solitary Genius* (New York and Oxford: Oxford University Press, 1991) and Marjorie Stone and Judith Thompson, "Contexts and Heterotexts: A Theoretical and Historical Introduction," in their *Literary Couplings: Writing Couples, Collaborators, and Construction of Authorship* (Madison: University of Wisconsin Press, 2006), pp. 3–37. Of the instances of collaboration discussed in these books, I have focused on those applicable especially to Dickens's early career.

59 I am indebted to Victoria Ford Smith for this and the Margaret Gatty example. There is no reference to Barbauld by Dickens in his correspondence and speeches or by his principal biographers, Forster, Johnson, Ackroyd, and Slater. So Dickens may never have encountered the Fairborne family, or if he did, the acquaintance was so perfunctory that it did not stay in his memory. My point is that the set-up for the *Clock* does have at least one precedent, and probably more, and that subconsciously Dickens might have been influenced by the notion of stored stories brought out and read aloud to a group of friends who originated the tales. "The Black Bag" appears in *Aunt Judy's Letters*, originally published in 1862.

60 References to the *Clock* texts are complicated. Where *Clock* material is included with the Clarendon edition of *The Old Curiosity Shop*, page citations appear parenthetically in the text (Charles Dickens, *The Old Curiosity Shop*, ed. Elizabeth M. Brennan [Oxford: Clarendon Press, 1997]). Where *Clock* material appears in John Bowen's Penguin edition of *Barnaby*

*Rudge*, the same principle applies (Charles Dickens, *Barnaby Rudge*, ed. John Bowen, Penguin Classic [London: Penguin Books, 2003]). But there are cases where the material quoted appears only in the weekly parts, gathered into three volumes, of the original edition. Then the citation is to number of the part and page.

61 Garrett Stewart accepts the identification of Nell with Mary Hogarth, and in a searching rhetorical analysis of frame narrators and tale tellers demonstrates the variety of ways in which Dickens in the *Clock* models and conscripts readers who are inducted "through the psychodynamic relays of character- ization and narration." "[T]he determinants of such reading," he continues, "go well beyond that privately eroticized and incognito mourning performed by Dickens. The novelistic issue concerns, instead, the more generally fetishized suffering of Nell's story – of nubile distress as the virgin page of ripe (written) but as yet unenjoyed (unread) text" (*Dear Reader: The Conscripted Audience in Nineteenth-Century British Fiction* [Baltimore and London: Johns Hopkins University Press, 1996], pp. 211–12). Given that Dickens's letters, written during the composition of the first seventy chapters, "provide no evidence that his thoughts . . . ever turned to his dead sister-in-law," and that Dickens's state of mind through the writing of the *Shop* was "buoyant and cheerful" (*Letters* 11:xii), I don't dwell on the novel as "incognito mourning" to which readers are conscripted. But I do see it, and the multiple narrators and narrative perspectives through which the story is seen (in text and illustrations) and related, as releasing, and then renormalizing and thus containing, a great deal of libidinal energy that evidently inspired similar psychological events in readers' minds.

62 James R. Kincaid is one of the first, and most acute, at countering the myth that the whole novel is about Nell's death. He resurrects Dick Swiveller, "the heart of the rejuvenated comic center," in "Laughter and Pathos: *The Old Curiosity Shop*," in Robert B. Partlow Jr., ed., *Dickens the Craftsman: Strat- egies of Presentation* (Carbondale and Edwardsville: Southern Illinois Univer- sity Press, 1970), pp. 65–94, 94. The chapter is enlarged in Kincaid's *Dickens and the Rhetoric of Laughter* (Oxford: Clarendon Press, 1971), pp. 76–104.

63 Audrey Jaffe maintains that Kit, by treating Nell's story as legend and foregrounding his own role, works through the traumas of the material and legitimately "conveys a sense that present and continuing life outweighs past sorrows" (*Vanishing Points*, p. 70). In my *Plot in Charles Dickens' Early Novels, 1836–1841*, Ph.D. dissertation, Princeton University, April 1965, and more authoritatively in Elizabeth Brennan's edition of the *Old Curiosity Shop*, the similarities between the plot of Dickens's novel and those redacted in the Rev. Edward Caswall's *Morals from the Churchyard; in a Series of Cheerful Fables. With Illustrations by H. K. Browne* are pointed out (p. lviii). Caswall's book was published by Chapman and Hall in 1836, and Dickens had been writing sequels to Caswall's *Sketches of Young Ladies* for several years.

64 Bowen, *Other Dickens*, p. 156.

65  On this novel's sentimental comedy as socialized feeling, feeling directed by outside considerations, see esp. Marcus, *Dickens*: "we call sentimentality when what we allow ourselves to *believe* we are feeling is shaped somehow to what we want to feel, to what we ought to feel, to what we think we deserve to feel – to a kind of self-deception" (pp. 159–60).

66  Occasionally the unnamed narrator intrudes, not to tell the plot, but to render judgment: see the last sentences of chapter 12, commending Kit's "kind and generous spirit" (pp. 99–100), or correcting the use of "childish" to apply to Nell's grandfather's feverish mania (p. 102).

67  And the illustrations quite remarkably place the viewer in a similar position of unapparent oversight. Commenting on Boz's observational activity in *Sketches by Boz*, Audrey Jaffe remarks that "eighteenth-century benevolence encounters both nineteenth-century anxiety about social mobility and a nineteenth-century perception of the poor as requiring governmental scrutiny and regulation" (*Vanishing Points*, p. 44). The prying done by characters in the *Shop* extends beyond these motives – it becomes the means to discovering their own and others' origins.

68  Well, "inconceivable" within the story. As James R. Kincaid pointed out nearly two decades ago, if the Victorians make the child into "an object of desire," that simultaneously creates "the one who desires." That desiring subject "acts out the range of attitudes and behaviors made compulsory by the role we have given the child." The mixture of "projection and denial" that constitutes the attitude of so many within the story and without seems to acknowledge this analysis. As I discuss a bit later in this chapter, the avidity of Dickens's readers for news about Nell's fate indicates a huge and complex investment in her condition. James R. Kincaid, *Child-Loving: The Erotic Child and Victorian Culture* (New York and London: Routledge, 1992), p. 5.

69  Strictly speaking, "eschatology" speaks of the end of history, the Last Judgment, the apocalypse. I'm using it figuratively in this sentence to refer to another "end," the end of Eden, which is the beginning of history but the end of innocence. I do mean, however, in referring to the "eschatological resonance" of this novel, that it is obsessed with death – but a death often depicted as the death of innocence (the schoolmaster's pupil, Nell; in an analogical way, Dick Swiveller's end of a kind of innocence that looks like predatory guilt, and the birth in him of another kind of transformative innocence in the society of the Marchioness). There is another sense in which the novel narrates the end of innocence. Hilary Schor points out that Nell's bloody footsteps betoken the onset of menstruation (Hilary Schor, *Dickens and the Daughter of the House* [Cambridge University Press, 1999], pp. 41–42). And there's an Abel in a Garland if not garden who is also an innocent. Even Sally Brass starts out the novel "in a state of lawful innocence, so to speak" (p. 280), though she has had a child out of wedlock and participates already in her brother's dubious law practice. Dickens excels in taking a motif and transforming it into all facets of its potential signifying power.

70 There is a disconcerting analogue to this scene earlier in the novel, when Nell
slips into bedrooms occupied by two men – Sampson Brass in the store-
room and Quilp in "her own little chamber" (p. 105). Whereas Nell is silent
and awake watching her grandfather steal in, Quilp is noisy and asleep.
Whereas her grandfather steals money, Nell steals the key that allows them to
escape from the Old Curiosity Shop. Surely Nell's family are not thieves, and
Nell should not be compared in any way to her grandfather or Quilp, and yet
in all cases it seems necessary secretly to penetrate the bedroom of the
opposite sex and steal their treasure in order to survive.

71 Cf. Audrey Jaffe: "while the novel is committed to Nell's inviolability and
purity, it is also continually involved in the attempt to uncover her, to violate
her privacy" (*Vanishing Points*, p. 63). In *The Literary Use of the Psychoanalytic Process*, Meredith Anne Skura reads the novel as composed of "recurring
configurations from the primal fantasy situation," which she identifies with
the child's "fiercely ambivalent" interaction with a mother and fantasies of
victimization. She thinks that the first third of the novel dramatizes the
loving/devouring parent and innocent/deathly child through human relationships that are dynamic and lively; the second third translates these
tensions into static art (Punch, waxworks); and the third reduces to primary
images of devouring (fire) and death that collapse and vitiate the energy. The
fantasy play also informs the relation between tale and tellers ([New Haven
and London: Yale University Press, 1981], pp. 58–124.

72 *Letters* II:181–82, 182.

73 *Letters* II:xii.

74 *Letters* II:ix–xii.

75 Theodor W. Adorno, "On Dickens' *The Old Curiosity Shop*: A Lecture," in
Rolf Tiedemann, ed., *Notes to Literature*, vol. II, trans. Shierry Weber
Nicholsen (New York: Columbia University Press, 1991), pp. 171–77; the
lecture was delivered ca. 1930 and first published in the *Frankfurter Zeitung*,
75, 285 (April 18, 1931), pp. 1 ff. under the title "Rede über den Raritätenladen
von Charles Dickens."

76 See Dickens's memorandum on the brothers, transcribed on p. 595.

77 Albert D. Hutter, "Nation and Generation in *A Tale of Two Cities*," *PMLA*
93 (1978): 448–62, connects embedded stories especially about biological
origins to the accounts of novels' origins. Steven Marcus notes (*Dickens*)
the relations between primal scenes, Dickens's inversions of them, and his
own accounts of his authorial origins. Dianne F. Sadoff, *Monsters of Affection: Dickens, Eliot & Bronte [sic] on Fatherhood* (Baltimore and London:
Johns Hopkins University Press, 1982), understands Freud's "primal scene"
as a metaphor for the novelists' explorations of their own origins, and focuses
on the role that fathers and daughterly redemptions play in these narratives.
John Bowen takes the Freudian reading a step further. In *Other Dickens* he
points out, using Freud's essay on "Dostoevsky and Parricide," that Nell's
grandfather's debts (and, though he doesn't mention it, Nell's father's
improvidence as well) "can be read as a material manifestation of

psychological guilt at a repressed or unacknowledged sexual desire" (p. 139). Grandfather's gambling is imbricated in his desires for Nell, for placing her at the head of his little state, as he says, "beyond the reach of want for ever" (p. 32). When she becomes desirable to Quilp and Dick as well, he punishes himself and her for this eruption of the repressed, flees from the danger that he brings along with him, and puts her into the very fatal situation that at another level he wishes to avoid (cf. Bowen, *Other Dickens*, pp. 139–40).

78 Matthew Rowlinson observes that money in this novel "does not function primarily as a store of value or as a means of exchange, but rather as the *wager* in a series of elaborate games of bluff and counter-bluff" (p. 177). His chapter on *The Old Curiosity Shop* in *Real Money and Romanticism* (Cambridge University Press, 2010), pp. 156–88, combines Marxian and psychoanalytic analyses of capital; I regret that the book arrived too late to be incorporated more deeply into my own discussion. It is an important contribution to comprehending the symbolic and material forms of wealth in Romantic and early Victorian literature.

79 The images here refer to Hablot K. Browne's wrapper design for *Dombey and Son*, which foretells the fall of the House of Dombey by means of rising and setting suns.

80 Gérard Genette's observation, in the epigraph to this chapter, that biographical renown catches up with literary renown applies to many of the "narrators" of the stories in *Master Humphrey's Clock* as well as to the two signed "authors" of the whole: "Boz" and Charles Dickens. In these cases the biographical overtakes whatever pseudo-identity the author or narrator of the story fashions for his auditors and readers. Thus Master Humphrey is eventually reconstituted as the younger brother of Nell's grandfather, and from hints dropped about his early life Jack Redburn may be Edward Chester. Dickens, once his biography is known, becomes the grieving survivor of Mary Hogarth reimagined as little Nell, etc.

81 Leah Price, *The Anthology and the Rise of the Novel: From Richardson to George Eliot* (Cambridge University Press, 2000).

82 Chittick demonstrates that throughout Dickens's early career the multiple reviews of his works were more likely to excerpt passages than to define his art. Chesterton thought *Nickleby* could have been simply "a book of sketches" comprising "A Yorkshire School," "A Provincial Theatre," etc. (*Appreciations and Criticisms*, pp. 30–31).

83 Patten, "'The Story-Weaver at His Loom': Dickens and the Beginning of *The Old Curiosity Shop*," in Partlow Jr., ed., *Dickens the Craftsman*, pp. 44–64.

84 Patten, "The Story-Weaver," pp. 53–59.

85 [Thomas Hood], Review of *Master Humphrey's Clock*, vol. 1, *The Athenaeum*, November 7, 1840, pp. 887–88, 887.

86 The same statement appears in the 1858 Library edition and the 1867 Charles Dickens edition, so the post-hoc structuring of the allegory after the original

opening chapter had been published substituted for virtually all Dickens's readers his retrospective and somewhat borrowed conceptualization for the initial composition (which might have been for a single installment, not a continued narrative or allegory).

87  *Letters* II:233n5, undated letter to Forster in Lytton Papers.

88  Marcus, *Dickens*, p. 143.

89  Eliot, *Some Patterns and Trends*, pp. 44–46.

90  The very size of the *Old Curiosity Shop* page might bespeak its appeal to a higher class of book buyer. There was still some tendency to distinguish the quality of a book by its format: folios and quartos were more prestigious than octavos and duodecimos for some subject matter. The standardization of format for particular kinds of materials – three-volume novels, for instance – occurs later in the century.

91  Price, *The Anthology*, p. 155.

92  See my *Plot in Charles Dickens' Early Novels*. By the 1840s reviewers sometimes preferred fictions in which characters and history drove the plot, rather than novels in which the plot was a matter of ingenious contrivance. Fiction that had some recognizable relation to contemporary life, and that explored dilemmas arising from personality and faith rather than from lost wills and secret enemies, gained ground in critical estimation, if not always in sales.

93  Leah Price points out that Victorian reviews alternated excerpts with plot summaries (*The Anthology*, p. 139). What was picked out as representative of a text might thereby become exceptional. I would add that, depending on the disposition of the reviewer or editor or publisher of the journal, the passage quoted could be a good example of an otherwise bad book, a bad example of an otherwise good book, a bad example of a bad book, or a good example from a good book, or it could indeed be unrepresentative of the book as a whole.

94  A point made by many critics, from G. K. Chesterton to Elizabeth M. Brennan; see the Clarendon edition of the novel, p. xxvii.

95  G. K. Chesterton, "Introduction" to the Everyman edition of *The Old Curiosity Shop* (London: J. M. Dent, 1907), p. ix.

96  Forster, *Life of Charles Dickens*, p. 150. Steven Marcus makes one of the most sustained cases for Dickens's personal investment in the story, assimilating Dickens's own failures in 1822–24 with the death of Mary Hogarth and the deaths of friends' children in the late 1830s.

97  John Bowen's chapter "Nell's Crypt: *The Old Curiosity Shop* and *Master Humphrey's Clock*," in *Other Dickens*, provides an excellent recent analysis of the work of incomplete mourning this novel performs. Audrey Jaffe is acute on the narratorial displacements as signs of Dickens's own investment: distancing himself from his own pain "gives rise to a series of further displacements in which the story of the self is told, over and over, as another's. And this series of displacements accounts for the novel's narrative structure, and for the phenomenon of the narrator motivated solely by curiosity" (*Vanishing Points*, p. 52).

98  Patten, *Publishers*, p. 110.

99  Quoted in Clarendon edition, pp. xxxvi–vii.

100  The Midlands fire is a kind of reel to its custodian: "It's like a book to me," he tells Nell, "the only book I ever learned to read; and many an old story it tells me" (p. 344).

101  See Appendix B of the Clarendon edition for "Dickens's Number Plans and Memoranda," pp. [591]–95.

102  The dream material may be too threatening for the dreamer to acknowledge ownership, and yet the material can be productive of extensive fantasies; see Skura, esp. her definition of *fantasy*: "fantasy does not replace adult experience but instead brings the intensities of childhood experience to bear on current adult life. It adds depth by evoking the unconscious remnants of infantile experience, without substituting that experience for an adult one" (*Literary Use*, pp. 73–74). Dickens's dreams in *The Old Curiosity Shop* are his effort to bring infantile experiences, reawakened by recent events, into some kind of concord with his adult life and faith. But, I am arguing, in the *Shop* he can neither author nor authorize that concord.

103  In his many commentaries on *The Old Curiosity Shop*, Chesterton repeatedly identified Dick as the hero of the story. Insofar as Dick makes a short story elevating a little child he is, like his name, a shorter version of Dickens.

7 UNWRITING BOZ (1841): *MASTER HUMPHREY'S CLOCK* AND *BARNABY RUDGE*

1  *Letters* II:191n2.

2  Kathleen Tillotson, in her undated "Introduction" to the New Oxford Illustrated Dickens edition of *Barnaby Rudge*, originally published in 1954, says that since "Dickens went to see Bedlam in 1836 . . . [it] suggest[s] that the outline of his main design was already formed" (p. vii; this Introduction was substantially incorporated into chapter 4 of Butt and Tillotson, *Dickens at Work* [1957]). Volume 1 of the Pilgrim edition of the *Letters*, published in 1965, however, prints two June 1836 letters from Dickens to Macrone projecting such a visit, but notes that no Bedlam sketch was ever written and that there is "no evidence that the visit took place" (153n1). Dickens did write "A Madman's Manuscript" for the July *Pickwick*, but as the Macrone letters are dated after mid-June, when presumably the text for the July number of *Pickwick* was being readied for, if not in the hands of, the printer, it is more probable that Dickens thought of visiting Bedlam after writing that intercalated story rather than before. Thus any projected visit to the madhouse may have had more to do with *Sketches* than anything Dickens was contemplating in the summer of 1836 for *Barnaby*.

3  Butt and Tillotson, *Dickens at Work*, p. 84 and n6.

4  *Letters* 1:648–49.

5  *Letters* 1:164–65.

6  *Letters* 1:194.

7 Ellis, *Ainsworth and His Friends*, 1:305–7 for a fuller account, and *Letters* 1:209 and nn.

8 *Letters* 1:652 and n6.

9 *Letters* 1:652n6.

10 *Letters* 1:666–74, 670. For the early sheets Carey, Lea and Blanchard paid Dickens £107.10 (*Letters* 1:652n7). Thomas J. Rice, in "The Politics of *Barnaby Rudge*" (in Robert Giddings, ed., *The Changing World of Charles* Dickens [London: Vision; Totowa, NJ: Barnes and Noble, 1983], pp. 51–74), convincingly lays out some of the political contexts relevant to the novel's gestation and publication; among other points, he demonstrates that Bentley's advertisements connected the "forthcoming" book to the Newport riots (November 1839; Bentley's notice in *Morning Chronicle*, December 14) and to contemporary treason trials ("a case of opportunism," Rice says, since Bentley was pretty sure Dickens wasn't writing the novel, but he nevertheless advertised it in the *Morning Chronicle* on February 20), pp. 59 and n26.

11 Butt and Tillotson, *Dickens at Work*, p. 82.

12 Quoted in Mary J. Hickman, "Integration or Segregation? The Education of the Irish in Britain in Roman Catholic Voluntary-Aided Schools," *British Journal of Sociology of Education* 14, 3 (1993): 285–300, 295; Hickman herself depends substantially on J. Murphy, *The Religious Problem in English Education: The Crucial Experiment* (Liverpool University Press, 1959), from which these quotations were taken.

13 Rice, "Politics," p. 57.

14 James Kincaid is particularly acute at identifying and explaining John Willet's centrality to the novel's rebellions, and at demonstrating how the comedy of the first part of the novel, at the Maypole, is darkened and reversed in the second part (*Rhetoric of Laughter*, pp. 104–31).

15 Quotations from the novel are to John Bowen's edition; here, to p. 343. Subsequent references will be cited parenthetically in the text.

16 There are many kinds of family secrets, but in these early novels, as we have seen, the mysteries about conception and birth are foregrounded. A Freudian explanation, while pertinent and applicable, doesn't sufficiently cover all the motivations for keeping these secrets, or being so curious as to discover them.

17 *Letters* 11:338n1.

18 Mircea Eliade, *Patterns in Comparative Religion*, trans. Rosemary Sheed (1958; New York: New American Library, 1963), p. 419. That there are many allusions to "devils" and others participating in the riots may remind readers of the "spirits" that appear in fairy or ghostly forms as early as *Pickwick*. Dickens does seem to conceptualize life as both material and transcendent, what Kermode terms "*aevum*" time (cf. Chapter 3). Eliade's conception of metaphysical paradox is more complicated than indicated here: see John Valk, "The Concept of the Coincidentia Oppositorum in the Thought of Mircea Eliade," *Religious Studies* 28, 1 (March 1992): 31–41.

19 Ronald Paulson, *The Art of Riot in England and America* (Baltimore, MD: Owlworks, 2010), p. 63.

20 *Letters* 1:618–19, 619.

21 *Letters* 1:618n2.

22 A draft of this Agreement, July 1840, is printed in *Letters* 11:475–77.

23 No Agreement for *Rudge* as serialized in the *Clock* or published separately thereafter now exists, nor is there reference to negotiations about this change of plans in the surviving correspondence. So it is presumed, though not proven, that the transfer of ownership, publication venue, and format was amicably concluded.

24 *Letters* 1:562–65, 564.

25 Edgar Allen Poe had much to say about Dickens's incompetence in managing the novel's mysteries; see later in this chapter.

26 Paulson, *Art of Riot*, pp. 59–61, 60.

27 Paulson, *Art of Riot*, p. 59.

28 A notable contrast to the women who play such a prominent role during the Revolution in *A Tale of Two Cities*, and to the symbol of Liberty and the triumph of the Republic, Marianne, developed to contrast the principles of liberation and reason against the male regime of King, Church, and Parlement.

29 *Letters* 11:198; Dickens was writing the first new chapter in a year. As with *Oliver* and *Nickleby*, the eponymous hero and the title of the book are often conflated in Dickens's correspondence.

30 See *Letters* 11:207, 214–15, and 224–26 and nn. Despite advice not to do it, Dickens placed a notice in the principal London papers on March 8 in which his solicitors, Smithson and Mitton, declare that "no person whatever has any right, title, or authority to make promissory notes, acceptances, or other pecuniary securities, payable either at the private residence of the said Charles Dickens, or at his publisher's or banker's; and ... such bills made payable as aforesaid will not be paid." Moreover, they gave notice that Dickens would not pay any debts save those he himself contracted (*Letters* 11:225n1).

31 *Letters* 11:253 and nn3, 5.

32 *Letters* 11:303–4, 304.

33 *Letters* 11:336–37 and 337nn1, 2.

34 *Letters* 11:323–26, 325.

35 *Letters* 11:342 and n1.

36 *Letters* 11:351 and n6.

37 *Letters* 11:356 and n3.

38 *Letters* 11:352–53, 352 and nn.

39 *Letters* 11:238–39, 238.

40 *Letters* 11:238–39, 239.

41 For this information about the banquet, I have relied on the *Letters* 11, K. J. Fielding's edition of Dickens's *Speeches*, pp. 8–15, Isobel Murray's entry on Scotland in Schlicke's *Oxford Reader's Companion*, and the crisp summary in Slater's biography, *Charles Dickens*, pp. 166–67.

42 *Letters* 11:345–46.

43 *Letters* 11:471–75 for the final Agreement with Bentley, and 11:346.

44 *Letters* 11:464–71, 464.

45 *Letters* II:348–51, 349 and n3.
46 Chapman Deed, *Letters* II:482–86; sent in late May, declined May 26.
47 *Letters* II:488–89.
48 *Letters* II:487–88, 488.
49 *Letters* II:345–46, 345.
50 *Letters* II:489–90, 490.
51 *Letters* II:478–81.
52 *Letters* II:364–67, 366.
53 *Letters* II:416.
54 *Letters* II:376 and nn.
55 *Letters* II:377.
56 *Letters* II:357 and n1.
57 Forster, *Life of Charles Dickens*, pp. 191–92.
58 *Letters* II:358.
59 In addition to his job as chief justice of the Court of King's Bench, Mansfield served in the House of Lords for decades.
60 *Letters* II:385.
61 Rice, "Politics," p. 53.
62 *Letters* II:383.
63 *Letters* II:385.
64 *Letters* II:389n1.
65 *Letters* II:410–11, 411.
66 *Letters* II:419 and nn.
67 *Letters* I:428n1.
68 *Letters* I:631–32 and 632nn.
69 *Letters* I:369–70, 370.
70 *Letters* II:364–67, 364; n4 identifies the "trash and rot" as "[a]nother reference to the imitators of his monthly parts," but it may also allude to the Newgate novel controversy and more obliquely to the problematics of writing historical fiction, discussed hereafter.
71 I am grateful to Kara Marler-Kennedy, who in a chapter of her doctoral dissertation, *Mourning, Violence, and the Historical Novel in Nineteenth-Century Fiction*, Rice University, 2010, embeds Bulwer's theory of historical fiction, especially as exemplified in *Rienzi*, into her larger survey of Victorian efforts to memorialize the past.
72 *Letters* II:224–26 and 225nn4, 5.
73 *Letters* II:294–95. There was documentary evidence for his reading of Gordon; see the Pilgrim notes to this letter.
74 *Letters* II:296. In one way this is simply a smart-alecky throwaway boast, but below the surface lie more serious implications: first, that Dickens identifies with Gordon, and second, that his own "Riot" might be "better" – implying, certainly, less destructive and mindless, but also perhaps more effective in motivating readers to religious tolerance and civic reform.
75 Donald Hawes, *Who's Who in Dickens* (London and New York: Routledge, 1998), s.v. Gashford.

76 Hardy, *Dickens and Creativity*, p. 76.

77 For a classic analysis of the advantages and limitations of the apprentice-master system, see Peter Laslett, *The World We Have Lost: England Before the Industrial Age*, 2nd edn. (London: Methuen, 1971).

78 The phrase "to cost an arm and a leg" may derive from the charges painters made for portraits; to add limbs increased the price of the picture. But there are other derivations implying that some objective, particularly in wartime, might be worth the sacrifice of a few extremities.

79 Myron Magnet, in *Dickens and the Social Order* (Philadelphia: University of Pennsylvania Press, 1985), is the principal spokesperson for the view that patriarchal authority is essential to civilization, and must be respected; he tends to downplay Dickens's descriptions of it as "despotic" and while acknowledging, especially in Barnaby's case, a perfect Freudian Oedipal situation sides with repression rather than generational rebellion: "if you want to have civilization, then you must resign yourself to enduring the repression, often enough excessive, out of which civilization is born and by which it is perpetuated" (p. 65). Magnet specifically disagrees with Jack Lindsay about Barnaby and Gordon in particular representing "the future striving to be born, the wild confusion of hopes and desires which can as yet be articulated only in the tones of 'wild animals, in pain'" (Jack Lindsay, *Charles Dickens: A Biographical and Critical Study* [London: Dakers, 1950], p. 101). Magnet also picks up on the similarity of the name Warren's Blacking to the Warren, but doesn't speculate extensively on Dickens's possible psychological investment in burning the latter down.

80 As the Bowen edition only summarizes the closing paragraphs, I quote from a first edition of the third volume of the *Clock*, pp. 421–26.

81 Edgar Allen Poe, review of *Barnaby Rudge* in *Graham's Magazine* 19 (February 1842): 124–29, repr. in Collins, *Critical Heritage*, pp. 105–11; quotations taken from pp. 106–07.

82 Dickens reconsiders this figure in *The Uncommercial Traveller* (1860–69).

83 Foucault, "What Is an Author?" p. 117.

84 Slater, *Charles Dickens*, p. 183.

85 Slater, *Charles Dickens*, p. 181, quoting a description in the *Worcester Aegis*.

86 Both quoted in Slater, *Charles Dickens*, p. 182.

# Bibliography

Ackroyd, Peter. *Dickens* (London: Sinclair-Stevenson, 1990; repr. paperback, New York: HarperCollins, 1992).

Adams, Thomas and Nicolas Barker. "A New Model for the Study of the Book," in Barker, ed., *A Potencie of Life: Books in Society* (London: British Library, 1993), pp. 5–43.

Adorno, Theodor. "On Dickens' *The Old Curiosity Shop*: A Lecture," in Rolf Tiedemann, ed., *Notes to Literature*, vol. ii, trans. Shierry Weber Nicholsen (New York: Columbia University Press, 1991).

Allen, Michael. *Charles Dickens' Childhood* (Houndmills: Macmillan, 1988).

"New Light on Dickens and the Blacking Factory," *The Dickensian* 106, 1 (Spring 2010): 5–30.

Altick, Richard D. *The English Common Reader* (Chicago and London: University of Chicago Press, 1957).

*Paintings from Books* (Columbus: Ohio State University Press, 1985).

*The Presence of the Present: Topics of the Day in the Victorian Novel* (Columbus: Ohio State University Press, 1991).

*American Quarterly Review* 16 (1834): 507.

Anon., "Novel Writing," *The Athenaeum* 315 (November 9, 1833).

Auden, W. H. "Dingley Dell and the Fleet," in *The Dyer's Hand and Other Essays* (New York: Random House, 1962), pp. 407–38.

Barham, R. H. D. *The Life and Letters of the Rev. Richard Harris Barham*, 2 vols. (London: Richard Bentley, 1870).

Barthes, Roland. "The Death of the Author," published in English in *Aspen* 5–6 (1967); repr. in Stephen Heath, ed. and trans., *Image Music Text* (New York: Hill and Wang, 1977), pp. 142–48.

*The Preparation of the Novel*, trans. Kate Briggs (New York: Columbia University Press, 2011).

Baudelaire, Charles. "The Painter of Modern Life" (1863), in *Baudelaire: Selected Writings on Art and Literature*, trans. P. E. Charvet (London: Penguin Books, 1972), pp. 390–435.

Bayley, John. "Oliver Twist: 'Things as They Really Are,'" in John Gross and Gabriel Pearson, eds., *Dickens and the Twentieth Century* (University of Toronto Press, 1962), pp. 49–64.

Besant, Walter. *The Bell of St. Paul's* (London: Chatto and Windus, 1890).

Bevis, Matthew. "Temporizing Dickens," *Review of English Studies* 52, 206 (2001): 171–91.

*The Art of Eloquence: Byron, Dickens, Tennyson, Joyce* (Oxford University Press, 2007).

Birrell, Augustine. *Seven Lectures on the Law and History of Copyright in Books* (London: Cassell, 1899).

Blayney, Peter W. M. "The Publication of Playbooks," in John D. Cox and David Scott Kastan, eds., *A New History of Early English Drama* (New York: Columbia University Press, 1997), pp. 383–422.

Bodenheimer, Rosemarie. *Knowing Dickens* (Ithaca and London: Cornell University Press, 2007).

Bolton, H. Philip. *Dickens Dramatized* (London: Mansell; Boston: G. K. Hall, 1987).

Booth, Wayne C. *The Rhetoric of Fiction* (University of Chicago Press, 1961).

Boswell, James. *Boswell's Life of Johnson*, ed. George Birkbeck Hill, rev. and enl. L. F. Powell, 6 vols. (Oxford: Clarendon Press, 1834).

Bourdieu, Pierre. *The Field of Cultural Production: Essays on Art and Literature*, ed. Randal Johnson (New York: Columbia University Press, 1993).

Bowen, John. *Other Dickens: Pickwick to Chuzzlewit* (Oxford University Press, 2000).

"Collins's Shorter Fiction," in Jenny Bourne Taylor, ed., *The Cambridge Companion to Wilkie Collins* (Cambridge University Press, 2006), pp. 37–49.

"Boz *versus* Dickens," *Parker's London Magazine* 1 (February 1845): 122–28.

Bradsher, Earl L. *Matthew Carey Editor, Author and Publisher*, Columbia University Studies in English (New York: Columbia University Press, 1912).

Briggs, Asa. *The Age of Improvement* (London and New York: Longmans, Green and Co., 1959).

Brooks, Peter. *Reading for the Plot: Design and Intention in Narrative* (Oxford: Clarendon Press, 1984).

Burke, Seán. *The Death and Return of the Author: Criticism and Subjectivity in Barthes, Foucault, and Derrida* (Edinburgh University Press, 1998).

Butt, John and Kathleen Tillotson. *Dickens at Work* (London: Methuen, 1957).

Calé, Luisa. "Dickens Extra-Illustrated: Heads and Scenes in Monthly Parts (The Case of *Nicholas Nickleby*)," *Yearbook of English Studies* 40 (July 2010): 8–32.

Carlton, William J. "Mr. Blackmore Engages an Office Boy," *Dickensian* 48, 4 (September 1952): 162–67.

Carlyle, Thomas. *Chartism* (London: James Fraser, 1840).

*"The Hero as Poet,"* in *Lectures on Heroes, Hero-Worship, and the Heroic in History* (London: J. Fraser and Chapman and Hall, 1841).

Carnall, Geoffrey. "The Monthly Magazine," *Review of English Studies* n.s. 5, 18 (April 1954).

Chartier, Roger. "Figures of the Author," in *The Order of Books: Readers, Authors, and Libraries in Europe Between the Fourteenth and Eighteenth Centuries*, trans. L. G. Cochrane (Stanford University Press, 1994), pp. 25–59.

ed. *The Culture of Print: Power and the Uses of Print in Early Modern Europe*, trans. Lydia G. Cochrane (Cambridge: Polity Press, 1989).

Chesterton, G. K. *Charles Dickens: A Critical Study* (New York: Dodd, Mead, 1906).

"Introduction," *The Old Curiosity Shop*, Everyman Edition (London: J. M. Dent, 1907).

*Appreciations and Criticisms of the Works of Charles Dickens* (London: J. M. Dent, 1911).

*Charles Dickens* (London: Methuen, 1906; 10th edn., 1914).

Childers, Joseph W. "*Nicholas Nickleby*'s Problem of *Doux Commerce*," *Dickens Studies Annual* 25 (1996): 49–65.

Chittick, Kathryn. *The Critical Reception of Charles Dickens 1833–1841* (New York and London: Garland Publishing, 1989).

*Dickens and the 1830s* (Cambridge and New York: Cambridge University Press, 1990).

Cleere, Eileen. *Avuncularism: Capitalism, Patriarchy, and Nineteenth-Century English Culture* (Stanford University Press, 2004).

Cohen, Jane R. *Charles Dickens and His Original Illustrators* (Columbus: Ohio State University Press, 1980).

Colby, Robert A. *Fiction with a Purpose: Major and Minor Nineteenth-Century Novels* (Bloomington and London: Indiana University Press, 1967).

Collins, Philip. *Dickens and Education* (London: Macmillan, 1963).

ed. *Dickens: The Critical Heritage* (New York: Barnes and Noble, 1971).

"Copyright Case in America," *Westminster Review* 24 (January 1836): 187–97.

Cotsell, Michael. "Nicholas Nickleby: Dickens's First Young Man," *Dickens Quarterly* 5, 3 (*Nicholas Nickleby* 150th Anniversary Issue, September 1988): 118–28.

Cronin, Mark. "Thackeray's First Fashioned Response to Dickens: *The Yellowplush Papers* Cast a Cynical Eye on the 'Admiral Boz's' *Pickwick Papers*," *Dickens Quarterly* 10, 4 (December 1993): 191–202.

Cunningham, Valentine. "Unto Him (or Her) that Hath," *Times Literary Supplement*, September 11, 1998, pp. 12–13.

Curtis, L. Perry. *Apes and Angels: The Irishman in Victorian Caricature* (Newton Abbot: David and Charles, 1971).

Darnton, Robert. "What Is the History of Books?" in *The Kiss of Lamourette: Reflections in Cultural History* (New York: W. W. Norton, 1990), pp. 107–35.

Davies, James A. *John Forster: A Literary Life* (Totowa, NJ: Barnes and Noble, 1983).

Derrida, Jacques. *Dissemination*, trans. and ed. Barbara Johnson (University of Chicago Press, 1981).

Dexter, Walter. "The Pickwick Dedications and Prefaces," *Dickensian* 32, 237 (Winter 1935–36): 61–64.

"The Reception of Dickens's First Book," *Dickensian* 32, 237 (Winter 1935–36): 43–50.

Dickens, Charles. "Our School," *Household Words*, October 11, 1851, pp. 49–52.

*Nicholas Nickleby*, Charles Dickens Edition (London: Chapman and Hall, 1867).

*Speeches*, ed. K. J. Fielding (Oxford: Clarendon Press, 1960).

*Letters*, ed. Madeline House, Graham Storey, Kathleen Tillotson, *et al.*, The Pilgrim/British Academy Edition, 12 vols. (Oxford: Clarendon Press, 1965–2002).

*Barnaby Rudge*, ed. Kathleen Tillotson, New Oxford Illustrated Edition (Oxford University Press, 1966).

*Oliver Twist*, ed. Kathleen Tillotson, The Clarendon Dickens (Oxford: Clarendon Press, 1966).

*The Pickwick Papers*, ed. Robert L. Patten (Harmondsworth: Penguin Books, 1972).

*Nicholas Nickleby*, ed. Michael Slater, Penguin English Library (Harmondsworth: Penguin Books, 1978).

*David Copperfield*, ed. Nina Burgis, The Clarendon Dickens (Oxford: Clarendon Press, 1981).

*Nicholas Nickleby*, ed. Michael Slater, facsimile edition, 2 vols. (Philadelphia: University of Pennsylvania Press, 1982).

*The Pickwick Papers*, ed. James Kinsley, The Clarendon Dickens (Oxford: Clarendon Press, 1986).

*Sketches by Boz*, ed. Dennis Walder (London: Penguin Books, 1995).

*The Old Curiosity Shop*, ed. Elizabeth M. Brennan, The Clarendon Dickens (Oxford: Clarendon Press, 1997).

*Nicholas Nickleby*, ed. Mark Ford, Penguin Classics (London: Penguin Books, 1999).

*Barnaby Rudge*, ed. John Bowen, Penguin Classics (London: Penguin Books, 2003).

Donaldson, Ian. *Jonson's Magic Houses* (Oxford: Clarendon Press, 1997).

Donohue, Joseph. *Theatre in the Age of Kean* (Totowa, NJ: Rowman and Littlefield, 1975).

Drew, John M. L. *Dickens the Journalist* (Houndmills: Palgrave Macmillan, 2003).

Easson, Angus. "Who is Boz? Dickens and his Sketches," *Dickensian* 81, 1 (Spring 1985): 13–22.

"Emotion and Gesture in *Nicholas Nickleby*," *Dickens Quarterly* 5, 3 (September 1988): 536–51.

Eckel, John C. *The First Editions of the Writings of Charles Dickens and Their Values: A Bibliography* (London: Chapman and Hall, 1913).

Edgar, David. "Adapting *Nickleby*," in Robert Giddings, ed., *The Changing World of Charles Dickens* (London: Vision Press; Totowa, NJ: Barnes and Noble, 1983), pp. 135–47.

Eigner, Edwin M. *The Dickens Pantomime* (Berkeley, Los Angeles and London: University of California Press, 1989).

Eliade, Mircea. *Patterns in Comparative Religion*, trans. Rosemary Sheed (1958; New York: New American Library, 1963).

Eliot, George. *Letters*, ed. Gordon S. Haight, 9 vols. (New Haven: Yale University Press, 1954–78).

Eliot, Simon. *Some Patterns and Trends in British Publishing, 1800–1919* (London: Bibliographical Society, 1994).

Ellis, S. M. *William Harrison Ainsworth and His Friends*, 2 vols. (London and New York: John Lane, 1911).

Feather, John. *A History of British Publishing* (London and New York: Routledge, 1988).

    *Publishing, Piracy and Politics: An Historical Study of Copyright in Britain* (London: Mansell, 1994).

Finkelstein, David and Alistair McCleery. *An Introduction to Book History* (New York and London: Routledge, 2005).

Fitzgerald, Percy. *The History of Pickwick* (London: Chapman and Hall, 1891).

Fitz-Gerald, S. J. Adair. *Dickens and the Drama* (London: Chapman and Hall, 1910).

Forster, John. *The Life and Times of Oliver Goldsmith*, 2 vols., 5th edn. (London: Chapman and Hall, 1871).

    *Diaries*, ed. William Toynbee, 2 vols. (New York: G. P. Putnam's Sons, 1912).

    *The Life of Charles Dickens*, ed. J. W. T. Ley (New York: Doubleday, Doran and Company, [1928]).

Foucault, Michel. "What Is an Author?" first delivered as a lecture before the Society at the Collège de France, 22 February 1969, and published in the *Bulletin de la Société française de Philosophie* 63, 3 (1969): 73–104, then repr. in Donald F. Bouchard, ed., *Language, Counter-Memory, Practice*, trans. Bouchard and Sherry Simon (Ithaca: Cornell University Press, 1977), pp. 113–38.

    "The Discourse on Language," in Hazard Adams and Leroy Searle, eds., *Critical Theory Since* 1965 (Tallahassee: Florida State University Press, 1986).

Frye, Northrop. "Comic Fictional Modes," in Robert D. Denham, ed., *Anatomy of Criticism: Four Essays*, The Collected Edition of the Works of Northrop Frye, ed. Alvin A. Lee, *et al.*, vol. XXII (Toronto, Buffalo and London: University of Toronto Press, 2006), pp. 40–49.

Fuchs, Barbara. *Mimesis and Empire: The New World, Islam, and European Identities* (Cambridge University Press, 2001).

Gallagher, Catherine. *The Body Economic: Life, Death, and Sensation in Political Economy and the Victorian Novel* (Princeton University Press, 2006).

Garcha, Amanpal. *From Sketch to Novel: The Development of Victorian Fiction* (Cambridge University Press, 2009).

Gardiner, Juliet. "Recuperating the Author: Consuming Fictions in the 1990s," *Papers of the Bibliographical Society of America* 94, 2 (June 2000): 255–74.

Garnett, Kevin, Gillian Davies, and Gwilym Harbottle, eds. *Copinger and Skone James on Copyright* (London: Sweet and Maxwell, 2009).

Garrick, David. "Impromptu Epitaph," in Ian Ousby, ed., *Cambridge Guide to Literature in English* (Cambridge University Press, rev. edn. 1993).

Genette, Gérard. *Paratexts: Thresholds of Interpretation*, trans. Jane E. Lewin, foreword Richard Macksey (Cambridge University Press, 1997).

Gettmann, Royal A. *A Victorian Publisher* (Cambridge University Press, 1960).

Gillies, Mary Ann. *The Professional Literary Agent in Britain, 1880–1920* (Toronto and Buffalo: University of Toronto Press, 1997).

Gillman, Susan and Robert L. Patten. "Dickens: Doubles::Twain:Twins," *Nineteenth-Century Fiction* 39, 4 (March 1985): 441–58.

Gilmour, Robin. *The Idea of the Gentleman in the Victorian Novel* (London: Allen and Unwin, 1981).

"Between Two Worlds: Aristocracy and Gentility in *Nicholas Nickleby*," *Dickens Quarterly* 5, 3 (*Nicholas Nickleby* 150th Anniversary Issue, September 1988): 110–18.

Gissing, George. *Critical Studies in the Works of Charles Dickens* (New York: Greenberg, Publisher, Inc., 1924).

Glavin, John. *After Dickens: Reading, Adaptation, and Performance* (Cambridge University Press, 1999).

Goldsmith, Oliver. *The Vicar of Wakefield and Other Writings*, ed. Frederick W. Hilles (New York: Modern Library, 1955).

*An Inquiry into the Present State of Polite Learning in Europe* (1759), in A. Friedman, ed., *The Collected Works of Oliver Goldsmith*, 5 vols. (Oxford: Clarendon Press, 1966).

Grant, James. *The Newspaper Press: Its Origin – Progress – and Present Position*, 2 vols. (London: Tinsley, 1871).

Gray, Donald A. "A List of Comic Periodicals Published in Great Britain, 1800–1900, with a Prefatory Essay," *Victorian Periodicals Newsletter* 15 (March 1972): 2–39.

Grego, Joseph. *Pictorial Pickwickiana: Charles Dickens and His Illustrators*, 2 vols. (London: Chapman and Hall, 1899).

Griffin, Robert J. "Anonymity and Authorship," *New Literary History* 30, 4 (Autumn 1999): 877–95.

*"The Faces of Anonymity": Anonymous and Pseudonymous Publication from the Sixteenth to the Twentieth Century* (New York and London: Palgrave Macmillan, 2003).

Grillo, Virgil. *Charles Dickens' "Sketches by Boz": End in the Beginning* (Boulder: Colorado Associated University Press, 1974).

Grossman, Jonathan H. *The Art of Alibi: English Law Courts and the Novel* (Baltimore and London: Johns Hopkins University Press, 2002).

Hall, Samuel Carter. *Retrospect of a Long Life, from 1815 to 1883*, 2 vols. (London: Berkeley and Son, 1883).

Hardy, Barbara. *Dickens and Creativity* (London and New York: Continuum, 2008).

Harvey, John R. *Victorian Novelists and Their Illustrators* (New York University Press, 1971).

Hauck, Richard. "The Dickens Controversy in the 'Spirit of the Times,'" *PMLA* 85, 2 (March 1970): 278–83.

Hawes, Donald. *Who's Who in Dickens* (London and New York: Routledge, 1998).

Hemstedt, Geoffrey. "Inventing Social Identity: *Sketches by Boz*," in Ruth Robbins and Julian Wolfreys, eds., *Victorian Identities: Social and Cultural Formations in Nineteenth-Century Literature* (London: Macmillan; New York: St. Martin's Press, 1996), pp. 215–29.

Hepburn, James G. *The Author's Empty Purse and the Rise of the Literary Agent* (London and New York: Oxford University Press, 1968).

Hickman, Mary J. "Integration or Segregation? The Education of the Irish in Britain in Roman Catholic Voluntary-Aided Schools," *British Journal of Sociology of Education* 14, 3 (1993): 285–300.

Hollingsworth, Keith. *The Newgate Novel, 1830–1847: Bulwer, Ainsworth, Dickens, and Thackeray* (Detroit: Wayne State University Press, 1963).

Hollington, Michael. "Dickens the Flâneur," *Dickensian* 77, 2 (1981): 71–87.

"Nickleby, Flanerie, Reverie: The View from Cheerybles," *Dickens Studies Annual* 35 (2005): 21–44.

Holway, Titiana M. "The Game of Speculation: Economics and Representation," *Dickens Quarterly* 9, 3 (September 1992): 103–14.

Hood, Thomas. "Copyright and Copywrong," *The Athenaeum*, April 15, 1837, pp. 263–65.

[Hood, Thomas]. Review of *Master Humphrey's Clock*, vol. 1, *The Athenaeum*, November 7, 1840, pp. 887–88.

Hutter, Albert D. "Nation and Generation in *A Tale of Two Cities*," *PMLA* 93 (1978): 448–62.

Ingham, Patricia. "The Name of the Hero in Oliver Twist," *Review of English Studies* 33, 130 (May 1982): 188–89.

Iser, Wolfgang. *The Act of Reading: A Theory of Aesthetic Response* (Baltimore: Johns Hopkins University Press, 1978).

Jaffe, Audrey. *Vanishing Points: Dickens, Narrative, and the Subject of Omniscience* (Berkeley, Los Angeles, and Oxford: University of California Press, 1991).

James, Louis. *Fiction for the Working Man 1830–1850* (London: Oxford University Press, 1963).

Jauss, Hans Robert. *Toward an Aesthetic of Reception,* trans. Timothy Bahti (Minneapolis: University of Minnesota Press, 1982).

Jerdan, William. *Autobiography,* 4 vols. (London: Arthur Hall, Virtue and Co., 1853).

Johns, Adrian. *Piracy: The Intellectual Property Wars from Gutenberg to Gates* (Chicago and London: University of Chicago Press, 2009).

Johnson, Samuel. *Letters,* ed. Bruce Redford, 5 vols. (Princeton University Press, 1992–94).

Johnstone, Christian Isobel. "Decline of the Drama," *Tait's Edinburgh Magazine* 21 (February 1838): 112–15.

Jordan, John O. "The Purloined Handkerchief," *Dickens Studies Annual* 18 (1989): 1–17.

"'Faithfully Yours, Charles Dickens,'" address to the Dickens Universe, University of California, Santa Cruz, August 2005.

Jordan, John O. and Robert L. Patten, eds. *Literature in the Marketplace* (Cambridge University Press, 1995).

Jowitt, Claire. *The Culture of Piracy, 1580–1630: English Literature and Seaborne Crime* (Farnham, Surrey, and Burlington, VT: Ashgate, 2010).

Kaser, David. *Messrs. Carey and Lea of Philadelphia* (Philadelphia: University of Pennsylvania Press, 1957).

Kennedy, James, W. A. Smith, and A. F. Johnson, *Dictionary of Anonymous and Pseudonymous English Literature (Samuel Halkett and John Laing)*, 7 vols. (Edinburgh and London: Oliver and Boyd, 1926).

Kermode, Sir Frank. *The Sense of an Ending: Studies in the Theory of Fiction; with a new epilogue* (1966; Oxford and New York: Oxford University Press, 2000).

"Fiction and E. M. Forster," condensation of the Clark Lectures delivered in Cambridge in March 2007, *London Review of Books* 29, 9 (10 May 2007): 15–24.

Kincaid, James R. "Laughter and Pathos: *The Old Curiosity Shop*," in Robert B. Partlow Jr., ed., *Dickens the Craftsman: Strategies of Presentation* (Carbondale and Edwardsville: Southern Illinois University Press, 1970).

*Dickens and the Rhetoric of Laughter* (Oxford: Clarendon Press, 1971).

*Child-Loving: The Erotic Child and Victorian Culture* (New York and London: Routledge, 1992).

Kitton, Frederic G. *Charles Dickens by Pen and Pencil* (London: Sabin and Dexter, 13 initial parts and 5 supplementary ones, 1889–90, then in one volume).

*Dickens and His Illustrators* (London: George Redway, 1899).

Lane, William Guerrant. *Richard Harris Barham* (Columbia: University of Missouri Press, 1967).

Langford, Paul. *Public Life and the Propertied Englishman, 1689–1798* (Oxford: Clarendon Press, 1991).

Langton, Robert. *The Childhood and Youth of Charles Dickens* (London: Hutchinson, 1891).

Laslett, Peter. *The World We Have Lost: England Before the Industrial Age*, 2nd edn. (London: Methuen, 1971).

Leary, Patrick and Andrew Nash. "Authorship," in David McKitterick, ed., *The Cambridge History of the Book in Britain*, vol. VI: *1830–1914* (Cambridge University Press, 2009), pp. 172–213.

Lester, Valerie Browne. *PHIZ: The Man Who Drew Dickens* (London: Chatto and Windus, 2004).

L'Estrange, A. G., ed. *Life of Mary Russell Mitford*, 3 vols. (London: Richard Bentley, 1870).

Lewes, George Henry. "Dickens in Relation to Criticism," *Fortnightly Review* o.s. 17 (January–June 1872): 141–54.

Lindsay, Jack. *Charles Dickens: A Biographical and Critical Study* (London: Dakers, 1950).

Linton, Joan Pong. *The Romance of the New World: Gender and the Literary Formations of English Colonialism* (Cambridge University Press, 1998).

Lloyd, Horatio. "The Real Squeers," *Times Literary Supplement*, December 19, 2003, p. 17.

Loewenstein, Joseph. *The Author's Due: Printing and the Prehistory of Copyright* (University of Chicago Press, 2002).

*Ben Jonson and Possessive Authorship* (Cambridge and New York: Cambridge University Press, 2002).

Lopate, Philip. "Bachelorhood and Its Literature," in *Bachelorhood: Tales of the Metropolis* (Boston and Toronto: Little, Brown and Company, 1981), pp. 249–81.

Mackenzie, R. Shelton. *Life of Charles Dickens* (Philadelphia: T. B. Peterson and Brothers, 1870).

Macready, William Charles. *Diaries*, ed. William Toynbee, 2 vols. (New York: G. P. Putnam's Sons, 1912).

Magnet, Myron. *Dickens and the Social Order* (Philadelphia: University of Pennsylvania Press, 1985).

Marcus, Steven. *Dickens: From Pickwick to Dombey* (London: Chatto and Windus, 1965).

"Language into Structure: Pickwick Revisited," *Daedalus* 101, 1 (Winter 1972): 183–202.

Marler-Kennedy, Kara. *Mourning, Violence, and the Historical Novel in Nineteenth-Century Fiction*, Ph.D. dissertation, Rice University, 2010.

Matz, B. W. "When Found," *Dickensian* 21, 1 (January 1925): [3]–9.

Maxwell, Richard. "Dickens, the Two *Chronicles*, and the Publication of *Sketches by Boz*," *Dickens Studies Annual* 9 (1981).

McKenzie, D. F. *Bibliography and the Sociology of Texts* (London: British Library, 1986).

McKitterick, David, ed. *The Cambridge History of the Book in Britain*, vol. VI: *1830–1914* (Cambridge University Press, 2009).

Michie, Helena. "The Avuncular and Beyond: Family Melodrama in *Nicholas Nickleby*," in John Schad, ed., *Dickens Re-Figured: Bodies, Desires, and Other Histories* (Manchester and New York: Manchester University Press, 1996), pp. 80–97.

"From Blood to Law: The Embarrassments of Family in Dickens," in John Bowen and Robert L. Patten, eds., *Palgrave Advances in Charles Dickens Studies* (London: Palgrave Macmillan, 2006), pp. 131–54.

*Millar* v. *Taylor* (1769) 4 Burr. 2303, 98 ER 201.

Miller, Andrew. *Novels Behind Glass: Commodity Culture and Victorian Narrative* (Cambridge and New York: Cambridge University Press, 1995).

Miller, J. Hillis. *Charles Dickens: The World of His Novels* (Cambridge, MA: Harvard University Press, 1958, second printing 1959).

"Sam Weller's Valentine," in John O. Jordan and Robert L. Patten, eds., *Literature in the Marketplace: Nineteenth-Century British Publishing and Reading Practices* (Cambridge University Press, 1995), pp. 93–122.

Mudie, Robert. *The Copyright Question and Mr. Sergeant Talfourd's Bill* (London: William Smith, 1838).

Mullan, John. *Anonymity: A Secret History of English Literature* (London: Faber, 2008).

Murphy, J. *The Religious Problem in English Education: The Crucial Experiment* (Liverpool University Press, 1959).

Murphy, Peter T. *Poetry as an Occupation and an Art in Britain, 1760–1830,* Cambridge Studies in Romanticism (Cambridge University Press, 1993).

Murray, K. M. Elisabeth. *Caught in the Web of Words: James Murray and the Oxford English Dictionary* (New Haven: Yale University Press, 1977).

Neavill, Gordon B. "Bibliographic Evidence and Reader Response: The Modern Library Series," presented on July 9, 2003 at the Society for the History of Authorship, Reading and Publishing Annual Conference at Scripps College, Claremont, CA.

Newsom, Robert. *Charles Dickens Revisited* (New York: Twayne, 2000).

Nord, Deborah Epstein. *Walking the Victorian Streets: Women, Representation, and the City* (Ithaca and London: Cornell University Press, 1995).

Nowell-Smith, Simon. "Firma Tauchnitz 1837–1900," *Book Collector* 15 (1966): 423–36.

*International Copyright Law and the Publisher in the Reign of Queen Victoria* (Oxford: Clarendon Press, 1968).

Nunokawa, Jeff. *The Afterlife of Property: Domestic Security and the Victorian Novel* (Princeton University Press, 1994).

Ong, Walter J. *Orality and Literacy: The Technologizing of the Word* (New York: Methuen, 1982).

*Oxford Reader's Companion to Dickens,* ed. Paul Schlicke (Oxford University Press, 1999).

Paroissien, David. *The Companion to "Oliver Twist"* (Edinburgh University Press, 1992).

Patten, Robert L. *Plot in Charles Dickens' Early Novels, 1836–1841,* Ph.D. dissertation, Princeton University, April 1965.

"Capitalism and Compassion in *Oliver Twist,*" *Studies in the Novel* 1 (June 1969): 207–21.

"Portraits of Pott: Lord Brougham and *The Pickwick Papers,*" *Dickensian* 66 (September 1970): 205–24.

"The Story-Weaver at His Loom," in Robert B. Partlow Jr., ed., *Dickens the Craftsman: Strategies of Presentation* (Carbondale: Southern Illinois University Press, 1970), pp. 44–64.

*Charles Dickens and His Publishers* (Oxford: Clarendon Press, 1978).

"Autobiography into Autobiography: The Evolution of *David Copperfield,*" in George P. Landow, ed., *Approaches to Victorian Autobiography* (Athens: Ohio University Press, 1979), pp. 269–91.

*George Cruikshank's Life, Times, and Art,* 2 vols. (New Brunswick, NJ: Rutgers University Press; Cambridge: Lutterworth Press, 1992, 1996).

"The Dickens Archive and the Sotheby's Sale," *Dickensian* 95, 3 (Winter 1999): 257–58.

"When Is a Book Not a Book?" *BIBLION: The Bulletin of the New York Public Library* 4, 2 (Spring 1996): 35–63, revised for *The Book History Reader,* ed. David Finkelstein and Alistair McCleery, 2nd edn. (London and New York: Routledge, 2006), pp. 354–68.

Patterson, Lyman Ray. *Copyright in Historical Perspective* (Nashville: Vanderbilt University Press, 1968).

Paulson, Ronald. *Hogarth: His Life, Art, and Times*, 2 vols. (New Haven: Yale University Press, 1971).

    *The Art of Riot in England and America* (Baltimore, MD: Owlworks, 2010).

Peterson, Linda H. *Becoming a Woman of Letters: Myths of Authorship and Facts of the Victorian Market* (Princeton University Press, 2009).

Peterson, Richard S. *Imitation and Praise in the Poems of Ben Jonson* (New Haven and London: Yale University Press, 1981).

Podeschi, John B. *Dickens and Dickensiana* (New Haven: Yale University Library, 1980).

Price, Leah. *The Anthology and the Rise of the Novel: From Richardson to George Eliot* (Cambridge University Press, 2000).

    *Privilege and Property, Essays on the History of Copyright*, available free as of the end of June, 2010, online at www.copyrighthistory.org.

R. J. [C. J. Davids]. "Impromptu," *Bentley's Miscellany* 1 (March 1837).

Raven, James. *The Business of Books: Booksellers and the English Book Trade, 1450–1850* (New Haven and London: Yale University Press, 2007).

Ray, Gordon. *Thackeray: The Uses of Adversity* (New York: McGraw-Hill, 1955).

Reader, W. J. *Professional Men: The Rise of the Professional Classes in Nineteenth-Century England* (London: Weidenfeld and Nicolson, 1966).

Rem, Tore. "Melodrama and Parody: A Reading that *Nicholas Nickleby* Requires," *English Studies* 77, 3 (1996): 240–54.

    "Playing Around with Melodrama: The Crummles Episode in *Nicholas Nickleby*," *Dickens Studies Annual* 25 (1996): 267–85.

*Report of the Copyright Case of Wheaton v. Peters Decided in the Supreme Court of the United States* (New York, 1834).

Rice, Thomas J. "The Politics of *Barnaby Rudge*," in Robert Giddings, ed., *The Changing World of Charles Dickens* (London: Vision; Totowa, NJ: Barnes and Noble, 1983), pp. 51–74.

Room, Adrian. *Dictionary of Pseudonyms*, 3rd edn. (Jefferson, NC and London: McFarland, 1998).

Rose, Mark. *Authors and Owners: The Invention of Copyright* (Cambridge, MA: Harvard University Press, 1993).

Rowlinson, Matthew. *Real Money and Romanticism* (Cambridge University Press, 2010).

Sadleir, Michael. *Bentley's Standard Novel Series* (Edinburgh: for the *Colophon*, April 1932).

    *XIX Century Fiction* (1951; repr. 2 vols., New York: Cooper Square Publishers, 1969).

Sadoff, Dianne F. *Monsters of Affection: Dickens, Eliot & Bronte on Fatherhood* (Baltimore and London: Johns Hopkins University Press, 1982.

Sanders, Andrew. *Charles Dickens "Resurrectionist"* (New York: St. Martin's Press, 1982).

Saville, Julia F. "Eccentricity as Englishness in *David Copperfield*," *SEL Studies in English Literature 1500–1900* 42, 4 (Autumn 2002): 781–97.

Schlicke, Paul. *Dickens and Popular Entertainment* (London: Allen and Unwin, 1985).

Schor, Hilary M. *Scheherezade in the Marketplace: Elizabeth Gaskell and the Victorian Novel* (New York and Oxford: Oxford University Press, 1992).

*Dickens and the Daughter of the House* (Cambridge University Press, 1999).

Scott, Sir Walter. *Letters*, ed. H. J. C. Grierson, 12 vols. (London: 1932–37).

Seville, Catherine. *Literary Copyright Reform in Early Victorian England: The Framing of the 1842 Copyright Act* (Cambridge University Press, 1999).

"Edward Bulwer Lytton Dreams of Copyright: 'It might make me a rich man,'" in Francis O'Gorman, ed., *Victorian Literature and Finance* (Oxford University Press, 2007), pp. 55–72.

"Copyright," in David McKitterick, ed., *The Cambridge History of the Book in Britain*, vol. VI: *1830–1914* (Cambridge University Press, 2009), pp. 214–37.

Seymour, Mrs. [Robert]. *An Account of the Origin of the "Pickwick Papers"* (London; printed for private circulation, 1854; repr. for author, London, 1901).

Shakespeare, William. *Mr. William Shakespeares Comedies, Histories, & Tragedies* (London: Isaac Iaggard and Ed. Blount, 1623).

*The Norton Shakespeare*, ed. Stephen Greenblatt *et al.* (New York and London: W. W. Norton, 1997).

Sher, Richard B. *The Enlightenment and the Book: Scottish Authors and Their Publishers in Eighteenth-Century Britain, Ireland, and America* (University of Chicago Press, 2006).

Skura, Meredith Anne. *The Literary Use of the Psychoanalytic Process* (New Haven and London: Yale University Press, 1981).

Slater, Michael. "Introduction," *Nicholas Nickleby*, 2 vols. (Philadelphia: University of Pennsylvania Press, 1982).

*Dickens and Women* (London: Dent, 1983).

*Douglas Jerrold: A Life (1803–1857)* (London: Duckworth, 2002).

*Charles Dickens* (New Haven and London: Yale University Press, 2009).

ed. *"Sketches by Boz" and Other Early Papers, 1833–39*, vol. 1 of the Dent Uniform Edition of Dickens' Journalism (Columbus: Ohio State University Press, 1994).

Slater, Michael and John Drew, eds. *"The Uncommercial Traveller" and Other Papers, 1859–70*, vol. IV of the Dent Uniform Edition of Dickens' Journalism (Columbus: Ohio State University Press, 2000).

Sotheby's Sale L09209, July 15, 1999, "The Dickens Archive," lots 160–188.

St. Clair, William. *The Reading Nation in the Romantic Period* (Cambridge University Press, 2004).

Stein, Richard. *Victoria's Year: English Literature and Culture, 1837–1838* (New York and Oxford: Oxford University Press, 1987).

Stevens, Joan. "'Woodcuts Dropped into the Text': The Illustrations in *The Old Curiosity Shop* and *Barnaby Rudge*," *Studies in Bibliography* 20 (1967): 113–34.

Stewart, Garrett. *Dickens and the Trials of Imagination* (Cambridge, MA and London: Harvard University Press, 1974).

*Death Sentences: Styles of Dying in British Fiction* (Cambridge, MA and London: Harvard University Press, 1984).

*Dear Reader: The Conscripted Audience in Nineteenth-Century British Fiction* (Baltimore and London: Johns Hopkins University Press, 1996).

Stillinger, Jack. *Multiple Authorship and the Myth of Solitary Genius* (New York and Oxford: Oxford University Press, 1991).

Stone, Marjorie and Judith Thompson. "Contexts and Heterotexts: A Theoretical and Historical Introduction," in *Literary Couplings: Writing Couples, Collaborators, and Construction of Authorship* (Madison: University of Wisconsin Press, 2006), pp. 3–37.

Stonehouse, J. H., ed. *Reprints of the Libraries of Charles Dickens and W. M. Thackeray* (London: Piccadilly Fountain Press, 1935).

Story, Gladys. *Dickens and Daughter* (London: F. Muller, 1939).

Sutherland, John. *Victorian Novelists and Publishers* (London: Athlone Press, 1976).

Thackeray, W. M. "Horae Catnachianae," *Fraser's Magazine* 19, 112 (April 1839): 407–424.

"Going to See a Man Hanged," *Fraser's Magazine* 22 (August 1840): 150–58.

"A Grumble about the Christmas Books," *Fraser's Magazine* 35 (January 1847): 119.

*Letters and Private Papers*, ed. Gordon N. Ray, 4 vols. (Cambridge, MA: Harvard University Press, 1945).

Tillotson, Kathleen. "Pickwick and Edward Jesse," *Times Literary Supplement*, April 1, 1960, p. 214.

Tracy, Robert. "'The Old Story' and Inside Stories: Modish Fiction and Fictional Modes in *Oliver Twist,*" *Dickens Studies Annual* 17 (1988): 1–34.

Tucker, Herbert F. "Literal Illustration in Victorian Print," in Richard Maxwell, ed., *The Victorian Illustrated Book* (Charlottesville and London: University Press of Virginia, 2002), pp. 163–208.

Turner, Michael. "Political Leadership and Political Parties, 1800–46," in Chris Williams, ed., *A Companion to Nineteenth-Century Britain*, Blackwell Companions to British History and The Historical Association (Oxford and Malden, MA: Blackwell Publishing, 2004; paperback 2007), pp. 125–39.

Valk, John. "The Concept of the Coincidentia Oppositorum in the Thought of Mircea Eliade," *Religious Studies* 28, 1 (March 1992): 31–41.

Vanden Bossche, C. R. "The Value of Literature: Representations of Print Culture in the Copyright Debate of 1837–1842," *Victorian Studies* 38, 1 (Autumn 1994): 41–68.

Varese, Jon. *The Value of Storytelling: Dickens, Collins, Eliot, and the Business of Novel-Writing in the 19th Century*, Ph.D. dissertation, University of California, Santa Cruz, 2011.

Vincent, David. *Literacy and Popular Culture: England 1750–1914* (Cambridge University Press, 1989).

Vizetelly, Henry. *Glances Back Through Seventy Years: Autobiographical and Other Reminiscences*, 2 vols. (London: Kegan Paul, Trench, Trubner, 1893).

*Waterloo Directory of English Newspapers and Periodicals, 1800-1900*, Series 1, ed. John S. North (Waterloo, Ont.: North Waterloo Academic Press).

Wechsler, Judith. *A Human Comedy: Physiognomy and Caricature in 19th Century Paris* (University of Chicago Press, 1982).

Welsh, Alexander. "Waverley, Pickwick, and Don Quixote," *Nineteenth-Century Fiction* 22, 1 (June 1967): 19–30.

Wheeler, Burton. "The Text and Plan of *Oliver Twist*," *Dickens Studies Annual* 12 (1983): 41–61.

Wilkinson, Ian. "Performance and Control: The Carnivalesque City and Its People in Charles Dickens's *Sketches by Boz*," *Dickens Studies Annual* 35 (2005): 1–19.

Willis, Nat. *Dashes at Life with a Free Pencil* (New York, 1845).

Wilson, Edmund. *The Wound and the Bow* (Oxford and New York: Oxford University Press, 1941).

Wimsatt, William K. and Monroe K. Beardsley. "The Intentional Fallacy," in *The Verbal Icon: Studies in the Meaning of Poetry* (Lexington: University of Kentucky Press, 1954), pp. 2–18.

Xavier, Andrew. "Charles and Catherine Dickens: Two Fine Portraits by Samuel Laurence," *Dickensian* 92, 2 (Summer 1996): 85–90.

# Index

à Beckett, Gilbert Abbott 90
Ackermann, Rudolph 102
Ackroyd, Peter 336, 353
acting, Victorian style of 201
adaptations (stage/screen) 17, 204–6
  copyright in 341
  *see also* piracy; *titles of works*
Adorno, Theodor W. 264, 374
Agnew, Sir Andrew 109
Aikin, John 254
Ainsworth, William Harrison 54, 70, 81–82, 83,
    112, 151, 179, 191, 207, 219, 221, 237, 249, 252,
    254, 281–82, 294
  editorship of *Bentley's Miscellany* 234, 235–36;
    speed of appointment 232, 233; terms of
    appointment
  *Jack Sheppard* 170, 234, 247–48; (alleged)
    copycat crimes 250; new edition 243–51;
    stage adaptations 249–50
  *John Law, the Projector* 348
  *Rookwood* 170
  travels with Dickens 228, 231
Albert, Prince (Consort) 37
Allen, Michael 335
almanacs 5
Anne, Queen 8
  Act of Anne *see* Copyright Act 1710
anthologies 267–71
Aristotle 113
Arnold, Matthew 36
"Astley's" (sketch) 68
Athenaeum Club 180, 192
Auden, W. H. 101, 123
Austen, Jane 84
  *Mansfield Park* 319
Austin, Henry 100
author(s)
  compulsory naming (for copyright purposes)
    7, 33–34
  "death of" 17–19
  definitions 20, 91–92, 276, 324

"divine inspiration" 16, 18–19
earnings 10, 16–17
empowerment 19–20
hazardous nature of profession 241
improvements in status 13, 19, 224–25
"industrial-age" xvi, 19, 328
intent, critical attitudes to 17
low reputation / social status 2, 34, 35, 47–48,
    223–24
maintenance of day jobs 34, 83–84
professionalization 227, 332
protection of rights 7, 9
as publicity machine 333–34
publishing agreements 10–11
sale of copyright 9, 16
Aytoun, William Edmonstone 37

Ballantine, Serjeant 73
Ballantyne, Christian, née Hogarth 83, 310
Ballantyne, James 13, 82–83, 309–10
Ballantyne, John Alexander 309–10
Balzac, Honoré de 15, 43
Banks, E. W. 246
Banks, Percival Weldon 54
Barbauld, Anna Laetitia 254, 371
Barham, R. H. 37, 137, 162, 235, 236
*Barnaby Rudge* xv, xvii, 11, 25, 49–50, 187, 250
  advance publicity 191, 227, 250–51
  characters (non-historical) 295, 313–20
  commerce in bodies 320
  composition process 227–28, 230–31, 298–300,
    306, 308–9
  Dickens's appropriation of copyright 287
  Dickens's refusal to complete for Bentley 251–52
  evolution of concept 281–82
  expression of Dickens's personal frustrations
    287–88, 320
  "Gabriel Vardon" (draft title) 109, 248, 280–81
  generic definition 289
  ghostly elements 291–92, 378
  halt in composition 228–33, 250

illustrations 293–94, 299–300
inconsistencies 321–22
narratorial voice 288–90, 295–97, 321, 323–24; sympathies 289–90
non-human characters 292, 315, 320
Oedipal elements 320
opening 228, 280
original conception 280–81
publication 272
rewriting of conventions 293–97, 309, 323–24, 326
social/political background 282–84
social/political message 291
terms of contract 147
theme of bottled-up energies 290
transfer of rights 234–35, 251–52
treatment of family relationships 228, 284–86, 314–16, 320, 381
treatment of prison setting 294
treatment of violence 297–300
use of historical characters 312–13, 316
Barrow, John Henry 28
Barrow, Mary Allen 62
Barthes, Roland 18–19, 43, 274, 276, 334
Baudelaire, Charles 2, 43
Baum, L. Frank 37
Beadnell, Maria / Beadnell family 87, 273
Beal, Peter 143
Beard, Thomas 50–51, 138, 161–62, 180, 286–87
Beardsley, Monroe K. 17
Becket, Thomas (bookseller) *see Donaldson* v. *Becket*
Bedford, Duke of 250
Behnes, William 44, 217
Belgium, copyright law 15
"Bellamy's" (sketch) 59
*Bell's Life in London* 44–46, 52, 85
    readership 53–54, 342
Benjamin, Walter 43
Bentham, Jeremy 50
Bentley, George 287
Bentley, Richard 2–3, 25, 48, 54, 102, 110, 135–38, 150, 216, 243, 281–82, 320, 346, 362
    accusations of piracy against 235–36
    Agreements with Dickens 112, 135–37, 138, 142–47, 153, 180–81, 187–89, 228, 239, 241, 361; clashes/violations 141; severance agreement 234–35
    character flaws 188, 229
    consideration of injunction against Dickens 251
    Dickens's conflicts with 23, 24–25, 83, 88, 142, 143–44, 147, 149, 158, 160, 162, 187–92, 228–36, 250–52, 286–87, 353; attempts at repair 188–89; final breakdown 232
    termination of relations with Dickens 251–52

Bentley, Samuel 102
*Bentley's Miscellany* 24–25, 39, 88, 111
    Bentley's control over 136–37, 234
    choice of title 136–37
    editorial responsibilities 142–47
    offer of payment to keep Dickens's name 232, 233
    reuse of material in novels 146, 362
    severance agreement 234–35, 251–52
    "Song of the Cover" 152
Bentley's Standard Novels 360
Berkeley, Grantley 55
Besant, Walter
    *The Bell of St. Paul's* 358
    "The Death of Samuel Pickwick" 132–33
Bible, distribution of copies 13
biography xv, 227
Birrell, Augustine 171
Black, John 29, 50, 59, 70, 72, 180, 253
"The Black Veil" (sketch) 72–73, 293
Blackmore, Edward 28
Blackwood, William 12, 44
Blake, William 165–66
Blayney, Peter W. M. 331
*Bleak House* 267, 327
Blessington, Countess of 81, 180, 268
"The Bloomsbury Christening" (sketch) 51–52, 66, 156
"The Boarding House" (sketch) 68
booksellers
    associations (congers) 9–10
    control of Stationers' Company 6–7
    operational strategy 8
Booth, Wayne C. 344
Boswell, James 44
Bowen, John 129, 132, 259, 292, 297, 376
"Boz" (pseudonym) 36–46, 90–91, 111
    abandonment 2–3, 186, 193, 215–17, 323–26
    (alleged) derivation 37, 38–42
    alternation with other pseudonyms/real name 45–46, 109, 152–53
    authorial persona 43–44, 46, 58, 63–65, 68–69, 258, 295–96, 347
    collaboration with Cruikshank 74–76, 85
    conflation with Dickens 217
    correspondence signed with 325
    Dickens's reasons for adopting 34–36, 36–37, 44
    distinguished from Dickens 192, 296
    evolution xvi, 23, 73, 90–91
    first use 22, 48, 52
    generic use/imitations 76, 167, 221, 347
    as insurance against failure 38
    political non-alignment 56
    popularity 69, 133, 135–36, 151–52
    puzzle as to real identity 38, 44, 73–74, 152
    range of connotations 41–43

"Boz" (pseudonym) (cont.)
  resurrection (for *Master Humphrey's Clock*)
    245, 258, 268
  shaping of Dickens's creativity 22–23
  significance of quotation marks 152
  transference of narratorial role 64–65
  use of first-person plural 63–65, 104–5
  use within family 77
  *see also Sketches by Boz; titles of individual
    sketches*
*Boz's Annual Register and Obituary of Blue Devils*
    145, 153
Braham, John 109
Braybrooke, Lord 182
Brennan, Elizabeth M. 376
Briggs, Asa 118
Brodie, John 219
"The Broker's Man" (sketch) 61, 64–65, 343
Brontë, Charlotte, *Jane Eyre* 319
Brontë sisters 37, 84
Brooks, John Crosse 184
Brooks, Peter 135, 161
Brougham, Henry 96, 349
Brown, Andrew 80
Browne, Gordon Frederick 38
Browne, Hablot Knight ("Phiz") 38, 103, 138,
    179, 200, 237, 339, 341, 375
  illustrations for *Barnaby Rudge* 294, 299–300
  illustrations for *Master Humphrey's Clock* 244
  illustrations for *Nicholas Nickleby* 215–16, 366–67
  illustrations for *Pickwick* 107–8, 112, 160, 217–18
  travels with Dickens 183–84, 189
Browning, Elizabeth Barrett 84
Browning, Robert 84, 151
Buckstone, John Baldwin
  *The Bloomsbury Christening* (unauthorized
    adaptation) 51–52, 156
  *Jack Sheppard* 249
  *Rienzi* 81, 85
Bulwer, Edward Lytton xvii, 2, 80–81, 83, 180,
    270, 294, 347
  *England and the English* 80
  *Eugene Aram* 81, 247
  *The Lady of Lyons* 81
  *The Last Days of Pompeii* 80
  *Money* 81
  *Paul Clifford* 81, 247
  *Rienzi, Last of the Tribunes* 80–81, 311
Bulwer, Rosina, née Wheeler 80
Bunyan, John, *The Pilgrim's Progress* 13, 223, 273
Burdett-Coutts, Angela 183, 200
Burnett, Fanny *see* Dickens, Frances Elizabeth
Burnett, Henry 193
Burns, Robert 301
Buss, Robert William 102–3, 105, 107, 108

*Dickens' Dream* 103
Butt, John, and Kathleen Tillotson, *Dickens at
    Work* xiii, 282
Byron, George Gordon, 6th Baron 13

Caldwell, Erskine 17
Campbell, Thomas 13
Camus, Albert 203
Canada, copyright law 169
Canning, George 96
capital punishment *see* executions
Carey, Henry Charles 158
Carey, Lea and Blanchard (publishers) 158, 175
*Carlton Chronicle* 54, 85, 138
Carlyle, Jane, née Welsh 219
Carlyle, Thomas 16, 47, 177
  *Chartism* 209–14, 365
  *The French Revolution* 210, 281
  *Sartor Resartus* 161
  *see also* "cash nexus"
carnival, spirit of 345
Caroline (of Brunswick), Princess
    (later Queen) 55
"cash nexus" 209–10, 213, 225
Catholic emancipation, agitation for/against 283
Cattermole, George 244–45, 257, 299–300
Cervantes, Miguel de, *Don Quixote* 118, 184,
    218, 253
Chadwick, Edwin 180
Chapman, Edward 95–96, 102, 183, 237, 241, 252,
    253, 302–3
  *see also* Chapman and Hall
Chapman, Thomas 237
Chapman, William 149–50, 303–4
Chapman and Hall (publishers) 23, 25, 33,
    111–12, 320
  and *Barnaby Rudge* 251–52
  as booksellers 32
  call for acknowledgment of debt 303–4
  concern over financial situation 302–5
  Dickens's aggressive bargaining with 238–41,
    287
  Dickens's termination of relations with 147, 327
  friendly relationship with Dickens 148–50,
    175, 237, 286; breakdown 304
  inexperience 101–2
  and *Master Humphrey's Clock* 238
  problems with Dickens's timekeeping 88–89, 92
  publicity material 105
  purchase of *Sketches* copyright 154, 355
  raising of Dickens's pay 88, 104, 111–12, 149
  role in *Pickwick* 85–91, 92–95, 179
Chartier, Roger 329
Charyn, Jerome 125, 335
Chekhov, Anton 43

Chesterfield, Philip Stanhope, 4th Earl of 317–18
Chesterton, G. K. 79, 101, 118, 124, 126, 130, 180, 186, 192, 194–95, 273, 297, 328, 375, 376, 377
Childers, Joseph 196
children
  kidnapping of 168
  protests at living/schooling conditions 183–85
  Victorian attitudes to 373
  witnessing of 'primal scenes' 265, 374–75
Chittick, Kathryn 31, 32, 35, 36, 48, 153, 220, 336, 337, 367, 375
Christmas, (sentimentalized) treatments 128–29
*A Christmas Carol* 274, 320
  copyright disputes 169
chronicle, genre of 289
Civil War (1642–49) 7
Cleere, Eileen 179, 196–97
Colburn, Henry 25, 102, 154–55, 230, 234, 239–40, 243, 346
Collins, Philip 185, 363
Collins, Wilkie 28, 30, 260
  "The Last Stage Coachman" 132
commercial relations, treatments in fiction 165–66, 197–200
  bodies as units of 199–200, 320
  insubstantiality of capital 214–15
  *see also* "cash nexus"
communications industry
  interaction of various elements 3
  Oriental origins 330
  reorganization 12–13
  role of authors 3–5, 8, 17
  technological developments 3, 19
Condell, Henry 7
Conrad, Joseph 37
Constable, Archibald 12, 13, 83
Cooper, James Fenimore 170, 360
copyright 5–17
  Agreements 145–46, 150
  authorities 330–31
  case law 9, 10–12, 14, 332
  costs of legal action 169
  debates 223–25
  dramatic 7, 172, 354–55
  flaws in English law 5, 11, 12, 24, 157, 168–69, 332
  in illustrations 76
  international, (near-)absence of 15–16, 158, 169, 205
  legal basis 168–69, 171–72
  in other countries 14–16
  penalties for infringement 7
  perpetual 10–11
  prolongation via new editions 13–14
  royal monopoly 5–7, 14

statutory periods 9, 12–13; proposed increase 177
  *see also* piracy; plagiarism
Copyright Act 1710 (Act of Anne) 9, 11, 12–13
Coram, Thomas 223, 368
Courvoisier, François 250, 371
Covent Garden, Dickens's planned audition at 30, 49
Cronin, Mark 132
"Cross Purposes" (burletta) 35
Crossley, James 231
Crowquill, Alfred (Charles and Alfred Forrester) 37, 156, 158
Cruikshank, George 38, 43, 82, 85, 112, 160, 163, 179, 200, 244, 254, 310
  drawings of Dickens 183
  friendship with Dickens 237; ruptures in 189–90
  illustration of Newgate novels 248, 249, 370–71
  illustrations for *Oliver Twist* 138–40, 146, 147, 161, 190
  illustrations for *Sketches by Boz* 53, 65, 74–76, 87, 92, 110, 154
  "The Loving Ballad of Lord Bateman" 193–94, 237, 240
Cruikshank, Mary 237
Cruikshank, Robert 75, 156
Culliford, Thomas John 77
Curll, Edmund 10

Darnton, Robert 2, 3–5, 88, 224, 330
Darwin, Charles 19, 180
Davenport, T. D./Jean 364
*David Copperfield* 21, 28, 36–37, 68, 184, 252, 267, 327
  autobiographical elements 26–27, 28–29, 39, 48, 162, 307
  critical/commercial success 33
  prefigurings in sketches 73
Davidge, W. P. 249
death
  depiction of characters on eve of 70–72
  extension of narrative beyond 72–73
  "immortality" (of author/characters) 62–63, 324–25
  linked with authorship 62–63, 344
  as theme of Dickens's work 60–61, 70–73, 116–25, 130, 258–59, 293, 313, 343
  *see also The Pickwick Papers*
Defoe, Daniel 339
"Delta" *see* Moir, David MacBeth
Dennis, Ned (historical figure) 313
Derrida, Jacques 203, 364
Dickens, Alfred Allen (brother, 1813–14) 30, 62, 179

Dickens, Alfred Lamert (brother, 1822–60) 30, 180
Dickens, Augustus (brother) 30, 37, 39–42
Dickens, Catherine, née Hogarth 28, 200, 237,
 273, 286, 300, 301–2
 births of children 142, 187, 246
 Dickens's separation from 327
 engagement 183
 letters to 52–53, 70, 72, 85, 86–88, 90, 97–98,
 100, 207
 marriage 98
**Dickens, Charles:**
as author
 anti-Tory poems 306–7
 anxieties xvi, 22, 23–24, 35–36, 111, 305–6
 authorial persona 89, 100, 108, 140–41, 175,
 182, 193–94, 217, 220–22, 258, 301–2, 323,
 324–26, 327, 344
 autobiographical account (1847) 26, 33, 94
 campaign for authors' rights 14, 19–20, 326
 collaborative projects 253–54 (*see also The
 Pickwick Papers*)
 concern for customer satisfaction 221–22
 contemporary criticisms 179, 227, 274, 280
 (*see also* Thackeray)
 control of own image 20–21, 25–26, 32–33,
 327–28
 cultural status 224, 225
 defense of characters 301
 earliest published works 31–33, 49–50, 93
 failure to meet deadlines 98 (*see also* Chapman
 and Hall)
 friendships with other writers 81–82
 income *see* finances
 influence of childhood trauma on works 27,
 73, 94, 162–63, 358
 innovative proposals 238
 lack of control over product 154, 159–60,
 174–75, 193–94, 275–78
 narratorial choices 263–64
 need for appreciation 224
 overloaded schedule xv, 52–53, 110, 138–39,
 140–42, 150, 187, 227
 prefaces 346–47
 public readings 327
 publishers' agreements 23–24, 88–89, 150, 153,
 175, 193–94, 281–82; clashes between
 141–47 (*see also* Bentley, Richard)
 range of options 83–85, 108–12
 range of outlets/audiences 53–55
 renown, manipulation of 305
 rewriting of own history 21, 25–26, 32–33,
 92–94, 167, 208–9, 230–31, 275, 296–97
 role models 21, 79–83
 sources 21–22, 56–60
 theater writings, unpopularity of 140

treatment of "vocation" 21; analogy with
 medicine 73
 treatments of family relationships 285–86
 writer's block 230–31
 year-long break (1841–2) 304–5, 322–23
 *see also* "Boz"; *titles of works*
as editor 24–25, 42–43, 111, 135–38, 142
 cancellation of engagements 25, 137–38, 234–35
 departure from *Bentley's Miscellany* 233–35
 later career 327
 social status 176–77, 224
 workload 137, 154–55; overestimation of
 capacities 144
 *see also titles of periodicals*
employment (non-literary) 28–31
 in blacking factory 20, 22, 26–27, 162–63,
 335, 358
 focus on print culture 22
 lack of plan 26
 as lawyer's clerk 28, 48, 131
 plans for acting career 30, 49, 337
 plans for legal career 34, 252–53
 plans to stand for Parliament 322
 range of options 22, 29–30, 48–49
events of life
 education 22, 27–28; lack of formal learning 27
 emigration, contemplation of 307
 surgery 308
 travels *see* Scotland; United States
family life/relationships
 deaths of family members 62
 (*see also* Hogarth, Mary)
 marriage 83, 98
 residences 246–47, 296
 support for extended family 24, 29–30, 51,
 286, 343
 *see also names of relations*
finances
 debts 100, 302–6
 dissatisfaction with income 228–30
 income from authorship 52, 86, 87–88, 110–11,
 145, 146, 149, 159–60, 305, 341, 350
 modern equivalents 305, 357
 objections to newspaper misrepresentation 148
 payment dates 89
 unconcern with profits 287–88, 305–6
 value of estate at death 327
 *see also* Chapman and Hall
journalism xv, 28–29, 30–31, 35, 48–49, 109, 138,
 336–37, 342
 furnishing of material for sketches 56, 57, 60
 range of coverage 58
 relations with colleagues 30–31
 transcription skills 28–29
 working conditions 50–51

personal characteristics
 (alleged) anti-Semitism 41–42
 library 220
 mood swings 70, 100, 111, 229, 298, 308
 physical appearance 73, 219, 326
 political views 53–56, 58, 306–8
 signature 222–23
 wardrobe 82, 219, 326, 367
 portraits of 103, 182–83, 200, 223, 227, 361, 367
 *Nickleby* frontispiece 217–23
Dickens, Charles Culliford Boz ("Charley")
 (son) 159
 birth 142, 160
 christening 77, 81
Dickens, Elizabeth (mother) 28, 246, 286, 315,
 336, 368
 Dickens's portrayal of 27, 196
Dickens, Frances Elizabeth ("Fanny") (sister,
 later Burnett) 29, 41, 62, 84, 182, 246
Dickens, Frederick William (brother) 30, 51, 151
Dickens, Harriet (sister) 62
Dickens, Henry Fielding (son) 41
Dickens, John (father) 30, 39, 77, 181, 315, 318, 368
 debts/imprisonment 20, 41–42, 51, 62, 69, 117,
 196, 335
 Dickens's positive image of 27, 28, 286
 role in Dickens's career choices 22, 28, 29–30
 trading on son's fame/fortune 286, 312, 379;
 Dickens's efforts to prevent 298
Dickens, Kate (daughter) 229, 280
Dickens, Letitia Mary (sister) 30, 62
Dickens, Mary (daughter) 187
Dickens, Walter Landor (son) 298
"A Dinner in Poplar Walk" (sketch) 56–57, 65, 67
Disraeli, Benjamin 19, 102, 151, 210
Doctors' Commons, Dickens's employment at 29
*Dombey and Son* 75–76, 267, 274, 327, 375
 critical/commercial success 33, 94
*Donaldson v. Becket* (1774) 11–12
D'Orsay, Alfred 219
Dowling, Henry 157
Drake, Sir Fancis 169
Drew, John M. L. 342–43
Drummond, Rose Emma 183
Drummond, Samuel 182–83, 200
"The Drunkard's Death" (sketch) 72
Dryden, John, *Troilus and Cressida* 10

Easson, Angus 347
Easthope, John 84–85, 86, 108–9
Eden, Garden of 123–24, 373
Edgar, David, *Nicholas Nickleby* (stage
 production) 195, 212
education *see* children; Dickens, Charles;
 Yorkshire schools

Egan, Pierce 35–36, 248
 *Life in London* 75
 *Tom and Jerry* 205
"The Election for Beadle" (sketch) 60–61
Eliade, Mircea 285, 378
Eliot, George (Mary Ann Evans) 223, 268, 367
Eliot, Simon xv
Eliot, T. S. 17
Elizabeth I 6
Engels, Friedrich 80, 214
 *The Condition of the Working Class in
 England* 210
eschatology 373
*Evening Chronicle* 52, 58–60
 readership 53
*The Examiner* 236
executions (public), objections to 250, 346, 371
expectations, frustration of (as theme of
 sketches) 56–57, 68
expulsion, as comic theme 126

Fagin, Bob 162–63, 358
Faulkner, William 17
Feather, John 5, 9, 12
Fielding, Henry 55, 117, 179, 248, 295
 *Tom Jones* 276
Finden, William 219–20, 222
"The Fine Old English Gentleman" (satirical
 poem) 306–7
"The First of May" (sketch) 85
*flâneur*, figure of 2, 43, 63, 340
Flaubert, Gustave 62, 344
Fleischer, Frederick 158
Fletcher, Angus 301–2
Follett, Robert Bayly 147, 187, 228, 234, 287
Ford, Mark 195
Ford, Richard 190
Forrester, Charles/Alfred *see* Crowquill, Alfred
Forster, E. M. 130
Forster, John xiii, 2–3, 20, 26, 27–28, 35, 81, 83,
 151, 159, 163, 180, 182, 228, 252, 253, 258–59,
 264, 270, 298, 300, 368
 *The Life of Charles Dickens* 26, 41, 242–43, 275,
 302, 348, 369–70
 *The Life and Times of Oliver Goldsmith* 33, 40,
 41, 74
 negotiations with Dickens's publishers 187,
 189–90, 231–33, 235–36, 238, 243–44, 368
 professional jealousy 325
 review of *Pickwick* 117, 121
Foucault, Michel 18–19, 20, 62–63, 91, 117, 254,
 324, 334, 344
France
 copyright law 14–15, 16
 drama, English translations 205

France (cont.)
   literary theory 17–19
Franklin, Sir John 307
Freud, Sigmund 265, 374–75
Frith, William Powell 271
Frobisher, Martin 169
Frye, Northrop 124–25

Galignani (publishers) 158
Garcha, Amanpal 48, 209, 343
Gardiner, Juliet 333–34
Garrick, David 40
Garrick Club 180
Gaskell, Elizabeth 84
   *Cranford* 131–32
Gatty, Margaret, "The Black Bag" 254, 371
Gay, John, *The Beggar's Opera* 249
Genette, Gérard 179, 192, 329, 366
"gentleman," status of 174, 179, 223, 225
   redefinition 174
   treatment in *Barnaby Rudge* 317–18
   treatment in *Oliver Twist* 175–76
George IV 302
Germany, copyright law 15, 16
Gibbon, Edward 349
Giles, William 40
Gilmour, Robin 174, 180, 360
Gissing, George 179, 194, 280, 328
Glavin, John 337
Goldsmith, Oliver 10, 33, 43, 74, 238, 340
   links with Dickens 40–41, 43
   *The Bee* 40–41, 241
   *The Citizen of the World* 40, 41, 243
   *The Vicar of Wakefield* 37, 39–42
*Gone With the Wind* (1939) 17
Gordon, George, Lord (historical figure) 283, 312, 380
Gordon riots (1780) 11, 280, 283, 297–300
Gore, Catherine 102
Grant, Daniel/William 207, 208, 369
Grant, James 30–31
*Great Expectations* 131
   autobiographical elements 162
   influences on 20–21
Gregory, John Swarbreck 287
Grey, Lord 50–51
Grillo, Virgil 345
Grimaldi, Joey 154, 180–82, 216
   *see also Memoirs of Joseph Grimaldi*
Grossman, Jonathan H. 79, 125–26
Grosvenor, Robert, Lord 361
Grote, George 180
Gutenberg, Johannes 330

Hall, Anna Maria 185
Hall, Spencer 180

Hall, William 86–87, 102, 180, 183, 237, 241, 242, 308
   first visit to Dickens 33, 93
   *see also* Chapman and Hall
Hammond, W. J. 157
Hansard, T. C. 141
*Hard Times* 21
Hardy, Barbara 253, 315
Hardy, Thomas 268
Harley, John Pritt 355–56
Hazlitt, William 79–80, 182, 347
   decline/death 80, 83
   *Liber Amoris* 79–80
   *The Spirit of the Age* 80
Head, Sir Francis Bond, *Bubbles from the Brunnens of Nassau* 74
Heath, William 156
Heminges, John 7
Hemstedt, Geoffrey 345
Hennell, Sara 367
Hicks, Charles 179
Hill, Thomas 179
history, writing of 283–84
   relationship/competition with fiction 311–13
Hogarth, George (father-in-law) 29, 46, 52, 59, 70, 72, 74, 80, 82–83, 85, 99, 180, 253, 286, 309–10
   *Memoirs of the Musical Drama* 187
Hogarth, George, Jr. (brother-in-law) 308
Hogarth, Georgina (sister-in-law) 182, 200, 286
Hogarth, Mary Scott (sister-in-law) 69, 246–47, 286
   death 117, 128, 147, 149, 263–64, 273, 310, 372
Hogarth, William 55, 223, 248, 254
   *Industry and Idleness* 139
Holcroft, Thomas, *Narrative of the Late Riots* 281
Holland, J. B., Capt. 32, 338
Hollington, Michael 340
Hood, Thomas 2, 131, 253, 269, 270
Hope, Anthony 37
"Horatio Sparkins" (sketch) 67, 176
"The Hospital Patient" (sketch) 54
House, Madeline xiii
"The House" (sketch) 58–59
*Household Words* 42–43, 131, 222
Hullah, John Pyke 84, 109
Humphreys, Thomas/William 245
Hunt, Leigh 180, 219
Hurnall, Mary 298–99
Hurst, Blackett 13
Hutter, Albert 265, 374–75

illegitimacy (of children)
   in fiction 160, 314
   in law 171, 357
industrial age

authorship 3, 327–28; defined 3
   importance of written word 22
Ingham, Patricia 163
Irving, Washington 74, 170, 346
   *The Sketch Book of Geoffrey Crayon, Gent.*
      74, 367
   *Tales of the Alhambra* 243
*Is She His Wife? or, Something Singular* (burletta)
      338, 355–56
Italy, copyright law 15

Jackson, John 95, 102
Jacox, Francis 335
Jaffe, Audrey 344, 372, 376
James, G. P. R., *The Smuggler* 169
James I of England/VI of Scotland 7
Jarvis, Steven 349
Jeffrey, Francis (Lord) 34, 80, 177, 300, 301
Jephson, Emily 162
Jerdan, William 137, 144, 149, 179, 235
Jerrold, Douglas 137, 367
Jesse, Edward, *Gleanings in Natural History* 97
Johnson, E. D. H. xiii
Johnson, Samuel, Dr. 10, 12, 40, 177, 211, 365
Jones, Mary 289–90
Jones, William 27
Jonson, Ben 113, 332, 360, 365
Jordan, John O. 222–23

Kafka, Franz 62, 344
Kean, Edmund 201
Keeley, Mrs. 249
Kennett, Brackley, Lord Mayor 290
Kermode, Frank 79, 129, 130
Kidd, William, *Characteristic Sketches of Young
   Gentlemen* 355
Kincaid, James R. 372, 373, 378
Kitton, Frederic 28
Knight, Charles 244
Knopf, Alfred 17
Kolle, Henry 32, 46, 49, 253

"The Ladies' Societies" (sketch) 61
Lamb, Lady Caroline 80
Lamb, Charles 43
Lamert, George (aka James) 26
Landor, Walter Savage 236
Langdale, Thomas 312
Laurence, Samuel 182, 200, 218
lawyers, social status 174
Lea, H. C. 158
Leary, Patrick, and Andrew Nash, "Authorship" 2
Lee, John 157
Leech, John 74, 108, 346
Leopold I of Belgium 15

Lever, Charles 84, 243
Lewes, G. H. 162, 220
Ley, J. W. T. 182
*The Library of Fiction* 33, 86, 88–89, 92,
      102, 348
"The Lifted Veil" (sketch) 249
"The Lions of London" 254
literacy, rise in 3
*Little Dorrit* 131
Liverpool, anti-Catholic feeling in 283
Liverpool, Lord 55
Locke, John 8, 11, 210, 331
Lockhart, John Gibson 79, 81, 82–83, 301
   biography of Scott 309–11
London, as cultural center 84
"London By Night" 49
Longman, Thomas 12, 223–24, 240
Lover, Samuel 180
Lyttleton, George, 4th Baron 180

Macaulay, Thomas Babington, 1st Baron 19
Mackenzie, Henry 34
Mackenzie, R. Shelton 148, 155, 236
Maclise, Daniel 41, 245, 367
   frontispiece to *Nicholas Nickleby* 218–23
Macready, William 81, 179–80, 192, 195, 246
Macrone, John 25, 70, 72, 75, 76, 82, 85, 90, 100,
      109–10, 280, 281–82
   death 286, 355 (*see also Pic Nic Papers*)
   Dickens's problems fulfilling commissions for
      137, 138, 141
   proposed reissue of *Sketches* 151, 153–54, 155;
      prevention by buyout 154
   publication of *Sketches by Boz* 53, 74
   working relationship with Dickens 112, 286
Maginn, William 55, 81, 136, 152, 247, 352–53
Magnet, Myron 381
Mahony, Francis 37
Mansfield, Lord 11, 14, 136, 307–8, 380
Manzoni, Alessandro, *I Promessi Sposi* 311
Marcus, Steven 101, 125, 196, 228, 265, 270,
      374–75, 376
Marler-Kennedy, Kara 380
Marryat, Frederick, Capt. 186–87, 319
Martin, Theodore 37
*Martin Chuzzlewit* 64–65, 197, 206
Marx, Karl 214
Mary I, Queen 6
*Master Humphrey's Clock* xvi, xvii, 41, 118, 159,
      237, 253–59, 268
   (alleged) aims 296
   authorial voice 258, 268, 295–97
   circulation 273–74, 321
   collaborative creation 243–53
   contrasted with *Barnaby Rudge* 293

*Master Humphrey's Clock* (cont.)
  Dickens as sole contributor 244, 245, 256, 257–58
  Dickens's control over 241–42
  Dickens's proposals for 238, 300, 369–70
  Dickens's reasons for proposing 242–43
  illustrations 244–45, 370
  narrative framework 256
  narrative structure 256–57, 258
  negotiations 243–44, 303–4
  personnel 254–57, 267, 320–21, 323
  pricing 271–72
  proposed format 241
  proposed topics 243
  recycling of *Pickwick* characters 255–57, 258, 297
  serialization of *Barnaby Rudge* 287
  sources 269
  switch to third-person narration 257, 260–61
  target readership 271–73
  US publication 250–51, 253
  winding-up 25, 308, 320–23, 325; reasons for 321–23
Mathews, Charles 278
Maxwell, Richard 342
Mayhew, Henry 49
McKenzie, D.F. xiv–xv, 329
McKitterick, David xv, 334
Meadows, Kenny 156
"Meditations in Monmouth Street" (sketch) 69, 71–72, 113, 342
Melbourne, William Lamb, 2nd Viscount 55, 109, 118, 283
*Memoirs of Joseph Grimaldi* 153, 180–82
  criticisms 181–82
  sales 181
Michie, Helena 197
Middle Temple, Dickens's admission to 252–53
*Millar* v. *Taylor* (1769) 11, 14
Miller, J. Hillis 101, 195–96
Milnes, Richard Monckton (later Baron Houghton) 180, 371
Milton, John 8
  *Paradise Lost* 10
*The Mirror of Parliament* (report journal) 28–29
Mitford, Mary Russell 84, 162
Mitton, Thomas 51, 147, 187–88, 234, 246, 305, 310–11
Moir, David MacBeth ("Delta") 36, 301
Molloy, Charles 28, 48
Moncrieff, W.T. 204–5, 217, 249
  *Nicholas Nickleby* 204–5
  *Sam Weller; or The Pickwickians* 157, 204, 356
*Monthly Magazine* 31–32, 35, 44, 49–50, 56–57
Moore, Thomas 151

morality, novels as vehicles for 130–31, 224
More, Hannah 274
More, Thomas, *Utopia* 211
Morgan, Edwin S. 186, 189
Morland, George 340
*Morning Chronicle* 29, 44, 50–53, 58–60, 84–85, 108–9, 111
  political stance/readership 53
Morritt, John 34
Mozart, Wolfgang Amadeus
  *Abduction from the Seraglio* 170
  *The Magic Flute* 170
"Mrs Joseph Porter Over the Way" (sketch) 49
Mudfog (projected setting for sketches) 140, 353
Mudie, Robert 223
Murphy, Peter 168
Murray, Isobel 302
Murray, James A. H. 171
Murray, John 12, 44, 74, 102

names, use in *Sketches* 66–68, 343
  *see also Oliver Twist*
natural rights, theory of 8
Neal, Joseph Clay 155
New Poor Law *see* Poor Law Amendment Act
Newgate fiction 72, 81–82, 224, 225, 370–71
  (alleged) copycat crimes 250
  criticisms 247–50, 253, 312
  reworking of conventions in *Barnaby Rudge* 293–94
Niboyet, Eugénie 157–58
*Nicholas Nickleby* 24, 177, 263
  adaptations/imitations 204–5, 212
  attacks on piracy 204–6
  autobiographical elements 27, 203–4, 217, 364, 365, 366
  as career-defining work 186, 192, 204
  characterization 202–4, 207–8, 212, 213; real-life originals *see* Grant, Daniel/William
  contemporary criticism 208
  ending 285, 364
  generic definition 186–87
  illustrations 185, 366–67; frontispiece 217–23
  income from 228–29, 238–39
  inserted stories 213–14
  narrative framework 216–17
  paratexts 215–16
  prefigurings in *Sketches* 196
  process of composition 187, 237
  "Proclamation" 194
  publication agreement 149–50
  range of issues 225
  RSC production *see* Edgar, David
  social critique 194, 212–14
  structure 195–97

theatricality 195, 196, 201–4, 253, 363
treatment of commerce 197–200, 214–15, 221;
alternatives to 206–9
treatment of employment 212–13, 366
treatment of portraiture 183, 200
use of humor 186
Nord, Deborah Epstein 340
North, Christopher *see* Wilson, John, Prof.
*Norton* v. *Melbourne* (1836) 109, 116
novels
competition for literary audience 271
readers'/reviewers' preferences 376

O'Connell, Daniel 109
*The Old Curiosity Shop* 253, 257
autobiographical significance 273, 276–77,
372, 376
characterization 266
comic elements 259–60, 373
commercial success 273–74, 288; in US 272
conclusion 288
death of Nell 258–59, 301
deletion of material from *Master Humphrey's
Clock* 269–70
dream motif 276–77, 377
generic characteristics 269, 278
illustrations 245, 256, 273–74, 373
interweaving of themes 274–75
Marxist interpretations 264
narrative voice 263–64, 277
narratorial voice/identity 259–63, 267, 268,
274–75; problems of 260–61
page format 376
prefaces 270, 275–78, 375–76
publication 272
setting 267
sexual implications 261–63, 265–67, 374–75
structure 272–73
theme of spying/overhearing 261–62, 373
theme of tale-telling 278
treatment of money 375
O'Leary, Joanna 358
Oliphant, Margaret 118
*Oliver Twist* xvii, 23, 40–42, 49–50, 74, 128, 158,
215, 359
advertising of other works by association
with 251
attacks on 247–48; Dickens's defense 248–49
authorial credit 2–3, 173, 191–93, 216
autobiographical elements 162–64
"coffin" motif 358–59
composition 117, 146
copyright 143, 145–46, 159, 234–35; transfer of
251–52
Dickens's income from 228–30

disputes over 189–92, 207
dramatizations 157
echoes/contrasts in later works 208–9, 294,
295, 314
generic definition 186
historical/social context 174–75
illustrations 146, 161, 190
origins 139–40, 160–61
prefigurings in *Sketches* 54, 69, 70, 73, 79,
167, 342
publication 147, 187
significance of names 163–64, 167, 193
social critique 69, 160–62, 175–76, 183,
198–99, 211
stories, telling of 164–66; as commercial
transaction 165–66
treatment of identity 163–64, 167–68, 172, 173,
206, 285
treatment of plagiarism 172–73
unsuitability for *Bentley's Miscellany* 135,
161–62, 249
Ollier, Charles 312
Onwhyn, Thomas 156, 158
Orczy, Baroness 341
origins, Dickens's interest in/treatment of
285–86
Osgood, James Ripley 355–56
*O'Thello* (Shakespeare burlesque) 49
*Our Mutual Friend* 131
"Our Next-Door Neighbours" (sketch) 65
"Our School" (1851 article) 27

paratext xiv
defined 329
"A Passage in the Life of Mr. Watkins Tottle"
(sketch) 61
Paulson, Ronald 286, 294
Pavese, Caesar 43
Payne, J. H., *Clari* 49
Peel, Sir Robert 55, 249, 322
Perkins, Maxwell 17
Petrarch 80
"Phiz" *see* Browne, Hablot Knight
physiognomy, as key to character 200
*Pic Nic Papers* (benefit publication for Macrone's
widow and family) 154–55, 187, 230,
239–40, 355
Pickering, Ferdinand 227
*The Pickwick Papers* xvii, 23, 55, 66, 79, 111, 135,
140, 200, 228–29, 250, 262, 281
Address from the Publishers (Part III,
June 1836) 105
advance Prospectus 89–91, 94–95
authorial credit 23, 76, 192
celebratory dinner (Nov. 17, 1837) 179–80

*The Pickwick Papers* (cont.)
  challenges facing author 108–21
  chancy nature of venture 101, 106–7
  characterization 64–65, 96–97, 112–15, 113–15, 124–25; formed around language 114–15; Jingle 107; Sam Weller 114–15; use of stock types 114
  collaborative nature of project 95–96, 97, 98, 253
  commercial success 107–8, 149, 151, 162, 179–80
  conclusion 130, 259
  conflicts, internal/intergenerational 120–21, 125–26
  critical analyses 101
  dates, significance of 125–26, 351–52
  death, as theme 91, 119–25, 126–27, 133; background of real-life deaths 117–18; metaphoric presence 122–23
  dedication 177
  Dickens's (claimed) control over 91–94, 100, 101
  Dickens's contribution to illustrations 97, 99–100, 350
  Dingley Dell Christmas episode 128–29
  "Dying Clown" episode/illustration 98–100, 107, 350
  echoes/contrasts in later works 133, 167, 208–9, 213
  eighteenth-century models 90
  Fleet Prison chapters 69–70, 117, 128
  foreign pirate editions 157–59
  Garden/Fall motif 123–24
  generic definition 118, 130, 186
  genesis 89–91, 94–96; mythologized version 91
  illustrations *see* Browne, H. K.; Buss, R. W.; Seymour, Robert
  increase in length of installments 103–4, 111–12
  integration of darkness and comedy 128
  narrative framework 116–17
  Notice to Correspondents 106
  parodies/reworkings 131–33, 154, 155–57
  plot development 108, 116–21
  poor early sales 101, 103
  Postscript from the Editor (Part III, June 1836) 105–6
  Preface to 1847 edition 32, 39, 42, 92–94, 337–38, 352
  prefigurings in *Sketches* 73, 79, 96, 98–99, 128
  publication agreements 148–50, 149–50, 159
  publication schedule 142
  readers' correspondence 105–7
  recycling of characters 255–57, 258, 297, 324–25
  reduction of illustrations 103–4
  sources of comedy 124–28; reworking of comic conventions 124–26
  stage adaptations 156–57
  switch of narrative direction 107
  transformations 127–28
  treatment of family relationships 120, 121, 285
  treatment of law 125–26, 252
  treatment of male–female relationships 116, 120, 121
  treatment of social class 175
  treatment of time 129–30, 133
piracy 11, 169–70, 359
  Dickens's attacks on 157, 170, 173, 204–6
  efforts at restriction 170
  remedies 170
  romantic connotations 169–70
plagiarism 171–73
  Dickens accused of 355
  distinguished from piracy 169, 171
  gravity of offence 173
  in *Oliver Twist* 172–73
Plato, *Republic* 211
Poe, Edgar Allan 321–22
Poor Law Amendment Act 161–62, 174–75, 180, 209
Pope, Alexander 10–11
Pope-Hennessy, Una 188
population shifts 167–68
Potter (clerk) 28
Powell, Anthony 118
Prescott, W. H. 188
Prest, T. P. 76
Price, Leah 267–68, 272, 376
prison, Dickens's visit to/use of as setting 70–72
professions, aspirations to status of gentleman 174, 225
property, law of 171
Protestant Association 283
Protestant work ethic 21
Proust, Marcel 62, 344
pseudonym(s) 192, 339
  advantages 33–36
  in fiction 67
  popularity 34, 37–38
  *see also* "Boz"; "Sparks, Timothy"; "Tibbs"; "W"
publishers, role in communications industry 12

Quiz (Edward Caswall), *Sketches of Young Ladies* 153

Rabelais, François, *Gargantua* 37
rape (implied), treatments 261–63, 374
Raven, James 34
Reade, Charles 84
realism, conventions of 130
reception history/theory xvi
Rede, William Leman, *Peregrinations of Pickwick* (musical adaptation) 156–57, 356

Reform Act 48–49, 55, 180
Reynolds, George W. M., *Pickwick Abroad* 156
Reynolds, Sir Joshua 200
Rice, Thomas J. 283, 308, 378
Richardson, Samuel 10, 268
Rogers, Samuel 81
Room, Adrian 34
Rousseau, Jean-Jacques 211
Rowlinson, Matthew 375
Rushton, William 157
Ruskin, John 274
Russell, Lord John 51
Russell, Lord William 250

Salisbury, Dowager Marchioness of 51
Salmon, Frederick 309
"Scenes and Characters" 52
Schlicke, Paul 196
Schor, Hilary M. 131
Scotland
    copyright law 11
    Dickens's visit to (1841) 299, 300–302, 304;
        celebratory dinner (June 25, 1841) 300–302
Scott, John 79
Scott, Sir Walter 13–14, 34, 82–83, 90, 169, 182,
    224, 254, 301
    Dickens seen as heir to 301
    financial misfortunes 82–83, 242, 309–10
    influence on *Barnaby Rudge* 309–11
    *The Heart of Midlothian* 280
Selby, Charles 238
Seville, Catherine 81
Seymour, Jane, née Holmes 93–94, 95, 100–101, 349
Seymour, Robert 66, 86–87, 88, 89, 90, 200
    Dickens's posthumous tribute 93
    illustrations for *Pickwick* 94–101, 108, 113, 350
    suicide 100–101, 102, 104–5, 109, 112,
        116–17, 121
Shakespeare, William 80, 115, 253
    *As You Like It* 125
    First Folio 7, 331
    *Hamlet* 140–41, 285
    *Henry V* 42
    *King Lear* 66, 203
    *A Midsummer Night's Dream* 125
    *Othello* 49, 151
    *Romeo and Juliet* 202–3
    *The Tempest* 125
    *Twelfth Night* 125
Shaw, William 184–85
Shelley, Mary, *Frankenstein* 20–21, 44
Shelley, Percy Bysshe 16
Sheridan, Richard Brinsley 57
Sibson, Thomas 156
Simmons, Samuel 10

*Sketches by Boz* xvii, 23, 45, 57, 58–61, 65, 79, 82, 90,
    100, 109, 110, 111, 112, 114, 135, 141, 221, 241, 263
    common themes 66–73
    echoes in later works *see titles of novels*
    illustrations 74–75
    popularity 91, 138
    projected reissue (1837) 151, 153–54, 155
    reviews 55, 62–63, 79, 85, 100
    studies 345
    "Sketches from Our Parish" 58–59, 60–61, 217
    "Sketches of London" 49, 52, 58–60, 108–9
*Sketches of Young Couples* 153, 237, 369
*Sketches of Young Gentlemen* 135, 153, 180
Skura, Meredith Anne 374, 377
Slater, Michael 53, 74, 335, 337
slavery, profits from 225, 319–20
Smith, Sydney 44, 57
Smith, Victoria Ford 371
Smithson, Charles 303–4
Smollett, Tobias 179
"Solomon Bell the Raree Showman" 138, 153
Solomons, Ikey 247
Spain, copyright law 15
"Sparks, Timothy" (pseudonym) 109, 153
*The Spectator* 243
St. Clair, William xv, 329
Stallworthy, Jon xiv
Star Chamber 6, 7
Stationers' Company 6–9, 169
    booksellers' control of 6–7
    extent of authority 6
    loss of monopoly 8–9, 331
    registration requirements 7
"The Steam Excursion" (sketch) 68
Stein, Richard, *Victoria's Year* 167–68
Stendhal (Henri-Pierre Bayle) 43
Stewart, Garrett 71, 132, 227, 352, 372
Stirling, Edward 156, 205
"The Story Without a Beginning" 53
Strachey, Lytton 328
*The Strange Gentleman* (musical play) 110, 140,
    354–55
    author credit 152
"Street Sketches" 58–59
"The Streets – Morning" (sketch) 69–70
subscription, publication by 10
*Sunday Under Three Heads* (political satire) 109
Surveyor of the Press, office of 7
Swift, Jonathan 36
    *Gulliver's Travels* 243

*A Tale of Two Cities* 293, 379
Talfourd, Thomas Noon 16, 23–24, 177, 180, 223,
    252, 322, 333
    *Ion* 177

Tauchnitz, Bernhard 159
Taylor, Robert *see Millar* v. *Taylor*
Taylor, Weld 182
Tegg, Thomas 138, 153
Tennyson, Alfred, 1st Baron 19, 84
Thackeray, William Makepeace 37–38, 108, 130,
   190, 193–94, 250, 367, 371
   criticisms of Dickens 227, 247–50, 253, 273;
     Dickens's response 248–49
   *Catherine* 247
   "Horae Catnachianae" 247–48
   *The Yellowplush Correspondence* 132
theater *see* acting; *Nicholas Nickleby*
Thompson, T. J. 225
Thomson, C. E. Poulett 16
Thomson, James, *The Seasons* 11
"Thoughts About People" (sketch) 59–60
"Tibbs" (pseudonym) 44–46
Tidd, William, *Practice of the Court of King's
   Bench* 28
Tillotson, Kathleen xiii, 190, 315, 377
   *see also* Butt, John
Tilt, Charles 32, 193, 237, 239–40
Tonson, Jacob 10
transformation, as comic theme 127–28
"Trio Club" 365
Trollope, Anthony 118
   *Orley Farm* 174
Trollope, Frances 102
Trollope, Thomas Adolphus 84
Tudor period, copyright laws/institutions 5–6
"The Tuggses at Ramsgate" (sketch) 66–67, 85
Turpin, Dick 82, 170
Twain, Mark 164, 358

*The Uncommercial Traveller* 175
United States
   copyright law 15–16
   Dickens's visit to 24, 308, 326
   "pirated" editions of British authors 169
universities, copyright privileges 6

*Valentine and Orson* (anon.) 285
Van Diemen's Land (Tasmania) 307
Vanden Bossche, Chris 223, 224–25
Varese, Jon 197

Verdi, Giuseppe, *Rienzi* (uncompleted) 81
Victoria, Queen 15, 118, 237
*The Village Coquettes* (operetta) 73, 84, 109–10,
   139, 140, 349
   author credit 152
"A Visit to Newgate" (sketch) 72, 82, 99, 249
Voltaire (François-Marie Arouet) 339

"W," pseudonym 306
Wagner, Richard, *Rienzi* 81
Warren's Jet Blacking 26–27, 29, 274, 335
Watson, Robert 312–13
   *The Life of George Gordon* 281
Wellington, Arthur Wellesley, 1st Duke of 55
Wellington House Academy 27–28, 39
Wheeler, Burton 160
Whitehead, Charles 86, 348
Wilde, Oscar 328
Wilkie, David 301
Wilkinson, Ian 345
Wilks, Thomas Egerton 154
William IV 53, 55
   death 117–18
Williams, Samuel 245
Willis, Nat 70, 82, 348, 367
Wills, W. H. 43
Wilson, Edmund 335
Wilson, John, Prof. 300–301
Wimsatt, William K. 17
Winter, Gilbert 207
*The Wizard of Oz* (1939) 17
Wood, Mrs Henry, *East Lynne* 341
Woodvine, John 195
Woolf, Virginia 328
Wordsworth, William 13
working classes, renderings of speech
   64–65

Xavier, Andrew 361

Yates, Edmund 155
Yates, Frederick 205
Yorkshire schools
   court cases involving 184–85
   Dickens's attacks on 183–85, 194
Young, Robert 341